BRITISH INTELLIGENCE, STRATEGY AND THE COLD WAR, 1945–51

BRITISH INTELLIGENCE, STRATEGY AND THE COLD WAR, 1945–51

Edited by Richard J. Aldrich

London and New York

First published in 1992 by
Routledge
11 New Fetter Lane, London EC4P 4EE

Simultaneously published in the USA and Canada
by Routledge
a division of Routledge, Chapman and Hall, Inc.
29 West 35th Street, New York, NY 10001

Phototypeset in 10/12pt Garamond by
Intype, London
Printed in Great Britain by
TJ Press (Padstow) Ltd, Padstow, Cornwall

British Library Cataloguing-in-Publication Data
British intelligence, strategy and the Cold War
1945–51
I. Aldrich, Richard J.
327.1241

Library of Congress Cataloging-in-Publication Data
also available

ISBN 0 415 07851 2

Contents

CONTENTS

Part II Strategy

Notes on contributors

Richard J. Aldrich is a Lecturer in International Relations at the University of Nottingham. He is Assistant Editor of *Intelligence and National Security* and is the author of *The Key to the South: Britain, the United States and Thailand during the approach of the Pacific War.*

Robert Cecil, CMG, served for over thirty years in the British Diplomatic Service before becoming Reader in Contemporary History at the University of Reading. He was Personal Assistant to the Chief of SIS, 1943–6. His publications include *The Myth of the Master Race, Hitler's Decision to Invade Russia* and *A Divided Life: A Biography of Donald Maclean.*

Alex Danchev is Professor of International Relations at the University of Keele. He is author of *Very Special Relationship, Establishing the Anglo-American Alliance* and a forthcoming study of the philosopher-statesman Oliver Franks.

Saki Dockrill is a Research Fellow at King's College, University of London. She is the author of *British Policy for West German Rearmament* and is completing studies of Eisenhower's New Look Military Doctrine and of the Pacific War.

Anthony Gorst is a Lecturer in History at the Polytechnic of Central London and was a Research Fellow of the Institute of Contemporary British History. He is presently completing a study of British post-war defence policy and is also co-director of a major documentation programme focusing upon twentieth-century Britain.

Karl Hack is a Senior Scholar at St Hugh's College, University of Oxford. He is conducting research on nuclear strategy and on British defence policy in Asia, 1949–60.

Beatrice Heuser is a Lecturer in War Studies at King's College, University of London. She is the author of *Western Containment Policy: The Yugoslav Case, 1948–53* and is presently working on European security.

John Kent is a Lecturer in International History at the London School of Economics. He is completing a study of British imperial strategy and the origins of the Cold War, 1944–9, and is editing the Middle East volumes in the forthcoming series of British documents on the end of Empire.

Sheila Kerr is Director of the MA programme in Intelligence and International Relations at the University of Salford. She has written widely on intelligence and the Cold War and is completing a study of the Foreign Office spy, Donald Maclean.

W. Scott Lucas is a Lecturer in History at the University of Birmingham. He is the author of *Divided We Stand: Britain, the United States and the Suez Crisis* and is presently preparing a study of post-war propaganda.

C. J. Morris is a doctoral student in the Institute of Communication Studies, University of Leeds, and is undertaking a study of British propaganda in Africa and the Middle East, 1945–60.

Bradley F. Smith is Professor of History at Cabrillo College, California. He is the author of many books including *The Road to Nuremberg, Shadow Warriors: OSS and the Origins of the CIA, The War's Long Shadow: World War II and its Aftermath.*

John W. Young is Professor of Contemporary History and Politics at the University of Salford. He is the author of *Britain, France and the Unity of Europe, 1945–51, France, the Cold War and the Western Alliance, 1944–9* and *Cold War Europe, 1945–89: A Political History.*

John Zametica is a Research Fellow at the International Institute of Strategic Studies, London, and has lectured at the Universities of Oxford and Cambridge. His publications include *British Officials and British Foreign Policy, 1945–50* and a forthcoming study of security in South East Europe.

Foreword

Robert Cecil

When, in the middle of the Potsdam Conference, Clement Attlee took over from Winston Churchill, he faced a future scarcely less precarious than that which had confronted his predecessor. The menace of Germany had indeed ended and Japan was already putting out peace feelers; but on Britain's flanks were two newly-fledged superpowers, neither of which was showing signs of wishing to project the wartime alliance into the post-war world. The USSR was showing in Poland, Iran and elsewhere that the four-year alliance had been no more than a truce in the perennial struggle of Communism against capitalism. The USA was only marginally more sympathetic to non-Marxist socialism of the British variety which was imperfectly understood in Washington. The abrupt cancellation of Lend-Lease, soon to be followed by rejection of the understandings about post-war nuclear development, as agreed between Churchill and Roosevelt, did not augur well. The spectre of American isolationism, as in 1919, walked abroad. Moreover both superpowers, if in differing degrees, were hostile to the British imperial tradition. It is true, as Alex Danchev points out in Chapter 9, that by 1952 Britain and the USA were both conscious of sharing a global commitment together (*Schicksalagemeinschaft* might be the best term), but this could not be foreseen in 1945. There were a few knights errant in the US State Department, who might be willing to save British damsels in distress, but there were also plenty of dragons on Capitol Hill.

How the ministers, who had assumed responsibility for Britain's foreign and defence policy, faced up to these grave problems is the theme of the chapters that follow. Overseas difficulties were, of course, much aggravated by domestic ones, most of which were economic; after nearly six years of war the cupboard was bare. Public opinion, however, had little understanding that the country, despite so many sacrifices, had emerged from war victorious, but without the economic and financial underpinning that alone would have made possible retention of Great Power status. As the Cold War developed, there came to light another illusion tending to distort public opinion. Labour ministers, like Bevin and Dalton, who had been members of the wartime coalition, had been able discreetly to monitor the signs that the death of some 20 million Soviet people had not assuaged Stalin's appetite for domination; but no intimation of this had leaked out to the public at large. On the contrary, official propaganda since 1941 had continued to praise the Red Army and its leaders and that this propaganda had been effective had been demonstrated by the failure of Churchill's attempt to sound the anti-Communist tocsin during the short election campaign of 1945. For some it seemed that the charter of the United Nations held out hope of international harmony. Between the wars many supporters of the Labour Party and of the League of Nations Union had displayed an inclination to believe that a pact on paper offered better security than a battleship, besides coming a good deal cheaper. Wishful thinking of this kind had survived the war.

It is clear to historians, as they survey the rocky coastline and the mounting waves, that there could not have been a happy landfall, whatever policies had been adopted. All that historians can hope to depict is a retreat: not, like Dunkirk, a quick retreat *pour mieux sauter*, but a slow, inexorable withdrawal from world power, however much it was mitigated by co-operation with the USA in defensive pacts, such as NATO and SEATO. It began in 1947 in the eastern Mediterranean with abandonment of support for Greece and Turkey, and continued in the following year with relinquishment of the mandate in Palestine. Indian independence, it is true, had made it less necessary to maintain all the traditional links through the Mediterranean to the subcontinent; but British reliance on Middle East oil had in no way diminished at a time when relations with the Arab world had become acutely unstable.

Worse was to come, as Mao's army evicted Chiang Kai-shek from the Chinese mainland and the Cold War embraced a new land-mass and a new ocean. In a partitioned world it was in the partitioned countries, Korea and Germany, that a 'Third World War' threatened to break out. A few experts suggested there were differences between Mao's and Stalin's Communism, but no one could predict the future Sino-Soviet split. When South Korea was invaded, it looked as if a monolithic world Communism was on the march: if North Korea was so aggressive, might not East Germany provide a springboard for invasion of occupied, but unarmed, West Germany? This faced the Labour government with the thorny problem of German rearmament, which is tackled by Saki Dockrill in Chapter 8. Barely five years after Hitler's self-immolation in Berlin Germans were called upon again to take up arms.

Here we leave the reader, much in the way that writers of popular weekly serials whet readers' appetites for the next instalment. The hero lies gagged and bound in the cellar and the water is rising. How will he make his escape? It is only necessary to turn the pages that follow in order to find that escape depicted with a wealth of research and a high level of insight.

Acknowledgements

Transcripts from Crown-copyright records in the Public Record Office and at the India Office Library and Records appear by permission of the Controller, Her Majesty's Stationery Office. Quotations from the Alanbrooke papers and Myers papers appear by permission of the trustees and the Liddell Hart Centre for Military Archives, Kings College London. Quotations from the Montgomery papers appear by permission of the trustees and the Imperial War Museum.

Abbreviations

ABC	American-British-Canadian
ACAS(I)	Assistant Chief of the Air Staff (Intelligence)
ALFPMO	Allied Land Forces Paramilitary Operations
ALFSEA	Allied Land Forces South East Asia
ANZIM	Australia, New Zealand, India, Malaya
ANZUS	Australia, New Zealand, United States
ASIO	Australian Security Intelligence Organization
ASIS	Australian Secret Intelligence Service
BAOR	British Army of the Rhine
BBC	British Broadcasting Corporation
BDCC	British Defence Co-ordinating Committee (Far East)
BJSM	British Joint Services Mission
BMEO	British Middle East Office
BRUSA	British-American Signals Intelligence Agreement
C	Chief of the Secret Intelligence Service
CAS	Chief of the Air Staff
CDT	Combined Development Trust
CI	Counter-intelligence
CIA	Central Intelligence Agency
CIC	Commanders in Chief
CIGS	Chief of the Imperial General Staff
CIPC	Colonial Information Policy Committee
CLC	Communities Liaison Committee (Malaya)
CNS	Chief of the Naval Staff
COS	Chiefs of Staff
CRPO	Combined Research and Planning Organization
DMI	Director of Military Intelligence
DNI	Director of Naval Intelligence
DO	Cabinet Defence Committee
DPM	Dominion Prime Ministers meeting
EDC	European Defence Community
elint	electronic intelligence
FBI	Federal Bureau of Investigation

FO	Foreign Office
FPS	Future Planning Staff
GCHQ	Government Communications Headquarters
GRU	Glavnoe Razvedyavatelnoe Upravlenie (Chief Intelligence Directorate of the Armed Forces)
IDC	Imperial Defence College
IMEMO	Institute of World Economics and International Relations
IMP	Independence of Malaya Party
IPD	Information Policy Department
IRD	Information Research Department
ISLD	Inter-Service Liaison Department (SIS)
JCOSA	Joint Chiefs of Staff Organization Australia
JCS	United States Joint Chiefs of Staff
JIB	Joint Intelligence Bureau
JIC	Joint Intelligence Committee
JIC CCG	Joint Intelligence Committee, Control Commission Germany
JIC ME	Joint Intelligence Committee, Middle East
JIC FE	Joint Intelligence Committee, Far East
JPS	Joint Planning Staff
JSIC	Joint Scientific Intelligence Committee
JTIC	Joint Technical Intelligence Committee
JSM	Joint Staff Mission, Washington
JTIC	Joint Technical Intelligence Committee
JTWC	Joint Technical Warfare Committee
KGB	Komitet Gosudarstvennoi Bezopasnosti (Committee of State Security)
MCP	Malayan Communist Party
MEC	Middle East Command
MI	Military Intelligence
MI5	Security Service
MI6	Secret Intelligence Service (SIS)
MP	Member of Parliament
MPAJA	Malayan People's Anti-Japanese Army
MSS	Malayan Security Service
NSC	National Security Council
OPC	Office of Policy Co-ordination
OSO	Office of Special Operations
OSP	Office of Special Projects
OSS	Office of Strategic Services
PHPS	Post Hostilities Planning Staff
PM	Prime Minister
PPS	State Department Policy Planning Staff
PRU	Photographic Reconnaissance Unit
PUSC	Permanent Under-Secretaries Committee

PUSD	Permanent Under-Secretaries Department
PWE	Political Warfare Executive
RAF	Royal Air Force
RC	Foreign Office Russia Committee
RCMP	Royal Canadian Mounted Police
SAC	Strategic Air Command
SAS	Special Air Service
SEAC	South East Asia Command
SEATO	South East Asia Treaty Organization
SHAEF	Supreme Headquarters, Allied Expeditionary Force
SHAPE	Supreme Headquarters Allied Powers in Europe
SIFE	Security Intelligence Far East
sigint	signals intelligence
SIME	Security Intelligence Middle East
SIS	Secret Intelligence Service (MI6)
SOE	Special Operations Executive
TUC	Trades Union Congress
UKUSA	American-British-Commonwealth Signals Intelligence Agreement
UMNO	United Malay's National Organizations
UN	United Nations
USAF	United States Air Force

DOCUMENTARY REFERENCES

ADM	Admiralty
AIR	Air Ministry
CAB	Cabinet
CCC	Churchill College, Cambridge
CO	Colonial Office
DBPO	*Documents on British Foreign Policy*
DEFE	Ministry of Defence
DO	Dominions Office
FO	Foreign Office
FRUS	*Foreign Relations of the United States*
HSTL	Harry S. Truman Library, Independence, Missouri
IOLR	India Office Library and Records, Blackfriars, London
IWM	Imperial War Museum
KCL	King's College, University of London
NARA	National Archives and Records Administration, Washington
PRO	Public Record Office, Kew Gardens, Surrey
RG	Record Group
T	Treasury
TOP	*Transfer of Power*
WO	War Office

Introduction
Intelligence, strategy and the Cold War

Richard J. Aldrich

> I know the term 'Cold War' is much disliked in the Foreign Office as tending to misleading analogies, in the matter of methods and machinery, with a military war. But it is so commonly used nowadays even officially . . . and in any case it is very expressive of a state of affairs which undoubtedly exists.[1]

In the 1980s it was often remarked, with justification and satisfaction, that the importance of Britain's role in the Cold War had at last been recognized.[2] Certainly as late as 1975, the American historians who dominated this field of study, whether traditionalist, revisionist or post-revisionist, appeared to understand the Cold War as a narrowly bipolar phenomenon.[3] Indeed, even the term 'bipolar' is perhaps an over-generous description for some of this scholarship, for much of it interpreted the international system as all but synonomous with United States foreign policy.[4] In 1978 D. Cameron Watt urged British historians to employ the documentation recently opened to public inspection in various archives to end the American near-monopoly upon the interpretation of the early Cold War.[5] There has followed a flood of publications examining the place of Britain and other European countries in this conflict.[6] Consequently, not only Attlee and Bevin but also senior Foreign Office officials such as Roberts, Sargent and Strang now loom large on the Cold War landscape.[7]

Yet historians have been slower to address the non-diplomatic dimensions of Britain's Cold War and consequently, in two important areas, much of the terrain remains unexplored. First, there is as yet no study which offers a comprehensive analysis of British defence policy during the formative period 1945–51, nor indeed the sort of valuable synthesis which integrates the diplomatic and military dimensions of British policy in the manner of J. L. Gaddis's magisterial *Strategies of Containment*. Fortunately, significant studies of military themes have begun to appear, but much of this complex area remains opaque.[8] Second, while there is a clear consensus that accepts the recent work of British historians engaged on the study of intelligence as 'essential' to our understanding of the Second

1

World War, scholars have been remarkably slow to turn their hand to intelligence in the post-war period. By contrast, historians of American post-war policy have been quick to ask about the nature of American information regarding the Soviet Union, or to analyze the significance of covert activities within the wider framework of American concepts of containment.[9] Moreover, in the context of intense controversy over the publication of official documentation (*FRUS: Foreign Relations of the United States*) for the 1950s, leading American historians have expressed their conviction that the covert dimension is an essential component of our understanding of policy. It is in the area of intelligence that American historians have often shown interest in Britain's Cold War.[10]

Given the role of the Foreign Office as the co-ordinating department for Britain's overseas policy, a role that increasingly embraced intelligence and other covert activities from 1948, close attention to diplomats and their documents is undoubtedly of central importance. Yet at the same time there exists something of an imbalance in favour of diplomacy within the current literature. A collection of essays cannot hope to redress this, still less achieve a satisfactory overview of either British intelligence or strategy during the late 1940s. However, it can address some key non-diplomatic themes and emphasize the importance of these areas in achieving a sophisticated understanding of Britain's Cold War.

Intelligence and strategy are not the only areas that merit closer attention. Despite the expansion of media history, economic, cultural and domestic approaches to the Cold War have also languished. While Britain did not experience the absurdities of the McCarthyite period that have rendered domestic and cultural approaches so attractive to American historians, nevertheless the work of Peter Weiler, Peter Hennessy and Keith Jeffrey has indicated that the domestic dimension of Britain's Cold War merits sustained attention.[11] In particular, official apprehension at, and indeed active attempts to counter, the influence of Soviet-dominated front organizations upon British society has been little studied. As early as July 1946 a British official engaged in countering such bodies reported:

> Enquiries are on foot about the management of the NUS [National Union of Students]: whether besides the Secretary and the Executive Committee there exists a governing body, and whether any of this personnel might be induced to work for the creation of a body of opinion within the delegation of the Union to balance the extremists.[12]

In the late 1940s British officials in the Foreign Office and elsewhere demonstrated an ingenuity for pursuing the non-diplomatic dimensions of the Cold War that British historians have so far failed to match.

If British historians have focused primarily upon Cold War diplomacy, then, in one important sense, this is understandable. A quite remarkable number of documents relating to both strategy and intelligence for the period 1945–51 are closed to public inspection. A significant proportion of the minutes and memoranda of the Cabinet Defence Committee, the Chiefs of Staff (COS) Committee and their labyrinthian subcommittees not only have been heavily 'weeded' but also are often closed in their entirety, even for the period 1945–6. In the 1940s the engine-room of British strategic planning was the Joint Planning Staff (JPS), a subcommittee of the COS, consisting of the three Service Directors of Plans, but surprisingly their minutes are not extant. The most authoritative statement of British defence policy during the late 1940s, DO (47) 44 'Future Defence Policy', was opened to public inspection only in 1990 and its successor in 1950, DO (50) 45 'Defence Policy and Global Strategy', remains closed.[13] Consequently, those historians examining intelligence and strategy have been required to display an uncommon ingenuity in tracking down additional circulated copies of closed Cabinet papers and other documents that remain open in the voluminous low-level files of various ministries. Julian Lewis in his study of British strategy and Bradley F. Smith in his volume on SOE (Special Operations Executive) and OSS (Office of Strategic Services) were early and formidable practitioners of this technique.[14]

While historians of intelligence and strategy are often required to adopt the same archival methodology, the historical problems they address are crucially different. The COS strategic planning machinery represents a remarkably well-ordered and self-contained subject, while in contrast the term 'intelligence' is commonly employed to denote a plethora of separate if related organizations responsible for a product consumed by many different Whitehall departments. Unlike Britain's strategic planning machinery, the central records of Britain's more significant intelligence services are closed in their *entirety* for the post-war period.[15] Therefore, in Britain, the intelligence dimension of the Cold War is best pursued through the papers of the departments which consumed intelligence. As such, while the quantity of open papers relating to post-war British intelligence has hitherto been greatly underestimated, their distribution is erratic to say the least. Paradoxically, in one important respect, the closure of the archives of the individual intelligence services has done historians a service, directing them away from the minutae of case studies and organizational histories, and towards the interaction of intelligence and high-level policy. This reflects the extent to which intelligence material can be found among the papers of the Cabinet Office, Foreign Office, Treasury and Service ministries. The closed archives of SIS (Secret Intelligence Service, or MI6) and GCHQ (Government Communications Headquarters) doubtless contain fascinating materials, but it is equally certain that only a small percentage of this influenced high policy.

Similar archival problems and solutions are perhaps the least notable points of commonality which link intelligence and strategy, identifying them as complementary themes in this volume. As Wesley Wark and Christopher Andrew have demonstrated, in Britain during the late 1930s and early 1940s a sophisticated and well-managed organizational dialogue was created between intelligence appreciation and strategic planning. The need for efficient exploitation of the invaluable 'Ultra' decrypts of Axis communications for operational planning lent the highest importance to the careful integration of intelligence and strategy.[16] Moreover, towards the end of the war the development of weapons of mass destruction and also revolutionary means of strategic delivery, such as the V–2, bringing with them the prospect of what the COS termed a 'nuclear Pearl Harbor', lent a new importance to advanced warning of surprise attack and to 'national' intelligence concerning Soviet strategic capabilities.

The period 1945–51 served only to confirm the intimate linkage between intelligence and strategy. It was intelligence penetration that initially persuaded the Soviets to devote resources to their own wartime atomic programme, contributing to the production of a Soviet bomb in 1949, to the surprise of many in the West.[17] Moreover, intelligence reports of a Soviet atomic explosion in 1949 were one of the key factors that triggered the recasting of British strategy in the period 1950–2. Nevertheless, the interplay between strategy and intelligence continues to be underemphasized by historians. Typically, despite the attention that has been given to the wartime body concerned with Britain's post-war strategic requirements, the Post Hostilities Planning Staff (PHPS), the espionage dimension has been largely ignored.[18] Meanwhile, the Australian historian, Robert Manne, has convincingly demonstrated that by 1945 the Soviets were receiving copies of these 'explosive' PHPS papers, including outspoken reports on the future of Germany, from Soviet agents within the Australian Foreign Service.[19]

It is important not to confine the interpretations of 'intelligence' and 'strategy' to the dialogue conducted inside the, admittedly labyrinthian, COS committee structure. Within this volume the term 'intelligence' is employed in a wide sense to denote not only the collection and interpretation of information but also other forms of covert activity including subversion, special operations, clandestine or 'black' propaganda and internal security. Arguably, it is in some of these operational areas that we find interesting developments in the thinking about containment under the Labour governments of 1945–51. There are similar dangers in pursuing British strategic concepts through the rarefied papers of the COS without reference to wider defence policy. Even a cursory consideration of Britain's economic predicament during this period reveals the gulf that yawned between strategic ideas and the reality of military resources.

If the terms 'intelligence' and 'strategy' are understood in a broad sense, then it is clear that these two areas increasingly overlapped in the late 1940s. Certainly by 1946, and perhaps earlier, British officials in various departments were considering a 'defensive-offensive' political strategy, including propaganda, in order to counter what they perceived as a Soviet campaign against Britain. By 1948, Foreign Office officials such as Robert Hankey, Head of the Northern Department, who only two years earlier had expressed the strongest reservations about provoking the Soviets with covert activities, were advocating a 'liberation' strategy directed towards the Soviet Union's eastern satellites. The Foreign Office, encouraged by the COS, began to consider extensive planning machinery for the control of propaganda and subversive activities. In the late 1940s, covert activities were increasingly perceived as an important aspect of Britain's Cold War strategy. As if to underline this blurring of political and military operations, in November 1948 General Sir Ian Jacob, attending the Russia Committee (RC) in his capacity as director of the BBC's European Services, recommended that the Foreign Office should now have its own Director of Plans in common with the three Service departments.[20]

These developments cast light, not only upon British policy, but also on our understanding of the term 'Cold War'. Since the 1950s many historians and political analysts have employed this term as something of a catch-all, sometimes to denote all international developments during an indeterminate post-war period, or as shorthand for ideological conflict between East and West, or indeed in many other ill-defined senses. But in 1948 the officials that constituted Britain's Russia Committee can be found using this term in a more precise sense to denote the more operational and often clandestine aspects of the struggle between East and West. In November 1948 these officials advocated establishing a new body to manage these activities entitled the ' "Cold War" planning subcommittee'. Tedder, Chief of the Air Staff, who attended the meeting, was using the term 'Cold War' in precisely this sense when he warned: 'That unless we reformed our machinery for conducting the "Cold War", we might lose it in which case the Services would have to conduct a hot war, which was the last thing they wanted to do.'[21] Parallels can be drawn between these developments and the role of George Kennan's Policy Planning Staff.[22] In both Britain and the United States, historians have yet to establish how far this advocacy of a forward 'Cold War' strategy progressed towards implementation.

Many of the themes discussed above are explored within this volume. In the first part which concerns itself with intelligence, Richard Aldrich (Chapter 1) questions the existence of a coherent intelligence community, adapted to post-war conditions, before 1949. Thereafter the Foreign Office, albeit reluctantly, assumed increasing importance in the higher direction of intelligence and special operations through new planning machinery. Bradley F. Smith (Chapter 2) explores the extent to which, by the end of the Second World War, Britain's intelligence community depended more upon its extensive personal experience of the Soviets, rather than analysis, when producing assessments of the Soviet Union. This chapter addresses the hitherto unexplored area of Anglo-Soviet intelligence co-operation on the eve of the Cold War.

The extent of Britain's commitment to the concept of 'liberation' during the late 1940s is examined in two complementary chapters dealing with operational themes. First, Beatrice Heuser (Chapter 3) analyzes the place of the Anglo-American programme of special operations against the Eastern block within Western containment policies. Second, Scott Lucas and C. J. Morris (Chapter 4) seek to establish the importance of the rapid expansion of British covert propaganda during the late 1940s. They demonstrate the ubiquitous nature of this programme which addressed not only Britain's Cold War adversaries, but also her allies and domestic audiences at home and in British overseas territories. The complex linkage between intelligence and propaganda is further underlined in Chapter 5 by Sheila Kerr's detailed consideration of the importance of Donald Maclean, the high-level Soviet source in the Foreign Office, and of other post-war British defectors as Cold War propagandists. This chapter reveals the importance that both East and West have attached to the replaying of contradictory versions of Cold War history, often through the medium of defectors, as key instruments of the same conflict.

The second part of this volume, with its focus upon strategy, opens with an iconoclastic essay by Anthony Gorst (Chapter 6). The unrealistic nature of the British strategic planning is exposed by contrasting elaborate planning with the dismal pattern of available resources. It is argued that the COS deliberately ignored the economic reality of Britain's position during the 1940s. In addressing British strategy and the Western Union, John Kent and John Young (Chapter 7) demonstrate that, while Britain continued to seek the short-term assistance of the United States, nevertheless Bevin hoped to create a separate 'third force' in the form of a Euro-African bloc that would be independent of both the United States and the Soviet Union. Consequently, prior to 1948, Britain sought to obstruct comprehensive Euro-American defence links in pursuit of an alternative pattern of British hegemony. Further confirmation of Europe's growing significance in the last years of the Attlee governments is provided by Saki Dockrill (Chapter 8), who examines the vigorous debate over British strategy and the rearmament of Germany. These European themes stand in contrast to the continued importance of personal relations within the Anglo-American relationship. Alex Danchev (Chapter 9) demonstrates that the United States displayed a marked preference for avoiding strategic discussions with third parties in favour of an Anglo-American dialogue.

The rise and decline of the Middle East as a central component of British strategy is examined in Chapter 10 by John Zametica and Richard Aldrich. Despite bitter resistance by Attlee, in 1946 Bevin and the COS advanced a strategy for a future war dependent upon an air offensive against the Soviet Union from Middle East bases. However, by 1949, a wide range of developments questioned Britain's ability to implement this strategy, not least wavering American support. Two further chapters explore British defence policy east of Suez during the late 1940s: Richard Aldrich (Chapter 11) examines the contradictions that confronted the Attlee government as it attempted at once to escape from the ignominy of colonial rule on the Indian subcontinent, while hoping to retain extensive strategic facilities there. Karl Hack (Chapter 12) explores the perennial nature of the dilemmas posed by Britain's strategic commitments in South East Asia and draws out the ironic parallels between 1939–41 and 1949–51 both in planning against attack on Malaya from the north and in Anglo-Australian defence relations.

Inevitably, there are many additional themes that could have been pursued within this volume; however, there has been a deliberate attempt to avoid rehearsing those subjects which have been examined exhaustively elsewhere. The negotiations leading up to the formation of the North Atlantic Pact, for example, have already received very considerable attention from both American and European historians and the flow of literature on this subject shows no sign of abating. Equally, while the Korean War is discussed obliquely by a number of contributors as one of the key factors that triggered a major reconsideration of British defence policy after 1950, nevertheless the specific issue of British strategy in North East Asia has already been discussed extensively elsewhere.[23]

There remain a wide range of subjects that have not been addressed within this volume because they await the concerted attention of historians. Some of these areas are awkward, but not impossible, to investigate because of the paucity of available documentation. An illustrative example is the question of the relative significance of the British chemical and biological warfare programmes during the late 1940s, alongside the drive to create an independent British nuclear capability. Given that much British thinking concerning strategic air power during the late 1940s was of a long-term nature (assuming war to be unlikely before 1957), their presumption of British access to 'weapons of mass destruction' was understandable. However, more curious is the assumption within even *short-term* emergency planning papers for 1948 and 1949 that Britain would have access to such weapons. Undoubtedly this reflected hopes that the United States would make atomic weapons available, and indeed conduct much of the air offensive herself (although American stocks of atomic weapons were themselves low).[24] Another answer may lie in Britain's definition of 'weapons of mass destruction' as not only atomic but also chemical and biological weapons.[25] The Second World War had witnessed important developments in these other fields.[26] This included the German discovery of nerve gas and American work on Brucella or Malta fever. The potential of these new weapons was fully recognized by the COS in 1945.[27]

In order to understand British interest in chemical and biological weapons in the late 1940s it is important to view this in the context of the devastation of Germany by conventional bombing with which British occupying forces had to contend after 1945. Few were more conscious of this problem than the new Chief of the Imperial General Staff (CIGS), Montgomery, who had commanded the 21st Army as it advanced into Germany's shattered heartland. His remarks in April 1947 to defence scientists on the nature of a future war should be interpreted in this sense:

> The likely effects of biological weapons require equally careful consideration. . . . Since the materials used in the production of bio-logical bombs are relatively plentiful, there is no reason why they should not be used in quantity. . . . It is my opinion that in bacterio-logical warfare we have a weapon that is relatively humane compared to atomic bombs, and which can produce the effect required without any great destruction to inanimate property.[28]

Montgomery's thoughts were shared by the Joint Technical Warfare Committee, who considered biological weapons 'very humane by comparison with atomic bombs' and also relatively free of production problems.[29] Atomic research had also raised the question of using radioactive gases. In 1946 it was noted that these were 'far more deadly, persistent and difficult to counter than any yet known'. In war they would have a use 'parallel to that of the atomic bomb itself but with the advantage that large areas could be rendered uninhabitable without wholesale destruction of buildings etc'.[30] It seems probable then that chemical and biological weapons were seen as complementary to atomic weapons, particularly during a period when the latter might be in short supply. In the late 1940s Britain was spending significant sums on chemical and biological development, particularly given the low cost of this work compared to atomic research. Nevertheless, the drive for atomic weapons remained the top priority.[31]

Certainly the major planning exercises held at the Staff College at Camberley from 1946 presumed possession of a limited number of both atomic and biological weapons 'which it is proposed to employ primarily against enemy industry and morale'.[32] Extensive trials were conducted during the late 1940s on the effectiveness of both chemical and biological weapons.[33] As a result, by 1952, chemical and biological programmes were important aspects of both offensive and defensive planning. One report noted:

1 *Offence*
   Since the war the main activity has been on nerve gases, which are the greatest advance yet made by Chemical Warfare, and it

now has been shown conclusively that these gases would have an outstanding value in the offensive role . . .

2 *Defence*

A new design of respirator for the civilian population, incorporating a big advance as regards both comfort in wear and protection against chemicals and bacteria, has been completed. Mass production of this new design in the many millions required by the Home Office will commence shortly.

3 *The Manufacture of Nerve Gases*

A pilot plant (1 ton/week) for the manufacture of nerve gases is being erected at Nancenuke, Cornwall.[34]

Yet the problem with any attempt to assess the *relative* importance of chemical and biological weapons against the drive for an atomic capability is that their detailed consideration was heavily compartmentalized and conducted by committees whose papers remain closed to public inspection. References within operational planning documents to such subjects as 'the chemical and biological plan for the Middle East' suggest, but cannot confirm, their significance.[35]

While such detailed planning is undoubtedly interesting, chemical and biological weapons may well hold more significance for the understanding of the general development of British post-war strategic thought. For if, after 1945, British planners were thinking in terms of all types of 'weapons of mass destruction', rather than specifically atomic weapons, then their concept of deterrence may have derived less from abstract speculation regarding the atomic bomb and more from almost half a century of practical experience with chemical and biological weapons.[36]

British intelligence during the early Cold War period also offers a wide range of unresolved questions. The opportunities for serious research have been underlined by a number of recent studies relating to Soviet espionage and British security during the 1940s. Typically, careful analysis of the available documentation now suggests that, contrary to the assertions of a number of improbable studies, Roger Hollis, who headed one of the divisions of MI5 during the late 1940s and was later its chief (1955–65), was not a Soviet spy.[37] Meanwhile much can be learnt from a careful examination of the material that passed through the hands of figures such as Donald Maclean and Alec Cairncross.[38] Nevertheless, awkward methodological problems remain, not only in identifying precisely what British material the Soviets received, but also more importantly, what information the Soviets believed and how effectively they interpreted and acted upon it. It is instructive to note that other historians, in examining Soviet intelligence in the 1930s and early 1940s, have demonstrated the depths of Soviet suspicion regarding material obtained by espionage.[39]

Questions of this nature, while awkward, may not be insoluble for the opportunities for research in the East continue to improve.[40]

Finally, in closing the editorial for a volume of this nature, it is customary, indeed almost obligatory, to offer vigorous criticism of the present official policy of withholding many documents relating to intelligence or strategy for the first half of the twentieth century. There can be no doubt that, at the highest level of government, attitudes to this question still persist that are at once so absurd and entertaining that they have recommended themselves as a separate subject for serious academic study. Yet, less conventionally, it might also be remarked that government is not uniformly obstructionist. On the contrary, the great volume of interesting materials at the Public Record Office can hardly be explained in terms of perpetual lapses on the part of the officials that review files before release. More material is available than is commonly suspected and tirades by historians concerning the activities of 'the weeders' are sometimes a substitute for meticulous research. Therefore, this is an appropriate place to thank the staff of the Air Historical Branch, the Foreign Office Library and Records Department and the Cabinet Office Historical Section for their kind and unfailingly helpful attitude in attempting to locate documents for these and other chapters.

NOTES

1 Sterndale Bennett, 25 March 1949, N3357/1051/38, FO 371/77616, PRO.
2 For further discussion of these historiographical shifts see A. Deighton, 'The "Frozen Front": the Labour Government, the Division of Germany and the Origins of the Cold War, 1945–7', *International Affairs* Vol. 63, No. 3 (summer 1987) pp. 449–65; R. Smith, 'A Climate of Opinion: British Officials and the Development of British Soviet Policy, 1945–7', *International Affairs* Vol. 64, No. 4 (autumn 1988), pp. 631–47. For further examples of assertions of Britain's importance see R. Frazier, 'Did Britain Start the Cold War?', *Historical Journal* Vol. 27, No. 3 (1984) pp. 715–27; A. Schlaim, 'Britain, the Berlin Blockade and the Cold War', *International Affairs* Vol. 60, No. 1 (winter 1983/4) pp. 1–14; D. Cameron Watt, 'Britain, the Historiography of the Yalta Conference and the Cold War', *Diplomatic History* Vol. 13, No. 1 (winter 1989), pp. 67–99.
3 For overviews of Cold War historiography see J. L. Gaddis, 'The Emerging Post-revisionist Synthesis and the Origins of the Cold War', *Diplomatic History* Vol. 7, No. 3 (summer 1983), pp. 171–90, and also 'The Corporatist Synthesis: A Skeptical View', *Diplomatic History* Vol. 10, No. 4 (Fall 1986), pp. 357–63; M. J. Hogan, 'Corporatism: A Positive Appraisal', ibid, pp. 363–72; J. S. Walker, 'Historians and Cold War Origins', in G. K. Haines and J. S. Walker (eds) *American Foreign Relations: A Historiographical Review*, (Pinter: London, 1981), pp. 207–36; G. Warner, 'The Study of the Origins of the Cold War', *Diplomacy and Statecraft* Vol. 1, No. 3 (November 1990), pp. 13–26.
4 Even those American historians who have examined European archives have, all too frequently, employed them as a source of new light on American policy rather than as means to a more sophisticated understanding of the Cold War. See for example T. H. Anderson, *The United States, Great Britain and the Cold War, 1944–47* (Columbia: University of Missouri Press, 1981).
5 D. Cameron Watt, 'Rethinking the Cold War: a letter to a British historian', *Political Quarterly*, Vol. 49, No. 4 (1978), pp. 446–56. See also D. Cameron Watt, 'Britain, the United States and the Opening of the Cold War', in R. Ovendale (ed.) *The Foreign*

Policy of the British Labour Governments. 1945–51 (Leicester: Leicester University Press, 1984), pp. 43–61.

6 Two path-breaking studies were A. Bullock, *Ernest Bevin: Foreign Secretary* (London: Heinemann, 1983); V. Rothwell, *Britain and the Cold War, 1941–7* (London: Cape, 1982). Examples of recent work dealing with France include B. Heuser, *Western Containment Policies and the Cold War: The Yugoslav Case* (London: Routledge, 1989); J.W. Young, *France, the Western Alliance and the Cold War, 1944–9* (Leicester: Leicester University Press, 1990).

7 See, for example, J. Zametica (ed.) *British Officials and British Foreign Policy, 1945–50* (Leicester: Leicester University Press, 1990).

8 J. L. Gaddis, *Strategies of Containment* (New York: Oxford University Press, 1982).

9 Z. Steiner, 'Deception and its Dividends', *Times Literary Supplement*, 7–13 December 1990, p. 1,310. For examples of recent American studies see Immerman, *The CIA in Guatemala: The Foreign Policy of Intervention* (Austin: University of Texas, 1982); G. Treverton, *Covert Action: The Limits of Intervention in the Post War World* (New York: William Morrow, 1987); J. E. Miller, 'Taking Off the Gloves: The United States and the Elections of 1948', *Diplomatic History*, Vol. 7, No. 1 (Winter 1983), pp. 35–56; J. Prados, *The Soviet Estimate: U.S. Intelligence Analysis and Soviet Strategic Forces* (New Jersey: Princeton University Press, 1982).

10 J. L. Gaddis discusses Britain at length for the first time in the context of his recent essay, 'Intelligence, Espionage and Cold War Origins', *Diplomatic History*, Vol. 13, No. 2 (Spring 1989), pp. 191–213. See also D. Cameron Watt, 'Intelligence and the Historian: A Comment on John Gaddis's "Intelligence, Espionage and Cold War Origins" ', *Diplomatic History*, Vol. 14, No. 2 (Spring 1990), pp. 199–204.

11 See, for example, P. Weiler, *British Labour and the Cold War* (Stanford, Calif: Stanford University Press, 1988); P. Hennessy and K. Jeffery, *States of Emergency: British Governments and Strikebreaking Since 1919* (London: Routledge & Kegan Paul, 1983).

12 Montagu-Pollock memorandum, 28 July 1946, N9929/5179/38, FO 371/56885, PRO.

13 Aside from the many specific minutes and memoranda that are closed the entire papers of the following committees are closed: Deputy Chiefs of Staff (after 1945), Defence Research Policy Committee, Transition to War Committee, Joint Intelligence Committee, Chemical Warfare Committee, Bacteriological Warfare Committee. DO (47) 44 is now available at CAB 21/1800, PRO.

14 J. Lewis, *Changing Direction: British Military Planning for Post War Strategic Defence* (London: Sherwood, 1988); B. F. Smith, *Shadow Warriors: OSS and the Origins of the CIA* (London: André Deutsch, 1984).

15 The policy regarding the eventual release remains unclear: W. K. Wark, 'A Visit to Never Never Land: the British Intelligence Archives', paper to the joint convention of the International Studies Association and the British International Studies Association, London, 29 May 1989.

16 W. K. Wark, *The Ultimate Enemy: British Intelligence and Nazi Germany, 1933–1939* (London: I. B. Tauris, 1985); C. M. Andrew, 'Churchill and Intelligence', *Intelligence and National Security*, Vol. 3, No. 1 (July 1988), pp. 181–93.

17 C. M. Andrew and O. Gordievsky, *KGB: The Inside Story* (London: Hodder & Stoughton, 1990), pp. 253–9.

18 On PHPS see Lewis, *Changing Direction*, pp. 98–122; A. Gorst, 'British Military Planning for Postwar Defence, 1943–45', in A. Deighton (ed.) *Britain and the First Cold War* (London: Macmillan, 1990), pp. 91–108; Rothwell, *Britain and the Cold War*, pp. 114–23; M. Kitchen, *Britain and the Soviet Union, 1941–5*, (London: Macmillan, 1986), pp. 198–204 and 215–18; J. Baylis, 'British Wartime Thinking About a Post War West European Security Group', *Review of International Studies*, Vol. 9, No. 4 (1983), pp. 273–7.

19 R. W. Manne, *The Petrov Affair: The Politics of Espionage* (Sydney: Pergamon, 1987). Lewis has made some most interesting remarks regarding the circulation of PHPS papers to Donald Maclean, *Changing Direction*, p. 135.

20 cf. pp. 21–2.

21 RC (27) 48, minutes, 16 December 1948, N13677/765/38, FO 371/71687, PRO. cf. p.82 n.20.

22 Gaddis, *Strategies of Containment*.
23 The literature on the birth of NATO now defies comprehensive footnoting: the more prominent works are listed in the bibliography. On Korea see P. Lowe, *The Korean War*; J. Cotton and I. Neary, *The Korean War in History* (Manchester: Manchester University Press, 1989); R. Foot, 'Anglo-American Relations in the Korean Crisis: The British Effort to Avert an Expanded War, December 1950-January 1951', *Diplomatic History*, Vol. 10, No. 2 (Winter 1986), pp. 43–59.
24 G. Herken, *The Winning Weapon: The Atomic Bomb in the Cold War, 1945–50* (New York: Alfred Knopf, 1980).
25 COS (47) 87 (0), 'Future Defence Policy', 23 April 1947, DEFE 5/4, PRO.
26 Lewis, *Changing Direction*, pp. 178–242; see also the important remarks on Churchill on pp. 388–406.
27 TWC (46) 15, 'Future Weapons and Methods of War', 6 July 1946, DEFE 2/1252, PRO.
28 Montgomery, address to the scientists of the Ministry of Supply, 10 April 1947, WO 216/206, PRO.
29 TWC (45) 45, 'Future Development of Bacteriological Warfare', 6 December 1945, DEFE 2/1252, PRO.
30 ICCDS/7, 'Chemical Warfare Problems', April 1946, L/WS/1/990, IOLR.
31 DCOS (46) 224 (Final), 'Service Estimates for the Financial Year 1947/8: Defence Research and Development Programmes', 14 November 1947, L/WS/1/993, IOLR; ICCDS/8, 'Bacteriological Warfare Problems', April 1946, L/WS/1/990, IOLR.
32 Furthermore, for planning purposes it 'will be assumed that gas has already been used in the war', memorandum on the background to CIGS exercises, Camberly, 25 September 1946, WO 216/785, PRO.
33 Ministry of Supply to Colonial Office, 7/Gen/459, 28 October 1948, CO 537/2702, PRO; DCOS (45) 107, 'Chemical Warfare Research in the Tropics', 7 November 1945, L/WS/1/992, IOLR; ICCDS/17 (Final), Annex E, 'Location of Facilities for the Investigation of Bacteriological Warfare Problems', 4 July 1946, ibid.
34 Controller of Supplies memorandum, 'Some Results of Research and Development for the Army Since the End of the War', July 1952, WO 216/648, PRO.
35 COS MELF memorandum, 'Digest on Anglo-American Planning in the Middle East', 27 May 1949, WO 216/312, PRO. In May 1949 Churchill, now in Opposition, expressed dismay that some of Britain's wartime stocks of gas had been loaded into ships and scuttled. He enquired of the CIGS whether all stocks had indeed now been destroyed, Churchill memorandum, 10 May 1949, WO 216/311, PRO.
36 COS (47) 87 (0), 'Future Defence Policy', 23 April 1947, DEFE 5/4, PRO; E. Spiers, *Chemical Warfare* (London: Macmillan, 1986).
37 S. Kerr, 'Roger Hollis and the Dangers of the Anglo-Soviet Treaty of 1942', *Intelligence and National Security*, Vol. 5, No. 3 (July 1990), pp. 148–58.
38 S. Kerr, 'The Secret Hotline to Moscow: Donald Maclean and the Berlin Crisis of 1948', in A. Deighton (ed.) *Britain and the First Cold War* (London: Macmillan, 1990), pp. 71–87; Andrew and Gordievsky, *KGB*.
39 The classic study is B. Whaley, *Codeword BARBAROSSA* (Cambridge, Mass.: MIT Press, 1973). See also G. Gorodetsky, 'Churchill's Warning to Stalin: A Reappraisal', *Historical Journal*, Vol. 29, No. 4 (1986), pp. 979–90.
40 An archival project was recently established in Washington DC by the National Intelligence Study Consortium under Dr Roy Godson to hold historical materials from the archives of Eastern bloc intelligence and security services.

Part I

INTELLIGENCE

THE 'COLD WAR'

The Directors of Intelligence ... set about it in no uncertain way. Their paper reviewed Communist policy, emphasized that the keystone of this policy was the inevitability of a struggle in order to establish Communism throughout the earth, and summed up the Communist policy by saying that the only method of preventing the Russian threat from ever materializing is by utterly defeating Russian Communism.

For the first time in our history a totalitarian organization of states is attempting to impose its will upon us by undiplomatic means other than armed conflict – conveniently described as 'cold war'. We could not win the 'cold war' unless we carried our offensive inside Russia and the satellite states. In fact what was required was a worldwide offensive, using every available agency. To date we had failed to unify our forces to oppose Soviet 'cold war' aggression.

It was agreed ... that the whole question of intelligence about Russia should be reviewed.... Perhaps at this late hour there will be a proper set-up to control and direct this very important aspect of our national defence. It must also be hoped that the clock is not on the point of striking.

(Montgomery, September 1948)

1

Secret intelligence for a post-war world: reshaping the British intelligence community, 1944–51

Richard J. Aldrich

It has been argued that a coherent and relatively well-ordered British intelligence 'community' emerged only during the Second World War, in no small part due to the efforts of Winston Churchill.[1] In this chapter it will be suggested that attempts to perpetuate this overall coherence beyond 1945 lost their way in the bureaucratic and political upheavals at the end of the war. These upheavals found their focus not only within Whitehall and Westminster but also in remarkable public exchanges during the election campaign of June 1945. The process of reshaping Britain's intelligence community remained *ad hoc* and incremental until the emergence of controversial centralized 'Cold War planning' mechanisms in late 1948.

Because of the absence of any comprehensive restructuring, the late 1940s were a period of continuity rather than radical change for the intelligence community. Confronted with the unfamiliar problems of an East-West conflict conducted 'by all means short of war', Whitehall gradually returned to the doctrines of the wartime subversive organizations, the Special Operations Executive (SOE) and the Political Warfare Executive (PWE), for a response. Elements of SOE and PWE were revived on an *ad hoc* basis even before they had reached a state of complete dissolution. Important continuities of personnel and doctrine were thus facilitated. Similar observations could be made regarding inter-allied co-operation: the Cold War spurred the elaboration of a network of pre-existing wartime agreements between the English-speaking powers. Meanwhile, the nature of the changes that *did* occur in 1945 and 1946 can also be seen as a legacy of the war, leaving a variety of bureaucratic scores to settle within Whitehall. These often found their expression in the individual post-war reviews conducted within each separate intelligence service.

In 1945 the recognition of the increased danger of surprise attack due to the advent of weapons of mass destruction and also ballistic rockets ensured that there was no possibility of the rapid contraction of intelligence services, as had occurred in 1919. The Chiefs of Staff (COS) now gave a high priority to 'national' or 'strategic' intelligence with Soviet strategic weapons development as the highest priority intelligence target. Thus intelligence appears to have suffered less under post-war austerity than other aspects of defence. As early as 1945, Victor Cavendish-Bentinck, the retiring chairman of the Joint Intelligence Committee, persuaded the COS of the principle that the intelligence structure should remain intact.[2] In May 1947, as austerity began to bite hard, the COS reaffirmed this in their definitive statement of 'Future Defence Policy', DO (47) 44. They insisted that within the Soviet Union

> the high standard of security achieved renders our collection of intelligence difficult and makes it all the more likely that Russia will have the advantage of surprise at the outset. . . .
>
> It is of the greatest importance that our Intelligence organisation should be able to provide us with adequate and timely warning. The smaller the armed forces the greater the need for developing our Intelligence Services in peace to enable them to fulfil this responsibility.[3]

But, for a variety of complex reasons that will now be explored, this sense of high importance was never translated into a comprehensive attempt to review and recast Whitehall's intelligence system to meet new conditions.

INTELLIGENCE AT THE TOP

One of the most important legacies of the Second World War was a relatively integrated intelligence community, rather than a coterie of separate agencies. Until the late 1930s, Britain lacked not only an organization that oversaw the systematic collation, evaluation and interpretation of intelligence, but also any central body responsible for the co-ordination of the various services. The mechanism which increasingly addressed these functions after its reorganization in July 1939 was the Joint Intelligence Committee (JIC), a COS subcommittee, albeit chaired by a senior Foreign Office official. During the war the JIC undertook not only interpretation but also a managerial role, being instructed to 'improve the efficient working of the intelligence organisation of the country as a whole'. This extended to resolving arguments between different intelligence services.[4] Changes in the role of the JIC in the post-war period offer important insights into the problems of reshaping intelligence for peacetime duties.

After 1945, the JIC remained the focus of strategic intelligence and an important link between the military, the diplomats and the intelligence community. Chaired by the head of the Foreign Office Service Liaison Department, the membership of the JIC included the heads of Service intelligence departments and of SIS and MI5 (the Security Service), with others in regular attendance.[5] Although the JIC received a new charter on

17 February 1948 emphasizing its established military role, 'giving higher direction to operations of defence intelligence and security', in practice its remit remained wider.[6] Significantly, in 1948 and at the suggestion of the Foreign Secretary, Ernest Bevin, the JIC membership was expanded to incorporate a Colonial Office member, reflecting the growing insurgency problems in areas like Malaya.[7] The extent to which the JIC continued to be the primary form of work-a-day intelligence co-ordination was underlined by the decision to retain the subordinate regional JICs that had developed within wartime commands in Europe, the Middle East and Asia.[8]

The co-ordinating work of the JIC was supplemented by a plethora of additional mechanisms. Wartime dissatisfaction with liaison between SIS and its political master, the Foreign Office, had led to the appointment of a Foreign Office official, Patrick Reilly, as Personal Assistant to Sir Stuart Menzies, the Chief of SIS, in 1942. In 1943 Reilly was succeeded by Robert Cecil, who remained until 1946. In addition the London Signals Intelligence Board and Committee co-ordinated signals intelligence matters while the London Controlling Section dealt with deception: all three survived into the post-war period. Meanwhile much business was conducted at the informal level in the clubland of Pall Mall (especially Whites).[9] As such, the JIC, until 1949, remained the hub of a complex wheel.

Economic austerity was an important motive behind the creation of a new topographic intelligence centre serving the JIC, the Joint Intelligence Bureau (JIB) headed by Eisenhower's wartime intelligence chief, General Strong.[10] Its inter-Service nature was intended to 'prevent overlapping and achieve economy', while obtaining its information 'from all overt sources and SIS'.[11] The JIB defined its role in grandiose terms, but in reality the JIB merely collated topographic and economic intelligence along with political background of the sort required for operational planning at the inter-Service level.[12] Their initial tasks included surveys of Empire ports and of the Persian Gulf. At their first meeting in 1946 they declared their intention of establishing regional JIBs along the lines of the JIC.[13] The result was a JIB Middle East and a JIB Australia covering the Far East with a small outstation at Singapore.[14]

Despite this elaboration of the JIC system, problems remained. The JIC had, above all, been established as part of the machinery for the higher strategic direction of the war, assisting in the incorporation of 'ultra' signals intelligence material into command decisions. But it was less effective in co-ordinating and adjudicating between the myriad intelligence services and organizations tasked with subversive activities such as propaganda (PWE) and guerrilla warfare (SOE), a role the JIC shared with a number of Foreign Office committees.[15] Co-ordination was complicated by the fact that SOE came under its own separate ministry.

Consequently, in wartime Whitehall, as the diaries of senior figures such as Cadogan, Dalton or Lockhart testify, these subversive organizations had quickly become a byword for back-biting and administrative confusion.[16]

Arguably, until 1945 this co-ordination problem had been ignored because subversion, while not insignificant, was nevertheless peripheral compared to the grand strategic direction of the war. But subsequently, in the context of an East-West conflict conducted by all means short of war, subversion and other forms of covert action would increasingly constitute central instruments in this struggle. Particularly with the advent of the Soviet Cominform in the autumn of 1947, the Foreign Office moved towards a containment policy that included elements of 'offence' as well as defence, requiring it to resolve the familiar wartime problem of the co-ordination of a wide range of clandestine agencies and their activities, particularly unacknowledged or 'black' propaganda. In 1948 pressure from the COS and from permanent officials in the Foreign Office prompted discussions on the need for a 'permanent Cold War planning staff' to manage this clandestine effort. Subsequent moves to establish a central planning apparatus, albeit reluctant and dogged by acrimony, constituted a critical turning-point in the higher direction of the British intelligence community.

This process began with the discussion of an important JIC report prepared in January 1946 analysing Soviet capabilities and intentions.[17] Responding to this JIC paper, Frank Roberts, a relatively junior but influential diplomat in Moscow (like his American counterpart George Kennan), suggested that the Soviet Union was pursuing a global policy, not least because of 'the ubiquitous activities of the communist parties directed, if not controlled in detail from Moscow'. Roberts remarked that this problem should be analysed by a new body that could overcome the geographical separation of Foreign Office departments and co-ordinate a global British response.[18] Once constituted, this new body, the Russia Committee (RC), was concerned with analysing the development of all aspects of Soviet policy and propaganda throughout the world, giving particular attention to the Soviet campaign against Britain. During its weekly meetings it was also required to make policy recommendations. The committee was to maintain close contact with the JIC 'with a view to co-ordinating intelligence and policy at every stage'.[19] Yet it might well be asked, was the JIC not already providing this sort of analysis through its regular reports on Soviet capabilities and intentions?

There appear to have been at least two reasons why the Foreign Office opted for its own separate analytical committee in parallel to the JIC. First, as Smith and Merrick have made clear in correcting a previous erroneous discussion of the RC, senior officials, such as Christopher Warner of the Northern Department, were anxious to establish a key committee not under the Cabinet or the COS, but controlled by the

Foreign Office.[20] This decision seems to reflect unhappy wartime experiences with two interdepartmental committees shared with the military in the context of a fierce debate over future Soviet intentions. In 1944, amid much acrimony, the Foreign Office withdrew from one of these committees, responsible for framing Britain's future strategic requirements, when it began to advocate the use of Germany as a bulwark against a post-war Soviet threat.[21] Subsequently, the Foreign Office appears to have used its chairmanship of the JIC to blunt the anti-Soviet thinking of the military.[22] Although by 1946 the distance between diplomatic and military perceptions of Soviet intentions had narrowed, the diplomats had had their fill of interdepartmental committees with the COS.[23] The RC, formed in 1946, offered the Foreign Office *independent* high-level appreciation.

The second reason that the JIC would not suffice was that the RC was also required to plan Britain's counter-strategy, the response to what Warner described as 'the Russian Campaign Against this Country'.[24] At its formation the Permanent Under-Secretary, Sir Orme Sargent, noted that 'it would be valuable to have a Joint Planning Committee of this kind for matters concerning the Russians since the Russians themselves clearly planned their campaign and therefore it made sense to try and assess their plan and make joint office counter-plans'.[25] Therefore, while desiring 'independence' from the JIC and other COS subcommittees, at the same time the many diplomats who regularly attended COS meetings admired their business-like approach to planning. Sir William Hayter, who chaired the JIC between 1947 and 1949, recalls that he pressed for a planning section within the Foreign Office precisely because he was impressed by the COS system.[26]

In 1946 senior officials clearly envisaged the RC as the planning centre for a 'defensive–offensive' strategy which would form a response to the Soviets. In May, in support of this, the RC instructed an official called Ivone Kirkpatrick to draw up a programme for a propaganda offensive, which involved the BBC, Chatham House and the Press. His recommendations drew on his own wartime experience of subversion by SOE and PWE:

> The V sign was emblazoned all over the world. But at the same time we acted. We parachuted men, money and arms into occupied territory. We were not inhibited by fear that the Germans would find out what we were doing, or that they might react or that we might be criticised. Propaganda on the larger scale was co-ordinated with our policy. The result was a success.

Sargent, the Permanent Under-Secretary, was convinced that Kirkpatrick's proposal was on the right lines but Bevin, never an enthusiast of covert activities, resisted.[27] Even after Bevin acceded to more rigorous propaganda in 1947 in response to the formation of the Cominform, he remained at best lukewarm in his attitude towards offensive policies.[28]

Kirkpatrick's proposals not only were important in prefiguring a later 'liberation' strategy towards the Eastern bloc adopted by the Western allies during late 1948, but also were critical in reshaping the control of subversion. During the war diplomatic opinion had wavered between those who, like Eden, periodically declared that SOE must come under direct Foreign Office control and those, like Cadogan, who railed against the idea of the Foreign Office becoming 'a department store' with co-ordinating responsibility for all sorts of 'fantastic' activities.[29] Kirkpatrick, more than most diplomats, understood co-ordination problems, having worked closely with both SOE and PWE as wartime controller of the BBC European Services. Kirkpatrick had been vitriolic in his criticism of the management of both organizations at the end of the war.[30] Consequently, he was among those determined to extend future Foreign Office control over subversion.

The prospects for Foreign Office control improved in the autumn of 1947. Confronted with the activities of the new Soviet Cominform, Bevin softened his reservations regarding covert propaganda. Significantly, rather than expanding the remnants of wartime PWE, a new body was created within the Foreign Office to conduct propaganda, the Information Research Department (IRD).[31] The importance of IRD is clearly difficult to overestimate. Before 1950, when defence programmes were being cut and the intelligence services were pleased to hold their programmes steady, IRD was expanding rapidly. By the early 1950s the IRD, working closely with SIS, constituted one of the Foreign Office's largest departments. Propaganda remains perhaps the most inadequately explored aspect of Britain's Cold War. Accordingly, IRD is examined at length elsewhere within this volume.[32]

But the strongest impetus for a co-ordinated counter-strategy came not from Warner and Kirkpatrick, but from the military. By 1948 the COS were enduring a twofold sense of frustration. First, they believed that the Cold War was being lost through an insufficiently rigorous approach on the part of the Foreign Office. Second, they believed that possible Soviet political gains in Europe or the Mediterranean would leave them in an untenable strategic position at the outbreak of war, or might even require them to initiate a war for which they were not yet prepared. The COS had voiced their concern at the West's lack of initiative in both December 1947 and May 1948, contributing to the pressure for the creation of IRD.[33] However, in August 1948, and to Bevin's dismay, accelerating tensions prompted the COS to press hard for both a centralized Cold War planning staff *with military participation* and offensive measures far beyond propaganda.

On 6 August the COS began by requesting a 'forecast of Russian moves' from the Foreign Office. However, they paid more attention to a parallel paper by the Directors of Intelligence of the three Services that warned in the strongest possible terms of a coming struggle to 'establish Communism throughout the earth'. Their prescription for counteraction was radical,

> the only way of preventing the Russian threat from materialising is by utterly defeating Russian Communism. . . . We couldn't win the 'cold war' unless we carried our offensive inside Russia and the satellite states. In fact what was required was a world wide offensive, using every available agency.

They called for a body that not only would oversee the higher direction of the conflict, but also was capable of 'controlling all executive action'.

On 9 and 10 September the Minister of Defence, A. V. Alexander, the COS and Kirkpatrick (representing the Foreign Office) considered these two papers at an extraordinary two-day staff conference. On the first day Lord Tedder, speaking for the COS, deplored the present conduct of the Cold War as 'completely inadequate' and called instead for the employment of all measures 'short of actual shooting'. Suggesting an interdepartmental planning body to do this, he qualified this thinly veiled attack upon Bevin and his officials by adding that this body 'should not be taken out of the hands of the Foreign Secretary'. Alexander, taken aback, suggested that these views should be 'watered down' before they were conveyed to Bevin. The following day Alexander reported that he had done so, but taking care to emphasize 'that the COS would be the last to criticize or embarrass' him.

On the second day Kirkpatrick also explained to the COS that they were 'incorrect' in presuming that IRD was the only Cold War mechanism, adding that 'the Russia Committee is in fact the Cold War Planning Staff'. In propaganda they were assisted by IRD 'and by the Head of the European Service of the BBC'. It was generally agreed that COS membership of RC was now required. But in two senses the military faced impediments in their efforts to stiffen Britain's conduct of the Cold War. First, their initiative, albeit watered down by Alexander, was clearly an attack upon Bevin and was unlikely to receive a sympathetic hearing. Second, while many permanent officials in the Foreign Office accepted the military prescription for an offensive 'using every agency', Bevin did not. Kirkpatrick categorically warned the staff conference that 'The Foreign Secretary was inclined to the view that covert activities would not pay a dividend'.[34]

The COS met with initial success in the autumn of 1948 since senior Foreign Office officials were agreed on the danger of 'losing the Cold War' and that their response should be accelerated. The RC was now expanded to include Tedder as the COS representative, thus constituting the 'Cold War planning staff' that the military had called for.[35] On 25 November 1948 the enlarged RC met for the first time to consider a paper by Robin Hankey, head of the Northern Department, entitled 'British policy towards the Soviet orbit in Europe'. Their subsequent recommendations indicated substantial agreement between the diplomats and the COS and called for

1 loosening the Soviet hold on the orbit countries and ultimately enabling them to regain their independence.
2 pending the attainment of this relatively long-term objective, we should aim at promoting civil discontent, internal confusion and possibly strife in satellite countries so that they will be a source not of strength but of weakness to Russia.

At the centre of this discussion was the use of 'PWE and SOE' methods. Tedder, in bombastic mood, looked forward to the collapse of the Soviet regime 'in the next five years'. To this end, Tedder suggested forming 'a small permanent team which would consider plans which would subsequently be executed by ourselves and the Americans'. Tedder's proposal met with general agreement, as did his contention that 'it was important to bring in the Americans at as early a stage as possible'. At a further meeting of the RC in December 1948, General Ian Jacob, head of the BBC European Services also suggested that for such operations the Foreign Office 'like the Service Ministries should have a director of plans'. A permanent 'Cold War subcommittee' of the RC was thus established.[36] The control of subversion during the possible future 'hot war' was also under discussion.[37]

Bevin came under further pressure from the military in the form of an initiative by Slessor, Commandant of the Imperial Defence College (IDC). His report in November 1948 revealed that senior strategists had employed the IDC as a forum for detailed discussion of the prosecution of the Cold War, calling, like the COS, for expanded machinery and a planning section for 'day-to-day operations'. In March 1949 the ever-tactful Alexander forwarded some of the less acerbic sections of Slessor's report to Attlee, who subsequently raised these points with Bevin. The Foreign Office were clearly stung by the implied rebuke, noting that Alexander's action 'in writing to the PM criticizing Foreign Office internal machinery is . . . decidedly odd'. They saw this as a 'revival' of the criticisms by the COS that had caused Bevin 'concern' in late 1948.[38] In the short term, Bevin appears to have resisted both attempts to allow a larger military role in Cold War planning, and any widespread offensive programme. Instead he permitted a special committee limited to consideration of activities to destabilize Albania only. More elaborate developments awaited the outbreak of the Korean War and advent of Herbert Morrison as Foreign Secretary.[39]

In 1949 the Foreign Office continued to develop its long-term planning machinery, but with care to avoid an interdepartmental element. Interest was also taken in George Kennan's State Department Policy Planning Staff (PPS), established in 1947. The result was the formation of the Permanent Under-Secretaries Committee (PUSC) in February 1949 wherein there was no COS representation. The PUSC, which met frequently, normally consisted of the Permanent Under-Secretary, Lord Strang, a junior minister and the Deputy and Assistant Under-Secretaries including an official specifically responsible for security and intelligence.[40] Many of the papers generated by this committee remain closed and its precise remit cannot be determined. However, it is clear that this new body, supported by a complete department (PUSD), absorbed some important machinery including the Service Liaison Department and also worked closely with the RC. By the early 1950s, PUSC/PUSD had to some extent displaced the JIC in its wartime role as a co-ordinating body for intelligence and subversion. In 1954, when a programme of economies was being imposed upon the British intelligence community, it was the PUSD that prepared an interdepartmental report for consideration not only by PUSC but also by the COS. Had this sort of exercise been undertaken even in 1947 it would undoubtedly have fallen to the JIC.[41]

Consequently, in the late 1940s intelligence at the top was characterized by two contradictory trends: continuity, represented by the survival of the JIC system as the ultimate authority on the interpretation of intelligence; but also change, denoted by a contemporaneous drive on the part of some diplomats and the COS for better co-ordination of subversion. This advanced in parallel with pressure from the COS for a more aggressive policy towards the Eastern bloc. The incremental nature of these changes begs the awkward question: when did Britain's 'liberation' activities actually begin? In the Foreign Office files the conceptual origins seem to lie with Kirkpatrick and Warner in the spring of 1946, albeit these ideas found little concrete expression other than propaganda before 1949. But the extent to which these ideas may have been prefigured elsewhere in Whitehall confounds any suggestion of orderly evolution. On the one hand, Tom Bower, on the basis of aural evidence, has established that officers of the Secret Intelligence Service (SIS) were already introducing a small number of agents into the Baltic states as early as the autumn of 1945. On the other hand, this early Baltic episode may have amounted to no more than an attempt to gather intelligence. Moreover, in the field the boundary between intelligence and subversion is rarely clear.[42] What is certain is that SIS, which was under direct, but not always close, Foreign Office control, had turned its attention to forming a new Soviet section as early as the summer of 1944. It is to these precocious developments that we must now turn.

SIS (MI6): THE SECRET INTELLIGENCE SERVICE

In the post-war period SIS retained its traditional role of intelligence gathering and of counter-espionage duties outside British territory. The reorganization of SIS after 1944 merits early consideration for it illustrates how significant reforms often emerged as a result of uncoordinated initiatives from within each service. SIS is also of special interest because, along with certain military planners under the COS, and in contrast to the Foreign Office, it was quick to embrace the concept of a future Soviet adversary, certainly no later than the summer of 1944. Remarkably, these developments were observed by the Soviets with limpid clarity by virtue of Kim Philby's central role in the reform of SIS.

By 1944 SIS officers were enjoying a good war, basking in the reflected glory of the triumphs of GCHQ and 'Ultra', over which they exercised control. Moreover, signals intelligence had also facilitated SIS work against the Axis secret services. Thus under Colonel Cowgill, the SIS counter-espionage department, Section V, had expanded from a handful of staff to a complement of 250 by 1944. This expansion resulted in friction with MI5, which was responsible for counter-espionage within British territory. In 1944 the focus of this expanded SIS counter-espionage effort began to change. Kim Philby, a rising star in Cowgill's Section V, recalled that 'senior officers in SIS began to turn their thoughts to the next enemy . . . and a modest start was made by setting up a small section, known as Section IX, to study past records of Soviet and Communist activity'. The exact source of this initiative is not clear. However, at a time when the corridors of SIS were full of forecasts of post-war reorganization this held attractions for senior SIS officers, for it seemed to hold out the prospect of a continued SIS foothold in post-war counter-espionage work.[43]

The management of the 'modest' Section IX was offered to Philby, rather than Cowgill. By late 1944 Philby was recruiting new staff for his section which was not yet operative, including Robert Carew-Hunt, who prepared background papers on Communism.[44] Recently, in an important essay, Robert Cecil, who was the Foreign Office Personal Assistant to the Chief of SIS, has made clear that far from attempting to strangulate the Soviet section, Philby sought to expand his new province. Robert Cecil recalls:

In February or early March 1945 there arrived on my desk the . . . charter for Section IX. It included a substantial number of [positions in] overseas stations to be held by officers under diplomatic cover, who would be directly responsible to the Head of Section IX. . . . Quite apart from his covert aims, it is also clear that he foresaw more plainly than I the onset of the Cold War, bringing with it more menacing surveillance and making necessary more permanent use of diplomatic cover. My vision of the future was at once more opaque and more optimistic; I sent the memorandum back to Philby suggesting that he might scale down his demands. Within hours Vivian [the Deputy Chief of SIS] and Philby had descended on me, upholding their requirements and insisting that these be transmitted to the Foreign Office. . . . I gave way; but I have since reflected with a certain wry amusement on the hypocrisy of Philby who . . . demanded a larger Cold War apparatus, when he could have settled for a smaller one.[45]

Thus, in 1944 SIS had begun to re-equip itself with a specifically Soviet section, albeit under the direction of Kim Philby.

In early 1945 SIS, like other services, was subjected to a somewhat toothless general inquiry into the Whitehall intelligence structure headed by Brigadier Sir Findlater Stewart. This inquiry had little impact upon SIS, or indeed anything else, and instead SIS chose to appoint their own Reorganization Committee in September 1945. This committee, consisting of senior SIS administrative staff, Philby and a representative of GCHQ, were responsible for the post-war shape of SIS. The fundamental question which they confronted was whether SIS should be organized along lines of geographical specialization, by country, or along lines of functional specialization, focused upon subjects such as economic, political and scientific intelligence. A compromise was adopted. SIS would henceforth be divided into five sections. The two most important sections were: Production (Section II) – responsible for the operational gathering of intelligence and organized on *geographical* lines with regional controllers; and Requirements (Section III) – responsible for analysis and distribution which was organized on *functional* lines. Under this new system Philby commanded the key part of Requirements (R5) devoted to world-wide Communism. The other elements were Section I, for Administration and Finance; Section IV, for Training and Development, addressing the growing demand for technical resources; while Section V dealt with planning for a future war. This basic pattern of organization remained unchanged for many years.[46]

Overseas, equally sweeping (if less uniform) changes were underway. During the war SIS had attached regional headquarters to the theatre commands in the Middle East and Far East. Although SIS retained these after 1945 they were eventually moved from military to diplomatic accommodation. In the Middle East this was accompanied by a decision to abandon the long-compromised local cover name for SIS, the 'Inter-Service Liaison Department' (ISLD) and to adopt the new cover name, 'Combined Research and Planning Organization' (CRPO: pronounced 'Creepo'). Accordingly, CRPO moved from the 'Grey Pillars' compound of GHQ Middle East to the Sharia Tolumbat compound, where it shared the diplomatic facilities of the British Middle East Office (BMEO).[47] Similarly, in Singapore, the SIS Regional Director was located alongside the new Foreign Office Special Commissioner for South East Asia.[48] In contrast to Cairo and Singapore, an entirely different system was employed in Germany and Austria, where SIS operated very large stations, under the cover of the Political Division of the Control Commissions and also the Civil Affairs and intelligence sections of formations such as the 21st Army Group. For both SIS and the CIA, Germany constituted the front line of the European Cold War.[49]

These regional SIS centres enjoyed a strong local identity: so much so that in 1945 the Middle East Defence Committee called for the creation of an entirely separate and specialist Middle East Intelligence Service. Certainly in the Persian Gulf, SIS often found itself dealing with local political issues far removed from those of the Cold War.[50] No Middle Eastern service was created but the JIC recognized that while the head of CRPO 'was responsible directly to SIS in London', nevertheless, in practice, he would more frequently fulfil 'local intelligence requirements'.[51]

Perhaps the greatest source of satisfaction for SIS in the immediate post-war period stemmed from its success in absorbing its wartime sister service, SOE, which had been responsible for special operations. Although SOE lobbied hard for an independent post-war existence their tendency to play a 'semi-lone hand' and to develop their own foreign policy had made many enemies in the Foreign Office and in Whitehall generally. Meanwhile commanders in the field had complained of too many different agencies 'all with direct access to the great, too often crossing each other's wires and cutting each other's throats'.[52] In contrast they pointed to the USA's wartime secret service (OSS) which combined both secret intelligence and special operations functions.[53] Therefore in January 1946 Sir Stuart Menzies, the Chief of SIS, supported by the Chief of the Imperial General Staff and the chairman of the JIC, decided that SOE should be pared down to form a small and subordinate section of SIS, the 'Special Operations Branch'.[54] While this solution suited the bureaucratic politics of Whitehall, invaluable SOE expertise was lost. Peversely, in 1949, when SIS was called upon to conduct special operations in support of 'liberation' strategies against the Eastern bloc, they found their in-house capabilities inadequate and so were forced hastily to reassemble old SOE sections. Equally, outside Europe, some elements of SOE were considered too valuable to be dispensed with and were pressed into service in a counter-insurgency context in Palestine, Greece and Malaya. Yet others were kept in place in Austria and Germany as possible 'stay behind' parties in case of a Soviet invasion.[55] However, while significant parts of SOE fought on into the post-war period, the transfer of personnel and doctrine from SOE to SIS was anything but ideal. Reflecting on this episode Robert Cecil has noted: 'SOE was liquidated with almost indecent haste. If relations with SIS had been more cordial, one first-class organization could have been created out of the best of two elements but the chance was missed'.[56]

Another competitor in the special operations field at the end of the war was the Special Air Service (SAS). However, although the War Office completed a favourable investigation into special operations and their relation to SIS activities, financial stringency ensured the abolition of the two regular SAS regiments.[57] Only vigorous lobbying on the part of senior SAS officers ensured the formation of a territorial SAS regiment, thus securing a vital nucleus for expansion during the 1950s. Meanwhile, having absorbed SOE and created its own war planning section, SIS now seemed to hold the monopoly on special operations in both peace and war.[58]

SIGNALS INTELLIGENCE AND SCIENTIFIC INTELLIGENCE

At what point in the 1940s Britain recommenced its pre-war work on intercepting and breaking Soviet communications remains a mystery. Britain's codebreaking organization (GCHQ) operated under formal SIS control until 1946 and, as we have seen, SIS slowly began to redirect its own attention towards the Soviet Union as early as 1944. But it has been asserted by Professor Hinsley, in his magisterial official history of British intelligence, that work on Soviet communications ceased with Germany's attack on the USSR in June 1941 for the duration of the war. However, in one sense at least, Britain was regularly reading Soviet communications, albeit at second hand, as early as 1943. In the initial stages of the war, Britain had broken the cipher key used by the German Air Force's own signals intelligence organization, who listened to Soviet communications on the Eastern Front. Consequently, when the German Air Force transmitted this intelligence material back to Berlin, it was also collected by GCHQ. As a result, as early as 1943, the JIC were able to produce detailed and accurate reports on the capabilities of the Soviet Air Force, based on Soviet material decrypted by the Germans.[59]

Britain enjoyed no post-war equivalent to the extraordinary achievements of 'Ultra' in decrypting Axis signals during the war. In direct contrast when GCHQ recommenced work against Soviet communications the results were poor. The Soviets, like the British, employed a 'One Time Pad' system based upon random numbers which, if employed correctly, was impenetrable. Soviet operators' errors allowed the West to make painfully slow (but nevertheless invaluable) progress with some KGB communications traffic as early as 1947, but this success was exceptional.[60]

Nevertheless, GCHQ's wartime reputation had ensured adequate funding for its post-war activities, an essential prerequisite as code-breaking had begun to enter the expensive 'mechanized' era with primitive computers constructed at the laboratories of the Post Office Research Department at

Dollis Hill in North London. It was no coincidence that in 1945, with GCHQ having outgrown its curious collection of Nissen huts at Bletchley Park, its director, Sir Edward Travis, should have chosen to move his organization to a site only a few miles away from Dollis Hill at Eastcote in the suburbs of north-west London. Here it remained until 1952 when it relocated to Cheltenham, reportedly chosen for less utilitarian reasons.[61]

GCHQ's priority intelligence target in the late 1940s, Soviet strategic weapons development, was dictated by Britain's perceived vulnerability to the new weapons of mass destruction. Other Soviet military activities (including espionage) and Soviet diplomacy constituted second and third priorities.[62] The extent to which Britain and indeed, the United States, were surprised by the Tito-Stalin split in 1948 and by the first Soviet atomic bomb in 1949, confirms that GCHQ enjoyed little success against high-level Soviet communications during the late 1940s.[63] Major advances were not made until the interception of Soviet landlines in the 1950s.

After 1945 GCHQ was also reorganizing to attack the communications of states with more vulnerable cipher systems. The JIC required GCHQ to examine, albeit with a lower priority, subjects such as 'Arab nationalism and relations of Arab states with UK and USA', the 'Attitude of Soviet Union, France, Italy and Arab states towards future of the ex-Italian colonies, especially Libya' and the 'Zionist movement including its intelligence services'.[64] Information on these GCHQ activities is sparse, but Alan Stripp, in his valuable memoir, recalls that at the end of the war in Asia he was quickly redeployed to the Iranian border to work on Iranian and indeed Afghan communications during the Ajerbaijan Crisis of 1946.[65]

If GCHQ's success against Soviet ciphers was modest, their political fortunes were more impressive. Not only did GCHQ escape from the direct control of SIS in 1946, coming instead under the Foreign Office, but also GCHQ gained control of the new field of electronic intelligence or 'elint', the analysis of the emissions of radars and air defence systems. This was undertaken with the help of the RAF Central Signals Establishment at Watton and was often conducted from specially modified Lincoln or Washington aircraft which operated in both Europe and the Middle East. By 1949 work was underway on a specialist elint aircraft. Much effort was also directed towards low-level Soviet voice traffic in the Eastern bloc.[66]

Although the COS were determined that, despite post-war austerity, GCHQ would not be allowed to slip into decline, nevertheless its increasingly expensive technical work clearly encountered resource problems. This was also the case for the RAF's photographic reconnaissance units (PRUs). In 1946 the Admiralty complained of staff shortages for signals intelligence leading to a review by Air Chief Marshal Sir Douglas Evill on behalf of the COS. The problem remained unresolved and in April 1949 the Admiralty Board were still lamenting that naval intercept stations were 'more than 10% short of their authorized personnel complements'. Moreover, while they recognized that valuable results could be achieved by mobile intercept stations in wartime there was presently 'little effort in this direction'. The disparity between increasing costs and Britain's defence budget lent added urgency to Anglo-American-Commonwealth signals intelligence co-operation, offering shared costs as well as information. Western co-operation in this area is one of the most significant developments of the 1940s and is therefore addressed below in some detail.[67]

Arguably, scientific intelligence should have received enormous post-war emphasis in Britain, not only because of its extraordinary wartime achievements, but also because of the significance of new strategic weapons. However, this crucial area was initially neglected by the COS, while the internal reform of scientific intelligence was left to another *ad hoc* committee and proved to be extremely ill advised. It is indicative of this neglect that the first post-war COS report on 'Future Developments in Weapons and Methods of War' (produced in July 1945) was roundly condemned by R. V. Jones, the head of RAF scientific intelligence, for its minimal attention to this subject.[68] Slessor, who would eventually replace Tedder as Chief of the Air Staff, was equally scathing on its failure to mention the need for 'a very efficient organisation for Scientific and Technical intelligence' for use, if necessary, against Britain's allies as well as her adversaries. The development of atomic weapons and ballistic rockets, he continued, underlined the 'vital importance of maintaining a really efficient Secret Intelligence Service and developing long range stratospheric Photo Reconnaissance aircraft'.[69] Despite these stern criticisms, a redrafted version of this paper in June 1946, taking account of new information on atomic warfare, was not much better. By March 1947 Sir Stuart Menzies, the Chief of SIS, was expressing concern to the COS regarding the weakness of scientific and technical intelligence.[70]

R. V. Jones, in his autobiographical accounts of this period, has condemned the post-war reorganization of Britain's scientific intelligence as an unmitigated disaster. New documents recently opened to public inspection bear him out. In the spring of 1945 the initiative was taken by the Admiralty, who suggested the formation of a special JIC subcommittee on the matter, to be chaired by the scientist P. M. S. Blackett. The other members were Edward Gollin, the scientist in the Naval Intelligence Department, Charles Ellis, the War Office scientist, and R. V. Jones. In May 1945 R. V. Jones put his own paper up to this committee. Never shy of confronting major questions, he rejected the 'lessons of our war experience' as a guide to post-war organization, pointing out that captured enemy documents and personnel would no longer be available and that they would now depend largely on human agents and signals intelligence.

Both these sources were under SIS control in 1945 and so he suggested that scientific intelligence should reside there.[71]

However, R. V. Jones's proposals were rejected by Blackett in favour of an inter-Service organization theoretically focused upon the consumers of its intelligence, the Service departments, rather than the producers, SIS. Each Service intelligence department was to have a scientific section headed by a scientific intelligence adviser to liaise with research programmes. Also SIS's 'Scientific Intelligence Section should include a Scientific Intelligence Adviser, independent of all three Services and, as assistants to the latter, such other scientists as "C" may find necessary'. All four advisers were to sit together to constitute a subcommittee of the JIC to be known as the Joint Scientific Intelligence Committee (JSIC). A Joint Technical Intelligence Committee (JTIC) was to operate in parallel.[72] The Service technical and scientific intelligence sections were located together at Bryanston Square with Strong's new Joint Intelligence Bureau.[73]

But in practice they sat next to neither the producers nor the consumers of intelligence. Bryanston Square was not only a shabby building, noted for its rotting linoleum, but also situated far from Whitehall. Scientific intelligence had 'been exiled . . . north of Marble Arch' and so the Services looked upon it as a 'trash bin for misfits'. The rotating chairmanship of the two committees ensured that scientific intelligence lacked the firm direction required to improve its status. Reforms were attempted by Francis Crick in 1948, but scientific intelligence remained in such disarray that in 1952 Churchill was obliged to recall R. V. Jones to undertake a major overhaul. Remarkably, it was only in 1952 that Britain finally appointed one authoritative director of scientific intelligence with a seat on the JIC. The new arrangements for intelligence on atomic matters, hitherto part of scientific intelligence, were no better. In 1945 Sir John Anderson, the director of the British component of the allied 'Tube Alloys' atomic effort, transferred atomic intelligence to the Foreign Office and the Ministry of Supply in an attempt to mirror the American system and thus facilitate co-operation. The result was a technical success – the Anglo-American Combined 'Tube Alloys' Intelligence Organization. However, the lapse in Anglo-American atomic co-operation in 1946 quickly rendered this useless. Thereafter the crucial area of atomic intelligence lacked any coherent focus. As with scientific intelligence, *ad hoc* and uncoordinated changes, albeit well intentioned, had caused great damage.[74]

MI5: THE SECURITY SERVICE

The absence of any comprehensive attempt to restructure the British intelligence community after 1945 is underlined by the remarkable variance in the post-war fates of MI5 and SIS. As we have seen, SIS emerged from the war with enhanced prestige, turning to address the Soviet question in the summer of 1944 and undergoing a thorough reorganization by early 1946. In contrast MI5, despite an equally successful war, contrived to emerge from the war under a dark political cloud the precise nature of which remains unclear. This resulted in the selection of a new director from outside of the service who was strong on democratic values but lacked professional leadership. No serious reorganization of MI5 was undertaken until 1952 and the Soviet section of MI5, consisting of only a few officers, was being run down even at the end of 1945. Positive vetting was resisted by the Cabinet. In the late 1940s MI5 was thus a demoralized service preoccupied with two areas: first, Communist Party members within government, particularly in technical areas; second, the unrest associated with the end of Empire in the Middle East, Africa and Asia. There was little incentive for innovative searches for penetration in the inner circles of the British Establishment.

The private diaries written by Britain's policy-making elite in 1944–5 betray intense disquiet concerning the political future of MI5. This may have been no more than a reaction to the suffocating blanket of security thrown over southern England in preparation for D-Day; however, by November 1944, Alanbrooke was clearly alarmed and noted:

Long talk with P. J. Grigg [Minister for War] on future of MI5 and the dangers attending the future should it fall into the wrong hands. . . .

Finally Lennox who controls [War Office liaison with] MI5 to discuss the future of this organisation and the grave danger of it falling into the clutches of unscrupulous political hands of which there are too many at present.[75]

Disquiet was also in evidence elsewhere. Cadogan's diary suggests that some sort of inquiry into MI5 was being considered in November 1944. Early the following year, when a wide-ranging (but ultimately toothless) review of the entire British intelligence community was under consideration, MI5 clearly feared the participation of Churchill's immediate political entourage. This general disquiet was even detected by junior officers within MI5 such as Yves Tangye, who recalled 'a strong current of prejudice against MI5 in many prominent circles' at the end of the war.[76]

These private concerns were paralleled by wider public controversies over future intelligence and security agencies in both Britain and the United States in 1945. During the election campaign of June 1945 in a major election broadcast, Churchill warned that a future Labour government

would have to fall back on some form of Gestapo, no doubt very humanely administered in the first instance . . . and where would the

31

ordinary simple folk – the common people as they like to call them in America – where would they be, once this mighty organism had got them in their grip?[77]

Churchill added 'Socialism is inseparably interwoven with Totalitarianism'. In any case Labour harboured their own long-standing suspicions of secret services dating back to the Zinoviev letter and the collapse of the MacDonald government in the 1920s. When asked to perpetuate the existence of SOE as a useful adjunct to peacetime foreign policy Attlee replied that he was not prepared to preside over a British version of the Comintern.[78] This general atmosphere of circumspection towards clandestine services found expression in a decision to bring in a respected outsider to head MI5.

Within MI5, Guy Liddell was the favoured successor, but no thought was given to internal candidates.[79] Instead a wide variety of respected wartime figures seem to have been considered for the post including 'Pug' Ismay, Kenneth Strong of SHAEF (Supreme Headquarters Allied Expeditionary Force) and William Penney, Mountbatten's highly regarded intelligence chief.[80] However, contrary to some accounts, the specific appointment of Percy Sillitoe, Chief Constable of Kent, was not a political decision by Attlee, but instead the result of general consensus among senior officials. When interviewed, Sillitoe simply outperformed the other candidates. In his diary for 9 November 1945 Cadogan recorded a 'beastly meeting on MI5' at 4.00 p.m. to interview Penney and Strong. Cadogan preferred Strong 'but didn't much plump for either of them.' Cadogan was more impressed on 14 November 1945: '[3.00 p.m.] meeting in Bridges' room [the Cabinet Secretary's office] to interview candidates for succession to MI5. We were unanimous in choosing Sillitoe, Chief Constable. I thought he certainly seemed good'.[81] Guy Liddell, MI5's rising star, was appointed as Sillitoe's deputy. Nevertheless the appointment of an outsider as Chief was regarded with dismay as a vote of no confidence within MI5. It appeared to be a decision to opt for a show of democratic control rather than professional competence. Sillitoe himself candidly recalls that

> the prospect suddenly before me caused me qualms that would not have been occasioned by the offer of any straightforward police work. . . . I had no way of gauging my potential ability to direct the Security Service. In common with the vast majority of the public, I knew very little about the work of MI5, and virtually nothing about the duties of its chief.[82]

Sillitoe probably exaggerates his ignorance of security matters;[83] however, even his sympathetic biographer did not regard the appointment as a success. Sillitoe expressed an open distaste for the university-educated intellectuals who headed five of MI5's six divisions, while conversely the majority of MI5 regarded Sillitoe with derision. Nevertheless, many individuals recall with approval 'his trenchant views on the dangers of police states and the importance of restrictions on police power'.[84]

MI5 retained its old pattern of organization as it moved into the post-war period, being divided into six 'divisions', mostly based in Curzon Street off Mayfair. The most prestigious part of MI5 was B Division, hitherto under Guy Liddell, whose B1(b) section had run the famous double-cross deception effort against Germany. Significantly, the small but elite and secretive B5(b) section of the Division, under Maxwell Knight, which had kept a wartime watch on Communism and its links with Soviet espionage, was now in decline. Sillitoe reportedly disliked the secrecy and relative autonomy of this small unit based in Dolphin Square. Consequently, they were broken up and transferred back to Curzon Street. Thus Yves Tangye recalls 'there were only two or three people in the Russian section of MI5'. This was in sharp contrast to SIS who, as we have seen, had begun to create a new Soviet section in 1944.[85] Meanwhile MI5 lost the benefit of wartime security powers, including blanket postal censorship, a valuable source of security intelligence.[86]

If Attlee was initially wary of MI5 then the embarrassing exposure of British atom spy, Alan Nunn May and, as a partial consequence, the severing of Anglo-American atomic co-operation in June 1946, nevertheless underlined the need for effective security. Faced with this and also growing industrial unrest, Attlee constituted a Cabinet committee on subversive activities (GEN 183) which met for the first time on 16 June 1947. Thereafter, Attlee was the first Prime Minister to visit MI5 headquarters and held several discussions with staff on subversion.[87] The Alan Nunn May case focused attention primarily upon the problem of Communist Party members who had found wartime work in sensitive scientific programmes.[88] Screening personnel even in this narrow area 'presented Departments and the Security Service with a formidable problem'. As others have demonstrated, the result was a low-key process of 'negative vetting', which resulted in the movement of some two dozen officials with a record of Communist or Fascist sympathies to non-sensitive posts.[89]

By Christmas 1949, even Attlee, by no means a Russophobe, had begun to attribute industrial disputes to Communist elements and by 1950 MI5 had been called in to investigate the possible sabotage of power stations. In the same year the director of the BBC was unsuccessfully approached in the hope of obtaining more favourable coverage of labour disputes.[90] Meanwhile, officials at the Foreign Office increasingly concerned themselves with Soviet 'front organizations' such as the World Federation of Trade Unions and the World Federation of Democratic Youth.[91] Nevertheless, Attlee refused to embark on the scale of security purge that was in full swing in the United States, despite the urging of some back-benchers in Westminster. Even in the wake of the Klaus Fuchs spy case in 1950, Attlee resisted strong pressure from the United States and Canada, from the small Foreign Office security section, as well as from senior officials such as Sir Norman Brook, the Cabinet Secretary, and John Winnifrith, to introduce the active investigation of the background of all officials in sensitive positions or 'positive vetting'. However, in 1951 the further spy cases of Pontecorvo, Burgess and Maclean swept aside even Attlee's reservations. Thus the introduction of positive vetting was one of the last actions of the Attlee administration. Only with this and a subsequent thorough MI5 reorganization following an inquiry by Sir Norman Brook, did British security begin to escape the doldrums.[92]

The domestic Cold War was not MI5's only concern. The late 1940s was also a period of massive expansion in MI5's overseas responsibilities. First, MI5 found itself partly responsible for security in occupied areas, particularly Germany, where a large Soviet espionage effort was underway. One British official lamented in July 1946:

> The number of low grade Russian agents who have recently arrived in our Zone [of Germany] is so large as to make it burdensome to keep tally of them. Attempts to suborn those who are serving us or working with us have increased markedly.[93]

Second, these occupational problems merged into insurgencies often in the context of the 'end of empire' in Burma, Greece, Indo-China, Indonesia and Palestine. In 1948 the pace accelerated with riots in West Africa and the outbreak of the Malayan Emergency. Although the Army and colonial police bore the brunt of these disturbances, British territories overseas now presented MI5 with severe organizational problems.

Malaya offers a good illustration of the confused state of colonial security in the late 1940s. Here the colonial government insisted on retaining its own separate but inadequate Malayan Security Service (MSS) alongside MI5, Military Intelligence and the Special Branch. In London the Colonial Office believed that the MSS were badly out of touch, a view vindicated by the fact that in May 1948, shortly before the outbreak of the Emergency, the MSS concluded that there was no evidence of trouble brewing in Malaya. Sillitoe visited Malaya in 1948 where, he claimed, he was 'instrumental' in setting up a new intelligence organization, presumably the new format for local MI5 organization, known as Security Intelligence Far East (SIFE).[94] But the formation of SIFE failed to address the fundamental problems of duplication and poor co-operation between the myriad security intelligence organizations. Compounding this problem, SIS also maintained a separate office in Singapore. It was symptomatic of the abiding duplication and rivalry that, despite requests from the governors of Singapore and Malaya, the director of the MSS was not permitted a seat on the authoritative JIC FE.[95] In 1950 Sir William Jenkin, a retired

Indian Police official, was brought in to overhaul the Malayan police but clashed with both the military and with SIFE before departing swiftly. Intelligence in Malaya was not placed on a rational footing (focused upon the Special Branch) until the arrival of General Sir Gerald Templer in 1952.[96]

MI5 faced increasing difficulties in almost every British overseas territory between 1945 and 1951, but nothing compared to the scale of the Emergency. In Cairo, Security Intelligence Middle East (SIME), like SIFE, was first and foremost responsible to MI5 in London and enjoyed relative quiet after the withdrawal from Palestine.[97] Thereafter, they were preoccupied with the problem of transferring expertise to successor states. The police forces in Egypt and elsewhere in the region had previously been dominated by British advisers who were now being sent packing. As early as 1946 officials complained of the return of 'oriental slackness' to Egyptian security.[98] Similar problems of a larger scale were faced in India in 1946 where the advent of an interim government of Indian officials immobilized much of Britain's intelligence apparatus on the subcontinent. MI5 held urgent conferences with SIS on how this espionage gap could be filled. The transfer of British security organizations to the successor states was of the highest importance, for India and Pakistan could be permitted to participate in high-level defence planning only if London and, more importantly, Washington, could be assured of their administrative security. Such issues underline the multiple preoccupations of MI5 in the Middle East and Asia in the late 1940s, at once concerned with the end of Empire, the Cold War and preparations for a possible future 'hot war' in which many thought the Middle East would be the key theatre.[99]

ALLIES AND WAR PLANNING

Without any question the most significant development of the late 1940s was the continuing integration of the British intelligence community with those of her post-war allies. Although important links had existed before the war, particularly with the Commonwealth, by 1941 the need for a global intelligence system in support of allied grand strategy had resulted in a formidable English-speaking intelligence alliance of an entirely new order. Thereafter, the perception of Communism as a centrally directed global threat, combined with the geographical requirements of signals intelligence collection, ensured that this integration continued. This post-war trend was further facilitated by the good working relationships that had developed between those who had served in joint wartime commands. For Britain there were added incentives during a period of financial austerity, for allied intelligence systems, even more than inter-Service systems, offered economy. However, any premature remarks about an emerging

'Western intelligence community' must be tempered by a recognition of the disruption resulting from British and Commonwealth security scandals.

By 1945 integration was most advanced in the field of signals intelligence (sigint). Churchill had been a driving force behind such co-operation which had begun in earnest even before Pearl Harbor and in 1943 Britain and the United States cemented their co-operation by means of the BRUSA agreement. This laid down regulations for the exchange of sigint personnel and for the secure distribution of 'Ultra' material. The much discussed post-war Anglo-American UKUSA agreement on sigint, now dated to 1948, to which Australia, New Zealand and Canada were second parties, was in many senses an elaboration of these prior agreements.[100]

Yet while the UKUSA agreement is correctly viewed as a post-war landmark of English-speaking intelligence co-operation, nevertheless it is clear that many of the UKUSA countries had committed themselves to continued full post-war co-operation as early as 1945. Policy-makers at the highest level had become accustomed to a world in which allied intelligence co-operation had rendered enemy intentions almost transparent and they were not about to relinquish that privilege willingly. Thus as early as November 1945, Andrew Cunningham, the Chief of the Naval Staff, recorded in his diary the essence of a critical British COS meeting: 'Much discussion about 100% co-operation with the USA about SIGINT. Decided that less than 100% was not worth having'.[101] Similarly, in Canada, George Glazebrook, the diplomatic representative on the Canadian JIC, opened a debate on post-war sigint co-operation in August 1945, by recommending that Canada make a big independent sigint effort to ensure her future place in a co-operative system. 'It is paramount' he insisted 'that Canada should make an adequate contribution to the general pool'.[102]

Australian signals intelligence had worked closely with GCHQ since the 1930s; indeed Australia established her own separate organization, the Special Intelligence Bureau, only in 1940. Here Anglo-Australian integration was already a reality and Australia's new post-war agency, the Defence Signals Bureau, inaugurated in 1947, was overseen by a GCHQ officer who arrived from Britain with a twenty-strong contingent. During the winter of 1946–7 an imperial sigint conference was held in London, chaired by Sir Edward Travis of GCHQ. This laid the basis for the Commonwealth Sigint Organization, headed by GCHQ, within which Australia, New Zealand, Canada and Britain outlined their spheres of cryptographic influence. With this and the BRUSA treaty of 1943 it was only a short step to the comprehensive UKUSA agreements of 1948.[103]

Nevertheless in a rush to emphasize these key landmarks on the road to integration, insufficient attention has been given to coexisting draconian restrictions governing information exchange, particularly in the atomic field. In February 1946 the United States was rocked by public revelations of Soviet espionage within the wartime allied atomic programme by Alan Nunn May, a British scientist. Fear of inadequate British security, along with ignorance of wartime agreements on co-operation, prompted the United States Congress to pass the McMahon Act 1946, which imposed drastic restrictions upon the exchange of all atomic information with foreign states. This had a severe impact on the exchange of intelligence relating to Soviet strategic developments, the very area which, as we have seen, the British COS had designated the top priority for GCHQ's post-war effort. Indeed, in 1949 the United States informed Britain of its suspicions that the Soviets had detonated an atomic device only after considerable deliberation. Their hesitancy was the direct result of the provisions of the McMahon Act and full exchange was restored only in 1958. Meanwhile, Washington developed the general conviction that the Commonwealth governments were not secure.[104] Indeed, efforts to improve security in the late 1940s, particularly in Australia, can be explained largely in terms of an attempt to restore full Anglo-American-Commonwealth information exchange.

Wartime co-operation had already resulted in similar Commonwealth systems and both Canada and Australia employed a JIC and later a JIB.[105] However, the main impetus for Commonwealth co-operation after 1945 was well-grounded American fears regarding Commonwealth security. The British COS often lamented that American reluctance to permit the association of a third party with Anglo-American planning discussions was 'notorious'.[106] Canada, initially the focus of grave security concern following the Gouzenkou spy case of 1945, enjoyed close liaison between the Royal Canadian Mounted Police (RCMP) and MI5. This and the formation of a Canadian Internal Security Panel in 1946 seemed to re-establish confidence in Canadian security.[107] This was not true of Australia and on 27 January 1948 Hillenkoetter, director of the CIA, wrote to President Truman:

> Indications have appeared that there is a leak in high government circles in Australia, to Russia. This may, in magnitude, approach that of the Canadian spy exposé of last year insofar as high Australian Government officials are concerned. The British Government is now engaged in extensive undercover investigations to determine just where, in the Australian Government, the leak is.[108]

From rare breaks into Soviet cypher traffic, it had become clear that, since 1943, documents had been passed to Soviet intelligence by Australian officials, including copies of controversial British PHPS reports dealing with future British strategy and the future of Germany.[109] As a result, the flow of much American information to Australia all but ceased, and co-operation with Britain became erratic for fear that information would be shared in the context of Anglo-Australian projects. The United States was further alarmed by Attlee's insistence that the new Dominions, India and Pakistan, should join in Commonwealth defence planning.

Such were the potential repercussions of this problem for Anglo-American relations that in 1948 Sillitoe, the head of MI5, was dispatched to Australia with a powerful team. This included Roger Hollis, head of C Division, concerned with protective security and vetting (but often mistakenly identified as head of B Division). In early 1947, in the context of joint rocket trials in Australia, Britain had asked for an expansion of Australia's fledgling Commonwealth Investigation Service and better liaison with MI5. However, the leaks identified in 1948 called for effort of a different order. In the summer of 1948, following discussions with Attlee and Sillitoe during the Commonwealth Prime Ministers' Conference, Australian Prime Minister Chifley accepted British proposals for a new and comprehensive Australian Security Intelligence Organization (ASIO) along the lines of MI5 and under British guidance.[110]

Despite these efforts the United States remained sceptical. In April 1949, a month after the formation of ASIO, Shedden, the Australian Defence Secretary, visited Washington in an attempt to convince the United States that Australia was now secure. Attlee was as concerned as Shedden for Australia's rehabilitation. In April 1949 he wrote to Truman pleading Shedden's case: 'I am most anxious for you to know' he began, 'that I have received most reassuring reports of the creation of ASIO'.

it will henceforth be possible for highly confidential and delicate investigations to be undertaken. . . . Throughout the past twelve months, officers of the British Security Service have been aiding and advising the Australians towards this end and it is from these reports to me that I have felt able to send you this encouraging account.[111]

However, the United States was not convinced and chose to reserve judgement upon Australia. In 1950 Britain dispatched Gerald Templer, Vice-Chief of the Imperial Staff, to Washington in an attempt to resolve the problem of information exchange and the Commonwealth. The subsequent achievement of the Templer-Burns Agreement was a major step forward, but this was overshadowed by news of Britain's Klaus Fuchs spy case which, to Templer's dismay, broke only days before his arrival in Washington.[112]

The establishment of the Australian Secret Intelligence Service (ASIS) in May 1952, under the guidance of the British SIS, was the result of British requests of a rather different nature. In the context of war-planning, Britain had asked in 1947 for the establishment of a base and then, in 1950, for an organization for special operations in the Far East.[113] This led to the establishment of ASIS in Australia which proceeded smoothly. By contrast, in Europe and the Middle East the question of joint war planning with other foreign services was very awkward, further illustrating the problems of third party co-operation.

It is often forgotten that the role of Britain's SIS after 1945 was not only to assist in the conduct of the Cold War but also to plan for special operations in any future 'hot war'. During 1948 the Berlin Crisis appeared to increase the possibility of open conflict, lending this planning a higher priority. The same events during 1948 also served to consolidate the emerging Western bloc. It therefore followed that special operations planning would now become part of inter-allied war planning. How would Britain react to the prospect of sharing SIS war plans with her allies?

Co-ordination with the United States was already a major post-war industry. Britain's liaison staff in Washington is often associated with Kim Philby, who served as *a* but not *the* British CIA liaison officer between 1949 and 1951. In practice Washington teemed with British officials serving as CIA liaison.[114] Meanwhile, with the end of wartime operations, the British Joint Staff Mission (JSM) in Washington increasingly turned its hand to the exchange of intelligence.[115] Arguably, the British required numerous liaison personnel, if only to keep track of the bewildering changes within American intelligence between 1945 and 1951.[116]

Although SIS had concluded several general agreements with the CIA in the 1940s, comprehensive discussions on war plans began only in the wake of the outbreak of the Korean War. In November 1950 the United States suggested to the British COS that organization of 'such US–UK planning as is necessary for wartime special (covert) operations' be devolved to the theatre level.[117] But the COS held out for an overall agreement on the 'control and organization of Allied clandestine affairs in wartime', adding

> a senior representative of M.I.6 [SIS] (General Sinclair) would visit Washington in the near future to present to the Central Intelligence Agency (CIA) the currently held British views on the question of organisation and control of special (covert) operations in wartime.[118]

In late November 1950 Sinclair was deputy chief of SIS and was soon to succeed Menzies as chief of SIS.[119] Sinclair's visit, made in December 1950, was successful and by February 1951, SIS and the CIA had agreed on a memorandum of understanding entitled 'Views on Wartime Organisation and Peacetime Planning'.[120] They then issued parallel directives on plans for the Middle East, Germany and Austria.[121]

However, in mid-1951, as if to disrupt this bilateral accord, SHAPE (Supreme Headquarters Allied Powers in Europe) created a Clandestine Committee, with French representation, to discuss the very same questions. Britain was alarmed and suggested to the Americans that their joint directives on Germany and Austria be withheld from SHAPE, 'particularly as the directives did not take account of the French'. Both the CIA and

SIS were equally wary of a similar committee under a proposed Allied Middle East Command, 'probably including French and Turkish members'.[122] While there remained some fundamental differences between SIS and the CIA, differences that would increase with time, these paled in comparison with their mutual fears of French insecurity and indeed of a further body, the Clandestine Planning Committee of NATO Standing Group, also formed in 1951.[123]

Predictably, a counter-intelligence (CI) conference, held at SHAPE headquarters in Paris in the autumn of 1951, also met with British reticence. Attended by the British, American and French security services it was designed to agree a joint counter-espionage organization for war. Again the French were regarded as insecure.[124] Yet for all Britain's ambivalence towards France in the Cold War context, on another front, the 'end of Empire', MI5 were simultaneously eager to court French security co-operation. Typically, in June 1948, in the wake of the Gold Coast riots, J. C. White and Alex Kellar of MI5's E Division (overseas/colonial matters) attended a meeting at the Colonial Office to announce that they were opening an MI5 office at Accra to effect closer liaison with French security at Dakar and Duala. Indeed they gave the impression of wishing to monopolize security relations with the French, stating that 'in West Africa, the MI5 representative should be the central point for the exchange of security information with the French security officers in West Africa'. Even wider co-operation was sought in the African context for MI5 proposed to appoint a further representative to Salisbury, who would effect liaison with South Africa, Portuguese territories and perhaps the Belgian Congo.[125] Consequently, intelligence relations with allies depended less on the particular service in question and more upon their geographical context.[126]

CONCLUSION

Although many aspects of Britain's intelligence community in the immediate post-war period remain poorly understood, nevertheless the overall architecture is increasingly clear. As late as 1948, its organizational pattern remained largely a Churchillian legacy. Continuity was assured by the absence of any serious attempt at comprehensive reform after 1945. Instead *ad hoc* changes were implemented by individual services, not only to accommodate themselves to the demands of a new conflict, but also to settle old bureaucratic scores. This resulted in serious deficiencies, not least in scientific and atomic intelligence. Strategic appreciations remained well managed under the familiar JIC and in 1948, as subversion achieved a higher profile within an emerging conflict by 'all means short of war', the diplomats and the COS moved, albeit uncertainly, to establish a much needed system of improved co-ordination in this area which resembled similar American machinery. This latter episode created serious tensions between Bevin, his senior officials and the COS. Meanwhile, a comprehensive review of Whitehall's intelligence requirements remained far distant.

At the same time, it must be emphasized that despite this internal incoherence, the grave mistakes of the inter-war period were not repeated. In terms of resources, intelligence fared better than most other areas of Britain's post-war defence forces. Moreover, it might well be asked, had the British intelligence community been radically re-cast in 1945, would the nature of Britain's post-war requirements have been clearly understood at that early stage? In 1944 the COS were still debating (albeit with a self-conscious air of unreality) the intelligence requirements of a future United Nations world force. Only in 1948 was the texture of an accelerating Cold War conflict, and indeed the parallel problems of the end of Empire, with their own complex intelligence requirements, becoming clear.

ACKNOWLEDGEMENTS

I am indebted to Robert Cecil, E. H. R. Harrison and Sheila Kerr for commenting on earlier drafts of this chapter. Responsibility for errors remains with the author.

NOTES

1 C. M. Andrew, 'Churchill and Intelligence', in *Intelligence and National Security* Vol. 3, No. 3 (July 1988), pp. 190–2. See also F. H. Hinsley, *British Intelligence in the Second World War: Its Influence on Strategy and Operations* (London: Her Majesty's Stationery Office, 1979), Vol. 1, pp. 160, 513–14; D. Cameron Watt, 'Intelligence and the Historian', *Diplomatic History* Vol. 14, No. 2 (spring 1990), p. 200.

2 K. Strong, *Men of Intelligence: A Study of the Roles and Decisions of Chiefs of Intelligence from World War II to the Present Day* (London: Cassell, 1970), p. 123.

3 DO (47) 44, 'Future Defence Policy', 22 May 1947, CAB 21/1800, PRO. DO (47) 44, the definitive statement of British strategy in the period 1947–9 has been thoughtfully reproduced by Julian Lewis in his important study *Changing Direction: British Military Planning for Post-war Strategic Defence, 1944–7* (London: Sherwood, 1988), pp. 370–87.

4 Hinsley, *British Intelligence*, Vol. 1, pp. 37–42.

5 The Service Liaison Department, headed by Victor Cavendish-Bentinck, then Harold Caccia and finally William Hayter, was finally absorbed by the machinery of the Permanent Under-Secretaries Department.

6 JIC (48) 19 (0) (2nd Revised Draft), 'Charter for the Joint Intelligence Committee', 27 February 1948, L/WS/1/1051, IOLR.

7 COS (48) 138th mtg (5), 27 September 1948, DEFE 4/16, PRO.

8 In 1948 the JIC Middle East (JIC ME), like its London counterpart, was chaired by a diplomat, the head of the British Middle East Office. The other members included the local Service intelligence chiefs and the regional MI5 and SIS directors along with those responsible for topographic and economic intelligence. One of the major attractions of the regional JICs and their Joint Intelligence Staffs which supported them was their inter-Service nature, avoiding duplication and saving personnel. However, Britain's withdrawal from India in 1947 resulted in an expansion of the JIC ME's geographical area of responsibility: the result was 'a great increase in staff'. At Singapore a JIC Far East was instituted on the same lines, chaired by the Deputy Special Commissioner for South East Asia and serving the British Defence Co-ordinating Committee, Far East. In Europe

this was paralleled by a JIC Control Commission, Germany. On this matter see JIC (48) 60 (Revised Final) 'Review of Intelligence Organisation in the Middle East', 12 November 1948, L/WS/1/1051, IOLR; JIC (46) 105 (0) (Final), 'Organisation of Intelligence in South East Asia', 9 December 1946, L/WS/1/734, IOLR. For earlier ideas on post-war intelligence in South East Asia see JIC (45) 280, 'Organisation of Intelligence – HQ SACSEA', 6 October 1945, 5/24, Papers of Major-General Penney, Liddell Hart Centre for Military Archives, King's College, London (hereafter KCL).

9 R. Cecil, 'The Cambridge Comintern', in C. M. Andrew and D. Dilks (eds) *The Missing Dimension: Governments and Intelligence Communities in the Twentieth Century* (London: Macmillan, 1984), p. 179. On these various boards and committees see Hinsley, *British Intelligence*, Vol. 2, pp. 618–19.

10 Strong himself noted that the JIB was partly designed to avoid the duplication of intelligence personnel, Strong, *Men of Intelligence*, pp. 121–2.

11 P.J.P. minute, 10 September 1946, L/WS/1/1088, IOLR.

12 Strong (JIB) to Monteath (IO), JIB/G/4, 28 August 1946, ibid.

13 Earle (JIB) to Carter (IO), JIB/0/2, 30 October 1946, ibid.; Earle (JIB) to Carter, 24 October 1946, ibid.; JIB (46) 1st mtg, 20 September 1946, ibid.

14 JIC (48) 60 (Revised Final), 'Review of Intelligence Organisation in the Middle East', 12 November 1948, L/WS/1/1051, IOLR.

15 COS 935 (JIC), 4 July 1939, CAB 59/51, PRO. For examples of the work of the JIC in co-ordinating intelligence and special operations see for example: JIC (42) 156 (0), 29 April 1942, CAB 84/85, PRO; JIC (43) 325 (0), 1 August 1943, CAB 79/63, PRO; JIC (45) 105 (0), 30 March 1945, CAB 79/31, PRO. In addition the Foreign Office Permanent Under-Secretary, Sir Alexander Cadogan, presided over SOE–SIS meetings in a further attempt to co-ordinate this area.

16 D. Dilks (ed.) *The Diaries of Sir Alexander Cadogan, 1938–1945* (London: Cassell, 1972); K. Young (ed.) *The Diaries of Sir Robert Bruce Lockhart: Vol. 2, 1939–65* (London: Macmillan, 1980); B. Pimlott (ed.) *The Second World War Diary of Hugh Dalton* (London: Cape, 1986) *passim*. In 1944, in the wake of several JIC reports which attempted to deal with SOE–SIS controversies in Europe, Churchill resigned himself to 'the warfare between S.I.S. and S.O.E. which is a lamentable, but perhaps inevitable, feature of our affairs', Churchill to Ismay, 10 February 1944, D41/4, CAB 120/827, PRO.

17 JIC (46) 1 (0) (Final Revise), 22 February 1946, referred to in JIC (46) 38 (0) (Final Revise), 14 June 1946, DO 35/1604, PRO.

18 R. Smith, 'A Climate of Opinion: British Officials and the Development of British Soviet Policy, 1945–7', *International Affairs*, Vol. 64, No. 4 (autumn 1988) p. 635.

19 Russia Committee T of R, 12 April 1946, N5170/5169/38, FO 371/56885, PRO.

20 R. Merrick, 'The Russia Committee of the British Foreign Office and the Cold War, 1946–47', *Journal of Contemporary History* Vol. 20, No. 3 (July 1985), pp. 454–5; Smith, 'A Climate of Opinion', p. 636. Others mistakenly attribute the formation of the RC to the JIC, see H. Thomas, *Armed Truce: The Beginnings of the Cold War, 1945–6* (London: Hamish Hamilton, 1986), pp. 550–1.

21 On this see the full account in Lewis, *Changing Direction*, pp. 98–178.

22 ibid., p. 136. An example of the relatively benign view of the Soviet Union emerging from the JIC towards the end of the war, reflecting Foreign Office rather than military views, is JIC (44) 467 (0), 'Russia's Strategic Interests and Intentions from the Point of View of her Security', 18 December 1944, CAB 80/89, PRO by Sir A. Noble of the Foreign Office. On 30 August 1944, after the JIC had completed another benign analysis of future Soviet intentions, a rueful military planner recorded: 'We have now received the JIC appreciation concerning Russian potentialities . . . it represents rather a setback for the would-be drinkers of Russian blood. The proposed world-wide appreciation of our war against Russia is to be dropped'. PHPS Secretary, Patrick Davidson, to Brigadier Cornwall Jones, 30 August 1944, CAB 122/1566, PRO.

23 Warner to Cavendish-Bentinck, 19 December 1944, N678/20/38, FO 371/47860, PRO; Roberts to FO, 18 March 1946, N4157/97/38, FO 371/56763, PRO.

24 Warner memorandum, 'The Soviet Campaign Against this Country and Our Response to it', 2 April 1946, N5169/5169/38. FO 371/56885. PRO.

25 Warner to Jebb, 22 November 1948, N12649/765/38, FO 371/71687, PRO cited in Smith, 'A Climate of Opinion', p. 636.

26 Sir William Hayter, *A Double Life*, pp. 82–3. For a rare account of a JPS meeting see Turnbull to Monteath, 13 September 1946, L/WS/1/1045, IOLR.

27 Memorandum by Kirkpatrick, 22 May 1946, P449/1/907, FO 930/488, PRO; minute by Sargent, 23 May 1946; minutes by Bevin, undated, ibid., all cited in Smith, 'A Climate of Opinion', pp. 636–9. cf. p.90.

28 For other examples of Bevin's general discomfort when contemplating a forward policy, see B. Heuser, *Western 'Containment' Policies in the Cold War: The Yugoslav Case* (London: Routledge, 1990), pp. 44–6 , 76–81; R. Aldrich, 'Unquiet in Death: The Special Operations Executive and British Post War Special Operations, 1945–51', in A. Gorst and W. S. Lucas (eds) *Politics and the Limits of Policy Making* (London: Pinter, 1991). Others have mistakenly asserted that Bevin was a covert action enthusiast, see for example, A. Verrier, *Through the Looking Glass: British Foreign Policy in an Age of Illusions* (London: Cape, 1983), p. 53; A. Cavendish, *Inside Intelligence* (London: Collins, 1990), p. 54.

29 COS (44) 381st mtg (6), Confidential Annex, 27 November 1944, CAB, 79/83, PRO; Eden to Churchill, PM/44/74, 23 November 1944, ibid.; Dilks (ed.) *Cadogan Diary*, diary entry for 24 November 1944, p. 683.

30 In April 1945, during a dinner with Will Codrington, in charge of Foreign Office security, Kirkpatrick gave 'a damning account of SOE and PWE' adding that an 'open investigation of such organisations by Parliament' would be 'invaluable', Colville, *Fringes of Power* (London: Hodder & Stoughton, 1983), diary entry for 3 April 1945, pp. 581–2. Kirkpatrick was a persistent critic of the control of PWE and SOE and had expressed similar sentiments to Cadogan, who recorded: 'I. K. [Ivone Kirkpatrick] about P. W. E. which is a *scandal*', diary entry for 12 May 1944, Dilks (ed.) *Cadogan Diary*, p. 628. Interestingly, Kirkpatrick himself had been moved to a 'planning' job as Deputy Commissioner for Germany in May 1944 which Cadogan described as 'King Planner', diary entries for 14 April, 18 April and 15 May, 1944, ibid., pp. 618, 621, 629.

31 The Political Warfare Executive was not entirely disbanded at the end of the war. Typically, in Iran, the British Embassy retained Dr Robert Zaehner of PWE in 1945 for the purpose of 'bribing the Persian press', Young minute, 16 June 1945, E4569/1630/65, FO 371/45272, PRO.

32 See Chapter 4 in this volume. The literature on this illusive subject is growing: P. M. Taylor, 'The Projection of Britain Abroad, 1945–51', in J.W. Young and M. Dockrill (eds) *British Foreign Policy, 1945–1956* (London: Macmillan, 1989), pp. 9–30; W. Wark, 'Coming in from the Cold: British Propaganda and the Red Army Defectors, 1945–52', *International History* Vol. IX, No.1 (February 1987), pp. 48–73; R. Fletcher, 'British Propaganda Since World War II: A Case Study', *Media, Culture and Society* Vol. IV, No. 9 (1982), pp. 97–109; L. Smith, 'Covert British Propaganda: The Information Research Department, 1944–77', *Millenium* Vol. 9, No.1, (1980) pp. 67–83.

33 cf. pp. 92–4.

34 Montgomery diary, BLM/1/186/1, June-September 1948, Section D, 'The "Cold War" ', IWM.

35 Price minute, 25 November 1948, N12751/765/38, FO 371/71687, PRO.

36 Tedder's optimism regarding guerrilla activities in the east was not unqualified. He was 'very sceptical of the value of SOE unless followed up by military action. He likened these operations to a barrage laid down before an attack by troops; if it were laid down too far ahead your friends were simply annihilated'. In the light of events in Albania in 1949 these were prescient remarks. Minutes of RC (16) 48, 25 November 1948, N13016/765/38, FO 371/71687, PRO; Annex A, 'Russia Committee: T of R for a "Cold War" subcommittee', ibid.; minutes of RC (29) 48, 16 December 1948, F13677/765/38, ibid.

37 In mid-July 1948, with a 'hot war' now a distinct possibility, officials including Robert Bruce Lockhart and John Slessor, Commandant of the IDC, 'evolved a scheme for wartime control whereby P.W.E., S.O.E., Deception and S.I.S. should have their own executive heads but should be co-ordinated under a very high and efficient official who would have a seat on the Chiefs of Staff'. Diary entry for 14 July 1948, Young (ed.)

Lockhart Diaries, pp. 662–3. Interestingly, Lockhart also suggests that IRD emerged through the initiative of the IDC.

38 IDC Report by Slessor, and Annex A, 'The Cold War', 29 November 1948, N3355/ 1051/38G, FO 371/77616, PRO; Alexander to Attlee, 7 March 1949, ibid.; Attlee to Bevin minute, M69/49, 10 March 1949, ibid.; Hankey and Jebb minutes, 23 March 1949, N3356/1051/38G, ibid. cf. pp. 99–102.

39 Minutes of RC 49, 17 February 1949, N1727/1052/38G, FO 371/77623, PRO.

40 Strang to Bevin, 9 May 1949, W3113/3/50G, FO 371/76384, PRO; Lord Strang, *Home and Abroad* (London: André Deutsch, 1956), p. 279. On the more overt aspects of PUSC/PUSD see A. Adamthwaite, 'Britain and the World, 1945–9: The View from the Foreign Office', *International Affairs* Vol. 61, No. 2 (spring 1985), pp. 234–5; R. Ovendale, 'William Strang and the Permanent Under Secretaries Committee', in J. Zametica (ed.) *British Officials and British Foreign Policy, 1945–50* (Leicester: Leicester University Press, 1990), pp. 212–14.

41 Thomas, 'British Signals Intelligence', p. 107.

42 T. Bower, *Red Web* (London: Aurum Press, 1988), pp. 50–65.

43 Counter-intelligence work was also facilitated by the increasing volume of Axis security records that had begun to fall into allied hands. K. Philby, *My Silent War* (London: MacGibbon & Kee, 1968), p. 52; F. H. Hinsley and P. Simkins, *British Intelligence* Vol. 4, pp. 131–41; R Cecil, 'C's War', *Intelligence and National Security* Vol. 1, No. 2 (May 1986), p. 178.

44 Diary entry for 11 June 1945 in J. Ferris, 'From Broadway House to Bletchley House: The Diary of Captain Malcolm Kennedy, 1934–46', *Intelligence and National Security* Vol. 4, No. 3 (July 1989), p. 442; Philby, *My Silent War*, pp. 70–9. Other staff included Jane Archer transferred from MI5 who was engaged in traffic analysis on Eastern European liberation movements. It should be noted that Philby's memoirs should be treated with care for they imply that Section IX was operational before 1945. *This was not the case.*

45 This quotation is taken from the definitive account of the formation of the new SIS anti-Soviet department, Section IX, given in an autobiographical essay by Robert Cecil, the Foreign Office Personal Assistant to the Chief of the Secret Service (PA/CSS). R. Cecil, 'The Cambridge Comintern', pp.180–1.

46 D. Stafford, *Britain and the European Resistance, 1939–1945* (London: Macmillan, 1983), p. 203; Philby, *My Silent War*, pp. 86–8; Cavendish, *Inside Intelligence*, pp. 39–40. Another official recalled at this time: 'My own section is being abolished and amalgamated with the remnants of Philby's organisation under a new nomenclature', diary entry for 19 January 1946 in Ferris, 'The Diary of Captain Malcolm Kennedy', p. 443.

47 JIC (48) 60 (Revised Final), 'Review of Intelligence Organisation in the Middle East', 12 November 1948, L/WS/1/1051, IOLR; Troutbeck to Bevin, 9 June 1949, E7480/ 1026/65, FO 371/75054, PRO.

48 JIC (FE)/5501, Appendix B 'Draft Charter for JIC (FE)', 5 January 1948, L/WS/1/1050, IOLR.

49 Mack (Allied Commission for Austria) to Oliver, 3 May 1945, C2226/141/G3, FO 371/ 46609, PRO, reproduced in H. Thomas, *Armed Truce*, Appendix VIII, 'SIS in Austria', p. 565; Hankey minute, 28 October 1945, C7716/72/G3, FO 371/46604, PRO.

50 Middle East Defence Committee to COS, CCL/52, 23 August 1945, FO 371/45272, PRO. See, for example, details of the Bushire secret service grant in Prior (Political Resident) to India Office, 6 April 1946, (Coll. 30/160 PII(S)), L/P&S/12/3896B, IOLR.

51 JIC (48) 60 (Revised Final), 'Review of Intelligence Organisation in the Middle East', 12 November 1948, fo. 21, L/WS/1/1051, IOLR.

52 See for example COS(45) 304, 'Evaluation of Lessons Learnt During the War', memorandum by Gubbins (SOE), not foliated, AIR 20/7958, PRO; Aldrich, 'Unquiet in Death', pp. 306–9.

53 Mountbatten in particular considered the American OSS 'very good' because of its ability to cover both intelligence and special operations, all of which, he contended, were 'inextricably mixed up' with propaganda and civil affairs. However, he continued, unlike OSS, any future organization needed to be 'joined in at the roots with the general direction of the war', Mountbatten to Ismay, SC5/1676/I, 20 August 1945, CAB 127/

25, PRO. I am indebted to Michael Coleman of Clare College, Cambridge, for drawing my attention to this document.

54 Entry for 23 January 1946, Alanbrooke diary, Liddell Hart Centre for Military Archives, KCL; COS (46) 9th mtg (6), 17 January 1946, (17003) L/WS/1/970, IOLR.

55 COS (45) 461 (0), 'Future of SOE Activity in the British Zone of Austria', 16 July 1945, WO 193/637A, PRO; COS (45) 572, 'Future of SOE Activity in the British Zone of Austria', 10 September 1945, C6072/72/G3, FO 371/46604, PRO.

56 R. Cecil, 'C's War', p. 182.

57 'Control of Special Units and Organisations', T1/1/1054, [presumed July 1946], WO 106/6024, PRO.

58 J. D. Ladd, *SAS Operations* (London: Hale, 1986), p. 103; Brigadier J. M. Calvert (SAS) memorandum, 'Future of SAS Troops', 12 October 1945, reproduced at Appendix 5 of J. Strawson, *A History of the SAS Regiment* (London: Secker & Warburg, 1985).

59 JIC (43) 64, 15 February 1943, annexed to COS (43) 55, CAB 80/39, PRO; Hinsley, *British Intelligence* Vol. 2, pp. 618–19; R. Aldrich and M. Coleman, 'The Cold War, the JIC and British Signals Intelligence, 1948', *Intelligence and National Security* Vol. 4, No. 3 (1989), pp. 538–40.

60 R. Manne, *The Petrov Affair* (Sydney: Pergamon, 1987) pp. 179–80; C. M. Andrew, 'The Growth of the Australian Intelligence Community and the Anglo-American Connection', *Intelligence and National Security* Vol. 4, No. 2 (April 1989), p. 227; Aldrich and Coleman, 'JIC and British Signals Intelligence', p. 535.

61 RAF Signals Directorate diagram detailing liaison (Signals 2b) with GCHQ Eastcote, [July 1948?], AIR 20/2794, PRO; R. Lewin, *Ultra Goes to War: The Secret Story* (London: Hutchinson, 1978) pp.129, 132–3; R. V. Jones, *Reflections On Intelligence* (London: Cape, 1989), p. 15.

62 JIC (48) 19 (0) (2nd Revised Draft), 'Sigint Intelligence Requirements – 1948', 11 May 1948, L/WS/1/1196, IOLR.

63 Aldrich and Coleman, 'JIC and British Signals Intelligence', pp. 539–41; R. M. Blum, 'Surprised by Tito: The Anatomy of an Intelligence Failure', *Diplomatic History* Vol. 12, No. 1 (winter 1988), pp. 39–57.

64 JIC (48) 19 (0) (2nd Revised Draft), 'Sigint Intelligence Requirements – 1948', 11 May 1948, fo. 2, L/WS/1/1196, IOLR.

65 A. Stripp, *Codebreaker in the Far East* (London: Frank Cass, 1989) pp. 50–62; A Stripp, 'Breaking Japanese Codes', *Intelligence and National Security* Vol. 2, No. 4 (October 1987), pp. 141–3; Jones, *Reflections On Intelligence*, p. 14–16.

66 ibid.; Thomas, 'British Signals Intelligence', p. 104.

67 C. M. Andrew, *Secret Service: The Making of the British Intelligence Community* (London: Heinemann, 1985), p. 488; Thomas, 'British Signals Intelligence', p. 103; Aldrich and Coleman, 'JIC and British Signals Intelligence', p. 541. On photo reconnaissance see AIR 8/1475, PRO, *passim*.

68 R. V. Jones, ADI (Sci) minute, 14 August 1945, AIR 2/12027, PRO; COS (45) 402 (0) 'Future developments in Weapons and Methods of War', 16 June 1945, ibid.

69 Slessor (AMP) minute, 16 July 1945, ibid.

70 TWC (46) 15 (Revise), 'Future Developments in Methods and Weapons of War', 6 July 1946, DEFE 2/1252, PRO, on this notable paper see Lewis, *Changing Direction*, pp. 178–242; COS (47) 42nd mtg, 19 March 1947, DEFE 4/3, PRO.

71 Jones, *Reflections On Intelligence*, pp. 7–8; R. V. Jones memorandum, 'An Improved Scientific Intelligence Service', 2 May 1945, AIR 20/1714, PRO.

72 JIC (45) 229, 'Organisation for Scientific and Technical Intelligence', 26 July 1945, fo. 5, ADM 1/20088, PRO.

73 CE 53323/46, 'Organisation of Scientific and Technical Intelligence', 1 November 1946, ibid.; Jones, *Most Secret War*, p. 497. R. V. Jones's accounts add much to our understanding of these changes; however, some details are confused, for example Jones conflates the Joint Science and Technical Intelligence Committees into one body, Jones, *Reflections on Intelligence*, p. 497.

74 Ironically, when firm links were re-established in the 1950s the British discovered that American atomic intelligence had been reorganized and placed within the CIA's Office of Scientific Intelligence. However, it should be noted that, throughout this period, SIS

maintained its own atomic intelligence section, R9 [requirements 9] staffed by Eric Welsh and Michael Perrin, ibid., pp. 6–8, 12, 16–17; Jones, *Most Secret War*, pp. 492–7, 517, 525.

75 Entries for 1 and 2 November 1944, Alanbrooke diary, 5/9, Liddell Hart Centre for Military Archives, KCL. Later Alanbrooke noted in his diary that: 'During the afternoon I had to see Croft who is worried about the security of MI5 and 6 [SIS], so am I!', diary entry for 16 May 1945, 5/10, ibid.

76 In October 1944 Cadogan's diary records a conversation with Menzies, head of SIS, followed by a further conversation with Sir Edward Bridges, the Cabinet Secretary, during which he 'talked to him about jurisdiction for an enquiry into MI5', diary entry for 24 October 1944, Cadogan Diary, ACAD 1/13, Churchill College, Cambridge. However, Cadogan may have been referring to the general inquiry into the structure of post-war intelligence conducted by Sir Findlater Stewart in the summer of 1945. In early 1945 Cadogan and Sir James Grigg, Secretary of State for War, had a discussion 'about enquiry into SIS and MI5'. Cadogan noted that MI5 were 'nervous' of Grigg conducting such an inquiry because he worked in an area where Churchill and his immediate circle 'snoop around too much', diary entry for 9 January 1945, Cadogan Diary, ACAD 1/15, ibid. D. Tangye, *The Way to Minack* (London: Michael Joseph, 1968), pp. 142–3.

77 *The Times*, 5 June 1945, quoted in K. O. Morgan, *Labour in Power, 1945–51* (Oxford: Oxford University Press, 1985), see also M. Gilbert, *Never Despair* (London: Heinemann, 1988), pp. 32–5. Colville, who divided his time as private secretary more or less equally between Churchill and Attlee at this point noted in his diary 'I helped draft both the charges and the counter-charges' during the election, Colville, *Fringes of Power*, p. 612. On the 'Gestapo' debate in the United States see J. Ranelagh, *The Rise and Decline of the CIA* (London: Weidenfeld & Nicolson, 1986), Ch. 3.

78 C. M. Andrew, *Secret Service*, pp. 301–16; M. R. D. Foot, *SOE: The Special Operations Executive, 1940–1946* (London: BBC, 1984), p. 245.

79 Philby, *My Silent War*, p. 51.

80 Entry for 8 November 1945, Cadogan Diary, ACAD 1/15, Churchill College, Cambridge; Browning to Penney, 19 November 1945, Papers of General Penney, 5/33, Liddell Hart Centre for Military Archives, KCL.

81 Entries for 8, 9 and 14 November 1945, Cadogan Diary, ACAD 1/15, Churchill College, Cambridge.

82 Sir Percy Sillitoe, *Cloak Without Dagger*, (London: Cassell, 1955), xiv.

83 Sillitoe, in the process of emphasizing his democratic credentials (the foreword to his autobiography by Clement Attlee strikes the same note) remarked: 'I had occasionally succumbed to the temptation which almost everyone finds irresistible – that of making fun of the "cloak and dagger boys" who one imagines as heavy handed British blimps'. However, it seems quite improbable that, as Chief Constable of Kent during the D-Day preparations, he should have been ignorant of security matters; indeed, these would probably have preoccupied him, bringing him into regular contact with security authorities in London. Sir Percy Sillitoe, *Cloak Without Dagger* (London: Cassell, 1955), xv–xvi. On Overlord security see Hinsley and Simpkins, *British Intelligence*, Vol. 4, pp. 247–61.

84 Andrew, *Secret Service*, p. 489; Jones, *Reflections On Intelligence*, p. 21.

85 Administrative and support services (A Division), the glamorous counter-espionage section (B Division), protective security and vetting (C Division), liaison with the Services (D Division), aliens and security in British overseas territories (E Division), political surveillance (F Division). F Division was headed by Graham Mitchell after 1945, while Maxwell Knight, a veteran expert on Communism, edged into semi-retirement. Meanwhile, Roger Hollis, Mitchell's predecessor, moved on to run C Division, which concerned itself with protective security and vetting. A. Masters, *The Man Who was M: The Life of Maxwell Knight* (Oxford: Blackwell, 1984), pp. 178–81; D. Tangye, *The Way to Minack* (London: Michael Joseph, 1968), p. 141.

86 Minutes of 2nd meeting on the revision of censorship regulations, attended by Colonel Valentine Vivian (Deputy Chief, MI5), A. Grogan (MI5) and David Boyle (SIS), 4

December 1945, T 222/10, PRO. See also MG (46) 1, 'Future of Postal and Telegraphic Censorship', 28 January 1946, ibid.

87 M. Gowing, *Independence and Deterrence: Britain and Atomic Energy, 1945–52*, Vol. 1, (London: Macmillan, 1976), pp. 104–12; P. Hennessy and G. Brownfeld, 'Britain's Cold War Security Purge: The Origins of Positive Vetting', *Historical Journal* Vol. 25, No. 4 (1982), pp. 965–75; Andrew, *Secret Service*, p. 490; P. Hennessy and K. Jeffrey, *States of Emergency*, Ch. 7 passim.

88 There was a general impression, arising out of the Gouzenkou affair, that the Soviet Union 'worked almost exclusively through the Communist party and by means of Communist Cells', see for example Butler to Sargent, n.d., N10772/10772/38, FO 371/56912, PRO.

89 Hennessy and Jeffrey, *States of Emergency*, pp. 216–18; Hennessy and Brownfeld, 'Cold War Security Purge', pp. 965–75. For a contrary view see Gaddis who asserts that no 'quiet "purge" ' took place in Britain, 'Intelligence and Cold War Origins', *Diplomatic History* Vol. 14, No. 1 (April 1989), p. 197.

90 Bevin held more robust views on the question of domestic Communism, Hennessy and Jeffrey, *States of Emergency*, p. 147.

91 'The Soviet Campaign Against this Country and Our Response to it', N6344/605/38, FO 371/56832, PRO; Ward minute, 6 June 1945, N7080/605/38, FO 371/56833, PRO.

92 Hennessy and Brownfeld, 'Britain's Cold War Security Purge', pp. 965–75; Cecil, 'The Cambridge Comintern', pp. 181–2. For analysis of Foreign Office Security problems during the 1930s see D. Dilks, 'Flashes of Intelligence: The Foreign Office, the SIS and Security before the Second World War', in Andrew and Dilks (eds) *The Missing Dimension*, pp. 101–26; D. Cameron Watt, 'Francis Herbert King: A Soviet Source in the Foreign Office', *Intelligence and National Security* Vol. 3, No. 4 (October 1988), pp. 62–83.

93 'The Soviet Campaign Against Britain in Germany', 27 July 1946, N10929/5769/38, FO 371/56885, PRO.

94 A. Short, *The Communist Insurrection in Malaya, 1948–60* (London: Muller, 1975), pp. 80, 86–7, 145, 155, 229–30, 275–6, 335, 358 n. 18; R. Stubbs, *Hearts and Minds* (Kuala Lumpur: Oxford University Press, 1989), pp. 19, 67–8. Until 1947, MI5 had participated in Mountbatten's Counter-Intelligence Combined Bureau, a composite organization, which had also included SIS Section V, that had performed security tasks for South East Asia Command's post-war regional administration, see JIC (46) 105 (0) (Final), 'Organisation of Intelligence in Southeast Asia', 9 December 1946, fo. 90, L/WS/1/734, IOLR.

95 BDCC (FE) 2nd mtg (6), Appendix C to JIC (FE)/5501, 17 January 1948, L/WS/1/1050, IOLR.

96 A. Short, *The Communist Insurrection*, pp. 335, 358, n. 18.

97 JIC (48) 60 (Revised Final), 'Review of Intelligence Organisation in the Middle East', 12 November 1948, L/WS/1/1051, IOLR.

98 Smart minute, 16 March 1946, FO 141/1009, PRO. For a rare glimpse of SIME in the late 1940s see Cavendish, *Inside Intelligence*, pp. 15–35.

99 JIC (47) 2 (0) (Final), 'India – Organisation for Intelligence', 4 January 1947, L/WS/1/1050, IOLR. Typically, during wartime SIME would expand to a complement of 177 personnel, of whom only 25 would be from MI5. The bulk of the personnel for SIME HQ in Cairo and its thirteen 'outstations' were to come from the Army which was scheduled to produce 90 staff, 'Report of Working Party to JIC', BM 7660(1), 25 March 1947, ADM 1/20379, PRO. By 1949 a subcommittee of the Defence Transition to War Committee had been created to oversee wartime security measures, see ADM 116/5719, PRO *passim*.

100 Andrew, 'Churchill and Intelligence', p. 192; Andrew 'Australian Intelligence Community', p. 222; Bamford *Puzzle Palace*, pp. 314–17.

101 Entry, 21 November 1945, Cunningham diary, MSS 52578, British Library.

102 W. K. Wark, 'Cryptographic Innocence: The Origins of Signals Intelligence in Canada in the Second World War', *Journal of Contemporary History* Vol. 22, No. 4 (October 1987), pp. 558–9.

103 The fullest and most authoritative treatment of this matter can be found in Andrew

'Australian Intelligence Community', p.224. See also Bamford, *Puzzle Palace*, Ch. 8; Richelson and Ball, *The Ties that Bind*, pp. 141–5.

104 Aldrich and Coleman, 'The JIC and British Signals Intelligence', pp. 540–1. For a refreshing departure from orthodoxy on the question of the exchange of scientific information, see F. Cain, 'Missiles and Mistrust; US Intelligence Responses to British and Australian Missile Research', *Intelligence and National Security* Vol. 3, No. 4 (October 1988), pp. 7–8.

105 In 1945 Australia and Canada were also persuaded to follow Britain in establishing JIB systems to co-ordinate their Service intelligence. In the Far East Britain saw an opportunity to delegate the costs of a regional JIB to Australia. Brigadier Penney from SEAC visited Australia to explore this and suggested that in the Far East it should be Australia rather than Singapore 'centralising and covering intelligence for the whole area' talking also of a parallel sigint organization. The Australian system was further rationalized with the creation of the Joint Intelligence Organization in 1947. British COS to Australian COS, 026635, 6 November 1945, fo. 6A, WO 106/4988, PRO. See also, JIC (45) 293 (Final), 'Manpower Requirements for Post War Intelligence Organisation', 13 October 1945, CAB 79/40, PRO.

106 COS(49) 17th mtg (2) Appendix, 2 February 1949, DEFE 4/19, PRO.

107 SANAAC 206/29, 'Disclosure of Classified Military Information to Foreign Governments', 15 June 1948, RG 330, NARA, cited in Cain, 'Missiles and Mistrust', p. 12; L. R. Aronsen, ' "Peace Order and Good Government" during the Cold War: The Origins and Organisation of Canada's Internal Security Program', *Intelligence and National Security* Vol. 1, No. 3 (September 1986), pp. 360–1.

108 Hillenkoetter, (Director of Central Intelligence), 'Memorandum for the President', 27 January 1948, Truman papers, Harry S. Truman Library, Independence, Missouri, quoted in Cain, 'Missiles and Mistrust', p. 13.

109 Manne, *The Petrov Affair*, pp. 180–1. The papers lost included PHP (45) 6 (0), 'Security in the Western Mediterranean and the Eastern Atlantic', May 1945, and PHP (45) 15 (0) Final, 'Security of India and the Indian Ocean', May 1945, CAB 81/46, PRO.

110 Andrew, 'The Anglo-American Connection', pp. 227–9; Sir Percy Sillitoe, *Cloak Without Dagger* (London: Cassell, 1955), pp. 11–12. New Zealand continued to depend on her Special Branch, albeit heavily reorganized in 1948.

111 Attlee to Truman (personal), 4 April 1949, (A-Attlee File), Box 170, PSF Subject File, Truman papers, Harry S. Truman Library, Independence, Missouri.

112 DO (50) 5th mtg (2), 5 April 1950, CAB 131/8, PRO; J. Cloake, *Templer: Tiger of Malaya* (London: Harrap, 1985), p. 180.

113 Andrew, 'The Anglo-American Connection', pp. 230–1; Richelson and Ball, *Ties That Bind* pp. 42–3.

114 P. Faligot and P. Krop, *La Piscine: The French Secret Service* (Oxford: Blackwell, 1989), pp. 62, 302, n. 2.

115 See for example Rowe (British Liaison Officer, Foreign Documents Branch, CIA) to Secretary JIC London, 14 June 1948, L/WS/1/1051, IOLR. For the Army section under Colonel Chapman intelligence exchange became the central task, British Army Staff (JSM Washington) memorandum, pt. III, 'Intelligence', August 1946, WO 202/917, PRO.

116 After the abolition of the wartime OSS in 1945, various components survived as Research and Intelligence (State Department), Strategic Services Unit (War Department) or as the short-lived Central Intelligence Group. Even after the formation of the CIA in 1947, there remained a separate body, OPC for covert action. Ranelagh, *Rise and Decline of the CIA*, Chs 3–4, *passim*.

117 JCS 1933/21, 'Arrangements for Covert Operations Military Planning with the British', Enclosure A, cited in JSPC 808/81, 'Special Operations in Support of Emergency War Plans', 18 December 1951, 385 (6-44-46) Sect. 120 SO, RG 165, NARA.

118 RDC 1/73, 'British memorandum for the US JCS', ibid.

119 Major-General John Sinclair had been DMI during the period 1944–5 and Vice-Chief of SIS from 1945 before succeeding Sir Stuart Menzies as Chief of SIS. There is some dispute as to the precise date of Sinclair's succession. Richelson and Verrier suggest that Sinclair succeeded in 1953 while West opts for 1952. Andrew asserts that Sinclair took

over at the end of 1951. Richelson and Ball, *The Ties that Bind*, p. 340; Verrier, *Through the Looking Glass*, p. 99; N. West, *The Friends: British Post War Secret Intelligence Operations* (London: Weidenfeld & Nicolson, 1988), xv; Andrew, *Secret Service*, p. 493.

120 GG1/3537/451, 'View on Wartime Organisation and Peacetime Planning', 9 February 1951 cited in JCS 1735/132, 'Clandestine Operations' Enclosure A, 24 June 1952, 385 (6-4-46) Sect. 42 SO, RG 165, NARA.

121 Britain submitted three draft directives to the US JCS who, while requesting 'certain changes', found themselves in general agreement with their contents, RDC 1/7, 'British memorandum to US JCS', enclosed in JCS 1833/26 cited in JSPC 808/81, 'Special operations in Support of Emergency War Plans', 18 December 1951, CCS 385 (6-44-46) Sect. 120 SO, RG 165, NARA.

122 RHB 1/48, 'British memorandum to US JCS', enclosed in JCS 1969/14, 8 November 1951, ibid.

123 Typically the US JCS resolved that '[NATO] Standing Group interest in special operations will be limited to general policy, direction and broad guidance and should not extend to operational details such as the determination of targets within theatres of operations. Furthermore, its interests will be limited to those special operations which support NATO military operations'. In short, Standing Group was most unwelcome, SPDM–384–51, 'Draft Report on Special Operations', 17 October 1951, 385 (6-4-46) Sect. 26 SO, RG 165, NARA.

124 JIC 566/4, 'Guidance for the US Military Delegation to the Shape Counter-intelligence Conference' 2 October 1951, 385 (6-4-46) Sect. 25 SO, RG 165, NARA. Sayer and Botting, in their study of the American CIC remark that the French intelligence service in Germany – particularly the positive arm, the Deuxième Bureau – was considered so riddled by pro-Soviet Communists that it was viewed as virtually a hostile organization second only to the intelligence organization of the USSR, I. Sayer and D. Botting, *America's Secret Army: the Untold Story of the Counter Intelligence Corps* (London: Grafton, 1989), p. 318.

125 Minutes of a meeting held at the Colonial Office attended by J. C. White (MI5) and Alex Kellar (MI5), 9 June 1948, fo. 15, CO 537/2760, PRO.

126 Remarkably, Verrier's respected account suggests that relations between SIS and the Israeli secret service were developing as early as 1948, Verrier, *Through the Looking Glass*, p. 97.

2

Anglo-Soviet intelligence co-operation and roads to the Cold War

Bradley F. Smith

In an ideal world, intelligence organizations, like Prussian kings, would be enlightened first servants of the state, gathering and collating information useful to their political and military masters. But in the actual world of the mid-twentieth century, intelligence organizations do not simply serve up value-free information or 'objective' assessments to their superiors. They are huge bureaucracies with their own operational dynamics, outlooks and visions of self-interest. They also have significant collective experiences and collective memories which can, and frequently do, exert strong influence on what advice they proffer.

When intelligence agencies are called upon to appraise the situation and intentions of another state at a critical moment in history, their judgement is based not merely on the overt and collective data which they have secured about that state, and the collective insight and wisdom which they have brought to bear upon it. The kinds of experiences which the members of the agency have had with the foreign state and its intelligence organs also profoundly shape the assessment of conditions and prospects which will finally be forwarded to the decision-makers.

In 1945, after five years of mortal struggle with *Abwehr* and *Gestapo/SD*, it is not surprising that many sections of the British intelligence community were not well inclined towards Germany or that they harboured grave doubts about whether defeat marked the demise of German expansionist aspirations. Even if the aura of efficiency and technical mastery which usually clung to all things German had been undermined in the inner sanctum of British intelligence by the knowledge that the German Enigma had been undone by the British Ultra.

At the other end of the belligerency scale, by VE Day (Victory in Europe, 8 May 1945) and VJ Day (Victory over Japan, 15 August 1945) the intelligence establishment in Britain enjoyed an unusually sympathetic and comradely relationship with the USA and its various intelligence practitioners. British and American intelligence personnel had experienced four years of close co-operative experience ranging from the Combined Intelligence Committee to Bletchley Park. National differences and egos still rankled and bumped from time to time, and severe difficulties had had to be overcome especially in centralizing intelligence assessment and in perfecting formal integrated systems for producing and sharing most secret (Ultra-Magic) intelligence. But the important phenomenon in 1945 was that the intelligence communities in both countries saw these developments as valuable achievements to be preserved in the post-war period. So while other formal aspects of wartime Anglo-American co-operation were allowed to end after VJ Day (especially the Combined Chiefs of Staff), the intelligence communities in both countries convinced their superiors that sigint and other forms of most secret intelligence co-operation should continue.

The preservation of wartime Anglo-American intelligence co-operation, especially its sigint aspects, is the clearest possible indication that the experience, collective opinion and memory of intelligence communities can prompt major foreign policy decisions. The agencies had been far from passive in this matter. On the contrary, the pressure to continue close intelligence co-operation had come from them, and once the governments responded positively to that pressure, Britain and the USA were probably bound more tightly together in the post-war era than could have been achieved by any conventional treaty.[1]

The early phase in the development of British post-war policy toward her other wartime superpower ally, the Soviet Union, also throws up interesting instances of the role of the intelligence community's collective memory in the shaping of high policy. British intelligence relations with the Soviet Union were far more circumscribed, and far less successful, during the Second World War than those enjoyed with the USA.

From June 1941 to October 1945, a British three-Service military mission was stationed in Moscow, with naval auxiliary stations in the far north and the Black Sea, operating for substantially the same period as the central mission in Moscow. Over this time, a comparable Soviet two-Service mission was established in London. Both the Soviet and British missions carried on various functions related to the organization and delivery of supplies to Soviet Russia, as well as concerning themselves with assorted administrative and personnel matters such as the processing of escaped and liberated prisoners of war.

From the very beginning, however, Whitehall considered the collection and exchange of intelligence to be one of the primary functions of both the British and Soviet military missions. When the first head of the British military mission to Moscow, Major-General Noel Mason Macfarlane, was appointed in the fourth week of June 1941, his orders specified that he was to act as a conduit for the communication of intelligence to the Soviet General Staff and to acquire all possible information which would help the intelligence agencies in London to assess the Soviet Union's power, her capacity to withstand the German assault, and her ability to inflict serious damage on the invader.[2] In addition, the authority designated in Whitehall to act as the mission's primary contact point was the office of the DMI (Director of Military Intelligence).[3]

Although the public records contain much less information regarding British liaison arrangements with the Soviet mission in London than they do regarding the directions given to the British mission in Moscow, the high place accorded intelligence in that relationship is also clear. Long accounts produced by the Liaison Group listing intelligence provided to the Soviet mission, and decrying the Soviet failure to reciprocate, begin at least as early as 1942, and continue on until the end of the war.[4]

Despite great efforts and considerable torment and soul-searching, the British hope for a profitable wartime intelligence partnership with the Soviet Union was never fully realized. Much of the reason for this disappointment arose from the repressive, secretive and suspicious features of the Stalinist regime, which are now common knowledge. British officials made numerous efforts to overcome or circumvent these limitations, but in the end they always failed, and in their minds most, if not all, of the failures which occurred in their intelligence relationship with the USSR during the war were due to these negative aspects of the Soviet regime.

From a forty-year vantage point it is clear that although the various horrid and unpleasant aspects of Stalinism bore a generous share of the responsibility, there were many other significant causes of the shortcomings and failures that occurred in the effort to achieve East–West intelligence co-operation.

First among them was the opinion, which seems to have grown stronger among British officials as the war progressed, that intelligence co-operation between allies is both simple and natural. The ease with which they acquired intelligence from the allied governments in exile in London may have played a significant role in the rise of this belief although we know very little about this aspect of the intelligence history of the Second World War. What clearly, and demonstrably, played a major part in the British idea of the naturalness of intelligence co-operation were the arrangements which were made with the USA, especially the sigint agreement with the United States Navy of 1 October 1942 and the BRUSA agreement with the United States Army of 17 May 1943. After these had been achieved it was easy for British intelligence officials to ease into a rhythm of normalizing inter-allied intelligence co-operation, and to perceive hiccups in this flow as peculiar, or perhaps sinister.

In addition to such overly rosy expectations by British intelligence officials regarding allied intelligence co-operation and the formidable obstacles which Stalinism placed in the way of any such closeness with the USSR, the British government made a series of misjudgements or bad calls following 22 June 1941 which lessened further the prospects for a flourishing intelligence trade between Moscow and London.

One of the most important of these, which would cast a long dark shadow over all of Britain's efforts to collaborate with the USSR between 1941 and 1945, was the assumption held throughout Whitehall in June 1941, and formalized in the directives for the mission to Moscow, that the Soviet Union's effort to withstand the Nazis was doomed to quick failure. Mason Macfarlane's primary assignment was to urge the Soviets to do the best they could and hold out as long as possible – prolong resistance 'by a few days' – but the British consensus held that the USSR was unlikely to last more than two to three months. After the inevitable quick collapse of resistance, the mission was instructed to try to get the Soviets to destroy everything which might be of value to the victorious Germans and, due to the special urgings of the DNI (Director of Naval Intelligence), to scuttle the Red Fleet. Once these bits of self-inflicted devastation had been completed, the mission, and any Soviets who were prepared to carry on the fight, were invited to scatter to the four winds and to try to make their way to Britain. Mason Macfarlane himself was told that he should go a thousand miles south and then work his way on foot over the mountains to India.[5]

This ringing vote of no confidence in Soviet capabilities, though certainly understandable in the light of Hitler's smashing victories in 1940 and early 1941, as well as the British lack of information about Soviet economic and military assets, was not the best way to encourage feelings of comradeship with the Soviet government.

By the end of July 1941 Mason Macfarlane and the DMI did begin to change their minds about Soviet prospects, but not until September was the Air Ministry prepared to concede that it had underestimated the Red Air Force. Three months later the great victory before Moscow provided the Foreign Office with an opportunity to castigate its military colleagues for having abysmally underestimated Soviet power, but as soon as the German spring offensive began to roll in 1942, the JIC immediately issued more dire warnings of Soviet disasters, and the Chiefs of Staff were even less optimistic about the USSR's chances.[6]

That the Soviets saw this as dark and denigrating pessimism about their chances and abilities is understandable. The offence was compounded by the British conviction that they had come to Moscow to act as teachers to the fumbling and doomed military leaders of the USSR. The mission's initial orders included the duty to assist the Soviets by sharing with them 'our experience' in fighting the Germans. But within a week of his arrival Mason Macfarlane discovered that the Soviets were not the least interested in 'our experience', and by 2 July his primary Soviet liaison contact was complaining that the British were talking too much and 'not doing enough fighting'.[7]

The initial War Office reaction to such charges was one of righteous indignation; a colonel in MO 1 contemptuously dismissed them on 10

July with the observation that 'we're doing quite nicely' in fighting the Germans, a remark which, coming as it did on the heels of the loss of Crete and the defeat of Operation 'Battle Ax' in the Western Desert was, at best, optimistic. But by August, Whitehall had reversed position and repeatedly tried to portray Britain as poor and weak as possible in order to parry limitless Soviet requests for more material aid and some form of second front. In September a Foreign Office official conceded resignedly that the only thing the Soviets believed they could learn from the British Army was 'the art of evacuation'.[8]

Even this abrupt fall from grace and confidence would not have been such a severe blow to the image and bargaining position of British officials had they not unwittingly done many things to convince the Soviets that the military mission was made up of arrogant enemies of the USSR intent on gaining intelligence about the Soviet system.

The first aspect of this image problem was the extensive use of personnel in the mission, and the liaison organization dealing with the Soviets in London, who had previously fought with the British forces in the Russian campaign of 1919. Such officers were given these assignments between 1941 and 1945 because no one in the War Office seems to have thought it was a problem, and because they were the only people in the British armed forces who could speak Russian and had Russian experience.

The result was a whole series of unfortunate incidents, as well as bitterly hostile reports sent back to the War Office from Moscow. All of this culminated in 1943 in a public scandal over a former head of mission making anti-Soviet speeches and a painful controversy concerning General Burrows's desire, when presenting his credentials as the new head of mission, to wear the decorations which he had won while fighting with the Whites against the Soviets in 1919.[9]

Even many of the officers sent to the Soviet Union, who did not have a 'White' past, did little to disguise their dislike for the USSR. They were, of course, in a highly difficult assignment, isolated, frequently treated rudely, with little to do, and in constant companionship with members of the Soviet secret police. The mission reports abound in negative comments on the USSR and the Soviet people – 'men of peasant stock disguised as officers', and so on. Interdepartmental crises occurred repeatedly as the Foreign Office tried to lessen the worst effects of what one Army officer temporarily assigned to the Moscow mission described as the basic fact that there were many there 'who dislike Russia and Russians, and don't try to hide it.'[10]

On the other hand, what the mission did try to conceal were a series of clumsy attempts to get around the Soviets' espionage paranoia and the country's formidable security restrictions. That the first head of the mission, Mason Macfarlane, had twice served as a military attaché and, as the Soviets were told, had been the Army's MI chief in France during the

54

disastrous campaign of 1940, did nothing to lessen Soviet suspicions. The trouble was compounded by repeated attempts to insert intelligence personnel into various areas of the Soviet Union to gather data on the USSR and its war effort. The British succeeded in placing naval people in Archangel, Murmansk and the Black Sea ports, but their attempt to put intelligence people within a mission to the Caucasus in 1941–2 were largely thwarted, as was the intelligence aspect of the abortive plan to place an Anglo-American air force in southern Russia in late 1942.[11]

The most long-lasting, and in Soviet eyes probably most suspicious of these futile intelligence projects, was the perennial proposal to place a naval intelligence officer in Vladivostock. The British vainly badgered Moscow to permit a Siberian mission throughout the period July–November 1941, revived the idea and tried again in July 1942, and when that failed came back to make a third, and equally unsuccessful attempt in February 1943.[12]

Given the range and depth of Soviet suspiciousness, these British efforts to spread an intelligence network over sensitive areas of the USSR (in all of which the allies had encouraged White opposition to the USSR in 1919–20) certainly put serious obstacles in the way of Soviet intelligence co-operation with the United Kingdom. When the other negative factors cited above are added in – Stalinist repression and paranoia, the appearance of British arrogance and lack of confidence in Soviet power, as well as a marked disregard for Soviet sensitivities – it seems quite remarkable that any intelligence co-operation at all occurred between Britain and the Soviet Union in the Second World War.

But military necessity does indeed make strange bedfellows. The Soviets spent most of the period from June 1941 to December 1942 in a fight for survival, and even after Stalingrad, they were obviously in need of all possible outside assistance. Britain had a clear interest in the Soviet Union blocking Hitler's advance and then tearing the heart out of the German Army. Co-operation was in Britain's military interest and, since through the middle period of the war the British public was smitten with the USSR, Whitehall also had no political choice except to make a serious effort to assist Russia, including making some attempt to aid her with useful intelligence.

Therefore immediately after the start of Operation Barbarossa in June 1941 the intelligence authorities agreed that the overall responsibility for providing intelligence to the USSR would be shared between the JIC and MI6. Each Service department would supply its own section of the mission in Moscow with routine intelligence but MI6 would control all most secret material including Ultra, and all such material would go to the mission only on MI6 communications circuits. All Ultra-based material was 'tightly wrapped up' with specific points often mixed in with less sensitive general material and attributed to the proverbial vague sources such as a 'most reliable and occasional' agent, or an agent in the German General Staff, etc. Very soon it was found necessary to divide the Ultra-based material into three categories: those items to be given to the Soviets, those intended exclusively for the senior members of the mission, and a category of 'hot' Ultra operational items (also suitably disguised as to source) which were to be given to the Soviet authorities immediately upon receipt.[13]

Mason Macfarlane took an assortment of intelligence items with him in June 1941 and immediately after presenting himself to his Soviet hosts he began to pass over intelligence, including items from various 'highly reliable' and 'occasional' most secret agents. The Soviets quickly responded to these welcome gifts in three ways: they expressed their gratitude, they asked for more, and they provided the British with some Soviet intelligence materials in exchange. Aside from the thankfulness, the other two features of the Soviet response would plague the Anglo-Soviet effort at intelligence exchange for four long years.

The first, most pressing, and most tormenting aspect of the Soviet reply to Britain's gift of intelligence was that it raised the question of how much Ultra should be given to the Soviets and under what conditions. All the old doubts and adverse opinions about the Soviets which lurked in White-hall were brought immediately into play, together with a caveat about heaping treasures on dying camels. But another feature peculiar to sigint greatly increased this tendency toward caution. The British authorities knew that Soviet codes were insecure. On 22 June 1941 a basic memor-andum set forth the fact that the Finns had read at least a portion of the Soviet codes during the Winter War of 1940 and presumably had continued to do so. This information was quickly supplemented by direct evidence from Ultra that the Germans were also reading some Soviet codes, and on a number of occasions in 1941–2 the military mission notified the Russians that some of their codes had been compromised.[14]

However, Whitehall could not solve its Ultra sharing problem by simply saying no, for as Mason Macfarlane soon forcibly indicated to London, high-grade intelligence was about all he had to give to the Soviets in the summer of 1941 and Soviet resistance, as well as the standing of the British military mission, needed all possible assistance.[15] Furthermore, as the summer wore on, it became obvious that Soviet resistance had been bent but not broken, and London was tempted to take bigger risks in supplying high-grade intelligence to the Soviets at critical moments in the Soviet, and allied, struggle for survival.

In consequence, London bounced back and forth between its desire to give, its fears of source compromise and the limitations imposed by the spotty quality of the intercepts it was obtaining from the Eastern Front. During the summer and early autumn of 1941 two crises occurred in Ultra transmission policy, both prompted by urgent pleas from the military mission for permission to give more Ultra information to the Soviets, and both ended in reiteration of the muddled formula that Ultra would not be given to the Soviets on a regular basis, coupled with the claim that the mission was already receiving everything available, and that specified 'hot' items could be handed over when 'C' gave his approval.[16]

The disappointed reaction of the mission to this confusing situation is easily traceable in the records, while the Soviet response can be almost as clearly inferred from the mission's reports on the meetings which occurred with Soviet officials. The Soviets immediately concluded that the British were holding back on them and badgered the mission to be more generous, spicing their requests with barbed observations that the much-vaunted British intelligence service was either overrated or dissembling.[17]

This situation was obviously not conducive to an effective exchange of intelligence but it had a further, and perhaps more serious effect as well. By giving the Soviets bits and pieces of Ultra material at irregular intervals, the British authorities created ideal conditions for misassessment of the intelligence data. The isolated 'hot' items given to the Soviets were analagous to the much more numerous 'golden eggs' which Churchill treasured, and whose impulsive use and misinterpretation by the Prime Minister, were a constant torment to 'C' and GCHQ. But in the Soviet case the risks of misassessment were even greater because Stalin did not have the British JIC reports and the like, which at least gave Churchill a fighting chance to get things right. Inevitably the Soviets got things wrong, and unfortunately they got the meaning of the Ultra titbits wrong in relation to the important issue of where and when the Germans were concentrating in the centre of their September attack line, that is the movements in preparation for the assault on Moscow.[18]

Stalin himself took the British ambassador to task in the third week of September, accusing the British military mission of providing erroneous high-level intelligence. The mission, the DMI, 'C' and a host of other officials subsequently strove to prove to their British masters that they had had it right and that Stalin had somehow got it wrong. But whatever the merit of the British intelligence establishment's explanations, the 'hot' Ultra delivery system had serious weaknesses which were never corrected and always left the Soviets with the feeling that they were being short-changed and on occasion not being given the true story.[19]

But if the British 'hot' Ultra response to the Soviet request for more high-grade intelligence after the initial delivery of 19 June ultimately left the Soviets confused, dissatisfied and even more suspicious than usual, the Soviet offer to share intelligence with the British released a comparable tide of confusion and disappointment in the military mission and in London. The intelligence which the Soviets provided was low in volume, came in dribs and drabs, and was never as showy as the Ultra 'hot' flashes which the British provided. Mason Macfarlane's response to the first Russian delivery – 'meagre' he called it – would be repeated *ad nauseam* both inside the mission and in London over the next four years. That Mason Macfarlane would also add near the end of his 30 June 1941 dispatch that the Russian materials included 'nevertheless some quite useful stuff' was also a precursor of a series of often grudging addenda that although the Soviets never provided 'hot' items they frequently included materials which were useful.[20]

Throughout the late summer and early autumn of 1941, amid the normal refrain that Britain gave more and better intelligence than she received, the Soviet items were of sufficient quality and quantity to lead Mason Macfarlane to observe that the two sides were conducting 'good business', enjoying 'excellent relations', and that in regard to order of battle exchanges the results were 'most satisfactory'.[21]

Yet such was the nature of the Soviet regime, and the ebb and flow of the tides of war, that the intelligence co-operation followed a complex and erratic course. Arrangements were gradually made in August 1941 for specialized co-operation on two important subjects: German order of battle (OB) and 'Y' matters. Each of these specialized areas followed a different course in regard to effectiveness and longevity. Some exchange of OB on Japan continued from August 1941 until January 1943, and after a fourteen months' hiatus, was resumed in a stunted form through the efforts of a special American OB mission to Moscow which shared its acquisitions with the British.[22]

Y co-operation also began in August 1941, but had a shorter duration, for the Soviets broke contact on army and air force Y in December 1942. The Royal Navy continued to operate a Y collection station in north Russia until the end of the war, and a few spasmodic Y exchange contacts seem to have been made on the Royal Navy side, and through a Y contact in the British embassy, in 1943–4. But overall, Y co-operation had a short life and was very frustrating for the British authorities due to Soviet hesitation and secrecy.[23]

British and Soviet interchanges on German OB were, as might be expected, the longest lasting, and probably the most beneficial sector of exchange between the two powers. But here too, the co-operation was uneven with the British giving more than they received, and the Soviets blowing hot and cold; being most generous and demanding on the eve of decisive battles and most tight-fisted and uncooperative after great triumphs such as Stalingrad and Kursk. The British were also angered by what they saw as Soviet politicizing of the exchanges, withholding information when relations between the two countries were clouded and 'rewarding' the British with extra OB treats on such occasions as the ratification of the Anglo-Soviet alliance, or the very eve of Overlord.[24]

Other more restricted areas of intelligence exchange occurred with rhythms that were equally bewildering and irritating to the British authorities. In general the Soviets were very cautious about sharing technical intelligence about their own or German equipment. But for no obvious reason they allowed an RAF test pilot to fly four models of Soviet front-line combat aircraft in August 1941, and among other less noteworthy incidents of erratic and unpredictable openhandedness in a broad field of secrecy regarding technical intelligence, after Kursk the Red Army gave the British mission technical details and actual samples of the new German Panther tank and Ferdinand self-propelled gun at a time when the Germans had not employed these weapons against the Western powers in North Africa or Sicily.[25]

When looking at the broad sweep of intelligence material which Britain and the USSR supplied to each other in the course of the Second World War a number of significant features stand out: and some of these had an important bearing on Britain's early post-war vision of the USSR. Overall, the British gave the Soviets far more, and especially more high-grade, intelligence than they received, but leaving aside the weighty question of how much intelligence would have to be supplied to balance out the value of what the Soviet military machine did to the Germany army, the Soviets did give as well as take. However, from late 1943 both sides reduced the flow of information, especially high-grade intelligence, which they supplied to each other, and by 1945, except for occasional bursts of isolated generosity, the exchange consisted of relatively low-grade, routine information.

This situation invited invidious comparison in London between the scanty Anglo-Soviet and the burgeoning Anglo-American co-operation which was expanding at an enormous rate during the last phase of the war.

Over and over again as one reads through the records from 1941 to 1945 a common pattern repeats itself; at the moment of receipt British officers on the spot often expressed gratitude for what had come to them from the Soviets, but the higher up the chain of command one moved (even at the time) the smaller was the value placed on the Soviet contribution. In a parallel pattern, the longer the war lasted, the stronger and more universal became the Whitehall litany that the Soviets had not co-operated effectively on matters of intelligence.

This was clearly due to the fact that only at the top, and only near the end of the conflict, was it possible to grasp the big picture and place an appropriate value on the Soviet informational contribution. In addition, as the subtitle of the official British history of intelligence in the Second World War ('its effect on operations') makes clear, Whitehall emphasized intelligence which immediately helped its operations; viewed from that perspective most of what the Soviets passed over, in fact most of what they probably possessed, was of marginal value to a Britain fighting halfway around the world in close union with the USA.

But since this pattern of downgrading Soviet intelligence material persisted in Whitehall throughout the war, and was often couched in angry and resentful language, it is reasonable to assume that more was involved than merely an effort to sift wheat from chaff. It was also the product of the anti-Soviet and anti-Russian sentiments rumbling within the armed service high command which perplexed and tormented the Foreign Office until at least the winter of 1944–5, when its own worries about future relations with the USSR inclined it to let the Whitehall anti-Communist dogs alone.[26]

A survey of the main efforts made by the Chiefs of Staff and the JIC to summarize military relations with the USSR, and the intelligence dimensions of that relationship between November 1943 and early October 1945 (six weeks *after* VJ Day), will indicate how the most negative possible view of the Soviet intelligence-sharing effort was gradually formalized and then served as the basis for a general conclusion that prospects for 'post-hostilities' co-operation with the USSR were extremely bleak.

In November 1943 Colonel Firebrace, the head of the London office of the British liaison unit dealing with the Russians (himself a veteran of the 'White' campaign of 1919), drew up a four-page report on 'our military relations with the USSR'. The report consisted solely of intelligence matters, and was divided into three segments: equipment and technical exchanges, intelligence exchanges regarding the Germans and Japanese, and visits to each other's fronts and installations. Under all three headings he concluded that the British had shared generously and 'done our best to play the game', while the Soviets could claim 'no credit for co-operation'.[27]

Not everyone in British intelligence agreed with Firebrace's analysis. Colonel F. Thornton in MO 1, for example, noted on 7 November 1943 that the report 'condemns the Russians too strongly', for although they had given less than they had received, they had provided a 'fair' amount, especially of technical information.[28]

But such cautionary views had no impact on Firebrace's report nor on its reception by the JIC. Firebrace concluded not only that the Soviets had 'done little to reciprocate our efforts or to co-operate with us', but contended that such non-co-operation was the result of a 'deliberate political policy' to grab everything possible from the Western powers and give nothing in return.[29]

In February 1944 a subcommittee of the JIC printed Firebrace's report and accepted most of its negative conclusions about co-operation with the USSR. The Service members of the committee agreed with Firebrace's report 'as a whole', but the Foreign Office thought it was too negative and called for a softer conclusion.[30] In March came the full JIC's turn to act. The committee stressed the 'continuous flow' of information 'of the highest value' which had been provided to the Soviets, while the latter had supplied only 'scanty' information in return. But faced with the imminence of Overlord and the fact that in that context it was 'of the highest importance to persuade the Russians to discuss their strategy, plans and intentions' with the West, the JIC eschewed Firebrace's advocacy of a 'get tough' policy with the Soviets, and did not indulge in dire judgements about Soviet political practices or intentions. None the less, the JIC, like its subcommittee before it, did attach as an appendix the highly critical report on Soviet practice and 'political policy', which had been written by Colonel Firebrace.[31]

Throughout the remainder of 1944 and on into the spring of 1945, in virtually every policy discussion reflecting fears of Soviet intentions or 'getting tough with the Russians', the JIC and JIC subcommittee reports were cited by those calling for a strong line. Firebrace's vision of the dire results of having tried to co-operate with the Soviets continued to be exhibit A for those who wished to move toward greater assertiveness or at least harder bargaining.

When the shooting stopped in Europe the JIC's inclination to establish a formula for being tougher with the Soviets – based on the view that 'open-handed' intelligence relations during the war had failed – rapidly expanded. On 23 May, two weeks after VE Day, the JIC issued a paper which consisted of a special subcommittee report on 'Relations with the Russians'. This paper specifically excluded any 'questions of high policy', considering 'mainly the type of negotiation hitherto carried on – i.e. the exchange of military intelligence, technical information exchange and the grant of facilities'. The JIC's basic premise, based on what might be called the 'Firebrace version' of the history of these three aspects of Anglo-Soviet wartime relations, was the predictable one that as negotiators the Russians were characterized by 'suspicion', 'an obsession with security and prestige', 'centralization of control', 'hard bargaining', and a tendency toward 'the multiple or indirect approach' (continuing 'their tactics of asking for the same thing at different levels'). The paper also drew the obvious conclusion that henceforth Britain should follow a policy of giving nothing 'to the Russians gratuitously'; all Soviet requests should be co-ordinated in London, all replies should be standardized, and 'the issues on which we are prepared to be really tough should be carefully selected'. Most important of all, 'no Russian request should normally be granted unless some request of ours to which we attach importance is granted in connection with it'.[32]

Once again, this JIC subcommittee report used a distorted picture of wartime intelligence co-operation with the Soviets to paint a dismal picture of the prospects for the future, and it too enjoyed a wide circulation, and was frequently cited by those trying to point British 'post-hostilities' policy toward the USSR into a more 'realistic' and assertive direction.

The last chapter in the story appeared in October 1945, six weeks after VJ Day, when the British military mission in Moscow was withdrawn. The last head of mission, Lieutenant-General J. A. H. Gammell, wrote a final report which, when circulated by the JIC and the Chiefs of Staff, recapitulated all the arguments of its predecessors and drew even colder conclusions for the future. Characterizing the Soviet attitude as one of 'get all the information you can, and give nothing – or at least, the barest minimum – in exchange', Gammell had no hesitation about drawing wide-ranging conclusions from his observations:

> Study of previous Soviet policy and mentality seem to indicate that, had they the sole use of the atomic bomb, the Soviet leaders would not hesitate to use it to further their own interests. It would be unfortunate if the Russians were allowed to gain the impression that the U.S.A. and ourselves were not prepared to do the same in defence of policies which we believe to be right and vital to our own security.[33]

Obviously this is as chilly an early Cold War picture of future East–West relations and methods as one is likely to discover, but it should not be taken as more than it was. Its tone was harsh in part because Gammell seems to have had the most difficult time of any of the British mission chiefs in Moscow. He exchanged little with the Soviets at a time when the West depended less on Soviet military power and looked on Soviet policies in Eastern Europe with rising fear and suspicion.

None the less, the Gammell report was the culminating feature of a special trend in British policy-making toward the USSR which had been gathering momentum since late 1943. From the Firebrace report of November 1943 to the Gammell report of October 1945, three basic points were repeated with rising passion and urgency:

1 the Soviets had not played fair in intelligence sharing
2 a tougher policy on the part of Britain (and the USA) would probably yield better results
3 this experience and this conclusion should be seen as a weathercock for helping to determine future Western policy toward the USSR.

Therefore, even though the JIC has received considerable attention from scholars when examining Britain's route to the Cold War, when dealing with such organizations it is not enough to study policy trends, ideological currents, or economic and strategic considerations.[34] Bureaucratic experience and bureaucratic memory were also significant factors. In this regard intelligence experience should not be overlooked, nor should the 'professionalism' of the intelligence community provide it with a free pass from careful examination at all possible levels of inquiry.

NOTES

All sources, unless indicated to the contrary, are from the Public Record Office, Kew, Surrey.

1 B. F. Smith, 'Sharing Ultra in World War II', *International Journal of Intelligence and Counter Intelligence* Vol. II, No. 1 (1988), pp. 59–72.

2 Noel Mason Macfarlane papers, Box 2, Folder 31, Imperial War Museum; CIGS instructions for the mission, WO 193/645A.

3 Most of Mason Macfarlane's main reports are so addressed, see for example the series in WO 193/645A, such as that of 3 July 1941.

4 See for example JP (41) 523, 6 July 1941, WO 193/659; 3 March 1943 report, WO 208/4115, and 26 July 1941 report in CAB 122/101.

5 Mason Macfarlane's papers, Box 2, Folder 31, 'Draft', Imperial War Museum; Naval orders, 22 June 1941, ADM 223/252 and MI 14 conclusion, 23 June 1941, WO 193/644, as well as the basic orders cited above. Two sample glimmers of light in the dark corner of allied intelligence co-operation are J. Herman, 'Agency Africa: Rygor's Franco Polish Network and Operation Torch', *Journal of Contemporary History* Vol. XXII, No. 4 (October 1987), pp. 681–706 and F. Moravec, *Master of Spies* (London: 1975). But no extensive effort has been made even to collate the overall references to acquisition of intelligence material from the governments in exile that are in the general correspondence series of the Foreign Office, FO 371.

6 See Mason Macfarlane to CIGS, WO 32/15548; Air Mission to Air Ministry, 12 September 1941, AIR 8/564; JIC (42) 200 (final) 1 June 1942, CAB 79/21.

7 22 June 1941 orders, ADM 223/252 and Head of Mission talk with M. Zhukov, 29 June 1941, FO 371/29485/N3277; Head of Mission to DMI, 3 July 1941, WO 193/654A.

8 10 July 1941 note, WO 193/654A; 24 August 1941, Colonel Firebrace and DMI comments, WO 32/15548; V. Cavendish-Bentinck comment 12 September 1941, FO 371/29563/N5219.

9 Warner note. May 1944, FO 371/43420/N3365. See also FO 371/43288/N1208.

10 Admiral Miles report, 31 December 1942, ADM 223/252; Warner to Clark Kerr, 1 July 1943, FO 800/301, frame 55.

11 On the Caucasus see the whole of FO 371/29594; Air forces in southern Russia, Chargé to Foreign Office, 11 February 1942, FO 181/96437.

12 See FO 371/29563, especially N4976 and N5219; FO 371/32955/N3889, and Exham to Clark Kerr, 13 February 1943, FO 800/301, frame 10–11.

13 The main characteristics of the system's operation are in F. H. Hinsley, E. E. Thomas *et al.*, *British Intelligence in the Second World War*, Vol. 2, (London: HMSO, 1981) pp. 58ff.

14 ibid. and FO to Moscow, nr. 662, 22 June 1941, FO 371/29358/N3048. Smith, 'Sharing Ultra in World War II'.

15 Mason Macfarlane to CIGS, 15 August 1941, WO 32/15548.

16 Hinsley *et al. British Intelligence*, Vol. 2, pp. 58f. The designation for the director of MI6 was 'C'; in the Second World War 'C' was Sir Stewart Menzies.

17 See for example Mason Macfarlane's report of 8 September 1941, WO 193/649.

18 An echo of this crisis appears in Volume 2 of the official history, Hinsley *et al.*, *British Intelligence*, Vol. 2, p. 60 (note).

19 Mason Macfarlane to COS, 22 September 1941, WO 193/645A.

20 Mason Macfarlane to War Office, 30 June 1941, WO 32/15548.

21 See especially the Mission War Diary for this period, WO 178/25.

22 The first Soviet delivery of Japanese OB material occurred on 26 August 1941, that is three and a half months *before* Pearl Harbor, WO 193/649. Y involves the interception of wireless traffic, its study by 'traffic analysis', and frequent breaking of low-grade combat codes.

23 Hinsley *et al.*, *British Intelligence*, Vol. 2, p. 63, states that the first Y officer was sent to the Soviet Union in the summer of 1941, but the first documentary evidence of a direct contact with the Soviets seems to be 11 September 1941, AIR 8/564.

24 Discussion of German Army OB began at least as early as 3 July 1941, and naval OB discussions by 9 July 1941, WO 178/25 and COS (41) 133 (0) 9 July 1941, CAB 80/58.

25 Collier to Air Ministry, 11 August 1941, AIR 8/564; 25 July 1943 summary, WO 208/1835.

26 See for example V. Cavendish-Bentinck comment, May 1945, FO 371/47849/N5116.

27 COS (43) 729 (0) 24 November 1943, CAB 122/942.

28 CAB 122/942.
29 COS (43) 729 (0) 24 November 1943, CAB 122/942.
30 See notes on p. 1, JIC (44) 81 (0) (final), 8 March 1944, FO 371/43289/N2914.
31 ibid.
32 JIC (45) 163 (0) Revised Final, 23 May 1945, FO 371/47849/N6045.
33 AIR 20/8061.
34 Two excellent short pieces on the subject are D. Cameron Watt, 'British Military Perceptions of the Soviet Union as a Strategic Threat, 1945–1950', in J. Becker and F. Knipping (eds) *Power in Europe? Great Britain, France, Italy and Germany in a Postwar World, 1945–1950* (Berlin and New York, 1986) pp. 325–38 and R. Smith, 'British Officials and the Development of British Postwar Soviet Policy', *International Affairs* Vol. 64, No. 4. (autumn 1988), pp. 631–47.

3

Covert action within British and American concepts of containment, 1948–51[1]

Beatrice Heuser

It was in 1948 that the United States and Britain conceived the policy which later came to be called 'roll-back'. Towards the end of that year the United States first attempted to implement the policy of liberating Eastern Europe from Soviet domination. This policy had been approved at the highest level in both Washington and London, by the successive US Presidents Harry Truman and Dwight Eisenhower, and by the British Foreign Secretary, Ernest Bevin (and presumably also the Prime Minister, Clement Attlee).[2] The US and British governments wanted to realize their plans not only by supporting East European resistance movements through propaganda and arms aid, but also by infiltrating exiles who were trained to organize insurrections. As anti-Communist propaganda campaigns were complemented by such clandestine operations which were mainly planned and staged by the British and American secret services, it is often difficult to find hard evidence for these policies, and very rarely is it possible to prove their implementation. Even so, enough pieces of the jigsaw can be found to put together the outlines of this liberation policy and of the attempts to execute it.[3]

Within two or three years after the end of the Second World War, Western foreign policy makers began to feel threatened by their former Soviet ally. Leaving aside any discussion of whether this was an accurate assessment, it is important to note that the British and US governments, alarmed by their military advisers[4] and their Moscow embassy staffs,[5] began to regard Stalin as set on extending his sphere of influence beyond the areas already controlled by him in 1945. While they regarded world domination as the Soviet Union's ultimate goal, and were convinced that Stalin would use subversion, civil war and political blackmail in pursuit of it, they did not believe that he would wittingly start a real war of a limited sort, let alone a world war. Yet in Anglo-American appreciations, a deliberate initiation of war by Stalin was not dismissed totally for the time when the USSR would have developed its own atomic bombs, thereby ending the US atomic monopoly.[6]

Based on the assumption of this threat, Britain and the United States in parallel developed a general political strategy, which was dubbed 'containment policy' in the USA, but which equally existed in Britain. Both governments held a remarkably similar view of the Soviet threat at the time, and reacted similarly;[7] if anything, it was the British Labour government that led the way.[8] It was to a large extent due to Bevin that Truman was persuaded to go beyond an interpretation of 'containment' which precluded military commitments in the form of defence pacts in peacetime. While Bevin found understanding and sympathy in Washington, particularly on the part of the Secretary of State Dean Acheson, the North Atlantic Pact in its present form would hardly have come into existence without Bevin and his French colleague, Georges Bidault.[9]

Nevertheless, certain differences between the attitudes of Britain and the United States continued to exist until the end of 1948,[10] and once again after 1951.[11] Churchill had implicitly accepted the concept of spheres of influence with the Moscow percentages agreement of 1944, in which he made an agreement with Stalin about which areas of Europe their two countries should dominate. The British Prime Minister had consulted neither his Cabinet nor Parliament,[12] but his thinking was rooted deeply in centuries of British foreign policy, when only a direct threat to British interests was seen as cause for conflict, and arrangements with other powers were never excluded for ideological reasons only. As British Foreign Secretary, Anthony Eden had also been involved in the Moscow deal. He did not regard it as a case of 'appeasing dictators': neither he nor Churchill thought of the percentages agreement as a sign of British weakness in a conflict with an ideological adversary, but as a pragmatical arrangement between two Great Powers. In 1944 Churchill and Eden still thought it possible or even likely that Stalin would keep to his own sphere of influence and that he would not threaten the areas of the world dominated by the British empire.

By 1947–8 this no longer seemed to be true, and Stalin was seen as challenging Western control or at least Western democracy in several areas beyond the Iron Curtain. By mid-1948 the Labour government under Bevin and Attlee, who had followed Churchill and Eden in office, was ready to commit itself to defend the states situated along the periphery of the Soviet empire against a military-*cum*-ideological threat, but had not yet conceived of the idea of challenging Stalin's rule within his own empire. This British attitude is exemplified by the 'Bastions Paper' of the summer of 1948.[13] The Bastions Paper does reflect British fears that Stalin would not be content with controlling his own sphere of influence alone but would attempt to seize areas beyond the Iron Curtain. But its hallmark was also a defensive stance which aimed at stopping Soviet expansion without engaging in full ideological conflict.

This implicit acknowledgement of the concept of spheres of influence did not correspond to the prevailing American attitude. The politics of successive US governments were rooted in a different tradition, hailing back to the Pilgrim Fathers, which had led Americans to believe in the intrinsic superiority of their own moral belief-system. The long isolation from the corrupt Old World, enshrined in the Monroe Doctrine, had been founded on the premise that American ideals of freedom and democracy could survive only if the USA were not contaminated by the pernicious influences of the Old World. But American isolationism and the recognition of spheres of influence by the USA before the First World War and during the inter-war years could not be maintained in the face of global conflict. If the Old World forced war upon the USA against its will, then this world had to be changed: in the famous words of Woodrow Wilson, the world had to be made safe for democracy. It was thus thought in Washington that only the adoption of American ideals and governmental procedures would improve the world and would make perpetual peace possible.[14].

In addition the political value-system of the United States was based on the firm conviction that given the choice, all humankind would prefer Western democracy to the 'yoke of communism and totalitarianism', in the US jargon of the Cold War.[15] The United States saw itself as the standard-bearer of Western values. This American missionary spirit contained aspirations no less global than those of the Soviet Union: as we shall see, the democratization of the world according to Western ideals became the explicit long-term aim of US foreign policy.

The US policy of containment with its proselytizing spirit after 1947 reached far beyond what was then referred to as 'the free world', let alone the Western hemisphere. If world peace was threatened by the USSR, everything had to be done to prevent Soviet expansionism, but beyond that, the Soviet Union itself had to be weakened until it was forced to withdraw from its own sphere of influence.[16] Afterwards the 'liberated' areas should be converted to democracy. Thus the US Secretary of State, George Marshall, briefed a group of US ambassadors on 17 March 1948:

> [The] ultimate United States objective toward Sov[iet] Balkan satellites – Yugoslavia, Albania, Bulgaria, Rumania and Hungary – may be summarized as [the] establishment [of] those states as democratic independent members [of the] family of nations, under conditions guaranteeing [their] people's [sic] effective enjoyment [of] human rights and non-discrimination against US interests and interests of other peace-loving states.

The Secretary of State emphasized that the Americans were hoping for the liberation of Eastern Europe from the 'totalitarian Soviet Balkan hegemony' which 'has thwarted [the] democratic will of [the] majority of [the] peoples, infringed [their] independence and sovereignty and subjugated them to [the] domination of Moscow'.[17] This supposed discontent was being fuelled by the US government through the radio broadcasts of the Voice of America.[18]

But the American activities were not confined to such broadcasts. Harry Truman approved a policy paper of the National Security Council (NSC 7 of 30 March 1948) which was entitled 'The Position of the United States with Respect to Soviet-Directed World Communism'. Here it says

> the USSR is attempting to gain world domination . . . a defensive policy cannot be considered an effectual means of checking the momentum of communist expansion and inducing the Kremlin to relinquish its aggressive designs. . . . As an alternative to a defensive policy the United States has open to it the organization of a world-wide counter-offensive against Soviet-directed world communism. . . . The United States should [aim] at undermining the strength of the communist forces in the Soviet world. . . . the United States should . . .
> – Develop a vigorous and effective ideological campaign.
> – Develop and at the appropriate time carry out a coordinated program to support underground resistance movements in countries behind the iron curtain, including the USSR.
> – Establish a substantial emergency fund to be used in combatting Soviet-directed world communism.[19]

This policy paper must be seen in connection with NSC 10/2 of 18 June 1948, creating the new CIA Office of Special Projects. It was given the task of planning and conducting covert operations in peacetime:

> covert operations are understood to be all activities . . . which are conducted or sponsored by this government against hostile foreign states or groups or in support of friendly foreign states or groups but which are so planned and conducted that any US Government responsibility for them is not evident . . . and that if uncovered the US Government can plausibly disclaim any responsibility for them. Specifically, such operations shall include any covert activities related to: propaganda; economic warfare; preventive direct action, including sabotage, anti-sabotage, demolition, and evacuation measures; subversion against hostile states, including assistance to underground resistance movements, guerillas and refugee liberation groups.

Acts of open aggression were excluded, however.[20] It has to be emphasized that this strategy, formulated during the presidency of Truman, was repeatedly applied during his years at the White House (as will be demonstrated), although Eisenhower and his Secretary-of-State-designate, Dulles, created the myth in their election campaign of 1952 that Truman's idea of containment had been purely passive and defensive.

In 1948 the US administration thus adopted a policy which was consciously modelled on that of their Soviet opponent. The National Security Council thought that the only way to deal with the 'world-wide Fifth Column' of 'Soviet-directed world communism' was a 'world-wide counter-offensive, as a defensive policy by attempting to be strong everywhere runs the risk of being weak everywhere'.[21] This conviction was based on the assumption that all Communist Parties were Stalin's tools, with which he was trying to break countries such as France or Italy out of the 'free world', bringing them under his own Communist domination. By the standards of the same interpretation, the Greek Civil War was seen in London and Washington as Communist subversive action supported by Stalin,[22] the sort of action, in fact, which was now being planned by the US government: it was probably impossible at the time to recognize that this was a crucial misinterpretation. Thus apart from having an important ideological element, the American policy of liberation was seen as a tit-for-tat in international affairs.[23]

While the British were ahead of the United States in formulating defensive policies against the Soviet threat, it was only several months after the USA that they developed a policy of liberation. But perhaps even more than the USA, they understood it as a counter-offensive. In doing so, the Labour government departed from Churchill's spheres-of-interest thinking as manifested in the percentages agreement, but they did so with the conviction that Stalin himself was not abiding by the agreement, as the evidence of Greece and some other cases seemed to show.

On 25 November 1948 Robert Hankey, a high-ranking official in the British Foreign Office, introduced the outline of a new policy to his colleagues on the Russia Committee (RC). It suggested that British policy should no longer be purely defensive when dealing with the 'Soviet Orbit in Europe', but Britain should take the offensive without, however, triggering a 'hot war'. Hankey's proposals met with agreement on all sides. The militant atmosphere of this meeting is best reflected in the postulation of the Chief of the RAF Staff, Lord Tedder, that 'we should aim at winning the "cold war" (by which he meant the overthrow of the Soviet régime) [sic] in five years time'.

In the course of this discussion, the one of the highest-ranking diplomats present, the Deputy Under-Secretary of State, Sir Ivone Kirkpatrick, pointed out that Britain's economic constraints and public opinion made it advisable initially to restrict any offensive action to a small area, and what he had in mind was Albania. Might not a civil war be started there? He was very explicitly arguing in terms of copying the Greek civil war (as all present assumed that the Soviet Union had started it). Sir Gladwyn

Jebb, like Hankey an Assistant Under-Secretary of State, and the chairman of the committee, pointed to the danger that the UN observers of the Greek Civil War might hear about such operations in Albania, and might publicize them. Kirkpatrick thought Western involvement would not become obvious if Albanian resistance movements were to be used to execute this plan. The committee liked the proposal and it was agreed to discuss it with the Americans.[24]

Thus the British government also adopted a liberation policy. The joint Anglo-American operation in Albania became the best-known attempt to implement it: in mid-February 1949 Ernest Bevin gave the green light for the project of severing Albania from the Soviet orbit by overthrowing its government.[25] Julian Amery, one of the three main organizers of this undertaking on the British side, emphasized the vindictive character of this endeavour: 'Stalin was trying to overthrow the pro-Western govern-ment in Athens, so I think we had every right to try and overthrow the pro-Soviet government in Tirana, or indeed in Sofia if we so wished.'[26]

It may have been the British who first suggested this plan to the Americans. The Greek Minister of War knew about US involvement in some 'indirect operation in Albania' by the end of March 1949.[27] The earliest published American document on this operation contains the minutes of a meeting of the Policy Planning Staff of the US State Depart-ment, dating from 1 April 1949. There it was decided to launch operations to establish a regime in Albania – and, if possible, elsewhere as well – which would be 'anti-communist and therefore pro-western'. For this purpose, extensive use was to be made of refugee groups

> representing the various free movements within the satellite countries. Assistance and, wherever possible, support should be given to elements within the captured countries which represent a weakness in the political control within the Russian orbit.[28]

These plans obviously fitted neatly into the context of the liberation policy, as formulated in Washington. But there was no mention here of replacing the Communist regimes in Eastern Europe with democratic governments: the US government would apparently have contented itself with any anti-Communist regime. The Albanian exiles, for example, wanted to re-establish the pre-war autocratic monarchy.[29]

On 14 September 1949 the plans concerning Albania (apparently called 'Operation Valuable'[30]) were discussed in Washington at a meeting between Ernest Bevin and his US counterpart, Dean Acheson.[31] Their realization, however, which was attempted over a period of four years, miscarried with disastrous effects for virtually all the Albanians involved. Most of the exiles who were parachuted into Albania were discovered immediately, killed on the spot or else captured and dragged off to be tortured before being humiliated in show trials, followed by executions on charges of treason.[32] The spectacular lack of success has been attributed to the betrayal of the operations by the Soviet agent Kim Philby, who represented the British Secret Intelligence Service in their planning and co-ordination with the Americans.[33] Yet there was also an element of reprehensible dilettantism, and Anglo-American (and internal departmental) rivalry also threw a spanner into the works.[34]

Operation Valuable dragged on until the end of 1953, but already by the end of 1950 the Foreign Office and the State Department began to feel unhappy about it. It was feared by the two foreign ministries that the operations in Albania might rekindle the flames of the Greek Civil War which had come to an end only in late 1949, or that they might serve Stalin as a pretext for taking military action against the adjacent Yugoslavia.[35]

There probably was another reason why Operation Valuable failed so miserably. There was little readiness on the part of the Albanian population itself to get organized for the overthrow of the government. In two CIA reports dating from September and December 1949 the conclusion was that no spontaneous Albanian insurrection was likely nor would such an insurrection have any chance of success unless it were given substantial aid from the outside.[36] Nor did the reports of the only Western embassy in Tirana, namely that of France, contain any evidence of resistance movements against the Communist government.[37]

The relative apathy of the population did not, however, fit into the Anglo-American understanding of the world at the time, based as it was on the assumption that all peoples of the earth were yearning for democracy (rather than peace), and that Eastern Europe was riddled with anti-Communist Fifth Columnists, happy to risk their lives for freedom and a form of government the majority of them had never experienced in their own countries. Walter Bedell Smith, first US ambassador in Moscow and head of the CIA from 7 October 1950 (and thus also responsible for the liberation policy), saw the Iron Curtain 'as a dike holding in check the churning torrents of the pent-up emotions of Eastern Europe'.[38] In reality there is little reason to believe that a sizeable proportion of the Eastern populations would have been willing once again to risk their own and their families' lives: after years of war they wanted food and fuel more then democracy and freedom of speech. Kim Philby commented cynically that the Albanian exiles found no arms open to welcome them.[39]

Another operation about which we have some information has all the trappings of a tragic comedy. It probably even constituted the first American 'roll back' operation.

In June 1948 the Yugoslav Communist Party had been expelled from the international Communist co-ordinating organization, the Cominform. Probably the main reason why Stalin humiliated the Yugoslav Communists in this way is that they had followed too radical a foreign policy, thereby provoking the Western powers unduly (who in turn thought that the

Yugoslavs were acting at Stalin's behest). The Yugoslav Communists, led by Tito, were taken by surprise by this excommunication, as they thought they had indeed been acting in the interests of world Communism (and thus of Stalin). For the best part of a year they continued to plead their innocence, begging Stalin for a reconciliation.[40]

The Western powers misunderstood these events to a considerable degree. Assuming that Stalin's autocracy was less palatable for the Communist governments of Eastern Europe than the political influence of the West, they thought it had been Tito who had broken free from the Kremlin's control.[41] What Western foreign policy analysts tended to overlook was the fact that the anti-Communist propaganda of the Voice of America made it quite clear to East European Communists who was their main enemy, and they certainly saw no alternative to co-operation with the Soviet Union.[42]

Against the background of this misinterpretation, the governments in Washington and London decided within days of the Yugoslav expulsion from the Cominform to support Tito against Stalin if necessary. In the view of Western diplomats only a more subservient Communist leader could realistically replace Tito. Both foreign ministries were convinced that any attempt to overthrow the Communist regime in Yugoslavia would create a welcome pretext for Soviet military intervention.[43] Moreover, it was believed that in the long term tactful support for Tito would encourage other East European governments to shake off Stalin's dictatorship.

This view was recorded by the US National Security Council (NSC) at the beginning of July 1948, and confirmed by President Truman.[44] It came to be the basis for many years of US economic and financial aid for Tito. A new aspect of the liberation policy had thus come into being: the US had stated its willingness in principle to support any Communist (and in this case certainly oppressive) regime as long as it was anti-Stalinist. While this was a pragmatic policy to assume, it was also a step away from the purely moral and ideological rationale of US foreign policy, which wanted to convert the world to freedom, the respect for human rights, and to peace.

Nevertheless, the decision of the NSC and, more important still, of the US President, to support Tito, did not stop the CIA half a year later from attempting to overthrow Tito. The CIA tried to infiltrate monarchist exiles into Yugoslavia, mainly the Serbian Chetniki,[45] who had fought against Tito's Partisans in a particularly bloody civil war during the Second World War. These men had been put into US Air Force uniforms, and it seems that, just like the Albanians later in Operation Valuable, they were arrested immediately by the Yugoslav secret police,[46] and taken off to concentration camps. Their journey there took them to the main railway station of Belgrade, where some of the former Chetnik leaders were recognized. Diplomats from the French embassy, who had received information about this, asked their stupefied American colleagues what on earth they were up to.[47]

This was apparently the first time that the US ambassador in Belgrade, Cavendish Cannon, had heard of the CIA operations. His following actions reflect his state of mind: he must have been both horrified at so much stupidity, and furious at this sign that his past advice was being disregarded. He cabled to the State Department that they should once and for all bury the notion that Tito's overthrow would result in anything but his replacement by a Soviet puppet: there were enough signs that Moscow was prepared to intervene given the slightest excuse.[48] To make sure that his views did not go unheard this time, Cannon informed his British colleague, Sir Charles Peake, about what he had found out. Peake in turn informed Whitehall, where the condemnation of 'this idiotic American behaviour' was unanimous all the way up to the Foreign Secretary. Bevin in a telegram to Washington echoed Cannon's views, admonishing the US administration to wind up the CIA operations in Yugoslavia immediately.[49] It does indeed seem as though the CIA had acted without the approval of the NSC or the US President.[50] Thus what was probably the first attempt to implement the liberation policy came to an end which was symptomatic of the entire policy.

Another predominantly British operation which seems to have been equally unsuccessful was carried out within the same year. The chief of MI6, Menzies, obtained the British government's authorization for his Secret Intelligence Service to try to contact resistance movements within the USSR, and the choice for a first operation seems to have fallen on Latvia. An ex-MI6 agent records one such operation in his memoirs: as a member of the British liaison staff, he helped organize the transport of groups of Latvian *émigrés* back to the shores of their native country. This was done with German S-boats with German crews and British liaison staff based at the northern German port of Bückeburg. The operations he witnessed came to grief; the Latvian agents, like the Chetniks and the Albanians before them, were picked up by members of the security services, in this case, the KGB.[51] The individual instance reported by the former British agent formed part of a much greater pattern: British operations of this sort were implemented from 1949 until 1956 against all three Baltic states, and extensive use was made of former German naval staff. The East Germans later based an anti-Western propaganda film on these operations, entitled *Rottenknechte* (Band of Knaves).[52]

It is probably of interest to note that these operations in the Baltic started in 1949,[53] and were thus conceived and authorized at roughly the same time as the Albanian operation, that is when British and American thinking was largely in unison about this way of countering Soviet Communism.

The year 1950 saw the beginning of the Korean War with its strong impact on Western perceptions of Soviet intentions. Once again it is of little importance for the purposes of this chapter to establish whether Stalin had ordered the attack by North Korea on the South, but this is what was believed in the West.[54] The attack on South Korea occurred after the Western intelligence services had predicted an increased belligerency on the part of the Soviet Union. The attack seemed to constitute an impressive confirmation of this forecast.[55] The most important decision-makers in the USA, Britain and France assumed not that the Korean War was the first step to a deliberately initiated world war, but that it was likely to be the first step in a series of world-wide Moscow-led acts of aggression.[56] It was largely believed in the West that this war was ushering in a new phase in Soviet foreign policy.[57] Attacks on Finland, West Germany, Yugoslavia, Greece or Iran were feared.[58]

Western reactions to the Korean War have been discussed many times: in US ambassador Averell Harriman's words, the Korean War 'put the "O" into NATO',[59] that is it resulted in the militarization of what had hitherto been little but a political alliance. Although plans for the militariz-ation of the pact had existed in the American and British planning staffs before the outbreak of war in the Far East, it is doubtful whether they could have been implemented if it had not been for the parliamentary approval given to these plans under the shock of the Korean War.[60] There was unanimity among the NATO partners about the urgent need for defensive measures to counter the Soviet threat. Agreement was also reached at the United Nations concerning a joint effort to defend South Korea.

Nevertheless, disagreements arose within six months of the outbreak of war about the form of this defence, and about the risk of escalation that should be incurred, particularly as the operation was entrusted to the command of the US General MacArthur: the British and the French came to regard MacArthur's strategy as unduly provocative in relation to Mao's newly established People's Republic, which soon entered the war on the side of North Korea.[61] Truman's public refusal of 29 November 1950 to exclude the possibility of using atomic weapons in Korea was also regarded as unnecessarily provocative in France, Britain, and throughout the Commonwealth.[62]

In the following year the disagreement between France and Britain on the one hand and the United States on the other emerged clearly. The French ambassador in Moscow, Yves Chataigneau, diagnosed a Soviet fear of encirclement by the Western powers, which was fuelled by the nego-tiations for the admission of Greece and Turkey into NATO.[63] In London the risky Far Eastern policies of Truman and MacArthur even caused the very architect of the US alliance with Europe, Ernest Bevin, and the Prime Minister, Clement Attlee, to have misgivings about US intentions; they wondered whether Washington was actually trying to provoke a general

East–West conflagration. The two politicians thought it necessary, in Attlee's words, to 'put the brakes on the bleachers'.[64] This was a remarkable dissonance in the 'special relationship' between the British and the US governments, whose policies towards and perceptions of the Soviet Union had been virtually identical until this point.[65]

This dissonance cannot be explained purely in terms of the United States' Far Eastern policies, although these were probably the first and main reason for the slight jarring of the harmony of European-American Cold War policies.[66] For in addition to the pushy Far Eastern policies, the United States also intensified its roll-back operations. The stepping up of this aggressive side of containment had also been planned prior to the outbreak of the Korean War, but like the other rearmament plans, it owed its approval by the US President to the scare caused by the attack on South Korea.[67] On 15 January 1951 the US Joint Chiefs of Staff not only asked the administration to increase their military procurement programme, but also urged them to fight 'A coordinated and integrated crusade against Kremlin-dominated communism everywhere' by adopting 'a large-scale program of psychological warfare, including special operations'. Just in case Truman had not got the message, the JCS added that 'crusade is used in the sense of a vigorous and aggressive movement for the advancement of an idea or cause'.[68]

The US National Security Council accepted this advice and incorporated it in its policy paper NSC 100, providing for the expansion of the subversive measures that had been adopted before the outbreak of war in the Far East. Thus anti-Communist propaganda was stepped up, and in addition to the Voice of America, Radio Free Europe and Radio Liberty were set up in 1950 and 1951 respectively, to broadcast to Eastern Europe and the Soviet Union. They received the vast bulk of their funding from the CIA.[69] The president of the Committee for a Free Europe, which ran Radio Free Europe, C. D. Jackson, described the mission of his broadcasting station as being 'to create conditions of turmoil in the countries our broadcasts reached'. General Lucius D. Clay, who is likely to have known about the beginnings of Western operations as chief of the US military authorities in Germany (1945–9) and was an intimate of Eisenhower's during the election campaign of 1952 which was partly fought over this 'roll-back' strategy, said the aim of the broadcasts was to 'help those trapped behind the curtain to prepare the day of liberation'.[70] The financing of this side of containment was secured with the help of the Mutual Security Act of May 1951, which earmarked funds for the support of resistance groups within the Soviet orbit.

In the following year, the CIA's Office for Special Operations (OSO) was merged with the Office for Policy Co-ordination (OPC), which in 1949 (before it had been brought under CIA control) had had a staff of 302. At the time of the merger, the OPC's staff had increased to 2,812 in the USA alone, and 3,142 abroad.[71] The OSO reached a strength of about 6,000 by January 1953.[72]

The number of covert operations organized by the CIA increased sixteenfold between January 1951 and January 1953.[73] The training and financing of the *émigrés* involved in these operations was organized through these agencies with Mutual Security Aid funding. The *émigré* groups were now organized into military units.[74] The largest unit among them was headed by the Polish Second World War veteran General Wladislaw Anders. Captured by the Soviets in 1939, he had organized Polish forces under Soviet command in 1941–2, and after being transferred to the command of General Eisenhower as supreme commander of the Allied European Forces, his forces were used against the Fascists in North Africa and Italy, contributing to the allied conquest of Montecassino in 1944. Anders now headed an army that numbered a staggering 239,000 *émigrés*, among them Poles, Bulgarians, Hungarians, Romanians and Czechoslovaks. With his experiences of Second World War operations, he claimed to be able to mobilize some 6,250,000 men behind the Iron Curtain, once a general East–West war were to break out: it was thought that his *émigré* forces could form cadres for larger forces integrating new refugees as they moved along. The US administration considered turning Anders's forces into an international brigade under the NATO Supreme Allied Commander in Europe, in the same way in which they had been under SHAEF (Supreme Headquarters Allied Expeditionary Force) command in the Second World War.[75]

In addition to the British operations in the Baltic area, there were important Anglo-American and purely American operations in the Ukraine and in the Caucasus.[76] But the main characteristic of the support given by the two Western powers to the Ukrainian nationalist movement (under the Ukrayinska Viyskova Orhanizatsiya) was that it started too late, at a time when the Soviets had all but eradicated any organized resistance in the Ukraine. The operations in the Ukraine got under way only in 1951 and ran on unsuccessfully until 1954.[77]

Most of the CIA's activities, however, were concentrated on the Far East. Originating in the context of the Korean War, these operations consisted mainly of paramilitary campaigns against mainland China which went on intermittently until Nixon's presidency.[78]

The French especially were none too happy about the expansion of the US liberation policy in 1951–2. Unlike their Anglo-American partners, they had never developed such a policy, and it is by no means certain that they were always kept informed about the activities of CIA and SIS. In a memorandum of 31 August 1951, the West European (Sub-) Department of the Quai d'Orsay noted its disapproval with the policy of trying to increase the number of rebels in Eastern Europe by means of radio broadcasts and other propaganda measures. In the opinion of the department's officials, it was an act of 'dishonesty' to tell the East Europeans that the hour of their liberation was nigh, as the West was ultimately *not* prepared to start a full-scale world war to defeat Stalinist oppression. The department urged the French government to point out to Washington the grave danger of prematurely inciting Stalin's East European vassals to start a civil war. This was none of the West's business: consensus among the Western powers, as the memorandum said, was based on NATO and its *defensive* quality, not on any *aggressive* policy.[79]

The head of the European Department, François Seydoux, agreed with this memorandum: NATO's security was based on the belief of the Western European populations in the moral integrity of their cause, which in turn would inspire them with the necessary moral strength to resist Soviet political pressure, and ultimately military aggression, should this occur. The moral strength of NATO would be undermined, however, if NATO's most important member, the United States, was conducting operations against the Soviet Union which could not be called defensive even by the most sympathetic of the USA's allies. In Seydoux's view, the strength and cohesion of NATO depended to some considerable extent on the moral conduct of US foreign affairs.[80]

François Seydoux's views were paralleled increasingly by senior members of the British Foreign Office. In January 1951 the Permanent Under-Secretary in the Foreign Office, Sir William Strang, advocated a policy to 'deflect the Americans from unwise and dangerous courses'.[81] The Foreign Office staff on several occasions showed its concern about the liberation policy. They thus anticipated the change of government at the end of 1951 with the return of Churchill and Eden to office. The British withdrawal from the Albanian operation at the beginning of 1952 is indicative of this change in British government attitudes.[82]

Both the French and the British foreign ministries regarded the emphasis put by Eisenhower and John Foster Dulles on the liberation of Eastern Europe in their election campaign as most unsalutory. A Foreign Office commentary on one of Eisenhower's election speeches on the policy of liberation put forward the same argument as the Quai d'Orsay's West European (Sub-) Department, namely that such talk was dangerous in view of the false hopes it would awaken in Eastern Europe.[83] In February 1953 the Eastern European (Sub-) Department of the Quai d'Orsay stated their worries about this American rhetorical emphasis on rolling back Soviet Communism. The French diplomats involved in drafting this memorandum thought the negative effects of the roll-back talk on the cohesion of NATO outweighed by far the scant effects of American policy on the Soviet orbit: there they saw few signs of an increased activity since the change of administration in Washington.[84] Indeed, it seems as though Eisenhower's and Dulles's policy towards Eastern Europe did not differ significantly from that of Truman, in that little more was done in the field of subversive activities than under the previous administration.[85]

Once back in government, Churchill steered British policy towards the Soviet Union back on to the course of negotiations. Churchill continued to believe in dealing directly with Stalin, rather than trying to corner him through indirect measures. In view of the Soviet restraint practised in Greece the possibility cannot be dismissed that direct talks with Western leaders were indeed a form of communication that Stalin took seriously. But the summit hankered for by Churchill did not come off during the lifetime of the old dictator.[86]

After Stalin's death in March 1953 the British government seems to have taken the view that a vociferous pursuit of a liberation policy would make an amelioration of relations with Stalin's successors impossible. On 3 July 1953 the acting Secretary of State, Lord Salisbury, drew his Cabinet colleagues' attention to what he regarded as a dangerous American tendency of regarding the 'situation behind the Iron Curtain as already very shaky', and of advocating 'the early liberation of the satellite countries'. This he thought unrealistic and provocative, and he felt that the British ought to 'counsel prudence and restraint.'[87] Salisbury and his Cabinet colleagues therefore favoured the Churchillian idea of a summit meeting with the new Soviet leadership.[88] The French also agreed with this approach, and Salisbury and his French colleague Bidault put this proposal to Dulles.

Surprisingly, the US Secretary of State gave Salisbury the impression that he was in agreement with the two Europeans.[89] This may be indicative of a lull in US roll-back activities. Already the last National Security Council papers of the Truman administration on the subject (such as those of August 1952)[90] had contained a note of caution with regard to the dangerous reactions which might be provoked on the part of the Soviet Union. NSC 141 of January 1953 temporarily stopped the steady increase of funds for subversive operations against the Soviet empire.[91] Immediately after coming to office, Eisenhower and Dulles seem temporarily to have practised restraint in their policy towards Eastern Europe.[92] Thus the US government did nothing to support the uprisings in the German Democratic Republic (GDR) and in Poland after Stalin's death, which must have experienced some stimulation from Radio Free Europe's broadcasts and promises of Western help. In the case of the East German uprising of 17 June 1953 it became particularly clear that the USA had not actually prepared any realistic plans for such an event. The total confusion with which Washington reacted to Stalin's death shows how little the Americans could have done at this stage to organize practical support for the resistance. Thus French and British prophesies concerning the false hopes engendered by US broadcasts in Eastern Europe were tragically fulfilled.[93]

Towards the end of 1953, however, the US liberation policy underwent a revival. Once again it claimed in an NSC paper that it was the ultimate aim of the United States to remove Soviet influence from Eastern Europe by all means available, short of all-out war.[94] At the same time the United States extended their activities to other parts of the world. Thus there is evidence of US subversive activities in Latin America in 1954 (Guatemala), and the operations against the People's Republic of China continued unabated.[95] At the same time the hopes of Eastern European resistance movements for Western help were kept up, but they were destined to be disappointed most bitterly once again, when Soviet tanks crushed the Hungarian fight for self-determination in 1956 while the Western powers looked on passively.[96]

Yet this was not the end of the US anti-Communist liberation policy of the type of the roll-back operations, even though we no longer have any clear evidence of activities in Eastern Europe. But the unsuccessful and embarrassing landing in the Cuban Bay of Pigs in 1961 was planned and conducted by the CIA along the same patterns as the European operations known to us. Once again, anti-Communist *émigrés* were trained and taken back to their native country in order to organize the supposedly already extant resistance movements, to start an insurrection and ultimately to overthrow the Communist government. The 1960s saw further large paramilitary operations of this sort in Laos and Indo-China. These gradually grew into the involvement of regular US forces in the Vietnam War, leaving the grey area of covert activities. It seems that with the *détente* of the Nixon era these activities were moved from the Far East to Africa. Various US projects in Latin America which are going on in the 1990s probably still have their roots in the 'special operations' for the 'containment' of Communism.

Looking back at the period 1948–53, it seems as though the policy of liberation had been based on false assumptions. The Americans (and, for a while, the British) overestimated the degree of readiness on the part of the Eastern Europeans to throw off the yoke of Communist totalitarian oppression during Stalin's lifetime. After the death of the *Bolshoj Vozhd* certain emancipatory tendencies did form in these countries. But as the United States was ultimately not ready to risk a world war to give support to the native East European movements of national liberation, all those opponents of the Soviet system who in 1953, 1956 and 1968 risked their lives to rise up against Moscow, relying on the promise of US support, were betrayed.

While the revolutions of 1989 have demonstrated that the majorities within the populations of the East European countries do seem to prefer Western-style democracy and the promise of Western-style prosperity to the Soviet jackboot, the chaos and misery of planned economies, and authoritarian one-party rule, they cannot be blamed for having postponed their revolutions until a time when Soviet weakness made non-violent liberation possible. Also, it must be remembered that the link between Western democracy and prosperity is very close in the minds of East Europeans today, a link which has only been forged by forty years of West European economic success and increasing prosperity.

Once it had become clear in the late 1950s that the United States could not carry the banner of liberation into Eastern Europe (because this would have meant large-scale war with the USSR, something neither the Americans nor their allies wanted), the focus of US subversive activities shifted to less sensitive areas of the world. Yet it is equally difficult to find examples of American success outside Europe (the Anglo-American operation against Mossadegh in Iran, 'Operation Ajax', could be termed a success, but it is difficult to classify this as a roll-back operation).

Instead, from 1951 at the latest, the policy of liberation began to undermine the cohesion of NATO. The pact was born from a common fear of Communist subversion and Soviet aggression; it was designed to prevent war, not to challenge the Soviet Union. Accordingly, the allies of the United States assigned great importance to the integrity of the foreign policy of each individual member state (above all, the leading nation, USA), which could be measured by the objective criteria of the UN Charter, to which all NATO members had subscribed.[97] However popular the policy of liberation may have been among the East European lobbies and other parts of the electorate in the USA, it was a destabilizing factor for NATO. As the first alliance formed by independent nations on the basis of free choice and common values, which included the common interest in the preservation of peace in Europe, NATO was and is particularly dependent on the support of public opinion in all member-states. If any member seemed to have adopted a policy more likely to endanger peace than preserve it, this weakened the cohesion of the alliance. Yet until this day, the security of Western Europe has been the corner-stone of US policy.[98] With their policy of liberation successive US administrations were ultimately acting against their own interest. The British, nearer to the area where war might have broken out, noticed this dilemma earlier, and therefore abandoned the liberation policy less than a decade after they had developed it.

NOTES

1 An earlier version of this chapter first appeared as 'Subversive Operationen im Dienste der "Roll-back" Politik, 1948–1953' in *Vierteljahreshefte für Zeitgeschichte* No. 2 (1989) pp. 279–97. The author gratefully acknowledges the permission of the editors of that journal to print it again. This research was made possible through the financial support of the North Atlantic Council, St John's College, Oxford, the British Economic and Social Research Council, and the Harry S. Truman Library.
2 See p. 70.
3 For valuable literature on this topic, see B. Kovrig, *The Myth of Liberation:* (Baltimore, Md: Johns Hopkins University Press, 1973); J. Yurechko, 'From Containment to

Counteroffensive' (MS PhD Berkeley, Calif., 1980). Yurechko's work is of crucial importance and deserves much greater publicity! N. Bethell, *The Great Betrayal: The Untold Story of Kim Philby's Biggest Coup* (London: Hodder & Stoughton, 1984) treats the Albanian case. Harry Rositzke, who himself worked for the CIA, wrote about American operations in *The CIA's Secret Operations: Espionage, Counter-Espionage and Covert Action* (New York: Reader's Digest Press, 1977) and in 'America's Secret Operations: A Perspective', *Foreign Affairs* Vol. 53, No. 2 (1975), pp. 344 ff. See also J. Prados, *The Presidents' Secret Wars: CIA and Pentagon Covert Operations from World War II through Iranscram* (New York: W. Morrow, 1986) pp. 13–78 for an extremely interesting but scantily documented account of CIA and SIS operations; and J. Ranelagh, *The Agency: The Rise and Decline of the CIA* (New York: Simon & Schuster, 2nd rev. edn, 1987) for an organizational history of American covert activities.

4 E. Barker, *Churchill and Eden at War* (London: Macmillan, 1978), Part IV, esp. pp. 246ff.; cf. also J. Lewis, *Changing Direction: British Military Planning for Postwar Strategic Defence, 1942–47* (London: Sherwood, 1988); D. Yergin, *The Shattered Peace* (London: André Deutsch, 1978), pp. 67ff.; V. Rothwell, *Britain and the Cold War, 1941–1947* (London: J. Cape, 1982). pp. 85 ff., esp. p. 115.

5 *Foreign Relations of the United States* (henceforth *FRUS*) 1946, Vol. VI, pp. 969 ff., Kennan's 'Long Telegram' of 22 February 1946; and for the influence of Kennan's British colleague Sir Frank Roberts, see E. Barker, *The British Between the Superpowers, 1945–1950* (London: Macmillan, 1983), pp. 44 f.; Rothwell, *Britain*, pp. 247 ff.; R. Merrick, 'The Russia Committee of the British Foreign Office and the Cold War, 1946–1947' *Journal of Contemporary History* Vol. 20, No. 3 (1985) pp. 453–68; J. Zametica, 'Three Letters to Bevin: Frank Roberts at the Moscow Embassy, 1945–7', in J. Zametica (ed.) *British Officials and British Foreign Policy, 1945–50* (Leicester: Leicester University Press, 1990), pp. 39–98; S. Greenwood, 'Frank Roberts and the other Long Telegram', *Journal of Contemporary History* Vol. 25, No. 1 (January 1990), pp. 103–25.

6 Rothwell, *Britain*, pp. 255ff.; the US National Security Council's report of 30 March 1948, *FRUS* 1948 Vol. I, Pt. 2, p. 546; the British Foreign Office's Bastions Paper of July/August 1948 in Public Records Office, Richmond, Surrey (henceforth PRO), FO 371/72196, R 10197/8476/G.

7 J. L. Gaddis, *Strategies of Containment* (New York: Oxford University Press, 1982), Chapters 2 and 3; Barker, *The British*, pp. 79ff., Merrick, 'Russia Committee', pp. 453ff.

8 cf. P. Boyle, 'The British Foreign Office and American Foreign Policy, 1947–1948', *American Studies* Vol. 16, No. 3 (1982), pp. 373–89.

9 cf. Boyle, 'Foreign Office'; Barker, *The British*, Chapters 5 and 6; A. Bullock, *Ernest Bevin, Foreign Secretary, 1945–51* (Oxford: Oxford University Press, 1983), Part IV; M. Folly, 'Breaking the Vicious Circle: Britain, the United States and the Genesis of the North Atlantic Treaty', *Diplomatic History* Vol. 12, No. 2 (1988), pp. 59ff.; J. W. Young, *France, the Cold War and the Western Alliance* (Leicester: Leicester University Press, 1990), p. 172.

10 J. W. Young and J. Kent, 'British Policy Overseas: The 'Third Force' and the Origins of NATO', in B. Heuser and R. O'Neill (eds) *Securing Peace in Europe, 1945–52: Thoughts for the 1990s* (London: Macmillan, 1992).

11 Ritchie Ovendale, 'Britain and the Cold War in Asia', in Ovendale (ed.) *The Foreign Policy of the British Labour Governments, 1945–1951* (Leicester: Leicester University Press, 1984), pp. 121–48.

12 M. Gilbert, *Winston Churchill Vol. VII: Road to Victory, 1941–1945* (London: Heinemann, 1986), pp. 991ff.; D. Carlton, *Anthony Eden: A Biography* (London: A. Lane, 1981), pp. 244f.

13 A document which has hitherto not been given sufficient attention, cf. B. Heuser, *Western Containment Policies in the Cold War: The Yugoslav Case, 1948–1953* (London and New York: Routledge, 1989), Chapter 1.

14 For the logic of George Kennan's ideas of containment, see NSC 20/1 of 18 August 1948 in T. Etzold and J. Gaddis (eds) *Containment: Documents on American Policy and Strategy, 1945–1950* (New York: Columbia University Press, 1978), pp. 173ff.; for a similar interpretation, see J. L. Gaddis, 'The United States and the Question of a Sphere of Influence in Europe, 1945–1949', in O. Riste (ed.) *Western Security: The Formative*

Years (Oslo: Norwegian University Press, 1985), pp. 60–91. B. Kovrig, 'Spheres of Influence: A Reassessment', *Survey* No. 70/71 (winter/spring 1969), pp. 102–20 underestimated the Truman administration's abandonment of spheres-of-influence thinking.

15 F. Ninkovich, *The Diplomacy of Ideas* (Cambridge: Cambridge University Press, 1981), pp. 8ff. and 61ff.

16 ibid., pp. 164ff.; cf. NSC 7 of 30 March 1948, see p. 68.

17 George Marshall to the US ambassador in Yugoslavia, 17 March 1948, *FRUS* 1948 Vol. IV, p. 312.

18 Kovrig, *Myth of Liberation*, pp. 80ff.

19 *FRUS* 1948 Vol. I, Pt 2, pp. 546ff., and see Ninkovich, *Diplomacy*, pp. 139ff.

20 Etzold and Gaddis, *Containment*, pp. 125 ff. NB that the Chatham House definition of the Cold War was 'all mischief short of war'. Royal Institute of International Affairs, *Defence in the Cold War, the Task for the Free World* (London: RIIA, 1950).

21 Etzold and Gaddis, *Containment*, p. 166.

22 cf. the Bastions Paper, PRO, FO 371/72196, R 10197/8476/G

23 cf. Ninkovich, *Diplomacy*, pp. 164ff.

24 PRO, FO 371/71687, RC(16)48 of 25 November 1948.

25 Bethell, *Great Betrayal*, p. 9.

26 ibid., p. 38.

27 Report of the French military attaché in Athens, 26 March 1949, Service Historique de l'Armée de Terre, Château de Vincennes, Paris (henceforth SHAT), File Grèce', No. 56.

28 *FRUS* 1949 Vol. V, pp. 12f.

29 Bethell, *Great Betrayal*, pp. 57, 183f.

30 Prados, *Presidents' Secret Wars*, p. 45.

31 *FRUS* 1949 Vol. VI, p. 415.

32 Bethell, *Great Betrayal*, pp. 127ff.

33 Bethell, *Great Betrayal*, passim.

34 ibid., and see H. A. R. Philby, *My Silent War* (New York: Ballentine Books, 1968), p. 161.

35 *FRUS* 1950 Vol. IV, p. 365f.

36 Quoted in Prados, *Presidents' Secret Wars*, pp. 49–50.

37 Ministère des Affaires Etrangères (henceforth MAE), Série Z Europe and EU Europe, Albanie, passim.

38 W. Bedell Smith, *Moscow Mission, 1946–1949* (London: Heinemann, 1950), p. 179.

39 Philby, *Silent War*, p. 62.

40 A. R. Johnson, *The Transformation of Communist Ideology: the Yugoslav Case* (Cambridge, Mass.: MIT Press, 1972).

41 cf. B. Heuser, 'Western Perceptions of the Tito–Stalin split', *The South Slav Journal* Vol. 10, No. 3 (1987), pp. 1–21.

42 A hope which was formulated explicitly in NSC 18/2 of 17 February 1949, US National Archives, Washington, DC (henceforth USNA), NSC documents series.

43 cf. the reports of G. T. C. Campbell from Belgrade in June and July 1948, PRO, FO 371/72579 and –/72583.

44 *FRUS* 1948 Vol. IV, p. 1,079ff.

45 PRO, FO 371/78715, R 2160, Bateman's comments of 17 February 1949.

46 For an obviously less than fictional account of this incident, see Lawrence Durrell, *White Eagle over Serbia* – wrongly regarded as something of a *Boy's Own* story. Lawrence Durrell served as British intelligence officer in Belgrade at the time.

47 SHAT, Yougoslavie, Relations Extérieures, French military attaché to the Ministry of Defence, 14 January 1949.

48 *FRUS* 1949 Vol. V, pp. 858f.

49 Comments by Bateman, Sargent, Roberts, on telegram No. 2057 of the Foreign office to Washington, PRO, FO 371/78715, R 2160/10345/92G.

50 cf. *FRUS* 1948 Vol. IV, pp. 1,079ff., and NSC 18/2 of 17 February 1949, USNA, NSC documents series.

51 Anthony Cavendish, 'The Imperfect spy', *Observer* (9 July 1989), pp. 17–19.

52 I am grateful to Dr Hans-Georg Wieck for this information (letter to the author, 21

August 1989, when he was president of the German equivalent of MI5), which I have found confirmed in unattributable interviews with retired German naval officers.

53 And not in 1950, as Cavendish remembers, 'The Imperfect Spy'.

54 PRO, FO 371/86756, NS 1052/68 of 1 July 1950, 'The Soviet Union and Korea'; cf. also the reports from the French embassy in Moscow of 3 July 1950, MAE, EU 31–9–1, Vol. 47; Rosemary Foot, *The Wrong War* (Ithaca, NY: Cornell University Press, 1985), pp. 58f. For the following see also Heuser, *Western Containment*, pp. 125–54.

55 R. Jervis, 'The Impact of the Korean War on the Cold War', *Journal of Conflict Resolution* Vol. 24, No. 4 (1980), p. 580; see also B. Heuser, 'NSC 68 and the Soviet Threat: a New View on Western Threat Perception and Policy Making', *Review of International Studies* Vol. 17, No.1 (January 1991).

56 e.g. *FRUS* 1950 Vol. I, p. 361.

57 C. Bohlen, *Witness to History 1929–1969*, (New York: W. W. Norton, 1973), p. 292.

58 H. S. Truman, *Memoirs Vol. II Years of Trial and Hope*, (London: Hodder & Stoughton, 1956), p. 359; PRO, DEFE 7/743 Item 39, 18 July 1950.

59 Acheson, *Present*, p. 399.

60 R. Osgood, *NATO, the Entangling Alliance* (Chicago, Ill.: University of Chicago Press, 1962), pp. 68 ff.; Etzold and Gaddis, *Containment*, pp. 389 and 442; W. Schilling, P. Hammond and G. Snyder, *Strategy, Politics and Defence Budgets*, (New York: Columbia University Press, 1962), the articles by Schilling and Hammond; S. Wells, 'Sounding the Tocsin, NSC 68 and the Soviet Threat', *International Security* Vol. IV, No. 2 (1979), pp. 116–58; J. L. Gaddis, 'NSC 68 and the Problem of Ends and Means', *International Security* Vol. IV, No. 4 (1979/1980), pp. 164ff.; K. Morgan, *Labour in Power, 1945–1951* (Oxford: Clarendon Press, 1984), p. 424; K. Harris, *Attlee*, (London: Weidenfeld & Nicolson, 1982), p. 455.

61 See for example MAE, EU 33–20–5, Généralités, Vol. 95, Sous-Direction d'Europe Orientale, 31 August 1951; and EU 31–9–1, Vol. 48, passim.

62 cf. Bullock, *Bevin*, p. 791; P. Lowe, *The Origins of the Korean War* (London: Longman, 1986), pp. 206ff.; R. O'Neill, *Australia in the Korean War Vol. 1 Strategy and Diplomacy* (Canberra: Australian Government Publishing Service, 1981), pp. 143–59.

63 MAE, EU 31–9–1, Vol. 48, reports by the French embassy in Moscow of 30 March and 22 October 1951.

64 PRO, FO 371/92067, F 10345/2 G of 3 January 1951 and PREM 8/1439, PM/51/4 of 12 January 1951; Harris, *Attlee* p. 455. See also M. Dockrill, 'The Foreign Office, Anglo-American Relations and the Korean War'. *International Affairs* Vol. 62, No. 3 (1986), pp. 459–76.

65 cf. R. Morgan, 'The Transatlantic Relationship', in K. Twitchett (ed.) *Europe and the World* (London: Lane, 1976).

66 For Anglo-American disagreements about Far Eastern policies, see J. T. H. Tang, 'Alliance under Stress: Anglo-American Relations and East Asia, 1949–51', in B. Heuser and R. O'Neill (eds) *Securing Peace in Europe*.

67 cf. NSC 68 of April 1950, in Etzold and Gaddis, *Containment*, pp. 434f., 440.

68 *FRUS* 1951 Vol. I, p. 63.

69 V. Marchetti and J. D. Marks, *The CIA and the Cult of Intelligence*, (New York: Laurel, 1980), pp. 152–6, cited in Ranelagh, *The Agency*, p. 216.

70 Quoted in Kovrig, *Myth of Liberation*, pp. 93ff.

71 A. Karalekas, 'Final Report of the Select Committee to Study Governmental Operations with Respect to Intelligence Activities', in US Senate, 94th Congress, 2nd session, Report No. 94–755, *Supplementary Detailed Staff Reports on Foreign and Military Intelligence* Book IV, pp. 31f. I should like to thank Dr Wolfgang Krieger for having brought this report to my attention.

72 Ranelagh, *The Agency*, p. 220.

73 ibid.

74 Yurechko, 'From Containment', pp. 65f., 90ff., 300.

75 MAE, EU 33–20–5, Généralités 95, VII, memorandum by François Seydoux of 20 August 1951.

76 Rositzke, 'America's Secret Operations', pp. 335f.; Philby, *My Silent War*, pp. 163f.; and

see Archives Nationales, Paris, Archives Bidault, Chataigneau's note for the President, 20 January 1953, with regard to the activities in the Ukraine and the Caucasus.

77 Prados, *Presidents'*, pp. 52–60.

78 Karalekas, 'Final Report', p. 36; Prados, *Presidents'*, pp. 61–78.

79 MAE, EU 33–20–5, Généralités 95, VIII, memorandum of 31 August 1951.

80 MAE, EU 31–9–1, vol. 48, Seydoux, 23 August 1951.

81 PRO, FO 371/92067, F 10345/2 G of 3 January 1951.

82 Bethell, *Great Betrayal*, pp. 180ff.

83 PRO, FO 371/102180, WY 1052/38 G of 11 September 1952.

84 MAE, EU 31–9–1, Vol. 50, no number, 18 February 1953.

85 Yurechko, 'From Containment', p. 134; M. Guhin, *John Foster Dulles, a Statesman and his Times* (New York: Columbia University Press, 1972), pp. 155ff.

86 Carlton, *Eden*, pp. 331ff.; J. W. Young, 'Churchill, the Russians and the Western Alliance: the three-power conference at Bermuda, December 1953', *English Historical Review* (1986), pp. 889ff.

87 PRO, CAB 129/61, C(53)187 of 3 July 1953.

88 PRO CAB 128/26, CC(53)39th of 6 July 1953, Item 3, and A. Seldon, *Churchill's Indian Summer* (London: Hodder & Stoughton, 1981), pp. 396ff.

89 PRO, CAB 128/26, CC(53)44th of 21 July 1953, Item 4.

90 e.g. *FRUS* 1952–1954 Vol. II, pp. 82ff., NSC 135/1 of 15 August 1953.

91 NSC 141 of 19 January 1953, see King's College, University of London, Liddell Hart Archives, JCS papers Microfilm No. 73.

92 For the period after Stalin's death our scarce sources on the liberation policy become fewer still, leaving us to formulate risky conclusions from *argumenta ex silentio*.

93 Yurechko, 'From Containment', pp. 217ff.

94 USNA, NSC series, NSC 174 of 11 December 1953.

95 Karalekas, 'Final Report', p. 49; Prados, *Presidents'*, pp. 98–100.

96 Kovrig, *Myth of Liberation*, Chapter 5.

97 Ninkovich, *Diplomacy*, pp. 168ff. NB the discrepancy, stressed by Ninkovich, between the political intolerance of the McCarthy era and the US campaign for freedom of thought in other parts of the world.

98 Western Europe was seen as the strategically most important area for the defence of the USA. See e.g. NSC 7 in Etzold and Gaddis, *Containment*, p. 168, which describes the strengthening of Western Europe as the most essential part of resisting the Communist threat.

4

A very British crusade: the Information Research Department and the beginning of the Cold War

W. Scott Lucas and C. J. Morris

HMG is pushing its objectives by a great variety of means ranging from military and naval measures, diplomatic representations, and various forms of international negotiation and participation in international bodies. . . . Publicity has a part to play in the support of many of these activities, and if it is to succeed, it is essential that it should be integrated with them and not independent of them. Actions speak louder than words, and words are most effective when they support actions.

(Foreign Office memorandum, July 1946)[1]

The world balance of power at the present time depends as much on the ideas in men's minds – in the mind of the Italian civil servant, the Vietnamese peasant, or the London docker – as on the weapons in the hands, or even the money in the pockets.

(Christopher Mayhew, Parliamentary Under-Secretary at the
Foreign Office, 1950)[2]

The dramatic changes in Eastern Europe since 1989 have been portrayed as the triumph of Western ideology over Marxist-Leninist systems. For the historian of the Cold War, this poses a problem. Given the Soviet ideological 'offensive' against the West since 1945, including sponsorship of Communist organizations in Western Europe and support for 'nationalist' and 'anti-colonial' movements, how did the West repel the Soviet onslaught and win the battle for men's minds? As *glasnost* and the lifting of the 'fog of war' allow increased access to Soviet records, providing information not only about Moscow's activities but also about Soviet perceptions of Western policies and operations, the time has come to consider Britain's own ideological offensive.

An essential component of British foreign policy after the Second World War, 'projection' (propaganda and political warfare), has been overlooked, largely because British records are closed. Examination of this ideological element leads to a review of British policy towards the Soviet Union in the early stages of the Cold War. Who formed that policy: the Cabinet, the Foreign Secretary (Ernest Bevin), the military, the permanent officials in Whitehall, or a combination of these? Did British defence of her interests prescribe partnership with the USA or could she rely upon her influence in the Commonwealth, Empire, and other areas of the world to pursue her own 'grand strategy', either unilaterally or as part of Western Europe? How did Britain, with her limited resources, contemplate confrontation with Moscow? Was British policy, supported by propaganda, 'defensive', by projecting British values and institutions, 'offensive', by criticizing the Soviet system and its ideology and actions, or even 'subversive', by attempting to loosen the Soviet hold on areas outside her borders?

Almost every participant in policy-making, minister and civil servant alike, agreed on the need to maintain British prestige and influence in the reshaping of the post-war world. They also recognized, however, that Britain's physical power had been diminished. She could not match the military personnel of the Soviet Union or the technological advantages of the United States, and demobilization would test the British ability to fulfil existing commitments, let alone accept new ones. Britain had used or lost more than 25 per cent of her assets during the war; the demands of post-war reconstruction, social and industrial, prohibited substantial expenditure overseas. Therefore, propaganda became essential to the maintenance of Britain's status. In the short term, it would mask British weakness; in the long term, it would encourage other countries to look to London for moral and ideological leadership and to resist incorporation into the Soviet bloc, without demanding a significant increase in British military and economic commitments. The psychological conflict called the Cold War would be fought with psychological methods.

More than forty years after its creation in 1948, most activities of the Information Research Department (IRD) of the Foreign Office are secret. The innocuous, official description of IRD stated that it was responsible for 'the compilation of information report for H. M. Missions abroad', yet all of its records, save seventy-nine 'briefing' papers on the Soviet Union between 1948 and 1954 and a few digests for the media, are withheld from the public. Even the 1948 file listing the work and staff of the IRD is 'missing before transit to the Public Record Office'.[3]

Examining the establishment of the IRD, three stages can be discerned in the evolution of British foreign policy, inextricably linked to propaganda. Before 1948, a general programme of 'defensive' propaganda attempted to maintain Britain's position through the projection of British moral and ideological superiority, while 'offensive' propaganda attacked Moscow in areas where the Soviets directly threatened British interests. In 1948 adoption of a general 'defensive / offensive' programme was wedded to a new tenet of British foreign policy, the 'positive' projection of the 'Third Force', a British-led Western European bloc linked to the Empire and Commonwealth and independent of both the Soviet Union and the USA. In January 1948 the Assistant Under-Secretary, Christopher Warner, summarized the IRD's organization:

1 an *offensive* branch attacking and exposing Communist methods and policy and contrasting them with 'Western' democracy and British methods and policy;
2 a *defensive* branch, which would be concerned with replying to Soviet and Communist attacks and hostile propaganda;
3 a *positive* branch which would deal with the 'build-up' of the Western Union conception.[4]

This second 'stage' was soon replaced by a third. By 1949 Britain had dismissed the viability of the 'Third Force' and accepted a long-term commitment to an Atlantic Pact. At the same time, the 'offensive' element of propaganda and policy was modified. Britain would not only attack the Soviets to defeat Moscow's challenge to British interests but also subvert the Soviet position in Eastern Europe.

The IRD's evolution also illuminates the developing machinery of British policy-making in the Cold War. Its creation reflected a policy that was not simply the product of Foreign Secretary Bevin and his working relationship with Prime Minister Attlee or even a co-ordinated reaction to Soviet expansion. Rather, it was the culmination of a campaign waged since 1946 by permanent officials of the Foreign Office, later supported by the military, for the adoption of a general 'defensive/offensive' strategy against the Soviets. Bevin delayed implementation of the strategy, primarily because of his need to maintain Cabinet and Labour Party unity on foreign affairs. However, because of the persistence of officials like Warner and the Assistant Under-Secretary, Ivone Kirkpatrick, both of whom opposed 'appeasement' of Germany in the 1930s and feared a revival of that policy after the war, and through the linking of an 'offensive' campaign to the positive projection of the 'Third Force', Bevin was persuaded to present the strategy to the Cabinet in January 1948.

Finally, the IRD's evolution in the late 1940s illustrates the shortcomings of Britain's Cold War policy. Bevin, to maintain exclusive Foreign Office control of foreign policy and to avoid Cabinet conflict about the policy of subverting the Soviet bloc, blocked the creation of an interdepartmental body to oversee operations. With no formal co-ordination between the Foreign Office, the military, the intelligence services, and other departments, the IRD became a 'service department', on call to support the intrigues and anti-Soviet projects of other agencies. Moreover, the IRD was soon used not only against the Soviet Union but also for *any* propaganda 'offensive', notably against nationalist insurgencies threatening Britain's colonial position, against non-Communist countries who were perceived as 'anti-British', and later within Britain against 'republicans' in Northern Ireland.

THE DEVELOPMENT OF BRITAIN'S COLD WAR POLICY AND PROPAGANDA

By the autumn of 1945 Bevin and his officials had concluded that Britain could not make any concessions to the Soviets over questions such as the future of Africa and the Middle East. As early as January 1946 Bevin told the Cabinet, 'The best means of preventing the countries of Southeastern Europe from being absorbed into an exclusive Soviet sphere of influence was to provide a steady stream of information about British life and culture'.[5] However, it was only in March that the Foreign Office considered establishing an organization to implement a comprehensive policy against Moscow. The Chiefs of Staff did not foresee a war with the Soviets within the next five years, but the Joint Intelligence Committee concluded that Moscow would use all means, short of war, to challenge Britain, especially in Greece, Turkey, Iran and the Middle East.[6] The Soviets refused to withdraw their troops from northern Iran, as had been agreed in the 1942 Anglo-Soviet Treaty; the Soviet leader, Joseph Stalin, announced a new Five Year Plan, implying that the Soviets would achieve reconstruction and industrialization without Western assistance, and Attlee's predecessor, Winston Churchill, made the 'Iron Curtain' speech at Fulton, Missouri. The British chargé d'affaires in Moscow, Frank Roberts, noted in a series of letters to Bevin that 'increasing attention was devoted [in the Soviet Union] to the renewed Marxist-Leninist ideological campaign. Britain, as the home of capitalism, imperialism, and now of social democracy, is a main target'.[7]

On 18 March a meeting was convened in the office of the Permanent Under-Secretary, Sir Orme Sargent, to brief the new British ambassador to Moscow, Sir Maurice Peterson. After a long discussion of Soviet aims, especially in the Middle East, the importance of which the Foreign Secretary, Bevin, 'rated . . . very highly', Warner, who supervised the work of the Northern Department, interjected:

The Soviet Government was actively favouring the development of Communism outside the borders of the Soviet Union. It was not just a question of Turkey or Persia. They were pushing much further afield. The probability was that their aim was not either economic or defensive or illegal, but all three combined.

The difficulty of implementing political, economic and psychological methods, including counter-propaganda, to fight the spread of Communism was recognized, particularly since the support of the Americans and British public opinion could not be taken for granted, but the officials assumed that a sterner British policy required more assertive propaganda. The Assistant Under-Secretary, Harold Caccia, argued 'We ought to go all out for the defence of our interests in the areas which the Chiefs of Staff eventually declared to be of vital importance', and Kirkpatrick concluded, 'Counter-propaganda would be easy to arrange if the Government decided to fight Communism – but not otherwise'. Sargent asked for a paper clearly identifying the aim of a counter-propaganda campaign.[8]

Asked for his opinion, Roberts repeated the assessment in his letters to Bevin. Although he agreed with the Joint Intelligence Committee's estimate that the Soviets would not provoke a war, in view of the Soviets' willingness to use all non-military means to challenge Britain's position, Britain should adopt similar measures.[9] On 2 April the Under-Secretaries formed the 'Russia Committee', whose object was to hold weekly meetings to assess Soviet action and define policy. Warner told the committee that 'it was clear [that the Soviet Union] had returned to pure Marx-Leninism, was becoming dynamic and aggressive [sic] and had opened an offensive against Great Britain as the leader of social democracy in the world'.[10] On the same day, he produced the paper requested by Sargent, 'The Soviet Campaign Against This Country and Our Response to It'. He recommended implementation of the 'defensive/offensive' policy while avoiding direct confrontation with Moscow

> by directing our campaign against Communism, as such, which we should frankly expose as totalitarianism, rather than against the policy of the Soviet Government. . . . We could, in every country, where social democrats, 'liberals', progressive agrarian parties, etc, are fighting a battle against Communism, give our friends all such moral and material support as is possible, without going so far as actually to endanger their lives or organisation.[11]

Bevin and Attlee endorsed the general principle of Warner's paper;[12] Kirkpatrick, chairing a working party of the Russia Committee, produced a detailed programme. At home, the BBC Home Service would be approached, as would the Royal Institute of International Affairs 'with a view to the inclusion of certain material in their publications', and the Foreign Office would 'endeavour to influence the home press and foreign correspondents in the right direction'. Abroad, the Foreign Office should 'enlist the cooperation of the BBC foreign services', who were 'much more amenable than the Home Service', the Central Office of Information would be asked to include 'suitable material' in items for its London Press Service, feature articles, and newsreels and documentaries. Political lecturers would be dispatched on overseas tours, books and pamphlets posted to the libraries and reading rooms of British embassies, and foreign trade-union leaders, politicians and publicists invited to Britain on VIP visits.[13]

Most importantly, in May 1946 Kirkpatrick went beyond Warner's vision of 'offensive' propaganda, linking it to a policy of subversion of the Communist bloc:

> Our defensive measures must include doing our best to counter the Soviet Government's policy and propaganda. . . . We have a good analogy in our very successful campaign during the war directed towards stimulating resistance movements in Europe. The V sign was blazoned all over the world, but at the same time we acted. We parachuted men, money, and arms into occupied territory. . . . Propaganda on the largest possible scale was coordinated with our policy.[14]

Kirkpatrick had gone too far. Many ministers and back-bench Labour Members of Parliament (MPs) were opposed to confrontation with the Soviets.[15] As late as November 1946, 130 of 352 Labour MPs declined to vote against an amendment criticizing the government's foreign policy.[16] Bevin was anxious to prevent the British press from undermining the government's diplomatic position against Moscow, personally complaining to *Times* editor Robin Barrington-Ward in March 1946 of the paper's 'jellyfish attitudes' on 'matters of foreign affairs', such as Greece;[17] however, the Foreign Secretary was himself opposed to subversive operations and sceptical about a general 'offensive' programme. When Sargent recommended Kirkpatrick's memorandum, Bevin fell back upon the 'defensive' projection of Britain:

> The more I study this, the less I like it. I am quite sure that the putting over of positive results of British attitudes will be a better corrective.[18]

The officials tried again, Assistant Under-Secretary R. G. Howe communicating a recommendation from the British embassy in Iran that, to defeat the Soviet-backed Tudeh Party, 'we should shortly pass over to a general counter-offensive . . . broadcast, press, pamphlets and so on'.[19] Sargent added, 'Our publicity is confined to telling what we are doing in this country, but this alone is hardly enough when it is a question of giving encouragement to our friends abroad who are resisting communism at the risk of their political lives', but Bevin stood firm: 'I am not going to commit myself to the whole of Kirkpatrick's scheme in order to tackle Persia . . . but I quite agree we should go all out in Persia'.[20]

On 4 June the Russia Committee accepted Bevin's verdict,[21] but it established a Publicity Subcommittee, which included Kirkpatrick and Warner, to consider other propaganda measures. Acting on a suggestion of the Parliamentary Under-Secretary, Kenneth Younger, the subcommittee recommended the transmission of reviews of the Soviet press to a selection of public or private bodies. . . . Before this was done, the Prime Minister should be asked to give an intimation to the Press that he did not wish newspapers to refrain from stating the plain truth about Russian propaganda regarding this country.[22]

The initiative was blocked by the Russia Committee, which recognized, with the Paris Conference of Foreign Ministers on peace treaties with East European countries in progress, that it was an inopportune time to ask Attlee to approach the press.[23]

However, zeal for the 'defensive/offensive' strategy was undiminished. On the contrary, Warner urged his colleagues to stand firm. He wrote to Roberts in May:

We have foreseen that the Russians would pretty soon realise how clumsy they have been in the last few months and would attempt to pull a velvet glove over their iron hand; and that public opinion and many important people both here and in America might well be misled into thinking quite erroneously that the iron hand had been discarded, or even that it had been a figment of the imagination of wicked Foreign Office and Foreign Service officials.[24]

Warner's memorandum of 2 April was circulated to British missions, almost all of whom endorsed the conclusions.[25] *Ad hoc* projects, such as the purchase of the Canadian Blue Book on trials of Soviet spies for distribution to the British public and publicity of Soviet sponsorshop of illegal Jewish immigration into Palestine, were pursued.[26] Kirkpatrick suggested that information officers 'give indirect replies [about Soviet affairs] by stressing certain aspects of British policy' and the diplomatic correspondent of the London Press Service 'could watch the Moscow trends and angle his Service accordingly'.[27] He told an interdepartmental meeting on overseas information, 'The stage of winning admirers and friends for Great Britain had now passed, and the time had come to persuade each country to take specific action'.[28]

Moreover, Bevin's identification of Persia as an exception to the rule against 'offensive' operations encouraged his officials to propose action on a case-by-case basis.[29] While a Colonel Wheeler was dispatched to Tehran to organize a 'Propaganda Department', collaborating with the British foreign intelligence service, MI6, 'to enquire into certain fields of Persian opinion',[30] Kirkpatrick identified the Middle East as the area where Bevin was most likely to authorize a campaign against the Soviets. Despite the Foreign Secretary's reservations that there was 'too much emphasis on anti-Communist propaganda', rather than 'the positive features of British theory and practice', and that it was a 'mistake to rouse Communist enthusiasm by excessive attacks on Communism',[31] Kirkpatrick's proposals for the Middle East were approved in October. On the 'defensive' side,

Britain would stress that its policy was 'progressive', not 'reactionary', leading 'the way in social reform' through its 'democratic system of government, social services, organization of industry, and liberal administration of justice'. On the 'offensive' side, publicity would be given 'to the real state of affairs in Russia, the system of government, the oppression of the workers, the inequality between the governing classes and the masses, the tyranny of the police state' and to 'those issues on which we are standing up to Russia, to Russian diplomatic reverses, and to any indications of the loss of Communist influence in other countries'. A separate department was not necessary to implement the directive, 'as it would tend to over-emphasize points selected by the Russians for attack and tend to lead to debates' about the counter-propaganda campaign.[32] The programme was so secret that the US government was not told about its 'offensive' element.[33]

The Foreign Office was especially careful to co-ordinate its efforts with the 'independent' BBC. In February 1946 the Cabinet rejected government control of the corporation, Bevin stating that 'he was anxious to establish the independent status of the BBC, particularly since he was relying on the BBC to build up a trustworthy foreign news service'.[34] However, General Sir Ian Jacob, the controller of the BBC's European Service, approached Sargent in September 'for guidance' on the British policy towards the Soviet Union. Sargent responded by inviting Jacob to attend the Russia Committee, and the committee changed its meetings from Tuesday to Thursday to fit Jacob's schedule.[35]

The ambiguity of the BBC's 'independence' was soon exposed. When the Russia Committee discussed Kirkpatrick's directive for the Middle East, Jacob warned: 'Once the publicity machine was set to act to a directive, it was extremely difficult to control the degree of propaganda which was injected into the broadcasts'. Kirkpatrick replied, 'The BBC should be able to pull up those compiling the foreign programmes when it considered that they were pushing their propaganda too hard'. The committee agreed that Kirkpatrick should discuss the matter with Sir William Haley, the director-general of the BBC.[36] Sargent subsequently minuted, 'The BBC are over the whole foreign field extremely helpful and cooperative'.[37]

Having succeeded in devising a general 'defensive' campaign and 'offensive' activities in specific areas, officials were, in the short term, content. Negotiations with Moscow over possible revision of the 1942 Anglo-Soviet Treaty began in early 1947, and ministers were preoccupied with the issues of India, Palestine, Greece and Turkey. In June 1947, however, after the Soviets consolidated political control of Hungary, Ambassador Peterson called for reconsideration of Warner's 'very good draft directive for political warfare against Communism'.[38] Warner noted that, with the Soviets invited to discussions of the Marshall plan for European recovery, an offensive could not be launched but added that 'a certain amount' of 'offensive' propaganda had 'been done piece-meal in so far as it falls within the exclusive scope of the Foreign Office'.[39]

After the Soviet withdrawal from the Marshall plan talks in July, Kirkpatrick again asked the Russia Committee to consider a general 'defensive/offensive' campaign. The committee declined, this time because of the forthcoming Conference of Foreign Ministers in Moscow. 'In view of the risk of a split within the Labour Party', Warner noted, 'we could expect no overall directives or public statements'. He was optimistic, however, that 'the hope of a change of heart on the part of the Russians was so slight that alternative plans must be prepared'.[40]

Warner and Kirkpatrick now found an important ally in the Parliamentary Under-Secretary, Christopher Mayhew. Writing to Bevin in October 1947, Mayhew took up the idea of a 'propaganda counter-offensive' and recommended that a separate Foreign Office department supervise the programme.[41] More importantly, he added a new dimension to the campaign, telling Sargent, Kirkpatrick and Warner that Britain 'shouldn't appear as defenders of the status quo but should attack Capitalism and Imperialism along with Russian Communism'.[42] Bevin had often advocated the 'Third Force' concept during the first years of the Attlee government. In January 1946 he summarized at a press briefing: 'You have two great imperialisms [Soviet and American] without, I am afraid, quite all the experience that this stupid old country has got'.[43] The idea had been muted because of British dependence, at least in the short term, upon American economic aid and strategic co-operation in Europe. However, a new British moral and ideological crusade overseas not only would give the Cabinet a mission comparable to 'social reconstruction' at home, but also would assuage back-bench Labour opinion, notably the members of the 'Keep Left' group led by Richard Crossman, Michael Foot and Ian Mikardo, who wished to avoid overt Atlantic partnership and proposed 'Third Force' as the Socialist alternative to 'balance of power' politics. Mayhew's emphasis on the 'positive' projection of Britain was married to the officials' priority of an 'offensive' against the totalitarian nature of Soviet Communism. Mayhew advised Bevin, in a letter of 6 December, to 'proceed quietly at first [with the campaign], being careful to stick to the truth and to balance anti-Communist with anti-capitalist arguments so as to reassure the Parliamentary Labour Party'.[44]

Whether Bevin actually believed that a British-led Western European bloc, supported by colonial possessions in Africa, was feasible or whether it was a device to win ministerial support, the 'defensive/offensive' strategy could now be presented to the Cabinet. On 5 October the Soviets had announced the formation of the Cominform, perceived by British officials as the vehicle for subversion of Western European democracies. Bevin informed the Cabinet on 25 November that, 'if the proceedings at' the

Moscow Conference of Foreign Ministers 'confirmed his fears, he would have to ask the Cabinet to consider a fresh approach to the main problems of our foreign policy'.[45] After the Conference collapsed in December, Bevin discussed military co-operation and the Western European 'bloc' with French Foreign Minister Georges Bidault.[46]

On 30 December Mayhew, Sargent, Kirkpatrick, Warner, A. A. Dudley, the head of the Information Policy Department, and A. E. Lambert of the Northern Department considered the presentation of the strategy. Mayhew, authorized by Bevin and Attlee to develop his ideas on 'Third Force Propaganda', recommended a 'Communist Information Department', which would only be 'concerned with the provision of information about Russia, about Communist tactics and about the current lines of Communist propaganda which needed to be offset'. Dissemination of British propaganda would be carried out by 'the existing information machinery'. Sargent countered with the argument for the creation of a special organization for the 'offensive' against the Soviets, as the Chiefs of Staff had been 'urging the desirability of reviewing political warfare machinery and undertaking certain "black" secret operations'. Mayhew finally accepted the combination of 'positive' and 'offensive' propaganda operations within a new Foreign Office department.[47]

The meeting then linked the new propaganda campaign to Bevin's proposal for a British-led 'spiritual union of the West', which was being drafted by Kirkpatrick:

> The principal common element in the two ideas was that this country should provide leadership to other nations with a similar point of view and that, by emphasising this, we could avoid the political difficulties connected with either advocacy of or unfavourable reflections on the American way of life.[48]

The officials also seized the opportunity to unveil the new strategy *before* it was presented to the Cabinet. Attlee, scheduled to broadcast to the nation on 3 January about British foreign policy, asked Sargent about a passage 'on the role of Great Britain in relation to the Communist offensive'.[49] After consulting Bevin, the Prime Minister told the nation:

> At one end of the scale are the Communist countries; at the other end the United States of America stands for individual liberty in the political sphere and for the maintenance of human rights, but its economy is based on capitalism, with all the problems which it presents and with the characteristic extreme inequality of wealth in its citizens . . . .
>
> Great Britain, like the other countries of Western Europe, is placed, geographically and from the point of view of economic and political theory between these two great continental states. . . . Our

task is to work out a system of a new and challenging kind, which combines individual freedom with a planned economy, democracy with social justice.[50]

On 8 January Bevin presented Mayhew's memorandum, 'Future Foreign Publicity Policy', Kirkpatrick's paper, 'The First Aim of British Foreign Policy', and two other memoranda, 'Policy in Germany' and 'Review of Soviet Policy', to the Cabinet. He concluded:

Provided we can organise a Western European system . . . backed by the resources of the Commonwealth and the Americas, it should be possible to develop our own power and influence to equal that of the United States of America and the USSR. We have the material resources in the Colonial Empire, if we develop them, and by giving a spiritual lead now we should be able to carry out our task in a way which will show clearly that we are not subservient to the United States or to the Soviet Union.[51]

Therefore, 'a small section in the Foreign Office' would be established

to oppose the inroads of Communism, by taking the offensive against it, basing ourselves on the standpoint of the position and vital ideas of British Social Democracy and Western civilisation, and to give a lead to our friends abroad and help them in the anti-Communist struggle. . . . We should seek to make London the Mecca for Social Democrats in Europe.

Britain would also attack 'the inefficiency, social injustice, and moral weakness of unrestrained capitalism', although she should not 'appear to be attacking any member of the Commonwealth or the US'.[52] While noting 'it was important that in the execution of the policy [of Western European Union] too much emphasis should not be laid on its anti-Soviet aspect', the Cabinet approved the policy and established the IRD, to be funded by secret vote in the same manner as the security and intelligence services, MI5 and MI6.[53]

When Warner informed the Russia Committee on 15 January of the Cabinet decision, Jacob emphasized that Attlee's speech must be followed by other ministerial pronouncements so the BBC could easily promote the government's line.[54] He had no reason to worry: the Foreign Office had already planned the next step in the campaign with Bevin's speech in the foreign affairs debate in the House of Commons on 22 January. The Foreign Secretary stated:

The free nations of Western Europe must now come together. . . . I am not concerned only with Europe as a geographical conception. Europe has extended its influence throughout the world, and we have to look further afield. . . . The organisation of Western Europe must be economically supported. That involves the closest possible collaboration with the Commonwealth and with overseas territories, not only British but French, Dutch, Belgian, and Portuguese.[55]

THE ORGANIZATION AND METHODS OF THE INFORMATION RESEARCH DEPARTMENT

Kirkpatrick was responsible for recruiting 'contract' staff for the IRD, including writers with wartime experience in propaganda and East European *émigrés*. Eight permanent officials, including the Soviet spy Guy Burgess and Robert Conquest, later an academic authority on the Soviet Union, supervised the work. The head of the department was Ralph Murray, who had served with the Political Warfare Executive in the Second World War and worked with the Control Commission for Germany and Austria before becoming head of the Far Eastern Information Department in 1946. Separate desks were established for geographical areas such as Eastern Europe, Africa, China and Latin America as well as for fields like economic affairs.

The IRD's work was divided into two categories. Category A consisted of analyses, not to be published, of intelligence collected by other agencies and Foreign Office departments, while Category B consisted of 'briefings' disseminated to the media, academics, trade union leaders and foreign officials for their own use.[56] Under Category A, the IRD produced regular reviews for the Russia Committee of 'The Trends of Communist Propaganda' and of Soviet-supported activities in areas such as Latin America. In turn, the Russia Committee would present the evaluations, through the Foreign Secretary, to the Cabinet and the Defence Committee. In certain cases, the IRD's conclusions would be transmitted to 'friendly' heads of state.[57]

The IRD's first priority under Category B was the production of 'factual background' papers on the ideology of 'Stalinism', conditions within the Soviet Union, and Soviet aims and activities throughout the world.[58] One of the earliest papers, 'The Real Conditions in Soviet Russia', set the pattern for the briefings. A series of concise, hard-hitting paragraphs, each under a subheading, laid out the argument.

PROPAGANDA AND THE REALITY – THE CONSTI-TUTIONAL FACADE – THE REALITY: FREEDOM FOR THE COMPLIANT ONLY – FREEDOM OF ASSOCIATION IN **ONE** PARTY ONLY – TRADE UNIONS ARE GOVERNMENT INSTRUMENTS. NO REDRESS FOR WORKERS – THE EXTRA-CONSTITUTIONAL, UNCONTROLLED SECRET POLICE – COMMUNISM=TYRANNY=FASCISM

The reader was left in no doubt about the Stalinist terror:

All Soviet citizens who are suspected of political heresy – actual or potential – are in constant danger of arbitrary arrest and sentence without public trial to exile and forced labour in concentration camps under conditions at least as terrible as those . . . in Dachau or Belsen. . . . Many well-informed Soviet officials have estimated the number of these slaves at twenty millions – or one in ten of the whole population.[59]

In July 1948 the dissemination of briefings was supplemented by the weekly production of 'digests'.[60] The cover of the work, marked 'Confidential', summarized its purpose:

This Digest is designed to present periodically in convenient form significant items of information on current relations with Soviet Russia, her satellites, and with the principal national and international agencies or organisations involved. It seeks particularly to record items which may not be common knowledge and which may be of local interest or of value as background information. It is prepared under official auspices and all the material in it may be published on the responsibility of the user. Unless explicitly stated to be so, items do not constitute official statements and may not be quoted as such.

The digest had two sections: Part A on general 'news' and Part B on specific areas such as Labour Affairs, the Islamic and Christian Worlds, Asiatic Affairs and the Iron Curtain. The first digest concentrated on 'The Potsdam Story: Soviet Allegations Examined and Refuted', but it also had items on the condemnation of Islamic customs by a leading Turkestan Communist, an attack on the Pope and the Catholic Church by a Moscow periodical, poor attendance by non-Russian students at schools in Tajkistan and Kazakhstan, and the shortage of goods in the Soviet Union. It concluded with a book review from *Pravda*:

Our people are the true guardians of universal culture. For this reason, only Soviet biographers have been able to give a faithful picture of outstanding foreigners. While English students of Shakespeare attempt to prove that Shakespeare's plays were written, not by Shakespeare, but by some aristocrat or other – Bacon, the Earl of Rutland, or the Earl of Oxford, Mr. Morosov established beyond all doubts that these brilliant productions belong to the pen of the Great Dramatist.[61]

In 1946 the Foreign Office Research Department, the Central Office of Information, the Colonial Office, and other agencies had pooled 'information' on Communism and Soviet tactics when Kirkpatrick's propaganda campaign was launched in the Middle East.[62] Every relevant document was now forwarded to the IRD for possible use: items from foreign and British media, government decrees, speeches and statements by public figures, and reports from British embassies and intelligence services. For example, in March 1948 the Foreign Office Research Department produced a paper on restrictions of political liberties in the Soviet zone of Germany. The report was carefully drafted to protect intelligence sources, and Murray asked that the German Political Department allow release of the information to the press. The IRD subsequently produced a briefing paper on 'Soviet Suppression of Liberty in Germany's Eastern Zone'.[63] The IRD even seized upon the British policy of encouraging the defection of Soviet soldiers to generate anti-Soviet publicity.[64]

The IRD quickly developed channels to disseminate its work. In late 1946 the Russia Committee had authorized

> machinery whereby factual reports and despatches analysing current problems should be made available to the Labour Party . . . through the Parliamentary Undersecretary [Mayhew]. . . . As regards the TUC [Trades Union Congress], the proposal was to establish a rear link in the Foreign Office with the Labour Attaches at H. M. Missions abroad, and this link [would] establish contacts with trade unions in this country . . . to furnish them with any information for which they might ask.[65]

Thus Mayhew's friendship with Denis Healey, the International Secretary of the Labour Party, became an important link for the IRD. Healey, a former Communist, was an important source of information on European Communist movements.[66] Norman Reddaway, Mayhew's private secretary, passed Soviet material on trade unions and the Labour movement to Healey, and the IRD regularly sent its briefings to him.[67]

The IRD also drafted 'speakers' notes', not only for ministers but also for back-bench MPs, public figures in business and other professions, and foreign statesmen.[68] Publicity material was sent to leading members of the TUC, including Herbert Tracey. With Mayhew, Tracey ran the anti-Communist organization 'Freedom First', which was subsidized by the IRD to distribute its newsletters to several hundred key trade union organizers.[69] The BBC agreed to 'temper its broadcasts to accord with the national interest' and considered the IRD's idea to 'plant' stories 'to draw [the Soviets] out on subjects to which we should like to know the answers'.[70] The IRD's items were placed not only with journalists, including the editor of the *Daily Herald*, and the BBC but also with news services, notably the Arab News Agency, which had been established by British intelligence services.[71] Eventually the IRD established a publishing company, Ampersand, to print anti-Communist books.[72] The British were exchanging information on 'publicity' with the State Department and US missions by March 1948 and with France and the Benelux countries by

November.[73] Co-operation was established in 1949 with French and Belgian authorities in Africa to counter nationalist movements in colonial territories.[74]

FROM PROPAGANDA TO POLITICAL WARFARE

The Cabinet decision of 1948, while empowering the IRD to implement a 'defensive/offensive' programme, did not authorize it to conduct subversive operations. Without a year, however, the department had been transformed into a peacetime version of the Political Warfare Executive. The 'positive' element disappeared, to be replaced not only by the anti-Communist crusade but also attacks against any country perceived to be 'anti-British'. There were three reasons for this transformation.

First, the worsening of relations with the Soviet Union in spring 1948 led to emphasis on IRD's 'offensive' role. On 5 March Bevin, in the aftermath of the Soviet-backed coup in Czechoslovakia, submitted a memorandum to the Cabinet on 'The Threat to Western Civilization'. He summarized:

> Not only is the Soviet Government not prepared at the present stage to co-operate in any real sense with any non-Communist or non-Communist-controlled Government, but it is actively preparing to extend its hold over the remaining part of continental Europe and, subsequently, over the Middle East and, no doubt, the bulk of the Far East as well.

Bevin recommended the immediate formation of the Western European bloc with the signing, with France, of treaties with the Benelux countries while involving the USA and the Commonwealth in the co-ordination of efforts for Western defence.[75] The Cabinet reiterated the 'positive' goal of British policy, 'We should use U.S. aid to gain time, but our ultimate aim should be to attain a position in which the countries of Western Europe could be independent both of the U. S. and of the Soviet Union', but ministers added, 'It should be possible to recruit, fairly rapidly, experienced staff for service in an organisation on the lines of the Political Warfare Executive'.[76]

Mayhew has claimed that IRD's 'first major operation occurred in the United Nations' in October 1948.[77] In fact, the department had been on the offensive for several months. Responding to the Cabinet decision in January, British authorities in Berlin suggested a propaganda directive promoting the British way of life and its guarantee of democracy, economic freedom and civil liberties, but they also wanted 'documentary proof' to present Communism as a 'hindrance to international cooperation and peace'. They concluded, 'The general directive . . . implies a state of political warfare'. Murray minuted that the programme was 'reasonable to us', and Warner thought Berlin's recommendations 'a good document', although he noted that the Foreign Office had been 'instructed not to use the phrase "political warfare" '. Berlin settled for the expression 'very active anti-Communist publicity'.[78]

In July a new directive combining the 'defence' of the British system with the 'offensive' against the Soviet Union was sent to Middle Eastern posts. British propaganda would

> stress that British and Western political thought emphasises the role of the individual and is essentially humanitarian. . . . In a Communist-controlled state the individual has no rights, but is at the disposal of the Politburo, the machine of the Communist Party (a small minority) and the secret police.

The false 'workers' paradise' of the Soviet Union would be compared with the high living standards of Western European and American workers and British efforts 'to help improve social and economic conditions without threatening the country's independence or imposing or advocating a system which suppresses the freedom of the individual'. Britain's 'traditional respect for Islam' would be contrasted with 'the anti-religious character of Communism'.[79] Similar instructions were sent to the Far Eastern missions.[80]

Second, by the end of 1948 the 'positive' side of British policy, the projection of the 'Third Force', was obsolete. The large cuts in defence spending since 1945 meant that Bevin was unable to underwrite the formation of a Western European political pact with a British military commitment. With the Berlin crisis of 1948, emphasis shifted from a British-led Western European bloc to an Atlantic Pact underpinned by American economic and military strength and the atomic bomb. Economically, Britain was unable, amidst the demands of industrial and social reconstruction, to re-establish the pound as a strong international currency, and the 1949 devaluation crisis finally ended hopes of a sterling bloc to rival American economic power. Politically, the 'Keep Left' group, after the Berlin crisis, accepted partnership in an Atlantic Pact.[81]

In December 1947 Warner and Kirkpatrick had been sceptical about the 'Third Force', and even pro-Europeans like Gladwyn Jebb were hesitant, but they deferred to ministerial wishes to obtain Cabinet acceptance of the 'defensive/offensive' campaign and the establishment of the IRD.[82] However, by April 1948, Warner, amending the propaganda directive for British authorities in Berlin, questioned whether 'positive' projection of the 'British way of life' should be replaced by projection of 'Western . . . principles and practices'.[83] In early 1949 the newly established Permanent Under-Secretaries Committee of the Foreign Office (PUSC),[84] in its first paper for long-term planning, concluded:

A weak, neutral Western Europe is undesirable and a strong, independent Western Europe is impracticable at present and could only come about, if at all, at the cost of the remilitarisation of Germany. The best hope of security for Western Europe lies in a consolidation on the lines indicated by the Atlantic Pact.

Bevin agreed with the preliminary views of the committee in March, and the final paper was accepted in May.[85]

The abandonment of 'Third Force' allowed the IRD to concentrate on 'offensive' propaganda while leaving a 'positive' programme, now vaguely defined, to other departments, notably the Information Policy Department (IPD), and semi-official bodies like the British Council. Murray concisely noted, after a wrangle with the IPD over British publicity in the colonies, 'This is *your* baby, not mine. . . . Positive, not negative'.[86] A typical IRD operation was undertaken in early 1949 when the Foreign Office received reports of a forthcoming Soviet 'peace offensive' in Europe. The department counterattacked with 'information' exposing Soviet hostility and intransigence, especially in the United Nations with the 'veto on peace', used by the Soviets in the Security Council twenty-eight times since 1946.[87]

Third, the British government failed to establish an interdepartmental body to set general guidelines for the IRD and to co-ordinate its work with that of other departments and agencies. An *ad hoc* ministerial committee was convened in May 1948 to consider 'anti-Communist propaganda', but it met only three times during the Attlee government.[88] Meanwhile, the Chiefs of Staff, excluded from the Russia Committee, agitated for an interdepartmental 'planning staff', not only for long-term strategy but also for day-to-day supervision of the anti-Soviet campaign. General Leslie Hollis, the Secretary of the Chiefs of Staff Committee, considered, with Sir Stewart Menzies, the head of MI6, and Warner and William Hayter of the Foreign Office 'what form of organization was required to establish a satisfactory link between the Chiefs of Staff and Foreign Office on matters connected with the day-to-day conduct of anti-Communist propaganda overseas'. A formal committee was rejected in favour of informal arrangements.[89]

After the Berlin crisis began, the Russia Committee accepted a Chiefs of Staff representative at its meetings and the question of planning of Cold War operations and strategy was placed on the agenda. In September 1948 the Foreign Office corresponded with General Hollis about arrangements for psychological warfare,[90] and on 25 November the Russia Committee considered a paper by Robin Hankey, the head of the Northern Department, on British policy towards the Soviet bloc. Kirkpatrick immediately reintroduced the idea of linking 'offensive' propaganda to subversive operations within the bloc:

In the present state of our finances and in view of public opinion, he thought that it would be best to start any kind of offensive operations in a small area and suggested for consideration, in this regard, Albania. Would it not be possible to start a civil war behind the Iron Curtain and, by careful assistance, to produce a state of affairs in Albania similar to the state of affairs that the Russians had produced in Greece?

Other officials questioned the wisdom or feasibility of provoking civil war in Eastern Europe, but the Russia Committee 'decided that our aim should certainly be to liberate the countries within the Soviet orbit short of war'.

The decision led to consideration of the proposed terms of reference for a 'Cold War Committee'. The Chief of the Air Staff, Air Chief Marshal Sir Arthur Tedder, attending the Russia Committee for the first time, argued:

> We should aim at winning the 'Cold War' [by which he meant the overthrow of the Soviet regime] in five years' time. . . . There should, in any case, be a small permanent team which would consider plans which would subsequently be executed by ourselves and the Americans.

Jebb, chairing the meeting, hesitated, 'If we were not going to establish a PWE [Political Warfare Executive] or an SOE [Special Operations Executive, responsible for covert operations in the Second World War] it was not evident . . . what any further machinery would do'. The committee agreed that a subcommittee should further study the question of a planning staff.[91]

On 16 December the Russia Committee accepted the subcommittee's recommendation of 'a small permanent planning section under the Foreign Office', that is the Permanent Under-Secretary's Committee (PUSC). The section, however, was responsible only for long-term planning and did not supervise implementation of policy. The question of a body to plan an immediate 'counter-offensive' against the Soviets was left for further study.[92]

Bevin approved the PUSC's formation in February 1949, but he balked at a committee supervising operations. Always wary of any interdepartmental body that threatened his control of foreign policy, he also feared the proposals would be coolly received by ministers who did not want to encourage subversion within the Soviet bloc. Moreover, exposure of the plans would be inopportune at a time of sensitive negotiations over the formation of the North Atlantic Treaty Organization. On 17 December 1948 Sargent warned Foreign Office Under-Secretaries:

> The Secretary of State would not agree to an offensive policy involving the encouragement of subversive movements and such activity that would require the revival in peacetime of the PWE and SOE;

still less would he allow the Defence Committee to run foreign policy on these lines.[93]

In February 1949 the Russia Committee held two meetings about operational planning. Frank Roberts, now private secretary to Bevin, communicated the Foreign Secretary's views:

> The rather far-reaching general objectives . . . for anti-Soviet action on a wide front might not commend themselves to the Defence Committee, particularly in view of the uncertainty at present surrounding the Atlantic Pact. . . . A committee set up to handle such a wide and intangible range of subjects might only spend a great deal of time and energy without achieving any concrete result.

Bevin had identified three immediate objectives for the Foreign Office: first, 'more energetic steps', with the USA, to save Greece from the Soviet orbit; second, discreet encouragement of the Yugoslav leader Tito; and third, 'detaching Albania from the orbit'. He did not believe it necessary to submit these objectives to the Defence Committee or an interdepartmental committee; instead he would simply ask Attlee for authority 'to study the best way of putting them into effect in consultation with any other Government departments concerned'. After discussion, Jebb concluded that the first two of Bevin's objectives were already being pursued within the Foreign Office, although, for the third, 'special machinery would have to be set up'.[94]

The Chiefs of Staff tried again in early March. Through the Minister of Defence, A. V. Alexander, they submitted to Attlee the recommendation of the Commandant of the Imperial Defence College, Air Chief Marshal Sir John Slessor, for 'an optimum technique of defence, which should be counter-offensive in nature, making use of all appropriate economic and political weapons', supervised 'by a specially qualified staff'.[95] Hankey and Jebb, at the request of the new Permanent Under-Secretary, Sir William Strang, drafted a submission for Bevin for 'reconsideration of his previous decision', and Strang proposed 'a small secret committee', including Jebb and Sir Maurice Dean of the Ministry of Defence.[96]

Bevin's reaction is in a file which is missing from the Public Record Office.[97] There is no evidence that the 'small secret committee' was established: instead, *ad hoc* groups considered the development of 'subversive propaganda'. In June 1949 the journalist and MP Vernon Bartlett, after a tour of Yugoslavia, Czechoslovakia, Bulgaria and Poland, met Mayhew, Reddaway, Robert Conquest of the IRD, and other officials. Bartlett 'had been told that the BBC and Voice of America made the mistake of prematurely encouraging elements hostile to the present regimes, which had no effect except to endanger [the elements]'. Mayhew explained that there was an important decision to be made 'between trying to overthrow satellite regimes altogether and trying to prise them away from Moscow without altering their Communist complexion'. Sir Anthony Rumbold, the head of the Southern Department, added, 'Although we did not want potential rebels to go off at half-cock, it was also important to keep them in good heart by a vigorous propaganda which would show that we . . . were alive to what was going on behind the Curtain'.[98]

The *ad hoc* ministerial committee on anti-Communist propaganda agreed in December 1949 that all restrictions on subversive propaganda in Communist countries should be removed and endorsed 'propaganda in other countries designed to stimulate subversive activities in the Soviet orbits'.[99] A paper by the PUSC, circulated to ministers, concluded:

> Every opportunity should be taken to weaken Russian control over the satellite states, although actions involving a serious risk of war or likely to encourage fatal resistance should be avoided. The first steps to this end might be to [establish] a *modus vivendi* with Yugoslavia, to detach Albania form the Soviet orbit, and to encourage the emergence of 'national deviationism' in other countries.[100]

The scant information available on the British effort to 'liberate' Albania from the Soviet bloc in 1949–50 indicates that the plan was pursued with 'special machinery' on the lines of the Second World War operations of the Political Warfare and Special Operations Executives. Bevin authorized Britain's foreign intelligence service, MI6, to smuggle *émigrés* into the country to organize a coup. Psychological warfare was conducted through 'black' radio stations, probably using material collected and disseminated by the IRD.[101]

The Albanian operation failed, partly because its betrayal by Kim Philby, MI6's liaison in Washington with the Americans, to the Soviets led to the capture of the *émigrés*.[102] However, the essential link between political warfare and subversive operations had been established by British officials. Arguably, in the long term, even the Albanian operation, by contributing to an atmosphere of suspicion, retribution and repression within the Soviet bloc, weakened ideological support for Eastern European regimes. This, in turn, gave the West opportunities to project the 'terror' and 'brutality' of Communist systems.

The IRD had become a service department, 'on call' to support the latest anti-Soviet projects of other departments and agencies. Although the Cabinet Overseas Information Committee noted in 1951, 'All experience shows that negative propaganda fails largely in its effect unless it is accompanied by at least as great a volume of positive material showing what is going on in the Western democracies',[103] the anti-Soviet 'offensive' was dominant. While the budgets of the 'overt' information services responsible for the 'positive' projection of Britain were cut by 25 per cent in real terms between 1948 and 1951,[104] the IRD, funded by the secret vote, expanded, with sixty staff, permanent and contract, in the Soviet section and 300 in all by the mid-1950s.[105]

The IRD was soon used for propaganda 'offensives' outside the Communist bloc. Initially, IRD desks were established to monitor Communism in different geographical areas but the 'geographical' approach encouraged department staff to target non-Communist groups as well. In July 1948 the Colonial Information Policy Committee (CIPC) was established by the ministerial committee on anti-Communist propaganda to co-ordinate programmes in Britain's colonial possessions. The CIPC, chaired by Mayhew, consisted of Parliamentary Under-Secretaries from the Foreign, Colonial, and Commonwealth Relations Offices, a representative from the Central Office of Information, and General Jacob of the BBC.[106] Its existence was a secret, even from other departments in Whitehall.[107] Initially, ministers doubted the wisdom of 'offensive' propaganda in the colonies and advocated emphasis 'on the positive advantages and achievements of the British way of life'.[108] However, in November 1948, Bevin warned Attlee 'that sooner or later the Russians will make a major drive against our position in Africa, and we ought to take steps now to counter it'. Murray subsequently minuted, 'I think that, in the propaganda field, we may have a [greater] chance of decisive action than in that of security'. Action already taken had been reported to the CIPC.[109] So much material was being sent by the IRD to African posts by the end of 1948 that the Governor of Gambia cabled that he 'should be grateful if the supply could be reduced'.[110]

In 1949 the IRD established a regional office in Singapore, in addition to the office existing in Hong Kong, to provide material for use throughout South-east Asia, embarking upon operations with MI6.[111] In December 1949, after Communists seized power in China, a propaganda directive, drafted by the Colonial Office and modified by the IRD's Adam Watson, linked propaganda against the Soviet bloc to the fight against Malayan insurgents:

We consider Communism to be the means whereby the Russians seek to expand and to dominate all Asian territories. As such Communism is the enemy of all genuine nationalists, since it seeks the domination of nationalism by alien influences.

Watson overruled Colonial Office opposition to the identification of the Malayan Communist Party with international Communism.[112] IRD notes on 'Stalin on Marxism and the National and Colonial Questions' were distributed not only to British posts in the colonies but also to 'emerging' countries like Indonesia.[113]

The overthrow of the Mossadegh government in Iran, the 'counter-insurgency' efforts, supervised by Alex Peterson and Hugh Carleton Greene, a future director-general of the BBC, in Malaya,[114] Cyprus, and the Arabian Peninsula, campaigns against 'nationalist' leaders throughout the Middle East and Africa, and the conflict with the Irish Republican Army have all been supported by the IRD's activities. In 1956, after the increased use of 'black' radio stations in the Middle East, the IRD was formally converted into a Political Warfare Executive, when the Information Co-ordinating Executive was established under military command during the Suez Crisis with Egypt.[115] Two years later, the evolution of the IRD from 'anti-Communist' to 'anti-anti-British' was recognized organizationally when the IRD was split into two sections, one for the Soviet bloc and the other for areas outside Eastern Europe.

CONCLUSION

In December 1950 Colonel James Hutchinson MP tabled a Parliamentary Question 'to ask the Prime Minister, whether he [would] reconstitute the Political Warfare Executive in order to combat Communist doctrines'. The reply drafted for Prime Minister Attlee was blunt; 'No, Sir', but it added an answer for any supplementary questions: 'The efforts of our existing Information Services, coupled with the Overseas broadcasts of the BBC, ensure that the Communist threat to the Free World is effectively exposed and that all possible encouragement is given to our friends on both sides of the Iron Curtain'.[116]

This ambiguous reply satisfied Parliament, which had never been informed of the IRD's creation, but in practice, if not name, the Political Warfare Executive was not only resurrected but also operating without interdepartmental control. The Russia Committee did not supervise operations and was virtually disbanded in 1951 by the Foreign Secretary in the Churchill government, Sir Anthony Eden.[117] Under Churchill, the Defence Committee met infrequently and considered general policy rather than operational details. An 'active' Foreign Secretary like Bevin or Eden might maintain informal control of subversive operations, but there was no guarantee that successors would do the same.

While the IRD's development provides some insight into the evolution of British foreign policy against the Soviet Union in the late 1940s, it raises other questions. Why are the records of an organization, ostensibly existing only to provide 'information', retained after more than forty years? How much of the material in the 'independent' British press and the BBC was 'planted' by a government body that was not accountable to Parliament or, arguably, the Cabinet? At what point did 'anti-Soviet' operations turn into 'anti-anti-British' campaigns? Who controlled the implementation of 'subversion': the Cabinet, the Foreign Secretary, permanent Foreign Office officials, MI6, or another group? Finally, did Britain's strategy for propaganda and political warfare assist in the securing of Western Europe against the Communist threat and the unleashing of ideological forces that eventually overwhelmed Eastern European regimes? Even if the British psychological 'crusade' in the Cold War is now acknowledged by historians, its nature and purpose await further research.

NOTES

1 Public Record Office, Kew, Surrey (hereafter cited as PRO), INF 12/61, Foreign Office memorandum for 'Projection of Britain' interdepartmental meeting, July 1946.
2 C. Mayhew, 'British Foreign Policy since 1945', *International Affairs* (1950), p. 477.
3 Several newspaper articles were written in 1978, soon after the IRD was replaced by the Overseas Information Department and a few authors have described some of the IRD's work. See L. Smith, 'Covert British Propaganda: The Information Research Department, 1947–1977', *Millennium* (1980), pp. 67ff.; R. Fletcher, 'British Propaganda since World War II – A Case Study', *Media, Culture, and Society* (1982), pp. 97ff.; W. Wark, 'Coming in from the Cold: British Propaganda and Red Army Defectors, 1945–1952', *International History Review* (1987), pp. 48ff.
4 PRO, FO371/71687/N765/765/38G, Russia Committee meeting, 15 January 1948.
5 PRO, CAB128/5, C.M.5(46), 15 January 1946.
6 PRO, DO35/1604, JIC(46)1(0)(Final Revise), 22 February 1946, cited in JIC(46)(38)(0)(Final Revise), 14 June 1946.
7 J. Zametica, 'Three Letters to Bevin: Frank Roberts at the Moscow Embassy, 1945–1946', in J. Zametica (ed.) *British Officials and British Foreign Policy, 1945–1950* (Leicester: Leicester University Press, 1990), p. 74.
8 PRO, FO371/56832/N5572/605/38G, Record of Foreign Office meeting, 18 March 1946.
9 cf. R. Merrick, 'The Russia Committee of the British Foreign Office and the Cold War, 1946–47', *Journal of Contemporary History* (1985), pp. 453ff, and Zametica, pp. 74ff.
10 PRO, FO371/56885/N5169/5169/38G, Russia Committee meeting, 2 April 1946.
11 PRO, FO371/56832/N6344/605/38G, Warner memorandum, 2 April 1946.
12 PRO, FO371/56784/N6733/140/38G, Sargent minute, 20 May 1946.
13 PRO, FO371/56885/N6092/5169/38G, Kirkpatrick memorandum, 15 May 1946.
14 PRO, FO930/488/P449/1/907, Kirkpatrick minute, 22 May 1946.
15 cf. PRO FO371/56784/N6733/140/38G, Howe to Sargent, 17 May 1946.
16 A. Bullock, *Ernest Bevin: Foreign Secretary, 1945–1951* (New York: Norton 1983), p. 329.
17 PRO, FO800/498/PRS/46/25, Henderson minute, 11 March 1946.
18 PRO, FO930/488/P449/1/907, Bevin minute, undated.
19 PRO, FO930/488/P449/1/907, Tehran to Foreign Office, Cable 749, 26 May 1946.
20 PRO, FO930/488/P449/1/907, Sargent to Bevin, 28 May 1946, and Bevin minute, 29 May 1946. cf. p. 19.
21 PRO, FO371/56885/N7515/5169/38G, Russia Committee meeting, 4 June 1946.
22 PRO, FO371/56886/N9930/5169/38G, Publicity Subcommittee meeting, 29 July 1946.
23 PRO, FO371/56886/N11284/5169/38G, Russia Committee meeting, 28 August 1946.
24 PRO, FO181/1023, Warner to Roberts, 1 May 1946.
25 cf. PRO, FO181/1023/File and FO371/56786/File.
26 PRO, FO371/56886/N10901/5169/38G, Russia Committee meeting, 20 August 1946, N11284/5169/38G, Russia Committee meeting, 28 August 1946, and N12335/5169/38G, Russia Committee meeting, 17 September 1946.
27 PRO, INF12/61, Foreign Office information officers conference, 14–18 October 1946.
28 PRO, INF12/61, interdepartmental meeting, 9 July 1946.
29 PRO, FO371/56784/N7199/140/38G, Warner to Dening, 29 July 1946.
30 PRO, FO371/62037/E2240/2240/34, Pyman to Howe, 10 March 1947.
31 PRO, INF12/61, Kirkpatrick minute, 3 October 1946, and subsequent minutes.
32 PRO, FO371/56887/N15609/5169/38G, Kirkpatrick memorandum, 14 October 1946.
33 PRO, FO371/61114/AN3997/3997/45G, Wright minute, 16 October 1947.
34 PRO, CAB128/5, C.M.16(46), 21 February 1946.

35 PRO, FO371/56886/N12335/5169/38G, Russia Committee meeting, 17 September 1946, and N12615/5169/38G, Russia Committee meeting, 24 September 1946.

36 PRO, FO371/56886/N13583/5169/38G, Russia Committee meeting 17 October 1946.

37 PRO, FO371/66370/N8114/271/38, Sargent to Peterson, 28 July 1947.

38 PRO, FO371/66370/N7457/271/38, Moscow to Foreign Office, Cable 1374, 20 June 1947.

39 PRO, FO371/66370/N7458/271/38, Warner to Sargent (draft), 25 June 1947.

40 PRO, FO371/66371/N9345/271/38G, Russia Committee meeting, 31 July 1947, and N9549/271/38G, Russia Committee meeting, 14 August 1947.

41 L. Smith, p. 68.

42 ibid.

43 PRO, FO800/498/PRS/46/1, Bevin press conference, 1 January 1946.

44 L. Smith, p. 70.

45 PRO, CAB128/10, C.M.90(47), 25 November 1947.

46 cf. J. Kent and J. W. Young, 'The "Western Union" Concept and British Defence Policy, 1947–8', Chapter 7 in this volume.

47 PRO, FO371/71648/N134/31/38G, Foreign Office meeting, 30 December 1947.

48 ibid.

49 PRO, FO800/502/SU/48/1, Sargent to Attlee, 2 January 1948.

50 *The Times*, 5 January 1948, p. 4.

51 PRO, CAB129/23, C.P.(48)6, 'The First Aim of British Foreign Policy', 4 January 1948.

52 PRO, CAB129/23, C.P.(48)8, 'Future Foreign Publicity Policy', 8 January 1948.

53 PRO, CAB128/11, C.M.3(48), 3 January 1948.

54 PRO, FO371/71687/N765/765/38G, Russia Committee meeting, 15 January 1948.

55 *Hansard*, Vol. 446, HC Deb. 5 S., Cols 395–8.

56 cf. Fletcher, p. 100.

57 cf. PRO, FO371/86751–86760/File.

58 cf. PRO, FO975/File.

59 PRO, FO975/1, 'The Real Conditions in Soviet Russia', undated.

60 cf. PRO, FO371/71713–71714/File.

61 PRO, FO371/71713, IRD Digest No. 1, 27 July 1948.

62 PRO, FO930/539/P1026, Routh to Scott, 30 November 1946, and subsequent minutes.

63 PRO, FO371/70552/C6308/44/18, Murray minute, 4 March 1948, and subsequent minutes.

64 cf. Wark, op. cit.
   The IRD's 'test case' for the handling of defections, Lieutentant-Colonel Grigori Tokaev, illustrated the problems of publicity. A press conference, held in London on 3 September 1948, nearly degenerated into violence between British officials and Soviet journalists. More significantly, Tokaev 'wrote' a series of articles for the *Sunday Express* in January 1949 which were so virulently anti-Communist that their effect was questionable. Jebb minuted, '**Not** very impressive to my mind', and Mayhew added, 'Too highly contrived or unoriginal to carry conviction'. It is a mystery whether Tokaev collaborated with the *Express* on his own initiative. The IRD 'handled' him without consulting Jebb and Mayhew, or another British agency arranged the articles. (Wark, op. cit.; PRO, FO371/77609/N135/1024/38, *Sunday Express* article, 2 January 1949, and N553/1024/38, *Sunday Express* article, 16 January 1949, and subsequent minutes.)

65 PRO, FO371/56886/N14607/5169/38G, Russia Committee meeting, 7 November 1946.

66 PRO, FO371/86761/NS1053/1G, Russia Committee meeting, 9 January 1950, and subsequent minutes.

67 cf. FO371/71632A–71632B/File; D. Healey, *The Time of My Life* (London: Michael Joseph, 1989), p. 106.

68 IRD's only apparent problem was meeting Minister of State Hector McNeil's request to find examples of Soviet 'abuse of children's books for stirring up international hatreds' (PRO, FO371/71629/N2123/1/38, Roberts minute, 7 February 1948).

69 L. Smith, pp. 70ff.

70 PRO, FO371/71632A/N13368/1/38G, Rae to Hankey, 27 December 1948, and subsequent minutes.

71 Fletcher, pp. 102ff.; N. West, *The Friends: Britain's Post-War Secret Intelligence*

Operations (London: Weidenfeld & Nicolson, 1988), p. 96.

In March 1949 Colonial Secretary Arthur Creech-Jones obtained IRD's publicity directives from Murray and circulated them to colonial posts to show 'the way in which anti-Communist propaganda is being spread throughout the world by means of news agencies, the BBC, and the London Press Service' (PRO, CO537/6549, Murray to Blackburne, 7 February 1949).

72 L. Smith, pp. 75ff.

73 PRO, FO371/71687/N8167/765/38G, Russia Committee meeting, 1 April 1948; PRO, CO537/5124, Foreign Office to Paris, Cable 1040, 11 November 1948.

74 cf. PRO, CO537/5124/File and CO537/5129/File.

75 PRO, CAB129/25, C.P.(48)72, 'The Threat to Western Civilisation', 3 March 1948.

76 PRO, CAB128/14, CAB19(48)N.C.R., 5 March 1948.

77 L. Smith, pp. 71ff.; C. Mayhew, *Time to Explain: An Autobiography* (London: Hutchinson, 1987), pp. 110ff.

78 PRO, FO371/70478/C2182/1/18, Garran to Dean, 23 February 1948, and subsequent minutes.

79 PRO, CO537/6549, Foreign Office to Cairo, Cable 83 Saving, 6 July 1948.

80 PRO, CO537/6549, Bevin circular cable 0116, 31 July 1948.

81 cf. Kent and Young, op. cit., and K. O. Morgan, *Labour People – Leaders and Lieutenants: Hardie to Kinnock* (Oxford: Oxford University Press, 1989), pp. 155ff.

82 PRO, FO371/66375/N14892/271/38G, Russia Committee meeting, 18 December 1947.

83 PRO, FO371/80748/C2182/1/18, Warner minute, April 1948.

84 For the establishment of the PUSC, see pp. 22–3.

85 PRO, FO371/76384/W3114/3/500G, PUSC(22)Final, 9 May 1949, and Bevin minute, 27 March 1949.

86 PRO, FO953/136/P4577, Murray to Dudley, 26 April 1948.

87 PRO, CO537/6549, Foreign Office to Paris, Cable 136, 22 January 1949; PRO, FO975/33, 'The Communist Peace Offensive', 30 August 1949.

88 PRO, CAB130/37/File.

89 PRO, CAB130/37, GEN231/2, 'Anti-Communist Propaganda – Liaison between the Foreign Office and Chiefs of Staff', 4 May 1948.

90 PRO, DEFE5/12, COS(48)218, Foreign Office to Hollis on psychological warfare, 24 September 1948 (retained).

91 PRO, FO371/71687/N13016/765/38G, Russia Committee meeting, 25 November 1948.

92 PRO, FO371/71687/N13677/765/38G, Russia Committee meeting, 16 December 1948.

93 PRO, FO371/77623/N171/1052/38G, Foreign Office meeting, 17 December 1948.

94 PRO, FO371/77623/N1388/1052/38G, Russia Committee meeting, 3 February 1949 (retained), and N1727/1052/38G, Russia Committee meeting, 17 February 1949.

95 PRO, FO371/77617/N3355/1051/38G, Commandant, Imperial Defence College, report, 29 November 1948, and Alexander to Attlee, 7 March 1949.

96 PRO, FO371/77616/N3356/1051/38G, Jebb minute, 22 March 1949, and FO371/77617/N3413/1051/38G, Strang minute, 4 April 1949.

97 PRO, FO371/77616/N3358/1051/38G (missing).

98 PRO, FO371/77389/N6556/1053/63, Falla minute, 24 June 1949.

99 PRO, CAB130/37, GEN231/3rd meeting, 19 December 1949.

100 PRO, FO371/77622/N11007/1051/38, 'British Policy Towards Soviet Communism', 28 July 1949.

101 cf. D. B. G. Heuser, *Western 'Containment' Policies in the Cold War; The Yugoslav Case* (London: Routledge, 1989); West, op. cit.

102 K. Philby, *My Silent War* (London: MacGibbon & Key 1968), pp. 117ff.

103 PRO, FO953/1051/P1011/94, 'Information, Propaganda, and the Cold War', 10 December 1951.

104 ibid.

105 L. Smith, p. 69; J. Bloch and P. Fitzgerald, *British Intelligence and Covert Action* (London: Junction, 1983), pp. 90ff.

106 PRO, CAB130/37, GEN231/4, 'Anti-Soviet and pro-British Colonial Propaganda', 16 June 1948.

107 PRO, CO537/5130, Morgan to Keith and others, 12 October 1949. The records of CIPC are retained in PRO, CAB21/1691–1693.
108 PRO, CAB130/37, GEN231/2nd meeting, 22 July 1948.
109 PRO, FO371/71660/N12163/51/38, Bevin to Attlee, 6 November 1948, and Murray minute, 15 November 1948.
110 PRO, CO537/6549, Governor of Gambia to Colonial Office, Cable 70, 30 December 1948.
111 Fletcher, p. 101.
112 PRO, FO76005/F17630/1017/61, Morris to Hibbert, 28 November 1949, and Watson to Morris, 1 December 1949.
113 PRO, FO371/76139/F5394/10111/62, Cloake minute, 11 May 1949, and subsequent minutes.
114 cf. West, p. 96.
115 cf. W. S. Lucas, *Divided We Stand: Britain, the U.S., and the Suez Crisis* (London: Hodder & Stoughton, 1991).
116 PRO, CAB21/2371, Parliamentary Question by Colonel James Hutchinson, and subsequent minutes.
117 Lord Gladwyn, *The Memoirs of Lord Gladwyn* (London: Weidenfeld & Nicolson, 1972), p. 227.

5

British Cold War defectors: the versatile, durable toys of propagandists

Sheila Kerr

It is forty years since Guy Burgess and Donald Maclean defected to the Soviet Union in 1951, and over twenty years since Kim Philby and George Blake followed them behind the Iron Curtain in the 1960s. During this time the images of these defectors have been etched on to the British consciousness by the ebb and flow of the Cold War, and particularly by British, American and Soviet Cold War propaganda.

The story of the defectors is a human story of men whose private political convictions had profound personal and international repercussions. What questions ought the historian to ask about the role they played in the post-war period? Within the literature about the Cambridge spies two interrelated themes are apparent; the effect of the defection upon the balance of power between East and West during the Cold War, and the moral and political questions concerning the defectors' decisions to put their ideological convictions before their loyalty to their country.[1]

Because the defectors became the toys of Cold War propagandists, perhaps the first impulse of the historian is to disentangle the facts from the fiction about the defectors. This process was begun by British journalists who fought against official censorship and challenged government statements about Maclean, Burgess and Philby. When the Soviets began to use these men as channels for their propaganda Western officials, academics and journalists retaliated by exposing and challenging Soviet propaganda. British and American writers have created additional myths by sensationalizing the exploits of these men. These myths are important because they had very real effects upon Anglo-Soviet and Anglo-American relations and, arguably, most impact upon British political culture.

The aim of this chapter is to examine how the Soviets have employed the defectors to disseminate their propaganda and to wage psychological warfare, and furthermore, to consider to what extent Soviet propaganda has influenced British attitudes towards the defectors and the issues of loyalty and security.

Let us begin by considering the significance of this subject, its place in existing scholarship and the further avenues of study offered by other

111

aspects of the defectors' lives. While the notoriety of the spies has attracted a high level of popular interest, it is only recently that they have been studied seriously. Burgess, Maclean and Philby became synonymous with the Cold War. Now that the ideological battle has ceased with the rejection of Communism in Eastern Europe and the Soviet Union's faltering steps towards reform, it is necessary to explain why the Soviets still feature the defectors in their propaganda against Britain.

This chapter has a historical perspective of nearly half a century, but has a narrow focus upon Soviet propagandists' employment of the British defectors in their attempts to influence British society. It is thus a useful case study of Soviet propaganda, which can be enhanced by examining British counter-propaganda.[2]

There are other interesting questions to consider. Hugh Trevor-Roper, Robert Cecil and Noel Annan have most eloquently and incisively exposed the propaganda in Philby's memoirs.[3] It would also be profitable to examine the memoirs of the defectors to measure the proportion of truth to falsehood, and to assess how much information the Soviets released about Western intelligence to challenge official British censorship. The defection of Burgess and Maclean was perceived by the British government as a tremendous 'loss', in terms of British prestige among its allies rather than a 'loss' of information. In the atmosphere of the Cold War this 'loss' was considered to be an automatic gain for the Soviets. But was this so? Did Soviet behaviour after the defection justify the view that they benefited from information from Burgess and Maclean, either by gaining advance warning of Western plans or by understanding Western behaviour more accurately? The issue of the 'loss' of information was disputed between British and American officials and was publicized in the press. The Soviets could not gloat publicly about their 'gains' as this would direct the public's gaze to their intelligence services and scupper their attempts to present the defectors as political refugees rather than spies.

While there is a prolific literature written by defectors, there has not been an assessment of their role in international relations. An extensive comparative study of the domestic and foreign uses of defectors during the Cold War could also illuminate the differences and similarities of British, American and Soviet political cultures. Both Communist and capitalist countries regard those who defect from their own countries as traitors, but defectors from enemy countries are welcomed and rewarded. There are interesting differences in the way spies are treated: the Soviet Union punishes its traitors with a sentence of death, while British traitors face that punishment only during wartime; moreover Burgess and Maclean were both allowed to be buried in Britain. Rewards are more public in the Soviet Union: they commemorate their spies on stamps, while Soviet defectors in Britain are rewarded privately. Another interesting project would be to continue the work that Niels Erik Rosenfeldt began with his comparative study of the testimonies of defectors, which shed new light on Stalin's government. This exercise would be useful given the number of defector accounts now available.[4]

This chapter focuses on how the Soviets presented the defectors to the British public and how the British have responded to Soviet propaganda in the post-war period. Studies of Soviet propaganda often focus on the size of the Soviet propaganda machine and its output, thus giving the misleading impression that its omnipresence signifies a powerful effectiveness. So it is essential to study Soviet propaganda in the context of the society it seeks to influence, with regard to the cultural and political resistance it must overcome and the counter-propaganda it has to withstand.

Defectors have many 'uses' to the country they defect to, and the potential to cause damage to the country they have betrayed. They are valued for their information and ability to interpret the enemy country. Soviet defectors who have published their memoirs or written articles also have a value as propagandists who publicize the evils and shortcomings of the Soviet system and praise Western democracy. They have contributed to the ideological battle between East and West during the Cold War.[5]

PROBLEMS OF EVIDENCE AND INTERPRETATION

There are three problems concerning the evidence for this study. First, the records of British and Soviet propaganda organizations are not available to show their involvement with the defectors. For the most part the origin of the information about the defectors is obvious. The interviews that the defectors gave to British journalists were instigated and controlled by the KGB; meanwhile statements from British and American government officials show the official line. Given the secrecy of the British anti-Communist propaganda organization, the Information Research Department (IRD), and the informal networks through which it worked, it is difficult to identify official propaganda without access to the records of IRD and the intelligence services.[6] In contrast, information which originated from Soviet sources can be confidently labelled propaganda. Superficially the driving force behind revelations about these men appears to have been the struggle by journalists and others against official secrecy. The secret and intermittent engine of these revelations, however, was the intelligence services. Peter Wright of MI5 and his friends leaked information about internal security investigations to the journalist Chapman Pincher.[7] The Soviets have been suspected of leaking information to Western journalists and authors who could then reveal more information about the spies than the government preferred.[8] We must therefore deduce from the propaganda in newspapers, books and films, the propagandists' perceptions, aims and tactics.

The second problem is that there is a lack of data to research British attitudes towards the defectors and the questions they raise about loyalty, patriotism, security and the individual's rights and responsibilities towards the state. Opinion polls have not asked specific questions about the defectors. Data which reveals changes in the public's attitudes towards the perceived threat from the Soviet Union, opinions about the USA, or public trust or distrust of the government and the media, may offer an oblique angle on the subject.[9] We can, however, study the content, intensity and timing of the manifestations of Soviet propaganda, trace its progress within the media, and make a general appraisal of how effective the Soviet message has been, even though evidence of British attitudes is patchy.

Finally there is a problem of accurately labelling Soviet propaganda. Statements by Soviet officials, organizations such as the Communist Party and the defectors are Soviet propaganda. Friends of the defectors, such as Tom Driberg and Graham Greene, and sympathetic journalists, such as Philip Knightley, have helped to disseminate Soviet information yet they are not on the Soviet payroll. Soviet propaganda about the defectors has been successful in influencing a group of influential people. In the British case, similarly statements by British officials show the official line. Because official secrecy has been employed to limit the damage of the defections, the counterattack against Soviet propaganda has been carried out by former colleagues of Philby's who write independently but presumably exercise some self-censorship to remain within the Official Secrets Act. With the cosy lobby system journalists risk becoming channels of official propaganda, but it is difficult to distinguish the tactful official word from the normal if sometimes over-zealous anti-Communism in some newspapers. The media – newspapers, books, broadcasts, film and television – have been the battlefield for the psychological confrontation during the Cold War between British, American and Soviet propagandists.

Mass opinion remains difficult to assess, but it is possible to trace the influence of Soviet propaganda upon the intelligentsia. Furthermore, by tracing the origins, development and repetition of Soviet propaganda and the British response it is possible to study the 'situation' the Soviets sought to influence and also to identify factors which seem to help or hinder the influence of their propaganda in Britain.

There are several approaches to studying Soviet propaganda. Alexander George suggested a two-stage process to understand propaganda, first to summarize what is said, and then to interpret the intentions, strategy and the calculations behind the propaganda.[10] These calculations include the psychological foundations of the propaganda, the prejudices, motivations, passions and complexes that propagandists hope to play upon. Alternatively, Jacques Ellul suggested propaganda can be seen as not just something made by certain people for specific purposes, but as a socio-logical phenomenon illustrating the broad and complex spectrum of opinion and apathy which propagandists hope to influence by changing opinions, and identifying and intensifying existing societal trends in order to lead people into action.[11]

The type of Soviet propaganda that the British defectors broadcast was 'white' or overt propaganda because its source, the Soviet Union, was known. Walter Winchell aptly described Maclean as 'Moscow's Lord Haw Haw'.[12] Using British traitors to influence British opinion at first seems inept, because these men had broken British laws and were regarded as traitors by the majority of the British public, thus their adherence to this view immunized them against Soviet talk which sought to descredit Western policies, and the British government. Yet by using the defectors the possibility that their propaganda would be effective was increased because the defectors, unlike the Soviets, understood how to communicate with a British audience. There was a small minority who were sympathetic to the defectors, and the Soviets hoped to increase the number of people who did not see the defectors as traitors to a hostile power, and who rejected what the Soviets termed 'bourgeois values'. In this way they hoped to improve their own image and weaken Britain from within.[13]

Soviet opportunities to use the defectors as propaganda weapons were not related to their value as informants, because what mattered were British perceptions of the defectors. The British public was the target of Soviet propaganda. For the British government the opportunity to use the defectors to reinforce anti-Communism at home and abroad was a tiny compensation considering the damage they experienced from the defection.

Soviet propaganda strategy aimed to influence members of the intelligentsia who could then explain the message in British terms to the masses.[14] The broad aims of Soviet propaganda have remained constant: to foster a favourable or complacent attitude towards the Soviet Union, to divide and discredit their enemies, stimulate belief in the inevitability of Communism as a world force and the unavoidable decline of capitalism, to attract recruits to the party and sustain the party faithful. In the post-war period, propaganda focused on attacking the USA, the main enemy. It portrayed the USA as an aggressive, militaristic, imperialist power responsible for every international conflict. The Soviets wanted to isolate the USA from its friends, especially its NATO allies, and to discredit US and NATO military and intelligence establishments.[15] These aims would be reflected in the words of the defectors.

It is widely recognized that the effectiveness of Soviet propaganda is difficult to assess. Observers from the target group are liable to fall into one of two extremes of opinion, either refusing to accept that Soviet propaganda can have any effect on a free society or attributing 'almost superhuman cunning, skill and effectiveness' to the propaganda. Soviet propagandists themselves may indulge in wishful thinking and take credit for shifts in public opinion which are not due to them.[16]

115

The Soviets regard propaganda as an essential tool in the preservation and maintenance of Soviet power at home and abroad. While it has proved its worth at home, abroad its effectiveness varies depending upon the historical circumstances. Jacques Ellul found it remarkable that foreign propaganda and psychological warfare have evoked the greatest interest even though it represents the weakest form of propaganda. Foreign propaganda is usually less effective than that within the home group, because it is immediately recognized as foreign, and often as hostile. Also the foreign propagandists are ignorant of the attitudes, interests and presumptions of its target audience. To some extent the Soviets overcame this through national Communist Parties and by using other nationals such as the defectors.

Ellul also challenged two commonly held views which directly affect our attempts to understand the impact of Soviet propaganda. First, that it is easier to disseminate propaganda in a democratic country than in a dictatorship. While this is true in the sense of there being open access to the British public, this advantage is strongly mitigated because overt foreign propaganda is immediately recognized and distrusted, and while there is interest in the Soviet point of view, there is less of an appetite for information. This latter point does not apply to the case of the defectors because successive British governments employed official secrecy to limit the damage of the defections and thus created hungry appetites for information within Britain that the Soviets then fed. In contrast, in totalitarian societies it is more difficult to reach public opinion, but most people before they are fully integrated want to know what is forbidden so that foreign propaganda is likely to exert a very powerful influence.

Given the difficulty in assessing the effectiveness of Soviet propaganda, Ellul suggested bearing in mind four possible effects that may be observed: a certain ambiguity in the thoughts and feelings of the British public, a disturbance of pre-existing ideas, beliefs and judgements. It may show up certain claims of domestic propaganda as false and create a certain amount of bad conscience.[17] Soviet propaganda has been successful in the past when it has played on Western fears of war or when it stood against a 'manifest evil' such as Hitler's regime, or encouraged anti-Western nationalisms. It has been unsuccessful when it was centrally co-ordinated as Western listeners found this type of propaganda 'boringly repetitious, obviously propagandist and dull'.[18] Lastly the effectiveness of Soviet propaganda also depends on its ability to withstand British counter propaganda.

THE BRITISH AND SOVIET RESPONSES TO THE DEFECTION

The British government knew that Burgess, Maclean and Philby were genuine defectors. They tried to limit the damage of the defection by saying that the two diplomats had not enjoyed access to top secret information: Burgess was too junior, and Maclean, although head of the American Department, had no access to information on the most sensitive issues of the day – Korea, NATO, and the Japanese peace treaty.[19] Twelve years later when Philby defected, the government again said as little as possible but announced that Philby had been the 'Third Man' and a Soviet agent before 1946.[20] Shortly before his defection MI6 deliberately fed him information hoping to disinform the Soviets.[21] Therefore secrecy and censorship were employed to limit the damage to the government's reputation at home and abroad and to confuse the Soviets.

For the KGB it was vital to remove Maclean before he was interrogated in case he jeopardized Philby, Blunt, and his former Soviet contacts. The successful rescue of three of their most important agents was a brilliant success for the KGB, a boost for their morale and their reputation within the Soviet elite. Stalin's government was silent after the defection, which perplexed the British, who expected the Soviets immediately to use the defectors as propaganda weapons.[22] Why were the Soviets silent? They denied themselves a major propaganda coup. Without access to Soviet records five reasons can be mooted. Perhaps one reason for silence was to protect Philby and Blunt: any loud propaganda campaign welcoming two ideological spies would make Philby's position much more difficult. Secrecy was the operating principle in the Soviet government just as in Whitehall; this gave them time to consider what to do, and increased their freedom of action.[23] If it was decided to 'eliminate' them, it was prudent not to admit they had ever been in the Soviet Union so the defectors were hidden in Kuibyshev away from Western journalists.[24] Given that the Korean War was seen in Britain largely as a Soviet-inspired aggression, this was a difficult moment for the Soviets to try and pose as a refuge for Western political refugees, even though their propaganda had little difficulty in reconciling its peace message with Soviet aggression and expansion. Lastly, it was not safe in Moscow because Stalin was about to launch another purge, and a faction in the KGB believed the Cambridge spies were double agents and should be 'eliminated'.[25]

Western fears and anxieties may have increased because Soviet silence was perceived as sinister. If the Soviets had launched a noisy propaganda campaign Britain and the USA were likely to have united and employed their co-ordinated propaganda units against them, and thus lessened the damage to Anglo-American relations and the Western alliance. It may be that Soviet silence was due to both confusion in the Kremlin and Stalin's predilection for secrecy, because while the Soviets had used other defectors in their propaganda those who were involved in espionage like Bruno Pontecorvo, Burgess and Maclean were left alone. Under Khrushchev this changed and the defectors who had been spies were employed in propaganda. The former 'spies' were presented to the West as 'political refugees' from the evil, oppressive and war-mongering capitalist countries.[26]

The FBI (Federal Bureau of Investigation) files contain a curious document which suggests that the Soviets may have intended to portray Maclean as an ideological defector. It consists of a letter addressed to the US ambassador, signed 'From an old pal of Maclean', and seems to be a 'deposition' from Maclean to his pal on the day before he left England. Maclean had apparently written, 'I am haunted and burdened by what I know of official secrets, especially . . . high level Anglo-American conversations. The British government . . . have betrayed the realm to the Americans, . . . to incinerate and destroy it in their own interest'. He claimed that the British and Americans were planning to use NATO to launch an assault on the Soviet Union, and that the Americans had arranged the Korean War. His 'duty to his country' lay in disclosing this information to Stalin, who could alert the British people. The FBI made no comment as to whether they thought the deposition was genuine, and the name of the person who sent the letter was deleted.[27]

It seems unlikely that Maclean was the author, as the political views seem crude and the tone is melodramatic. The fact that the letter was sent to the Americans and not the British suggests that the sender thought the Americans were more likely to publish it than the British. It seems most likely that the letter was either of Soviet origin or from a fellow traveller not under strict Soviet control, as the letter aimed to discredit British and American foreign policy. But it would also reveal that Maclean had gone to Moscow, and thus upset Soviet secrecy. Had the Americans decided to publish the letter on 12 June, it would have caused an uproar and made it impossible for the British to pretend that the missing diplomats were off on a spree, and were not escaping spies. Although Hoover (director of the FBI) hated the British, the letter would have also damaged the Americans. In order to make an educated guess it is necessary to know when the letter was posted to the US embassy but this vital piece of information is absent from the FBI published records.[28]

THE INFORMATION EQUATION

The mental outlook of Cold Warriors in the 1950s determined that the short-term loss of information through the defectors was an automatic and potentially dangerous gain to the Communists. This outlook was refined when it was recognized that much of the Cold War confrontation was caused and exacerbated by mutual misperceptions. Just as Soviet defectors helped the West to understand the Soviets, arguably, Burgess and Maclean could help the Soviets to understand Western behaviour and thus ease tensions.[29]

Philby's memoirs give some indication of the type of information he gave them, but without access to KGB archives we can only speculate on the contents of the debriefing reports on the defectors, and the utilization of this information. The KGB valued its Cambridge spies,[30] but had to establish if the defectors were genuine or 'plants' who would disinform the KGB, by carefully checking their information. Probably they discussed the escape and the danger Philby and Blunt faced. Next came questions about current Soviet concerns, for example, US policy in Korea, and Germany, and also information relating to the personalities of policy-makers.[31] Burgess and Maclean had been prolific collectors of intelligence and possibly their case officer had questions arising from past information. The KGB also helped the defectors to settle in.[32]

The qualities of the defectors which probably determined their value can be identified and compared. The information that defectors possess is their 'meal ticket' but is a 'wasting asset'.[33] Top-grade, current information was required, and this depended on the defectors' access to information, their job, and their connections to senior policy-makers. Also of value was the defectors' experience of the enemy country, their ability to explain its behaviour accurately in the future, and to resist the temptation to fabricate information. Personality was also important: defectors had to adapt to their new life, and a mental breakdown or alcoholism would lessen their value.

While in Kuibyshev, Maclean and Burgess took on new names, respectively Mark Petrovich Fraser and Jim Andreyvich Eliot. All three defectors drank excessively. Maclean drank suicidally, recovered and then took a job in a language institute, before he fully adapted to Soviet life, learned the language and became an academic at the prestigious and influential Institute of World Economics and International Relations (IMEMO).[34] Burgess dissipated his considerable talents. He had the extra burden of being a homosexual, and a social butterfly with nowhere to flutter. He became utterly depressed by the Soviet utopia.[35] Philby worked intermittently for the KGB, continuing to play his 'game' against the West. He resorted to drink when the KGB ceased to employ him during the period 1967–71, but was then rescued by Rufa, whom he married. Subsequently the KGB took a renewed interest in his services.[36]

From the KGB's perspective the information on strategic and diplomatic policy from these three might earn them points within the Soviet ruling elite. Their first priority, however, was to 'know' the enemy intelligence agency and thus Philby, even with twelve-year-old information on the procedures, personnel and operations of MI6 and the CIA, was perhaps most valued, and not least because he was a fellow intelligence officer. Next in importance would be Maclean because of his current information, and his sixteen years' experience in senior posts in the Foreign Office. Burgess had followed a peripatetic career in British intelligence, the BBC and the Foreign Office, where he stayed for seven years mainly at a junior level. Perhaps his heady social life and knowledge of Whitehall's clubland enabled him to identify vulnerable people whom the KGB could bribe and blackmail.

From a Western perspective, their order of importance is similar to that posited for the Soviets, although different departments in Whitehall may have had different opinions. Philby's mischief-making from Moscow was much more of an annoyance to the Anglo-American intelligence community than the loss of old information. As each year passed the defectors became less useful as their knowledge of British politics and international relations became more academic. Part of Philby's legend was his claim that he was still useful years after his debriefing ended in 1967.[37] He may have continued to remember fresh details about his career but it is unlikely that these memories were useful to the KGB.

Soviet obituaries offer a particularly useful window upon Soviet opinion about the defectors: as officially approved epitaphs, they had some propaganda value at home and abroad. In contrast the British obituaries were not government approved, but expressed disapproval of the defectors' treachery.[38] This analysis may exaggerate the significance of the obituaries. Burgess's and Maclean's obituaries were written when Soviet government censorship was strict, while Philby's was written with the controls relaxed, but it seems likely that the KGB wrote his obituary.

If the approximate length of the obituary was a sign of value then the Soviets valued Maclean most highly as his obituary was 210 words long. Philby's was half as long at 101 words, while Burgess's was only 78 words long. The positions of the obituaries in the newspapers were approximately equal: Philby and Burgess were on page 4 of *Izvestia*, while Maclean was on page 6.

Philby's and Maclean's careers and contributions to Soviet society were fully described, but no mention was made of Burgess's previous career except the platitude that he had devoted his whole life to the cause of peace and the struggle for a better future for humankind. This reflected Soviet peace propaganda rather than paying tribute to Burgess. The brevity and vagueness of Burgess's obituary perhaps indicates official disapproval because his defection had ended Philby's career, and because of his homosexuality, his decadent life-style and his tendency to tangle with Western correspondents. Unless of course his obituary was Soviet disinformation! Maclean's obituary in 1983 also echoed Soviet peace propaganda: he had 'dedicated his entire life to social progress, humanism, and peace'. By 1988, when Philby died, the old-style Soviet ideological propaganda had all but vanished: Philby had just found 'genuine human happiness' in the Soviet Union.

The honours that Soviet governments bestowed on the defectors were an important indication of their value. Philby and Maclean received many medals. Philby's Red Banner seems to have been awarded to counter the British withdrawal of his OBE in 1965; this award was very prestigious during the war but afterwards it was awarded more frequently.[39] Significantly Burgess, according to the obituary, was not decorated and this casts doubt upon the value of his services to the Soviet Union before and after he defected. Maclean's obituary was the most detailed and seemed to be a warm tribute from several colleagues in contrast to the sparse official tone of the statement on Philby.

THE DEFECTORS AS PROPAGANDA WEAPONS: THE COLD WAR 1951–64

Before examining how the Soviets used the defectors in their propaganda, it is important to recognize that the intelligence agencies can be the hidden undercurrent that influences the events we study. We may never know exactly how the British, American and Soviet intelligence services used the defectors in their secret war, and if or how this influenced the visible propaganda battle, but a few instances have emerged. The CIA spread two rumours to make life difficult for Philby. They suggested that Israeli intelligence had known that Burgess, Maclean and Philby were Soviet agents, that CIA and SIS had used them to send false information to the KGB, and hinted that Philby could return to England.[40] The KGB played similar games: Philby tried to entrap Nicholas Elliot of MI6, by luring him to a secret meeting.[41] MI6's treatment of Philby after 1951 was designed to make the KGB think that Philby was a double agent, but this had the unfortunate side-effect of increasing American suspicions of MI6.[42]

The watershed year in this period was 1956 when, after five years of Soviet silence and frenzied Western speculation, Burgess and Maclean suddenly appeared at a press conference in Moscow. Previously the Soviets denied all knowledge of Burgess and Maclean, but allowed them to contact their families. After the press conference the Soviets used the defectors openly, the British responded and the propaganda battle became noisier. The permanent aim of the British government was to say as little as possible about the defectors. They fought a war of words on three fronts, against the Soviets, against curious British journalists, and against some American officials and politicians who tried to use British security lapses as a rationale to curtail the 'special relationship' in the fields of atomic energy and intelligence.

Before the conference it was the British press who shouted about the defectors. They had been starved of information and began a determined search to find out where Burgess and Maclean were and the true story behind their disappearance. They correctly speculated that the men had been Soviet spies and had fled to Moscow. As the British government would neither confirm nor deny any rumours the press was full of all kinds of wild speculation, and papers competed with each other to publish the juiciest stories. In hindsight these stories seem like a chaotic farce with

Burgess and Maclean popping up in every European capital, one step ahead of the journalists who followed them. Opinions were divided as to whether Burgess and Maclean were happy or sad, alive or dead, important advisers to the Soviets or rotting in a Soviet gaol.[43] But the Cold War was in deadly earnest, and these stories possibly increased public anxiety about the Soviets, and also strengthened anti-Communism in Britain. Although the Burgess and Maclean case was a very sensitive and volatile issue, we cannot dismiss the likelihood that some of these stories originated from the Foreign Office because they served the government's anti-Soviet propaganda.

Under Stalin, stories about Burgess and Maclean being spies, defectors and advisers to the Soviet government were ignored, perhaps because a denial might give the accusations some credibility. The East German Premier Otto Nusche, however, responded to Western accusations about the defectors when he told journalists that Burgess and Maclean had been kidnapped by the CIA. Western diplomats exposed this as just a pathetic ruse to avoid being questioned about the kidnapping of a West German lawyer by East German security police.[44] This may have been a deliberate statement designed to test Western reaction or just Nusche's spontaneous annoyance.

In September 1953 Khrushchev became the leader of the Soviet Union, and under his regime the Soviet people experienced a period of transitory reforms. The West perceived this 'thaw' but subsequently his foreign policy became as heavy-handed and dangerous as Stalin's. Later at the Twentieth Congress in 1956, de-Stalinization began. Khrushchev rejected the theory of the inevitability of war, but the main themes of Stalin's propaganda were continued and revitalized in a more extensive and intense propaganda and psychological warfare campaign against Western ideology and policy. The peace movement was recognized as the most important weapon against the west.[45]

Khruschev's new era was marked dramatically on 11 September 1953, when Melinda Maclean and her three children 'disappeared': everyone assumed (correctly) that she had joined Donald in the Soviet Union. In response the British press renewed their attack on the incompetence of the British security services. Some journalists suspected that the Soviets timed Melinda's disappearance to scupper British attempts to forge a new atomic energy agreement with the Americans, but it seems more likely that with Stalin dead, Melinda could go to Moscow.[46]

The next month, as if to deny any responsibility in Melinda's disappearance, the Soviets broke their silence to say there was no connection between the disappearance of the two diplomats and the Soviet Union, and blamed the capitalist press, diplomacy and intelligence for using the case to aggravate the international situation and to sow suspicion.[47] The first part of this statement was a lie, but the second part was true because during this period British anti-Soviet propaganda in the newspapers frequently featured Burgess and Maclean.

The defection of Vladimir Petrov on 5 April 1954 changed the stakes for both Britain and the Soviet Union. The Soviets knew what information Petrov possessed, but could not control what he told the Australian and British authorities nor how these countries' propagandists would utilize their new spokesman and his information. On 28 April Petrov revealed that Burgess and Maclean were advisers to the Soviet government, that Mrs Maclean had been blackmailed into joining her husband and that the Soviets would use the family in anti-Western propaganda.[48] Without Melinda's testimony it is not possible to know if she was blackmailed.

Petrov's defection was not a simple advantage to the British government, but a liability, because his disclosures put Burgess and Maclean back on to the front pages of British and (more alarmingly) American newspapers. Moreover, his claim that Burgess and Maclean were long-term penetration agents was widely believed and showed that the government had lied about the case in 1951. The British government defended its version of the case, by attempting to undermine Petrov's credibility. Selwyn Lloyd, the Foreign Secretary, said Petrov's information was no more than hearsay – an astonishing example of the British government doing the KGB's job of challenging the credibility of a Soviet defector. Petrov's revelations were instrumental in persuading the government to issue a formal explanation in a White Paper; moreover, the government took over a year to consider their response.[49]

Soviet propagandists took up a new instrument in March 1955: Bruno Pontecorvo, an Italian scientist who had worked on the Anglo-American atomic project, until he defected in 1950. He suddenly resurfaced and trumpeted Soviet propaganda. He urged a ban on nuclear weapons and claimed that Soviet scientists worked only on peaceful projects. He described how he left Britain because of his 'moral suffering' after Hiroshima, and the 'systematic blackmail' of British police authorities. Was this an opportunity to test Western reaction, before taking up their British instruments Burgess and Maclean? The British answered Pontecorvo's peace overture by promptly withdrawing his British citizenship.[50]

Later that year two rumours circulated, apparently from Soviet sources which claimed that Burgess and Maclean were valuable advisers to the Soviet and East German governments and lived outside of Moscow.[51] But a few months later, Khrushchev privately told Harold Wilson that he knew nothing about the defectors.[52] Then the next month, on 13 February, Burgess and Maclean suddenly appeared at the press conference and read prepared statements, causing a brief international sensation.[53] Why did Khrushchev decide to end the mystery of the disappearing diplomats in this dramatic way? Was this a belated attempt to counter Petrov, and show off to the foreign Communist Parties assembled in Moscow for the Twentieth Congress, and at the same time have the world's attention for some peace propaganda?

Burgess and Maclean said they had appeared because the doubts about

123

their whereabouts and speculations about their past activities were being exploited by the opponents of Anglo-Soviet understanding. They denied that they had been Communist agents. They claimed they had gone to Moscow only to seek a better understanding between the Soviet Union and the West, because the official information in their possession convinced them that neither the British nor the Americans were working for peace. What is striking about this statement is its caution and restraint. This was not a diatribe against Western policy, the specifics of the conflict between East and West were downplayed, their espionage was glossed over by simply stating that the information they knew had caused them to go to the Soviet Union. Having tested the waters of Western opinion, Maclean then publicized the Soviet line in a letter to the *Daily Herald*. He contradicted previous government statements that he had not dealt with NATO, and deplored the militaristic statements of NATO's military leaders, their war readiness and their desire to arm NATO forces with nuclear weapons. Socialist societies were, he claimed, entirely peaceful.[54]

The British response was combative: in the House of Commons, Selwyn Lloyd criticized the 'consistent lack of candour of the Soviet authorities in their statements about these men', which showed the difficulties of establishing relations of mutual trust which the Soviet Union professed to desire. He told the Soviets that they would not succeed in using Burgess and Maclean to drive a wedge between Britain and the United States. He was greeted with enthusiastic cheers from MPs. In Washington this theme was repeated by the British ambassador, Roger Makins, who said, 'Burgess and Maclean are no longer an issue between Britain and America'. Petrov joined in pointing out that Burgess and Maclean were instruments of Soviet propaganda. These themes were repeated in the newspapers.[55]

The results of the press conference were mixed. The dramatic appearance of the defectors not only reopened the wounds in the Anglo-American partnership but also drew the partners together. There was perhaps more damage to the government's reputation at home than abroad. This particular Soviet propaganda stunt was unlikely to convince anyone except the party faithful because there was abundant evidence of Soviet aggression. Instead of 'clearing the air' with the British, relations worsened.

Burgess's and Maclean's statements were published in Soviet newspapers. Soviet domestic propaganda aimed to reassure the people of its peaceful intentions and convince them that the West was aggressive and planning a war, which was the rationale for economic and political privations. Burgess and Maclean's defection also implied the superiority of Soviet to Western society because they had chosen to live in the Soviet Union for ideological reasons. What the average Soviet citizen thought about their preference for the Soviet Union is an interesting if elusive question.

In British newspapers stories about Burgess and Maclean became more aggressive after their appearance in Moscow. These stories sometimes contradicted each other: for example Maclean and Burgess were described as being very useful to the Soviets, and also an embarrassment and a barrier to better relations with Britain. They were also a barrier to increasing Anglo-American co-operation. In 1955 a US Senate Security Committee probed Maclean's espionage and discussed General MacArthur's accusation that Maclean had sabotaged the war effort by leaking to the Soviets the crucial information that UN forces would not take all-out action against the Chinese if they invaded Korea; the Soviets passed it to the Chinese. The accusation was based on the twenty-one-day gap between Maclean becoming head of the American Department on 6 November 1950, and 26 November when Chinese Communists broke through the Korean stronghold and shattered the UN line. The British argued (correctly) that Maclean could not have told the Communists anything because he had been appointed four days after the Korean attack had begun.[56]

The last Soviet propaganda initiative in this period was also the first major attempt to challenge the orthodox view of the defectors as traitors; this was Tom Driberg's book, *Guy Burgess, Portrait with Background*. The KGB allowed Burgess to tell his story to Driberg, a well-known left-wing, homosexual MP who had known Burgess in London and was sympathetic to him. Burgess had written to Driberg asking him if he thought Anglo-Soviet relations would be improved if he told his story, and he also said that he would very much like to show a British socialist around Moscow; Driberg accepted Burgess's offer. Driberg combined some obvious and heavy-handed KGB propaganda with some plausible 'legends', and a sophisticated attack upon the orthodox view of Burgess and Maclean as traitors. Driberg's concept of treason rested not in the act itself, but in the motives of the act. Therefore to sell state secrets for money was treason, but to give state secrets to an enemy was justifiable if the individual had for ideological reasons transferred his loyalty to the enemy. He drew a moral equivalence between the lies that government officials and politicians sometimes told and the lies that Burgess and Maclean continually told in order to cover up their allegiance to Stalin. He also suggested that Burgess and Maclean might be 'far-seeing patriots', if their espionage had eased East–West tensions. He suggested that the atom spies promoted peace because their information enabled the Soviets to catch up with the Americans in the arms race. Driberg attacked the moral principle of loyalty to the state and then provided evidence to suggest that Soviet espionage had been beneficial to Britain.[57] These notions were absorbed by other members of the British intelligentsia in the following years. The Soviets used Burgess and Driberg in their sophisticated psychological war against 'bourgeois values'.

Two examples of obvious propaganda were Burgess's opinion of Dzerzhinsky as a 'Polish humanist' who supported the Bolshevik revolution, despite his role as chief of the blood-thirsty secret police, the

Cheka. Philby would repeat this refrain later. Burgess praised the Soviet nationalities policy, and ignored the interminable tragedy for the ethnic groups who were suppressed, deported or massacred. Burgess also boosted his own image by presenting himself as a 'roving expert Englishman' who advised the Soviets.[58]

Burgess continued to be a channel for Soviet anti-American propaganda which aimed to drive a wedge between Britain and the USA. The 'peaceful utopian Soviet Union' was favourably compared to a war-mongering USA which dominated its weak-kneed ally Britain.[59] This view would find a receptive audience not only in Communist and left-wing circles but also among Conservatives who resented American power; however, Conservatives and most Labour politicians were unlikely to listen to Burgess.

The fact that Driberg was a well-known left-winger and the propagandist tone of the book both guaranteed a hostile reception in centre and right-wing political circles, but on the left it was received almost uncritically.[60] The book was a 'Christmas choice' for the *New Statesman*, hardly cheering reading for those angered and saddened by the Suez débâcle! But for those people who saw Suez as a symbol of everything that was rotten in England, Burgess's book was grist to their mill. This book marked the opening phase of the defectors as weapons in Soviet psychological warfare. Clewes noted that during the 1950s the Soviet line was uncompromising and its supporters were easily identifiable. In the next decade this distinction became blurred as Soviet propaganda became more complex and Soviet 'auxiliaries' were harder to spot.[61] Furthermore the atmosphere of *détente*, the rise of anti-Americanism and the nihilistic and rebellious youth culture combined to erode the Cold War consensus, and created more favourable conditions for the influence of Soviet propaganda.

BREZHNEV AND *DÉTENTE*: 1964–85

The main source of antagonism and mistrust between East and West during this period was that Western governments misunderstood the Soviet policy of 'peaceful coexistence' and *détente*'. For the West *détente* was a relaxation of tension; for the Soviets it was, 'the steady strengthening of . . . the socialist camp and a defeat for imperialist forces'. '*Détente* was an offensive Soviet strategy to disseminate Communist ideology and socialist values.[62] The KGB served this policy, and increased their activities in the West.[63] The defectors were a highly visible instrument of this policy but were used sparingly, possibly to increase their impact, and because the KGB did not want to focus Western attention on their past espionage activities while they paid lip-service to *détente*. During this period differences between the projected images of Philby and Maclean became apparent. Both defectors gave interviews and published books. Maclean became an academic and retreated from view, while the KGB began to build Philby's image as the masterspy of the century.

Maclean wrote three articles under the auspices of IMEMO, before *The Times* in January 1967 drew attention to what they erroneously described as Maclean's 'first article' on 'British and American "special relations" at the present stage'. *The Times* was hostile to Maclean, labelled his article 'Stalinist', and asked whether his journey to Moscow had been worthwhile either for himself or for the Soviets. Maclean criticized the pro-American orientation of Harold Wilson's foreign policy because it conflicted with London's effort to increase its influence in Europe, and increased public disquiet about the government's support for US 'aggression' in Vietnam.[64]

In the 1950s the British perceived Maclean and Burgess as instruments of Soviet psychological warfare. Later, when journalists discovered Philby was a translator for *Sputnik*, an English language magazine, they feared his knowledge of British culture would sharpen the Soviets' 'psychological attack' on Britain.[65]

As media interest in the defectors continued to grow in Britain, the defectors became the object of circulation wars between newspapers and thus created a larger audience for Soviet propaganda. In 1967 journalists from the *Sunday Times* published a book on Philby and the KGB seized the opportunity to use Philby for anti-Western propaganda. Philby's interviews with two journalists, Roy Blackman and Murray Sayle, contained the first expression of the themes of KGB propaganda that became Philby's 'Western serenade', designed to embarrass and discredit Western intelligence services, upset the Anglo-American intelligence partnership, and to establish the Philby legend.[66]

Philby carried Soviet propaganda to a new phase because he commanded more media attention than his fellow defectors; as a former trusted and respected MI6 officer he knew how to attack the West, and seemed intent on wounding his former employers and some of his former colleagues. In Philby's hands the Soviet attack on the West became personal, intense and spiteful, and also somewhat childish. For example, he repeatedly boasted about the brilliance and superiority of the KGB, insulted former colleagues, and gleefully chanted, 'our spies are better than your spies!'

The *Daily Express* warned its readers (in bold type) that Philby was a traitor, and that the interview was a KGB attempt to discredit British intelligence services. In a Moscow restaurant, Philby characteristically indulged in food and wine, became boorish, and boasted about his exploits as a spy. He had no regrets and said he was sure there were more young men like him in Britain. He admitted he made mistakes and wondered how many of these the British and American intelligence services could identify! He told Roy Blackman to ask George Blake about the recent changes in British intelligence and cheekily asked how Blake had escaped from prison, which must have made his former colleagues in the intelligence world wince. Philby broadcast the orthodox Soviet line which aimed to weaken the Anglo-American alliance by exacerbating internal policy divisions in the Labour Party, which was then in power: 'Must the Americans run amok indefinitely in Asia, and South America, seriously endangering us? Must a Labour government support them indefinitely just to ensure US support for sterling?'

Philby took the same line with Murray Sayle and added two new elements: he claimed he was a serving officer in the KGB and justified his treachery by saying that he always placed political concerns before private concerns, 'To betray you must first belong. I never belonged.' Philby taunted British and American intelligence agencies by saying that he had taken precautions against any 'rough stuff' from Western intelligence who might disrupt their meeting, and he mischievously offered to withdraw his book if the Krogers were exchanged for Gerald Brooke.[67] In April 1968 Hugh Trevor-Roper, a former wartime colleague of Philby's, counterattacked and warned that with Philby's reappearance and the publication of four books about him, including his memoirs, there was a danger of Philby becoming a legend. The KGB were deliberately building Philby's image as a super-spy: there was more to this than just praising and protecting their agent; this was a personality cult designed to attack British and American intelligence services.[68]

Philby's memoirs lent his new image some permanence: there were five reprints of the paperback edition. Graham Greene (another wartime colleague) billed Philby's memoirs as 'far more gripping than any novel of espionage I can remember'. Here was one 'legend in his own time' building a legend for his friend Philby.[69] Greene's sponsorship of Philby was arguably an important factor in proselytizing the Philby legend. Later, much of Philby's sabotage would be exposed by former officials and academics.[70] Philby's book, however, is cleverly written and sifting the truth from the falsehoods requires care and specialized knowledge of the Anglo-American intelligence community.

In contrast, Maclean's book was largely well received. Professor D. Cameron Watt considered that Maclean had put his exile to much better advantage than Burgess and Philby. Maclean shared the same prejudices of any middle-aged, middle-class, left-liberal member of the intelligentsia. Objectivity had been accomplished by glossing over the issues where British and Soviet policy conflicted. Gordon Brooke Shepherd disagreed and detected Soviet propaganda in chapters on Britain and the Third World, a task usually undertaken by 'the blunt Tass trowel', but for once left to the 'rapier of the qualified defector'.[71] The book has become required reading for students of British foreign policy. It is possible to believe that the book was not influenced by the KGB. However, its attack on the US domination of Britain and Europe, and its predictions of the disintegration of the Anglo-American alliance, NATO and the Commonwealth complemented the policy objectives of *détente* and its publication fitted in with the 'openness' of *détente*.

Thereafter, there was silence from the defectors until 1982, and during this period British interest in their spies dramatically increased. Andrew Boyle revealed that Anthony Blunt was the 'Fourth Man' in the Cambridge spy ring. Blunt was stripped of his knighthood, hounded by the press and died a few years later.[72] The next scandal to grip Whitehall was caused by Peter Wright, a disgruntled former employee of MI5. He gave Chapman Pincher information about the internal security investigations that had torn MI5 apart as they hunted for a super-spy, a 'Fifth Man', the elusive 'Elli', first identified by Igor Gouzenko in 1945. The scandal returned in full force when Wright published his memoirs and the British government attempted to ban the book. The government was attacked from both sides of the political spectrum. There can be little doubt that the '*Spycatcher* affair' temporarily did more damage to Britain's image abroad than the KGB could have inflicted.[73]

The witch-hunt for Sir Roger Hollis and the related Peter Wright fiasco were both generated by British officials. Wright's conviction that Hollis was the spy in MI5 was due in part to his near-religious faith in the testimony of Soviet defector Anatoli Golitsyn, and his certainty that another defector, Yuri Nosenko, was a plant. It seems likely that both defectors were genuine, but Golitsyn began to fabricate information and was the victim of his own conspiratorial nightmares. The suspicions which worried British intelligence and paralysed the CIA were largely of their own making, though the KGB may also bear some of the responsibility.[74] When the Hollis controversy became public the KGB were confused because they knew he was innocent and deduced that this was a dastardly British plot.[75]

Ironically, while those convinced of Hollis's guilt sought more stringent security procedures, their campaign has paradoxically decreased public trust in the security services and increased demands for the reform of official secrecy. The pursuit of Hollis is an English variant of McCarthyism: it utilized McCarthy's favourite techniques – guilt by association, guilt by geographic proximity, and guilt if you cannot prove your innocence. Just as Soviet propagandists twisted the truth, these popular books distorted reality by abandoning normal standards of historical scholarship in favour of a mind-numbing labyrinth of interlocking unsupported accusations. The influence of these popular books seems to be widespread, but perhaps signifies the British public's keen appetite for books about spies and scandals rather than any desire for serious understanding.[76]

In 1982, after twelve years of silence, the Soviets issued an exaggerated report of Maclean's illness which deflected press attention away from a GRU captain, Anatoli Zotov, who had been expelled from Britain.[77] Maclean died the following year. His last interview was published after his death; he seemed composed, dignified and sad, while the journalist reminded readers of his past as a British traitor and Soviet spy.[78] The old story about Maclean helping to 'get the Chinese into the war in Korea and keeping the Soviets out' resurfaced in two places: the *Sunday Telegraph* quoted 'a reliable Soviet source', and Roy Medvedev, who had known Maclean in Moscow, recalled he had heard him boast about his 'spy coup'.[79] Perhaps this is an example of the Soviets and perhaps even of Maclean (who was not prone to boast about himself) picking up an attractive story that had originated among General MacArthur's supporters. This story was seen by experts as an attempt to encourage the US view that Britain cannot be trusted and to demonstrate the role one individual can play in countering Western imperialism. Sir David Hunt squashed this story in the same way that British officials had responded when it first appeared in 1956.[80] Maclean's death was not an occasion for extensive Soviet propaganda, while Philby's death was to be their *pièce de résistance*.

THE GORBACHEV ERA

The influence of the KGB increased when their candidate, Mikhail Gorbachev, won the succession contest after Chernenko's death.[81] Gorbachev initiated a new spirit of reform and freedom which backfired on the KGB. It became a target of forceful public criticism, and found itself required to defend its right to exist. It responded by opening up a little, but this fed the public's appetite for reform.[82] The KGB became increasingly image conscious, and turned to the British defectors as a means of advertising their 'best' qualities. On the defensive at home, abroad the KGB faced a situation in some ways similar to the years of *détente*. The atmosphere was favourable for collecting information and making contacts, but Western governments were more suspicious of the KGB.[83] In these unsettled conditions, the KGB brought British defectors Philby and George Blake back into play. Their propaganda was directed equally at domestic and foreign audiences in contrast to the past when they focused mainly on the West.

Resurgent nationalism in the Republics threatened to cause disintegration within the Soviet Union. Philby, now in his dotage, was put into harness to explain away troubles in the Baltic as the handiwork of Western intelligence agencies who had caused trouble in this area during the Cold War.[84] These appearances served the KGB's domestic propaganda purposes of glamorizing their organization, justifying its existence, and blaming internal problems on foreign intelligence agencies. With hindsight these appearances seem to lead to the climax of Philby's career as a propagandist, that is his interviews with Philip Knightley, serialized in the *Sunday Times* and later incorporated into a book, *Philby: The Life and Views of the KGB Masterspy*.[85]

Philby had mellowed, the abrasive tone of his previous interviews had gone, but the 'song' was all too familiar, and perhaps more persuasive because of its amiable tone. Philby withdrew his claim to have been a colonel in the KGB, but said that he retained a colonel's privileges. He repeated that British intelligence had deliberately allowed him to escape in order to avoid a scandal. He still had 'no regrets', and justified his treachery by arguing the primacy of politics above people.

Initially Philby dismissed the view that Hollis was a Soviet spy, but then threw a tasty morsel to those in pursuit of Hollis. He recalled a meeting with Hollis and Anthony Blunt: Hollis had turned towards Blunt and called 'Oh Elli', Blunt did not bat an eyelid, and Hollis resumed the conversation. This anecdote was quickly absorbed as evidence that Hollis was a Soviet agent.[86]

Philby's testimony was immediately challenged. David Owen, MP and former Foreign Secretary, dismissed Philby's claim that MI6 had deliberately let him go, saying 'Common sense tells you that Philby would have caused far less damage to Britain had he been convicted and locked up for the past forty years'. Noel Annan wrote a decimating rebuttal to all the excuses that Philby and his supporters have adopted, and criticized Knightley for being a passive cypher for Philby. Knightley recognized the problem about the conversations – 'How much of what Philby said was the man speaking and how much the serving KGB officer?' – but perpetuated the myth that Philby was a KGB officer! Knightley made an attempt to place Philby's testimony in a critical context but applied a critical eye selectively and thus some of Philby's myths were given a new lease of life in the book.[87]

The next KGB propaganda coup was Philby's funeral. He was given an official funeral, which was broadcast by all the major networks, and pictures of his open coffin with his wife bidding him farewell were on the front pages of most newspapers. It was very much a hero's death, designed to annoy Western intelligence and advertise to future recruits how well the Soviets looked after their own.[88]

The advantage of Philby as an instrument of Soviet propaganda is that he was and remains 'the sort of man who won worshippers'.[89] The homosexuality of Burgess and Maclean counted against them; also Burgess was perhaps too outrageous and bohemian and Maclean was too bookish. Despite the considerable efforts of academics and retired civil servants, the Philby legend still gains new converts. The most recent 'convert' to the Philby legend was columnist Julie Burchill, who eulogized Philby as her 'hero', and commended his alcoholism, his philandering and his ability to lie successfully, attributes which are usually disapproved of. Following in the footsteps of Driberg and Greene she excused Philby's treachery by saying that 'in a world of betrayals Philby's treachery was small beer'.[90] How seriously should we take Burchill as evidence of a new generation of converts to the Philby cult? Perhaps not at all, because Communism is discredited and the Soviet Union is adopting capitalist ways; it seems unlikely they will attract ideological converts until they have something superior to offer Western youth. Significantly both Knightley and Burchill belong to a new and separate generation from the previous supporters of Philby who were his friends or contemporaries. The legend therefore lives on.

A few months after Philby's reappearance, the Blake case resurfaced when Pat Pottle and Michael Randall confessed that they had helped Blake to escape in 1966. In the 1970s Sean Burke, a cell-mate of Blake's, claimed that supporters of CND had helped Blake to escape. At the time this was not widely believed, but now the rumour appeared to be true. Pottle and Randall were members of CND who had been imprisoned with Blake; they saw Blake as a 'prisoner of war in a sordid underground battle between rival intelligence industries' and felt that his sentence was unjust.[91] Once they confessed, the authorities were faced with a decision on whether or not to prosecute them; this led to a distasteful episode in which MI5 was accused of deliberately allowing Blake to escape and pretending not to know who had helped him.[92] This issue was discussed in the newspapers and also in a television programme, *The Blake Escape*. This matter has since been resolved in favour of Pottle and Randall. The Blake case drew attention yet again to the secrecy of the British government and the inadequacies of the intelligence and security services.[93]

In 1990 the KGB cast Philby's image in celluloid, and brought George Blake into play: he appeared in a television programme and published his memoirs, again for both domestic and foreign audiences.[94] The aim of the documentary on Philby was to perpetuate his image as a super-spy, and to justify their own existence by appearing as sympathetic figures and also successful intelligence professionals, and perhaps also to earn some hard currency.[95] The Soviet version of the film was twice as long as the version shown in Britain and the USA, an indication of the KGB's efforts to improve their image at home. This did not preclude some well-designed mischief to upset Western intelligence. In the publicity for the film a Soviet spokesman sought to discredit the British government by comparing their secrecy with the *glasnost* of the KGB as they had released documents about Philby to the film-makers.[96] Furthermore, the KGB officials who had run Philby as an agent appeared and gloated over their success, which probably infuriated Western intelligence officers. One KGB officer meddled in the Fifth Man controversy, and said that the Fifth Man was not known to British intelligence. Possibly this was an attempt to pre-empt Oleg Gordievsky, who was shortly to reveal the identities of the Fifth Man and 'Elli'. Former British and American intelligence officers spoke against Philby, but the overall impression of the programme was of a salute to Philby the masterspy. The film lingered over Philby's funeral, and the programme ended sentimentally to the music of Frank Sinatra singing 'My Way'!

British reviewers were quick to spot the laughable errors in the film, which cast doubt upon the efficiency and knowledge of the KGB. For example, photographs of Maclean and Burgess were mixed up, so that Maclean appeared as Burgess and vice versa. The KGB claimed that Philby set up the CIA, and seemed to think that MI6 was MI5, and that the wartime headquarters of SOE in Baker Street were the headquarters of MI6.[97] So long as one read a review of the programme, these errors and the KGB's motives were explained, but people who knew little about the subject may have been misled. Significantly, in boosting Philby, the KGB belittled Burgess and Maclean. How much impact this visual image of Philby will have, only time will tell.

Since the 1950s the images of the defectors have become established, and there are specific groups of authors who write about the spies, and members of the media and intelligentsia who believe that the defectors were not traitors and did no harm. The KGB has to work far less hard to stoke controversies today than it did in the 1950s. For example the KGB tried to discredit Gordievsky by suggesting that he had not had access to important information.[98] When his book was published, the KGB's work was done for them by a group of authors, with a vested interest in keeping the mystery unsolved, who attacked Gordievsky far more savagely than the KGB.[99] It is always prudent to suspect the testimony of a defector especially when he solves a particularly irksome mystery for successive British governments. But it is very odd that these writers refuse to accept the new evidence even when some of Gordievsky's testimony has been corroborated by two former KGB officials in Moscow.[100]

George Blake aligned himself with those who favour reforms in the KGB, thus contributing to the image that Gorbachev and the KGB wish to project of a Soviet Union on the path of reform.[101]. He was treated in a firm and resolute manner by Tom Bower, who interviewed him for the BBC, unlike the sympathetic hearing that Philby always received from Philip Knightley. Blake wrote that both the KGB and Western publishers persuaded him to write his memoirs, while Knightley in his introduction does not mention KGB involvement. Peter Hennessy reviewed Blake's book and noted that it lacked the literary attractions of Philby's memoirs, and was therefore unlikely to be such powerful disinformation.[102] It does seem to be Blake's own work, and in stark contrast to the KGB he eulogized Maclean, but not Philby. Blake asks us to reappraise Maclean's life; perhaps Maclean and even Burgess will be rehabilitated in the future.

CONCLUSIONS

Before concluding, it is necessary to place this study of the British defectors in perspective. First, in the post-war period the number of Soviet defectors has far exceeded the number of British or Western defectors who headed East. The security services of the Eastern bloc have therefore been less successful than those of the West in this respect. Thus the propaganda agencies of the West have had more opportunities to use Soviet defectors than their Eastern bloc rivals. Second, while the British defectors have had a very high profile in the Western media, they are but a small if powerful channel for propaganda, in contrast to the much larger and persistent efforts of Soviet propagandists who control the dissemination of the main messages such as the peace campaigns.

This study of how Soviet propagandists have used the defectors confirmed what we know about the aims and tactics of Soviet propaganda and psychological warfare in this period. They used the defectors to communicate the Soviet message in British terms to the intelligentsia, and to left-wing political circles, in order to reach the masses. The messages served Soviet policy and were broadcast persistently. Helped by Philby and by Western paranoia the KGB has been fairly successful in building up its image as a powerful elite force, an image which has only recently been corrected by the memoirs of Soviet defectors.[103] In the same period 'anti-Americanism' grew, but other historical factors were also at work here. Philby is seen as the 'masterspy', but the majority of people still regard him as a traitor, all the more distasteful for being so successful.

Without precise data it is impossible to assess how far Soviet propaganda has affected British attitudes towards the issues of loyalty and security. The 'strategy' behind the use of the defectors seems to be a combination of challenging the orthodox view of the balance between individuals' freedom of conscience and their responsibility or loyalty to the state or the country, and more characteristic attempts to discredit the policies and government agencies of Britain and the USA, and to cause friction between the two allies. The defectors thus attempt to appeal to our belief in democracy, and our sense that an individual has the right to freedom of conscience. The emphasis on the failures of our security services and government secrecy finds a deep resonance with the British propensity to criticize the government – often with good reason. As Knightley noted, the class-consciousness of the British also drew attention to Burgess, Maclean and Philby, who were all sons of the Establishment, yet Blake has not been able to command the same fascination, perhaps because he came from a different class. Apathy has not been a problem because the British public has remained keenly interested in the defectors. The testimony of not only the British defectors but also the Soviet defector Petrov has shown that the government's story was not the whole truth; thus they have caused a certain amount of bad conscience, and an ambiguity in beliefs and ideas. The existing trends in society, which enhanced the defectors' message, were growing disillusion and distrust of the establishment and official secrecy, the partial disintegration of the Cold War consensus, and growing demand for more open government.

Soviet propagandists were helped by Philby's friends in Britain, and more importantly by official secrecy which allowed rumours to circulate, and by the public perception of a declining 'threat' from the Soviet Union, which underpinned public disapproval of the defectors. As Noel Annan noted, public criticism had shifted from the spies being a danger to national security, to a more general attack on the Establishment.[104] Soviet propaganda has been fairly consistently challenged but in a free country it is not possible nor desirable to enforce conformity. It seems that the counter-attack against Philby was less strong in the 1960s and 1970s than it was in the 1950s and 1980s, which may have helped Philby's image. There will always be sympathizers for these defectors, even now when the Soviet Union is in disarray and Communism discredited, and discussions of the rights and wrongs of these spies seems anachronistic, except to historians.

What contemporary lessons should we draw from the defectors? The KGB's continued use of Philby is but one relatively minor indication that the organization has not shaken off its past. It is arguably unwise of the Soviets to be conducting propaganda campaigns and to use Philby to embarrass the government and remind the British public of a nasty scandal, when they want the West to believe that they are genuinely on the road to reform and want to be friends. The perpetuation of the Philby legend seems to be as important to the KGB at home as it is abroad. If Maclean through his work at IMEMO has in any way influenced the new thinking within the Soviet elite then he will deserve a favourable epitaph. Burgess seems to have been unhappy with himself and with Moscow.

These three men will always be notorious historical figures. Their lives symbolize the rise and decline of Communist ideology Soviet style, and the paths they chose to take as history unfolded instruct us about the important events and moral questions of that time. Arguably there are more honourable men and women who would be more sympathetic and worthy symbols.[105] In the 1930s they dreamed of being the architects of the new Communist utopia; instead they became the servants of a state dominated by Stalin's paranoia and megalomania. The ideology they believed in is today 'no more than a spectre';[106] they became the victims rather than the creators of historical change.

This chapter has begun to address the question of the use of these very British defectors in Cold War propaganda which contributes to our understanding of their historical significance. A research agenda has emerged, which consists of four questions: what role did Burgess, Maclean and Philby play in the formulation of Soviet propaganda towards Britain and possibly the USA? Were the British journalists justified in their fears that the defectors improved the effectiveness of Soviet propaganda? Did Soviet propagandists and/or the KGB conduct a covert campaign about the defectors either to play with the perceptions of British and American intelligence services or to ensure that information about the defectors became public knowledge? Lastly, what role did official British propagandists play in countering the Soviets? Some aspects of these questions may well have to await the opening of archives in both Britain and the Soviet Union.

Burgess, Maclean and Philby illustrate an odd, deviant, tragic and occasionally humorous aspect of British history.[107] In 1968 Hugh Trevor-Roper tried, unsuccessfully, to forestall the developing Philby cult by exposing Soviet propaganda, and by stating that 'Philby, Burgess and Maclean are now altogether irrelevant. They are the fossils of the past'. Thirty years later Philby, Burgess and Maclean seem irrelevant to the awesome problems facing Soviet leaders today, but they are not yet fossilized. Significantly, Philby has recently been commemorated on a Soviet stamp, so perhaps at last this process has now begun.[108]

NOTES

1 Most of the books appraise the significance of Burgess, Maclean and Philby as spies; much less has been written about them as defectors, see especially R. Cecil, *A Divided Life: A Biography of Donald Maclean* (London: Bodley Head, 1989); R. Cecil, 'The Cambridge Comintern', in C. Andrew and D. Dilks (eds) *The Missing Dimension* (London: Macmillan, 1983); S. Kerr, 'NATO's First Spies: The Case of the Disappearing Diplomats', in R. O'Neil and B. Heuser (eds) *Securing Peace in Europe, 1945–1982* (London: Macmillan, 1991).

2 C. Rose, *The Soviet Propaganda Network: A Directory of Organisations serving Soviet Foreign Policy* (London: Pinter, 1988). A helpful book, which deals with defining propaganda and offers an explanation of the propaganda process, is B. A. Hazan, *Soviet Propaganda: A Case Study of the Middle East Conflict*, (London: Keter Publishing House, 1976). Other examples are *Soviet Anti-Semitic Propaganda (1975–1978)*, (London: Institute of Jewish Affairs, Narod Press, 1978); G. Wettig, *Broadcasting and Detente: Eastern Policies and their Implications for East West Relations*. (London: C. Hurst, 1977).

3 H. Trevor-Roper, 'The Philby Affair, Espionage, Treason and Secret Services', *Encounter* (April 1968); R. Cecil, 'Legends Spies Tell', *Encounter* (April 1978); N. Annan, 'The Spy With No Excuses', *The Independent* (13 May 1989); N. Annan, 'The Upper Class and the Underworld', *New York Review* (13 April 1989); N. Annan, *Our Age: Portrait of a Generation* (London: Weidenfeld & Nicolson, 1990).

4 For lists of Soviet, British and American defectors, see N. West, *Games of Intelligence, The Classified Conflict of International Espionage* (London: Weidenfeld & Nicolson, 1989). For an account of British use of Soviet defectors see, W. Wark, 'Red Army Defectors', *International History Review* (February 1987). Another means of understanding cultural differences is to examine the literature and films in a comparative and historical perspective. See *Spy Fiction, Spy Films and Real Intelligence*, special issue of *Intelligence and National Security* Vol. 5 (October 1990); N. E. Rosenfeldt, *Knowledge and Power: The Role of Stalin's Secret Chancellery in the Soviet System of Government* (Copenhagen: Copenhagen University Institute of Slavonic Studies, No 5, Rosenkilde & Bagger, 1978).

5 A useful guide to literature by and about defectors is R. G. Rocca and J. J. Dziack, *Bibliography on Soviet Intelligence and Security Services*, (Boulder, Col: Westview Press, 1985); W. Krivitsky, *In Stalin's Secret Service* (New York: Hyperion, 1979; first published 1939); I. Gouzenko, *The Iron Curtain* (New York: Dutton, 1948); P. Deriabin and F. Gibney, *The Secret World* (New York: Doubleday, 1959).

6 L. Smith, 'Covert British Propaganda: The Information Research Department 1944–1947', *Millennium* Vol. ix (1980).

7 C. Pincher, *Their Trade is Treachery* (London: Sidgwick & Jackson, 1981). The publicity for the paperback edition quoted a newspaper headline, 'Premier orders urgent probe into Pincher's sources'; P. Wright, *Spycatcher* (New York: Dell, 1987). See also H. G. Gelber, 'The Hunt for Spies: Another Inside Story', *Intelligence and National Security* Vol. IV, No. 2 (April 1989).

8 The CIA suspected that the Soviets had secretly helped the exposure of Blunt and Leo Long, *Daily Express* (3 November 1981); R. Cecil, Letter to *Daily Telegraph* (13 May 1990). For an insight into conspiracy networks in Britain see J. White, 'Yorkshire Terriers on the Conspiracy Trail', *The Independent* (16 April 1990).

9 See *The Gallup International Public Opinion Polls, 1937–1975*; *Index to International Public Opinion, 1985–86* (Survey Research, Consultants International, Westport, Conn: Greenwood Press, 1987).

10 A. George, *Propaganda Analysis* (Westport, Conn.: Rand Corporation, Greenwood Press, 1959).

11 J. Ellul, *Propaganda: The Formation of Men's Attitudes* (New York: Knopf, 1972) pp. V–VIII.

12 W. Winchell, 12 September 1954, US Broadcast, FBI Files, Philby, Burgess and Maclean, Serial 1–48. Had we been at war with the Soviet Union, Maclean might have been hanged, as was Lord Haw Haw.

13 The Soviets, like other non-Western countries and unlike the West, do not draw a distinct line between war and peace, or aims and capabilities. From their perspective the attack on 'bourgeois' values was an integrated part of their attack on capitalism. See A. Bozeman, 'Political Intelligence in Non-Western Societies: Suggestions for Research', in R. Godson (ed.) *Comparing Foreign Intelligence* (New York: Pergamon Brassey, 1988).

14 R. Godson and R. Shultz, *Dezinformatsia* (New York: Pergamon Brassey, 1988). Propaganda can be broadly defined as written or oral information which deliberately seeks to influence and/or manipulate the opinions and attitudes of a given target grouping, p. 34.

15 J. C. Clewes, *Communist Propaganda Techniques* (London: Methuen, 1964), Chapter 1; Godson and Shultz, *Dezinformatsia*, pp. 39–40.

16 F. C. Barghoorn, *Soviet Foreign Propaganda* (Princeton, NJ: Princeton University Press, 1964) p. 309; C. Andrew and O. Gordievsky, *KGB: The Inside Story* (London: Hodder & Stoughton, 1990), pp. 506–7.

17 Ellul, p. 295.

18 Barghoorn, pp. 301–5.

19 Kerr, 'Nato's First Spies'.

20 Keesings Contemporary Archives, 1 July 1963 19597A. See also P. Seale and M. McConville, *Philby, The Long Road to Moscow* (Harmondsworth: Penguin, 1978), pp. 317–18.

21 J. Ranelagh, *The Rise and Decline of the CIA* (London: Weidenfeld & Nicolson, 1982), p. 153.

22 A. Forbes, *Sunday Dispatch* (10 June 1951).

23 R. Hutchings, *Soviet Secrecy and Non-Secrecy* (London: Macmillan, 1987) pp. 3, 165.

24 Cecil, *A Divided Life*, p. 187; R. Medvedev, *The Times* (31 May 1983).

25 A. Nekrich and M. Heller, *Utopia in Power* (London: Hutchinson, 1982) pp. 600–2; M. Lubimov, *The Fifth Man*, Granada TV (16 October 1990).

26 Note that the later defections of two Americans followed a similar pattern to Burgess and Maclean: they deposited a pre-departure deposition in a safe deposit box, and also made statements at a press conference on 6 September 1960. W. G. Barker and R. E. Coffman, *The Anatomy of Two Traitors: The Defection of Bernon F. Mitchell and William H. Martin* (New York: Aegean Park Press, 1981) pp. 62–82; *Current Digest of the Soviet Press (CDSP)*, Vol. 15, No. 31, p. 23; *Izvestia* (31 July 1963).

27 FBI Burgess, Maclean, Philby file. For a review of these files see S. Kerr, *Intelligence Studies Newsletter* (July 1989) No. 1.

28 Information from Robert Cecil.

29 *Daily Express* (28 June 1956); a Western diplomat was quoted as saying it was a pity that the Soviets were not using Maclean (who was quite brilliant) to advise them on their diplomatic exchanges. *Evening Standard* (2 July 1963) 'If the object is to improve

Anglo-Soviet relations then the more they shatter Soviet illusions about our intentions and way of life the better'.

30 Andrew and Gordievsky, *KGB*, Chapters 6 and 8.
31 For a description of the Soviet mind set, see J. Erickson, 'Threat Identification and Strategic Appraisal by the Soviet Union, 1930–1941', in E. R. May (ed.) *Knowing One's Enemies* (Princeton, NJ: Princeton University Press, 1986) pp. 377–9.
32 J. Mather, *The Great Spy Scandal* (London: *Daily Express*, 1955), pp. 82–6, 93 (telegrams and letters the KGB allowed Burgess and Maclean to send home). P. Knightley, *Philby: the Life and Views of the KGB Masterspy*, (London: André Deutsch, 1988), p. 220.
33 Seale and McConville, *Philby*, p. 320.
34 Cecil, *A Divided Life*, p. 166. For a description of IMEMO's function and status, see B. P. McCrea, J. L. Plano and G. Klein, *The Soviet and East European Dictionary* (ABC CLIO Information Serices, 1984).
35 T. Driberg, *Guy Burgess: Portrait with Background* (London: Weidenfeld & Nicolson, 1956); Knightley, *Philby*, pp. 222–4. See F. Wheen, *Tom Driberg: His Life and Indiscretions* (London: Chatto & Windus, 1990).
36 Knightley, *Philby*, pp. 225–7, 234–8.
37 Knightley, *Philby*, p. 226.
38 Soviet obituaries: *CDSP/Current Digest of the Soviet Press*. Burgess, *CDSP*, Vol. 36, No. 23 (5 October 1963); Maclean, *CDSP*, Vol. 35, No. 12 (20 April 1987); Philby, *CDSP*, Vol. 40, No. 20 (14 May 1988).
39 Seale and McConville, *Philby*, p. 321. For a brief description of the meaning of Soviet medals, see A. A. Purves, *The Medals and Decorations of World War Two*, (London: J. B. Hayward and Sons, 1986).
40 T. Powers, *The Man Who Kept the Secrets: Richard Helms and the CIA* (New York: Knopf, 1970) pp. 349–50, note 23. Andrew and Gordievsky, *KGB*, p. 360; the KGB used a postcard from Burgess to facilitate meeting Blunt.
41 Knightley, *Philby*, p. 230; Andrew and Gordievsky, *KGB*, p. 360.
42 Ranelagh, *CIA*, pp. 157–9.
43 The newspaper references represent only a selection of available press cuttings, and are mainly from the Obituaries collection at the British Newspaper Library, Colindale. I am grateful to Peter Hennessy for some of these press references.
44 *Sunday Express* and *Sunday Graphic* (21 September 1952).
45 Neckrich and Heller, Chapter 10. Clewes, *Communist Propaganda*, pp. 52–68.
46 *Daily Express* (18 October 1955); Cecil, *A Divided Life*, p. 168.
47 *The Times* (5 October 1953); *New York Times* (4 October 1953).
48 Mather, pp. 74–8; Robert Cecil noted inaccuracies in Petrov's story which seemed to have been tailored for readers of the *People*, p. 153.
49 Mather, p. 76.
50 *The Times* (5 March 1955, p. 5; 11 March 1955, p. 8); 27 May 1955, 'Deprived of British citizenship'.
51 *Daily Mail* (4 November 1955).
52 'A jigsaw fits at last', *Sunday Express* (12 February 1956). This article reviewed the story since the defection.
53 See *The Times*, *Daily Telegraph*, and so on, 13–16 February 1956. The *Daily Worker* expressed views similar to those which Burgess and Philby would later express. Just after the defection, they focused on the panic in the Foreign Office, the Anglo-American row that developed, and alleged that the Americans wanted to take over MI5, which was in line with their aim of depicting Americans as warmongering and dominating their Western allies. With the reappearance of the diplomats in 1956, they criticized US foreign policy, charged that the diplomats were being used to widen the rift between East and West and under a banner headline of 'McCarthy Morrison' alleged that there would be an anti-Communist witch-hunt. By 15 February Khrushchev's report became the main interest.
54 Maclean to *Daily Herald* (24 February 1956, p. 35).
55 *Daily Express* (14 February 1956, Lloyd); *Daily Express* (28 February 1956, Makins); *Daily Telegraph* (13 February 1956, Petrov).
56 *Manchester Guardian* 'American Accusation, China got facts' (27 September 1955).

57 Driberg, p. 104.
58 Knightley, *Philby*, Sayle interview for Philby on Dzerzinsky.
59 'Burgess says: No return while cold war lasts' (21 October 1960); 'Burgess: I'm afraid Kim may have been killed' (5 March 1963), Colindale references, newspaper not specified.
60 A. Moorehead, *New Statesman* (1 December 1956). *The Economist*, October – December 1956, p. 963, criticized Driberg's 'unctuous and repellant narrative' and his 'slanted reporting', but did not mention the KGB.
61 Clewes, *Communist Propaganda*, p. 30.
62 Nekrich and Heller, p. 630. Definition of *détente* taken from Soviet *Short Political Dictionary*, the Party's propaganda encyclopedia.
63 J. Barron, *KGB*, pp. 38, 450–1. Andrew and Gordievsky, *KGB*, Chapters 12 and 13.
64 *The Times* (22 January 1967), 'Britanski Go Home'.
65 *The Times* (2 October 1967).
66 Blackman, *Daily Express* (5 November 1967). Sayle (17 December 1967), reprinted in Knightley, *Philby*.
67 There is a brief account of Gerald Brooke and the Krogers in C. Dobson and R. Payne, *The Dictionary of Espionage* (London, Harrap, 1984). The Krogers were swopped for Brooke in 1969. P. Shipley, *Hostile Action: The KGB and Secret Soviet Operations in Britain*, (London: St Martin's Press, 1989), pp. 135–6. See also Wright, *Spycatcher*, index.
68 Trevor-Roper, *The Philby Affair*; K. Philby, *My Silent War* (London: Granada, 1969), see pp. 19 and 226, Philby quotes from Graham Greene's novels.
69 N. Sherry, *The Independent* (8 December 1990). *The Life of Graham Greene part 1, 1904–1939* (Harmondsworth: Penguin, 1990).
70 Cecil, 'Legends Spies Tell'; Annan, 'The Spy With No Excuses'; C. Andrew, 'More Unreliable Memoirs from General Philby', *Daily Telegraph* (15 April 1988).
71 D. C. Watt, *Sunday Times* (3 May 1970); R. Stephens, *Observer* (3 May 1970); G. Brooke Shepherd, *Sunday Telegraph* (3 May 1970). R. Cecil, pp. 181–4.
72 *Daily Telegraph* (16 November 1979) 'Andrew Boyle names 25 spies'; (17 November 1979) 'Saga of Upper Class Deceit'; *Guardian* (16 November 1979) 'PM Ends 15 year cover upon Sir Anthony Blunt'; A. Boyle, *The Fourth Man* (New York: Dial Press, 1979); J. Costello, *Mask of Treachery* (London: Collins, 1988).
73 Pincher, *Their Trade is Treachery*; Wright, *Spycatcher*; N. West, *The Friends*, (London: Coronet, 1988), pp. 195–8.
74 For the spy scare in the CIA see D. Martin, *A Wilderness of Mirrors* (New York: Ballantine, 1981); T. Powers, *Richard Helms: The Man Who Kept the Secrets*, pp. 281–5. For MI5, see Wright, *Spycatcher*. For a penetrating insight into Angleton see T. Mangold, *Cold Warrior: James Jesus Angleton, The CIA's Master Spy Hunter*, (New York: Simon and Schuster, 1991).
75 Andrew and Gordievsky, *KGB*, p. XXIV.
76 D. Cameron Watt, 'Intelligence and the Historian', *Diplomatic History* Vol. 14, No. 2 (spring 1990) pp. 199–205. See also B. Levin, 'The Spy Writers who came in for a Killing', *The Times* (9 April 1990).
77 Cecil, *A Divided Life*, p. 187.
78 M. Frankland, 'The Last Testament of a Traitor', *Observer* (13 March 1983).
79 R. Medvedev, 'Maclean's Biggest Coup', *Sunday Telegraph* (27 March 1983).
80 Sir David Hunt, Letter to *The Times* (2 June 1983).
81 Andrew and Gordievsky, *KGB*, p. 508.
82 *CDSP* 1988, Vol. 40, No. 20 (7:1) 'Gorbachev's keynote speech'. *CDSP* 1989, Vol. 41, No. 17, (12:) 'KGB document to extend democracy in the work of the Chekists'. *CDSP* 1989, Vol. 41, No. 34 (32:1) 'Meeting held between victims of 1930s and 1950s repressions'. *CDSP* 1989, Vol. 41, No. 44 (27:2) 'Memorial Society sponsors "human chain" around KGB building'. *CDSP* 1990, Vol. XLII, No. 14, 'Dialogue on Dzerzhinsky Square', 23 March, 'A Group of People's Deputies met with the head of the KGB for a chat and tour of KGB HQ'. *Time Magazine* (13 February 1990) 'Inside the KGB'.
83 *Soviet Intelligence and Active Measures*, spring 1990.
84 *The Independent* (12 May 1988). Philby's appearances: 6 October 1987, Latvian TV;

21 November 1987, English Language Service of Moscow Radio, Latvian Documentary, *The Game*.

85 *Sunday Times* (13, 20, 27 March, 3, 10 April 1988).

86 W. J. West, *The Truth About Hollis* (London: Duckworth, 1989), p. 163.

87 D. Owen, *Sunday Times* (13 March 1987); Annan, 'The Upper Class and the Underworld'; Knightley replied to criticism of his biography *Sunday Times* (13 November 1988).

88 *The Times* 12 May, 1d, 14f, 20b. 14 May 1d.

89 Sir Robert Mackenzie, quoted in Knightley, *Philby*, pp. 118–19.

90 J. Burchill, *The Independent Magazine* (5 August 1990). See letters following week for readers' views.

91 S. Bourke, *The Springing of George Blake* (London: Cassel, 1970); D. Leigh, 'CND Men sprang spy Blake', *Observer* (13 November 1988).

92 *The Independent*, 'MI5 File says Police knew peace men helped spy escape'; *The Independent*, R. Gordon, 'A Case against state prosecutions' (11 May 1990). The Blake escape trial continued to be reported in the serious newspapers in July and November 1990.

93 *The Blake Escape*, ITV, 26 April 1989.

94 *Cutting Edge*, Channel 4, 14 May 1990; Tom Bower, *Inside Story, The Confession*, BBC TV, 19 September 1990.

95 Oleg Kalugin interview, 'Ex-Spy turns spotlight on KGB', *European* (10–12 August 1990).

96 *The Times*, 'Soviet Film on Philby keeps identity of Fifth man secret' (11 May 1990).

97 N. West, 'Philby Continues Making Mischief From The Grave', *Daily Telegraph* (16 May 1990); R. Payne, *European* (18–20 May 1990); R. Cecil, Letter to *Daily Telegraph* (13 May 1990).

98 *The Times* (23 March 1990, p. 8g) 'Publicity given to Defector attacked by Soviet envoy'.

99 *The Times* (6 November 1990) Letters by N. West, J. Rusbridger and C. Pincher. A. Glees, Letter to *Times Literary Supplement* (2–8 November 1990) and further correspondence (23–29 November, 7–13 and 14–20 December 1990).

100 *The Fifth Man*, Granada TV, 16 October 1990. Kalugin, former head of KGB Counter-Intelligence, confirmed to Granada that there was a Cambridge-educated Fifth Man. Lyubimov confirmed that the 'Fifth Man' had been awarded the Red Banner, that his initials are JC and that he had been a student at Trinity College, Cambridge, in 1934, all of which fitted Cairncross's past record exactly. 'Fifth Man Claim Backed by KGB', *Sunday Telegraph* (21 October 1990).

101 *European* (10–12 August 1990) 'British Double Agent Backs Reform'.

102 G. Blake, *No Other Choice* (London: Jonathan Cape, 1990); P. Hennessy, 'Debts Through Misadventure', *The Independent* (22 September 1990).

103 I. Dzhirkvelov, *Secret Servant: My Life with the KGB and the Soviet Elite* (New York: Harper & Row, 1987); V. Kuzichkin, *Inside the KGB: Myth and Reality* (London: André Deutsch, 1990); Andrew and Gordievsky, *KGB*.

104 Annan, 'The Upper Class and the Underworld'.

105 See for example W. Leonhard, *Child of the Revolution*, or works by Solzhenitsyn. A neglected story is that of the idealistic young Communists of the 1920s and 1930s who emigrated to the Soviet Union and have remained there since. See R. Nadelson, 'The Future That Didn't Work', *The Independent* (17 November 1990).

106 Kuzichkin, *KGB*, p. 395.

107 There have been several dramas about the Cambridge spies, but as far as I know only one musical comedy: The Natural Theatre Company, 'Spy Society, or Burgess, Philby and Maclean (The Musical)' in which 'Bing Philby, Frank Burgess and Grace (or is it Shirley?) Maclean sing their greatest hits and give away all their secrets (and everyone else's)'.

108 Trevor-Roper, *Philby*; *The Independent*, 'Philby-ately' (21 November 1990).

Part II

STRATEGY

We have talked about the atomic business; we have seen the difference it makes to technique and tactics and materials and everything.... Are we going to rely on being able to use the atom ... because if we do rely on it and the Government of the day says, 'Oh but you cannot possibly use that; you must not use that. If the other fellow uses it, all right, you can use it, but in the meantime you must not use it; you must use the ordinary decent weapons of incendiary and high explosive', where do we go from there?

(Tedder (CAS), 16 August 1947, AIR 8/1536)

6

'We must cut our coat according to our cloth': the making of British defence policy, 1945–8

Anthony Gorst

In comparison with the flood of publications based on archival research that examine British foreign policy between 1945 and 1948, the development of British defence policy in the same early critical Cold War period remains largely unexplored by historians. Although recent work has focused on the post-war strategic debate in Britain, little attention has been paid to the more fundamental question that bedevilled British defence policy in this period, the provision of forces to implement this strategy.[1] To achieve a clear understanding of British defence policy as it changed direction to address a post-war Soviet threat it is essential to place this strategic debate in the wider context of the reality of Britain's drastically reduced economic circumstances. Military planners were deliberately invited to prepare their appreciations without reference to budgetary limitations and the majority of the strategic planning papers produced during this period assumed a level of resources which neither the Prime Minister nor the Chancellor of the Exchequer had the remotest intention of providing. Only when the elaborate strategic concept had reached the final stages was there any attempt to reconcile it with economic reality. This inherently lengthy process was exacerbated by intense inter-service competition for scarce resources. Those who fail to take into account the disparity between those forces fondly hoped for by the military, and the reality of British forces in being, risk serious distortion of this period: in the immediate post-war period financial considerations lie at the very heart of *all* questions surrounding British defence policy.

With the sudden end of the Second World War in August 1945 the British military had to prepare a new defence policy that reflected the changed post-war environment. They were singularly ill-prepared to do so: despite three years of planning no coherent framework for a long-term post-war defence policy existed on the cessation of hostilities with Japan. The Post Hostilities Planning Staff (PHPS) had produced a series of regional strategic appreciations summarized in July 1945 in a digest entitled 'The

143

Security of the British Empire.' Based on the assumption, provided by the Joint Intelligence Committee (JIC), of a hostile Soviet Union ready to launch a premeditated general war in 1956, this outlined British strategic requirements for the post-war world.[2] The PHPS had wanted this paper to be approved as the basis for post-war defence policy but this was vetoed by the Chiefs of Staff (COS) and, as with previous PHPS papers, it was merely noted as a staff study. The COS did not disagree to any great extent with the conclusions of the PHPS: the Chief of the Imperial General Staff (CIGS), Field Marshal Sir Alan Brooke, thought it 'a very useful paper'. Although the PHPS was then dissolved and its functions transferred to the Joint Planning Staff (JPS), this was in accordance with previous decisions. The reluctance of the COS to forward the findings of the PHPS to higher authority was rooted in a recognition that the PHPS had only addressed grand strategy. The PHPS had recognized this short-coming and wished to include other vital elements such as the size and shape of the armed forces within its deliberations only to be told by the COS that this was undesirable as it opened the door to inter-Service controversy. Moreover in the summer of 1945 the work of the PHPS could not be used even for the limited purpose of giving short-term strategic advice as it was in need of immediate revision to take account of future developments in warfare and of the resources that could or would be allocated to the armed forces.[3]

An assessment of future weapons had been produced by early summer 1945 by the 'Tizard Committee' but its conclusions had to be re-evaluated by the Joint Technical Warfare Committee (JTWC) after the destruction of Hiroshima and Nagasaki.[4] No firm assessment of resources had been undertaken apart from a vague calculation produced for the Beveridge Report that allocated an arbitrary sum of £500 million per annum for defence.[5] Wartime planning by the individual Service departments had already sounded warning bells as they produced post-war estimates comfortably in excess of this figure.[6]

Nevertheless, the optimistic intention of the COS in the summer of 1945 was that the JPS should take the assumptions of the PHPS and extrapolate the post-war requirements of the Services. The JPS realized that this was not a simple matter as the peacetime armed forces would inevitably be governed by fiscal and personnel constraints. Further problems lay in creating armed forces that could carry out their immediate occupational commitments in areas such as Germany and Palestine while simultaneously preparing to meet the possibility of total war with the Soviet Union in the mid-1950s. The obvious solution put forward by the JPS was that, where these requirements did not conflict, the peacetime armed forces would provide a nucleus of cadre forces for rapid expansion for war when the only limitation would be available personnel and the amount of warning received of impending war. It was intended that an overall estimate of the size and composition of the forces required for war against the Soviet Union in the 1950s should be prepared, based on a strategic analysis by the JPS, an examination of the likely warning period by the JIC and a manpower assessment by the Ministry of Labour and the Ministry of Production. The JPS would then produce a plan for the peacetime cadre armed forces based on this blueprint. Only *then* would this plan be judged against resource constraints to produce peacetime armed forces.[7]

This lengthy process was soon derailed by events. The JTWC study of future weapons proceeded slowly and the JPS estimate for the mid-1950s, which was the backbone of their approach, had to be truncated to an interim projection to 1950.[8] Even this report, covering a shorter period where weapons and methods of warfare could be predicted with some degree of certainty, was never tabled as the COS told the Defence Committee that 'there are so many uncertain factors that we feel grave doubts as to whether even an approximate estimate for such a long period could be made.'[9] The long-term ordered approach desired by the COS was overwhelmed by discussions on the short-term size of the armed forces as the new Labour government immediately demonstrated an intense interest in all aspects of the defence of the United Kingdom. This was contrary to the wishes of the COS but in the face of pressure from their new political masters, particularly the Prime Minister, Clement Attlee, and the Chancellor of the Exchequer, Hugh Dalton, they had little choice.

NEW CHALLENGES: AUGUST 1945 TO MAY 1946

In August 1945 the Cabinet ordered that munitions production should be tapered off as quickly as possible while the Manpower Committee, chaired by the Foreign Secretary, Ernest Bevin, would urgently review personnel allocations for the armed forces. Although Attlee stressed that 'it was essential that there should be no avoidable delay in releasing men and women from the armed forces', Bevin was anxious to avoid 'a state of affairs similar to that of 1918–19 when the position of His Majesty's Government was seriously weakened by the rapidity with which the forces were demobilized'. The Cabinet therefore concluded that 'full weight must be given to the lessons learned at the end of the last war and to the heavy tasks which His Majesty's Government were still bound to discharge in connection with the occupation of ex-enemy countries'.[10]

These auspicious words were not borne out in practice. A JPS report on personnel requirements up to 30 June 1946 had asked for 2,267,700 men to fulfil the minimum strategic requirements of the armed forces, the provision of forces for occupation duties, garrison forces for the Empire, nucleus forces for home defence and protection of sea communications, and a strategic reserve.[11] This was noted by the Defence Committee but

Dalton took the opportunity of putting down a marker for the future by noting the importance of cutting personnel requirements and military expenditure overseas 'as quickly as possible'.[12] When the full Manpower Committee review was discussed in Cabinet even Bevin expressed his concern that the armed forces requirements were 'more than the country could afford' while Dalton noted that

> he was gravely disappointed that notwithstanding the ending of hostilities the amount proposed to be spent on the services in the remainder of 1945 was as high as the estimates which had been prepared on the assumption that the war would be continued.

The COS were therefore informed that it was essential to release at least 1.5 million personnel from the armed forces by the end of 1945.[13]

Worse was to follow. The Service ministers then asked the Defence Committee to give agreement in principle to target personnel figures which would allow volunteer enlistments to begin 'without prejudice to the ultimate strength and composition of the armed forces'. An acrimonious discussion ensued when Attlee, a convinced internationalist, argued that the committee was being asked to approve figures that were too high as 'it was our policy now to work in unison with other big powers and we should not therefore require such strong armed forces as before'. Despite the pleading of First Lord of the Admiralty Albert Alexander and Secretary of State for War John Lawson that 'there was a certain minimum level below which we could not fall' as 'a certain premium had to be paid for safety', nevertheless it was decided that the Service ministers' estimates had to be resubmitted with detailed costings.[14]

An ominous prospect began to open up for the military as short-term constraints called into question the whole basis of their ordered approach. This was confirmed at the end of October: having grudgingly approved an Air Ministry production programme that Dalton called 'fantastically excessive', the Defence Committee discussed 'a new approach to the problem of the size of the armed forces'. Bevin proposed that

> a global sum of money to cover the requirements of all three services should be decided upon in relation to the national income . . . it would then be for the Chiefs of Staff to work out balanced armed forces within this figure reporting on the role to be played by each service and the proportion allocated to each service.

Alexander, backed by the Chief of the Air Staff, Marshal of the Royal Air Force Sir Charles Portal, reacted with alarm and pointed out that

> it had always . . . been the practice for the Government to state their policy and plans and then to ask the Chiefs of Staff what forces were required to carry out their policy. The proposal to fix a global

figure would reverse this process and in his opinion would probably be an unsound way of proceeding.

None the less, Attlee overruled the military, pointing out that the old method had not worked in practice and that the government of the day 'always had cut their coat according to their cloth', and accepted this sensible procedure for the future.[15]

In the mean time, for the Service Estimates for the first peacetime fiscal year of 1946–7 the COS put forward personnel figures of 2,068,000 at 30 June 1946 and 1,440,300 at 31 March 1947. The COS stated baldly that these forces were the absolute minimum necessary and could be cut only if either existing commitments or force levels were reduced.[16] These were merely noted at the Defence Committee following another plea by Bevin not to weaken his hand in foreign policy, but Dalton again stated that 'the whole picture of defence manpower and expenditure appeared out of scale and if there was no quick drop . . . he could not promise anything but economic disaster'.[17]

Ten days later the COS ran into real trouble when the Defence Committee reviewed the COS personnel projections for March 1947. The newly elevated Viscount Alanbrooke opened bravely by pointing out that the figures before the committee represented a 75 per cent demobilization since VE Day. Attlee was unimpressed, responding that 'there was no doubt that the nation could not afford either the manpower or the money for forces of the size suggested by the Chiefs of Staff'. He therefore laid down personnel ceilings of 1.9 million for June and 1.1 million for December 1946 with the bulk of the cuts to fall on the Navy and the Air Force rather than on the Army, for the latter 'had a great number of commitments which could not be liquidated'. Attlee brushed aside protests by Alexander saying, 'as there was no-one to fight . . . a certain amount of inefficiency might have to be accepted'.[18]

In response the Services stated that they could meet these targets provided that the Defence Committee accepted certain conditions, including an 'abandonment of certain of our hitherto accepted commitments' and 'a general reduction in the efficiency of our armed forces . . . over the next two years which will make it impossible for the Services to deal with any emergency'.[19] The Defence Committee was unmoved and not only accepted the COS conditions but also imposed an arbitrary 10 per cent cut on the financial estimate, a cut confirmed by the Cabinet in allocating £1,091 million (not including terminal charges) for the needs of the armed forces in 1946–7.[20]

In the first six months of peace the COS had seen their stated requirements progressively whittled away: with no agreed long-term policy against which their demands could be judged, their estimates had proved vulnerable to short-term cuts imposed on purely economic grounds. The effect of these cuts on the armed forces was starkly revealed when, in discussing the temporary continuation of national service pending the institution of a permanent scheme of peacetime national service, Attlee again stressed that the armed forces had to be reduced 'to something approaching their pre-war status': the COS lost no time in pointing out that

> we have already carried the process of economy to a point which will constitute a grave risk to our security . . . if the process is carried further not only will it decrease the efficiency of our remaining forces but the risk to our security will be greatly accelerated.[21]

Significantly, while these debates on the size of the armed forces had been in progress, there had been no parallel discussions of long-term strategy, not only because the military had been absorbed in budgetary questions but also because the COS were awaiting the results of the JTWC report on future weapons technology. Attlee had already registered his disagreement with the underlying strategic assumptions of the COS on 15 February 1946 when he queried 'the strategic assumption that it was vital for us to keep open the Mediterranean . . . he did not see how we could possibly do this under modern conditions'. On 22 February 1946 he raised the question formally with the COS, noting that the view that control of the Mediterranean was vital to the Empire in peace and war owed more to 'historical factors' than to the conditions of modern warfare, and

> it may be that we shall have to consider the British Isles as an easterly extension of a strategic area the centre of which is the American continent, rather than as a power looking eastwards through the Mediterranean to India and the East.

In referring this challenge to the planners the COS made it plain that they expected their strategic advice to remain unaltered.[22]

In a paper inspired by Alanbrooke, the military responded to Attlee's challenge with the first full post-war statement of their strategic vision. Based on 'facts of geography and the distribution of manpower and natural resources which do not change' which would 'not be radically altered by new developments in methods or weapons of warfare' the planners refuted the arguments of the Prime Minister point by point. In the event of a major war with the Soviet Union, they argued that Britain needed to retain control of the 'Main Support Areas' of the British Isles, the United States, South Africa and the Pacific Dominions because of their personnel and industrial resources, the sea communications between them, and 'areas of strategic influence', which included the Middle East. In a sop to the concerns of the Prime Minister the military pointed out that the areas of strategic interest could be supported by diplomatic and economic measures and that 'it does not therefore follow that our strategic requirements . . .

would result in the maintenance of large-scale armed forces which it is quite clear the country cannot afford to maintain in peacetime'.[23]

In the Defence Committee Alanbrooke directly confronted the Prime Minister

> If we withdraw our influence from the Mediterranean, we should lack the essential depth in front of our vital areas to allow the necessary time for us to mobilize our own forces and for the resources of the United States to be brought into play. Moreover, we should be deprived of bases ... from which the threat of air action would be a deterrent to Russian aggression and from which we could at the outset of war conduct offensive operations.

The Prime Minister remained unconvinced, responding that 'it was very doubtful that we could provide the forces on such a scale as would be necessary to support a forward policy in the Middle East' but with Bevin supporting the COS, they succeeded in forcing Attlee to retreat and their strategy was accepted as a 'provisional basis for discussion' at the forthcoming Dominion Prime Ministers' meeting (DPM).[24]

In preparation for this meeting, the COS took this 'approved' strategic concept and refined it to include elaborate proposals for 'zones of defence' and liaison arrangements between the Commonwealth countries.[25] However, no progress was made at the DPM in securing agreement on the question of future Commonwealth defence arrangements or indeed on Commonwealth contributions to relieve the burden imposed on Britain by her defence obligations.[26]

TOWARDS A STRATEGY: MAY 1946 TO JANUARY 1947

This disappointment was followed in succeeding months by a reopening of the strategic debate as Attlee continued to question the centrepiece of the COS strategy, a continued role for Britain in the Middle East. A COS plea for the retention of full military rights and facilities in Palestine provoked an unwelcome response with the Defence Committee concluding, at the instigation of Attlee, that 'it was clear that our whole position in the Middle East required re-examination to determine our exact strategic requirements'.[27]

The COS responded with an unambiguous restatement of their position: 'it was essential to the security of the British Commonwealth to maintain our position in the Middle East in peace and to defend it in war'. It was a fundamental requirement to possess peacetime facilities in Egypt, Palestine and Cyrenaica from which to operate in war and which would also provide a visible token of a British presence to prevent Soviet infiltration.[28] As far as Attlee was concerned 'the complexities of international politics' meant that the preparation of military facilities on their vulnerable southern flank would be deemed provocative by the Soviet Union and, moreover, it was unlikely that Britain would be able to secure all its strategic desiderata in the Middle East purely by negotiation. It was therefore agreed that the conclusions of the COS would have to be re-examined after 'a further examination of the overall Commonwealth strategic concept . . . made in the light . . . of the latest developments in weapons and methods of warfare'.[29]

Two weeks before, this additional complicating factor had entered the strategic debate: after some nine months of concentrated effort, the JTWC finally delivered their evaluation of 'Future Developments in Weapons and Methods of War'. Its conclusion that the advent of atomic and biological weapons together with appropriate delivery systems constituted 'a major change in the nature of warfare' to which the United Kingdom was uniquely vulnerable, due to its geographical position, the concentration of its population and the lack of any foreseeable active air defence measures, demanded an assessment of whether the COS strategy remained appropriate.[30] Attlee had therefore turned one of the props of the preferred COS procedure against them and forced a re-evaluation of British long-term strategy.

This re-evaluation was to be carried out by a special section of the JPS, the Future Planning Section (FPS). Appointed by the COS specifically to look at long-term strategy, it gradually developed a wider brief which embraced a 'Review of Defence Problems' as it was also to examine the size and shape of the armed forces required to implement their strategy.[31] However, as the FPS went to work, the military again became embroiled in budgetary questions that, in the absence of an agreed strategy, had serious implications for their long-term plans.

Despite the success of the military in October 1946 in securing the agreement of the government to permanent peacetime conscription, the COS continued to find it difficult to get adequate allocations which would enable them to plan with a degree of certainty. When the COS submitted their personnel projections for 1947–8 they pointed out that by the end of 1946 'none of the three services will be able fully to meet their commitments' and that the forces were now 'too small and their state of efficiency too low to meet a major threat to our security'. Moreover, the COS argued that the matter was now urgent as it was essential that by March 1948 the forces should have begun their reconstruction so that they could provide forces for existing commitments, deterrent forces to dissuade the Soviet Union from precipitate action and nucleus forces for mobilization in an emergency.

The Services' initial bid for March 1948 totalled over 1 million personnel: although they indicated that they could work on reduced figures for the Navy and Air Force, the Army could not be reduced as its size was governed by existing occupational and security commitments. The

Navy and the Air Force placed more emphasis on long-term preparations: as they used increasingly complex equipment that demanded highly trained personnel, they could not improvise on the outbreak of war. The Navy therefore wished to build up to an active fleet of 4 battleships, 10 aircraft carriers, 19 cruisers, 71 destroyers, 34 escorts, 36 submarines and miscellaneous light forces in commission backed by a reserve fleet of 1 battleship, 16 light fleet carriers, 10 cruisers, 40 destroyers, 260 escorts and 50 submarines held in 'mothballs' at varying stages of readiness. This required a minimum personnel allocation of 164,000; even this would leave the active fleet short of 2 aircraft carriers and 27 destroyers. The Air Force was in an even worse plight: with a minimum strategic requirement of 150 squadrons (including an inadequate 27 fighter and 32 strategic bomber squadrons) to provide a deterrent force, an initial defence in case of war and a nucleus for expansion and training needs, it had nevertheless been reduced to 90 squadrons at 'an extremely low state of efficiency'. The RAF plan was therefore for these 90 squadrons to be fleshed out, which required 299,000 men but, in order to avoid overloading the training machine, 250,000 was acceptable.[32]

Despite this bleak picture in November 1946 the COS were again attacked in the Defence Committee by Dalton for the effect that their requirements would have on the British economy. Attlee therefore ruled that although this COS report was useful as a guide 'it would be quite wrong for the Committee to reach a decision on the Chiefs of Staff estimates without further scrutiny'. The COS had therefore again failed to secure the resources to begin the reconstruction of Britain's defence forces which would underpin their long-term strategic concept.[33]

The proposed scrutiny of Service Estimates proposed by Attlee was to be carried by Albert Alexander, the new Minister of Defence elect. An inquiry by a small *ad hoc* committee of ministers, including Attlee and Alexander, into the higher organization of defence in Britain had concluded in September 1946 that what was needed was better co-ordination rather than a 'drastic recasting of the . . . existing organisation'. The COS machinery would continue to provide strategic advice to the Defence Committee and the Service ministers would remain responsible for the administration of the three Services but a Minister of Defence with a small staff was to be superimposed on the existing structure specifically to supervise 'the apportioning of available resources . . . between the three services in accordance with the strategic policy laid down by the Defence Committee'.[34] The creation of an administratively weak Ministry of Defence did little to check the rising tide of Service department competition.

Even before these administrative changes went into effect on 1 January 1947 Alexander began his task by returning to first principles: on 17 December 1946 he called for a series of meetings with the COS as it would be helpful to all of us if at the earliest possible date we could reach some conclusions in general terms about future British Defence Policy as distinct from manpower and fiscal problems in 1947.

As this was in accordance with their preferred procedure of making strategic plans without detailed consideration of the complicating factor of resources, the COS 'warmly welcomed' this initiative by their new minister.[35]

The COS were well prepared for these discussions as the FPS had completed two papers on future strategy by late November 1946. The first of these papers considered how a major war might break out and confirmed, on JIC advice, that war in the short term was improbable while a planned war of aggression launched by the Soviet Union was not likely for another decade. The second paper attempted to give some strategic guidance on how a future war would be waged in the light of the JTWC conclusions on the importance of weapons of mass destruction. If the initial Soviet thrust into the Middle East and Western Europe could be held the question was then how to end the war: the answer, in so far as it could be foreseen, was to force the capitulation of the Soviet Union through the destruction of its war potential, the breaking of its morale and the defeat of its armed forces using a combination of an air offensive using weapons of mass destruction, political and psychological warfare and eventually a land campaign to mop up a defeated enemy in the throes of political disintegration. The FPS concluded that it was essential to have forces in being as well as rapid mobilization potential. Research and development and production programmes had to be maintained to retain the technical superiority of the West over the Soviet Union and intelligence-gathering machinery developed.[36]

Armed with this strategic projection the JPS attempted to derive some conclusions on the peacetime size and shape of the armed forces for use by the COS in the discussions with Alexander. It was axiomatic that balanced armed forces capable of rapid expansion on the outbreak of war had to be created, however, the JPS put their finger on the nub of the problem that had bedevilled them for the previous year:

> We are thinking of our defence policy in terms of war in some ten years time, while the armed forces, the strength of which is presently under consideration, are related to existing conditions and not to those which we believe may obtain in the future.

The central problem was therefore the post-war occupational duties of the Army. If the defence of the British Isles and of vital sea communications were to have first priority, the cuts in the Royal Navy and the Royal Air Force would have to be 'adjusted' so that they could carry out these essential commitments. The burden of any future reductions would have to fall on the Army: as its size was related to existing occupational commitments which bore no relation to its role in war, it could be progressively reduced to its peacetime cadre as these commitments were gradually liquidated.[37]

Alexander opened the first meeting with the COS on 23 December 1946 by putting forward a series of assumptions on possible allies and enemies that showed he agreed with the purely strategic assumptions that the JPS had put to the COS. Unfortunately the abrasive Chief of the Imperial General Staff, Field Marshal Montgomery, upset the atmosphere of the meeting by pointing out that decisions on the size and shape of the armed forces could not be delayed much longer or the Services would be so disorganized by 1948 as to be incapable of developing into a force capable of carrying out any strategy developed for the mid-1950s. This discordant note raised the question of resources that the meeting had been carefully avoiding and forced Alexander into an unambiguous statement of the Government's position:

Unless the fiscal and economic foundations of the country were re-established the remainder of the edifice would crumble. The immediate problem with which this Government was faced was that if the economic position of the country failed, the remaining structure in the form of foreign policy, the use of the armed forces, trade and our sphere of influence would be irreparably harmed. In the last resort therefore the question was of how much we could afford at the present time: this would govern the size of the forces in the near future, irrespective of a solution to our future defence policy.

The meeting ended by instructing the secretary, General Hollis, to prepare a paper for use at a Staff Conference to be attended by the Prime Minister and Foreign Secretary early in the new year.[38] This paper, while paying lip-service to the importance of building up a strong economy, nevertheless merely asserted that the three-pillar strategy codified by the FPS, the defence of the United Kingdom, the maintenance of sea communications and the retention of the Middle East, was the basis of British defence policy.[39]

Before this paper could be taken, the three-pillar strategy with its emphasis on the Middle East again came under attack by Attlee in a further Staff Conference held to discuss British policy towards Palestine, Greece and Turkey. The COS argued that these vital outposts for the defence of the British position in the Middle East had to be retained or 'our whole strategic position in the Middle East will be gravely prejudiced'.[40] Bevin supported the military strongly. Attlee responded with a comprehensive résumé of the position which he had held for the past year: such a stance would be interpreted by the Soviets as offensive in nature, it was inherently expensive and strategically outmoded, while potential allies in the region, such as Iraq, could not be relied upon. With Alexander backing his military advisers to the hilt and the support of the Foreign Secretary, the meeting nevertheless endorsed the COS recommendations. However, in a meeting with Bevin and Alexander two days later, Attlee continued to resist the final step of approving the COS strategy in full.[41]

Sensing the tide turning in their favour the COS pushed the Prime Minister for a full discussion of the Hollis paper on defence problems and strengthened the paper, stressing the importance of Palestine to the defence of Egypt and the importance of Egypt in the defence of the Middle East, which was, in turn, a key point 'in the defence of the Commonwealth and directly of the United Kingdom.'[42] Further pressure was put on by the CIGS, who, before the Staff Conference scheduled for the 13 January 1947, deployed the threat of resignation *en masse* by his senior military advisers. This had the desired effect on the Prime Minister.[43] When the CAS Marshal of the Royal Air Force Tedder opened the Staff Conference by laying down the three-pillar strategy as the 'fundamental fact' of British strategy, Attlee meekly capitulated, indicating his acceptance of the Middle East as part of the interdependent tripod that was the basis of British Defence Policy. At last the assumptions of the COS strategy had been approved.[44]

A 'FUTURE DEFENCE POLICY?': JANUARY 1947 TO JULY 1947

If the COS thought that this victory had secured them a breathing space in which the FPS could work out future defence policy in comparative peace, they were to be immediately disillusioned as they became embroiled in further budgetary debates. Only one day after the fateful Staff Conference the Defence Committee considered the Defence Estimates of £963 million and 1,094,000 men for the forthcoming year put forward by Alexander. Alexander stressed that 'any further cuts in the estimates ... would have such adverse effects that he would not be able to report to Parliament that the Services were either efficient or adequate to meet out obligations'. This implied threat left Attlee unmoved:

> while balanced and efficient nucleus forces must be preserved for expansion in the event of war and adequate military backing for our foreign policy must be maintained, the money and manpower allotted to the Services must be within the national resources.

It was agreed that the estimates would have to be reviewed by Cabinet.[45]

In the course of heated discussions Alexander stuck to his guns and secured the desired personnel allocations, arguing that any further reduction in the figures which he had put before the Cabinet would make it impossible for the Services either to discharge their present commitments or to evolve towards balanced forces.

On the financial estimates it was a different story: by careful pruning Alexander had been able to reduce the estimates by £20 million, but Dalton, with the support of other ministers, insisted on a further 10 per cent cut or 'the whole national economy would be in serious jeopardy'.

In reporting the effect of cuts of such magnitude Alexander emphasized that this would mean the cessation of nearly all new production, a virtual naval withdrawal from East of Suez, the loss of 100,000 men from the Army, and the closing of an operational command in the RAF; he reiterated that they

would have the most serious consequences on the efficiency and welfare of the forces, their ability to undertake . . . commitments and any plan for the establishment of balanced forces in future years.

In the face of this impasse a compromise was hammered out whereby Alexander offered a cut of 5 per cent or £40 million on the understanding that this did not set a precedent and that no difficulty would be made about a supplementary estimate. On this basis, total estimates of £899 million for the forthcoming year were approved. Once again the long-term demands of the armed forces had been sacrificed for economic recovery.[46]

After this dispute with his Cabinet colleagues over the short-term resources to be allocated to the armed forces, Alexander returned to battle with his military advisers on the long-term size and shape of the armed forces. He insisted that this should be projected for the next decade based on a budget of not more than £600 million per year and laid down the roles of the services: the Navy to give priority to anti-submarine and convoy escort work, the Army to develop a small regular field force backed by a Territorial Army for expansion in war and the RAF to concentrate on the air defence of the United Kingdom and the provision of a deterrent bomber force.[47]

The COS were also anxious to begin this process and agreed to discuss future defence policy as soon as the FPS had reported. Their concern to establish a stable long-term defence policy was based on apprehension at the implications for the strategic position of the Commonwealth of recent policy decisions on India, a worry that led them, at the instigation of Montgomery, to register their unease with the Defence Committee.[48]

By the end of March 1947 the FPS were ready to submit their report which

put forward concrete proposals for a Commonwealth Defence Policy which shall place us in a position, with our allies, to resist aggression by force with reasonable prospects of success.

To a large extent the report summarized the strategic discussions of the previous year. What was new was the 1 million men at £845 million per year that the FPS believed necessary for the armed forces to carry out the approved strategy. The FPS, despite all the evidence provided by the resource constraints of the previous year, believed this to be within the realms of possibility, although they admitted that 'whether we like it or not... Defence Policy in common with many other aspects of our national life, must be subordinated to economic recovery for the next few years'.[49]

Despite the belief of Tedder that 'there was not the slightest likelihood of this government, or indeed any government, accepting such a charge on the national economy in time of peace' preliminary discussions by the COS raised issues which were purely strategic, focusing on the implications of mass destruction weapons for the security of the British Isles and on whether the Middle East and its oil supplies could be denied to the Soviet Union. There was no reference to whether the United Kingdom could support the armed forces necessary to carry out the strategy put forward.[50] Consequently discussions with Alexander covered the same arid ground of the previous year. Even when Alexander suggested the institution of a Ten Year Rule on defence expenditure to reflect the likelihood of war, his proposal was dismissed by the COS on the grounds that any further short-term reduction in the armed forces would preclude the build up for the 1950s.[51]

Questions of resources were therefore deliberately excluded when draft terms of reference were issued to the JPS by the COS for their final report on Future Defence Policy: these made it explicit that 'it was not intended that the JPS should include in their report an attempt to evaluate priorities between the three Services' and should avoid 'becoming involved in the discussion of the size and shape of the armed forces'. In restricting the role of the JPS to merely assisting 'the Service Ministries in the preparation of an estimate of the size and shape of our forces' by providing 'some indication of the relative importance of the tasks of the armed forces in the event of a major war' the military made it inevitable that inter-Service competition for resources would continue and this would create the conditions for further conflict with the Prime Minister and the Chancellor.[52]

With this contentious question ruled out of their jurisdiction, the JPS were able to make rapid progress on their report: a draft was prepared by 7 May 1947, cleared by the COS with only minor amendments on 14 May 1947 and approved by Alexander for circulation to the Prime Minister and Foreign Secretary on 21 May 1947.[53] It began by stating that 'the supreme object of British policy is to prevent war, provided that this can be done without prejudicing our vital interests'. It noted, however, that the United Nations gave no security against a Great Power and the only deterrent against the Soviet Union was therefore 'tangible evidence of our intention and ability to withstand attack and to hit back immediately': the intention was to 'refashion our forces and our war potential to meet the needs of the future, but in the process, we must remain strong enough to demonstrate our ability to withstand and our intention to counter aggression at any time'. After stressing the interdependence of the Commonwealth in the face of the Soviet threat and the absolute necessity of an alliance with the United States, the paper then went over old ground, reaffirming the three-pillar strategy as the basis of British defence policy, pointing out the importance and vulnerability of the Middle East, the implications of 'New Weapons' for an increasingly vulnerable United Kingdom and the importance of an early air offensive from bomber bases in Britain, the Middle East and North-west India backed by an implied threat to use mass destruction weapons.

Only in the conclusions did the JPS 'indicate certain general principles which should govern the nature and size of our future forces'. Great stress was laid on the maintenance of technical superiority through research and development, particularly in the creation of a credible deterrent force. The RAF had to provide both the 'powerful offensive force essential to our security' and the complementary active air defence force, together with maritime air forces to assist the Navy in the control of sea communications, tactical air forces to support the Army in the Middle East and transport forces for a nucleus airborne assault force. The Navy was to furnish anti-submarine forces and anti-surface-unit task groups for control of sea communications, and forces to enable the Army to keep alive the art of Combined Operations. The Army was to provide forces for the anti-aircraft defence of the United Kingdom, including 'aid to the civil power', and a field force for the Middle East which 'must be given priority over the anti-invasion role in the United Kingdom'.[54]

There the military rested: the report was finally approved, after some further discussion of the Middle East, at a Staff Conference attended by Attlee and Bevin in mid-June 1947.[55] Despite acknowledging in their report on Future Defence Policy that 'the economy of the United Kingdom should be thoroughly sound and able to support a powerful war potential and adequate armed forces' the JPS had been precluded by their terms of reference from assessing the dilemma implicit within this statement which lay at the heart of the preceding eighteen months of debate; if the economy could not support adequate armed forces then what? Instead, the COS authorized the preparation of a separate paper 'setting out the ultimate size and shape of the forces immediately required on the outbreak of a future war': from this the Service Ministers would then assess the peace-time forces required to ensure that this target force could be achieved. The continuation of this piecemeal and inherently competitive process was to have disastrous results for the military.[56]

RESOURCES AND STRATEGIC CHOICES: JULY 1947 TO JANUARY 1948

The Army had already begun work on such an assessment and was therefore first off the mark: to fulfil the roles assigned to it on the outbreak of war, the Army needed no fewer than 350,000 personnel to defend the United Kingdom plus two divisions in the Middle East and a further three divisions as reinforcements, two brigade groups and one division to garrison the Far East and seven brigades plus anti-aircraft units for the defence of overseas ports essential for the control of sea communications. Not surprisingly this produced a terse reminder from Alexander that the military should bear in mind the £600 million per year limit that he had laid down in February.[57]

This warning shot had little effect on the Service departments; naval requirements for forces on the outbreak of war were assessed as 8 fleet aircraft carriers, 25 light fleet aircraft carriers, 1,200 carrier-borne aircraft, 4 capital ships, 35 cruisers, 135 destroyers and radar pickets, 332 escorts, 200 minesweepers, 80 submarines and 150 light forces with 382,000 personnel. The RAF put its requirements at 287 squadrons, including 75 bomber squadrons (65 of them equipped with long and medium-range strategic bombers) and 130 fighter squadrons, deployed mainly in the British Isles and the Middle East.[58]

When translated into peacetime estimates by the Service departments these produced astronomical results. Both the Navy and the Air Force stressed the need for forces in being: sea control forces on such a scale could not be improvised within the likely one-year warning of war period, while the primary deterrent to war, the bomber force, needed to be at a high state of readiness. Consequently the Navy, with around 40 per cent of its ships in commission, would need some £236 million and 213,000 personnel in 1948–9 rising to £465 million in 1954–5 as re-equipment and production for war reserves took effect; similarly, the Air Force required an average of £245 million per year between 1948 and 1950 rising to £550 million per year from 1955. Not to be outdone, the Army estimated its cadre forces at 368,300 personnel at a cost for a 'normal year' of £392 million.[59]

At a time when the COS were under insistent pressure from the Cabinet to make every possible economy in order to ease the Balance of Payments crisis of August 1947, these estimates, which with terminal charges, production and research and development would total well over £1,200 million, were clearly out of the question.[60] Although the COS warned that any reduction in the estimates 'would bear no relation to future war requirements' Alexander insisted that the requirements should be re-examined and an indication provided of where the cuts would fall and the attendant risks lie.[61]

All three Services agreed that in principle ruthless pruning would have to be undertaken: garrison forces and those with a defensive or limited offensive role would have to be eliminated in favour of a concentration on those forces, particularly RAF Bomber Command, which gave the best deterrent show of strength. However, while accepting Alexander's figures and his assumption that 'the risk of major war is negligible for the next five years and that the risk would only gradually increase during the following five years', the COS were adamant that any directive should be issued on the direct authority of the minister as it would be 'based entirely on political considerations and . . . was not in accord with current strategic thinking'.[62]

Despite this ruling, the 1948–9 estimates were prepared to different assumptions. The Air Ministry accepted the logic of Alexander's ruling and sought to reduce its administrative 'tail' in order to bring its estimates down to under £200 million in the short term: even so the front-line strength of Bomber Command, the core of the deterrent, would have to be cut by 20 per cent and would remain equipped with obsolete aircraft into the 1950s. The Admiralty submitted a five year plan that brought the 1948–9 estimate down to £185 million and postponed the much-needed refurbishment of the fleet until 1953. The War Office, however, despite paying lip-service to Alexander's thinking, made no attempt to prepare a long-term plan and simply argued that on existing commitments the 1948–9 estimates would be £330 million. When the COS considered these estimates, an acrimonious discussion ensued with the First Sea Lord Admiral Sir John Cunningham and Tedder pointing out that if the Army estimates stood, then the RAF and the Navy would have to bear a proportion of the cut which could not be justified by any strategic logic. Despite pleas from all the Services that they were already well below their minimum requirements, Alexander was forced to order further percentage cuts in the Service Estimates.[63]

This produced further unsatisfactory results. The Admiralty reported that it could find the stated £20 million savings only if it reduced expenditure on welfare and amenities for the fleet, closed one dockyard at home and another abroad and cut down even further on new construction and research and development, all of which 'would seriously impair the ability of the Navy subsequently to expand commensurately with its responsibilities if and when the risk of war increases'. The War Office stated baldly that it could not see any way to make a £60 million cut and any savings made through the cancellation of equipment and the disbanding of units would have 'the gravest effects on the Army in 1948/9 and for many years to come'. The Air Ministry simply reported that their previous calculations had been wrong and that the true cost would be £206 million for 1948–9; any further cuts would have to be found from works services or administration as the front-line strength of the RAF could be cut no further.

In the face of this impasse a fundamental change of approach was necessary and the COS agreed that the only way forward was to abandon the piecemeal process whereby the Service ministries submitted separate proposals; instead, the JPS were to prepare a rigorous review of long-term defence policy based on DO (47) 44 but with Alexander's ceilings of £600 million and 700,000 personnel per year in mind.[64] In discussing the terms of reference to be issued to the JPS, Montgomery wished to place the onus for unpalatable decisions squarely on the Minister of Defence. He was opposed by both Tedder and Cunningham who felt that 'the whole position of the Chiefs of Staff Committee would be undermined' unless full use was made of the joint staff structure before bringing the Minister of Defence further into the process. Despite his belief that the individual Directors of Plans would not go against the interests of their service in JPS discussions and that another deadlock would therefore result, Montgomery capitulated.[65] The JPS were themselves dubious that they could do what the Service ministries and the COS had signally failed to do and secured agreement 'to indicate modifications to this policy should it prove impossible to provide the forces required to fulfil it'.[66]

When Alexander put the Service Estimates for 1948–9 totalling £711 million to the Defence Committee, spelling out the reductions that had been made, particularly in the RAF and the Navy, he stressed that

> the strategic consequences of measures of this kind are extremely grave and must bring with them undesirable political consequences, especially in the virtual abandonment of our position in the Pacific and the serious weakening of our strength in the Middle East and Germany.

He received little sympathy from Attlee, who stated that 'there had not been sufficient appreciation of the need to bring the strength of the armed forces within the limits of what the country could afford' and queried why expenditure on the scale envisioned should none the less 'immobilise the armed forces'. With the support of Bevin, who reiterated that 'if the country was to have any influence in international affairs he must have an adequate backing of armed force', Alexander managed to secure provisional acceptance of the figures, subject to further scrutiny by Dalton before formal presentation to the Cabinet, but Attlee gave a clear sign that his patience was running out by stressing the urgent need for a long-term approach to produce balanced armed forces within a strict budget.[67]

It was to be mid-November before JPS figures were available; as Montgomery had foreseen, this delay was due to the inability of the JPS to solve the puzzle laid before them. When the COS discussed the JPS proposals it was clear that the forces envisaged would cost far in excess of £600 million per year to maintain, an overrun largely due to the fact that the estimates 'had not been prepared to a common basis'. The War Office had once more broken ranks by insisting that the Army estimates should be prepared on the basis of existing peacetime commitments. Tedder and Cunningham again condemned the War Office for 'not facing the changed type of warfare that modern weapons had already brought about' and pointed out that the remaining difficulty in drawing up a long-term defence policy was the insistence of the Army on providing figures geared to peacetime commitments rather than a programme leading to readiness for war in the 1950s. In particular, the maintenance of nine Territorial Army divisions in the United Kingdom as an anti-invasion force was indefensible as they had no foreseeable role under the conditions of modern warfare beyond aid to the civil power.[68]

Alexander was by now becoming anxious about the absence of a long-term plan which he could present to Parliament as the basis of the 1948 Defence White Paper. On 28 November 1947 he reported to Attlee that 'no real progress has been made' and sought his support in forcing a decision in order to 'enable the Government to take firm decisions'. Attlee backed his Minister of Defence with exceptional force:

> The method of giving the Chiefs of Staff a ceiling within which to work is the only satisfactory one. The Government, not the Chiefs of Staff, must decide what proportion of our resources can be devoted to defence. They may say that the amount is insufficient. They almost always do. They can either accept the decision of the Government or resign on the grounds that they refuse to take the responsibility. The Government must then take the responsibility and find other advisers ... the delay in producing them [the long-term figures] has been due to the failure of the Chiefs of Staff to agree. If they cannot agree, they must give way to those who can.[69]

On the same day that Attlee was conveying this warning to the Secretary of State for War, Shinwell, with its implied invitation for resignation echoing the COS's *démarche* led by Montgomery in January, the COS met to try and resolve their differences. Tedder and Cunningham again argued that the insistence of the Army on retaining an anti-invasion role was distorting the proposed defence budget and preventing an agreed paper being submitted to Alexander but the War Office was unrepentant.[70]

In the light of this the COS were forced to submit a 'collective report' to Alexander on the size and shape of the armed forces that was anything but, as it focused on the unresolved problems. The COS pointed out that the attitude of the War Office made it impossible to produce balanced forces within the limits specified by Alexander. An annual expenditure of £662 million (£42 million for research and development, £180 million for the Navy, £250 million for the Army and £190 million for the RAF) was the minimum that the forces could accept; even this would have to be increased after two or three years as the RAF and the Navy began a twelve-year rearmament programme to build up deterrent forces.[71]

A meeting between Alexander and the COS was held to clear the air but no progress could be made on shifting the Army from its entrenched position in the absence of Montgomery on an overseas tour. The Prime Minister was therefore called on to give rulings on the outstanding issues. Attlee gave the Army short shrift, accepting the arguments of the Navy and the RAF, and ordering concentration on the preparation of deterrent forces: he and Alexander agreed that it would be possible to reduce expenditure if the size of the Army was reduced by dropping any anti-invasion role and cutting Anti-Aircraft Command.[72]

The return of Montgomery made little difference. In January 1948, although Alexander recommended that while there were still occupational commitments for the Army to fulfil the Defence Committee should accept the different planning assumptions of the armed forces, this was on the understanding that 'this divergence will be reduced or eliminated as soon as possible'. The Services were ordered to reduce their requirements to £600 million and 650,000 personnel per year by 1949; any consequent cuts were to fall on the Army. Even so, Alexander found it difficult to contemplate the expenditure involved in the long-term programmes of the RAF and the Navy.[73]

At two Defence Committee meetings in early January 1948 where the new Chancellor of the Exchequer, Sir Stafford Cripps, agreed only reluctantly to the base figure of £600 million per year, it rapidly became apparent that the Army had lost the battle. Despite arguing that the nine Territorial divisions were essential not only for the defence of the United Kingdom but also for reinforcing the Middle East in the event of war, pending the arrival of American units, and for a possible continental commitment, Montgomery was unable to counter the arguments of ministers and his Service colleagues. The Prime Minister ruled in favour of Alexander's policy for the future size and shape of the armed forces.[74]

CONCLUSION

After two-and-a-half years of often bitter debate, Britain had finally formulated a post-war defence policy: a strategy had been drawn up, the roles of the Services established and priorities agreed within an overall budget. That this had taken so long was both a measure of the magnitude of the task facing British policy-makers as they tried to balance military needs against economic stringency and a reflection of the inadequacies of the higher organization for defence in post-war Britain, characterized by competing Service interests, which the creation of a weak Ministry of Defence had done little to resolve.

The demands of the three Services expressed through the individual heads of the armed forces in the Chiefs of Staff Committee paid only lip-service to the priority of economic recovery, being based solely on perceived strategic need. The inability of the Minister of Defence and the COS in their collective capacity as his advisers to enforce a common approach on the size and shape of the armed forces resulted in the development of British long-term defence policy being influenced as much by resource constraints as by strategic logic. The continual referral of policy issues to higher authority for decision meant that the Prime Minister and the Chancellor of the Exchequer were continually drawn into making what were essentially strategic decisions on fiscal and personnel grounds. Whatever the impact of defence expenditure on the British economy, there can be no doubt of the impact of economic constraints on the evolution of British defence policy.[75]

Ironically, in 1948, no sooner had some measure of agreement been reached than the accelerating Cold War raised serious questions about the assumptions underlying this policy. The Czech coup and the Berlin airlift introduced the spectre of a shooting war in the short term, something that the policy made no provision for, while the movement towards a Western defence organization reopened the debate on the role of the British armed forces within the three-pillar strategy. The awkward compromises within this defence policy were brutally exposed barely six months after it had been finalized and the Labour government was no nearer an agreed policy that satisfied all concerned than when it started its balancing act in August 1945.

NOTES

Unless otherwise stated all archival material is from the Public Record Office, Kew, Surrey. Crown copyright material in the Public Record Office is reproduced by permission of the Controller of Her Majesty's Stationery Office.

1 Many of the standard works on post-war British defence policy were published before the opening of the records under the thirty year rule; see, for example, C. J. Bartlett, *The Long Retreat* (London, 1972); F. A. Johnson, *Defence by Committee* (Oxford, 1960); R. N. Rosecrance, *Defence of the Realm* (New York, 1968); W. P. Snyder, *The Politics of British Defence Policy, 1945–1962*, (London, 1965). The most recent survey is M. Dockrill, *British Defence Policy since 1945*, (Oxford, 1989). On strategic planning see the pioneering J. Lewis, *Changing Direction: British Military Planning for Postwar Strategic Defence* (London: 1988).

2 British post-war strategic planning has been the subject of some scholarly debate in part because of the dramatic disagreements between the Chiefs of Staff and the Foreign Office over the threat posed by the Soviet Union. See Lewis; G. Ross, *The Foreign Office and the Kremlin* (London: 1984); V. Rothwell, *Britain and the Cold War 1941-7* (London: 1982); J. Baylis 'British Wartime Thinking about a Postwar European Security Group', *Review of International Studies* Vol. 9 No. 4; Wiebes and Zeeman, 'Baylis and Postwar Planning', J. Bayliss, 'A Reply', *Review of International Studies* Vol. 10, No. 3; A. Gorst, 'British Military Planning for Postwar Defence, 1943–1945', in A. Deighton (ed.) *Britain and the First Cold War* (London: 1990); G. Ross, 'Foreign Office Attitudes to the Soviet Union', in W. Laquer (ed.) *The Second World War* (London: 1982); J. Zamet-

ica, 'British Strategic Planning for the Eastern Mediterranean and the Middle East, 1944–1947', Cambridge DPhil 1986.

3 Gorst, pp. 97–9.

4 Lewis, pp. 188–91.

5 See for example WM(43)8, 14 January 1943, CAB 65/33.

6 Gorst, pp. 99–104.

7 JP(45)174(S)(TR), undated but probably mid-August 1945, WO 193/95.

8 Lewis, p. 246.

9 DO(45)29, 5 November 1945, considered at DO(45) mtg 13, 7 November 1945, CAB 69/7.

10 CM(45)18, 7 August 1945, CM(45)23, 16 August 1945 and CM(45)26, 30 August 1945, CAB 128/1.

11 JP(45)205(F) approved at COS(45) mtg 216, 6 September 1945, CAB 79/38, circulated as COS(45)565(0), 6 September 1945, CAB 80/97.

12 DO(45) mtg 6, 14 September 1945, CAB 69/7.

13 CM(45)36, 28 September 1945, CAB 128/1.

14 DO(45) mtg 7, 5 October 1945, CAB 69/7.

15 DO(45) mtg 11, 29 October 1945, CAB 69/7.

16 COS(46)5(0), 8 January 1946 and COS(46)9(0), 15 January 1946, CAB 80/99.

17 DO(46) mtg 1, 11 January 1946, CAB 131/1.

18 DO(46) mtg 3, 21 January 1946, CAB 131/1.

19 DO(46)20, 13 February 1946, CAB 131/2.

20 DO(46) mtg 5, 15 February 1946, CAB 131/1 and CM(46) mtg 16, 18 February 1946, CAB 128/5.

21 DO(46) mtg 12, 15 April 1946, CAB 131/1; DO(46)66, 10 May 1946, CAB 131/2.

22 DO(46) mtg 5, 15 February 1946, CAB 131/5; COS(46) 54(0), 22 February 1946, CAB 80/100 considered at COS(46) mtg 31, 25 February 1946, CAB79/45; JP(46)45(T.R.), 25 February 1946, CAB 84/79. On the role of Attlee in the strategic debate on the Middle East see R. Smith and J. Zametica, 'The Cold Warrior: Clement Attlee reconsidered, 1945–7', *International Affairs*, Vol. 61, No. 2.

23 JP(46)45(Revised Final), 31 March 1946, CAB 84/79, circulated as DO(46)47, 2 April 1946, CAB 131/2.

24 DO(46) mtg 10, 5 April 1946, CAB 131/1.

25 DO(46)46, 30 March 1946 and DO(46)54, 15 April 1946, CAB 131/2.

26 For the meetings of the Dominion Prime Ministers in April-May 1946 see CAB 133/86.

27 DO(46)67, 25 May 1946, CAB 131/2; DO(46)17, 27 May 1946, CAB 131/1.

28 DO(46)80, 18 June 1946, CAB 131/3.

29 DO(46)22, 19 July 1946, CAB 131/1.

30 TWC(46)15(Revise), 1 July 1946, DEFE 2/1252.

31 Lewis, p. 270.

32 DO(46)135, 8 November 1946, CAB 131/3.

33 DO(46) mtg 33, 20 November 1946, CAB 131/1.

34 CP(46)345, 11 September 1946, CAB 129/12 considered at CM(46)82, 17 September 1946, CAB 128/6.

35 Alexander to Hollis, 17 December 1946, Annex 1 to COS(46) mtg 184, 18 December 1946, CAB 79/54.

36 There are no paper numbers assigned to these papers dated 26 November 1946: they are annexed to a note by Mallaby to the Directors of Plans, 7 December 1946, AIR 9/267.

37 JP(46)229(F), 19 December 1946, CAB 84/86.

38 COS(46) mtg 187, 23 December 1946, CAB 79/54.

39 COS(47)5(0)(Final), 23 January 1947, DEFE 5/3.

40 DO(47)1, 1 January 1947, DO(47)2, 2 January 1947 and DO(47)3, 6 January 1947, CAB 131/4.

41 COS(47) mtg 6, 7 January 1947, DEFE 32/1; Smith and Zametica, p. 251.

42 COS(47) mtg 7, 8 January 1947, DEFE 4/1.

43 Chapter 33, 'Palestine', BLM178/1, papers of Field Marshal Viscount Montgomery of Alamein, Imperial War Museum. cf. pp. 246–53.

44 COS(47) mtg 9, 13 January 1947, DEFE 4/1. See also Smith and Zametica, p. 251, and Lewis, pp. 292–3.
45 DO(47)4, 7 January 1947 and DO(47)9, 13 January 1947, CAB 131/4 considered at DO(47) mtg 2, 14 January 1947, CAB 131/5.
46 CM(47)9, 17 January 1947, CM(47)10, 21 January 1947 and CM(47)13, 28 January 1947, CAB 128/9.
47 COS(47)33(0), 18 February 1947, AIR 9/268.
48 COS(47) mtg 35, 5 March 1947, DEFE 4/2; DO(47)23, 7 March 1947, CAB 131/4.
49 The relevant paper JP(46)164(F) dated 31 March 1947 is retained by department: Lewis, pp. 293–315, contains a summary of this paper with no indication of its location.
50 COS(47)72(0), 3 April 1947, COS(47)78(0), 14 April 1947, DEFE 5/4 and COS(47)79(0), 19 April 1947, AIR 9/268.
51 COS(47) mtg 54, 17 April 1947, AIR 9/268.
52 COS(47)79(0), 21 April 1947, COS(47)87(0), 21 April 1947 and COS(47)87(0), 23 April 1947, DEFE 5/4, considered at COS(47) mtg 57, 23 April 1947, DEFE 4/3. A fuller record of COS(47) mtg 57 is contained in AIR 9/268.
53 COS(47) mtg 64, 14 May 1947 and COS(47) mtg 66, 21 May 1947, DEFE 4/4.
54 JP(47)55(F), 7 May 1947, AIR 9/268 circulated as DO(47)44, 22 May 1947, CAB 21/1800.
55 The record of this Staff Conference, COS(47) mtg 74, 11 June 1947 is retained by department. Lewis has a summary, pp. 331–4.
56 COS(47) mtg 64, 14 May 1947, DEFE 4/4.
57 COS(47)106(0), 19 May 1947, COS(47)114(0), 30 May 1947, DEFE 5/4.
58 COS(47)142, 9 July 1947, DEFE 5/5.
59 COS(47)166(0), 13 August 1947, COS(47)167(0), 13 August 1947, COS(47)169(0), 15 August 1947, DEFE 5/5.
60 CM(47)67, 1 August 1947, CAB 128/10.
61 COS(47) mtg 105, 19 August 1947, DEFE 4/6; COS(47)173(0), 23 August 1947, DEFE 5/5.
62 COS(47) mtg 106, 20 August 1947 and COS(47) mtg 107, 21 August 1947, DEFE 4/6.
63 COS(47)178(0), 29 August 1947, COS(46)179(0), 29 August 1947 and COS(47)180(0), 29 August 1947, DEFE 5/5 considered at COS(47) mtg 112, 30 August 1947, DEFE 4/6.
64 COS(47)184(0), 1 September 1947, COS(47)185(0), 1 September 1947, COS(47)186(0), 2 September 1947, DEFE 5/5 considered at COS(47) mtg 114, 2 September 1947, DEFE 4/7.
65 COS(47) mtg 115, 3 September 1947, DEFE 4/7.
66 COS(47) mtg 120, 17 September 1947, DEFE 4/7.
67 DO(47)68, 15 September 1947, CAB 131/4 discussed at DO(47) mtg 20, 18 September 1947, CAB 131/5.
68 COS(47) mtg 143, 19 November 1947 and COS(47) mtg 147, 26 November 1947, DEFE 32/1.
69 Alexander letter to Attlee, 28 November 1947, Shinwell note to Alexander, 4 December 1947, Attlee notes for discussion with Alexander and Shinwell, 8 December 1947, PREM 8/659.
70 COS(47) mtg 152, 8 December 1947, DEFE 4/9.
71 COS(47)263(0), 11 December 1947, DEFE 5/6.
72 COS(47) mtg 156, 13 December 1947, DEFE 4/9.
73 DO(48)2, 5 January 1948, CAB 131/6.
74 DO(48) mtg 2, 8 January 1948 and DO(48) mtg 3, 14 January 1948, CAB 131/5.
75 See for example T. Geiger, 'The Next War is Bound to Come: Defence production policy, the Ministry of Supply and defence contractors, 1945–57', in A. Gorst, L. Johnman and W. S. Lucas (eds) *Politics and the Limits of Policy* (London: 1991).

7

The 'Western Union' concept and British defence policy, 1947–8

John Kent and John W. Young

A major area of interest surrounding the foreign policy of the Attlee governments is co-operation between Britain and Western Europe. Numerous writers have now demonstrated that the Foreign Secretary, Ernest Bevin, had a genuine interest in close links to the continent which, alongside links to the African colonies and Middle East (an area of British predominance), could form a 'third power' in world affairs. This is despite the widespread supposition that Bevin had little interest in European unity. But by late 1949 British foreign policy became based on co-operation with the United States and securing a special place within an American-dominated alliance.[1] Important reasons for this evolution lay in differences between Bevin's ministry and other Whitehall departments. The Treasury and Board of Trade showed less enthusiasm for a European customs union than did Bevin, while the Colonial Office had little liking for grandiose schemes for a 'Euro-African' combination.[2] The subject of this chapter is the relationship between the Foreign Office and military planners.[3]

The idea of a 'Western bloc' involving a permanent security arrangement between Britain and her continental neighbours was discussed during the Second World War and by 1944 had become popular in the Foreign Office. It would not only help to contain Germany and provide defence in depth on the continent, but also allow Britain to act as the representative of the West European democracies in world affairs.[4] Ernest Bevin was interested in co-operation with Western Europe from the moment he became Foreign Secretary in July 1945. He particularly hoped to develop economic and commercial links to the continent.[5] Yet in 1945–7 it proved impossible to pursue a Western bloc. This was partly because of fears of antagonizing the USSR through the pursuit of West European links, but there were also important differences between Britain and the most important of the continental democracies, France, on the German problem, and Bevin was suspicious of the Communist role in coalition governments in Paris. An alliance between them became possible only in March 1947.[6]

When the Anglo-French Treaty of Dunkirk was signed, Orme Sargent, Bevin's Permanent Under-Secretary, still hoped to create 'a European group which will enable us to deal on a footing of equality with our two gigantic colleagues, the USA and USSR'.[7] The actual form of the Dunkirk Treaty, however, was a narrowly drawn, anti-German security pact. The Foreign Office insisted that 'any suggestion that the Treaty was not directed primarily against Germany would arouse suspicion' from the USSR.[8] The Chiefs of Staff (COS), asked to comment on the Dunkirk text, were as cautious as the Foreign Office, but for different reasons. The military's Joint Planning Staff, in a paper submitted to the COS committee, wanted France to become 'the keystone of a strong western region of defence' but they also wanted to retain Britain's independence in deciding what aid was sent to the continent. The COS themselves also wanted to avoid any step which did not have American support, as the United States was regarded 'as the keystone on which our major strategy and planning are based'.[9] In May 1947, when Bevin again raised the idea of European links – this time to Belgium and the Netherlands – as a way to reinforce British strength *vis-à-vis* the USA and USSR, the COS continued to strike a cautious note. They were ready to give Belgium and the Netherlands priority in military supplies but were reluctant to make any British commitment to defend the two countries themselves from attack.[10] In military terms Belgium and the Netherlands hardly represented formidable allies and France was little better. The French Army, historically the backbone of any effective defence against Germany, was in a poor state after the war.[11] Any idea of matching the Red Army in Europe, however, was further undermined by the development of post-war military thinking on the defence of the British Empire.

Since 1944 British military leaders had attempted to define a global strategy for the defence of their world position. This was based upon the perception of the Soviet Union as the only potential threat to the British Empire and had to take into consideration Britain's much-diminished post-war resources; it had to come to terms not only with military uncertainties (over, for example, the impact of atomic weapons) but also with political uncertainties regarding the post-war international system, which made it impossible to disentangle military security from foreign policy issues. Britain needed a strategy which would provide the best possible means of conducting a major war, while ensuring the survival of the United Kingdom itself, as the heart of the Empire. As the Second World War had shown, Britain possessed neither the economic nor the military resources to do this, without the support of the Dominions, colonies and major foreign powers, such as the USA. Thus strategic plans had to aim at securing those 'support areas' in the world deemed essential, in terms of manpower and resources. Naval forces would guarantee sea communications between these areas, while foreign policy must aim at developing ties to nations whose support was vital for ultimate victory in a major conflict.

The precise policy, which the COS had fought long and hard to get accepted in 1945–7, was based primarily on the defence of the *Middle East*. The COS had defined the 'support areas' as Britain, Central and Southern Africa, the Western hemisphere and the antipodean Dominions. In order to defend Africa, however, and to reduce the likely success of a Soviet invasion of Western Europe, the COS argued that it was essential, above all, to secure the Middle East, which held a pivotal position between Europe, Africa and Asia and which was also vital as a source of oil. If airbases in the Middle East were used to launch bombing raids on the USSR, the weight of the Soviet assault on Western Europe could be reduced. If the Middle East was not defended the logic was that the 'support areas' both of Africa and (via the Soviet advance into Western Europe) the UK would be endangered. Ultimate victory would then be in jeopardy. In terms of priorities the defence of the Middle East was therefore more important than the defence of Western Europe. Bevin, keen to maintain imperial positions and increasingly determined to oppose the Soviets, had given valuable support to the COS views in 1945–7. Their arguments had won through only against strong opposition from the Prime Minister. The British military looked on close collaboration with Washington as the *sine qua non* for their own security and talks were held on Middle Eastern defence with the USA in October.[12] The success of the talks led the military planners to consider an extension of Anglo-American discussions to other areas in order to harmonize the strategic perceptions of the two countries. Since 1945 the ornate Anglo-American defence structure, created in wartime, had largely become defunct (although nominally the 'Combined Chiefs of Staff' still existed). The Joint Planning Staff, in looking at possible new areas for Anglo-American talks, argued that the Far East should be treated as being second in importance to the Middle East. But neither the Chief of the Imperial General Staff, Bernard Montgomery, nor the Chief of the Air Staff, Lord Tedder, accepted this. Montgomery and Tedder believed that *Western Europe* was more significant and should be the next area for Anglo-American talks. Meanwhile the question of co-operation with Western Europe had been made more urgent by events surrounding the breakdown of East–West relations, and particularly the division of Europe brought about by the Marshall plan.

French military planners had grown increasingly concerned at the East–West breakdown. They believed that French armed forces, unable to defend their own country or to maintain a position of neutrality in the Cold War, must co-operate with Britain and the USA.[13] In late October the official head of the French Foreign Ministry, Jean Chauvel, visited London and raised the question of Anglo-French military co-operation. He wanted to know what would happen if, as now seemed likely, Germany became divided between East and West, and the line of division had to be defended. Bevin and Sir Orme Sargent were evidently surprised by the sudden French interest in anti-Soviet, rather than anti-German, security preparations. Bevin said he wished to give East–West agreement one more chance to succeed, at the four-power talks on Germany planned for November; Sargent said that public concern could be aroused if Britain and France held military talks without the USA and that these should be put off for the present. The USA was, quite clearly, the most powerful Western state in military terms and, once again, the British were unwilling to move without her.[14]

Despite the caution of Bevin and Sargent regarding this first, serious proposal for Anglo-French staff talks after the war, Chauvel had succeeded in putting the item on the diplomatic agenda. The implication of his talks in London was that, if the East–West talks on Germany's future broke down, Western military co-operation would be considered. In mid-November the ambassador to Paris, Duff Cooper, wrote to Bevin complaining about a letter from the Director of Military Intelligence, Templer, to the military attaché in Paris which had discouraged the idea of staff talks. By now the French had proposed that their Army Chief of Staff, General Georges Revers, should visit London and Duff Cooper believed such a visit would be valuable. In the Foreign Office there was some sympathy for the military's reluctance to talk to Revers, who was seen as right wing, and lacking in good political sense. But Templer's letter was rather blunt in tone and Bevin himself minuted that 'what we must get into the heads of our people is Western security regionally and less anti-attitude [sic]'. Nevertheless immediate staff talks were ruled out for two reasons. One was that French security was suspect, because of the strength of Communist support in France; the other was that all British reports on the military situation in Western Europe were so discouraging that they would upset the French. Duff Cooper continued to argue that Britain must, through sheer military necessity, hold talks with the French; Bevin insisted that he *did* want military talks in due course and that the main problem was one of *timing*. In mid-December, when the four-power talks on Germany broke down as predicted, the Foreign Secretary assured the ambassador that 'we shall not postpone any longer than we should [the] discussion of future security arrangements between those of the Great Powers who are prepared to co-operate'.[15]

At the end of the four-power conference on Germany on 17 December, Bevin had a conversation with the French Foreign Minister, Georges Bidault, about future co-operation. Military links were an important theme. Bevin was now ready to welcome a visit from Revers but underlined the British view that actual war with the USSR was unlikely in the near future. The Soviets were still recovering from the last war and were technologically inferior to the Americans, who retained their monopoly of the atomic bomb. Rather than launch war, the Soviets would rely on strong Communist Parties in France and Italy to try to destabilize Western Europe *from within*. Bevin hoped that, once Western defences were built up, armed conflict with the USSR would become even less likely. Significantly, however, Bevin was also keen to involve the USA in European defence, possibly by sending a small Anglo-French military team to Washington. Bidault was interested in this idea. The same day, however, while informing the USA's George Marshall of the forthcoming visit by Revers, Bevin made it clear that he hoped to maintain close Anglo-American military co-operation independently of the French. Marshall said that he felt the French needed military equipment more than they needed military staff talks, and Bevin agreed on the importance of a modern French army, evidently hoping that France could again play the major role of defending Europe on land while Britain supported her with naval and air power.[16]

A few days later Bevin discussed the Revers visit with Montgomery, who seemed very keen on the proposal and agreed that the French Army must be strengthened.[17] A discussion by the COS on 23 December, however, showed that the proposed visit by Revers had not endeared them to Anglo-French co-operation. They felt that full-scale staff talks should be carried out only with the Americans. Although Western European countries should be encouraged to look to Britain for leadership, Britain's resources were still not sufficient to arm a continental alliance and US assistance would be required. For the moment the COS were prepared to do little more than continue established forms of co-operation with Europe (providing clothing, aircraft spares and the like).[18] What was particularly worrying for the British military was the prospect of European talks on the question of *overall* strategy. Not only did the British military's emphasis on the Middle East give different priorities from the French, but also the US Navy wanted Anglo-American planning of an operation, codenamed 'Dunkirk', which aimed at a rapid evacuation of US occupation forces in Germany. Such a response to a Soviet attack was unlikely to be well received in Paris![19]

The difficulty of reconciling strategic planning with the requirements of foreign policy was entering a critical phase because the period December 1947 to January 1948 marked the peak of Foreign Office enthusiasm for West European co-operation. Close links to the continent seemed to provide the means to solve so many of Britain's international problems: the containment of Soviet power and defeat of Communist influence within Western Europe; the control of Germany and the encouragement of US support for Europe; and the creation of a 'third force' to match the USA and USSR in world affairs.[20] Many historians have seen British interest in a Western European alliance at this time as being merely the 'preliminary' to a wider alliance involving the USA – what eventually became NATO.[21] But in his key memorandum to the Cabinet, 'The First Aim of British Foreign Policy' (4 January 1948), Bevin made clear that, although material assistance from the USA was vital, 'the countries of Western Europe . . . despise the spiritual values of America' and

> Provided we can organise a Western European system . . . backed by the resources of the Commonwealth and the Americas, it should be possible to develop our own power and influence to equal that of the United States of America and the USSR. We have the material resources in the Colonial Empire, if we develop them, and by giving a spiritual lead now we should be able to carry out our task in a way which will show clearly that we are not subservient to the United States or to the Soviet Union.

It is significant that, in explaining his views to the Americans later in January, Bevin sent an expurgated copy of this memorandum, carefully omitting all that has just been quoted. What Bevin did tell the Americans was that he wanted a Western European 'democratic system' which he called the 'Western Union'. He was not certain how exactly to create this in institutional terms but stated that 'there would be an understanding backed by power, money and resolution bound together by the common ideals for which the Western Powers have twice in one generation shed their blood'.[22]

In this situation the Foreign Office was extremely disappointed with the COS view of Revers's visit, and Sir Orme Sargent asked the military to reconsider. Bevin's officials conceded that *full* defence conversations with Paris might be impossible at present: Britain had yet to resolve the structure of its own military forces, and preliminary consultations with the Americans seemed desirable before any major commitments to Europe were made. But Bevin had promised meaningful talks to Bidault and anything less might upset the French. The Foreign Office felt that the time had come at least to take Revers into Britain's confidence, whatever the problems with French security and however bleak Britain's analysis of the military situation. Sargent hoped that the COS might set an agenda for Revers's visit to include an exchange on the general military situation in Europe, talks about any immediate French request for equipment, British views on the organization of modern 'armed forces' and the possibilities of standardizing West European military equipment – an idea which the Foreign Office believed could be taken up by Britain, France and the Benelux states. Faced by this strong plea the COS agreed on 7 January to adopt most of the suggested agenda, though it was decided to focus the talks narrowly on army co-operation, and doubts were again raised about France's trustworthiness with information. Admiral Sir John Cunningham also pointed out that Britain's reluctance to send a large land army to the continent, when war broke out, would prove embarrassing if discovered. The French ambassador, René Massigli, was therefore warned that, though Revers could raise whatever questions he wished during his visit, he might not receive an answer to them (!) and that it was too early to discuss the issue of military dispositions.[23]

The decisions in the Foreign Office on the new Western Union policy had coincided in early January with important discussions in the Defence Committee of the British Cabinet on the 'Size and shape of the armed forces'. Decisions were needed on the question in order to draw up the 1948 Defence White Paper, and one important point was that any commitment by the British Army to defend continental Europe was ruled out. This was despite arguments in favour of a European commitment by both Bevin and Montgomery. In the Defence Committee on 8 January the CIGS argued that the Army should at least treat the defence of Britain as one of its tasks but both the Air Force and Navy chiefs, Tedder and Cunningham, argued that the risk of invasion was negligible: the RAF and Royal Navy would prevent this. When the discussion moved on to the issues of sending an army to Europe in the event of war, according to the record:

> The Foreign Secretary pointed out the embarrassment that would be likely to arise with our potential European allies if our plans were based on the assumption that we did not intend to do this. Several ministers were, however, inclined to agree with the Chief of the Air Staff that the maintenance of a first-class navy and a first-class Air Force, together with an Army on a continental scale, was beyond our resources.

Indeed the COS had already ruled out the idea in principle. Six days later, in a further discussion, from which Bevin was absent, Montgomery again argued that the Army should be concerned with home defence and suggested that Territorial Army units could be expanded to fight on the continent but he was strongly opposed by the Minister of Defence. This defeat did not (as will be seen) prevent the CIGS from arguing in future weeks in favour of a continental commitment, but drafting of a White Paper now went forward on the basis of a very restricted budget of £600 million, with no provision for a continental army. This fact gravely undermined any later attempts to commit British forces to European defence.[24]

General Revers's visit to London finally took place on 20–4 January, ironically at the same time as Bevin's major speech to the House of Commons on 'Western Union', delivered on the 22nd. The speech publicly announced that, co-operation with Moscow having failed, Britain would now pursue a policy of co-operation with Western Europe, backed by links to the USA and the Commonwealth.[25] As seen in the Cabinet memorandum of 4 January, Bevin's long-term hope in early 1948 was to create a 'third force' in world affairs 'equal to and independent of the US and USSR'.[26] He talked ambitiously of organizing what he later referred to as the 'middle of the planet' – that is Western Europe, the Middle East and Africa – into a coherent whole,[27] within a wider 'spiritual union' of the West. But he was well aware that, in the short term, the 'middle of the planet' would rely heavily on US support to foster economic recovery and prevent the spread of Communism. Specifically, in the speech of 22 January, Bevin wanted to extend the Anglo-French Treaty of Dunkirk to the Benelux states. This was a well-established idea and the French had been pressing for an approach to Belgium for a treaty since late December.[28] In the Foreign Office there had initially been some doubt as to whether a military alliance with Belgium would 'help or hinder' Bevin's ideal of Western Union.[29] (In the US State Department too it was felt that Western Union must be more than 'just another framework of military alliances'.)[30] Bevin decided in early January that an alliance *should* be made with Belgium and the Netherlands,[31] but he was clear, in explaining his new policy to the French and Americans, that such an alliance must merely be the 'core' of a much wider arrangement involving political, economic and military co-operation with other European countries, the Middle East and the development of African resources. However, Bevin also told the British ambassadors in Paris and Washington:

> I am aware that if my proposals are to be realised it will be necessary to make provision for security in Western Europe, and that this can only be achieved with United States co-operation. I am considering how best to tackle this problem.[32]

This statement by Bevin reflected the fact that, a week before his Western Union speech to the Commons, the Foreign Office was fully aware of the practical problems facing any military alliance with Europe. The problem was admirably set out in a highly important minute by Ivone Kirkpatrick on 9 January:

> The Chiefs of Staff have . . . decided . . . that we shall not in a future crisis initially send a land expeditionary force to the Continent. If this policy is maintained . . . we shall eventually either have to admit it to our allies or refuse to disclose our intentions. Both courses are likely to discourage them to the point of refusing to associate themselves with us. In this predicament it seems to me that our only method of satisfying the need for security is to involve America as far as possible in the defence of Western Europe. It is quite likely that the Americans too will refuse specifically to commit their forces to the Continent of Europe; but if they would enter with ourselves into some general commitment to go to war with an aggressor it is probable that the potential victims might feel reassured as to eventual victory and hence refuse to embark on a fatal policy of appeasement.[33]

This was indeed a succinct and lucid statement of the problems that Bevin had to try to unravel in early 1948 to make Western Union succeed. How to maintain British leadership in Europe when the British military were unwilling to defend the continent; how to strengthen European resolve while refusing to reveal Britain's military plans; how to obtain a US commitment to Europe when the Americans too were unwilling to commit themselves to European defence – all these became major issues over the following months. However, what needs to be underlined at the outset is that the aim of Bevin and the Foreign Office in early 1948 was *not*, as is often stated, to use a 'sprat to catch a mackerel' (a description later used by Bevin himself). It was *not* that Bevin needed a European alliance in order to win a US alliance. The case was quite the opposite: a US alliance was needed in order to make a European-based system, the Western Union, effective. And Western Union was intended to maintain Britain's standing as a major power, independent of the United States. Bevin made it quite clear that a treaty with Belgium and the Netherlands 'should not be subject to [George Marshall's] approval'.[34]

This is not to say that a US alliance was unimportant. The Foreign Office, indeed, had already begun to study possible ways to secure a US guarantee and one official minuted 'that an arrangement which ties down the Americans in Europe must have higher priority than any other treaty'. Bevin himself, reluctant to offend the Soviets overmuch, was anxious to carry the USA along with any British action. As part of his Western Union policy, to secure closer military co-operation, he also knew that the COS 'would have to be educated' because the CIGS and some of the others were 'discussing the problem . . . as if it were the making of the Entente Cordiale and really this won't do'. Yet even Bevin believed that 'We do not want any more Dunkirks' and that 'it is going to be difficult for us to put troops on the continent'. One solution he felt would be 'to enter into a commitment in the air and on the sea [which] should be of a much greater kind than we had before'.[35] But it was not at all clear how such a solution could reassure the Europeans.

At first the reticence of the British over military co-operation was not damaging to Anglo-continental co-operation: the French too were anxious to involve the USA in European defence, extremely reluctant to antagonize the Soviets overmuch, and believed that it would be difficult to hold a Soviet attack on Western Europe. (The French in 1948 had their own plans for a 'Dunkirk' operation: they planned to retreat in war to North Africa.) Furthermore General Revers was quite pleased with his visit to Britain, largely because his most important talks, on 21 and 23 January, were with Montgomery, the one British military figure who was genuinely interested in continental co-operation. What particularly pleased Revers was that Montgomery seemed keen to defend continental Europe along the line of the Rhine, thus protecting the French border. One of the points which the French were most keen to establish at this time, assuming British and US forces were available, was the line along which Western Europe would be defended. Montgomery, carefully avoiding any promises to commit British forces to the continent, waxed lyrical about the need to build up West European forces, talked of France's central role in Western defence, and said that the USA – and even Spain – must be involved in Europe's defence. The British also conceded that, while the USSR might not want war, conflict could none the less occur by 'accident'; this possibility was of particular concern to the French, who knew that war with the USSR could quickly lead to the occupation of their homeland.[36]

Montgomery had for several months been considering both the military and political aspects of British security. Believing that war with the Soviet Union was inevitable and likely to break out between 1957 and 1960 he was eager to take all possible steps to prepare for such an eventuality. This meant developing the correct military strategy, utilizing German economic and military resources, and ensuring that Western Europe developed the political will to resist Communism and prepare for the inevitable military struggle. In the difficult post-war circumstances, Montgomery considered Western Europe in general needed something to build up its morale and to encourage people of the 'right' character to provide leadership against Communism. Such attitudes set him apart from all other important military leaders, who preferred to concentrate on strategic planning and the best use of scarce resources, had little liking for a continental commitment and gave priority to Middle Eastern defence.

Confronted with increasing Foreign Office demands for military talks with the French, for what were essentially *political* reasons – that is, to make Western Union succeed – the military reaction was to stress the importance of agreeing first with the Americans on political and military questions.[37] But Montgomery argued that before the military could discuss a defence policy for Western Europe with the United States it would be necessary to decide on specific British strategy in the event of a war with the USSR.[38] As it stood, the relationship of the Middle East to Britain and the other main support areas had only been defined in terms of 'three pillars' – the defence of the UK, the defence of sea communications and the defence of the Middle East. What *exactly* the British would do in the event of an attack by the Soviet Union had not been planned in detail. The lack of emergency planning reflected the military belief that a deliberate assault on the West was not being considered by the Soviets in the short term.[39] In January, however, with the military conceding that war could break out by 'accident', it was more urgent to co-ordinate Anglo-American plans and, as Montgomery suggested, to relate them to a strategy for Western Europe's defence.

The Joint Planning Staff, endorsed by the Chiefs of Staff Committee, argued that, although the Soviet conquest of Western Europe would mean the loss of Mediterranean communications and facilitate a direct attack on the UK, the idea of defending the region should be ruled out as impractical unless Germany was rearmed or the countries of Western Europe revived in both economic and military terms. Montgomery, however, rejected this.[40] He had discussed the idea of a continental commitment with Bevin earlier in January;[41] Montgomery, on Bevin's instructions, had ordered General Robertson, the British commander in Germany, to consult with the US and French zonal commanders, General Lucius Clay and General Pierre Koenig, about defence without apparently informing either the Navy or the Air Force.[42] In order to win support for his ideas Montgomery emphasized the importance of building up Western Germany as part of Western Union, but he was convinced that the only 'sure and certain solution to the economic problems of Europe is to develop a non-dollar economy in Africa and link it to Europe'. For this 'third world force' to succeed, however, Montgomery believed that it was essential to provide a commitment to fight on the Rhine.[43] This alone would give the continentals the necessary *psychological* reassurance to stand up to Communism. Planning for a new Dunkirk was quite useless: it would demoralize the continentals if discovered.

The Prime Minister, Clement Attlee, not surprisingly, was astonished to discover that, after two-and-a-half years of emphasizing the importance of defending the Middle East, Montgomery wanted a commitment to fight on the Rhine. Attlee was worried about rebuilding Germany and did not believe that the two British divisions – all that was available in Germany – would provide much encouragement when between thirty and forty were necessary to resist the Soviets.[44] He did not, apparently, point out the other flaws in Montgomery's argument, such as the danger of alienating the French by rebuilding Germany, and the difficulty of encouraging Germany to join a Western European organization while basing Western defence on the Rhine! Other opposition came from the Chief of the Naval Staff, Cunningham, who realized that the commitment to fight on the Rhine was being advocated for political rather than military reasons; for Cunningham it was pointless to try and defend the Rhine unless enough European support could be given to ensure its success.[45] Given the state of the French Army and the economic difficulties confronting Western Europe this was clearly impossible in the next few years. Bevin replied that Western Europe did have the necessary resources and that what each nation should provide had to be costed out on a budgetary basis. When British force levels were determined and there were land forces to spare, he could see no objection to them going to the continent to reinforce the two divisions already in Germany. But Bevin agreed that no decision to send land forces to the continent should be taken without further study. For his part Montgomery now suggested that a decision to fight on the Rhine was vital for the defence of the Middle East – thereby reversing the arguments used by the military since 1945. 'I consider', he wrote, 'that no single operation can produce a greater contribution, directly, to the security of the UK, and the maintenance of our sea communications, and, indirectly to the maintenance of our position in the Middle East'.[46]

One major dimension to Bevin's grand design, it has been seen, was the support of the United States. An American commitment to European security would boost morale in the struggle against Communism and allow Montgomery and Bevin to organize their third world force. There were, however, differences in the USA about the form which commitments to Europe should take throughout early 1948 and talks with the Europeans were not finally agreed until spring. Western Union was enthusiastically welcomed by John Hickerson (head of the Office of European Affairs in the State Department) and by George Kennan (of the Policy Planning Staff) who hoped that a successful 'third force' would resist Communism and be friendly towards the USA, without placing huge demands on US resources. Hickerson even 'envisaged the creation of a third force which was . . . strong enough to say "no" both to the Soviet Union and to the United States' and felt that the United States should be ready to enter a defence arrangement to back this up. Kennan was much less certain about becoming involved in military talks. However, both Hickerson and Kennan were determined that Western Union should be a European initiative and that, while the United States should be positive about requests for support, the Europeans must create a meaningful organization before Washington acted.[47] The Under-Secretary of State, Bob Lovett, fully agreed. Referring to Bevin's 'suggestion that the US might enter with Great Britain into a general commitment to go to war with an aggressor, thereby reinforcing the defense proposals envisaged for Western Europe', Lovett urged that only when there was evidence of European determination to defend themselves could the USA consider a role in support of Western Union. Such doubts led Bevin increasingly to fear a 'vicious circle' in Western co-operation: the British military insisted on achieving joint plans with the United States before embarking on a commitment to Western European defence, and without a military commitment to Europe the British were unlikely to be able to make Western Union a going concern; but Americans like Lovett were unwilling to commit themselves more firmly to European defence unless the Europeans acted first. This was ironic: the USA, like Bevin, wanted to see a strong, independent Europe; but Bevin, in order to make his vision of Europe a reality needed to compensate for British military weakness by obtaining US support; and the Americans refused to provide such support until they were certain that Europeans could act together on their own.

This concern about a 'vicious circle' was expressed to the Americans in exactly the same terms Kirkpatrick had earlier used, in his minute of 9 January, though the arguments were now said to be 'Bevin's': Britain could not commit herself to defend Europe; this situation was 'likely to land them in trouble'; but a joint Anglo-American commitment to defend the continentals could provide the necessary reassurance. At the end of January Bevin tried to press the USA for bilateral military talks about Western Europe, similar to those held on the Middle East the previous year but the Americans refused, insisting that a European alliance must be made first. When Bevin (referring to his talk with Marshall of 17 December) argued that he had begun Western Union only in the belief that Marshall would support him, Lovett – quite correctly – pointed out that the Americans had only ever been given a vague outline of Bevin's intentions and that Marshall had made *no* specific promises about entering a *military* alliance. Lovett even told the British ambassador, Lord Inverchapel, on 6 February, that the United States government 'does not have any very clear picture of exactly what Mr Bevin's proposals for a Western Union really are'. (Neither did the United States like the British policy of making *bilateral* alliances directed against Germany, with each of the Benelux countries at this time: the Americans and the Benelux countries themselves preferred – and eventually got – a *multilateral* treaty, directed against any aggressor.)[48]

The problem was worsened from the British point of view by the fact that the continentals wanted not mere 'paper' guarantees but concrete actions such as joint defence strategies, the pooling of resources and a combined response to a Soviet attack. In negotiations for the Brussels Treaty, for example, the Belgian Foreign Minister, Paul-Henri Spaak, repeatedly said that he wanted precise military conversations as part of the treaty negotiations.[49] The British military, of course, were very reluctant to reveal details of strategic planning or provide information on forces which the British were planning to send to the continent. One way out, certainly, was to adapt military planning to the requirements of foreign policy as Montgomery wanted, by a commitment to give the defence of Western Europe priority over the Middle East. (Another solution, proposed by Bevin, was not to get bogged down in a detailed examination of defence problems but to lift the Western Union idea to a 'higher' plan involving the examination of economic, spiritual and cultural problems.)[50] But the other Chiefs of Staff remained very reluctant to adopt Montgomery's approach.

A Cabinet meeting on 5 March produced a renewed commitment to the creation of economic and cultural links with Europe and the urgent completion of security pacts. The meeting took place in the wake of the Communist coup in Czechoslovakia and a few days after a telegram from the Washington embassy suggested that bold actions were required in Europe to win American support for Western Union.[51] As a result of the Cabinet discussion the Chiefs of Staff were asked to re-examine their defence policy, effectively in order to produce a military strategy to support

Bevin's foreign policy, a policy which now aimed to conclude treaties with the Scandinavian, Atlantic and Mediterranean powers as well as France and the Benelux. The COS's examination was to focus on two main concerns: actions required to support the diplomatic steps being taken to prevent the spread of Communism; and defence policy in Western Europe in the event of a future war.[52] This crucial meeting therefore launched military planning in a direction not related to Britain's resources (which it never actually had been) nor to an assessment of the Soviet military threat (which in any case was held to be unlikely to emerge) but to the requirements of foreign policy. Neither Tedder nor Cunningham was happy with such a situation. It made no military sense, the latter believed, to hold talks about military support for Europe until sufficient military forces existed. Equally absurd was the failure to consider what the Soviets might do. If war did break out by accident, Cunningham felt that Soviet forces would draw back rather than get involved in a total war, while Tedder believed that the Soviets were thinking of withdrawing East in any war rather than attacking West![53]

The real danger of war in 1948, according to the military planners, lay not in Soviet intentions to strike westwards but in Soviet misperceptions about Anglo-American policy: without a firm and united Western stance the Soviets would encourage internal subversion, particularly in France and Italy, which could force Britain to declare war. For the military the British task was to make the Soviet leaders realize that war *would* be the result if Communism spread westward. This was their first important rationale for any security pacts; the second was to enable anti-Communist forces to take action against their opponents in certain countries (especially France and Italy) without feeling they would provoke a Soviet response.[54] But as Bevin and Montgomery had already argued, these arguments did not go far enough, because *the confidence to resist Communist subversion could not be achieved without an alliance based on an agreement to fight on the Rhine.* A further consideration was that US support could be achieved only once European military co-operation was extended beyond the signing of pacts to the development of a common strategy involving a British continental commitment. By March it was clear that the French, like the Belgians, were not primarily interested in paper security pacts like the one being negotiated by Britain, France and the Benelux countries. They saw the proposed Brussels Treaty as a treaty of military assistance: it was the need for military assistance which had prompted not only Revers's visit, but also a later mission by General Lechères, who was personally instructed by the French President of the Council to discuss unofficially the air defence of Western Europe.[55] The French were attempting to find out if the British were really interested in the joint defence of Western Europe.

The March Cabinet directive forced the COS to define what was termed a 'stop line' for the defence of Europe (to be drawn as far east as possible) alongside the defence of the Middle East. Planning along these lines was related to three separate periods: the immediate future, 1948–50; 1950–6, when it was expected that more resources would be available; and the post-1956 period, when it was assumed that both East and West would have atomic weapons. But it was still argued that no decision could be taken to defend any part of Europe until American support was guaranteed.[56] When the Brussels Treaty was signed on 17 March the COS agreed with Bevin therefore that the next stage was to get the US to underwrite the pact. An Atlantic pact should be made, and to complete the organization of the middle of the planet, a Mediterranean pact should be concluded – though only on the assumption that the United States participated. Future policy, in military eyes, had to be based on a common Anglo-American strategy backed up by American military support.[57] Once the British knew what the United States was prepared to do they would be better equipped to decide which of their own forces would be available for Europe. An American military commitment therefore remained of key importance.

The Americans, however, had still not decided how to support Western Union. Top secret talks with the British and the Canadians had been held at the Pentagon between 22 March and 1 April,[58] and in their wake, General Hollis, Chief Staff Officer to the Ministry of Defence, reported that it was now certain the United States would underwrite the Brussels Treaty and become the leading member of the Atlantic area agreement. Yet there was still uncertainty about the precise form of American backing: would Europe be offered a treaty, a presidential declaration or military aid? Hollis, the military representative at the Pentagon talks, had been sent by the Chiefs of Staff to ask the United States to support one or all of the proposed three pacts – the Brussels Treaty, an Atlantic pact and/ or a Mediterranean arrangement; he was also to try to get US acceptance of both a 'stop line' in Europe 'as far East as possible' and the importance of defending the Middle East. On his return Hollis reported an American acceptance, in principle, of a 'stop line', and his belief that the United States would be willing to come in on any security arrangements that might be made between the European powers.[59] It was therefore a question of making arrangements to link military co-operation with the new security pacts.

At the same time as the Pentagon talks were being held the head of the British Joint Services Mission in Washington requested that the Joint Planning Staff should proceed to the US capital without delay. The idea was that discussions would be held on strategy for the three periods 1948-50, 1950-6 and post-1956.[60] It emerged at the subsequent talks in April that the Americans, with memories of Pearl Harbor, were determined to give priority to an emergency plan based on the resources available at 1 July 1948, and designed to respond to a pre-1950 Soviet attack. Hollis, who remained in Washington, reported a latent American fear that Britain was too weak to mean business, which further strengthened the US service chiefs' resolve to secure British co-operation on emergency planning before turning to long-term collaboration.[61] This presented problems regarding the defence of Western Europe as the British also knew that the 'Dunkirk' approach of January had not changed. For, at the Pentagon talks, General Gruenther emphasized that any American commitment to aid a victim of Soviet attack should *not* require that such aid would be delivered *locally*.[62] This of course was in line with the thinking of Tedder and Cunningham, who were prepared to go to war against the Soviets, but who were not willing to commit land forces to the defence of Western Europe. The Joint Planning Staff too continued to maintain that any emergency short-term plan should not involve a British commitment to fight on the continent.[63] The American and British military were prepared to sign paper treaties with European states, therefore, but they were not ready to defend them if war broke out.

Political demands may have forced the military to define a 'stop line' in Europe, but this was of very limited value since they had not produced an examination of how this line could be defended. In the nature of military thinking in 1948 this was not really surprising: after all, the prime aim was to build up French morale and define a zone in which military action should be taken against Communist regimes, rather than to defend Western Europe against a Soviet attack, which was deemed unlikely! But such logic did not resolve the dilemmas facing the British. For the French and Belgians wanted to know exactly what Britain would do in a war, and the State Department evidently wanted an 'emergency plan' drawn up before they would commit themselves to underwrite Western Union. When, on 10 April, the embassy in Washington reported Lovett's views that the Brussels Treaty would remain a piece of paper until its signatories got to work on active plans for their own defence, no steps had been taken towards serious military talks among the five powers; this was partly because of the British military's suspicion of the French, and partly because the French themselves reasoned that it was pointless to make any defence plans without the Americans, who alone had the resources to provide for the effective defence of Western Europe.[64] Five days later the US ambassador in London emphasized the State Department's position by explaining to Bevin that the integration of the defence plans of the five would impress the authorities in Washington and enable the Europeans to decide what they needed in terms of American support.[65] This support therefore increasingly seemed to depend on European co-operation on force allocation and short-term planning to meet a Soviet attack.

On 16 April the British learned of a State Department questionnaire to be sent to the five signatories of the Brussels Treaty requesting information on such issues as whether equipment would be pooled and standardized; whether the military organization would be structured on multilateral lines; and, most crucially, on what forces the five powers would assemble and what plan of action they would follow in the initial stages of the conflict before American help arrived.[66] That same day Bevin told Bidault he had reason to believe that the United States wanted the Brussels Treaty powers to make military arrangements without delay, and that this was likely to result in American participation in security arrangements. It is significant that Bevin also told Bidault he was opposed to American involvement *'from the beginning'* because they would 'tell us what we should do'. This shows that in April Bevin was still determined to build up Western European co-operation under British leadership *before* US involvement: Western Europe should prepare its *own plans* while securing US *support*. The French on the other hand saw value in military preparations only if the USA were directly involved in the initial stages. Bidault's response highlighted once again the 'vicious circle' in Western defence planning. For, before the Europeans began to make preparations, Bidault believed that the Americans should tell the Europeans what support they could provide.[67] The agreement reached by the Brussels powers reflected the French position more than the British; it stated that while the Europeans were ready to make arrangements for military talks, they would 'simultaneously require the assistance of the United States, in order to organize the effective defence of Western Europe'.[68] A Military Staff Committee of the Brussels Treaty Organization was then formed on 30 April and charged with 'preparing jointly the building up and the eventual use in the field of the forces of the Five Powers for the defence of Western Europe'.[69] More specifically this meant assessing what forces would be available and how the Europeans would use them in the initial stages of a conflict.

These issues had actually been considered on an Anglo-American basis at the military planning talks held in Washington in April. As a result of these discussions, which made each side aware of the other's thinking, the Joint Planning Staff eventually produced two parallel emergency plans, HALFMOON and DOUBLEQUICK. The British plan DOUBLE-QUICK was the first attempt to define in detail a response to a Soviet attack, but it was based on the evacuation from Europe of the occupation forces in Germany. An initial draft was available in early May and it contained a commitment to withdraw Anglo-American forces from the continent. This plan served only to highlight the problems Britain had become tangled in. It was drawn up because it was *militarily* essential to co-operate with the United States; but because it was also *politically* essential to co-operate with Western Europe, it was vital that the Western Europeans should *not* find out how the Anglo-Saxons intended to co-operate with them in military terms. This they would certainly do if the

British gave specific answers to the State Department 'questionnaire'. Bevin himself may not have grasped this essential point because he wanted answers provided and was interested in psychological reassurance for Europe. The COS, however, were unsurprisingly opposed to providing details of British planning, albeit on the grounds that they could not provide top secret information until they were satisfied with Western Union security arrangements.[70]

Whatever Bevin's commitment to Western Union as an idea, little had actually been done on the practical side to resolve the dilemmas and contradictions of its implementation. The Foreign Secretary considered that the organization of Europe as part of his 'grand design' should be done primarily by Britain and the Europeans and *underwritten* by a US security guarantee. But this required the building of greater European confidence in their ability to resist Communist pressure which itself required greater military co-operation with Britain and not merely a paper guarantee. This in turn, however, required a change in British strategy which, so most of the military argued, could be done only on an Anglo-American basis. Yet the Americans appeared unlikely to support a military strategy geared more to the continent of Europe. Worse, even a paper guarantee would not be given by the United States until Britain and the Europeans had evolved a short-term strategy for the defence of Western Europe; but if the British gave details of their emergency planning this would be disastrous for the political organization of Western Union because the British in blunt terms planned to abandon the continent to its fate – as indeed did the Americans. The fact that the Soviets were not expected to launch war as a deliberate act of policy was little comfort, because of growing concern about an 'accidental' conflict. British and US leaders may have believed that the Europeans *would* be given psychological reassurance by paper guarantees alone, but the continentals (especially the French) were clear that the only genuine 'psychological reassurance' was the creation of effective defences.

The emergence of these dilemmas in early May produced attempts to resolve the most obvious contradictions. The primacy of political requirements produced a ministerial decision to make a commitment to fight as 'far east in Germany as possible', although where that should be would have to be considered by the military. On 5 May the COS began to discuss it, with Montgomery arguing that British troops in Germany should stay and fight on the Rhine. On this occasion he got support from Tedder but met the expected resistance from Cunningham, who argued that this was not possible and therefore it would be sensible to continue with the realistic American policy of evacuation on which DOUBLE-QUICK was based. Yet Montgomery refused to see such things in terms of what was realistic. He actually conceded that in Western Union Britain was linked to something which 'militarily was a nonsense', but said this did not matter as, with the Soviets unlikely to start a war in the immediate future, an examination of the practicality of fighting was not really required. What was needed was to imbue the Western Europeans with the spirit to resist aggression and to reorganize their forces on the correct lines within the next ten years, when war would be more likely. One needed a paper *commitment* to stay and fight on the Rhine to boost European morale but *actual* resources were not needed. By 12 May the arguments had produced two results. The first was the revision of DOUB-LEQUICK in order to remove references to evacuation, and the revised version was sent to the Americans with an explanation of the change; it was hoped that the Americans would then incorporate the British amendment into their emergency plan, which would then look palatable to Europeans. Second, the COS decided that British forces would stay and fight on the Rhine 'unless and until pushed out'.

This tentative strategy, now geared to the political requirements of the 'stop line', was unlikely to boost the confidence of the Western Europeans on its own however, at least not unless reinforcements were provided. Yet the provision of British reinforcements was ruled out by both the CIGS and the Minister of Defence.[71] Montgomery may have been the British military leader most interested in European defence but as seen above this did not mean that he wanted to provide resources, in the short term, to defend the continent. He was hoping to build up European confidence for a war in ten years' time. Actually, however, Montgomery was not correct in thinking that a simple commitment to fight on the Rhine was all that was required. In terms of European morale such a commitment could not be divorced from emergency planning; if the conflict between military strategy and the goals of foreign policy was to be resolved in order to improve European security Anglo-American policy would have to change on both evacuation and reinforcement.

There was of course no inclination to do this, even on the part of Montgomery, and in consequence the reply to the State Department was vague on crucial issues and misrepresented British military thinking. The response provided by the Brussels Treaty Military Committee in fact told the State Department that they were preparing an inventory both of the total military resources 'mobilisable in the near future' and of 'the potential military forces' of the five powers. The aim was to fight as 'far east in Germany as possible', and to hold the Soviets on the best position, covering the territory of the five powers, to enable American military power to intervene.[72] The reply reflected British reticence and the desire of the Brussels powers to persuade the State Department that they were ready to fight. It was a vague document and the difference between its bold aims and the resources available to fulfil it was enormous.

In the State Department George Kennan's staff drew up papers in May advocating a policy which would produce US participation in the Military

Committee of the Brussels Treaty Organization 'with a view to: (a) concerting military plans for use in the event that the USSR should resort *in the short term future* to aggressive action in Germany, Austria or elsewhere in Europe, and (b) drawing up a coordinated military supply plan'.[73] Kennan's ideas on military co-operation reflected his opposition to formal military alliances or pacts; they were in line with French thinking, because Bidault was 'not interested in guarantees' but in practical, concrete measures to increase European security. This view was embodied in Lovett's message to the French ambassador in Washington explaining 'we are not thinking and have never thought of "guarantees", but we are thinking of practical measures to increase security'.[74] In the Foreign Office, the attempt to get American backing for Western Union was accompanied by what, since March, was a more urgent desire to create an Atlantic treaty organization. Bevin wanted a treaty, because he feared that a mere 'presidential declaration' by the USA would leave Britain waiting for aid in a new conflict as in 1939–41. But however many pacts were signed, they would not provide additional military resources on the outbreak of war as desired by the French. A pact might be better than a declaration, but it was still only a piece of paper and would not help to build up Western Union, especially if on the outbreak of war, American troops were going to 'evacuate' rather than reinforce Europe; that would mean 1940 all over again.

In early May the British Foreign Secretary was still grappling with the challenge of finding practical measures, based on Britain's military strategy, which would cement Western Union and achieve the desired impact on the French. But the task proved impossible. What Bevin hoped for was a satisfactory understanding about the unity of the military forces in Western Europe and a commitment to deploy them from the start of a conflict; he then wished to discover the strength of available forces so as to decide on strategy and the feasibility of defending the Rhine.[75] But this was simply obtuse, because it failed to recognize the inseparability of global military strategy and the availability of forces for Western Europe. The amount of troops which could be deployed would inevitably depend on what forces were allocated to other theatres, which, for Britain, meant primarily the Middle East, still deemed in strategic terms the most important region. Later in the year the French were to insist on the British providing full details of their military resources on a global basis, rather than those which Britain intended to commit to a European theatre. This met with a blunt refusal on the grounds that it 'would at once lead to arguments about our strategy which was no concern of the French'.[76]

In May the French, encouraged by the aims of the State Department, formally requested, through the Brussels Military Committee, that the Western Union powers take steps to prepare plans to meet a sudden emergency. Predictably the first British military response was to suggest misleading the French by telling them that Britain and the United States were still in the process of preparing such plans. Unfortunately this would only postpone the evil day, so it was suggested that the military governors of Germany should draw up plans for a withdrawal to the Rhine.[77] This idea sidestepped the fundamental problem of reconciling Anglo-American emergency planning with support for Western Union based on a common European strategy for its defence. As the Minister of Defence explained in early June, short-term planning to fight with what was immediately available was confined to Britain and the United States; only long-term planning was to be built around Western Union in conjunction with the Americans.[78] Moreover, as the British now became aware, French feelings were such that a commitment to stay and fight on the Rhine was neither here nor there: what the French required were reinforcements for the continent, and this the British had definitely ruled out in terms of both land and air forces. The British, so it was decided, could not therefore reveal to the Western Europeans details of any Anglo-American planning which did not cater for the dispatch of reinforcements to the continent.[79]

In June 1948, when the Berlin blockade began in earnest and brought greater danger of 'war by accident', the British military were opposed to integrating the Americans into a future command organization for Western Union until their attitudes were 'sorted out'.[80] As Templer explained later in the year, any exchange of information on operational planning would sooner or later lead to the disclosure of US intentions to retreat from Europe in a war, and this would help produce a situation where Britain was faced with the breakdown of Western Union or the virtual cessation of defence collaboration with the United States.[81] The Americans themselves obliged by joining the Brussels Military Committee merely as observers. But the contradiction between the political unity of Western Europe and the military response to an immediate Soviet attack was made more acute by the Berlin crisis. With even Cunningham now convinced that the five year rule for a future war was dead, and that short-term measures were required because of the greater risk of 'war by accident', the pressures for emergency planning were mounting. But the British military got even colder feet over Western Union largely because of their continuing fears of lax French security. This fear assumed a new dimension with the commitment to withdraw to the Rhine; if the Germans got wind of that it would be another blow to the concept of Western Union. In addition the military continued to claim that Communism was rife in the French government, in French military research establishments and in the French Service ministries; Cunningham argued that the integration of British and French forces would mean that British weakness would be known to the Soviets: if Western Union did that it would reduce, not increase, British security.[82] What is more, on the economic front there was a growing belief that the European Recovery Programme would not close the gap between

Europe's needs and her productive capacity within the allotted time. Here was another area in which difficulties were producing an apparent loss of impetus in proceeding with Western Union. The French economic planner, Jean Monnet, believed that the time was ripe therefore for an Anglo-French political federation. In the Foreign Office, Jebb, while accepting that this would improve the economic situation in Western Europe, believed that the political obstacles in the way of federation were too large. But with Bevin still interested in pressing ahead with Western Union some means of giving it fresh impetus would have to be found, or hopes of maintaining British equality with the USA and USSR would be dashed.

With the Washington talks on security beginning on 6 July, and pessimistic assessments of possible progress for Western Union on the political and economic fronts the onus was very much on the military aspects of Western Union. Given the attitudes of the Chiefs of Staff, Jebb concluded that an extension of the Brussels Treaty was neither practicable nor desirable and that, if it ever was to be extended, the entry by the United States into some larger system of Atlantic security would be a *conditio sine qua non*. In short, Britain could not provide the kind of military co-operation desired by the Europeans. Consequently, as Jebb pointed out, if Western Union was to succeed some form of military involvement by the United States would be necessary.[83] Moreover, as Kirkpatrick had stated in early January, a paper pact with US membership would look far more formidable than a European treaty and – even if the French remained desperate to get actual US military equipment, joint emergency planning and additional forces to defend the Rhine[84] – it could prove an important psychological boost to Western Europe. Another paper pact, even if it was again 'militarily a nonsense', would at least offer the prospect of papering over the divisions likely to be opened by attempts to co-ordinate practical measures to meet a Soviet attack. The Atlantic Pact was the result, and its birth therefore owed more to the difficulty of implementing Bevin's initial ideas on Western Union than to their successful realization.

Western Union was initially conceived, not as the first step towards NATO, but as part of a general long-term design to reassert British power and influence. Britain, by forging closer links with Africa, the Dominions and Western Europe, would organize the middle of the planet and this third force would then be underwritten by the United States; but initial American involvement in the mechanics of its organization was not seen as necessary or desirable. By July, however, as talks on an Atlantic Pact finally began, progress towards a Western Union under British auspices appeared increasingly problematic. In part this was due to the problems which arose in other areas of co-operation – European customs unions and colonial co-operation in Africa – but one of the most important reasons lay in the difficulty of creating the kind of military co-operation deemed necessary by the Western European powers. Historians, most of whom praise Bevin's Western Union policy for drawing the USA into European defence, have tended to confuse the political and military aspects of security, by failing to distinguish between the development of combined military planning and the provision of paper guarantees. When one surveys the details of military security talks in 1948, it is clear that British policy offered nothing more than paper guarantees, which were of limited use in reassuring the continentals about how an actual Soviet attack would be met. What the French, in particular, required was short-term joint planning geared to the provision of land forces to meet a Soviet attack in Europe. In the first half of 1948 the French military too believed that the only practical response to an immediate Soviet attack was withdrawal from Europe, but the French hoped that Britain would commit herself to European defence and help to win American support for a continental strategy, given that (as was universally recognized) only the Americans had the necessary resources to provide defence equipment. British military thinking was, however, based on co-operation with the United States on a global strategy in which reinforcements for the Middle East took precedence over those for Western Europe.

Although the reluctance of some leading military figures to accept *any* form of closer co-operation with the French was overcome by Bevin and Montgomery, daunting problems remained. Far from seeing emergency planning for war in Europe as a vital aim, Bevin hoped to boost French morale by embarking on a long-term scheme which would gear British military strategy and foreign policy aims more towards Europe. The problem was that Britain's limited resources and the US military's reluctance to co-operate in taking practical steps to defend Western Europe in 1948 made this difficult to achieve. It became even more difficult when the State Department and the Quai d'Orsay both linked Western Union to emergency planning and European decisions on the allocation of actual forces. Unfortunately paper pacts and vague statements were all that the British could offer, and these were of limited use when the French were obsessed with the dangers of war breaking out 'by accident'. Thus the French desire for an American alliance was strengthened by the British failure to make the Brussels Treaty into an effective military organization or a vehicle for genuine European co-operation.

From the British point of view the military rationale for Western Union was not the need to respond to a Soviet attack *in 1948*: nor did Western Union produce the kind of military co-operation that the French and the State Department required. As such the idea of Bevin successfully organizing European security arrangements with the aim of involving the United States in the defence of Europe requires substantial revision. An Atlantic treaty was certainly Bevin's idea, and from March 1948 its creation was deemed the most vital of the envisaged system of security pacts. But it has to be remembered that political moves to link the United States with

Europe in 1948 were often accompanied by British moves to keep the Americans and continentals apart, by restricting genuine military co-operation to an Anglo-American basis and refusing to tell the Europeans anything about this. One result was that when talks on an Atlantic Pact began in July 1948 the French and the Benelux states were unprepared for American thinking on security, and very disappointed that the USA (like Britain) would offer only a paper guarantee in the short term.[85] From the British records it emerges that Whitehall was never as keen as the State Department to encourage the kind of military co-operation favoured by the Quai d'Orsay: on that subject Britain's position was one of discouraging rather than promoting American involvement with Europe, while being unable to offer the Europeans the kind of support they required.

Contrary to Foreign Office fears France and the Benelux states *did* prove ready to make a security pact in 1948: indeed it was the French who pressed for a Belgian treaty in December 1947 and the Belgians who strove to make it into a meaningful and wide-ranging alliance. All these states also fully understood the need for US support and joined Bevin in making appeals for this. However, France and Belgium also wanted to begin military planning in earnest and here Bevin quite failed to provide the necessary leadership. By concentrating on the question of paper guarantees some writers have come to praise Bevin in early 1948 for 'breaking the vicious circle of American hesitancy and European lack of confidence' regarding Western security.[86] In fact the existence of a 'vicious circle' in February 1948 was due to Britain's failure to fuse its Western Union plans with what Europe required and what the Americans were able to give. As a result Bevin's own schemes for maintaining British power underwent a profound change. The original political goals of Western Union proved irreconcilable with closer military co-operation in the first seven months of 1948, and in the months following July 1948 Bevin turned from a policy based primarily on co-operation with Western Europe, and designed to maintain British influence in the world independent of the USA, to a very different policy where Britain became the USA's most loyal lieutenant in an Atlantic community.

NOTES

1 See especially S. Greenwood, 'Ernest Bevin, France and Western Union', *European History Quarterly* Vol. 14 (1984); J. Kent, 'Bevin's Imperialism and the Idea of Euro-Africa', in M. Dockrill and J. W. Young (eds) *British Foreign Policy, 1945–56* (London, 1989); G. Warner's essay in R. Ovendale (ed.) *The Foreign Policy of the British Labour Governments, 1945–51* (Leicester, 1984); J. W. Young, *Britain, France and the Unity of Europe, 1945–51* (Leicester, 1984).

2 Young, ibid., pp. 38–40, 48, 71–2, 87–8, 119–23; Kent, 'Bevin's Imperialism', 63–8.

3 In this account we have deliberately avoided detailed discussions on the making of the Brussels Treaty and the consideration of other paper guarantees, choosing to concentrate

on military planning. On the Brussels Treaty talks see especially A. Varsori, *Il Patto de Bruxelles* (Rome, 1988).

4 In general on the wartime debates about a 'Western bloc' see Sir L. Woodward, *British Foreign Policy in the Second World War, Vol. V.* (London, 1976), pp. 181–97.

5 See especially the various accounts of Bevin's special meeting with officials to discuss policy in Western Europe on 13.8.45: Public Record Office (PRO), FO 371/49069/9595 minutes and records of 13–21 August; Alexander Cadogan's diary, Churchill College, Cambridge, 1/15, of 13.8.45; Oliver Harvey's diary, British Library, London, of 13.8.45.

6 In general see Young, *Britain, France and the Unity of Europe* Chapters 2–5.

7 FO 371/67670/25, Sargent minute, 21.12.46.

8 FO 371/67670/723. Paris to FO, 18.1.47; Hoyar-Millar minute, 21.1.47. and Bevin to Duff Cooper, 23.1.47.

9 FO 371/67671/1662, 10.2.47 letter enclosing JP (47) 14; DEFE. 4/1, the JP paper.

10 FO 371/67724/4670 record of meeting, 7.5.47. and 5705, JP (47) 70 of 4.6.47.

11 On the post-war French army see especially the essays by J. Delmas, P. Lassalle, C. Lévy and J. Vernet, in Institut d'Histoire de Temps Present et l'Institut Charles de Gaulle, *De Gaulle et la Nation Face aux Problèmes de Defense, 1945–6* (Paris, 1983).

12 For the debate between Attlee and Bevin see R. Smith and J. Zametica, 'The Cold Warrior – Clement Attlee Reconsidered 1945–47', *International Affairs* Vol. 61, no. 2 (1985). More specifically *Documents on British Policy Overseas*, Series I Vol. 1, Document 179, and Vol. II, Document 18, and for the ideas of the military planners, JP(46) 45 Revised Final 31.3.46 in AIR9/267/DO(46) 80 18.6.46 in CAB 131/3 and DO(47) 23 7.3.47 in CAB 131/4 and COS(47) 5(0) Final 23.1.47 in DEFE 5/3, DO(46) 47 2.4.46 in CAB 131/2, DO(46) 80 18.4.46 in CAB 131/3 and for discussions in the Defence Committee DO(46) 22nd meeting 19.7.46 in CAB 131/1. On the defence talks in 1947 see FO371/61557–9. The military attitudes to Egypt are in CAB 84/81 JP(46) 100 Final 23.5.46 Annex 1.

13 For a fuller analysis see J. W. Young, *France, the Cold War and the Western Alliance 1944–9* (London, 1990), pp. 169–72.

14 FO 371/67674/9992, records of talks, 21.10.47 and 9376 Harvey minute 21.10.47.

15 FO 371/67674/10271, Duff Cooper to Bevin, reply, and Crosthwaite minute, 13, 21, 28.11.47 and undated Bevin minute.

16 FO 371/67674/10907, Duff Cooper to Bevin and reply, 5 and 17.12.47; FO 371/67674/11010, record of Bevin-Bidault talk, 17.12.47; FO 371/67674/11009, record of Bevin-Marshall talk, 17.12.47.

17 FO 371/67674/11125 Roberts minute, 22.12.47 and 11126 Montgomery to Bevin, 23.12.47.

18 COS (47) 162, 23.12.47 and annexed letter from COS Secretary to Foreign Office 24.12.47, copied in FO 371/67674/1127.

19 DEFE 4/10 JP (48) 4 Final, 6.1.48.

20 FO 371/62555/12502 minutes of 22.12.47–4.1.48.

21 A. Bullock, *Ernest Bevin, Foreign Secretary, 1945–51* (London, 1983). See also E. Barker's statement that Western Union was 'in one sense a sprat to catch a whale', in *The British between the Superpowers, 1945–50* (1983), p. 127, and see pp. 112–20 for one of the few discussions of British military planning in early 1948.

22 CAB 129/23 CP (48) 6. 4.1.48. And, on what was said to the Americans, see *Foreign Relations of the United States (FRUS), 1948, Vol. III* (Washington, 1974), pp. 4–6. We are grateful to one of our postgraduate students, Mr John Milloy, for analysing the differences between the Cabinet paper and the telegram to Washington. The established accounts of the making of NATO from the British side fail to point out the differences between these two documents, and so gravely underestimate the importance of the 'third force'. (They also tend to concentrate on the issue of military *pacts*, and so fail to note the impact of actual military *planning* on Bevin's policies.) See especially Bullock, *Ernest Bevin*, p. 517; J. Baylis, 'Britain the Brussels Pact and the Continental Commitment', *International Affairs* Vol. 60 (autumn 1984), p. 620 – an account which exaggerates Britain's 'continental commitment' in 1948; M. Folly, 'Breaking the Vicious Circle', *Diplomatic History* Vol. 12 (winter, 1988), p. 62 insists that 'British links would . . . be at least as strong with . . . the United States' as with Europe, but does later, pp. 64–5, give consideration to military planning.

23 FO 371/67674/11127 Sargent to Stapleton, 1 Jan. COS meeting and Kirkpatrick minute, 7.1.48 and Crosthwaite letter of 9.1.48. Also DEFE 4/10, COS (48) 3rd, 7.1.48.

24 CAB 131/5, DO (48) 2nd, 8.1.48 and 3rd, 14.1.48 and see DEFE 4/4, COS (47) 163rd, 23.12.47 on consideration of a continental commitment.

25 On the speech see Hansard, House of Commons debates, Vol. 446, cols 387–409.

26 This formula was used more than once.

27 The term 'middle of the planet' was used in a Commons speech in September. Hansard House of Commons Debates, Vol. 456, col. 106, and in a conversation between Bevin and Dalton in October. B. Pimlott (ed.) *The Political Diary of Hugh Dalton*, (London, 1986), p. 443.

28 On French pressure for a Belgian treaty: FO 371/73045/321, Sargent minute, 23.12.47, FO 371/67679/10969, Kirkpatrick to Rendel, 18.12.47.

29 FO 371/73045/322, Kirkpatrick minute, 30.12.47.

30 *FRUS 1948, III*, 7–8.

31 FO 371/73045/322, Roberts minute, 8.1.48.

32 FO 371/73045/273, FO to Washington and Paris. 13.1.48; *FRUS 1948, III*, 3–4. These telegrams were drafted by Ivone Kirkpatrick. But see especially FO 371/73045/353. Bevin minute, 12.1.48 on Bevin's plans.

33 FO 371/73045/323, Kirkpatrick minute, 9.1.48. Kirkpatrick shared the COS fears about French security.

34 FO 371/73045/353 Bevin minute 12.1.48 and see above note 21 on the 'sprat to catch a mackerel'.

35 ibid. and 354 Bevin minute, 12.1.48.

36 Service Historique, Armé de Terre, Vincennes, 4 Q 37, dossier 2, 25.1.48. On French views of the visit see also V. Auriol, *Journal du Septennat, Vol. II, 1948* (Paris, 1974) pp. 57, 64–5; Ministère des Affaires Etrangères, Paris, René Massigli papers, Vol. 93, reports by Massigli to Paris, 1.12.47–28.1.48.

37 DEFE 4/10 JP(48) 4. 6.1.48 'Subjects for Discussions with the Americans'.

38 DEFE 4/10 COS(48) 14th 28.1.48.

39 DEFE 4/11 J.P. (48) 28 (Final) 13.3.48, approved as COS (48) 59.

40 DEFE 4/10 COS (48) 15th 30.1.48. Discussions on JP (48) 16 (Final).

41 FO 800/452 Minute by Bevin 12.1.48. And see the memorandum sent by Montgomery to Bevin for approval *before* he put it to the other Chiefs of Staff.

42 FO 800/452 Montgomery to General Omar Bradley 8.3.48. Referring to Bevin's instructions given 'some time ago'.

43 DEFE 5/10 COS (48) 26 (0) 30.1.48.

44 DEFE 4/10 COS (48) 18th, 4.2.48.

45 DEFE 4/10 COS (48) 16th, 2.2.48.

46 DEFE 4/10 COS (48) 18th, 4.2.48; DEFE 5/10 COS (48) 30 7.2.48.

47 *FRUS 1948, Vol. III* (Washington, 1974), pp. 7–12.

48 ibid., pp. 12–16, 17–18, 19–20, 21–3.

49 FO 371/73047/1174 and 1250 Minute by W. N. M. Hog 12.2.48; Minute by H MacNeil 7.2.48.

50 FO 371/73048/1318 FO to Paris 16.2.48.

51 CAB 128/12 CM (48) 19th 5.3.48; FO 371/73050/1827 and 1778 Balfour to Wright 28.2.48 and Minutes by P. M. Crosthwaite 4.3.48.

52 DEFE 4/11 COS (48) 34th 9.3.48; DEFE 5/10 COS (48) 58 17.3.48.

53 DEFE 4/11 COS (48) 37th, 15.3.48; DEFE 4/11 COS (48) 39th, 17.3.48.

54 DEFE 4/11 COS (48) 41st, 18.3.48. Annex.

55 DEFE 5/10 COS (48) 65 25.3.48 Record of meeting with General Lechères.

56 DEFE 4/11 COS (48) 39th 17.3.48; DEFE 5/10 COS (48) 58 17.3.48. When Attlee questioned the Chiefs of Staff as to whether Communist coups West of the stop line would be regarded by them as a *casus belli* Montgomery's response was if France and Benelux were under Russian domination this would bring Britain almost to the point of war and the United States might feel Communist domination of Norway was equally dangerous. DEFE 4/11 COS (48) 42nd, 19.3.48.

57 DEFE 4/11 COS (48) 37th, 15.3.48; FO 800/452 Memorandum by the Chief Staff Officer

to the Minister of Defence 17.3.48. This order of priority was changed by Bevin on 18 March because of what was seen as a Soviet threat to Norway.

58 See *FRUS, 1948, Vol. III*, pp. 59–67, 69–75.
59 DEFE 5/10 COS (48) 75 7.4.48; COS (48) 75 Annex II Copy of General Hollis' Telegram 6.4.48; COS (48) 95 Annex Memorandum by Hollis 20.4.48.
60 DEFE 4/12 COS (48) 46th 31.3.48 Confidential Annex; JP (48) 35 30.3.48.
61 DEFE 5/10 COS (48) 75th 7.4.48 Annex II Copy of telegram from General Hollis 6.4.48; COS (48) 95th Annex Memorandum by Hollis 20.4.48.
62 *FRUS, 1948, Vol. III*, 70. Minutes of 4th meeting of US–UK–Canada Security Negotiations 29.3.48.
63 DEFE 4/12 COS (48) 46th 31.3.48 Confidential Annex.
64 FO 371/68068 A Washington to FO 10.4.48; on French attitudes see *FRUS 1948 Vol. III*, pp. 84–5 Caffery (US Ambassador in Paris) to Secretary of State 13.4.48 pp. 88–9 Douglas (US Ambassador in London) to Secretary of State 16.4.48 giving Bevin's view that the French were to blame for the delay.
65 FO 371/68068 A/1618 Bevin to Lord Inverchapel 15.4.48.
66 FO 371/68068 A/1664 Lord Inverchapel to FO 16.4.48 and *FRUS 1948 Vol. III*, Douglas to Secretary of State 14.5.48 123–6.
67 FO 371/73057/3413 Record of Bevin/Bidault Conversation 16.4.48.
68 *FRUS, 1948, Vol. III*, 91 Bidault and Bevin to Marshall 17.4.48.
69 *FRUS, 1948, Vol. III*, 147. The full directive is in DEFE 4/13.
70 DEFE 4.13 COS (48) 64th 10.5.48; COS (48) 56th 23.4.48; COS (48) 57th 26.4.48.
71 DEFE 4/13 COS (48) 62nd 5.5.48 Confidential Annex; COS (48) 64th 10.5.48; COS (48) 66th 12.5.48.
   The American plan HALFMOON, completed in July 1948, contained under the heading of 'Evacuation' a statement that the initial withdrawal would be to the Rhine, with a further retreat either to the Channel coast or the Pyrenees, see T. Etzold and J.L. Gaddis (eds) *Containment: Documents on US Policy and Strategy 1945–50* (1978), p. 318.
   The British study of whether it was feasible to defend the Rhine was not initiated until after the Berlin crisis began, and it concluded in September that it was totally impossible, see DEFE 4/16.
72 *FRUS, 1948, Vol. III*, p. 125, Douglas to Secretary of State 14.5.48.,
73 Ibid., 117 Kennan to Lovett 7.5.48. Enclosing a policy paper which emphasized that the Europeans must first plan their coordinated defence with the means *'presently available'*. See *FRUS, Vol. III* 140.
74 ibid., 121 Lovett to the embassy in France 14.5.48.
75 CAB 127/341 Record of Downing Street meeting between Bevin, Attlee, Alexander and Montgomery, 7.5.48.
76 DEFE 4/15 COS (48) 122nd 3.9.48.
77 DEFE 4/13 COS (48) 70th Annex 24.5.48; COS (48) 72nd 26.5.48.
78 DEFE 4/13 COS (48) 79th 9.6.48.
79 DEFE 4/13 COS (48) 72nd Annex II Copy of letter from General Hollis to Minister of Defence 25.5.48.
80 DEFE 4/13 COS (48) 83rd Annex 18.6.48.
81 DEFE 4/17 COS (48) 153rd 29.10.48.
82 DEFE 4/15 COS (48) 106th 28.7.48; DEFE 4/14 COS (48) 85th Annex 23.6.48.
83 FO 371/73060/5801 Sir Oliver Harvey to Sir Ivone Kirkpatrick 26.6.48; Minute by G. Jebb 2.7.48; Minute by F. K. Roberts 8.7.48; G. Jebb to Sir Oliver Harvey 12.7.48.
84 On French planning at this point see Young, *France, the Cold War and the Western Alliance*, pp. 181–3.
85 ibid., pp. 215–17.
86 Folly, 'Breaking the Vicious Circle', p. 77; and for a recent account see J. Baylis, *Britain and the Formation of NATO*, International Politics Research Paper, 7 November, UCW, Aberystwyth, 1989.

8

Britain's strategy for Europe: must West Germany be rearmed? 1949–51

Saki Dockrill

By 1949 there were no serious doubts in Whitehall about the need to assimilate West Germany politically and economically into the Western orbit. However, the resolution of the military implications of the German question, without contributing further to Cold War tensions and without precipitating the re-emergence of Germany as a threat to world peace, remained a major problem. This chapter will explain how Britain came to view the defence of Western Europe, which necessitated rearming the West Germans, as crucial to her security and yet why the British Labour government remained somewhat hesitant in its support for the remilitarization of West Germany.

BRITAIN'S INITIAL STRATEGY FOR EUROPE BEFORE 1949

Britain's political aim in Europe lay in consolidating the democratic Western European societies, including the three Western zones of occupied Germany, in order to counter the formation of a 'solid political and economic bloc' by the Kremlin.[1] This broad concept of Western Union was introduced to the Cabinet in January 1948 by the Foreign Secretary, Ernest Bevin, as a substitute for the Foreign Office's original aim of maintaining the wartime triumvirate of Britain, the United States and the Soviet Union in the post-war world.[2]

The urgent need for Western Union was reinforced by what Britain perceived as the increasingly aggressive behaviour of the Soviet Union so recently demonstrated by the Communist take-over of Czechoslovakia in February 1948. Bevin's initiative led to the establishment of the Brussels Treaty Organization (or the Western Union) in March 1948.[3] The military exploitation of German resources in the face of the potential threat of the Soviet Union had already been suggested by British military planners on the eve of the fall of Nazi Germany.[4] However, distrust of the Germans remained robust both in the Labour Party and in the country at large and the Cabinet at the end of 1948 confirmed the existing allied policy of transforming the three Western zones of Germany into a democratic state, which would be linked economically and politically to the West. Any consideration of West Germany for the defence of Western Europe was judged, in the words of Bevin, to be 'premature'.[5]

BRITAIN'S SEARCH FOR A MILITARY ROLE IN EUROPE AND THE FORMATION OF THE NORTH ATLANTIC TREATY IN 1949

From the strategic and military point of view Europe was regarded by both civilian and military leaders as 'only part of our overall strategy' until 1949.[6] Britain's aspirations for the retention of her global status and her remaining overseas commitments dictated that the Middle East be given the highest strategic priority.[7] Moreover, military planners did not expect the USSR to be in a position to resort to war with the West before 1957, given her technological backwardness and the exhaustion of an economy which had suffered enormous losses during the recent war.[8]

Consequently, there was no agreed British defence strategy for Europe, and the only deterrence to Soviet threats was provided by the American atomic bombs. Of course, the Chiefs of Staff were well aware that the defence of Britain would be greatly strengthened if her allies in Europe became capable of resisting the enemy 'as far to the East as possible' – probably on the River Rhine.[9] It was even more essential for Britain to secure early and full American military support on the continent.[10]

However, the Western European states, who had barely recovered from the Second World War, were unable to do much towards building up their defences. The morale of the French Army, whose reconstruction Britain considered to be the key to the defence of Western Europe, was low.[11] Nor did the USA make it clear how many troops and how much military equipment she was prepared to send to Europe if the Soviet Union should attack Western Europe. British leaders realized that Britain on her own could do little to defend Western Europe, given her own technological weakness and her inadequate resources, unless the Western Europeans and the Americans became more serious about their own defence preparations.[12]

The Prime Minister, Clement Attlee, warned his colleagues at a meeting of the Cabinet Defence Committee in February 1948 that once the British Army became involved in a continental war, 'previous experience had shown how Continental commitments initially small, were apt to grow into very large ones'.[13] Thus Britain's short-term European strategy was to fight on the continent with those British forces already stationed in occupied Germany, that is two and one-third divisions and a tactical air force of 141 aircraft.[14]

Since a British soldier, Field Marshal Montgomery, was chairman of the Commander-in-Chief's Committee of the Brussels Treaty, her continental allies naturally pressed Britain to reinforce her forces assigned to the Western Union. In June 1949 the Chiefs of Staff reluctantly agreed to send one infantry brigade group to support the Dutch armed forces in the event of war.[15] They also informed the Western Union that Britain would increase her military manpower by 1951, which would enable her to raise four additional infantry divisions and two armoured brigades three months after mobilization, provided that she could overcome her equipment difficulties. This force planning for the Western Union's interim plan did not substantially alter Britain's global strategy, as her defence role within the agreed Western Union strategy was to defend the Middle East but not to send substantial armed forces to Central Europe.[16]

The formation of NATO and the US Mutual Defence Assistance Bill enabled Britain to justify further reliance on American economic and military power for the defence of Western Europe. However, NATO's first 'strategic concept' in December 1949 did not require any drastic change in the existing Anglo-American commitment to Europe. While the United States continued her preparation for the strategic bombing of the Soviet Union in the event of war,[17] she rejected Britain's pressure to become a full member of three European regional groups which were to be set up within NATO for detailed defence planning.[18] Britain's main contributions to NATO were the defence of sea communications (in co-operation with the USA) and the security of the Middle East, while the other European allies, and particularly France, were to be responsible for building up ground forces in Central Europe.[19] There was no question of taking into account West Germany's possible defence role and indeed the NATO medium-term plan envisaged that NATO's defences would be based on the River Rhine, which meant writing off the territory of West Germany in the event of war with the Soviet Union.[20] Conversely, given the great gap between the reported Soviet 175 divisions and total allied forces of about 12 divisions in Central Europe, arguments about defence, whether on the Rhine or on the Elbe were academic: there were really insufficient forces to hold any line at all.[21]

CHANGES IN BRITAIN'S EUROPEAN STRATEGY MARCH–MAY 1950

Britain's declining confidence in the utility of the American nuclear deterrent after the successful Soviet atomic explosion in August 1949 made her anxious by October 1949 to 'withstand the greater concentration of power now stretching from China to the Oder'.[22] Britain was quicker than the United States to respond to this increased threat from the Communist camp. First, at the end of 1949, the Cabinet approved a defence budget of £780 million for 1950–1, a considerable increase on the average annual expenditure of £600 million between 1947 and 1949. This marked the

195

first sign of a move away from the low priority hitherto accorded to the nation's defence in favour of the recovery of the civilian sector of the economy.[23]

Second, the Cabinet Defence Committee accepted in March 1950 a Chiefs of Staff's recommendation that Britain should provide a corps of two infantry divisions as a reinforcement to the British Army of the Rhine (BAOR) in the event of a war with the Soviet Union. These two divisions were to be provided at the expense of reinforcements for the Middle East. While the Service chiefs noted that there was some risk of 'suffering a second Dunkirk' in the event of a serious reverse in Western Europe, they were united in the view that holding the Russians 'East of the Rhine' was now 'vital to . . . the defence of the United Kingdom'.[24] This meant a clear shift in Britain's global strategy from the Middle East to Western Europe.

The third shift was political. The creation of NATO, in which the United States had accepted a legal commitment to the security of Western Europe, meant that Bevin's broad concept of 'creating some form' of Western Union, 'backed by' the Americans in 1948 had been overtaken by events. Consequently, at a Cabinet meeting on 8 May 1950 British ministers gave their wholehearted support to Bevin's proposal calling for the replacement of the 'original conception of Western Union' by 'the wider conception of the Atlantic community'.[25]

BRITAIN'S INITIAL POLICY FOR A WEST GERMAN DEFENCE CONTRIBUTION, MAY 1950

Hence by 1950 Britain had decided that the problem of integrating the Western democracies must be dealt with in the wider context of the Atlantic alliance, while at the same time she adopted a Europe-first strategy. The definition of West Germany's future military role in the West now became more feasible than it had been in 1948.

The timing of Britain's deliberations about the German problem coincided with the formation of the Federal Republic of Germany out of the Western zones of Germany in September 1949, and of the German Democratic Republic in October 1949, in the Soviet zone of Germany. The Federal Republic, headed by the Chancellor, Dr Konrad Adenauer, was promised her progressive incorporation into the Western community economically and politically, but there was no alteration of the existing allied policy of maintaining the demilitarization of the Federal Republic of Germany.

Nevertheless there was considerable speculation in Europe after November 1949 that the three occupying powers might request a West German contribution to the defence of Western Europe. The German Chancellor did not want to create a German 'national' army, but believed that instead West Germany's security could be promoted by her assimilation with the

Western democracies by the contribution of 'a German contingent inside a European army and under European command'.[26] He regarded West Germany's rearmament as a useful political bargaining counter to achieve full sovereignty, while France, naturally enough, remained totally opposed to any plan which would make West Germany militarily strong.[27]

Britain's new-found willingness to consider the rearmament of West Germany stemmed from her increasing fears of the Soviet military threat. There now appeared to be a clear military need for securing Germany's resources for the defence of Western Europe. Politically, it seemed essential to avert Soviet domination of the whole of Germany by associating West Germany politically and militarily firmly with the Western community.[28] Britain also appreciated that the existing situation could not last for ever, since it was unlikely, as Attlee told Bevin on 2 May, that West Germany would 'settle down without some armed forces'.[29]

However, the powerful military and political arguments for rearming West Germany were not sufficient to enable Britain's leaders to resolve the question.[30] A lessened danger from the Soviet Union as a result of West Germany's contribution to the strength of Western Europe might be replaced by a renewed threat from a rearmed West Germany to Western Europe. Moreover, while the Soviet Union had already set up a paramilitary police force in her zone, she had not taken any steps towards bringing East Germany into any Eastern European version of NATO. The Chiefs of Staff, while they were more alive than the Foreign Office to the military necessity for a West German defence contribution to the West, advised against a hasty approach to the problem, since this 'might even terrify the Russians to the point of preventive war'.[31] What Britain feared most was the danger of a rearmed West Germany falling under Soviet influence.

Hence Britain insisted on strengthening the military capabilities of the Western European allies before considering the integration of West German military effectives in the West, in the belief that this would counter both a re-emergence of West German military preponderance on the continent and any violent reaction from the Soviet Union. Initial studies undertaken by military planners also suggested that sufficient restrictions should be imposed on German armed forces, for instance a ban on her possession of tanks and military aircraft, to allay fears of a future German military threat to Europe.[32] Britain thus preferred a gradual approach to the recovery of West Germany's military power, which, she anticipated, could not be completed before 1954.[33]

Another anxiety about West German rearmament concerned its consequences for Britain's long-term goal of the reunification of Germany. It is true that by the spring of 1950, Bevin, the Foreign Office and the Cabinet were in complete agreement with the Chiefs of Staff that negotiations with the Soviet Union were not worthwhile until the West had built up its military strength and had gradually drawn West Germany into its orbit.[34] However, this timetable for the rearmament of West Germany *before* the reunification of Germany was not a firm one. The Permanent Under-Secretaries Committee pointed out that the inclusion of a rearmed West Germany into the West would mean the hardening of the division of Europe, which in turn would make German reunification even more difficult to achieve. Moreover, Britain anticipated that it would be 'embarrassing' to reject any Soviet proposal for the resumption of four-power negotiations on Germany, given the strong pressure in West Germany for reunification.[35] The military recovery of West Germany allied to the West thus would depend on the course of developments and particularly on the attitudes of the Soviets and the Germans themselves.

There was also the problem of how France and the United States would react to the military implications of West Germany's integration into the West. Bevin's new-found enthusiasm for the Atlantic alliance entailed a double-edged strategy not only for the Cold War but also for a future rearmed West Germany. The Cabinet on 8 May fully endorsed Bevin's argument that West Germany should be rearmed within NATO. Unlike the Western Union, NATO involved the United States, and as such was regarded as a more reliable and stronger body to contain any military threat from a rearmed West Germany.[36]

However, Britain suspected that France would prefer to involve West Germany in a purely European arrangement, such as that proposed in the Schuman plan of May 1950.[37] Even more irritating to London, Washington fully supported the French scheme for closer ties with West Germany, which might eventually create a climate favourable to the solution by the Europeans themselves of the military problem of West Germany.[38]

In any case at this stage Washington preferred to concentrate on strengthening NATO, accepting that the time was not ripe for formal consideration of a future place for West Germany in the defence of Western Europe, a view which was supported by her European allies in a series of meetings in the NATO Council conference in London in May 1950.[39]

THE OUTBREAK OF THE KOREAN WAR

The advent of the Korean War in June 1950 deepened Britain's fears about the weakness of Western Europe's defences. During the summer of 1950, as a result of considerable American pressure, Britain – now the leading European power in NATO, with the bulk of the French Army pinned down in Indo-China – made three major decisions designed to strengthen Western Europe's defence posture.

First, on 8 August 1950 the British government endorsed a large defence budget of £3,400 million over the period from 1950 to 1954. This ambitious programme, together with a subsequent decision to extend the period of national service from eighteen months to two years, was considered by the Chancellor of the Exchequer to be a manageable one, provided that the United States contributed the sum of £550 million in financial aid.[40]

Second, in July the Defence Committee authorized a further acceleration of the guided weapons programme. This decision stemmed not only from the precarious state of East–West relations, but also from the recent demonstration that the nuclear superiority of the United States had not deterred the Communist invasion of South Korea.[41]

This loss of confidence in deterrence led Britain to try to meet a third strategic requirement – the building up of her ground forces. On 1 September 1950 the Defence Committee proposed the strengthening of the BAOR by one division, from two and one-third to three and one-third. It was also agreed that this increase would not affect a previous decision of March 1950 that, in the event of war, two Territorial divisions would be dispatched to Europe after D+3 months (that is three months after the outbreak of war).[42]

Since the allied rearmament programmes would take some time to effect any major improvement in the West's military preparedness, Britain remained concerned about the possibility of a Korean-type conflict breaking out in Berlin or in West Germany. The East German military police force of about 52,500 men armed with machine-guns and Soviet T34 tanks, concentrated in the south-west and near Berlin, did not present a serious challenge to the allied garrison at this stage, but was believed by the West to be the nucleus for the formation of an East German army of 150,000 men by 1951.[43]

In this bleak situation the British were scarcely surprised that the West Germans had become demoralized and were in a mood of 'ohne mich' in response to the Korean War. Adenauer not only demanded that the allies reinforce their troops in West Germany but also repeated a request for the Federal government to be allowed to establish an armed police force of 150,000 men, a sharp rise on the figure of 25,000 men that he had proposed in April 1950.[44]

Renewed speculation about a future West German defence contribution to the West were reflected in the debates in the Council of Europe in mid-August, in which West Germany participated for the first time as an associate member. The final resolution, led by Winston Churchill, the Conservative Opposition leader, called for the creation of 'a unified European Army', which delighted European federalists and pleased Adenauer.[45] In fact, Churchill's concept for a European Army, while broad and vague in details, envisaged a coalition of about thirty-six divisions of different nationals, including fifteen French, six British, six American, and five West German divisions, to be created during the next six months as an emergency measure. As such it differed profoundly from the subsequent 'Pleven' plan put forward by the French for a European Army.[46]

199

Britain anticipated that the question of a West German defence contribution to the West would be raised at the NATO Council meeting in New York in September.[47] However, the outbreak of the Korean War did little to reduce Britain's fundamental distrust of a rearmed West Germany. The Foreign Office insisted, in the face of Britain's uncertainties about Soviet intentions in Europe after the Korean War, that any proposal to rearm West Germany would require even more cautious handling in order not to provoke the Soviet Union and East Germany.[48]

In May the Prime Minister, the Foreign Office and the Chiefs of Staff had agreed that the military planners should conduct a detailed study on military aspects of West German rearmament and by mid-August the study was approved by the Chiefs of Staff.[49] It called for the raising of a balanced West German army of twenty divisions with a tactical air force,[50] but the Chiefs of Staff made it clear to Bevin that they did not think it 'possible immediately to go ahead with the programme advocated in their paper' without overcoming various political objections to the rearmament of West Germany.[51]

By 1 September the Foreign Office and the Chiefs of Staff reached a consensus about Britain's policy for the rearmament of West Germany. There was to be no mention at this stage of an eventual formation of West German contingents within NATO, but some measures to relax allied occupation policy for the demilitarization and disarmament of Germany should be considered, including the cessation, with a few exceptions, of the industrial dismantling and demolition programme and, more importantly, the creation of a Federal police force of 100,000 men in response to Adenauer's recent request.[52]

Britain had been examining the possibility of establishing a Federal police force since the autumn of 1949. The Federal government was not empowered to establish central police forces. The allied occupation forces were therefore left with the sole responsibility for dealing with any internal unrest which the existing weak police forces of some 87,000 men organized on a local basis and equipped with pistols were unable to handle. The introduction of a strong Federal police force would certainly remove the bulk of this responsibility from the allies.[53] While there existed, prior to the Korean War, some differences between British civilian and military leaders over the exact function of such a Federal police force,[54] they were now united in the view that police units on a Federal basis should be organized on the model of the East German paramilitary police force to deal with not only internal but also external security problems.

Thus, on the eve of the opening of the New York Conference, Britain was prepared to take some steps towards rearming West Germans, albeit by covert means, which were judged to be less provocative towards the Soviet Union than any immediate moves towards the military integration of West Germany into NATO. This police scheme would enable the West to secure German personnel for Western European defence more quickly and would not threaten Europe with the revival of German militarism.[55]

THE NEW YORK CONFERENCE, 12–26 SEPTEMBER 1950[56]

The United States leadership saw the Korean conflict as a clear demonstration that the Soviet Union intended to use armed force to gain her ends and thus confirmed the warnings contained in NSC–68.[57] As a result, the Americans placed a 'one-package' proposal before the North Atlantic Council in New York in September 1950, a package which stemmed from the rather hasty and haphazard process of resolving what Dean Acheson, the Secretary of State, described as 'an ugly dilemma' facing the Pentagon and the State Department over how to bring about West German rearmament.[58] This made the fulfilment of an American promise both to reinforce their troops stationed in Western Europe and to appoint a US general as the NATO Supreme Commander in Europe, contingent upon NATO's agreement in principle to the formation of about four to ten West German divisions within NATO.[59]

Bevin was surprised by, and Robert Schuman, the French Foreign Minister, was furious about the way the USA urged her NATO allies to agree in principle to West Germany's rearmament.[60] A Cabinet meeting on 14 September remained opposed to the early inclusion of West Germany into NATO, but on the following day the Cabinet, having belatedly realized that the US demand for West German troops was a *sine qua non* of a further American contribution to the defence of Western Europe, reluctantly authorized Bevin to accept the one-package proposal in principle. The Korean War increased the importance in British eyes of preserving the close relationship with the United States in the defence of Western Europe. Furthermore, the ministers appreciated that even after agreement in principle had been reached to the rearming of West Germany within NATO, it would take some time to work out such details as 'the timing, announcement and method' of raising and integrating West German armed units into NATO.[61]

Apart from France, the other allies also accepted the US package proposal, with the tacit understanding that before West Germany could join NATO, a unified force of the other powers under a Supreme Commander must first be established. In other words, American troops and the Supreme Commander must arrive in Europe before the integration of West German military effectives into NATO could begin. But France would not agree even to this revised interpretation of West German rearmament and at the final Council session the finalization of the one-package proposal was suspended, pending further consideration by the NATO Defence Committee of the question of a West German contribution.[62]

The significance of the New York NATO Conference lay in the American initiative for the combining of the West European defence question with the West German rearmament issue. Britain's proposal for the formation of a Federal police force was pigeon-holed and, in the event, growing German opposition to such clandestine measures of utilizing West German manpower led Britain to abandon this scheme altogether.[63] The three Western allies and the Bonn government agreed instead on the creation of a small and lightly equipped *Land*-based mobile police force whose functions were limited to internal policing.[64]

THE FRANCO-AMERICAN DILEMMA OVER THE WEST GERMAN REARMAMENT QUESTION, OCTOBER–DECEMBER 1950

During this period, Britain was anxious to strengthen European defences by putting the American offers contained in the one-package proposal into operation as soon as possible, and this anxiety overshadowed her grave misgivings about accepting West German rearmament even in principle.

France, isolated in New York and feeling betrayed by Britain's acceptance in principle of the one-package proposal, produced a counter-proposal, the so-called Pleven plan, on 24 October 1950. This involved the setting up of a European Army, which later became known as the European Defence Community (EDC), comprising land, air and naval forces, on a supranational basis, financed by a common budget, under the leadership of 'a European Minister of Defence' and was, in effect, the application of the Schuman programme for pooling coal and steel among the six European partners (West Germany, France, the three Benelux countries, and Italy) to the European military sphere.[65]

The Pleven plan reflected 'primarily', as Evelyn Shuckburgh (the head of the Western Organization Department, Foreign Office) put it, 'the French obsession with the German menace'. Under this plan, West German military effectives would be fused with those of other European nationals 'at the level of the smallest possible unit'.[66] Thus, a single European Army consisting of the European members of NATO together with West German units would take its place alongside the national armies of those NATO countries, such as Canada and the United States, who would not participate in the European Army.

Britain suspected that the Pleven plan was a means to attain the French goal for European federation, and which was clearly the converse of London's aspirations for strengthening the Atlantic alliance.[67] It was evident that the Pleven plan, which would involve the time-consuming task of setting up a supranational organization, was a device to delay consideration of a German defence contribution and separate it from the rest of the package proposal.[68] Britain's initial official position was that while she would not openly reject the French proposal, she would not participate in such an 'unrealistic' scheme.[69]

The majority view at the Washington meetings of the NATO Defence Committee between 28 and 31 October was that the Pleven plan did not seem to be workable. However, the French insisted that they would not consider the German rearmament question except in the context of the French European Army scheme and as a result, the Americans refused to proceed with the rest of the package proposal for the general reorganization of NATO.[70] Attlee expressed his growing frustration with the ensuing stalemate at the Cabinet Defence Committee on 8 November.

> Valuable time was being lost: chances of substantial American reinforcements in Europe were being thrown away. . . . This dangerous situation was the direct result of the French attachment to an unworkable and unsound plan.[71]

Faced with 'this dangerous situation', Britain decided to expand further her rearmament programme. The August estimate of a four year (1950–4) rearmament plan costing £3,400 million was increased by £200 million in September, and on 16 November the Cabinet approved this target of £3,600 million, and reduced the completion period to three years.[72] Moreover, in mid-October 1950 the Defence Committee endorsed a COS proposal for an increase in the BAOR by a second armoured division in the autumn of 1951, thus bringing the total number of divisions up to four and one-third.[73]

This expansion was intended to demonstrate to her allies that Britain was contributing wholeheartedly to her NATO commitment, but her image as a leading NATO power was somewhat tarnished by her inability to exert much influence in the controversy between the French and the Americans about West Germany's participation.

Britain considered two alternative schemes intended to resolve the stalemate, both of which were either ill timed or ill considered. The Chiefs of Staff, suspecting that the French plan would not work, produced a compromise plan in mid-November, whereby the French would explore her European Army project with other European partners, while at the same time the American plan for including West German armed units directly into NATO would be adopted.[74] However, before this British plan could be discussed by the Cabinet, the NATO Council of Deputies were already contemplating a similar scheme which became known as the Spofford proposal.

The Foreign Secretary, however, stated that Britain could not 'afford to allow the European federal concept to gain a foothold within NATO' and wishing to 'kill' the French plan at once, formulated a proposal for an 'Atlantic Confederate Force'.[75] The gist of the plan was for a self-contained Atlantic system whereby an Atlantic Army not only would be subject operationally to the Supreme Commander but also would be controlled administratively by a higher authority under the NATO Council. In a sense, Bevin's Atlantic Army amounted to the expansion of the French European Army into the Atlantic area. This grandiose scheme was regarded by his Cabinet colleagues, including the Prime Minister, as impracticable.[76]

The Spofford plan, named after Charles Spofford, the American chairman of the NATO Council of Deputies,[77] was devised during discussions in the Military Committee and in the Council of Deputies of NATO between mid-November and mid-December 1950. It sought to bring together the US package proposal and the French European Army scheme so that the US project for a European integrated force would be put into operation, allowing for the recruitment and training of German troops so that they could participate, on a provisional basis, in NATO. Under this plan, two sets of negotiations concerning a West German defence contribution would ensue: one between the three occupying powers and the Federal Republic for the immediate raising of West German armed units, and the second for a conference in Paris on the setting up of a European Army.[78] The Spofford plan was intended to be a face-saving political arrangement to overcome the disagreement between the French and the Americans over the method and timing of a German defence contribution.

Britain did not regard the Spofford approach as an ideal answer to the German rearmament question, since it would provide the West Germans with the opportunity of exploring two methods of participating, either directly through NATO or within a European Army, and lead to the eventual creation of a powerful European Army, although ministers were more dubious than the Foreign Secretary about the latter possibility.[79]

In the face of increasing tensions in Korea as a result of the major Chinese offensive at the beginning of December, Bevin once again tried to undermine the Pleven plan by sending Attlee, who was conferring with President Truman in Washington, some recommendations which were designed to retard further progress on the West German rearmament question.[80] However, Attlee rejected Bevin's suggestions, and approved the Spofford plan, 'as a means of securing the early appointment of a Supreme Commander of the European integrated force, to which he and his Cabinet colleagues attached such great importance'.[81]

The two-day Conference of the NATO Council at Brussels on 18–19 December culminated in the unanimous acceptance of the Spofford plan.[82] Accordingly, the United States agreed to proceed with the one-package proposal: Truman announced the appointment of General Dwight D. Eisenhower as Supreme Commander and the US Congress began to debate the dispatch of US troop reinforcements to Western Europe.[83] NATO's acceptance of the Spofford plan also meant agreement in principle on West German rearmament, which would in turn require negotiations with Bonn.

Thus the Brussels Conference was successful in separating the German question from the urgent problem of setting up a European integrated force, a solution which Britain had sought in September.

ATTLEE'S FOUR CONDITIONS

The three allied powers began to negotiate with the West German authorities over the Spofford plan for West German rearmament on 9 January 1951, while in February, France opened the European Army conference in Paris with those powers who were to set up the Schuman Coal and Steel Community (although the Netherlands remained an observer until the autumn of 1951). Britain and the United States also sent observers to this conference. The advantage from Britain's point of view of this procedure was that, while these two sets of negotiations continued, it was unlikely that Britain would be pressed to go further than her 'moral commitment' to the Spofford plan.[84]

In an effort to prevent West German rearmament, the Soviet Union had in a note of 3 November 1950 asked the three Western occupying powers to resume the four-power negotiations on Germany. For the reasons already discussed Britain could not reject this Soviet overture outright, and the three Western powers agreed to the opening of four-power talks provided that the Soviets were prepared to discuss broader issues than just the German question in the hope that this would lead to a relaxation of Cold War tensions.[85] The threat of a German defence contribution to Western Europe might prove to be a useful bargaining counter in negotiating with the USSR and, until then, the Labour government was anxious to postpone any practical steps towards German rearmament.[86]

Hence Britain was in a better position in early 1951 than she had been hitherto to urge a cautious approach towards this controversial problem, and, in the House of Commons on 12 February 1951, the Prime Minister set out four British conditions for the acceptance of a German defence contribution to the defence of Western Europe. First, the rearmament of NATO countries must precede that of West Germany; second, allied forces must be significantly strengthened before West German armed units could be raised; third, West German units must be associated with the other NATO forces in such a way as to preclude the re-emergence of a West German military threat; and fourth, there must be agreement with the West Germans on the level of their contribution.[87]

While Attlee's four conditions did not represent a radical departure from existing government policy, the statement went some way towards reducing the opposition of left-wing Labour MPs to the haste with which the USA was pressing for West Germany's rearmament.[88] Attlee's initiative also provided guidelines for the Foreign Office and the Chiefs of Staff and calmed Bevin's worries about the subject.[89] Paul Addison has commented that

> As a politician Attlee resembled the frog who sits motionless on a stone, occasionally snapping up an insect with its tongue. If it came to the point he could take sharp decisions with no fuss or self advertisement.[90]

FROM REARMAMENT TO EUROPEAN UNITY: THE LABOUR GOVERNMENT'S SEPTEMBER 1951 DECLARATION

By the summer of 1951 a number of developments had led to some relaxation in European tension. Eisenhower formally set up the Supreme Headquarters Allied Powers in Europe (SHAPE) in Paris on 2 April 1951, while American troop reinforcements of four divisions began to arrive in Europe after May. The long-drawn-out and unsuccessful conference of the four-power deputies between 5 March and 21 June had not affected the solidarity of the three allies. European public opinion had greeted with relief the opening of the Korean armistice talks in July. As a result, the pressure for a costly rearmament programme was losing ground, and conversely, the political goal of furthering European unity was gaining in popularity.[91]

In January 1951 British defence expenditure had risen to £4,700 million over the next three years from the previous estimate of £3,600 million approved in November 1950.[92] However, by the summer of 1951 Britain, like the other European powers, was suffering from the effects of this ambitious rearmament programme on her balance of payments and on her rate of inflation, while the unity of the Labour Party was threatened by the resignations of the Minister of Labour, Aneurin Bevan, the President of the Board of Trade, Harold Wilson, and the Under-Secretary at the Ministry of Supply, John Freeman, in protest at Attlee's rearmament policy.[93] Britain could no longer take the lead in NATO in the field of rearmament: as the Chancellor of the Exchequer, Hugh Gaitskell, informed France and the United States, 'he did not see how the UK could do any more than it was doing, and it was doubtful that it could even carry out the [£] 4.7 [billion] program[me] on schedule'.[94]

Furthermore, in view of the tripartite meeting of the Foreign Ministers on Germany in mid-September, Britain could no longer reserve her decision on the timing and the nature of a West German defence contribution. The new Foreign Secretary, Herbert Morrison (who had succeeded Bevin early in March 1951), and the Minister of Defence, Emanuel

Shinwell, in a joint minute of 24 July 1951 appreciated that 'the stakes in the game far transcend the mere recruitment of a few German divisions'.[95]

Although this was all that the Americans had sought when they had put forward the one-package proposal in New York ten months before, since then the three occupying powers had agreed to a number of measures towards the restoration of West Germany's political freedom in preparation for the conclusion of a contractual agreement with her to replace the existing occupation statute and which would result in the setting up of a sovereign Federal Republic.[96]

Moreover, the Federal Republic made it clear during the negotiations in Bonn that she could not participate in NATO unless she was treated on the basis of equality with the other participants. This amounted to West Germany's rejection of the Spofford plan.[97] While the Bonn talks collapsed at the end of June 1951, the Paris Conference on the European Army began, in Morrison's words, 'to look as if it might result in an agreement'.[98] What became clear to Britain at this stage was that West Germany's price for her defence contribution was her political and military equality in the Western community, which made Britain hesitate to pursue the inclusion of West German armed forces directly into NATO.[99]

By the beginning of September, however, France made considerable efforts at Paris to convince Washington and Bonn of the viability of her proposed supranational military organization; the project secured the full support of General Eisenhower and, subsequently, of the Truman administration and of Adenauer. Growing enthusiasm for further moves towards European unity also contributed to gathering momentum in the Paris negotiations.[100]

Morrison, Shinwell, and the Secretary of State for Commonwealth Relations, Patrick Gordon-Walker, had already been disposed to support the European Army project by the end of July,[101] and the Prime Minister, in a minute for the Cabinet of 30 August 1951, agreed that 'the Foreign Secretary should give every encouragement to it [the European Army plan]' in the forthcoming Washington talks, a view which was approved by the Cabinet on 4 September 1951[102] While Britain as a global power did not wish to become too closely involved in European affairs, her anxiety to maintain her influence in Europe, a theatre of crucial importance to her security and political interests, meant that she could not afford to remain aloof from continental developments. Furthermore she could not and would not stand aside while the future of West Germany was being determined.

The European Army plan seemed the only feasible method of resolving the West German military question, and had been accepted in Paris, Bonn and Washington. Given the prospect of West Germany attaining political sovereignty through the allied contractual agreements, the European Army project appeared to be a safe forum in which West German soldiers could be firmly integrated into a European common defence force under NATO. Britain remained suspicious of continental federation schemes, the success of which might precipitate an early American retreat from Europe, but she hoped that the projected European Army, which was to be formed within NATO, would remain under the overall control of the SACEUR. Thus Britain had no choice but to encourage the European Army plan.[103]

At the end of the Washington tripartite Foreign Ministers' conference of 10 and 14 September 1951, Morrison defined Britain's position thus: 'The Government of the United Kingdom desires to establish the closest possible association with the European continental community at all stages in its development'.[104] This high-sounding pledge pleased Schuman and Acheson and as a result, the Washington conference reached a consensus on the contentious German question: the three Western powers agreed not only that West Germany should form a part of the projected European Army, but also that the West German rearmament question and the problem of her political sovereignty would be settled simultaneously 'in the developing process of achieving European unity'.[105]

A major shortcoming in Morrison's Washington statement was that this could be interpreted in two ways: either that Britain really intended to emphasize (as she actually did) her non-participation in the EDC or that she wanted to suggest that she might ultimately become a full member of the EDC – the words 'the closest possible association' could certainly be taken to mean the latter.

Conversely, from the standpoint of domestic party politics, there was some virtue in Britain's September declaration. The fact that the Labour government had hinted at its readiness to accept a British commitment to the EDC might complicate the Conservative Party's response to the question. Churchill, a fervent advocate (at least in Opposition) of European integration, could propose full British participation in the Paris Conference only if he wanted to outdo the Labour government. If he failed to do this, the Conservatives would have to adopt Labour policy on this question. If this was indeed their intention, Attlee and Morrison operated quite skilfully in handling this issue on the eve of the British general election.[106]

Since 1949, Western Europe had experienced dramatic changes: the American commitment to NATO alliance, the establishment of two German governments, the outbreak of the Korean War and the ensuing tensions in that theatre, the decision to strengthen NATO and finally agreement among the three occupying powers to the political and military recovery of West Germany and her full participation in the Western community. For Britain, the Cold War and the subsequent 'hot war' on the Korean peninsula compelled her to recognize once again the painful fact that Europe was much too close to be regarded as merely one among several security interests. Ironically, however, Britain's growing interest in European security and particularly in resolving satisfactorily the problem of West Germany's rearmament encouraged the Labour government to move decisively to the support of the Atlantic alliance, while dissociating itself from membership of any continental federation. While the United States, France and West Germany all shared, albeit from different perspectives, a common interest in the creation of a unified and stable Western Europe, their ideas about how to achieve this ran counter to those of Britain, in that they supported a federated Europe. Nevertheless, Britain gained most of what she had sought from the United States, that is the transformation of NATO into a fully fledged military organization under Eisenhower's command. Nor did she suffer from any serious diplomatic setbacks during the long negotiations over the one-package proposal, and was able to seize the opportunity to declare her readiness to co-operate with the European Army project.

NOTES

1 CP(48) 6, 46, 4 Jan., 10 Feb., 1948, CAB 129/23, 24 (Public Record Office, Kew, London)

2 CP(48) 6, ibid; see also CP(47) 326, CP(48) 5 & CP(49) 208, 10 Dec. 1947, 5 Jan. 1948, and 18 Oct. 1949, CAB 129/22, 23 and 37; A. Adamthwaite, 'Britain and the World, 1945–1949: the View from the Foreign Office', in J. Becker and F. Knipping (eds) *Power in Europe?* (New York and Berlin: Walter de Gruyter, 1986), p. 14.

3 CP(48) 5, 6 and 72, CAB 129/23 and 25; 2nd and 19th mtgs, CAB 128/2 and 12; for the Brussels Treaty see J. Baylis, 'Britain, the Brussels Pact and the Continental Commitment', *International Affairs* Vol. 60, No. 4 (autumn, 1984), pp. 615–29; J. Young, *France, the Cold War and the Western Alliance, 1945–1949* (Leicester: Leicester University Press, 1990), pp. 175–97ff. See also Kent and Young, Chapter 7 in this volume.

4 The Post Hostilities Planning (PHP) Committee report, PHP (44)17(0), 20 July 1944, CAB 79/78; COS(46)105, 5 Apr. 1946, CAB 80/101. See also D. Cameron Watt, 'British Military Perceptions of the Soviet Union as a Strategic Threat, 1945–1950', in *Power in Europe*, pp. 328–30; V. Rothwell, *Britain and the Cold War, 1941–47* (London: Jonathan Cape, 1982) p. 119; E. Barker, *The British between the Superpowers* (London: Macmillan, 1983), pp. 1–9.

5 82nd mtg, 22 Dec. 1948, CAB 128/13; G. Warner, 'Britain and Europe in 1948: the View from the Cabinet', in Becker and Knipping, *Power in Europe?*, p. 42; A. Bullock, *Ernest Bevin: Foreign Secretary* (London: Heinemann, 1983), p. 764; H. Dalton, *High Tide and After* (London: Frederick Muller, 1962), pp. 166–7, 269–70. For Britain's policy for Germany during this period, see A. Deighton, 'Cold-War Diplomacy: British Policy towards Germany's Role in Europe, 1945–9', in I. Turner (ed.) *British Occupation Policy and the Western Zones, 1945–55* (Oxford: Berg, 1989), pp. 15–34.

6 DO 16th mtg, 21 June 1949, CAB 131/8.

7 DO(46)40, 13 Mar. 1946, CAB 131/2; see also Watt, in *Power in Europe ?*, p. 331.

8 COS(47)173 and 227, 23 Aug. and 17 Nov. 1947, DEFE 5/5 and 6; 151st mtg, 30 Jan. 1948, DEFE 4/10; DO(48)46, 26 July 1948, CAB 131/6; DO(49)3, 7 Jan. 1949, CAB 131/7.

9 COS (46)105, 5 Apr. 1946, CAB 80/101; JP(48) 16 in COS 15th mtg, 30 Jan. 1948, DEFE 4/10.

10 23rd mtg, 10 Feb. 1947, DEFE 4/11; COS (47) 227(0), 17 Nov. 1947, DEFE 5/6; 16th, 18th and 42nd mtgs, 2 and 4 Feb., 3 Mar. 1948, DEFE 4/10, 10 and 11; CP(48)240, 2 Nov. 1948, CAB 129/30.

11 18th and 42nd mtgs, 4 Feb. and 19 Mar. 1949, DEFE 4/10, 11; DO(50)20, 20 Mar.

1950, CAB 131/9. See also M. L. Dockrill, 'British Attitudes Towards France as a Military Ally', *Diplomacy and Statecraft* Vol. 1, No. 1 (March 1990), pp. 55, 63.

12 16th and 18th mtgs, 2 and 4 Feb. 1948, DEFE 4/10; 16th mtg, 21 June 1949, CAB 131/8.

13 18th mtg, 4 Feb. 1948, DEFE 4/10.

14 DO(49)45, 17 June 1949, CAB 131/7; see also Barker, *The British Between the Superpowers*, pp. 115–20.

15 DO(49)3, 7 Jan. 1949, CAB 131/7.

16 DO(49)45, 17 June 1949, CAB 131/7.

17 For the Strategic Concept, see *Foreign Relations of the United States (FRUS) 1949 Vol. 4*, pp. 352–6.

18 'Record of a mtg held in Washington, on 14 Sept. 1949 on Atlantic Pact Machinery', FO 800/483; JP(50)17, 33, 14 Feb., 20 Mar. 1950, DEFE 6/12; *FRUS 1949 Vol. 4*, pp. 325–8; see also T. Ireland, *Creating the Entangling Alliance* (London: Aldwych Press, 1981), pp. 162–3.

19 DO(50)20, 20 Mar. 1950, CAB 131/9.

20 JP(49)156, 15 Mar. 1950. DEFE 6/11; COS(50)8, 10 Jan. 1950, DEFE 5/19.

21 DO(50)31, CAB 131/9; DO 17th mtg, CAB 131/8; Lord Ismay, *NATO: The First Five Years 1949–1954* (Netherlands: Bosch-Utrecht, 1954), p. 29; W. Poole, *The History of the Joint Chiefs of Staff Vol. 4* (Wilmington: Michael Glazier, 1979), p. 185; R. McGeehan, *The German Rearmament Question* (Urbana: University of Illinois Press, 1971), p. 11.

22 29th mtg, 8 May 1950, CAB 128/17.

23 72nd mtg, 15 Dec. 1949, CAB 128/16; see also COS (47) 173, 23 Aug. 1947, DEFE 5/5; 2nd mtg, 8 Jan. 1948, CAB 131/5; DO(48)46, 26 July 1948, CAB 131/16; Bullock, *Bevin*, pp. 798–9; K. Harris, *Attlee* (London: Weidenfeld & Nicolson, 1982), p. 455.

24 DO(50)20, 20 Mar. 1950, CAB 131/9; 5th mtg, 23 Mar. 1950, CAB 131/8; JP(50)22, 10 Mar. 1950, DEFE 6/12.

25 29th mtg, 8 May 1950, CAB 128/17; see also PUSC (50)9, 21 Apr. 1950, PREM 8/1203.

26 Adenauer, *Konrad Adenauer Memoirs 1945–53* trans. B. Rhum von Oppen (London: Weidenfeld & Nicolson, 1966) p. 268. For German views on their defence contribution, see N. Wiggershaus, 'Zur Frage der Planung für die verdeckte Aufstellung westdeutscher Verteidigungskräfte in Konrad Adenauers sicherheitspolitischer Konzeption 1950', in MGFA (ed.) *Dienstgruppen und Westdeutscher Verteidigungsbeitrag-Militärgeschichte seite 1945* Vol. 6 (Boppard: Harald Boldt, 1982), pp. 11–33; H. Speidel, *Aus unserer Zeit – Erinnerungen* (Berlin: Ullstein, 1977), pp. 249–57; M. Messerschmidt *et al.*, 'West Germany's Strategic Position and her Role in Defence Policy as seen by the German Military, 1945–1949', in *Power in Europe?*, pp. 353–67.

27 P. Mélandri, *Les Etats-Unis Face a l'unification de L'Europe, 1945–1954* (Paris: Pedone, 1980), p. 289; François Seydoux, *Mémoires – D'outre – Rhin* (Paris: Bernard Grasset, 1975), pp. 155–7; R. Massigli, *Une Comédie des Erreurs 1943–1956* (Paris: Plon, 1978), pp. 239–42; J. Frémeaux and A. Martel, 'French Defence Policy, 1947–1949', in O. Riste (ed.) *Western Security: The Formative Years* (Oslo: Norwegian University Press, 1985), pp. 96–9.

28 DO(50)67, 30 Aug. 1950, CAB 131/9; CP(50)8, 26 Apr. 1950, CAB 129/39.

29 PREM 8/1203.

30 For Britain's initial policy towards West German rearmament, see JP(49)156, 15 Mar. 1950, DEFE 6/11; COS(50)8, 10 Jan. 1950, DEFE 5/19; 52nd and 70th mtgs, 20 Mar. and 2 May, 1950, DEFE 4/30, 31; PUSC(49)62, 19 Apr. 1950, PREM 8/1203.

31 The COS report on 'Global Strategy' DO(50)34 of 1 May 1950 quoted in Gilchrist minute, 12 July 1950, FO 371/85050.

32 JP(49)156, 15 Mar. 1950, DEFE 6/11; COS(50)8, 10 Jan. 1950, DEFE 5/19; 52nd and 70th mtgs, 20 Mar. & 2 May 1950, DEFE 4/30, 31.

33 70th mtg, 2 May 1950, DEFE 4/31; see also CP(50)80, 26 Apr. 1950, CAB 129/39; 29th mtg, 8 May 1950, CAB 128/17.

34 JP(49)156, 15 Mar. 1950, DEFE 6/11; PUSC(49)62, 19 Apr. 1950, PREM 8/1203; 29th mtg, 8 May 1950, CAB 128/17.

35 PUSC(49)62 and PUSC(50)9, 19 and 26 Apr. 1950, PREM 8/1203.
36 CP(50)114, 19 May 1950, CAB 129/40; 29th mtg, 8 May 1950, CAB 128/17.
37 CP(50)92, 2 May 1950, CAB 129/39; 29th mtg, 8 May 1950, CAB 128/17; *FRUS 1950 Vol. 3*, pp. 60–2; A. K. Henrikson, 'The Creation of the North Atlantic Alliance, 1948–1952' *Naval War College Review* Vol. 32, No. 3 (1980), pp. 27–8.
38 NSC 71/1, 3 July 1950 in *Documents of the National Security Council 1947–1977* (Maryland: Microfilm Project of University Publications of America Inc., 1980) (hereafter cited as *DNSC*); M. Hogan, *The Marshall Plan* (Cambridge and New York: Cambridge University Press, 1987), pp. 26–53, 367–8.
39 For the JCS views, see NSC 71 (8 June 1950), *DNSC*; For the State Department view, see NSC 71/1 (3 July 1950), ibid.; Poole, *JCS Vol. 4*, p. 193; L. W. Martin, 'The American Decision to Rearm Germany', in H. Stein (ed.) *American Civil–Military Decisions* (Alabama: University of Alabama Press, 1963), p. 651. For the record of the NATO London meetings, see CP(50) 114, 115 and 118, 19, 22 and 26 May 1950, CAB 129/40; *FRUS 1950 Vol. 3* pp. 923–1,091ff.
40 14th mtg, 14 July 1950, CAB 131/8; 50th, 52nd, 53rd and 54th mtgs, 25 July, 1, 11 and 16 Aug. 1950, CAB 128/18; K. Morgan, *Labour in Power, 1945–1951* (Oxford: Clarendon Press, 1984), p. 423.
41 10th mtg, 25 May 1950, CAB 131/8; DO(50)52, 5 July 1950, CAB 131/9; see also B. Bond, *Liddell Hart: A Study of Military Thought* (London: Cassell, 1977), p. 199.
42 17th mtg, 1 Sept. 1950, CAB 131/8; Bevin to O. Franks, Washington, tel. 3946, 2 Sept 1950 in R. Bullen and M. E. Pelly (eds) *Documents on British Policy Overseas*, Series II, Vol. 3 (London: HMSO, 1989) (hereafter cited as *DBPO 3*), pp. 2–3.
43 For Britain's estimate on the strength of the East German police force, see Elliot minute, 31 Aug. 1950, CAB 21/1896; DO(50)66, 29 Aug. 1950, CAB 131/9; 126th and 140th mtgs, 11 and 31 Aug. 1950, DEFE 4/34, 35; DO 17th mtg, 1 Sept. 1950, CAB 131/8; see also Gilchrist minute, 26 July 1950, FO 371/85050.
44 Ivone Kirkpatrick (UK High Commissioner for Germany June 1950–1953) *The Inner Circle* (London: Macmillan, 1959) pp. 238–40; G. Mai, *Westliche Sicherheitspolitik im Kaltan Krieg* in MGFA (ed.) Militärgeschichte seite 1945 Vol. 4 (Boppard: Harald Boldt, 1977), pp. 99–141; Speidel, *Erinnerungen*, pp. 267–9; Adenauer, *Memoirs*, p. 279; see also Kirkpatrick, Wahnerheide to FO, tels 968 and 992, 29 June and 3 July 1950, FO 371/85049; Kirkpatrick, tels 239, 257, 1258 and 422, 19, 24, and 24 Aug 1950, all in CAB 21/1896.
45 E. Fursdon, *The European Defence Community: A History* (London: Macmillan, 1980), pp. 74–6; Speidel, *Erinnerungen*, pp. 257–69 ff; Masssigli, *Une Comédie*, p. 244. For the resolution see *Documents on International Affairs 1949–1950* (London: RIIA, 1953), p. 331.
46 Churchill to Attlee, 6 Aug. 1950, FO 800/456; M. Gilbert, *'Never Despair': Winston S. Churchill, 1945–1965* (London: Heinemann, 1988) pp. 542–5; see also *Parl Deb H of C* Vol. 478, Cols 984–6.
47 Younger minute (for Shinwell), 13 July 1950, FO 371/85050; FO to HM Representatives, tel. 161, 4 Aug. 1950, CAB 21/1896.
48 Ivone Mallet minute (for Bevin), 17 Aug. 1950, FO 371/85050; 130th mtg (Mallet present), 16 Aug. 1950, DEFE 4/34; DO(50)66, 29 Aug 1950, CAB 131/9.
49 70th mtg, 2 May 1950, DEFE 4/31; JP(50)46(S), 4 May 1940, DEFE 6/12; Elliot minute, 9 June 1950, CAB 21/1896; Shinwell minute (for Attlee), 13 June 1950, PREM 8/1203.
50 DO(50)67, 30 Aug. 1950, CAB 131/9.
51 Barclay minute, 30 Aug. 1950, FO 371/85053. For the detailed British debates during the summer, see S. Dockrill, *Britain's Policy for West German Rearmament* (Cambridge: Cambridge University Press, 1991), Ch. 2.
52 17th mtg, 1 Sept. 1950, CAB 131/8; 56th mtg, 6 Sept. 1950, CAB 128/18.
53 JP(49)156, 15 Mar. 1950, DEFE 6/11; CP(50)80, 114 and 115, 26 Apr., 19 and 22 May 1950, CAB 129/39 and 40.
54 Gilchrist minute and Gainer minute (for Bevin), 12 and 13 July 1950, both in FO 371/85050.
55 Gainer minute (for Bevin), 29 Aug. 1950, PREM 8/1429; DO(50)66, 29 Aug. 1950, CAB 131/9; *FRUS 1950 Vol. 3*, pp. 264–6.

56 For the record of the New York Conference, see FO 800/449 and *FRUS 1950 Vol. 3*, pp. 207–354.

57 For the American response to the Korean War, JCS 1924/10 and JIC 530/3, 30 June, 22 Aug. 1950 in *Records of the Joint Chiefs of Staff Part II, 1946–53* (Maryland: Microfilm Project of University Publications of America Inc., 1980) (hereafter cited as *RJCS*); *NSC 73/4*, 25 Aug. 1950, in *DNSC*; H. Truman, *Years of Trial and Hope* (New York: Doubleday, 1956) pp. 332–3. The National Security Council recommended in NSC 68 an all-round strengthening of US military capabilities to allow for an appropriate response at any level to a Communist assault upon the Western hemisphere. See Poole, *JCS Vol. 4*, pp. 4–14.

58 D. Acheson, *Present at the Creation* (London: Hamish Hamilton, 1970), p. 437; see also S. Dockrill, *Britain's Policy*, Ch. 2.

59 For the one-package proposal, see Acheson, *Present*, pp. 436–7; *FRUS 1950 Vol. 3*, pp. 211–19, 273–8; JCS 2124/6, 10 and 18, 26 Aug., 1 and 6 Sept. 1950, all in *RJCS*, L. Martin, *The American Decision*, pp. 653–7.

60 See the record of the mtg of Attlee, Bevin and Schuman of 2 Dec. 1950 in FO 800/465; Massigli, *Une Comédie*, p. 249.

61 58th and 59th mtgs, 14, 15 Sept. 1950, CAB 128/18; *DBPO3*, pp. 32–4, 45–6, 54–5.

62 Jebb, NY to FO, tel. 412, 26 Sept. 1950, FO 800/449.

63 Messerschumidt *et al.*, in *Power in Europe?*, pp. 358–9; Kirkpatrick, tels 1447 and 1454, 30 Sept. and 4 Oct. 1950, FO 371/85056; Gainer minute, 7 Oct. 1950, FO 371/85056; Dixon minute, 13 Oct. 1950, FO 371/85056.

64 *FRUS 1950 Vol. 4*, p. 726; Kirkpatrick to FO, tel. 1465, 7 Oct. 1950, FO 371/85056; FO to HM Representatives, tel. 244, 18 Nov. 1950, CAB 21/1898.

65 J. Monnet, *Memoirs*, (London: Collins, 1978) trans. R. Mayne, pp. 345–6; Seydoux, *Mémoires*, pp. 159–63; J. Moch, *Histoire de Réarmement Allemand depuis 1950* (Paris: Robert Laffont, 1965), pp. 90–1; Mélandri, *Les Etats-Unis Face*, p. 299; Massigli, *Une Comédie*, p. 254; *DBPO 3*, pp. 206–8; DO(50)95, 7 Nov. 1950, Harvey, Paris to FO, tel. 287, 24 Oct. 1950, CAB 21/1898.

66 *DBPO 3*, p. 217.

67 ibid., p. 217; 69th mtg, 30 Oct. 1950, PREM 8/1429.

68 Shinwell to PM and Bevin, tels 378 and 384, 29 Oct. 1950, PREM 8/1429; Acheson, *Present*, p. 459; Poole, *JCS Vol. 4*, p. 212.

69 69th mtg, 30 Oct. 1950, PREM 8/1429; Bevin conv. with Belgian Amb, 25 Oct. 1950, FO 800/483.

70 *FRUS 1950 Vol. 3*, pp. 415–27, 431–2, 439–40; Moch, *Histoire*, pp. 159–64.

71 21st mtg, 8 Nov. 1950, CAB 131/8.

72 162nd mtg, 5 Oct. 1950, DEFE 4/36; DO(50)81 and 91, 5 and 23 Oct. 1950, CAB 131/9; 19th mtg, 25 Oct. 1950, CAB 131/8; 72nd and 74th mtgs, 4 and 16 Nov 1950, CAB 128/18.

73 DO(51)21, 28 Feb. 1951, CAB 131/11.

74 JP(50)161, 14 Nov. 1950, DEFE 6/15; COS(50)474, 17 Nov. 1950, DEFE 5/25; 177th mtg, 9 Nov. 1950, DEFE 4/37.

75 DO(50)100, 24 Nov. 1950, PREM 8/1429.

76 22nd mtg, 27 Nov. 1950, CAB 131/8; see also 186th mtg, 24 Nov. 1950, DEFE 4/37; Dixon and Elliot minutes (for Bevin), 25 Nov. 1950, PREM 8/1429.

77 The NATO Council of Deputies was set up in London in May 1950 in order to discuss and determine policy between meetings of the NATO Council. See DO(51)35, 22 Mar. 1951, CAB 131/11.

78 Summary of the Spofford plan in CP(50)311, 12 Dec. 1950, CAB 129/43; see also *FRUS 1950 Vol. 3*, pp. 457–61, 501–5, 517–21, 531–47.

79 186th mtg, 24 Nov. 1950, DEFE 4/37; 22nd mtg, 27 Nov. 1950, CAB 131/8; CP(51)43, 7 Feb. 1951, CAB 129/44.

80 CP(50)311, 12 Dec. 1950, CAB 129/43; 193rd, 194th and 197th mtgs, 4, 4 and 5 Dec. 1950, DEFE 4/38.

81 85th mtg, 12 Dec. 1950, CAB 128/18; see also Attlee to Bevin, tel. 3309, 6 Dec. 1950, in *DBPO 3*, pp. 345–7; Bevin to Attlee, tel. 5524, 7 Dec. 1950, FO 800/456.

82 For the record of this conference, see CP(51)1, 43, 1 Jan., 7 Feb. 1951, CAB 129/44; *FRUS 1950 Vol. 3*, pp. 585–604ff.

83 ibid., pp. 604–5; see also T. Carpenter, 'United States' NATO policy at the Crossroads: the "Great Debate" of 1950–1951', *International History Review* Vol. 8, No. 3 (1986), pp. 389–415.

84 CP(51)43, 7 Feb. 1951, CAB 129/44.

85 For the November note, see *FRUS 1950 Vol. 4*, pp. 902–3 and Britain's responses see 71st and 73rd mtgs, CAB 128/18.

86 10th and 12th mtgs, 29 Jan. and 8 Feb. 1951, CAB 128/19.

87 CP(51)74, 9 Mar. 1951, CAB 129/44; Bevin to Kirkpatrick, tel. 77, 23 Feb. 1951, FO 371/93376.

88 Dalton diaries, 31 Dec. 1951, Dalton papers, Part I/38, British Library of Political and Economic Science, London School of Economics and Political Science (LSE); D. Hill (ed.) *Tribune 40* (London: Quartet Books, 1977), pp. 93–4; transcripts of interviews between Kenneth Younger and Richard Rose, 27 December 1961, Younger papers, Nuffield College; P. Williams, *Hugh Gaitskell* (Oxford: Oxford University Press, 1982), p. 168.

89 See Kenneth Younger diaries, 4 Feb. 1951 (by kind permission of Professor G. Warner).

90 P. Addison, *The Road to 1945* (London: Jonathan Cape, 1975), p. 113.

91 Mélandri, 'France and the Atlantic Alliance, 1950–1953', in *Western Security*, p. 272; Adenauer, *Memoirs*, p. 315; Poole, *JCS Vol. 4*, pp. 85–6, 93, 109; CP(51)230, 27 July 1951, CAB 129/47. For the four-power talks, see Davies report, 29 June 1951, FO 371/93349; Strang minute, 30 June 1951, FO 371/93349; CP(51)239, 30 Aug. 1951, CAB 129/47.

92 Morgan, *Labour in Power*, pp. 434–5; H. Pelling, *The Labour Governments 1945–1951* (London: Macmillan, 1985), p. 248.

93 B. Pimlott, *Hugh Dalton* (London: Macmillan, 1986), p. 598; Harris, *Attlee*, pp. 475–8; F. Williams, *A Prime Minister Remembers* (London: Heinemann, 1961) pp. 247–9; D. Hill, *Tribune*, p. 82.

94 *FRUS 1951 Vol. 3*, p. 1,289.

95 CP(51)233, CAB 129/47.

96 CP(51)74 and 240, 9 Mar., 30 Aug. 1951, CAB 129/44 and 47; B. Oppen (ed.) *Documents on Germany under Occupation, 1945–54* (London: Oxford University Press, 1955), pp. 550–3.

97 For the German views, see H. J. Rautenberg, Part 6 in MGFA (ed.) *Anfänge westdeutscher Sicherheitspolitik, 1945–1956 – Von der Kapitulation bis zum Pleven-Plan* (München: R. Oldenbourg Verlag, 1982), p. 813; Rautenberg and Wiggershaus, *Die 'Himmeroder Denkschrift' vom Oktober 1950* (Freiberg: MGFA, 1985) pp. 27–8, 43. Speidel, *Erinnerungen* pp. 287–90ff. For the record of the Bonn Talks see *FRUS 1950 Vol. 3*, pp. 990–1,047; CAB 21/1899 (9 Jan. and 18, 19 Feb. 1951); PREM 8/1429 (3 Feb.); CP(51)43 and 74, 7 Feb. and 9 Mar. 1951, CAB 129/44.

98 For the record of the Paris Conference between February and June 1951, see *FRUS 1951 Vol. 3*, pp. 755–98; for the less complete reports from Harvey, see CAB 21/1784; see also Massigli, *Une Comédie*, pp. 270–1. For Morrison's view, see CP (51)128, 8 May 1951, CAB 21/1784.

99 20th mtg, 26 July 1951, CAB 131/10; 56th mtg, 30 July 1951, CAB 128/20.

100 *FRUS 1951 Vol. 3*, pp. 800, 805–12, 837–46, 856–65; Speidel, *Erinnerungen*, pp. 292–3; CAB 21/1784 (23 July); H. Schwartz, *Adenauer – Der Aufstieg* (Stuttgart: Deutsche Verlags-Anstalt, 1986), p. 873; A. Bérard, *Un Ambassadeur se souvient* (Paris: Plon, 1978), p. 375; Massigli, *Une Comédie*, pp. 280–3ff; S. Ambrose, *Eisenhower Vol. 1* (London: George Allen & Unwin, 1984), pp. 501–8.

101 118th mtg, 20 July 1951, DEFE 4/45; CP(51)233, 24 July 1951, CAB 129/47.

102 CP(51)240, 30 Aug. 1951, CAB 129/47; 58th mtg, 4 Sept. 1951, CAB 128/20.

103 For the British views on the European Army plan, see CP(51)233, 239 and 240, 24 July, 30 and 30 Aug. 1950, CAB 129/47; 56th and 58th mtgs, 30 July and 4 Sept. 1951, CAB 128/20.

104 *FRUS 1951 Vol. 3*, p. 1,306.

105 ibid., pp. 1,268–71; CP(51)266, 22 Oct. 1951, CAB 129/49.

106 See Britain's commitment to the EDC during the Churchill govt, S. Dockrill, 'The Evolution of Britain's Policy towards a European Army, 1950–54', *Journal of Strategic Studies* Vol. 12, No. 1 (Mar. 1989), pp. 47–58.

9

In the back room: Anglo-American defence co-operation, 1945–51

Alex Danchev

'See what the boys in the back room will have...'
Frenchy (Marlene Dietrich) in *Destry Rides Again* (1939)

'Don't you think we can meet in the back room for the global business
and let the French continue in the North Atlantic Treaty Organization?'
This brazenly conspiratorial proposition was made by the Chief of Staff
of the United States Air Force (USAF), General Hoyt S. Vandenberg, at
a closed meeting of the American and British Chiefs of Staff in October
1950. It was recorded in the ramshackle US minutes but expunged from
the published record.[1] Post-war Anglo-American defence co-operation is
a will-o'-the-wisp. To pin it down one has to dig deep and sift carefully,
in the manner of the archaeologist, but also acculturate, like some intrepid
anthropologist, to a strange and secretive society whose intricate social
and professional networks are familiar to their members but quite baffling
to the outsider, whose currency is the informal understanding, and whose
transactions consist chiefly of unwritten and sometimes unspoken agreements or, failing that, ritual denunciation. For this exacting inquiry
Vandenberg's words are freighted with meaning. First of all, they convey
a certain attitude. It is well understood that the British actively sought a
'special relationship' with the United States in this period. There were
obvious reasons for them to do so – primarily, the sapping need for
financial support. It is not well understood that key American decision-
makers were open to suggestion. These men were susceptible to special
arrangements, if not to a special relationship *tout court*. The reasons for
this susceptibility were perhaps less obvious but no less real. They had
little or nothing to do with sentiment. Personal experience and personal
circumstances certainly played their part, but official USA was as unmoved
by the grandiloquent exhortation of Winston Churchill's 'fraternal association of the English-speaking peoples' as by the Pilgrim Society's maudlin
annual chorus of 'hands across the sea'. The US Secretary of State, Dean
Acheson – one of the most susceptible and also one of the most significant

– caught something of the general feeling in a characteristically direct speech to the British-American Parliamentary Group in London.

I shall not bother you by doing what is done so often on occasions like this, of talking about all that we have in common: language, history and all of that. We know all that. What I do wish to stress is one thing which we have in common, one desperately important thing, and that is that we have a common fate.[2]

Immediately after the Second World War no one else was in the global business. Coping with the Cold War was ineluctably an Anglo-American predicament.

If Vandenberg's proposition alerts us to the intriguing possibilities for clandestine co-operation, the way in which the proposition was made also signals the constraints felt (and imposed) by the Americans. Ideally, the British wanted a relationship that was not only special but also exclusive and avowed. They ached to jump 'the European queue', in the recurrent metaphor of the time; to be the full partner and not the poor relation of the United States – an aspiration dating from at least 1942.[3] Fearful of being jilted or simply ignored, the British required constant reassurance from Washington in the form of information, consultation and association. But the Americans were frustratingly undemonstrative. To them the relationship was a matter for consenting adults meeting in private. Specialness was stealthily conceded, but publicly disavowed. This was made distressingly plain in the celebrated case of the unmentionable paper of 1950. In preparation for a round of talks between Acheson and the Foreign Secretary, Ernest Bevin, in London in May, British officials had undertaken the Sisyphean task of codifying the nature of the special relationship in a discussion paper. The purpose of the exercise from the British point of view was encapsulated in the title of a later draft, 'Continued Consultation on and Co-ordination of Policy'. This version of the paper came before the ministers on 10 May 1950. Discussion began and ended with a short pronouncement from the Secretary of State.

MR. ACHESON said that he had read the paper before him and had been struck by two thoughts. The first was that he entirely agreed with the general content of the paper in its exposition of the need for close and continued consultation on all the parallel interests of the United States and the United Kingdom. The second was that it was quite impossible to allow it to be known that any such paper had been drawn up or that it had been agreed to.[4]

Some three years later, reviewing his State Department stewardship in the company of a number of close colleagues, Acheson gave full vent to his feelings. On arrival in London for the talks he had been 'shocked, horrified and overwhelmed to discover that there was a paper which spelled out this common law marriage in a way which I thought would utterly destroy us if it were ever known, either to our allies or to anybody in the United States'.[5] Just as the Roosevelt administration became increasingly sensitive to the appearance of what General Marshall called 'ganging up' on the Soviets, so the Truman administration became increasingly sensitive to the *amour propre* of its other European allies – the French in particular – especially after the North Atlantic Treaty, signed in April 1949, began to take shape as a genuine organization. The Standing Group of NATO's Military Committee, for example, was established in October 1949 with representatives from three, not two, countries: the USA, the UK and France. 'Special relationships', Paul Nitze has observed, 'can be poisonous' – or just embarrassing.[6] For his part, Acheson reflected that 'nothing has ever seemed to me truer than that [a special relationship] existed; nothing has ever seemed to me more dangerous than talking about it, and certainly writing it down'. He was determined that the paper should not be considered. 'You either talked about it and repudiated it, which was terrible; or you talked about it and agreed to it, which was bad; or you talked about it and got nowhere with it, which was worse'.[7] Unsurprisingly, Acheson had his way. The British paper was an aberration, a bid for unaccustomed definition. Its very existence transgressed the accepted norms of a closed society. The elders of Anglo-Saxondom knew this instinctively. Acheson's friend and confessor, the widely esteemed British ambassador Sir Oliver Franks, has noted shrewdly that throughout a remarkably close personal association the words 'special relationship' never passed their lips.[8] Thus the unmentionable paper provoked an almost pathological response. As the sound and the fury died away, the customary evasions supervened.

Such a pathology was not confined to Washington. Donald Cameron Watt has expressed it exactly: 'Both British and American elites, anxious that these issues should not be openly explored, entered therefore on a conspiracy to misrepresent their relationship'.[9] In consequence the extent and nature of post-war Anglo-American defence co-operation has continued to elude definition. A traditional reading of the relationship proposes a swollen wartime alliance disintegrating with surprising speed in 1945; little but recrimination in 1946; some movement in 1947; virtual reconstitution in 1948–9; and renewed irritation in 1950–1, assuaged somewhat by the reappearance late in the day of that old war man Winston Churchill.[10] On this view there was a hiatus in the special relationship, or more exactly a moratorium imposed by the United States, in whose gift it is thought to lie. The period of the moratorium varies in these accounts, but is often said to run almost three years, from the abrupt ending of Lend-Lease in August 1945 to the decision to counter the Berlin blockade in June 1948. At this juncture, it is argued, the United States relented and a special relationship was at once resumed, on a quasi-wartime basis, under the pressure of external events: as witness the Berlin airlift of 1948–9, a remarkably effective combined operation on the wartime model.[11]

Such an interpretation has the virtue of clear periodization and, implicitly, a proper recognition of defence co-operation (subsuming intelligence co-operation) as the heart and soul of Anglo-American relations. As an answer to the fundamental question of what endured and what vanished in the relationship after the Second World War, however, it is profoundly unconvincing. For one thing, how was co-operation immediately restored at many different levels during the Berlin crisis if relations had been quite so exiguous for quite so long? It seems that there was more to the 1945–8 relationship than meets the eye – a common Anglo-American phenomenon. The reality was both messier and richer than historians or indeed the principals themselves have been prepared to acknowledge. Why this was so is not something that a traditional reading can readily explain. Its monolithic picture of Washington policy-making cannot comprehend what Ernest May has called the peculiarities of the American system in this period: 'the newness of the apparatus of national power, the inherent fragmentation of the governmental apparatus as a whole, the burden of lessons drawn from recent history, and a extraordinary openness to influence from sources outside the nation'.[12] Chief among those sources were the British, who grasped the double opportunity of the inside track and variously handicapped rivals to 'work' Washington more diligently and more effectually than anyone else. Oliver Franks had no ambassadorial peer in this period; his access and influence at all levels of the State Department was unique. This was especially true of the Secretary's inner circle of philosopher-kings – men like Philip Jessup, Paul Nitze, Dean Rusk and, for a while, George Kennan – who regarded Franks as one of themselves: 'a useful member of the central team of the US government', as Nitze put it.[13] Marshal of the RAF Lord Tedder established a similarly privileged position with his American counterparts, as Chief of the Air Staff (1946–9) and, in an unusual but highly significant switch, chairman of the British Joint Services Mission in Washington (1950–1). As the sagacious Sir Ambrose Abercrombie says in Evelyn Waugh's 'Anglo-American tragedy', *The Loved One*, which first appeared in 1948, 'we limeys have a peculiar position to keep up, you know. . . . We can't all be at the top of the tree but we are all men of responsibility. You never find an Englishman among the underdogs – except in England of course'.[14]

Nor was the quality of the relationship simply determined by American whim. 'Magnanimity was not the issue at all'.[15] Certainly the British were reliant on the Americans, not only financially but strategically too. The gross asymmetry in disposable power meant that Bevin's preferred 'basis of partnership' with the United States was extraordinarily difficult to negotiate. As the editor of the official series of British diplomatic documents notes, with unofficial tartness, 'Whether such a "basis of partnership" could exist between a debtor nation and its major creditor was a question posed rather than answered'. In October 1945 Bevin himself remarked on the danger of the UK being 'plucked' like a chicken by her wartime allies.[16] But relative British weakness should not be exaggerated. There was also a gross asymmetry, never to be repeated, between the United Kingdom and any other potential ally. Even at the end of this period the UK was still easily the third greatest power in the world, and clearly *secundus inter pares* in the West. The USA was 'spread from hell to breakfast' throughout the international jungle: an environment full of traps for the unwary.[17] In the circumstances, reliance was not one-way. Paradoxically, at the apogee of its power the United States found itself in need of a well-placed friend. The assessment embodied in an internal State Department memorandum of March 1950 would have commanded widespread, if furtive, agreement:

> Certainly the UK is our closest friend and strongest and most dependable ally. The British and ourselves have far more worldwide interests than any other nation and are the only two in a position to fight anywhere in the world in the event of war or to wield much influence all over the world in peacetime. The British have much strategically located real estate which is of vital importance to us. Clearly and inevitably we must have a special relationship with the British, which must be the basic core of any wider grouping. This will continue to constitute an inevitable financial drain upon us.[18]

There is a suggestion here of that profound 'sense of political company' that was such an important factor in the post-war Anglo-American relationship.[19] Because this intangible element is an easy prey for the mythologist it is apt to deceive. Anglo-American affinities have been persistently mythologized, usually by the underdog British for their own selfish purposes. In themselves, of course, myths can express a potent political reality, as the career of the British mythologist-in-chief, Winston Churchill, makes very clear. Gallingly out of office during the 1945–51 period, Churchill busied himself in reinterpreting to an attentive public the greatest Anglo-American experience of his lifetime, the Second World War. He did so in six copious volumes of war memoirs published between 1948 and 1954, a carefully crafted testament to the special relationship that worked; and in the endlessly fascinating 'Iron Curtain' speech of March 1946, a remarkably candid adumbration of the special relationship that survived. 'Fraternal association', he explained to his American audience, 'requires not only the growing friendship and mutual understanding between our two vast but kindred systems of society', but also

the continuance of the intimate relationships between our military

219

advisers, leading to common study of potential dangers, similarity of weapons and manuals of instruction and interchange of officers and cadets at colleges. It should carry with it the continuance of present facilities for mutual security by the joint use of all naval and air force bases in the possession of either country all over the world. This would perhaps double the mobility of the American Navy and Air Force. It would greatly expand that of the British Empire forces and might well lead, if and as the world calms down, to important financial savings. Already we use together a large number of islands; many more will be intrusted to our joint care in the near future.[20]

In Churchill's declamatory style, myth and entreaty regularly jostled with fact. But the fact of 'intimate relationships', half-buried and regularly disclaimed, is indisputable. British and American elites, civil and military, were harnessed together. This was what a sense of company meant in practice. To probe the kind of company they kept, not only in Washington and London but also in embassies and outstations all over the world, is to appreciate the delicacy and complexity of Anglo-American defence co-operation in these years. One indicator of the strength of these ties is the amount of information exchanged between the two. A proxy for this, a crude index of 'specialness', is the existence of highly classified American documents in British archives, and vice versa. The results naturally vary (by region and department, for example), but overall the incidence of such documentary migration is impressively high – higher, probably, than for any other international pairing and higher than for any other period in Anglo-American relations, with the singular exception of 1942–5. But this is only an indicator. Human relations cannot be reconstructed from documents, not even from the transaction implicit in a fugitive copy. As John Lewis Gaddis has written,

> the traditional sources upon which [historians] depend – archives, memoirs, contemporary published materials – do little more than suggest the informal lines of influence that flow from close personal friendships or from intimate professional collaboration; conversations occurring in corridors or over the telephone, or at cocktail parties . . . can at times shape events more decisively than whole stacks of official memoranda that find their way into the archives.[21]

Much of this informal influence remains to be reconstructed. In the formative phase of the United Nations in 1945–6 little is known of the collaboration on the Executive Committee between Adlai Stevenson and Gladwyn Jebb, both destined for greater fame.[22] In the concoction of a European Recovery Programme in 1947 the extent of the 'friendly aid' offered by a cabal of key American diplomats to the British leadership has yet to be fully revealed.[23] In the progressive hardening of attitudes towards the Soviet Union in 1946 the influential 'collusion' between the American and British chargés d'affaires in Moscow, George Kennan and Frank Roberts, has at last been extensively analysed; but the equally happy relationship between Roberts and the US ambassador, the ulcerous General Walter Bedell Smith, is still widely unappreciated, in spite of the fact that the consultative practices thereby established assumed some operational importance during the Berlin crisis of 1948. Kennan joked with Roberts that it was rather a waste of time having two embassies when one would do. The arrangements were reminiscent of a small-scale and informal version of the vast integrated wartime theatre commands – the very system that Bedell Smith had organized and run so successfully for Eisenhower at SHAEF (Supreme Headquarters Allied Expeditionary Force).[24]

Perhaps the greatest legacy of the wartime period was the Combined Chiefs of Staff (CCS) organization, an intricate fretwork of specialist Anglo-American committees (planning, intelligence, communications, transport, production and the like) which managed the war effort under the executive direction of the CCS themselves, that is the American and the British Chiefs of Staff, or their representatives, sitting together.[25] This grand and unprecedented experiment in institutionalized co-operation had been in outward decline since mid-1944. Meetings of the CCS committee in Washington were no longer held weekly, as had been customary. Less and less information was exchanged as a matter of course, particularly after the death in November 1944 of the senior British member of the CCS, Field Marshal Sir John Dill, whose means of access to the diverse channels of the US military establishment were unsurpassed. Consultation by request increasingly prevailed. The requests were usually British: a disturbing pattern appeared to be emerging. When the war ended the CCS entered a kind of official limbo. It was not disbanded, nor was it active, as such. By December 1945 some combined committees had withered and died; others eked out a precarious existence on the coat-tails of the old Anglo-American wartime aristocracy. Yet the picture of decline should not be overdrawn. The organization was moribund; but the animating spirit was never completely quenched. At American behest, co-operation went underground. Substantive collaboration continued on research and development, standardization of equipment, tactical doctrine, operational analysis, officer training, scientific and technical information exchange (notably in the burgeoning field of electronic communications), intelligence assessments and operations, raw materials, and the sinister promise of biological and chemical warfare.[26]

Co-operation, therefore, did not cease but merely disappeared from view after the end of the war. Underground rather than open collaboration was effectively imposed on the British by the American Chiefs of Staff, who pleaded the political embarrassment of public recognition but used the strength of their bargaining position to try to control, and if necessary curtail, the collaborative process.[27] Political embarrassment, however, was not an entirely specious argument. It seems that the Truman administration was unaware of the extent of continuing collaboration – an early instance of the convenient mask of deniability. On the British side the picture is less clear, but it is likely that even the masterful Ernest Bevin, powered by a well-oiled Foreign Office machine, knew only part of the story; and certain that successive defence ministers (the acquiescent A. V. Alexander and the suspiciously doctrinaire Emanuel Shinwell) knew virtually nothing.[28] Anglo-American defence co-operation depended not so much on explicit political direction as on the strength and continuity of personal connections; on inter-Service and inter-agency calculation of the advantages to be had from making common cause; on the technical and strategic data of the day; and on the gravity and urgency of the perceived threat, for as Richard Ullman has reminded us, the Anglo-American enterprise was nothing if not a *pax anti-Sovietica* in inspiration.[29]

All of these factors were bound up in the strategic orientation of the two countries, a frame of reference perhaps best encapsulated by George Orwell in a novel written, presciently, in 1948 and published the following year.

> At this moment . . . Oceania was at war with Eurasia and in alliance with Eastasia. In no public or private utterance was it ever admitted that the three powers had at any time been grouped along different lines. Actually, as Winston well knew, it was only four years since Oceania had been at war with Eastasia and in alliance with Eurasia. But that was only a piece of furtive knowledge which he happened to possess because his memory was not satisfactorily under control. . . . Everything had been different then. Even the names of countries, and their shapes on the map, had been different. Airstrip One, for instance, had not been so called in those days: it had been called England, or Britain, though London, he felt fairly certain, had always been called London.[30]

'Airstrip One' expressed a fundamental truth: in this period British territory was central to American war planning and strategic capability. Those who found this truth unpalatable could reflect that Britain's position, literally and figuratively, was a wasting strategic asset. Those who coveted special ties, however, or merely saw the immediate need, could nurture the Airstrip One relationship with few regrets.

The basic US Emergency War Plans of these years – from PINCHER in April 1946 through HALFMOON in May 1948 to OFFTACKLE in November 1949 – all assumed that the Soviets could overrun the whole of the Eurasian land-mass more or less at will.[31] No direct defence was possible. Anglo-American occupation forces in Germany would simply abandon the continent when necessary. Re-entry was rightly assumed to be as problematical as in the previous war. OFFTACKLE was the first of these plans seriously to countenance an OVERLORD-type reinvasion of Western Europe, in the war's third phase, D+12 to D+24 months (that is one to two years after the outbreak of hostilities); even this was believed to be extremely dubious on logistic grounds alone.[32] The bleak assumptions of the US planners were shared by their British and Canadian counterparts. Contrary to the traditional interpretation, informal Anglo-American consultation on the implications of the war plans took place as early as mid-1946, often at American initiative. The pressing need to co-ordinate planning for evacuation operations and the doubtful feasibility of holding a bridgehead for this purpose led to a flurry of working-level meetings, involving both the British Joint Services Mission (BJSM) in Washington and American and British commanders in Europe.[33] At the Chiefs of Staff level, the Washington visit of the new CIGS, Field Marshal Montgomery, in September 1946 meant a good deal less than his extensive self-advertisement would have us believe. On the other hand the untrumpeted London visit of the new US Army Chief of Staff, General Eisenhower, in the following month was most productive.[34] The war plans themselves were discussed in detail by the American, British and Canadian planners during week-long talks in Washington in April and October 1948 and again in September–October 1949. Perhaps understandably, both the plans and the talks were earnestly kept from the French.[35]

The foundation of action in all American and British war plans was the early use of the 'absolute weapon' of which the United States then enjoyed a monopoly. HALFMOON, for example, envisaged 'a powerful air offensive designed to exploit the destructive and psychological power of atomic weapons against the vital elements of Soviet war-making capacity'.[36] Typically, the offensive would begin on D+15 (fifteen days after the outbreak of hostilities) or conceivably as soon as D+6. Targeting was far from being an exact science. There was in fact no calculated strategy for destroying Soviet war-making capacity. The type of target usually mentioned – centres of government, industrial areas, petroleum refineries, electricity power-plants and submarine building yards – in effect meant only one thing: bombing cities. In 1948 HALFMOON called for dropping fifty atomic bombs on twenty Soviet cities (the priorities being Moscow, Leningrad, Gorky, Kuybyshev and Baku) in the hope of causing 'immediate paralysis of at least fifty percent of Soviet industry'. Whether 50 per cent would be achieved, and if so whether it would be sufficient, were not questions which the authors of the plan were equipped to answer. As late as December 1950, when the eminent strategist Bernard Brodie was invited by Vandenberg to examine the target list he was astonished to find that the planners 'simply expected the Soviet Union "to collapse" as a result of the bombing campaign. . . . People kept talking about the "Sunday punch" '.[37]

Crude reliance on the Sunday punch was not simply a matter of intellectual shortcomings in the planning process. It was an indication of the primitive state of the nuclear deterrent.[38] In theory the United States had a tremendous advantage over the Soviet Union in the terrifying trial of strength that was the early Cold War. In practice there were a number of shocking deficiencies in American atomic capability. (British capability, in terms of a weapon system, was a nullity at this stage: a bomb 'with a bloody Union Jack on top of it', as Bevin said, was covertly sanctioned in January 1947 and successfully tested only in October 1952.)[39] The deficiencies were known at the time only to a privileged few. Shared secrets make a powerful bond; for those who knew, especially for a small Anglo-American coterie of atomically minded air force officers, collaboration was made a little easier.

In 1945 the only available delivery system for the bomb was the B-29 bomber, the Superfortress, specially modified for the purpose. At the time of the Berlin crisis in mid-1948 there were no more than about thirty of these 'atomic-capable' bombers in service, all in the 509th Bomber Group at Roswell Field, New Mexico. Combat-ready crews were at a premium. There was a stockpile of fifty bombs – no doubt the explanation for this requirement in the war plan – which was an enormous advance on the puny totals of nine in mid-1946 and thirteen in mid-1947, but as yet a relatively small arsenal. All of these bombs were the Mark III 'Fatman' type dropped on Nagasaki, weighing about 10,000 pounds, and believed to be as unreliable as they were unwieldy. The bomb canisters and their atomic cores were stored separately. To assemble each weapon and load it into the aeroplane might take a skilled bomb assembly team two days. (When the new Mark IV bomb became available in 1949 the time was halved, which still meant an inordinate delay.) The bomb then remained ready for forty-eight hours. After that it had to be partially disassembled in order to recharge the batteries powering the fusing and monitoring systems. In January 1949 there were but seven fully trained assembly teams in the United States.

Thus loaded, the B-29 had an effective combat radius of roughly 1,600 miles. It could not reach Soviet targets from the United States and return home. The domestic solutions to this strategic impasse tended to be both expensive and protracted. Flying one-way missions – deliberately planning to crash-land in enemy territory – immediately doubled the combat radius, but at terrible cost. Utilizing aircraft carriers for atomic bombers raised formidable technical difficulties surmounted only in the late 1950s, to say nothing of the political repercussions of deploying these 'floating fortresses' in remote and perhaps hostile waters. Increasing the range of the bomber itself by developing new variants or new techniques also took time: it was not until 1951 that the intercontinental though unproven B-36 became available in quantity or that in-flight refuelling was practised as a matter of course. By then, too, there were over 250 atomic-capable aircraft, a stockpile of some 400 bombs of improved design, and a sizeable complement of combat-ready ground and air crew. Nevertheless, throughout this period the essence of Washington's problem remained the same: the vaunted atomic air offensive was impossible for the United States to deliver unaided. The absolute weapon was absolutely dependent on the ample provision of forward airbases.

To satisfy their voracious appetite for bases the Americans turned inevitably to Britain. It was not only that Britain herself could resume her wartime role as 'unsinkable aircraft carrier' for US forces, but almost everywhere the Americans went they had to contend with the mother country. Malta, Gibraltar, Cyprus, Libya, Aden, Cairo, Suez, the Bahamas, Ceylon, Sudan, Iraq, Jordan, the Persian Gulf – the barbicans and tollgates of Empire gave access to a veritable fleet of 'aircraft carriers' all over the world, and more particularly around the Soviet Union. (Similar considerations impelled intelligence collaboration. In his mischief-making memoirs Kim Philby recalled a remark made by a US covert operations officer: 'Whenever we want to subvert any place we find the British own an island within easy reach'.)[40] Some bases were naturally more attractive than others: a complex calculation of distance from the target, security of the base area, available facilities, development potential, climatic conditions and diplomatic convenience, with cost very much a secondary consideration. The war plans told the results. The principal operating bases for the atomic air offensive were to be the UK, Okinawa in the Pacific, the Cairo–Suez area – a traditional cockpit of war, about which there were grave doubts – and at least until 1948 the Karachi-Lahore area of what became Pakistan (formerly North West India).

The greatest of these was the UK. The distance from London to Moscow is a feasible 1,500 miles; the tempting oilfields of Ploesti were also within range. Alternative bases could theoretically match this reach, but on every other consideration there was simply no contest. In the wake of the Berlin crisis American facilities in the UK mushroomed at an unparalleled rate: not only for bombers but also for fighters, aerial reconnaisance, navigation systems, storage and stockpiling, command, communications and, of course, intelligence. USAF bases alone increased from five in mid-1949 (with some 7,000 personnel) to forty-three in mid-1953 (with some 50,000 personnel).[41] The enduring weapons-for-bases relationship, famously begun in September 1940 with fifty superannuated destroyers, was triumphantly re-established in July 1948 with sixty atomic bombers.[42] Overnight, it appeared that Airstrip One had become a reality.

The appearance, however, was a little deceptive. In the first place, it is now common knowledge that none of the B-29s transferred to Britain in July and August 1948 had been modified for atomic operations. It is less often remarked that the bombs themselves remained in the United States.

To this extent the deterrent threat implicit in the arrival of the bombers in the European theatre was a hollow one. Their actual status was reported without comment in the American technical press.[43] Whether it was also reported to the Soviets by Donald Maclean from the British embassy in Washington is a matter for speculation. Those concerned with the operational details of the transfer would not have been misled; but incredible as it may seem, it is perfectly possible that there were some on both sides of the Atlantic who thought they were transferring truly atomic bombers when in fact they were not. So eager was London to accept them that in great secrecy on 29 June 1948 the US Secretary of State sent an unusually explicit caution to his British opposite number:

> With respect to the two B-29 groups which we contemplate sending to Britain . . . : before taking [the] final decision we wish to be absolutely certain that there is no British hesitancy in giving their consent and that Bevin has given full consideration to the effect which the return of US bomber forces might have on British opinion. Also we wish to be sure that Bevin has no concern that this action will constitute unnecessary provocation to the Soviets. In other words we do not wish to exercise pressure on the British unless they are anxious and willing to have these planes available.[44]

Bevin hesitated for a full two weeks. The Americans were then cordially invited in. There were no formalities, no conditions, no reservations. As the newly installed commander of the USAF declared, with unwonted candour, 'Never before in history has one first-class power gone into another first-class power's country without any agreement. We were just told to come over and "we shall be pleased to have you".'[45]

Modified B-29s began to arrive in the UK during the following year. Not until late 1950 were they all atomic-capable. Exactly when the bombs themselves were transferred remains something of a mystery, bound up with the internecine warfare within the US administration for effective control of the atomic weapon. Some components certainly arrived in 1950 after presidential authorization; officially they did not include the atomic cores, which were to be flown over in the event of an emergency – a bureaucratically convenient but strategically impractical arrangement clearly unsatisfactory to the respective air forces.[46] Those in a position to know cannot or will not say, but there is a suggestion that special arrangements may have been made through Service channels for a number of bombs, complete with 'the business end', to be stored in the UK at the same time as the arrival of the first aeroplanes capable of delivering them, in mid-1949.[47]

Such a suggestion is all the more plausible when it is realized that the much-trumpeted transfer of B-29s in 1948 was merely an augmentation of strength rather than a fundamental departure: a public occasion – even a declaratory gesture – rather than a new concord. The truth was that for all practical purposes the smuggled 'return' of US bomber forces to the UK had been accomplished some two years before the Berlin crisis erupted. In June–July 1946 the so-called Spaatz–Tedder Agreement provided for the preparation of five bases in East Anglia (Lakenheath, Mildenhall, Scampton, Marham and Bassingbourn) for emergency use by the USA, including two specially equipped with 'certain physical facilities' for the handling of atomic bombs; and for the inauguration of 'training flights' on a rotational basis by units of the newly formed Strategic Air Command (SAC).[48] Bomb assembly and loading facilities were ready by early 1947. Regular SAC rotational tours began, unsung, in July of the same year. Spaatz and Tedder were the respective Air Force Chiefs of Staff; as far as can be ascertained, they acted on their own initiative. Their informal agreement, embodied in a miscellaneous collection of elliptical memoranda, is little known and little understood; yet it is part of the basic infrastructure of post-war Anglo-American defence co-operation. The two men were old sparring partners; they had cut their strategic teeth on the combined organization in the Second World War. More importantly, they both understood the deficiencies of the deterrent. They knew that they could help each other, and at the same time help themselves. The atomic bomb was an air force weapon now – only after 1958 did it become a naval one – and it had to be safeguarded. SAC was grievously unprepared for large-scale combat operations; the RAF was overstretched and underfunded. The Red menace was gathering in the East. In many ways the situation of the two air forces in 1946–7 paralleled that of the two armies in 1941–2. As in the earlier period, the time was ripe for an understanding to mature.

There is abundant evidence that the Americans intended that their presence in the UK would become 'somewhat of an accepted fixture', in the hopeful words of the US Secretary of Defence, and that the British connived at this purpose.[49] British policy-makers were guilty of neither entrapment nor complaisance, as is sometimes alleged. In 1948 the arrangement (or lack of arrangement) was merely expedient for both parties. With the passage of time, however, Bevin in particular became increasingly anxious to regularize the position. British concern focused on the fundamental safeguards of termination and consultation. The first of these was addressed rather obliquely in what is known as the Ambassador's Agreement of April 1950, negotiated between the trusted US ambassador in London, Lewis Douglas, and the Parliamentary Under-Secretary of State for Air, Aidan Crawley. This informal agreement, little more than an exchange of letters, was an attempt jointly to regulate a substantial new construction programme for additional US bases in the Oxford area (Upper Heyford, Brize Norton, Fairford and Greenham Common) and to find a mutually acceptable formula for sharing the costs involved; it also provided that bases in the UK would be made available to the USAF 'so long as both governments considered it desirable in the interests of common defence'.[50] Of course, in the early 1950s no British government would have considered otherwise. Unilateral abrogation by the underdog was scarcely conceivable.

Consultation was at once more urgent and more difficult to achieve. London sought prior consultation with Washington not only on the use to be made of US bases in the UK, but also on the use (or threatened use) of US atomic weapons world-wide – in Korea for instance. The British interest was unpalatably plain: no annihilation without representation. Once upon a time, they recalled, there had been a marvellous collaborative mission.[51] British science and British scientists had fertilized the wartime 'Manhattan project' to build a bomb before the Germans did so. At Quebec in August 1943 Churchill and Roosevelt had signed an agreement not to use it against third parties without each other's consent – ostensibly, an absolute veto – and at Hyde Park, New York, in September 1944 an *aide-mémoire* on full collaboration for both military and commercial purposes after the war. But the fairy-tale promise of these developments never materialized. The perfunctory way in which British consent was requested for the dropping of the bomb in August 1945 bespoke the letter rather than the spirit of the Quebec agreement. The outcome of the Washington conference of November 1945 between the heirs to the wartime legacy, Attlee and Truman, was not encouraging.[52] The passage through Congress of the notorious McMahon Act in August 1946 formally severed the main arteries of atomic information exchange, the vital source of any genuine consultation.[53] Numb with shock, London lurched on alone.

Out of this packed history grew two fundamental beliefs, deeply at odds with each other. To the British, atomic consultation was a right, to be reclaimed as a matter of natural justice and shared risk. Under the draconian regime of the McMahon Act Washington was practising nothing less than atomic extortion. Compensation was deserved and overdue, just as it was in the matter of economic recovery. To the Americans, on the other hand, atomic consultation was a privilege, to be granted or withheld according to the dictates of Washington politics and state security. After Hiroshima, the constitutional authority of the President and Commander-in-Chief with regard to the absolute weapon would not be compromised by written commitments to allies, however special their relationship. In January 1948 the *modus vivendi* summarily removed the requirement for consent, made no offer to consult, and restored only limited technical atomic information exchange in return. Given that the Americans were nearly desperate to obtain agreement on an increased allocation of uranium for their own project, it was a very bad bargain for the British.[54]

An ever larger supply of uranium was indispensable to the expansionary

US atomic weapons project. Both London and Washington fancied that the key to this supply was held by the British. In June 1944 Churchill and Roosevelt had established a kind of global prospecting and procurement agency, the Combined Development Trust (CDT), to acquire as much uranium as could profitably be found.[55] At this juncture the only major source for the West was the rich ore of the Belgian Congo: the all-important contracts were negotiated by the British. The greatest potential source was believed to be South Africa: Washington relied upon British good offices to secure it. Britain's influence as procurator for the new atomic empire may have been, as Margaret Gowing has written, her 'one redeeming asset'.[56] Like her own geo-strategic position, however, it offered diminishing returns. By the early 1950s the United States and Canada were producing uranium of their own. Nevertheless, full collaboration in every aspect of raw materials continued, fretful yet unabated, throughout the McMahon years, a lifeline to both parties. Certainly the Americans got most of the available uranium; but the British got all they needed – the cheapest and highest grade of the 1946–7 Congo deliveries – and for sterling, with a timely 'dollar windfall' in the form of reimbursements from the USA for the extra American allocation. Without collaboration, it is most unlikely that the Americans would have got so much, so soon. In competition with the mighty dollar, the British might not have got any.

The UK did have another redeemable asset in this rarefied field. Certain individual British scientists were held to be virtually irreplaceable in the United States.[57] Ironically, the naturalized British atomic spy Klaus Fuchs worked at the very heart of the Manhattan project and left Los Alamos only in June 1946. At the first US post-war bomb test at Bikini in the Pacific in July 1946 Ernest Titterton, instrumentation group leader at Los Alamos as late as spring 1947, gave the countdown and detonation order; William Penney, whose presence had been specially requested for the purpose, played a leading part in the blast measurement and subsequent analysis. Penney remained *persona gratissima* in Washington throughout the period, as did the unassuming Nobel laureate James Chadwick. It was not all jam and kippers, as Chadwick once remarked, but it was something.[58]

The British position was unquestionably weakened, and American anti-Communist excitation worsened, by the revelation of a whole series of British security and intelligence failures. The most celebrated was the overnight disappearance in May 1951 of the diplomats Guy Burgess and Donald Maclean, the latter privy to some atomic information (though not as much as is commonly supposed) especially in his capacity as British secretary to the Combined Policy Committee in 1947–8. The corrosive effect of this astonishing farrago was permanent American suspicion of a 'Third Man', Kim Philby, who had occupied the extraordinarily sensitive position of SIS liaison with the CIA and FBI in Washington since September 1949, and who defected in his turn in 1963. The most damaging to atomic consultation was Fuchs's arrest in February 1950. Negotiations then in progress were abruptly suspended by the Americans as soon as the case broke. The interruption lasted for almost a year.[59] Suddenly, in December 1950, during a celebrated series of talks between Truman and Attlee in Washington, the old spectre reappeared. In the course of their fifth meeting, the President emerged from a brief *tête-à-tête* with the Prime Minister to announce cheerfully that they had been discussing the atomic bomb. He had apparently told Attlee 'that the governments of the United Kingdom and the United States had always been partners in this matter and that he would not consider the use of the bomb without consulting with the United Kingdom'. Attlee asked whether this agreement should be put in writing – an interesting question for Anglo-American defence co-operation – to which Truman made the characteristic response that 'if a man's word wasn't any good it wasn't made any better by writing it down'.[60]

With this textbook demonstration of back-room technique the British had to rest content. Acheson promptly remonstrated with his chief for going so far. The President's words were deleted from the American, though not the British, record of the talks. London maintained that an undertaking had been given. Washington was adamant that whatever passed between Truman and Attlee in private was an irrelevance: what mattered was the final communiqué, sanctioned by all. The communiqué was mute:

> The President stated that it was his hope that world conditions would never call for the use of the atomic bomb. The President told the Prime Minister that it was also his desire to keep the Prime Minister at all times informed of developments which might bring about a change in the situation.[61]

Despite this innocuous formulation, word of Truman's largess rocked the US delegation and provoked some dark muttering about being 'raped' by the British:

> I don't [know] which is worse, to have it in the communiqué, or to have Attlee tell the Commons about it, and make everybody think that Truman and Attlee made secret deals at which Truman lost his shirt. It will be like Yalta – a pretty and sweet communiqué, and then all the sordid details coming to light later.[62]

These forebodings were never realized. On his return to London the Prime Minister gave no hint of dissatisfaction with the assurances he had received. Nor did he attempt to exploit the ambiguities of his dealings with the

President.[63] Attlee was always an unlikely despoiler. The secrets of the back room were safe for the moment.

Thereafter the British struggled to catch the echo of Truman's words. Oliver Franks and the chairman of the BJSM in Washington (first Tedder, then Air Chief Marshal Sir William Elliot) had been accustomed to having informal and free-ranging 'politico-military' talks on a regular basis with a select few US officials led by Philip Jessup or Paul Nitze for the State Department and General Omar Bradley for the Joint Chiefs of Staff.[64] In September 1951, with the Attlee government at bay in a general election campaign, these men set themselves to defuse the political time-bomb of atomic consultation. An exhaustive discussion conducted with remarkable candour revealed that, though the Americans were prepared to meet the British position with regard to US bases in the UK, they were not prepared to make any concession on the wider issue. Thus the State Department summary concluded:

> On the question of whether we proposed to use UK bases without their consent, we stated, and General Bradley concurred, that prior consultation and agreement with them would obviously be required. . . .
> On the more general question of consultation . . . our position was that we wanted to talk to them frankly and in as broad an area as possible, but that we could not enter into any agreement or commitment or procedure that would imply a commitment, even a commitment to continue to talk or to follow any given procedure.[65]

Franks held out for more, but no more was forthcoming. A month elapsed. Election day loomed. Finally, following an earlier suggestion of Nitze's, he produced the Delphic formula which has become part of the essential grammar of the weapons-for-bases relationship, the foundation of all Anglo-American defence co-operation in the post-war period: 'The use of these bases in an emergency would be a matter for joint decision by His Majesty's Government and the United States Government in the light of the circumstances prevailing at the time'. This formula was immediately approved by the Americans. In addition, it was agreed that, if pressed on the issue of the bases, British ministers would reply 'there is naturally no question of their use in an emergency without our consent' – but only if pressed. Both governments also approved, but did not release, a statement drafted in Washington on 'Consultations on Atomic Warfare' which embroidered vacuously on the final communiqué of the Truman–Attlee talks.[66]

Taken together, these agreements appear to constitute the fabled 'Truman–Attlee Understandings', properly dated October 1951. They were confirmed by Winston Churchill during his own talks with Truman in January 1952. They have been regularly reaffirmed ever since. From the British point of view they surely leave a lot to be desired. And yet no one, not even Churchill, has been able to improve on them.[67] The only change effected by the ageing titan was the open publication of the 'joint decision' formula, an early indication of its supreme political serviceability for both London and Washington. The apparent weakness of the formula is in fact its great strength – it is open to interpretation.[68] Deliberate ambiguity can often cement an alliance, as the NATO strategy of 'flexible response' was later to show. From the Anglo-American point of view the Truman–Attlee Understandings attain an almost emblematic status. They mark the willingness of the policy-making elite of both countries to go tiger shooting together with surprisingly few qualms, something they were never prepared to do before the Second World War.[69] With all their tensions and tergiversations, their secrets and suppressions, the Truman–Attlee Understandings are the seminal product of a unique locus of power in the Cold War world, the Anglo-American back room.

ACKNOWLEDGEMENTS

The author held a Fellowship during 1989 at the Woodrow Wilson International Centre for Scholars in Washington DC and wishes to acknowledge the assistance of the Centre in researching this chapter.

NOTES

1 Approved Summary of Agreements and Conclusions, 23 October 1950, printed in *FRUS*, 1950, Vol. III, pp. 1,686–98. See items 10 and 11.
2 Talk to British–American Parliamentary Group, 26 June 1952, Acheson Papers, Box 67, HSTL.
3 'The queue' may have been Oliver Franks's coinage, much imitated in British official correspondence. See Franks to Attlee, 15 July 1950, FO 371/84089, PRO.
4 Record of 4th Bipartite Ministerial Meeting, 10 May 1950, printed in *DBPO*, Series II, Vol. II, doc. 84, pp. 288–94. See item VII. The paper is printed in ibid., doc. 67, pp. 242–4, and in *FRUS*, 1950, Vol. III, pp. 1,072–4. cf. R. Bissell, 'The Position of the UK and its Relations with the US', 22 March 1950, ECA, Special Assistant to Administrator, Box 1, RG 286, NA.
5 Princeton Seminars, 10 October 1953, Acheson Papers, Box 83, HSTL. cf. D. Acheson, *Present at the Creation* (New York: Norton, 1969), pp. 387–8.
6 Interview with Ambassador Paul H. Nitze, 31 May 1989. On the North Atlantic Treaty see A. Danchev, 'Taking the Pledge', *Diplomatic History*, Vol. 15, No. 2 (1991), pp. 199–219.
7 Princeton Seminars, *op. cit.* See also Acheson to Truman, 7 January 1953, Truman Papers, General File, Box 115, Churchill Folder, HSTL.
8 Interview with Lord Franks, 6 August 1987. On Franks see A. Danchev, *Founding Father* (Oxford: Oxford University Press, forthcoming); as ambassador, P. Boyle, 'Oliver Franks and the Washington Embassy', in J. Zametica (ed.) *British Officials and British Foreign Policy* (London: Pinter, 1990), pp. 189–211. 'The Anglo-Saxons' – de Gaulle's term – are subjected to critical scrutiny from left and right by C. Hitchens, *Blood, Class and Nostalgia* (London: Chatto, 1990), and H. Thomas, *Armed Truce* (London: Sceptre, 1988), pp. 285–327.
9 D. Cameron Watt, *Succeeding John Bull* (Cambridge: Cambridge University Press, 1984), p. 118.
10 For general surveys of Anglo-American relations in this period see R. Edmonds, *Setting*

the Mould (New York: Norton, 1986), pp. 87–224; R. Hathaway, *Great Britain and the United States* (Boston, Mass., Twayne, 1990), pp. 9–45; D. Dimbleby and D. Reynolds, *An Ocean Apart* (London: Hodder & Stoughton, 1988), pp. 162–202. For more on defence see J. Baylis, *Anglo-American Defence Relations* (London: Macmillan, 1984), pp. 29–64; I. Clark and N. Wheeler, *The Origins of British Nuclear Strategy* (Oxford: Clarendon, 1989), pp. 112–52; M. Gowing, *Independence and Deterrence*, Vol. 1 (London: Macmillan, 1974). Geoffrey Warner is almost alone in underlining the positive in 1945–7, in 'The Anglo-American Special Relationship', *Diplomatic History* Vol. 13, No. 4 (1989), pp. 479–99.

11 See A. Shlaim, 'Britain, the Berlin Blockade and the Cold War', *International Affairs* Vol. 60, No. 1 (1983–4), pp. 1–14; A. Tusa and J. Tusa, *The Berlin Airlift* (New York: Atheneum, 1988).

12 E. R. May, 'The American Commitment to Germany', *Diplomatic History* Vol. 13, No. 4 (1989), p. 456.

13 Nitze interview, 31 May 1989.

14 Evelyn Waugh, *The Loved One* (Harmondsworth: Penguin, 1951), pp. 12–13. 'An Anglo-American Tragedy' is the book's subtitle.

15 Cameron Watt, p. 118.

16 R. Bullen, preface to *DBPO*, Series II, Vol. II, p. ix; Bevin quoted in J. L. Gormly, *The Collapse of the Grand Alliance* (Baton Rouge: Louisiana State University Press, 1987), p. 85.

17 Robert Lovett, Oral History Interview no. 327, 7 July 1971, HSTL.

18 Achilles memorandum, 1 March 1950, 611.41/2–2851, RG 59, NA.

19 E. R. May and G. F. Treverton, 'Defence Relationships', in W. R. Louis and H. Bull (eds) *The Special Relationship* (Oxford: Oxford University Press, 1986), p. 181.

20 Churchill's speech, at Fulton, Missouri, on 5 March 1946, is exhaustively analysed in F. Harbutt, *The Iron Curtain* (Oxford: Oxford University Press, 1986). The quoted passage is on p. 187. cf. Churchill to Roosevelt, 28 May 1943, printed in W. F. Kimball (ed.) *Churchill and Roosevelt*, Vol. 2 (Princeton, NJ: Princeton University Press, 1984), pp. 222–7.

21 J. L. Gaddis, 'A Time of Confrontation and Confusion', *Times Literary Supplement*, 8 May 1987.

22 Interview with Lord Gladwyn, 28 June 1990; *The Memoirs of Lord Gladwyn* (London: Weidenfeld & Nicolson, 1972), p. 178.

23 M. Hogan, *The Marshall Plan* (Cambridge: Cambridge University Press, 1987), pp. 69–87; A. S. Milward, *The Reconstruction of Western Europe* (London: Methuen, 1987), pp. 69–89.

24 S. Greenwood, 'Frank Roberts and the "Other" Long Telegram', *Journal of Contemporary History* Vol. 25, No. 1 (1990), pp. 103–22; J. Zametica, 'Three Letters to Bevin', in Zametica, pp. 39–97.

25 See A. Danchev, 'Being Friends: the Combined Chiefs of Staff and the Making of Allied Strategy in the Second World War', in L. Freedman, P. Hayes and R. O'Neill (eds) *War, Strategy and Intelligence* (Oxford: Oxford University Press, forthcoming).

26 For the 1945–7 period in particular see T. H. Anderson, *The United States, Great Britain and the Cold War* (Columbia: University of Missouri Press, 1981), pp. 118–43; R. A. Best, *Co-operation With Like-Minded Peoples* (Westport, Conn.: Greenwood, 1986), pp. 27–109; R. Hathaway, *Ambiguous Partnership* (New York: Columbia University Press, 1981), pp. 263–75.

27 Eisenhower to Nimitz, 29 June 1946, and appended documentation, in L. Galambos (ed.) *The Papers of Dwight D. Eisenhower*, Vol. VII (Baltimore, Md: Johns Hopkins University Press, 1978), pp. 1,157–9; Lincoln memoranda, 12 and 14 February 1946, ABC 381 United Nations (1-23-42), section 9, RG 319, NA; Wilson to COS, 9 February 1946, CAB 105/51, PRO.

28 Shinwell's left-wing pedigree was disturbing to the US (and British) military establishment. See Acheson memorandum of conversation, 9 March 1950, 741.5/3–950, RG 59, NA.

29 R. H. Ullman, 'America, Britain and the Soviet threat in historical and present perspective', in Louis and Bull, pp. 103–14. *Pax anti-Sovietica* is Louis's expression (p. viii).

30 G. Orwell, *Nineteen Eighty-four* (Harmondsworth: Penguin, 1954), pp. 30–1.
31 See S. T. Ross, *American War Plans* (New York: Garland, 1988), a detailed exegesis of the original documents. Parts of HALFMOON and OFFTACKLE are printed in T. H. Etzold and J. L. Gaddis, (eds) *Containment* (New York: Columbia University Press, 1978), pp. 315–34.
32 K. W. Condit, *The Joint Chiefs of Staff and National Policy* Vol. II (Wilmington: Michael Glazier, 1979), pp. 290–4; Ross, pp. 118–19.
33 Forrestal diary, 3 September 1946, printed in W. Millis (ed.) *The Forrestal Diaries* (New York: Viking, 1951), p. 198; Leahy diary, 5 and 16 September 1946, Leahy Papers, LC; Lincoln to Norstad, 29 August 1946, P&O 381 TS, section III, case 66, RG 319, NA.
34 N. Hamilton, *Monty*, Vol. III (London: Hamilton, 1986), pp. 656–9; *The Memoirs and Field Marshal Montgomery of Alamein* (London: Collins, 1958), pp. 440–3; Leahy diary, 12 and 16 September 1946; Ismay to Eisenhower, and Lincoln memorandum, 10 October and 4 November 1946, P&O 091 Great Britain (October–November 1946), RG 319, NA.
35 Condit, pp. 280, 289; Ross, pp. 89–90, 95.
36 See D. A. Rosenberg, 'American Atomic Strategy and the Hydrogen Bomb Decision', *Journal of American History* Vol. 66, No. 1 (1979), pp. 68–75; 'The Origins of Overkill', *International Security* Vol. 7, No. 4 (1983), pp. 14–18.
37 Brodie to Rosenberg, 22 August 1977, quoted in Rosenberg, 'Overkill', p. 18.
38 The basic work on this key question is Rosenberg's. See his stupendous PhD thesis, 'Toward Armageddon', University of Chicago, 1983, and the articles drawn from it. cf. H. S. Borowski, *A Hollow Threat* (Westport, Conn.: Greenwood, 1982).
39 Sir Michael Perrin, quoted in A. Bullock, *Ernest Bevin*, Vol. III (Oxford: Oxford University Press, 1985), p. 352.
40 Frank Wisner, quoted in K. Philby, *My Secret War* (London: Panther, 1969), p. 182. For Anglo-American dealings on bases world-wide see papers in the JCS 570 series, CCS 360 (12-9-42), RG 218, NA.
41 D. Campbell, *The Unsinkable Aircraft Carrier* (London: Paladin, 1986); S. Duke, *US Defence Bases in the United Kingdom* (London: Macmillan, 1987). On the Asian and Pacific alternatives, see R. Aldrich and M. Coleman, 'Britain and the Strategic Air Offensive Against the Soviet Union', *History* Vol. 74, No. 242 (1989), pp. 400–26; L. J. Foltos, 'The New Pacific Barrier', *Diplomatic History* Vol. 13, No. 3 (1989), pp. 317–42.
42 On the destroyers-for-bases deal see D. Reynolds, *The Creation of the Anglo-American Alliance* (London: Europa, 1981), pp. 113–32.
43 'US Air Power Flowing Back to Europe', *Aviation Week*, 2 August 1948; confirmed twenty-six years later by Gowing, p. 311. cf. G. Herken, *The Winning Weapon* (Princeton, NJ: Princeton University Press, 1981), pp. 257–62.
44 Marshall to Douglas, 29 June 1948, 811.2340/6-2948, RG 59, NA.
45 General Leon Johnson, quoted in 'Notes of the Month', *World Today* Vol. 16, No. 8 (1960), p. 320.
46 Forrestal diary, 1 August–30 September 1948, typescript pp. 2,501–2, Forrestal Papers, Naval Historical Centre, Washington Navy Yard; R. G. Hewlett, and F. Duncan, *A History of the United States Atomic Energy Commission*, Vol. II (University Park, Pa: Pennsylvania State University Press, 1969), p. 521; Rosenberg, 'Toward Armageddon', pp. 173–4, 185–6. See also Webb to Truman, 22 July 1948, PSF, NSC Atomic Folder, Box 200, HSTL.
47 Interviews with General Leon Johnson and R. Gordon Arneson, 28 June and 15 August 1989.
48 The Spaatz–Tedder Agreement must be pieced together from the Spaatz–Bissell correspondence, June–August 1946, Spaatz Papers, Box 27, LC. See also the England Trip papers in Box 265. I am grateful to Tami Davis Biddle for helping me to reconstruct this documentation. Extracts are printed and discussed only in Duke, pp. 20–3, 195–6. cf. S. Menaul, *Countdown* (London: Hale, 1980), pp. 23, 46, 91.
49 Forrestal diary, 15 July 1948, in Millis, p. 457; NSC 36th meeting, 22 March 1949, PSF, NSC meetings, Box 220, HSTL; Douglas to Acheson, 1 December 1949, Acheson Papers, Box 64, HSTL; Shuckburgh memorandum, 'US Air Force Groups in the UK', 4 January 1950, DEFE 7/516, PRO; discussion at DO(50) 4th meeting, 15 March 1950, CAB 131/8, PRO.

50 Henderson memorandum, 31 August 1951, FO 371/90966, PRO. See Duke, pp. 50–6. The East Anglian bases were thought to be vulnerable to low-level attack from the east and north-east.
51 See the respective official histories, R. G. Hewlett and O. E. Anderson, *A History of the United States Atomic Energy Commission*, Vol. I (University Park, Pa: Pennsylvania State University Press, 1962); M. Gowing, *Britain and Atomic Energy* (London: Macmillan, 1964). The various agreements are also printed in Baylis.
52 Gowing, *Independence and Deterrence*, pp. 63–86; J. L. Gormly, 'The Washington Declaration and the "Poor Relation" ', *Diplomatic History* Vol. 8, No. 2 (1984), pp. 125–43.
53 The British badly underestimated the McMahon Bill (Gowing, *Independence and Deterrence*, pp. 105–11), very much a pattern in British atomic diplomacy. See A. Danchev, *Very Special Relationship* (London: Brassey's, 1986), pp. 99–108.
54 The handling of the negotiations by Roger Makins is open to criticism, implicitly acknowledged by J. Edwards, 'Roger Makins: Mr Atom', in Zametica, p. 33; and Gowing, *Independence and Deterrence*, pp. 252–4. Lord Sherfield (the former Roger Makins) sees it differently: 'Britain's Nuclear Story', *Round Table* No. 258 (1975), pp. 193–204.
55 Printed in Gowing, *Independence and Deterrence*, pp. 393–5.
56 ibid., p. 95. See also pp. 349–401.
57 ibid., pp. 112–13; J. Simpson, *The Independent Nuclear State* (London: Macmillan, 1986), pp. 26–7.
58 Chadwick quoted in Gowing, *Britain and Atomic Energy*, p. 237.
59 Makins to Bevin, 17 April and 10 May 1950, printed in *DBPO*, Series II, Vol. II, docs 19 and 87, pp. 52–3 and 299–301.
60 Minutes of 6th meeting, Truman–Attlee Conversations, 8 December 1950, printed in *FRUS*, 1950, Vol. III, pp. 1,774–82; Jessup and Arneson memoranda, 7 December 1950 and 16 January 1953, printed in *FRUS*, 1950, Vol. VII, pp. 1,462–64.
61 Arneson and Jessup memoranda, 16 January 1953 and 9 January 1951, printed in ibid., pp. 1,462–66; final communiqué, 8 December 1950, printed in *FRUS*, 1950, Vol. III, pp. 1,783–7. See the penultimate paragraph. Acheson liked to tell how he 'unachieved' what Attlee had achieved. *Present at the Creation*, p. 484, based on the Princeton Seminars (11 December 1953, Acheson Papers, Box 83, HSTL), differs slightly from the interview quoted in K. Harris, *Attlee* (London: Weidenfeld & Nicolson, 1982), pp. 464–5.
62 Anonymous [?Elsey] notes, [7 December 1950], PSF, Truman–Attlee Talks, Box 164, HSTL.
63 Attlee to Bevin, quoted Edmonds, p. 223; in Cabinet, 12 December 1950, CAB 128/18, PRO; in the Commons, 14 December 1950, *Hansard* Vol. 482, cols 1,355–7.
64 Bradley and Elsey memoranda, 26 and 27 July 1950, PSF, JCS Folder, Box 124, HSTL; records printed in *FRUS*, 1950, Vol. III, pp. 1,657–9.
65 Nitze and Matthews memoranda, 13 September 1951, printed in *FRUS*, 1951, Vol. I, pp. 883–91. Quotation on p. 890.
66 Arneson memoranda and US draft statement, 17 and 18 October 1951, printed in ibid., pp. 891–94. The 'joint decision' formula is quoted by a number of authorities, including Duke, p. 77.
67 Communiqué, 9 January 1952, in Department of State *Bulletin* Vol. 25 (1952), pp. 83–4. Harold Macmillan's claim to have initialled a 'regular' agreement with President Eisenhower in June 1958 which 'replaces the loose arrangement made by Attlee and confirmed by Churchill' has not been substantiated. See his *Riding the Storm* (London: Macmillan, 1971), p. 494.
68 cf. J. Baylis, 'American Bases in Britain', *World Today* Vol. 42, No. 8/9 (1986), pp. 155–9; T. Botti, *The Long Wait* (Westport, Conn.: Greenwood, 1987), pp. 84–7; D. Gates, 'American Strategic Bases in Britain', *Comparative Strategy* Vol. 8 (1989), pp. 99–123.
69 On the tiger shooting test in Anglo-American relations see A. Danchev, 'Tiger Shooting Together', *Reviews in American History* Vol. 18, No. 1 (1990), pp. 112–17. cf. Eden quoted in R. J. Barnet, *The Alliance* (New York: Simon & Schuster, 1983), p. 131.

10

The rise and decline of a strategic concept: the Middle East, 1945–51

Richard J. Aldrich and John Zametica

No satisfactory understanding of the development and context of British strategy as a whole in the early post-war period is possible without careful scrutiny of the planning process for the Eastern Mediterranean and the Middle East. The formulation and eventual adoption of strategic prescriptions on a wider scale during the late 1940s was to a large extent driven by controversial debates over issues, both long and short term, emanating from this region. This subject is lent greater significance because of the central role of the Prime Minister. The debate over Middle East strategy, leading to the adoption of Britain's first comprehensive statement of post-war strategy, 'Future Defence Policy', in May 1947, was in large measure originated by the iconoclastic vision of Clement Attlee. This debate was largely responsible for the dominant strategic concept in the late 1940s which aimed to achieve deterrence in peace and defence in war by planning for an Anglo-American air offensive against the Soviet hinterland, much of which was to be launched from the Middle East.

The adoption of this strategic concept, with the Middle East at its centre, was achieved only in the wake of repeated confrontations between Attlee, Bevin and the COS. Yet in retrospect, acceptance by Cabinet of this radical new strategy proved to be the least of its problems. While the underlying ideas may have been sound, the tendency of the COS to plan on the basis of geostrategic concepts rather than economic or political reality pointed to future trouble. By mid-1947 it was increasingly apparent that Britain was unable to marshal the resources to fulfil this strategy, leaving it dependent upon American and Commonwealth support for implementation. However, a firm American military commitment to this region remained elusive and while Commonwealth support improved after 1948, key states, including Australia, remained ambivalent.

The Cabinet Defence Committee reports of 1946, serenely planning on the basis of a 600-bomber air force that existed only on paper, give little indication of the gulf between the concept and the reality of British strategy during the late 1940s. Only in the late spring of 1948, with the prospect of open conflict over Berlin, were the exasperated COS forced to confront reality. The diary of the Chief of the Imperial General Staff (CIGS), Field Marshal Sir Bernard Montgomery, records the high temperature of staff conferences attended by the COS and ministers who, confronted with Britain's extreme strategic debility, were now 'really worked up' about their predicament.[1] Even if firm military commitments from the United States and the Commonwealth for the Middle East had been forthcoming, planning turned around perennially elusive base rights in Egypt. Meanwhile, financial stringency ensured that elaborate paper plans for duplicate facilities in Kenya, Cyrenaica, Cyprus and Saudi Arabia remained frozen until early 1950 when, in any case, international developments forced the reconsideration of Britain's entire strategy. By 1951, while the Middle East remained important, attention was increasingly diverted to Europe and the Far East. Therefore, throughout this period, the Middle East concept, although remarkable for its originality and foresight, remained largely dependent upon an increasingly elusive American air commitment for its implementation. As such it reflected the future hopes of strategic planners rather than the immediate reality of Britain's military power.

PESSIMISM AND 'DEFEATISM', 1945

British wartime thinking regarding her post-war strategy in the Middle East, begun as early as 1942, was not optimistic in tone.[2] Under the auspices of the Chiefs of Staff (COS) a number of planning bodies, culminating in the Post Hostilities Planning Staff (PHPS) in May 1944, began to consider long-term strategic requirements. As the outcome of the war became increasingly predictable the COS called for strategic backgrounds against which to consider Britain's future commitments, and for this purpose the PHPS identified the Soviet Union as the most likely post-war adversary. By July 1944 they had recommended that, if faced with a hostile Soviet Union, German help might prove 'essential' to Britain's survival.[3]

During 1944 and 1945 the PHPS came to the conclusion that, presuming a Soviet adversary, the Middle East was at once strategically vital to Britain and also indefensible against a concerted Soviet attack. On the one hand they emphasized not only the increasing importance of oil in modern war but also the traditional factor of the Suez Canal. Moreover, Egypt, at the centre of Britain's imperial communications, offered an ideal base for a strategic reserve or 'fire brigade'. But on the other hand the PHPS, and indeed the Joint Intelligence Committee (JIC), concluded that the Soviet Union would exploit the twin vulnerabilities of Britain's oil and communications in this region to concerted air attack. In a future war, they concluded, not only Turkey and Iraq but also Egypt would be lost. In addition Britain had to contend with Egyptian resentment of the presence of foreign troops.[4] By April 1945 the PHPS were recommending that

Britain take steps to reduce her dependence on this region for oil and communications, and gave the Middle East only third priority, below that of the Indian Ocean.[5]

This already pessimistic vision was further darkened by the predictions of defence scientists. In November 1944 the COS instructed a committee under Sir Henry Tizard to review future developments in weapons and methods of war. Like the PHPS, they pointed to the great difficulties posed by the growing importance of air power, particularly rockets and also submarines. Although reporting before the attacks on Hiroshima and Nagasaki, they were dubious about the possibility of defending Britain against atomic weapons.[6]

Middle Eastern prospects were also uncertain at the political level. There was no question of the commitment of Churchill's outgoing administration to the Middle East. Indeed, Churchill displayed a near obsession with the situation in Greece and had made attempts to reach a *modus vivendi* with Stalin over south-east Europe in October 1944. Eden was no less firm, asserting in April 1945 that it was here that Britain's imperial communications could be severed and accordingly, the defence of this region was a 'matter of life and death'. Meanwhile Foreign Office officials declared their intention to combat what they termed the widespread 'misconception' that Britain was in decline as a world power.[7]

The attitudes of Prime Minister Clement Attlee and many of his incoming Labour Cabinet in July 1945 were very different. Attlee in particular, for four separate but related reasons, was adamant that Britain should withdraw from her imperial position in the Middle East. First, he expressed scepticism about Britain's post-war economic potential; second, he was committed to rapid self-government for the colonies, particularly India; third, he believed that modern air power had rendered the Mediterranean route obsolete; and fourth, his firm belief in internationalism and support for the idea of the United Nations (UN). As wartime Deputy Prime Minister, Attlee had given Eden, Amery, Cranborne and a number of high-level officials a foretaste of these views during a discussion on post-war imperial defence in October 1942. Rounding on his colleagues he remarked tartly that after the war, the British people 'would not wish to have the exclusive privilege of paying for the defence of all these territories at the expense of their own standard of living and for the benefit of certain privileged classes'; instead, he continued, there should be a powerful world organization, for the 'international control and administration of these territories'. Attlee's views were consistently radical. In early 1945 in his capacity as chairman of the Cabinet Suez Canal Committee he submitted a short but pungent report suggesting international control for the Canal in line with Britain's public professions of support for the UN and its eventual purchase by Egypt.[8] In other committees he emphasized a greater role for both the UN and the United States in the

238

Middle East in the light of Britain's probable post-war financial and military weakness. A horrified Foreign Office denounced Attlee's views as 'defeatist in tone'.[9]

As Prime Minister, Attlee wasted no time in expressing his radical views at the Potsdam Conference in mid-July 1945. Here Attlee found both the Soviets and the British expressing a competing interest in Cyrenaica, a former Italian possession in North Africa. Eden perceived Cyrenaica as an alternative to controversial bases in Egypt. Attlee, however, wrote to both Eden and Churchill urging them to confront the Soviets, not with the needs of British imperial defence, but a future UN. He attacked their 'obsolete conception of imperial defence derived from the naval era' which took little account of air power and he questioned the 'continuing burden of heavy defence expenditure' implicit in their policy. These heretical views reverberated around Whitehall causing Sir Andrew Cunningham, Chief of the Naval Staff (CNS), to note in his diary: 'Atlee [sic] has apparently written what appears to be a damn silly letter [Attlee became PM himself a few days later] saying we ought not to oppose a great country like Russia having bases anywhere she wants them, What an ass!'[10] For the remainder of the Potsdam Conference Attlee took a back seat, leaving affairs to Ernest Bevin, the new Foreign Secretary, who entertained markedly more orthodox views. Nevertheless, this exchange at Potsdam pointed to future trouble.

EVOLVING A STRATEGIC CONCEPT

Although Attlee had made his own views on the Middle East abundantly clear during his first few days in office, no attempt could yet be made to formulate a Middle East strategy. At a general level, uncertainties abounded regarding Britain's post-war occupational commitments. These were compounded by the unexpected surrender of Japan and the developing debate over the future importance of atomic weapons. More specifically, in the Middle East, the future of Cyrenaica was yet to be resolved and Egypt continued to press for the withdrawal of troops from Britain's main regional base. It was these pressing political problems, or more specifically, Attlee's pronouncements upon them, that provoked the COS into producing their first coherent statement of post-war Middle East strategy. By mid-1946 the attempts of the COS to justify Britain's continued hold on the Middle East in terms of the defence of the United Kingdom increasingly placed this region at the centre of overall British defence policy.

The debate developed initially in the context of the captured Italian colonies in North Africa. The Foreign Office (FO) hoped that prospective British bases here offered the answer to the fraught political problems of retaining bases in Egypt.[11] Although the Joint Planning Staff (JPS), who served the COS, rejected this option on the grounds that Cyrenaica was too far from the Suez Canal, Bevin, the FO and the COS were all nevertheless agreed on preventing a Soviet presence there.[12] Attlee categorically rejected this conventional consensus dominated by Anglo-Soviet competition. The demonstration of the power of atomic weapons had not only reaffirmed his conviction that air power had now rendered the Mediterranean route valueless, it had also reinforced his commitment to international control of atomic weapons under the UN. He asserted

> The British Empire can only be defended by its membership of the UNO. If we do not accept this we had better say so. . . . If the new organisation is a reality, it does not matter who holds Cyrenaica or Somalia or controls the Suez Canal. If it is not a reality then we had better be thinking of the defence of England, for unless we can protect the home country no strategic position elsewhere will avail.

On 13 September 1945 Alanbrooke, the CIGS, privately recorded 'we . . . were shaken'. The debate continued in Cabinet with Bevin and the COS citing the lessons of the war. Only Attlee's absence from Cabinet on 11 September resulted in his temporary acquiescence.[13]

On the eve of the first Council of Foreign Ministers in September 1945, British strategy remained confused and reactive, responding only to the immediate political problems of the region. The COS and Bevin pursued Eden's established line on the Black Sea Straits, resisting a Soviet presence in the Mediterranean but happy to see the United States make the running in opposing Soviet requests. Meanwhile the advent of atomic weapons, a subject still under lengthy analysis, had paralysed the COS's attempts at formulating long-range strategy. The future of Egyptian bases looked increasingly uncertain, prompting Bevin and the military to cast around for alternatives in Cyprus or through some Middle East confederacy. Meanwhile, in Cabinet Defence Committee, Attlee and Dalton pressed for deep defence cuts. Only on 2 December 1945 did the JPS begin to show signs of concerted thinking on the Middle East by rejecting the advice of the now disbanded PHPS to abandon the Middle East. The JPS asserted that it should be held in peace and war, but as yet did not say why.[14]

Consequently, in early 1946 only Clement Attlee was possessed of a coherent defence policy. Attlee's fresh-minded and radical approach to the problems of Britain's post-war defence has been widely misunderstood. Attlee was in no sense a 'Cold Warrior', nor did his behaviour amount to superficial protestations of high-minded principles accompanied by private *Realpolitik* as some have chosen to assert. Such interpretations mistake entirely the fundamentals of Attlee's world view.[15] This is clearly illustrated by Attlee's attitude to atomic power during 1945 and 1946. Far from seeking a British capability in order to safeguard against future Soviet intentions, he sought an internationalist solution. Dalton recorded:

CRA [Attlee] is going to see Truman. We have had several meeting of the Inner Cabinet on this, and the outcome is that the only possible course, if the world is to be saved from further and great disasters, is to put all our force behind a real UNO, with power and determination to smash any aggressor by every means, including Atomic Bombs.

Attlee spared no effort in pressing these views on Truman. Truman, however, was not of the same mind and as early as September 1945, spoke of atomic weapons as a 'sacred trust', hinting at a future United States monopoly.[16]

Although Britain's growing difficulties in Greece and Turkey during late 1945 had set the British COS in search of American involvement in that area, these problems had failed to inspire any sort of grand strategic review. Equally, the confrontation with the Soviet Union in Iran does not appear to have impinged upon long-term planning. Concerted thinking on Middle East strategy by the COS was triggered only in February 1946 by Cabinet debate over the unresolved question of the Italian colonies.[17] In contrast to Bevin, whose attitude was dominated by matters of political prestige and mistrust of Soviet intentions, Attlee continued to advocate abandonment of the Middle East. Some, like Cunningham, the CNS, pronounced Attlee's attitude to be 'past belief'. Others, however, like Dalton recognized that Attlee understood the wider factors, not least India's move towards independence and a possible American return to isolationism:

> Attlee is fresh-minded on Defence. It was no good, he thought, pretending any more that we could keep open the Mediterranean route in time of war. That meant we could pull troops out of Egypt and the rest of the Middle East, as well as Greece. Nor could we hope, he thought, to defend Turkey, Iraq or Persia against a steady pressure of the Russian land masses. And if India goes her own way before long, as she must, there will be still less sense in thinking of lines of imperial communication through the Suez canal. . . . If, however, the USA were to become seriously interested in Middle Eastern oil, the whole thing would look different. Meanwhile the USA seems to be exactly repeating their post-last-war experience.

Dalton was hardly an impartial observer. These discussions were taking place alongside acrimonious exchanges over future levels of military manpower which found Attlee, Dalton and ministers with domestic portfolios ranged against Bevin and the COS.[18]

Attlee chose this moment to challenge the presumptions of the COS Mediterranean strategy of 'navalism' in a key paper on the Italian colonies, completed on 22 February 1946. In the era of air power, he asserted, the loss of Spain and Italy, or Greece and Turkey, would render this route impassable. Moreover, with India gone and the region's oil clearly indefensible, Australia and New Zealand remained the only rationale for maintaining such a route, which could be equally served by the Cape route. The COS, he concluded, were wedded to 'sentimental' ideas 'based on the past'. Clearly, this memorandum went far beyond the problem of the Italian colonies and offered a radical challenge to presumptions of the COS. Alanbrooke dismissed this paper as 'defeatist', but it now provoked serious thought among the Air Staff, perhaps because it emphasized air power.[19]

As if Attlee's astringent paper was not enough to awaken the COS to the need for coherent thought on the Middle East, the following month Bevin proposed moving Britain's 'imperial command post' for this region from Cairo to Mombasa in Kenya. Such a move, he argued, not only would resolve serious political problems by permitting military withdrawal from Egypt, Palestine and Cyprus, but also would offer a central position for the simultaneous defence of the Middle East, the Indian Ocean and South Africa. Moreover, he proposed a trans-African road to develop trade with West Africa, whose importance was growing due to uranium deposits. Despite the expense of abandoning the infrastructure of Egypt this found favour with Attlee, Dalton and, temporarily, even Alanbrooke. On reflection the COS concluded that facilities in Mombasa were inadequate but they had now been woken up to the urgent need for Middle East planning.[20]

Meanwhile, one of the few areas upon which Attlee, Bevin and the COS were in complete agreement, albeit for different reasons, was the importance of obtaining Commonwealth support for British defence policy. For Attlee, the Commonwealth, particularly with the addition of successor states in South Asia, appeared to offer a model of international co-operation. In addition there were the obvious attractions of financial burden sharing. Conversely, the COS sought support for a traditional role in the Middle East. Britain hoped to pursue a zonal policy, on the grounds that it was easier to persuade the Dominions to accept responsibilities 'in their own areas' than to secure some nebulous over-arching guarantee.[21] This approach had no success at the Dominion Prime Ministers' Conference in 1944, but made some headway at their subsequent meeting in April 1946. That all the Prime Ministers could not attend at the same time ensured that agreements were reached with Nash of New Zealand and Smuts of South Africa on the Middle East policy that would not have received the support of the Canadian Prime Minister, Mackenzie King. But while Smuts asserted that Britain should remain in Egypt by force if necessary, and Australia looked forward to a post-independence defence role for India in the Indian Ocean, they shied away from concrete commitments to defend the Middle East. This prompted Alanbrooke to remark bitterly upon 'Dominion Prime Ministers with mentalities limited to the normal horizon of a Whitehall charwoman'.[22]

Therefore by March 1946 the COS and their subordinates, the JPS, were faced with the necessity of responding in the broadest terms to the major issues raised by Attlee's iconoclastic remarks, and also by Bevin's ideas concerning Kenya. In responding to Attlee's paper of 22 February 1946 they found themselves preparing a report not on the strategic importance of the Italian colonies, but in effect on the strategic importance of the entire Mediterranean and the Middle East in relation to Britain's global defence. It was long overdue. Remarkably, despite the volatile nature of the Middle East during the last nine months, this report amounted to the first formal coherent consideration of Middle East strategy since June 1945.

By late March 1946 the Service departments and in particular the Air Staff had begun to prepare a startling response to Attlee's attack on the conventional Middle East wisdom of the COS. The intellectual origins of this response lay at a relatively low level, beginning with the comments of the Deputy Director of Policy (Air Staff), Group Captain M. R. MacArthur. By late March 1946 an early draft version of the JPS reply to Attlee was circulating in the Service departments.[23] Its stolid and conventional restatement of the importance of this region to imperial communications was greeted by MacArthur with disdain. While MacArthur had no doubt that Britain should retain her position in the Middle East, he nevertheless attacked this draft paper for reaching the right answers 'for the wrong reasons'. It did not, he remarked, do what the Prime Minister had requested, namely 'take account of modern weapons' and indeed 'it might well have been written in 1939 or even 1919'. He continued:

> It does not make nearly enough of our inevitable dependence through lack of manpower on scientific warfare as distinct from mass land attack. I consider that the paper as drafted at present runs the risk of being returned to the Chiefs of Staff by the Defence Committee on grounds of obsolescence.

Instead, MacArthur advocated confronting the Defence Committee with nothing less than the outline of the course of a future 'Third World War'.

Such a war, he postulated, would not be started by the USSR but by the West in response to continual Soviet absorption of territory. 'We', he declared, 'will be the ones to start the ball of a major war rolling.' Without sufficient manpower to facilitate a land attack on the Soviet Union in the early stages of such a war the only hope of success, or indeed of effective defence, would be air attack. Therefore both attack and defence would depend upon an ability to bombard strategic areas inside the Soviet Union. For reasons of this air offensive alone, in the Middle East and elsewhere, 'subsidiary base areas become vital to us'. The traditional naval reasons given in the early draft of the JPS paper, he continued, were 'important' but 'not unassailable'; however, the 'need for airbases is to my mind incontrovertible'. The Middle East, along with bases in North West India, offered the possibility that 'long range attack could be opened on the industrial areas of the Urals and Western Siberia'.[24]

The great impact of MacArthur's comments is easily understood when considering the final draft of this JPS paper on the 'Strategic Position of the British Commonwealth'. In addressing the 'fundamental issues' raised by Attlee, it began with the assumption that the Soviet Union was for the time being the only serious potential adversary and in such a war it would be 'vital' to have American support. The JPS then moved on to consider two factors: the holding of 'main support areas' on which the war effort would be based (including the communications between them) and also 'other areas of strategic importance' facilitating their defence. These main support areas were identified as the United Kingdom, the Americas, Africa south of the Sahara and Australasia. However, they continued, to concentrate on the defence of these areas alone might encourage the Soviets to move into areas of significant war potential including Western Europe and the Middle East. The United Kingdom would then 'be reduced to a Malta-type existence'.

The paper thus turned to the question of 'other areas' of strategic significance where MacArthur's influence was most evident. These additional areas served three wider strategic concerns: ensuring the security of the main support areas; denying their potential to the enemy; and attacking areas of importance to the enemy at the outset of war. What clearly preoccupied the JPS was the great numerical superiority of Soviet land forces in the event of war. Thus they looked to new scientific weapons, air and sea power and also defence in depth to allow time for mobilization. They continued: 'the threat of attack by air or long range weapons will be our one effective military deterrent to Russian aggression'. These 'other areas' included Western Europe, the Iberian Peninsula, North West Africa, the Middle East, India and South East Asia. The Middle East was identified as particularly valuable in bringing attacks to bear on Soviet oil producing and industrial centres. In an attached memorandum specifically for the Prime Minister, the JPS underlined their new contention that the Suez route was not essential, but instead on the 'broadest strategical grounds', Britain's position in the Middle East should be maintained.[25]

The place of the Middle East had, at last, received clear definition in British planning and this paper was therefore met with overwhelming enthusiasm within the Air Ministry. Dickson, soon to become Vice-Chief of the Air Staff, expounded:

We regard this paper as one of the very greatest importance. If it is accepted by the Defence Committee, it will form the basis of our future defence policy for a long time to come.... Broadly speaking ... conclusions can be summed up in one phrase – 'What we have we must hold.' We believe this to be the correct answer to the problems posed by the Prime Minister and we believe too ... that this policy is the only one open to us if we are to continue as a major power in world politics.

This paper appeared on 2 April 1947 as DO (46) 47 for discussion by the Defence Committee. Therein its reception was markedly less enthusiastic.[26]

Attlee was confronted with the new air concept at a meeting of the Defence Committee on 5 April 1946 and, predictably, offered a critical response, questioning the availability of sufficient forces to defend bases in the Middle East. However, Tedder, the CAS, replied that the delays required for mobilization could be imposed only by air action. Moreover, early American help was most likely to arrive in the form of air power for which bases would be required. Alanbrooke agreed, speaking for the first time of atomic attacks against not only industrial but also tactical targets. A Middle East garrison was a small premium to pay for time to mobilize. Bevin now joined the debate, broadening its context by addressing one of his favourite themes, the political and economic importance of the Middle East and Africa. Attlee, however, chose to end the meeting abruptly. Such were the far-reaching consequences of these issues, he insisted, that no decision could yet be taken. Instead he called for a special review of the vulnerability of the United Kingdom and of the potential of Africa.

Although DO (46) 47 had received only provisional approval as a document for the forthcoming Conference of Dominion Prime Ministers, Alanbrooke clearly thought that with Bevin's help, Attlee had been 'defeated'. This was not the case. Nor could the COS rely on Bevin, whose objectives lay primarily in the fields of foreign and economic policy, and also Africa. Moreover, the fluid political situation in the Middle East continually underlined the problem of base facilities. Thus the COS were still far from securing their new strategic concept. Nevertheless, DO (46) 47, albeit provisional, represented a remarkable development. Within only one week in late March 1946, the entire character of British planning had been transformed. Gone were the uncoordinated area studies without reference to any overarching global concept. Gone were lengthy imperial prognostications about the route to India. The Middle East now derived its value from its proximity to the Soviet Union and as a barrier guarding the main support area of Africa south of the Sahara. Defence in depth and early air attack were the twin pillars of COS Middle East strategy.[27]

CONFRONTATION AND SURRENDER

By mid-1946 it was increasingly apparent to the COS that, even if they convinced the Cabinet of their views on the Middle East, political conditions in the region might nevertheless thwart them. This uncomfortable fact was underlined in April by the departure of a British delegation to Egypt, headed by the Air Minister, Lord Stansgate, in order to discuss base rights. The COS had asked him to seek hopelessly elaborate concessions. Meanwhile, as Stansgate recognized, any refusal to withdraw from Egypt would be met by an embarrassing appeal to the UN. Good relations with Egypt and political *kudos* in the Arab world, he noted, 'can only be had at the expense of telling the Staff that they must look elsewhere for their base – and, in fact, that elsewhere does not exist'.[28] The perennial dilemma of base rights would become increasingly familiar over the next five years, throughout the Middle East and also in post-independence India.

While these diplomatic problems in Egypt turned Bevin's attention back to the unresolved future of Cyrenaica and its value as an alternative base, the possibility of abandoning Palestine arrived on the agenda of the Defence Committee. Egypt, Palestine and Cyrenaica had now begun to converge offering a combined threat to the COS's new Middle East strategy. In May 1946 the COS approved a gloomy JPS review of these developments. They concluded that only Egypt offered adequate facilities and that Palestine was essential to its northward defence; 'without both', they insisted, 'it would not be possible to defend any of our vital interests in the area'. As such their desiderata included the retention of full military rights in Palestine and emergency base rights in Egypt with further bases in Cyrenaica. Meanwhile East Africa was dismissed as too distant for locating a strategic bomber force, nor could they envisage any alternative to Egypt for a regional headquarters.[29]

Interestingly, Attlee had meanwhile been in receipt of very different advice from the military theoretician Basil Liddell Hart in the form of a paper entitled 'Africa or the Middle East?' Hart criticized the British position in the Middle East, which he identified as arousing Soviet suspicions and also indigenous political instability. Instead he favoured shifting Britain's centre of gravity to Africa and employing the Middle East as a buffer zone. These points echoed Attlee's own views and he was thus 'very interested' to read Hart's memorandum.[30]

At a further Defence Committee meeting on 27 May 1946, the cloud of political uncertainty that hung over military rights prevented any direct confrontation. Instead of challenging the air offensive concept Attlee chose to emphasize the undoubted obstacles now emerging to bases in the region. Bevin was pessimistic regarding Egypt and urged alternatives in either Cyrenaica or the Kenya/Sudan area. Echoing Liddell Hart, Attlee added that in any case a regional headquarters in Palestine or Egypt would 'advertise our intentions and promote suspicions'. The debate then slid sideways into a vague discussion of oil resources. These uncertainties permitted Attlee to impose delay and to request from the COS a further reconsideration of Britain's minimum strategic requirements in the region. However, a few days later Attlee wrote privately to the COS asserting that defence of Europe should take precedence over the Middle East.[31]

The COS did more than was requested of them. They now set out to rework their ideas on the Middle East in such a way as to link the defence of this region with the United Kingdom, thus directly addressing Attlee's intense concern regarding the 'home base'. They were greatly assisted in this task by the completion of a revised study of scientific methods of warfare which placed unprecedented emphasis on air power and weapons of mass destruction. There were other important developments: first, there now appeared to be no hope of wartime facilities in Egypt; second, the JIC had begun a series of pessimistic monthly reviews of Soviet intentions in the Middle East which forecast expansion 'by every means short of war'.[32]

Drawing upon the new report on scientific methods of war, the COS emphasized Britain's vulnerability to air attack, owing to her position and concentrated population. While local defence would prevent invasion, Britain would be devastated by air weapons against which there was no adequate defence. In their new paper, DO (46) 80, they argued that the only method of countering this was 'striking quick and hard at the vital centres of enemy war potential' to relieve this aerial pressure on Britain:

> Some of this counter-offensive could be undertaken from the United Kingdom, but if we regard Russia as the potential enemy many of her vital centres are out of range from the United Kingdom; her most vulnerable flank is the South-East, where most of her oil industry is located. It is only from the Middle East area that effective air action can be taken against this flank. Thus an offensive strategy conducted from bases both inside the United Kingdom and the Middle East area is an essential complement to the defence of the United Kingdom itself.

Therefore the COS had turned Attlee's criticisms against him, asserting that the defence of the home base was dependent on what was done elsewhere. By linking the Middle East directly to the defence of Britain, they attempted to raise the importance of this region to the highest level. The COS did not stop there. They increased the emphasis placed on oil and argued that, given the communication problems that would be encountered by any invading force, the resources required to defend the area would not be enormous. Conversely, drawing on recent JIC reports they concluded that the Soviet Union would quickly move into any vacuum left in the Middle East.[33]

The strength of Attlee's reaction to these propositions can be gauged by his decision to meet the COS in a staff conference at 10 Downing Street (the Prime Minister's office) before the paper reached Defence Committee. It might be noted here that Attlee was addressing a changed COS, with the arrival of Admiral Sir John Cunningham as CNS and the abrasive Field Marshal Sir Bernard Montgomery as CIGS. Like the COS, Attlee had been greatly influenced by the new report on scientific methods of war emphasizing the problem of aerial bombardment by rockets and weapons of mass destruction. Attlee was unnerved by the prospect of such weapons being massed across the Channel and doubted that an air attack from the Middle East against the dispersed facilities of the Soviet Union would prevent the rapid devastation of a small island such as Britain. Montgomery accepted the scale of the problem, but countered that, given Soviet manpower rendered mainland Europe indefensible, there was no other strategy. Moreover, attacks on oil supplies, an area of Soviet vulnerability, would eventually prevail. Cunningham, the new CNS, insisted that even looking forward many years to a robust 'Western bloc' the same Middle East strategy would remain an essential complement to its defence. Every argument was now brought to bear on Attlee: the need for bases for early American air reinforcements was underlined and Britain's potential for dispersal of her war production to the Dominions noted. At last Attlee appeared persuaded. Moreover, it was increasingly clear that Western Europe was regarded not so much as a strategic asset but as a liability.

Although it was now clear that COS thinking on the Middle East was developing into a blueprint for an overall defence policy, Attlee remained sceptical and launched a renewed attack in Defence Committee on 19 July 1946. Attlee now raised political objections noting that no country would offer Britain bases if they suspected an aggressive purpose, and furthermore, such preparations would increase Soviet suspicions, increasing the possibility of war occurring. All these questions pointed once more to the advantage of East Africa as an alternative base. Meanwhile, the uncertainties over bases and other political questions, not least due to the impending Paris Conference, allowed Attlee to secure 'general agreement' that firm decisions should be postponed, awaiting both political developments and further study of the alarming new weapons technology.[34]

The outcome of the Defence Committee meeting on 19 July 1946 represented a serious setback for the COS. No advance could now be made while international developments were awaited. Meanwhile their strategic concept was to be re-examined. Moreover the COS had been exhorted to take account of the danger of generating Soviet suspicion: a difficult task given that even Attlee, after reading the new report on scientific warfare, was inclined to take a pessimistic view of future Soviet capabilities. During the ensuing lull in the planning effort, several parallel developments were taking place: first, Bevin reaffirmed that British troops would be withdrawn from Greece as soon as possible, and second, the COS created a special section of the JPS, the Future Planning Staff (FPS) to examine the military situation characterized by radically new weapons in approximately five to seven years hence, and also to assist with the first stages of a tentative dialogue with the Americans on war plans. At the same time, the JPS began work on an interim report covering the next few years. Through what remained of 1946 this somewhat confused parallel process was further dogged by a plethora of unresolved political questions.[35]

Oil was also figuring more strongly in the calculations of the COS. This in turn increased Britain's reservations about offending Arab sentiment in any future settlement of the deadlocked Palestine question. Moreover, given the increasingly elusive nature of bases in Egypt, bases in Palestine appeared increasingly attractive. The Paris Conference failed to resolve the question of the Italian colonies. The Foreign Office and Stansgate (and later Mountbatten in India) found the Chiefs of Staff's desiderata increasingly irksome, noting: 'They merely look at maps and argue with perfect justice that freedom to move in the whole area and to establish themselves where they like is indispensable for a perfect war plan. Theoretically they are right, but in practice is such a thing possible?'[36]

In 1946 Greece and Turkey were also emerging as major issues. During July 1946 Bevin had been struggling to persuade the Cabinet to extend financial support for Greece until the following spring in the absence of any prospect of American aid in the area.[37] But in October 1946 matters brightened significantly during a conversation between James Byrnes and Albert Alexander on Greece and Turkey. Byrnes suggested that Britain supply military equipment while the USA did all she could to extend economic support.[38] Bevin was quick to pursue this offer during his visit to New York during November 1946. Attlee, however, never afraid to take an iconoclastic view, continued to ask whether American interest in a number of such strategic outposts, not least Canada, denoted not an emerging commitment to Western security, but a search for a 'glacis plate' of bases behind which the USA could safely return to isolationism.[39] Attlee also questioned whether Greece and Turkey could be rendered strong enough to resist the Soviets. Instead he continued to advocate the idea of the Middle East as a neutral zone, with a corresponding shift of British forces to Africa. Attlee, Bevin and indeed Truman all appear to have been unaware of the extent of Anglo-American military conversations at this stage.[40]

When the COS emphasized the importance of supporting Greece and Turkey if the Middle East were to be held, they encountered more than Attlee's familiar strategic reservations. In a staff conference on 23 December 1946 Alexander confronted the COS with Britain's growing financial problems. 'In the last resort', he said, 'the question was how much we could afford at the present time.'[41] As such, by the end of 1946 no aspect of British strategic planning for the region appeared to be near resolution. All political questions, including Greece and Turkey, appeared to be in flux, moreover the JPS and FPS had not completed their reports on, respectively, medium and long-term strategy. Yet within only a few weeks a dramatic unfolding of events would finally produce a decision on Britain's post-war strategy.

The final confrontation with Attlee was prompted by further consideration of the future of Greece and Turkey. In early January the COS put a paper to the Defence Committee asserting that the loss of Greece to the Soviet Union would weaken Britain's entire regional position and urged the pursuit of American assistance. In another paper, Bevin echoed the views of the COS on the strategic importance of the Middle East, going so far as to quote DO (46) 80, their most trenchant statement of the air offensive strategy. His emphasis upon the extent to which the United States shared these views reflected his discussion in Washington of the previous November.[42] Greece, Turkey and Palestine now required careful consideration. Bevin not only agreed with the COS over American aid to Greece, but also asserted that in the search for a solution in Palestine, British strategic requirements were the paramount consideration.[43] The COS in a further paper asserted not only that the defence of the Middle East was 'vital to the whole Commonwealth defence strategy' but also that Egypt was the 'essential base both for defence and for the air counter-offensive', adding that the defence of Egypt 'can only be conducted effectively against attacks from the north by holding Palestine'. Moreover, given the importance of general Arab goodwill, they added the rider that any future partition of Palestine should not give offence in this quarter.[44]

Attlee had never been impressed by the strategic concept outlined in DO (46) 80 and was quick to reply. Writing to Bevin he observed that aside from the inadequacy of Britain's economic and military resources to hold this region, she would be drawn into fierce economic and political competition with the Soviets. Bases in the Middle East were a provocation, while offering only a limited deterrent effect. He continued:

> Unless we are persuaded that the U.S.S.R. is irrevocably committed to a policy of world domination and that there is no possibility of her alteration, I think that before being committed to this strategy we should seek to come to an agreement with the U.S.S.R. after consideration with Stalin of all our points of conflict.

The key question to be resolved, he reasoned, was whether the Soviets could be persuaded that war with the United States was not inevitable. If so, then he was sure that the points of friction could be dealt with. Attlee's approach, ironically, had a distinctly Churchillian ring, looking hopefully for some sort of agreement on spheres and interests.[45]

This debate came to a head at a special staff conference on 7 January

1947 attended by the COS, Attlee, Bevin, Dalton and Alexander, thus constituting something of an inner Defence Committee.[46] This was primarily a confrontation between Bevin and Attlee within which the issue of the strategic concept formed only a part. Bevin opened the meeting with a long exposition on his aims and objectives. He emphasized not only the strategic importance of the region but also economic and political factors: the importance of oil, the need to develop the area as a source of food to replace India and its value as an export market. Turning to negotiations with the Soviets, Bevin expounded a view radically different from that of Attlee, 'amply proved', he noted, by weeks of unproductive meetings with Molotov in Paris. He concluded that firm Anglo-American policy had now resulted in a Soviet recognition that incursion into Greece and Turkey was dangerous. Conversely, withdrawal would indicate weakness, removing any incentive for the Soviets to negotiate. 'It was only by adopting a firm line', he insisted, 'that categorical Russian opposition could be overcome and a solution ultimately reached by compromise.' His grand objectives were now 'a full economic and military alliance with Egypt' prefacing a wider programme of 'similar alliance' with other Middle East states. Talks with Iraq were already under way. Bevin made frequent references, doubtless aimed at Dalton the Exchequer, to American economic support. On Palestine he aligned himself with the COS: 'Strategically, he was impressed with the need to retain the friendship and co-operation of the Arab States'.

Attlee would have none of this and did not hesitate to launch the broadest counterattack upon Bevin's prescription:

> Russia would regard our activities in that area as directed against herself. We should be required to expend a great deal of money on the Middle East States, who were backward and of little economic value. None of these States were true democracies, their social fabric was rotten, and Russian propaganda would make the utmost gain out of our support for them. Strategically the Chiefs of Staff looked upon the Middle East as an offensive base from which to attack Russia, but he was not convinced that . . . the Middle East was necessary to the defence of the Commonwealth.

Meanwhile he cast doubt upon the speed of American entry into any future war, and expressed doubt about access to the region's oil in wartime.

Dalton now interjected to underline Britain's 'very serious' economic position, and welcomed American assistance. He expressed hopes that any presence in the region could be retained without excessive cost and expressed interest in 'the development of Africa'. But his comments also revealed grave misconceptions on the part of his Treasury officials who were still assuring him that American and Canadian loans would not be exhausted for some time. Alexander and the COS aligned themselves with

Bevin, reassuring Dalton that their peacetime plans would 'not require large forces'. John Cunningham, CNS, added a further conciliatory note:

> The Prime Minister had suggested that we wished to retain our military position in the Middle East as an offensive threat towards Russia. This was true in a way, as the best form of defence was the ability to retaliate. He would describe our military policy in the Middle East more as a deterrent than a provocation.

The tone of the meeting was perhaps less acerbic than it might have been due to the absence of Montgomery in Moscow. No firm decision was reached. While the COS made some headway with an agreement to support Greece and Turkey, contingent on sufficient American aid, there was no decision on Palestine or Middle East strategy.[47]

However, the tide was now turning decisively against Attlee. First, on the political front both Bevin and the Foreign Office concluded that Attlee's idea of negotiation with the Soviets was unacceptable. Bevin now addressed the sharpest possible rebuke to the Prime Minister:

> It would be Munich all over again, only on a world scale, with Greece, Turkey and Persia as the first victims in place of Czechoslovakia. If I am right about Russian ideology, Russia would certainly fill the gap we leave empty, whatever her promises. Whatever we may think of the internal regimes of the Middle Eastern countries, they are all passionately attached to their national independence. If we speak to Stalin as you propose, he is likely to respect their independence as Hitler was to respect Czechoslovakia's and we should get as much of Stalin's goodwill as we got of Hitler's at Munich.

Bevin had bluntly accused Attlee of proposing a 'surrender'. The two met alone on the afternoon of 9 January. While Attlee conceded that at present, there would be no further withdrawals from the Middle East, he refused to accept that the area had any significance for Britain's overall defence.[48]

Matters now took a second and dramatic twist with the return of the impulsive Montgomery, CIGS, from Moscow. Although there are grounds for interpreting Montgomery's diary with care,[49] the evidence suggests that his account of what followed is accurate. Montgomery decided upon a direct confrontation and asked the COS whether they were prepared to resign rather than give way over the Middle East. Tedder and Cunningham 'agreed wholeheartedly' whereupon Attlee was privately informed of their resolve. Already, Attlee must have been shaken by Bevin's outspoken 'appeasement' letter and this second *démarche* now clinched the issue.[50] When the protagonists met again on 13 January 1947 it was to consider an uncompromising document prepared by the COS entitled 'Future Defence Policy'. This rehearsed the concept of an air counter-offensive and identified three interdependent principles: first, the defence and safety of the United Kingdom and its development as an offensive base, second, maintenance of sea communications, and third, a firm hold on the Middle East area. In a dramatic *volte face* and without protest, Attlee endorsed these three principles.[51] This central document summarizing ground that had been so bitterly contested for a period of almost twelve months became DO (47) 44, 'Future Defence Policy', the conceptual blueprint of British strategic thinking that was to stand until 1950. This document is notable not only for its trenchant reassertion of COS thinking on the Middle East, but also for the dismissive comments on Attlee's continental predelictions:

> There is now . . . no combination of European Powers capable of standing up to Russia on land, nor do we think that the probable military capabilities of an association of European states at present justify us in relying upon such an association for our defence.[52]

THE PROBLEMS OF IMPLEMENTATION, 1948–9

Attlee's resistance to the COS had been tenacious, capitulating only when subjected to overwhelming pressure. Yet, if the COS believed acceptance of DO (47) 44 'Future Defence Policy' marked the realization of their Middle East strategy then they were badly mistaken. Political approval of what Stansgate had sarcastically described as the COS's 'perfect war plan' was one thing, to obtain the economic resources and regional bases to implement it was quite another. Undoubtedly, the COS were guilty of deliberately disregarding financial considerations, but at the same time in early 1947 the Treasury itself was still remarkably optimistic about the sterling area. Britain's economic problems were wrongly perceived as short term. Attlee held a more realistic appreciation not only of economic matters and the depth of nationalist opposition to British overseas bases, but also of the divergent nature of American strategy. These and other factors would undermine COS thinking on the Middle East by 1950.[53]

After 1947 improvements in Commonwealth defence co-operation marked the only substantial achievement in a period of British reverses inside and, more importantly, outside the region. It was primarily economic weakness that undermined not only the Middle Eastern concept of the COS but also, as others have shown, Bevin's idea of a bloc incorporating Europe, the Middle East and Africa, which he had hoped would permit Britain to escape dependence on the United States. Events in Europe and Asia throughout 1949 and 1950 finally forced the recognition of Britain's weakness, heralding a reluctant shift to align British strategy with American and Western Union planning which emphasized not the Middle East but European continental defence. All this prefigured further revisions during 1951 and 1952.[54]

Despite continual wrangling over military expenditure and manpower, the COS's objectives in the Middle East appeared deceptively close to realization during 1947 and early 1948. Although the Council of Foreign Ministers in the autumn of 1947 failed to settle the question of Cyrenaica, Britain remained in occupation of the area and enjoyed American support. Palestine remained a major problem, but nevertheless, in early 1948 treaty talks with Egypt, moribund since 1946, showed signs of revival. Later that year the acceleration of tensions in Europe in any case determined the COS to remain in Egypt in the short term, regardless of the consequences.[55]

More importantly, given Britain's dependence on American atomic power for the implementation of her Middle East strategy, approval now seemed to be forthcoming from Washington. Growing American support for Greece and Turkey, culminating in the Truman Doctrine of March 1947, was followed by informal talks on the Middle East held at the Pentagon in October 1947. These achieved a remarkable degree of consonance on strategy. The British desired political support for their position in the region while the United States, conscious of its declining troop levels, wished to avoid military involvement by utilizing the British to prevent a vacuum in the area.[56] Britain's attitude also reflected Bevin's desire to avoid an increased American political role in the region, particularly in the Gulf where American economic intentions were viewed by the Foreign Office as 'sinister'. These meetings not only ended a period when Anglo-American strategic conversations had been in the doldrums, but also increased British resolve to hold bases in the region in the short term.[57]

By early 1948 British contingency planning for war in the Middle East not only depended upon American strategic air power, but also required bases in Egypt and the securing of sea lanes through the Mediterranean, thus providing bases for the American *tactical* air power and extensive logistic support required to hold this position.[58] The American Joint Chiefs of Staff (JCS) were confident of Britain's ability to 'take and hold' airbases in the Cairo area.[59] This Anglo-American strategic consensus, encapsulated in plan SANDOWN, reflected intensive discussions held in Washington during April 1948.[60] Here British planners had convinced their American counterparts to abandon the idea of launching airstrikes from captured airbases in Pakistan in favour of the British plan to use airbases in the Suez/Cairo/Khartoum area. This British influence was apparent in the subsequent American short-term War Plan HALFMOON.[61] By the late summer of 1948 detailed Anglo-American planning had progressed to the point of identifying specific roads, railways and refineries for demolition by special forces. Therefore, Plan SANDOWN was substantially in line with American thinking, albeit this alignment had been achieved only after considerable British badgering on the value of the Middle East in general and Egyptian airbases in particular.[62]

Although Britain now adopted a short-range war plan similar to the American HALFMOON (of which SANDOWN was the Middle East portion) these impressive documents disguised considerable Anglo-American disagreements.[63] A strong contingent in Washington favoured airbases in Europe and Asia over those in the Middle East, furthermore they desired a commitment to continental defence in Europe. The United States tended to emphasize short-term emergency planning while the British presumed that war was a more distant prospect.[64] Moreover, in June 1948, when these plans (which presumed a first strike) were circulated, Attlee questioned, not for the first time, their assumption that political permission would even be given for the use of atomic weapons. The deepening crisis over Berlin during the autumn of 1948 temporarily silenced these disagreements. Britain now placed more emphasis on short-term planning and found herself even more dependent upon Egypt where much of the logistics for SANDOWN were prelocated.[65]

During 1948 and early 1949 confident of some American support, Britain's strategic requirements in the Middle East remained extensive. Political uncertainty over peacetime rights in Egypt increased interest in Cyrenaica and indeed in South Asia. East Africa, a costly alternative favoured particularly by Bevin and Montgomery, was also the subject of recurring interest. Views on a continental commitment remained equally firm. Despite Montgomery's periodic enthusiasm for a continental commitment, his colleagues Tedder and Cunningham remained convinced that there was no prospect of defending Europe before 1957.[66]

The extensive regional facilities sought by the COS remained elusive. Stalemate in the talks on Egyptian bases was accompanied by political and, more importantly, financial problems in other territories. The depth of Arab hostility to foreign bases was underlined at an early stage by the case of Iraq. Here, even in January 1948, the recently signed Portsmouth Treaty, giving access to bases in war, was not only repudiated, but also resulted in riots which brought down the moderate government. This failure had wider repercussions given that the Portsmouth Treaty had represented Bevin's model for military partnership with other Arab states. Saudi Arabia was alarmed by developments in Iraq and refused to contemplate a similar arrangement.[67] Eventually Britain secured permission to examine the possibility of airfield development in Saudi Arabia, a scheme which quickly foundered because of the enormous cost. Only King Abdullah of Transjordan, known unkindly to the Foreign Office as 'Mr Bevin's little King', offered Britain the strategic compliance she sought. This was not an ideal relationship to display to other states in the region.[68]

Britain's fixation was Egypt meanwhile served to undermine more realistic alternatives in Cyrenaica. The possibility that base facilities in Egypt might still be agreed rendered British officials reluctant to go to the expense of duplicating them in Cyrenaica. Thus the envisaged cost of new bases strengthened the case for the unrealistic Egyptian option.[69] Cyrenaica was viewed only as an adjunct to Egypt, for the COS asserted

> without Egypt the Middle East could not be defended, and that if we did not obtain the right to enter Egypt in a war by negotiation we should have to go there by force . . . if we could not negotiate the right to enter Egypt in a war, the strategic facilities we required in . . . Cyrenaica, would be even more essential, for we should need them to enable us to enter Egypt by force.[70]

Financial stringency therefore reinforced politically unrealistic options.

Perhaps the most dramatic evidence that British Middle East planning was at odds with economic reality is provided by the case of strategic bases in Cyprus. As early as July 1947 the COS had examined and then rejected the alternative of constructing very heavy bomber bases on this island specifically on grounds of cost. Political difficulties with bases in Egypt and elsewhere forced the COS to reconsider during the spring of 1948. After all, they noted, there were no troublesome negotiations required since Cyprus was a formal colony and thus 'the only territory in the Middle East . . . unfettered by treaties'.[71] More importantly, Cyprus alone offered Britain a limited strategic capability *independent* of the United States. In 1948 Britain's most advanced bombers, a fleet of 160 Lincoln aircraft, possessed only a limited range (750 miles). Accordingly the proximity of Cyprus to the Soviet Union appeared invaluable:

> The strategic bombers we have at present, and which we are likely to have for the next few years, are scarcely able with a reasonable bomb load to reach worthwhile Russian targets from Egypt and are definitely unable to do so from Cyrenaica. From Cyprus on the other hand, a significant portion of Southern Russia is within range of our bombers, including much of the Dombas and Caucasian oil fields.

Clearly, in the short term, Cyprus was the only base option which allowed British participation in the air offensive (see Figure 1). Moreover, the JIC noted that in war, the Soviet Air Force would be preoccupied in Europe, leaving Cyprus relatively free from attack.[72] During 1948 much planning was devoted to the Cyprus option with the base at Famagusta selected for the storage of 'special cargoes'. However, by September 1949 all work had been suspended due to 'financial stringency'. In April 1950 Cyprus remained 'the favoured location' on 'all but financial grounds' but no more work was undertaken.[73]

Therefore throughout the late 1940s the major problems underlying Britain's Middle East strategy were primarily those of resources. Indian independence in 1947 and the resulting loss of the Indian Army exacerbated Britain's difficulties. Subsequently the outbreak of the Malayan

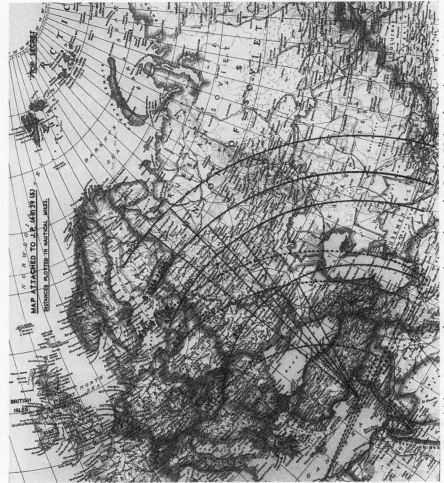

Figure 1 British target map for an atomic attack on the Soviet Union from bases in Cyprus, 1948, JP (48) 39, DEFE2/1654, PRO.

Emergency pushed Britain towards the return of conscription at a time when she could ill afford the loss of industrial manpower. Despite massive American assistance the economy recovered only slowly and by mid-1948, with the international situation deteriorating, the COS recognized the grave disparity between commitments and resources. Clearly, the Middle East could be held only with American and Commonwealth military assistance.[74]

'THE CENTRE OF THE WORLD': FEDERATIONS AND COMMONWEALTH DEFENCE

Britain's active search for increased Commonwealth defence co-operation in the Middle East during 1948 was driven by perceptions of an increasing Soviet threat. In 1946 the JIC had confidently asserted that the Soviet Union would not have recovered sufficiently to embark on a shooting war for ten years. In the Middle East the JIC suggested that the Soviets desired to acquire a security zone to cover their vulnerable southern flank, but concluded that they would only pursue this by 'all means short of war'.[75] The views of the JIC on Soviet methods altered only slightly during 1947, with growing emphasis upon 'political infiltration and the promotion of unrest'. The JIC now asserted that Soviet leaders believed 'the capitalist world is about to collapse'.[76] During the first six months of 1948, despite growing tensions over Czechoslovakia and Berlin, the JIC believed that the Soviets would continue to employ ' "cold war" methods rather than real war' because of the American atomic monopoly. However, at the same time the COS also considered that the danger of accident or miscalculation had increased so markedly 'that the risk of open war could not now be ignored'.[77] Moreover, the contemporaneous outbreak of the Malayan Emergency placed an unexpected strain on manpower resources. Commonwealth reinforcements for the Middle East would now be imperative in war.[78]

Britain had always perceived the Middle East as an Empire-Commonwealth responsibility. However, by 1948 the Commonwealth had not yet been acquainted with the thinking behind Anglo-American emergency plans. Talks on such matters could not be conducted through the usual system of low-level Commonwealth liaison officers based in London. The COS now desired high-level talks, hopefully leading to a concrete Commonwealth commitment to defend the Middle East, and acceptance of current Anglo-American strategy.[79] This objective was complicated by American scepticism regarding Commonwealth security with sensitive information.

Prior to 1948 Commonwealth defence co-operation had not been entirely stagnant, scientific research and intelligence were particularly well integrated, but joint strategic planning had progressed slowly. At the

Commonwealth Prime Ministers' Conference of October 1948, under the pressure of events in Berlin and Malaya, accelerated co-operation was agreed.[80] Pakistan expressed enthusiasm for Middle East defence, albeit partly motivated by antipathy towards Israel. South Africa was amenable, offering aircraft for the Middle East and for service in Berlin.[81] While the Prime Ministers were presented with a summary of the Anglo-American emergency planning, Attlee and the COS agreed that there should also be scope for Commonwealth input. The COS were delighted and noted: 'Much progress on [Middle East Plan] "Sandown" has been made'. Improved Commonwealth defence co-operation, combined with the advent of the Western Union in March 1948, was perceived as offering political as well as strategic advantages. Britain was now inclined to think of herself as the key interlocutor between these two organizations and the United States.[82]

The outcome of subsequent bilateral discussions with Commonwealth governments was by no means uniform. Canada would have nothing to do with Middle East defence, while in contrast New Zealand, perhaps the most Anglocentric Dominion, was happy to introduce conscription in the autumn of 1949 with the specific purpose of providing manpower for service in this theatre. Australian manpower, however, remained elusive. British planners visited Melbourne in August 1949 and the Australian Labour government appeared sympathetic, but gave no firm undertakings. Privately, Australia doubted Britain's ability to obtain base rights in Egypt and resolved to speed the development of Pacific defence links with the United States.[83]

By 1950 the objectives of Commonwealth defence in the Middle East had broadened, facilitating attempts to secure both a firmer American military commitment to the region and also Egyptian bases. Before departing for the Colombo Conference on economic co-operation in January 1950, Bevin and the COS resolved to raise defence matters between the formal sessions. Several objectives were identified. First, there would be a drive to persuade governments to endorse the plans agreed at the service level and Bevin would also press again for a formal Australian commitment to Middle East defence. Second, Bevin was actively considering 'some form of Regional Pact covering the centre of the world – the Middle East and the Indian Ocean': this would include the United Kingdom, Australia, New Zealand, South Africa, and 'certain Middle Eastern countries, notably Egypt'. But the primary objective was to involve the United States. They emphasized that

the approach of the Americans to the problem of Europe had been that they were prepared to help those who helped themselves. It was unlikely that the U.S. Authorities would have been willing to join the Atlantic Pact unless the nations of Western Europe had first proclaimed to the world their intention to defend themselves by setting up the Brussels Treaty Organisation. It was considered that the American approach to regional undertakings in other parts of the world would be on similar lines. The United States were more likely to enter into commitments in the Middle East and the Indian Ocean if there was already in existence some form of Regional organisation ... we should not wait until the United States were ready to join it.

The objective was clear: 'The ultimate aim should be to work for a Regional Pact ... which would include the United States'. As with so many aspects of Bevin's Middle East policy, an additional aim of this regional pact was to 'facilitate Egyptian negotiations' over the ever elusive base rights.

The problem of financial burden sharing was also discussed. The Foreign Office proposed asking the Commonwealth for a direct financial contribution of £60 million a year 'to be devoted to defence expenditure in peacetime in the Middle East'. The COS objected, noting that they desired contributions of manpower more than money. There were more fundamental objections. Commonwealth countries, they noted, would not 'agree to make a financial contribution unless they were given a considerable say in shaping our defence policy'. Not only would this entail 'a serious restriction on our freedom of action', but also 'the forces of the United Kingdom would tend to become the hired mercenaries of the Commonwealth, which would be placing us in a most invidious position'. It was therefore resolved to seek contributions in terms of manpower only, particularly from Australia.[84]

At the Colombo Conference, while there was a clear Australian will to endorse planning, the unconditional commitment of units remained elusive. Although an election in Australia had delivered a more amenable government, its attention was dominated by events in Malaya and China, soon to be compounded by the outbreak of the Korean War in the summer of 1950. In this context, and recalling Britain's 'great betrayal' of 1941, Australia was far happier committing troops for the defence of South East Asia than enmeshing herself in the Middle East. Slim, the CIGS, visited Melbourne in June 1950 to press this issue again, but the Australian Defence Committee evaded this initiative by undertaking to plan for both Malaya and the Middle East. By January 1951, prior to the Commonwealth Heads of Government Conference, the COS were optimistic enough to contemplate collective rather than bilateral discussions on the Middle East. Commonwealth co-operation, reinforced by the Korean War, offered an unusual success for a Middle East strategy otherwise beset by difficulties during the late 1940s.[85]

By 1950 American anxiety to use the Commonwealth to avoid increased

US military commitments in the Middle East resulted in a more relaxed attitude to the release of its planning to third parties. Hitherto, these restrictions had dogged efforts in areas as diverse as Anglo-Australian rocket research and planning between the Royal Navy and the navies of the Western Union. American concern had also resulted in the JIC arranging for the circulation of discreetly sanitized documents to India and Pakistan. This matter greatly irritated Attlee, for whom the construction of a New Commonwealth remained a high priority.[86] In December 1949 Slim visited Washington and pressed the American JCS hard on this issue, asserting that it placed Britain 'in an impossible position in our relations both with the Commonwealth and the Western Union'. American accommodation was underlined by a subsequent Anglo-American agreement on information security in January 1950.[87]

Bevin's hopes for a pact covering 'the centre of the world', expressed at the Colombo Conference, was but one example of Britain's fascination with artificial federations, regional organizations and defence pacts during the late 1940s. How far the Western Union was primarily designed to 'entangle' the United States remains unclear, but in the Middle East, South and South East Asia, part of the rationale for these proposed groupings was to elicit a firmer American commitment. Regional pacts also held out the appearance of egalitarian co-operation with successor states while at the same time hopefully maintaining British leadership and facilitating base rights. Britain's pursuit of both a regional pact and a proposed Middle East Command between 1948 and 1951 conformed to this general pattern.[88]

Although most British initiatives in the Middle East during the late 1940s were bilateral, vague ideas of some sort of regional defence pact had been voiced as early as 1948. Initially, little effort was expended in this direction for fear that a collective formula might fail to secure specific strategic desiderata. Moreover, the Foreign Office, conscious of the difficulties of persuading an economizing Republican Congress to accept the North Atlantic Treaty, was circumspect about further pacts.[89] There were also fears that Arab states would require a regional agreement to address the Israeli question (borne out by Egypt's Arab League).[90] Therefore British enthusiasm for regional pacts prior to 1950 was largely the result of hopes that an Anglo-American approach would secure allied access to Egyptian bases. By inviting the Egyptians to joint talks with Britain *and* the United States, the COS hoped to 'flatter' the Egyptians into acceptance of their requirements. Predictably, the Egyptians saw through this crude device and failed to take the bait. Britain's search for a regional pact took on greater urgency after the outbreak of the Korean War, but continued to founder, not least over British withdrawal from Egypt.[91]

From 1950 regional initiatives began to develop from an entirely different direction following Greek and Turkish attempts to join NATO. Alongside extremely complex discussions over a Middle East Command,

British and American views enjoyed a brief period of consonance as both envisaged their accession to NATO through some regional pact. The United States perceived Greece and Turkey in a European context as part of the southern flank of NATO, while conversely, Britain viewed them as an adjunct to Commonwealth defence in the Middle East. The issue was complicated by internal divisions in Washington. The State Department was increasingly aware that Britain required greater support if she was to remain in the region; however, the JCS were adamant that Turkey should look towards the Southern Mediterranean rather than be subsumed in a British-dominated Middle Eastern Command. These differences were symptomatic of a more alarming transatlantic divergence over the relative value of the defence of Europe and the Middle East which was increasingly difficult to ignore.[92]

MIDDLE EAST STRATEGY IN CRISIS, 1949–51

Between 1947 and 1949 the COS had embarked on a search for the political, geographical and above all the economic wherewithal to implement their Middle East strategy and had met with only limited success. Firm base dispositions and regional military commitments by allies remained conspicuous by their absence. From mid-1949 Britain's Middle East strategy began to confront problems of an entirely different order. Important developments in Europe and Asia now posed insuperable resource problems for Britain and the Commonwealth, and greatly exacerbated underlying differences in Anglo-American strategic thinking. All this pointed to a complete overhaul of British strategy. This trend towards fundamental revision was apparent even as early as the spring of 1949 when events in China raised the question of large troop commitments in South East Asia. By April this had been followed by a decision to hold Hong Kong against possible Chinese pressure. In August 1949 even the United States was alarmed by Britain's predicament and feared that she might abandon overseas commitments. The CIA concluded: 'Britain is now strained as nearly to capacity as a democratic nation has ever been in peacetime'.[93]

Meanwhile, in the spring of 1949, the new CIGS, Field Marshal Slim, revived his predecessor's interest in a military commitment to Europe, partly to facilitate British political leadership there. However, for Tedder, the CAS, the Middle East remained the key to a future air war and Slim's initiative was headed off with Bevin's assistance.[94] But the question of a continental commitment returned with greater force following the suspected detonation of a Soviet atomic device in the early autumn of 1949. Hitherto, the COS had accepted the advice of the JIC, that the Soviets might achieve an atomic capability by the early 1950s, probably 1952. Overnight, three years were removed from this most important planning horizon. Fears were exacerbated by the Klaus Fuchs atom spy case in early 1950 and the COS concluded that Soviet atomic development was now 'much more advanced than it was thought to have been'. They reflected with discomfort upon Britain's position now that a nuclear armed adversary might quickly reach the Atlantic seaboard in a future war.[95]

The United States, which had always placed less emphasis on the Middle East than Britain, now redoubled its focus upon Western Europe. This reflected not only increased Soviet, but also improved American capabilities. The development of American aircraft with longer range permitted a 'strategic air offensive . . . contemplating the use of heavy bomber air facilities in the UK, Alaska and Okinawa' rather than less secure bases in the Middle East.[96] This American shift in emphasis met with dismay on the part of British planners, and recalled Anglo-American wartime friction over the question of Mediterranean 'sideshows'. Divergence was especially evident at the ABC (American-British-Canadian) planning session in Washington during late September 1949. To the horror of the British representatives, the US JCS declared it more important to maintain a bridgehead into Europe than to hold the Middle East. By November 1949 there were even doubts about American air support for the region. Although by the end of the year revised British and American war plans, GALLOPER and OFFTACKLE respectively, were completed, their different emphasis rendered them all but incompatible.[97]

The speed of this American shift in favour of Europe took the COS by surprise. In December 1949 Slim, the CIGS, visited Washington and expressed his 'disappointment' that all the detailed planning for the Middle East, painstakingly worked out between British planners and the American Mediterranean Commander, 'had been shelved without warning'. The US JCS, by way of reply, confronted Slim with the worst of all possible worlds, a request for a continued British commitment but without American support:

> [The JCS] hastened to add that they did not in any way doubt the importance of the Middle East and agreed . . . that it should be held. Their only reservation was that they could not send troops to the Middle East at the outbreak of war as they judged Western Europe to be of more immediate importance.[98]

But without American support, the Middle East air offensive, outlined in DO (47) 44, 'Future Defence Policy', a dominant concept which had stood throughout the late 1940s, appeared increasingly impractical.[99]

These alarming developments contributed to Britain's subsequent decision to re-examine her own Middle East planning in the spring of 1950. Here Britain attempted to fudge the problem of American emphasis upon European defence by conflating this with one of the 'three pillars' of British strategy outlined in DO (47) 44, the defence of Britain. As Slim observed with some satisfaction, this blurring of Britain's attitude to a continental commitment was possible because, for the time being, any such undertaking was meaningless, for mainland Europe would be unlikely to hold out long enough for Britain to mobilize. *De facto* flexibility was therefore the order of the day and by January 1950 a larger proportion of forces designated for the Middle East were to be held 'in readiness' in Britain. Notwithstanding all this talk of flexibility, there was no escaping the fact that the US JCS now attached a lower priority to the Middle East. Meanwhile, British planners continued to value the region as second only to Britain. Attempts to secure changes in American strategy were complicated by disagreements between the JCS and the State Department.[100]

In 1946 it had been a lengthy debate over the increased importance of air power and weapons of mass destruction which had led to formulation of DO (47) 44 with its emphasis on the Middle East. In early 1950, as the COS reconsidered Britain's strategy, air power – in this case specifically the new Soviet atomic capability – was again a primary cause of reconsideration, now in favour of European defence. On 8 March 1950 the COS concluded that Britain must hold the Soviets on the Rhine, if only to permit Britain an adequate forward zone to provide early warning of air attack. On 11 May 1950 Slim put their views bluntly to the new Minister of Defence, Shinwell: 'The reason for this change in policy was that it was now considered that, if Europe was overwhelmed, the United Kingdom would be threatened as never before and might well not survive'.[101] In the summer of 1950 Britain's shift towards continental defence was encapsulated in a new paper, DO (50) 45, 'Defence Policy and Global Strategy', which confirmed Europe as 'the most important area'. This paper stood more or less unchanged until the advent of the second Churchill government in 1952.[102]

While the importance of the Middle East in British strategy was primarily undermined by economic and strategic factors emanating from outside the region, local difficulties proved as intractable as ever. Paradoxically, while the United States backed away from commitments in the Middle East, at the same time she pressed Britain to aim in war for the ambitious forward defence of Turkey and the Persian Gulf, rather than Egypt and Palestine. Problems arose over the Arab–Israeli conflict and the Foreign Office intervened to restrain the COS, who wished to supply arms to Arab states. The problem of honouring defence agreements with Iraq, Egypt and Transjordan in this context was actively discussed.[103]

Meanwhile, Britain remained eternally optimistic concerning Egyptian base rights. Talks reopened in June 1949, facilitated by Egypt's desire for arms in the wake of her confrontation with Israel in 1948. But the British objective, extensive British managed bases, was unrealistic. More moderate British requests in 1950 came up against the firm opposition of the newly formed nationalist government. Forcing the British out had now become a *sine qua non* for Egyptian politicians and relations deteriorated through 1950, accompanied by anti-British rioting in Cairo, Bevin's discussions with the Egyptian Foreign Secretary in December 1950 confirmed that Cairo would accept only total British withdrawal.[104] By July 1951 British planners had accepted American wishes that Turkey and Greece should enter NATO, provided that they simultaneously joined a Middle East Command (MEC). Underlying these complex negotiations over an MEC were futile British hopes that Egyptian participation would provide a framework for resolving the stalemate over bases. This unfounded optimism was dashed in the autumn of 1951 by the predictable Egyptian rejection of this allied ploy. Further complex reformulations and rejections followed in September and October 1951. Finally the 1936 Anglo-Egyptian Treaty was repudiated on 16 October 1951. Renewed rioting in Cairo exposed the bankruptcy of the British position, confirming American resolve to pursue privately a separate policy of support for the 'northern tier' – Greece, Turkey and Iran.[105]

Because of the atmosphere of crisis created by the Korean War, the United States gave her support to the British decision to stand rigidly on the terms of the repudiated 1936 treaty, permitting a presence until 1956. Nevertheless, the outlook for Britain's regional headquarters was hardly auspicious. British weakness was underlined by the crisis with Iran over oilfield nationalization. After toying with the idea of a show of force, (and there was no doubt that Britain had considerable regional military capability), Britain succumbed to American pressure for restraint.[106]

By 1951 the Commonwealth had joined the United States in questioning the wisdom of extensive Middle East commitments. Australia was prepared to offer considerable support in Malaya but the expanding conflict there and in Korea reinforced Australian reluctance to send forces further afield. During the Commonwealth Defence Ministers' meeting in late June 1951, Australia was urged to send more aircraft to the Middle East and in September 1951 Shinwell was still pressing this issue upon Canberra. In late 1951, as if to offer a definitive reply to these tiresome and repetitive British overtures, Australia offered a clear statement of her Pacific focus in the form of the ANZUS pact – a Pacific security agreement embracing Australia, New Zealand and the United States but not Britain.[107]

CONCLUSION

As late as 1949 the Middle East still lay at the centre of Britain's strategic concept. In April 1949 the authoritative Foreign Office Permanent Under-Secretaries Committee reviewed regional policy. All the arguments of 1946 remained in place: oil, the defence of Africa, communications and above all, the value of an air offensive against vulnerable areas of the Soviet hinterland. The need for American and Commonwealth support was recognized, the precarious nature of Britain's bases acknowledged, but there was no indication of diminished importance. Even in November 1949 the COS were firmly restating their case for the Middle East:

> We must find a way of holding the Middle East at the beginning of a war with our own resources and of developing offensive action against Russia from that area. We believe this can be done. It must be done.[108]

But this latter assertion was symptomatic, not of their determination, but of their frustration, in the face of a growing range of related obstacles and distractions: Soviet atomic power, British economic weakness and vulnerability, divergent American strategy, and new developments in Europe and Asia. The place of the Middle East was being inexorably undermined.[109]

Within Britain's revised strategy of 1950, encapsulated in DO (50) 45, the decline of the Middle East was not over-dramatic. The Middle East remained second only to the defence of Europe and the RAF hoped to expand its air capability in this region. In June 1951 this paper was updated, but other than increased emphasis upon South East Asia, its tone had changed little.[110] These papers represented less a new strategic concept and more a reluctant recognition of the reality which had prevailed during the late 1940s. Attlee's prescient remarks in 1946 about the paucity of resources, the problems of base rights and the vulnerability of the home base to attack from Europe were at last receiving concerted attention.

In one other important respect the inconoclastic perspective previously advanced by Attlee returned to confront the COS during 1950. In November 1946 Attlee had warned that the basing of American bombers in British territories might render it difficult not to follow American policy in any future crisis with the Soviet Union, 'while in return little protection would be afforded'. In 1950 the new dangers posed by the advent of a Soviet atomic capability combined with the increasingly abrasive policy pursued by the United States following the outbreak of the Korean War prompted the COS to reflect along precisely the same lines.[111] Meeting on 12 July 1950 to discuss the Sino-American confrontation over Formosa, the COS concluded: 'If we supported the Americans there seemed a most serious risk that we would provoke a world war'. They added: 'We were in no position to fight at the moment. If war broke out now, it was highly probable that both Western Europe and the Middle East would be overrun'. A little more than a week later, the COS decided to approach the United States regarding control over an air offensive from British bases. They wrote to Tedder in Washington:

> You are of course aware of the existence of an American plan in the

event of major war to initiate immediately an atomic attack on Russia from bases in this country. . . . The fact is all we, the Chiefs of Staff, know about this plan is (a) that it exists (b) certain broad details which our planners have been able to glean during their visit to America last year and (c) that there may be considerable difference of opinion about it not only between Strategic Air Command and the Air Staff in the Pentagon but also . . . between the airmen and the soldiers in America . . .

At present it is not unduly fanciful to imagine a situation in which Vandenburg or Lemay [US JCS] sends Johnson [USAF Commander, UK] an order to initiate the offensive while we may have to resist any action pending consideration by the Prime Minister and Government to Government discussions.[112]

During 1950, therefore, many of the basic assumptions that had underpinned British strategy during the late 1940s were undergoing revision. The centre-piece of this strategy, an Anglo-American air offensive from the Middle East, had encountered severe regional difficulties over matters such as Egyptian bases. But the main issues prompting the reconsideration of British strategy during 1950 and 1951 were on a much grander scale. Not only were the COS simultaneously confronted with new commitments in Europe and Asia, but also they were now required to address both a nuclear capable adversary and an increasingly unpredictable ally.

NOTES

1 Montgomery recorded on 7 September: 'Leaning across the table CIGS [Montgomery] then taxed the Minister with a direct and very blunt question. . . . Is the Government prepared to go to war for Berlin? . . . AVA [Alexander] was quite shattered'. Two days later he recorded: 'After the Chief of the Air Staff had got really worked up and AVA [Alexander] even more so, CIGS felt that the time had come for him to join in.' Entries for 30 May to September 1948, Montgomery diary, Ch. 71, BLM 1/185/1–186/1, Imperial War Museum, London (hereafter IWM).
2 The first body appointed to this task was the Military Sub-committee (MSC), see MSC (42) 3, PHHP/MSC/3, 'Post War Strategic Requirements in the Middle East', 11 December 1942, L/WS/1/1341, IOLR.
3 PHP (44) 17 (0) (Revised Draft), 'Security in Western Europe and the North Atlantic', 15 July 1944, U6791/748/70, FO 371/40741A, PRO. For the extensive literature on PHPS see p. 301, n. 7.
4 PHP (44) 16 (0) (3rd Draft), 'Policy Required to Secure British Strategic Interests in the Eastern Mediterranean and the Middle East', 5 January 1945, U181/36/70, FO 371/50774, PRO; PHP (45) 10 (0) (Final), 'Security in the Eastern Mediterranean and the Middle East', 27 March 1945, CAB 81/48, PRO; JIC (44) 467 (O) (Final), 'Russian Strategic Interests and Intentions from the Point of View of her Security', 18 December 1944, N678/20/38, FO 371/47860, PRO.
5 PHP (45) 29 (0), 'The Security of the British Empire', 2 April 1945, U3390/36/70, FO 371/50775, PRO. The COS accepted these conclusions, as a 'staff study' only, COS (45) 175th mtg., 12 July 1945, CAB 79/36, PRO.
6 COS (45) 402 (0), 'Future Developments in Weapons and Methods of War', 16 June 1945, CAB 80/94, PRO.
7 A. Resis, 'The Churchill–Stalin Percentages Agreement', *American Historical Review*

Vol. 83, No. 2 (1978), pp. 368–87; P. Tsakoyolannis, 'The Moscow Puzzle', *Journal of Contemporary History* Vol. 21, No. 1 (January 1986), pp. 37–57; WP (45) 256, memorandum by Eden, 'Defence of the Middle East', 13 April 1945, CAB 66/65, PRO; Sargent memorandum, 'Stocktaking After VE Day', 11 July 1945, U5471/5471/70, FO 371/50912, PRO.

8 The meeting was attended by ministers: Attlee, Eden, Amery and Cranborne. Minutes of a meeting held at the Foreign Office, (6584/3806/61), 16 October 1942, L/P&S/12/4628, IOLR; WP (45) 197, 'Future Defence Policy in the Suez Canal Area', 20 March 1945, CAB 66/63, PRO.

9 WP (45) 242, 'Compulsory Military Service', 12 April 1945, CAB 66/64, PRO; Ward minute, 13 April 1945, U2273/36/70, FO 371/, PRO.

10 Eden minute to Dixon, 13 July 1945, in R. Butler and M. E. Pelly (eds) *Documents on British Policy Overseas: Series I, Vol I, The Conference at Potsdam* (London: HMSO, 1984) (henceforth *DBPO*), No. 131, p. 270; Attlee to Eden, 18 July 1945, ibid., No. 179, pp. 363–4; Attlee to Churchill, ibid., No. 237, pp. 573–4; Entry for 23 July 1945, Cunningham Diary, MSS 52579, British Library, London.

11 Serious unrest and nationalist protests against the presence of British bases were exacerbated by the end of British influence over the police, see Fitzpatrick, Commandant Cairo City Police, 'Policy Memorandum', 12 November 1945, FO 141/1009, PRO. The protesters were given the opportunity to make their views personally known to Montgomery, Alanbrooke's successor, when he was caught up in a riot during his visit to Cairo later that year, entry for 23–24 November 1946, Montgomery diary, Ch. 19, BLM 1/176/6, IWM.

12 ORC (45) 21, 'The Future of the Italian Colonies and the Italian Mediterranean Islands', 25 August 1945, CAB 134/594, PRO; ORC (45), 4th mtg, 30 August 1945, ibid.

13 CP (45) 144, 'Future of the Italian Colonies', 1 September 1945, CAB 129/1, PRO; entry for 3 September 1945, Alanbrooke diary, papers of Field Marshal Lord Alanbrooke, 5/11, Liddell Hart Centre for Military Archives, King's College, London (hereafter KCL); CM (45), 27th mtg, 3 September 1945, CAB 128/1, PRO; CM (45) 30, 11 September 1945, ibid.; CP (45) 162, 11 September 1945, CAB 129/2, PRO.

14 JP (45) 233 (Final), 'Montreux Convention', 4 September 1945, CAB 84/75, PRO; CM (45) 38th mtg, 4 October 1945, CAB 128/1, PRO; DO (45), 6th mtg, 14 September 1945, CAB 69/7, PRO; Zametica, 'British Strategic Planning', pp. 50–6, 64–6. On Bevin and Eden, see P. Dixon, *Double Diploma* (London: Hutchinson, 1968) pp. 183–4; COS (45) 678 (0) Annex, 2 December 1945, CAB 80/98, PRO.

15 Harris, *Attlee* (London: Weidenfeld & Nicolson, 1982), p. 292; Gowing, pp. 70–7; Bullock, *Bevin*, pp. 185–8.

16 Entry for 7 November 1945, B. Pimlott (ed.) *The Political Diary of Hugh Dalton: 1918–40 and 1945–60* (London: Cape, 1986); Attlee to Truman, 25 September 1945, Box 170, PSF Subject File (A-Attlee), Harry S. Truman Library, Independence, Missouri, USA; Navy Day, 27 October 1945, *Harry S. Truman: Public Papers*, 1945 (Washington DC: US Government Printing Office, 1967), pp. 431–8.

17 JP (45) 292 (Final), 'Long Term Policy in Greece', 3 December 1945, CAB 84/76, PRO; Roberts to FO, 27 November 1945, N16025/18/38, FO 371/47858, PRO; COS (46) 30 (0), 'Future of the Italian Colonies', 31 January 1946, CAB 80/99, PRO.

18 J. Zametica, 'British Strategic Planning for the Mediterranean and the Middle East, 1944–47', PhD dissertation, University of Cambridge, 1986, pp. 84–90; CM (46) 14th mtg, 11 February 1946, CAB 128/7, PRO; entry for 16 February 1946, Cunningham diary, MSS 52579, British Library; H. Dalton, *High Tide and After: Memoirs, 1945–60* (London: Frederick Muller, 1962), p. 101; DO (46) 5th mtg, 15 February 1946, CAB 131/1, PRO.

19 COS (46) 54 (0) Annex, 'The Future of the Italian Colonies', 22 February 1946, CAB 80/100, PRO; entry for 18 March 1946, Alanbrooke diary, 5/11, Liddell Hart Centre for Military Archives, King's College, London; Dickson memorandum, 'Future of the Italian Colonies', 24 February 1946, AIR 9/267, PRO.

20 ibid.; DO (46) 40 Annex, 13 March 1946, CAB 131/2, PRO; DO (46) 8th mtg, 18 March 1946, CAB 131/1, PRO; COS (46) 96 Annex, 'Review of the Anglo-Egyptian

Treaty', 27 March 1946, CAB 80/100, PRO; COS (46) 51st mtg (4), 29 March 1946, CAB 79/46, PRO.

21 T. Burridge, *Attlee* (London: Collins, 1987), p. 322; the COS also looked to the Dominions as rear area bases, should wartime bombardment render Britain 'untenable', COS (46) 111, 'United Kingdom Military Representation in the Dominions', Annex II, 10 April 1946, L/WS/1/985, IOLR. See also JP (46) 82, 'Strategic Position of the British Commonwealth', 17 April 1946, ibid.

22 PMM (44) 14th mtg (2), April 1944, CAB 99/28, PRO; PMM (46) 6th mtg, April 1946, CAB 133/86, PRO; PMM (46) 13th mtg, April 1946, ibid.; PMM (46) 7, 'Australian Defence Committee', 23 April 1946, ibid.; Alanbrooke seems to have been thinking in particular of Prime Minister Evatt of Australia, entry for 26 April 1946, Alanbrooke diary, papers of Field Marshal Lord Alanbrooke, 5/12, Liddell Hart Centre for Military Archives, KCL.

23 This early draft paper, JP (46) 45 (Draft) is not extant, but its contents can be deduced from MacArthur's caustic criticisms.

24 MacArthur minute to Director of Plans, 25 March 1946, AIR 9/267, PRO.

25 JP (46) 45 (Final), 'Strategic Position of the British Commonwealth', and Annex, 27 March 1946, CAB 84/79, PRO.

26 Dickson ACAS (P), minute, 28 March 1946, AIR 9/267, PRO; DO (46) 47, 'Strategic Position of the British Commonwealth', 2 April 1946, CAB 131/2, PRO.

27 DO (46) 10th mtg, 5 April 1946, CAB 131/1, PRO; entry for 5 April 1946, Alanbrooke diary, 5/12, Liddell Hart Centre for Military Archives, KCL.

28 Appreciation, 20 April 1946, papers of Lord Stansgate, ST/188/8, House of Lords Record Office, London.

29 JP (46) 100 (Final), 'Strategic Requirements in the Middle East', 23 May 1946, CAB 84/81, PRO; COS (46) 82nd mtg, 24 May 1946, CAB 79/48, PRO; DO (46) 67 (Revised), 'Strategic Requirements in the Middle East', 25 May 1946, CAB 21/2086, PRO.

30 Liddell Hart memorandum, 'Africa or the Middle East', 20 March 1946 (dispatched 10 May 1946), papers of Liddell Hart, 1/28/14, Liddell Hart Centre for Military Archives, KCL; Rowan to Liddell Hart, 13 May 1946, 1/28/16, ibid.

31 DO (46) 17th mtg, 27 May 1946, CAB 21/2086, PRO; Attlee to COS, D15/46, 31 May 1946, CAB 21/2277, PRO.

32 TWC (46) 15 (Revise), 'Future Developments in Weapons and Methods of War', 6 July 1946, DEFE 2/1252, PRO; CM (46) 57th Conclusions, 6 June 1946, CAB 128/5, PRO; JIC (46) 38 (0) (Final) (Revise), 'Russia's Strategic Interests and Intentions in the Middle East', 14 June 1946, DO 35/1604, PRO. This JIC paper was the first of a series of monthly reviews of Soviet Middle East policy on which the JIC had started work in May 1946. An earlier draft of this paper was discussed at JIC (46) 90th mtg (3), 7 June 1946, L/WS/1/1050, IOLR.

33 DO (46) 80, 'British Strategic Requirements in the Middle East', CAB 131/3, PRO.

34 COS (46) 108th mtg, minutes of a staff conference at 10 Downing St on 12 July 1946, CAB 21/2086, PRO; DO (46) 22nd mtg, 19 July 1946, CAB 131/1, PRO.

35 CM (46) 54th Conclusions, 3 June 1946, CAB 128/5, PRO; COS (46) 96th mtg, 21 June 1946, PRO; entry for 26 June to 19 August 1946, Montgomery diary, Ch. 9, BLM 1/175/1, IWM; COS (46) 133rd mtg, 30 August 1946, CAB 79/51, PRO.

36 COS (46) 188 (0) 'Palestine: Anglo-U.S. Report – Military Implications', 10 July 1946, CAB 80/102, PRO; Zametica, 'British Strategic Planning', pp. 144–52; Stansgate to Sargent, 7 August 1946, papers of Lord Stansgate, ST/188/8, House of Lords Records Office, London.

37 DO (46) 23rd mtg, 22 July 1946, CAB 131/1, PRO; minutes of a meeting between Bevin and Byrnes, Paris, 26 April 1946, R6382/1/19, FO 371/58687, PRO.

38 COS (46) 259 (0), 'Greece, Turkey and the Persian Gulf; Interview between Mr A. V. Alexander and Mr Byrnes on Tuesday, 15 October 1946', 26 October 1946, R15933/15770/67, FO 371/58658, PRO.

39 Zametica, 'British Strategic Planning', pp. 153–5; R. Aldrich and M. Coleman, 'Britain and the Strategic Air Offensive: The Question of South Asian Air Bases, 1945–9, *History* Vol. 74, No. 242 (October 1989), pp. 406–8. The glacis plate option outlined by Attlee

was undoubtedly considered at a high level by US officials during this period, see for example, memorandum, 'Problems and Objectives of US Policy', 2 April 1945, Box 15, Conway File, Harry S. Truman Library, Independence, Missouri.

40 Attlee to Bevin, 1 December 1946, ME/46/22, FO 800/475, PRO. On preliminary strategic talks Tedder had recently advised Montgomery: 'American [Joint] Chiefs [of Staff] have so far kept the whole matter secret from the State Department and the President. We have consequently been compelled to do the same at this end for the present', Tedder to Montgomery (Washington), SALT 33, 10 September 1946, Montgomery papers, Ch. 14, BLM 1/175/31, IWM.

41 JP (46) 229 (Final), 'Discussions on Defence Policy', 19 December 1946, CAB 21/2096, PRO; COS (46) 187th mtg, 23 December 1946, CAB 79/54, PRO.

42 DO (47) 1, 'Future Policy Towards Greece and Turkey', 1 January 1947, CAB 21/1964, PRO.

43 DO (47) 2, 'British Strategic Requirements in the Middle East', 2 January 1947, CAB 21/2086, PRO.

44 DO (47) 3, 'Palestine – Strategic Requirements', 6 January 1947, ibid.

45 Attlee memorandum, 'Near Eastern Policy', M.15/47, 5 January 1947, ME/47/1, FO 800/476, PRO. On Churchill and the Mediterranean see n. 7.

46 COS (47) 6th mtg, 2.30 p.m., 7 January 1947, DEFE 32/1, PRO. The minutes of this meeting, in common with other sensitive COS material, were kept separate from the main COS records in the Standard File of the Secretary to the COS. Copies of the minutes were circulated only to the participants. Meanwhile a short anodyne account was entered in the main COS records at DEFE 4/1, PRO. The full minutes of this meeting were withheld from public inspection until 1990.

47 Meanwhile Attlee achieved an undertaking that bulk storage of oil reserves in the United Kingdom would be examined, ibid.

48 Bevin to Attlee, P.M./47/8, 9 January 1947, ME/47/4, FO 800/476, PRO; Dixon minute, 10 January 1947, ME 47/5, ibid.

49 R. B. Lockhart recorded the following, after a conversation with Kenneth Strong, Head of Intelligence at Eisenhower's SHAEF Command, to which Montgomery had been subordinate: 'Strong . . . regards Montgomery not only as a cad but as a crook, says the Americans will never trust him again and that he has done more harm to Anglo-American relations than any Englishman since Lord North. He accused Monty of not only boycotting and bypassing his chief, Eisenhower, to the detriment of the Allied cause, but also of keeping a fake and dishonest diary record of the war. According to Strong his secretary who keeps this diary was so disgusted by the gross egotism and untruthful nature of Monty's diaries that she resigned. He says that SHAEF Intelligence has her report.' Entry for 28 August 1945, K. Young (ed.) The Diaries of Sir Robert Bruce Lockhart: Vol. 2, 1939–1965 (London: Macmillan, 1980), p. 499.

50 Entry for 10 December 1946 to 3 February 1947, Ch. 33, Montgomery Diary, 178/1, IWM; Field Marshal Montgomery of Alamein, The Memoirs of Field Marshal Montgomery (London: Collins, 1958), p. 436. For a full consideration of this incident, see Smith and Zametica, 'Cold Warrior', p. 251.

51 COS (47) 7th mtg, 8 January 1947, DEFE 4/1, PRO; COS (47) 5 (0) Final, 'Future Defence Policy' 23 January 1947, CAB 21/2096, PRO; COS (47) 9th mtg, 13 January 1947, DEFE 4/1, PRO.

52 DO (47) 44, 'Future Defence Policy', CAB 21/1800, PRO. Although the authors were permitted access to this document in 1985, the file remained closed to public inspection until 1990. This document has been thoughtfully reproduced in its entirety by Julian Lewis in Changing Direction, Appendix 7, pp. 370–88.

53 cf. pp. 143–65. See also Clarke memorandum, 12 February 1946, in R. C. Clarke, Anglo-American Economic Collaboration in War and Peace, 1942–1949 (Oxford: Oxford University Press,1981), pp. 139–45; A.Cairncross, The Years of Recovery, (London: Methuen, 1984).

54 cf pp. 193–214; Kent, 'British Empire', pp. 180–1. Fortunately, many aspects of British defence policy and the Middle East in the period beyond 1948 have received close attention. See David Devereux's carefully documented study The Formulation of British Defence Policy in the Middle East, 1948–56 (London: Macmillan, 1990); and also J. G.

Albert, 'Attlee, the Chiefs of Staff and the Restructuring of Commonwealth Defence Between V. J. Day and the Outbreak of the Korean War', PhD dissertation, University of Oxford, 1986.

55 DO (48) 31, 'Former Italian Colonies', 27 April 1948, DEFE 4/10, PRO; Louis, *British Empire*, p. 302; COS (48) 130th mtg, 17 September 1948, DEFE 4/16, PRO.

56 JP (47) 130, 'Middle East: Brief for Discussions', 30 September 1947, CAB 21/2086, PRO; British memorandum, 16 October 1947, *FRUS*, 1947, Vol. 5, pp. 566–7; Bevin minute, 'Pentagon Talks', ME/47/15, 9 October 1947, FO 800/476, PRO. See also Louis, *British Empire*, pp. 109–15; Best, *Like Minded Peoples*, pp. 138–9.

57 A. Machmani, ' "It's a Matter of Getting the Mixture Right"; Britain's Post War Relations with America in the Middle East', *Journal of Contemporary History* Vol. 18, No. 1 (January 1983), p. 133; COS (47) 144th mtg, 21 November 1947, DEFE 4/8, PRO.

58 COS (48) 123, Plan SANDOWN, 16 October 1948, AIR 8/1603, PRO. Much of the detailed planning for SANDOWN is available in AIR 8/1603–5, PRO *passim*.

59 This is clear from talks on USAF plans in late 1948: 'Major General Saville: Assuming the opposition of the Egyptians, how much force would be required to take and hold the airdrome at Cairo, approximately? Major General Anderson: . . . We think the British can take care of any trouble there', presentation on Operation DUALISM, by Anderson, Maxwell Air Force Base, 6–8 December 1948 – Operation DUALISM file, 5–81–45, OPD 337, Sec. 2, RG 341, NARA.

60 JP (48) 35 (Final), 'Discussions with the Americans' 30 March 1948, AIR 20/8101, PRO. CNS Cunningham asserted that they should involve 'a full exchange with the Americans of JPS and JIC papers on plans to meet Russian aggression', COS (48) 62nd mtg (2), 5 May 1948, DEFE 4/13, PRO.

61 JP (48) 54 (Final), 'Use of Pakistan as an Airbase during the next Eighteen Months', 10 May 1948, DEFE 6/6, PRO; Plan HALFMOON, reproduced in T. H. Etzold and J. L. Gaddis (eds) *Containment: Documents on American Policy and Strategy, 1945–50* (New York: Columbia University Press, 1978), p. 315. British planners feared that capturing airfields at Karachi would alienate Arab opinion, Aldrich and Coleman, 'Strategic Air Offensive', pp. 418–19.

62 COS (48) 189 (0), 'Denial of Persian and Iraqi Oil and Demolition of the Trans-Persian Railway', 21 August 1948, DEFE 5/11, PRO; JP (48) 135 (Final), 'Destruction of Persian Communications and Neutralisation of Middle Eastern Oil Installations', 4 November 1948, DEFE 6/7, PRO. Talks should be held in Washington as 'American planners are more forthcoming and more decisive when they are playing on their own pitch', JP (48) 12 (Final), 'Discussions with the Americans on Middle East Planning', 28 January 1948, AIR 20/2463, PRO.

63 The British plan was codenamed DOUBLEQUICK. JP (48) 63 (Final), 'Western Union Defence', 26 June 1948, DEFE 6/6, PRO; COS 125th mtg (2), 9 September 1948, DEFE 4/6, PRO. See also Best, *Like Minded Peoples*, pp. 182–3; Leahy to Truman, 10 September 1946, CCS 360, (12–9–42), Sec. 27. RG 218, NARA; Entry for 16 February to 29 May 1948, Montgomery diary, BLM 1/184/1, IWM.

65 COS (48) 78th mtg (1), 9 June 1948, DEFE 4/13, PRO. On the question of a first strike see Clarke and Wheeler, *Nuclear Strategy*, pp. 100–1; DO (48) 14th (1), CAB 131/5, PRO.

66 JP (47) 60, 'British Strategic Requirements in the Arab World', 13 January 1948, DEFE 4/10, PRO; DO (48) 61, 14 September 1948, CAB 131/6, PRO; COS (49) 115, 'Strategic Requirements in the Middle East', 1 April 1949, AIR 20/2463, PRO; Louis, 'American anti-colonialism', pp. 403–4; Aldrich and Coleman, 'Strategic Air Offensive', pp. 415–19; entry for 9 August to 12 November 1947, Montgomery diary, Ch. 59, BLM 1/183/2, IWM; Montgomery memorandum, report on visit to Africa, 13–18 November 1948, 19 November 1948, DO 35/2380, PRO. JP (48) 16 (Final), 'Discussion on Policy for Western Europe', DEFE 4/10, PRO; COS (48) 43rd mtg (1), 22 March 1948, DEFE 4/11, PRO; Montgomery, *Memoirs*, pp. 500–1.

67 Louis, *British Empire*, p. 104; Albert, pp. 151–60; Ovendale, *English-Speaking Alliance*, p. 108; JP (48) 6, 'Saudi Arabia Strategic Facilities', 19 January 1948, DEFE 4/10, PRO.

68 Chief of Division of NEA memorandum, 26 January 1948, *FRUS* 1948, Vol. 5, pp.

217–18, COS (50) 28, 'Reconnaisance of Airfields in Saudi Arabia', 26 January 1950, DEFE 5/19, PRO; A. Schlaim, *Collusion Across the Jordan* (Oxford: Oxford University Press); Ovendale, *English-Speaking Alliance*, p. 98.

69 Devereux, *Middle East*, pp. 32–3; Louis, 'American anti-colonialism', pp. 403–9.

70 COS (48) 31st mtg (3), 3 March 1948, DEFE 4/11, PRO.

71 COS (47) 92nd mtg (11), 30 July 1947, DEFE 4/5, PRO; COS (48) 70, 3 April 1948, DEFE 2/1654, PRO.

72 JP (48) 39 (Final), 'Cyprus – Construction of a Very Heavy Bomber Airfield', 26 April 1948, ibid.

73 JAP/P (48) 16 Final, 'Cyprus – Implications of Development of a Very Heavy Bomber Airfield', Appendix 1, ibid; COS (49) 133rd mtg (2), 9 September 1949, ibid.; E. L. minute, 6 April 1950, ibid.

74 DO (49) 48, 'The Size and Shape of the Armed Forces: the Harwood Report', 21 June 1949, CAB 131/7, PRO; COS (48) 71st mtg, Annex III, 25 May 1948, DEFE 4/13, PRO.

75 JIC (46) 1 (0), 1 March 1946, discussed in Warner memorandum, 'The Soviet Campaign Against this Country and Our Response to it', 2 April 1946, N6344/605/38, FO 371/ 56832, PRO; JIC (46) 38 (0) Final Revise, 'Russia's Strategic Interests and Intentions in the Middle East', 14 June 1946, DO 35/1604, PRO; JIC (46) 64 (0) Final, 'Russia's Strategic Interests and Intentions in the Middle East', 6 July 1946, L/WS/1/1050, IOLR; JIC (46) 90th mtg, 7 June 1946, ibid.

76 JIC (47) 65 (0) Final, 'Summary of the Principal Factors Affecting Commonwealth Security', 29 October 1947, L/WS/1/986, IOLR.

77 JIC (48) 9 (0) Final, 'Russian Interests, Intentions and Capabilities', 23 July 1948 [70 printed pages], L/WS/1/1173, IOLR. See particularly Section III (iii) 'Avoidance of a Premature Major War', p. 29, ibid.; Tedder addressing PMM (48) 11th mtg, Confidential Annex, 20 October 1948, CAB 133/88, PRO.

78 DO (48) 16th mtg (3), 13 August 1948, CAB 131/5, PRO.

79 COS (48) 139th mtg (3), 29 September 1948, DEFE 4/16, PRO.

80 cf. pp. 35–40; C. M. Andrew, 'The Growth of the Australian Intelligence Community and the Anglo-Australian Connection', *Intelligence and National Security* Vol. 4, No. 2 (April 1989), pp. 226–9; Ovendale, *English Speaking Alliance* p. 119; COS (48) 34th mtg, 9 March 1948, DEFE 4/11, PRO.

81 Pakistan's Prime Minister, Liaqat Ali Khan, warned that a Jewish state in Palestine would be 'a meance to the integrity and independence of the Arab world and would become a hotbed of Russian and Communist intrigue'. He also called for a regional defence scheme for the Middle East. PMM (48) 4th mtg, 12 October 1948, CAB 133/ 88; PMM (48) 11th mtg, 20 October 1948, ibid.

82 ibid.; Albert, 'Commonwealth Defence', pp. 207–18; Stapleton memorandum, COS 1815/30/10/8, 30 October 1948, L/WS/1/1214, IOLR. See also JP (48) 117 (Final), 'Defence Appreciations as a Basis for Military Planning Between Liaison Staffs', 19 January 1949, ibid.

83 COS (49) 332, 'Liaison Between New Zealand Service Authorities and C. in C. Middle East', 7 October 1949, DEFE 5/16, PRO; Ovendale *English Speaking Alliance*, pp. 119–21.

84 COS (49) 190th mtg (1), attended by Michael Wright of the FO, 30 December 1949, AIR 8/999, PRO. See also Elliot memorandum, 29 December 1949, AIR 8/999, PRO.

85 COS (49) 190th mtg (1), Confidential Annex, 30 December 1949, DEFE 4/27, PRO; Devereux, *Middle East*, pp. 80–1; P. Edwards, 'The Australian Commitment to the Malayan Emergency, 1948–1950', *Historical Studies* Vol. 22, No. 89 (October 1987), pp. 604–16.

86 JIC (47) 63rd mtg (3), Draft Annex, 'Release of Military Information to the Common-wealth', 19 September 1947, L/WS/1/1046, IOLR; this stated 'steps are taken to see that they receive intelligence summaries which are, apparently, Top Secret, and are similar to those which go to other Commonwealth countries'. See also COS (48) 176th mtg (1), 9 December 1948, DEFE 4/18, PRO; COS (48) 139th mtg (3), 29 September 1948, DEFE 4/16, PRO.

87 COS (49) 182nd mtg (3), 8 December 1949, DEFE 32/1, PRO; cf. p. 38.

88 See for example, T. Remme, 'Britain and Regional Co-operation in Southeast Asia, 1945–9', unpublished PhD thesis, London School of Economics, 1990. On the search for regional defence see Devereux, *Middle East*, pp. 43–75; A. Jalal, 'Towards the Baghdad Pact: South Asia and Middle Eastern Defence in the Cold War, 1947–55', *International History Review* Vol. XI, No. 3 (August 1989), pp. 409–33; P. L. Hahn, 'Containment and Egyptian Nationalism: The Unsuccessful Effort to Establish a Middle East Command, 1950–3', *Diplomatic History*, Vol. 11, No. 1 (winter 1987), pp. 23–40.

89 COS (48) 8th mtg, 16 January 1948, DEFE 4/10, PRO; PUSC (19), 'Middle East', 30 April 1949, FO 800/455, PRO.

90 JIC (49) 6, discussed in COS (49) 115, 'Strategic Requirements for the Middle East', 1 April 1949, AIR 20/2463, PRO. See also JIC (47) 52 (0) Final, 'Possible Future of Palestine', fo. 01(1), L/WS/1/1162, IOLR; Devereux, *Middle East*, pp. 45–6; Aldrich and Coleman, 'Strategic Air Offensive', pp. 419–24.

91 COS (49) 8th mtg (7), Confidential Annex, DEFE 4/19, PRO; COS (49) 38th mtg (1), 7 March 1949, DEFE 4/20, PRO; Record of Anglo-American discussions on the Middle East, 7 May 1950, *DBPO*, Series 2, Vol. 2, Doc. 65i.

92 Hahn, 'Containment and Egyptian Nationalism', pp. 24–9; Devereux, 'Britain and the Failure of Collective Defence in the Middle East, 1948–53', in Deighton, *Britain and the First Cold War*, pp. 237–52; State–JCS meeting, 2 May 1951, *FRUS* 1951, Vol. 5, pp. 114–15.

93 COS (49) 13th mtg (6), 27 January 1949, DEFE 4/19, PRO; COS (49) 62nd mtg (2), 29 April 1949, DEFE 4/21, PRO; CP (49) 118, 'Defence of Hong Kong', 24 May 1949, CAB 129/35; PRO; ORE 79(–49) 'US Security and the British Dollar Problem', 31 August 1949, PSF Intelligence File, Box 256, Harry S. Truman Library, Independence. See also ORE 93 (–49), 'The Possibility of Britain's Abandonment of Overseas Military Commitments', 23 December 1949, Box 257, ibid.

94 COS (49) 57th mtg (1), 20 April 1949, DEFE 4/21, PRO; COS (49) 88th mtg (2), Confidential Annex, 16 June 1949, DEFE 4/22, PRO; DO (49) 16th mtg (1), 21 June 1949, CAB 131/8, PRO.

95 COS (50) 26th mtg, 13 February 1950, DEFE 32/1, PRO.

96 JIC 439/18, 'Joint Intelligence for Basic Evaluation of the Strategic Air Offensive', 16 December 1949, 373.11, (12–14–48), Sec. 2, RG 218, NARA; K. Condit, *The History of the Joint Chiefs of Staff: 1947–1949* Vol. 2 (Washington DC: Joint Chiefs of Staff, 1970), p. 300; M. A. Stoler, *The Politics of the Second Front: American Military Planning and Diplomacy in Coalition Warfare, 1941–3* (Westport, Conn.: Greenwood Press, 1977).

97 JP (49) 133 (Final), 'Visit of JPS to Washington, September–October 1949', 14 October 1949, DEFE 6/11, PRO; COS (49) 154th mtg (5), Confidential Annex, 19 October 1949, DEFE 4/25, PRO; JP (49) 126 (Final), 'Emergency Plans', Annex 1, 2 November 1949, DEFE 6/10, PRO; JP (49) 134 (Final), 'Plan Galloper', 1 March 1950, DEFE 6/11, PRO.

98 COS (49) 182nd mtg (3), 8 December 1949, DEFE 32/1, PRO. For the detailed planning that was 'shelved' see COS MELF memorandum, 'Digest on Anglo-American Planning in the Middle East', 27 May 1949, WO 216/312, PRO.

99 JP (49) 59 (2nd Revised), 'Strategic Background for Diplomatic Representatives in the Middle East', 20 July 1949, DEFE 4/22, PRO.

100 JP (49) 134 (Final), 'Plan Galloper', 1 March 1950, DEFE 4/29, PRO.

101 COS (50) 37th mtg (1), Confidential Annex, 8 March 1950, DEFE 4/29, PRO; COS (50) 74th mtg (2), DEFE 4/31, PRO.

102 DO (50) 45, 'Defence Policy and Global Strategy', 7 June 1950 is closed. However, a copy was located in Australia, by Ritchie Ovendale, see *English Speaking Alliance*, pp. 122–9. See also DO (51) 64, 'Defence Policy and Global Strategy: Revision of DO (50) 45', 7 June 1951, CAB 21/1787, PRO.

103 COS (51) 282, 7 May 1951, DEFE 4/16, PRO; Albert, p. 269.

104 U. Bialer, 'The Iranian Connection in Israel's Foreign Policy, 1948–1951', *Middle East Journal* Vol. 39, No. 2 (spring 1985), pp. 292–315; Devereux, *Middle East*, pp. 26–8; Bullock, *Bevin*, pp. 759–60; Louis, *British Empire*, pp. 709–20.

105 Middle East Conference, 14–21 February 1951, *FRUS* 1951, Vol. 5, pp. 56–60; PPS

memorandum, 23 May 1951, ibid., pp. 144–7; ibid., Vol. 3, pp. 725–30; Devereux, *Middle East*, pp. 56–9.

106 Minutes of discussion between Bevin and Saleh-el-Din, 4–9 December 1950, FO 800/ 457, PRO; Louis, pp. 716–18; W. R. Louis, 'Mussadiq and the Dilemma of British Imperialism' in W. R. Louis (ed.) *Mussadiq, Iranian Nationalism and Oil* (Austin: University of Texas, 1988), pp. 229–31; Ovendale, *English Speaking Alliance*, p. 132.

107 ibid., pp. 137–8; J. M. Siracusa and G. Barclay, 'Australia, the United States and the Cold War, 1945–51: From VJ Day to ANZUS', *Diplomatic History* Vol. 5, No. 1 (winter 1981), pp. 45–83; Edwards, 'Australian Commitment', p. 615; R. O'Neill, *Australia in the Korean War, 1950–3: Vol. 1, Strategy and Diplomacy* (Canberra, 1981), pp. 39–44.

108 PUSC (19), 'Middle East', 30 April 1949, FO 800/455, PRO; COS (49) 381, 'Strategic Implications of an Independent and United Libya', DEFE 5/18, PRO, quoted in Louis, 'American Anticolonialism', p. 405.

109 JIC (49) 23rd mtg, 9 December 1949, L/WS/1/1216, IOLR.

110 MDM (51) 2, 11 June 1951, CAB 21/1787, PRO; Devereux, *Middle East*, pp. 106–7.

111 Attlee to Bevin (Washington), 11 November 1946, CAB 21/1919, PRO; N. Wheeler, 'The Attlee Government's Nuclear Strategy, 1945–51', in Deighton, *Britain and the First Cold War*, pp. 137–8.

112 COS (50) 107th mtg, 12 July 1950, DEFE 32/1, PRO; COS to Tedder (Washington), DEF 604, 28 July 1950, ibid.

11

British strategy and the end of Empire: South Asia, 1945–51

Richard J. Aldrich

The Indian subcontinent is central to any consideration of the development of post-war defence policy. Until the second half of the twentieth century, this area was often the dominant rationale for strategic concepts that shaped defence policy from the Mediterranean to the Far East. Particularly after the demise of the Anglo-Japanese alliance in 1921, it was the Indian Army that constituted the basis of British military power in South East Asia and the Middle East and that facilitated campaigns in these regions during the Second World War. It is all the more puzzling, therefore, that in contrast to the Middle East, and more recently Africa, only limited attention has been paid to the role of South Asia in the strategic planning of the Labour governments, 1945–51. Hitherto, in so far as this issue has been considered, it has been interpreted as a political question, perhaps reflecting the emphasis of the available published documents, with correspondingly little attention to military records.[1] It has also been addressed narrowly in terms of India, rather than within the wider regional framework which informed the concepts of the British Chiefs of Staff (COS) and their subordinates: therefore only limited attention has been paid to Afghanistan, Pakistan, Ceylon, neighbouring Burma or indeed the impact of changes within this region upon broader aspects of British defence policy.[2] Moreover, South Asia has been all but ignored by most historians of Britain's Cold War and recent historical studies of British defence policy have focused upon Europe and the Middle East. Those specifically examining the question of Commonwealth and Cold War have often chosen to concentrate upon the role of Canada and Australia rather than that of the New Commonwealth.[3] In contrast, and perhaps prompted by developments in Afghanistan since 1979, historians in the United States have been quick to investigate the place of India and Pakistan in American strategy. They have also been more adept at exploring the links between this region and Middle East defence.[4]

This chapter seeks to examine South Asia through the eyes of Britain's strategic planners during the period 1945–51. Before the transfer of power negotiations and as late as 1949, the military concerned themselves with two primary objectives: post-independence defence collaboration between Britain, India and Pakistan and permission for Britain to use airbases in North West India (later northern Pakistan), within range of the Soviet hinterland, in any future war. Beyond 1949, as Anglo-American air strategy shifted its emphasis to airbases in Europe and the Far East, Pakistan was instead perceived as significant in terms of Middle East defence co-operation. Meanwhile, Indian political leadership was increasingly valued in the context of low-intensity conflicts emerging in Asia. This period was also marked by Anglo-American disagreements over proposed US security guarantees to Pakistan and over Asian security policy generally. Britain's desire to maintain an outwardly even-handed approach to these two Commonwealth states, along with her limited ability to offer material assistance, pointed towards the rapid eclipse of British influence by the United States in South West Asia. Yet throughout this period, a close and co-operative relationship with Ceylon ensured a range of facilities for a continued British presence in the Indian Ocean. Moreover, defence co-operation with Burma continued into the 1950s, albeit on an erratic basis, driven partly by the advent of a Communist China.

It is important to emphasize that the British COS also identified a crucial *negative* requirement in the region: that the subcontinent should not be dominated by a hostile power. The potential problems of a hostile India were given considerable thought and this possibility, combined with recognition of Britain's debility after 1945, ensured that the goodwill of successor states would always be given priority over attempts to drive a hard bargain for strategic desiderata. Indeed, what is most striking about Britain's defence relations with South Asian states prior to 1951 is the extent to which they stand in contrast to the Middle Eastern experience, particularly in Egypt, where Britain chose to perpetuate her presence regardless of indigenous opposition. In South Asia, and quite contrary to the assertions of some historians, it was quickly recognized that Britain's search for post-independence defence co-operation and facilities on the subcontinent would be conducted from a position of weakness.[5]

SOUTH ASIA AND STRATEGIC PLANNING, 1945–7

By the summer of 1946 five fundamental factors had come to determine the formulation of Britain's strategic thinking for the post-war period. First, the Soviet Union had been identified as Britain's most likely future adversary. Second, intelligence estimates suggested that, notwithstanding this, the Soviet Union would not be ready for war for ten years. Third, American assistance was deemed essential in any future war, supplemented by support from the Empire-Commonwealth and some future West European bloc. A fourth factor was the decision to retain many imperial defence commitments, reached after an acrimonious debate between Attlee, Bevin and the COS (which rumbled on into 1947). This dispute was lent additional dynamism by a fifth factor, the results of a study of the revolution in methods of war.

Prior to 1945, several committees were busily examining aspects of Britain's post-war strategy. Of these, perhaps the most widely understood is the Post Hostilities Planning Staff (PHPS), who were given the task of considering Britain's future strategic requirements; they were the first formally to identify Britain's post-war allies and adversaries. This body was responsible for Britain's most detailed wartime planning on India and the Indian Ocean in future strategy.[6] PHPS were, however, disbanded in the summer of 1945 and their work, although fascinating and sometimes influential, did not constitute a definitive blueprint of Britain's post-war strategy.[7] Indeed, their particular prescriptions for the Middle East and the Indian Ocean were rapidly overturned by the COS.

Of more lasting significance was the work of a committee of defence scientists led by Sir Henry Tizard examining new weapons and methods of war. Their report, completed on 16 July 1945, less than two months before the atomic attack on Hiroshima and Nagasaki, placed great stress on the recent development of ballistic rockets, new chemical and biological weapons and the development of atomic bombs.[8] A revised version of this paper, completed by the Joint Technical Warfare Committee (JTWC), taking into account lessons from the atomic attack on Japan and completed in July 1946, was particularly influential in terms of military thinking generally, and led to considerable emphasis being placed upon airbases in North West India. They concluded that atomic weapons had revolutionized warfare and even five or six bombs would significantly reduce the power of any country to make war, adding that 'the number of atomic weapons required to destroy a country would be materially reduced if bacteriological weapons were simultaneously used'. Equally significant were the observations of this report upon 'adequate means of delivery' of such weapons and the need for the development of aircraft with a range of 2,000 miles. In the short term the limited outward range of British aircraft in the late 1940s (750 miles) lent increased importance to imperial bases close to the Soviet Union, in the Middle East and also at Peshawar in India.[9]

The importance of India with particular regard to aircraft range had in fact been identified by the JTWC as early as November 1945 in a study of the problem of launching air attacks on Soviet cities with populations of over 100,000. Very little could be achieved from bases in the United Kingdom alone, but by also employing imperial bases at Nicosia in Cyprus and Peshawar in India, Britain's capabilities could be dramatically increased to offer coverage of 77 per cent of Soviet cities and greatly complicate the problems of Soviet air defence.[10] Even so, the problem of aircraft range was so great that these calculations were based on an outward range of

1,500 miles, requiring the crew of any bomber to bail out shortly after attacking their target. The report was unequivocal on this point, emphasizing 'that the actual bomber at least need not return and so will only have petrol for the outward journey'.[11]

India's strategic value in any future air war was also identified by the US Joint Chiefs of Staff (JCS), and as early as October 1945, James Byrnes, the US Secretary of State, made a verbal request to Ernest Bevin for American control of a variety of Empire bases, including some Pacific islands.[12] In February 1946 Byrnes reinforced his point in conversation with a senior British official in Washington. He stated

> If we and the British had use of these two Indian airfields (when I asked him to specify them he could not do so) my experts tell me that we should have no need to be so interested in the little old Pacific islands for defence purposes if there were trouble from this quarter. (Here he plumped the palm of his hand down on Siberia.)

However, the British Cabinet repeatedly asserted that this was a matter not for them, but for the future government of India.[13] This pious attitude did not, however, extend to the question of strategic minerals. In August 1945 Britain, Canada and the United States initiated a scheme to achieve a world-wide monopoly of strategic materials such as uranium. The Indian state of Travancore contained 'some of the richest deposits in the world' of thorium, a material 'of great importance' in the manufacture of atomic weapons. Negotiations with Travancore were scheduled for October 1946, amid considerable secrecy, in the hope of avoiding interference from the interim government of India.[14]

The wider importance of these technical surveys was underlined in 1946 as a bitter debate developed between Attlee, Bevin and the COS regarding the maintenance of a British military presence in the Middle East. This argument, of seminal importance for the development of British defence policy in the late 1940s, is analysed at length in Chapter 10 in this volume. It is sufficient to state here that Attlee was generally sceptical about the value of imperial defence commitments, not least on economic grounds, arguing instead in favour of internationalist solutions to Britain's defence problems.[15] In February 1946 he accused the COS of employing an outmoded and 'sentimental' Middle East strategy based upon extended imperial communications which had been rendered untenable by the growing significance of air power. In any case, he noted, the value of the Mediterranean route would soon be decreased by India's independence. The COS chose to reply in equally radical terms and drawing upon the work of the JTWC, they too now stressed air power. They argued that Britain's only hope of deterring Soviet aggression in Western Europe would be the threat of a reply in the form of an all-out air attack. Given that 'the United Kingdom as the sole base would be quite inadequate, since many areas of importance would be out of range', the COS emphasized additional bases in the Middle East and India. From the Middle East it would be possible to attack 'many ... important industrial areas of Russia' while airbases in North West India were, 'except for those in Iraq, the nearest we have to certain Russian industrial areas in the Urals and Western Siberia'.[16] Although Attlee initially remained obdurate in the face of this new rationale, during 1946 the COS continued to plan on the assumption of employing Empire bases (see Figure 2). In early January 1947 Attlee conceded, as a result of pressure from Bevin and of a *démarche* led by the Chief of the Imperial General Staff, Montgomery, in which the COS threatened to resign *en masse* in support of what they considered to be a critical issue.[17] However, as will be shown, over the question of Indian independence the boot was on the other foot. Here Attlee was able to persuade both Bevin and the COS of the primacy of political settlement over military considerations.

POLITICAL DIFFICULTIES, 1946 TO MAY 1947

Although future access to facilities on the Indian subcontinent was considered of great importance, it must also be emphasized that British officials were, even before the end of the war, conscious that their strategic desiderata constituted requests and not demands. Sir David Monteath, Permanent Under-Secretary of State at the India Office, had stressed repeatedly to the defence planners the precariousness of India's future place within post-war Commonwealth defence planning. In October 1944 he commented acerbically on one particularly optimistic batch of military papers that their value would be greater if the importance of strategic requirements is 'such that constitutional developments must be determined by them; in actual fact the tendency is the other way around'. By 1946 this message had been thoroughly absorbed by the COS. They stated

> [given Britain's weakness] we cannot afford to let the [independence] negotiations break down and therefore cannot classify any of our needs as essential, if by this it is meant we would rather abandon the negotiations than modify our requirements.[18]

Moreover, in October 1946 the COS noted that 'Past experience has shown, particularly in Egypt,' that even where military treaties were secured, their public nature rendered them ideal targets for expressions of nationalist sentiment. In the wake of difficulties in Egypt over military agreements, they were especially conscious of this. Presumptuous remarks are to be found within papers by Indian Army officers, but such individuals were on the periphery of British policy. The main strategic planning papers of 1946 and early 1947 are quite clear. In DO (47) 44, 'Future Defence Policy', the COS stated 'We should strive for an agree-

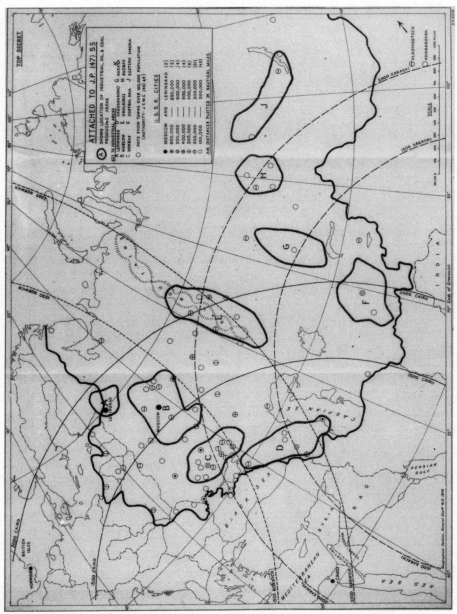

Figure 2 British target map for an atomic attack on the Soviet Union illustrating the value of Indian bases, 1947, JP (47) 55, AIR 9/297, PRO.

ment with India' but then added pointedly, 'We cannot, however, count on this at present'. Furthermore, the COS noted that but for this political uncertainty 'which may profoundly affect our Commonwealth strategic position' they would have included India with the essential 'three pillars' of Commonwealth strategy.[19] This circumspection was supported at the highest level by Clement Attlee who, emphasizing Britain's diminished resources, was a firm advocate of radical departures in imperial strategy.

This interpretation of both Britain's negotiating position and Attlee's priorities is contrary to the view advanced by some historians. For example, it has been suggested that Britain intended to concede independence only when she had been promised military facilities and co-operation. One historian has even asserted that

> a military treaty, which Indians might dislike, would be the price they must pay for achieving independence. Political agreement between the Indian parties would not be the final stepping stone to independence; the securing by the British of their own military concerns was. The condition of a military treaty would hang over the heads of the Indians, like a sword of Damocles, until they granted the British the facilities they wanted.[20]

Furthermore, Attlee's views have been compared to those of Leopold Amery, Churchill's Secretary of State for India: 'Neither for Amery, nor for Attlee ... was the transfer of power an end in itself' and 'Attlee believed that the main purpose of any treaty would be to secure British interests in the Indian Ocean area'; moreover, 'Labour's commitment to the maintenance of British power was obviously and understandably greater than its so-called commitment to Indian independence'.[21]

It will be suggested here that the above assertions have arisen from a wholly misplaced interpretation of Attlee's objectives, which were *internationalist* rather than imperialist in nature, seeking to ensure that India accepted both the rights and duties of independence, including responsibility for the defence of the subcontinent, thus taking her full place in the world community of states. Attlee viewed the achievement of this as 'a moral responsibility'.[22] India would be able to fulfil her obligations to the United Nations and the Commonwealth, which Attlee especially perceived as very distinct from British military interests.

The period 1946 to early 1947 saw contradictory developments in British strategy towards India. A number of factors, notably deteriorating East–West relations along with problems over bases in Palestine and Egypt, tended to add to India's future strategic importance. However, as even the planners recognized, the momentum of political developments within India raised the possibility that Britain would soon be denied any sort of military facilities on the subcontinent. The importance attached to future defence co-operation with India during the late 1940s was therefore ironic.

Approaching independence prompted the JPS to consider Britain's strategic desiderata on the subcontinent during early 1946. On 1 March they were asked by the India Office to prepare a brief for the ill-fated Cabinet mission which was about to depart for independence negotiations in Delhi.[23] The JPS emphasized access by Britain to Indian airbases, noting that 'airfields in North West India are the nearest we have to the industrial areas of the Urals and Siberia'. Also important was the need for internal stability in India; for an Indian Army capable of assisting Britain in the Middle East and of rapid expansion in wartime; and for a British presence sufficient to guarantee the efficiency of the armed forces and the defence of the North West Frontier.[24] Manpower was especially attractive with her short-term occupational commitments in Europe and Asia, and her long-term ambition to retain a military presence in the Middle East.[25]

Significantly, however, Attlee did not permit the COS to attend the meeting of the Cabinet mission at Chequers before its departure, indeed 'there was no soldier present'. Ignoring the litany of hopeful requests drawn up by the military, Attlee stated that Dominion status or independence would be conditional only upon India being able to defend herself, and in addition to taking on her traditional role in South East Asia within the Commonwealth or under the auspices of the United Nations. There was no reference to British strategic desiderata.[26] In any case India would require British help to maintain her armed forces after independence and thus it seemed likely that India would request defence co-operation at a later date.[27] At the same time there was an overwhelming desire to retain India within the Commonwealth. Not only was her military assistance desirable in the Middle East and Asia, but also in the context of continuing meetings of the Council of Foreign Ministers and of the United Nations, an Indian decision against Commonwealth membership would have been a heavy blow to British prestige. Bevin in particular emphasized this latter point along with that of trade. Thus they concluded that it was 'as nearly vital as anything could be' that India remain in the Commonwealth'.[28]

Political factors rendered even these limited objectives improbable. The seriousness of the situation in India itself was indicated by the failure of the Cabinet mission. Apart from considerable popular unrest, Pandit Nehru increasingly addressed the virtues of a non-aligned India, while Jinnah, the leader of the Muslim League, continued to press the cause of an independent Pakistan. As early as April 1946 two particularly able and prescient British officials, Croft and Turnbull, had noted with alarm that Jinnah's attitude suggested a subcontinent consisting of two hostile states. Moreover it was obvious to them that a defence agreement would be easier to achieve with a small and dependent Pakistan, than with a neutral India. By July Attlee's Cabinet was confronted with the possibility of a civil war in India. During the rest of 1946, while the JPS continued to review lists of strategic desiderata for use in future defence talks, they also recognized that these were a distant prospect.[29]

The possibility of a separate Pakistan dismayed British planners in London and Delhi alike. On the one hand any future Muslim state would inherit a disproportionate share of the geostrategic burden of defending the subcontinent against the Soviets, namely the North West Frontier and the border with Iran. Yet Pakistan was almost devoid of military and industrial facilities, not to mention an economy capable of supporting the substantial forces required. In any case, geographically, Pakistan lacked the defence in depth required to withstand a Soviet drive from the north. Consequently, in April 1946, military planners formulated a very considerable further objective: if India were to be partitioned, defence must nevertheless be retained under a common planning authority.[30]

The problem of possible partition, combined with accelerating East–West tension in the Middle East, also prompted the military planners to give considerable thought to the prospect of a neutral, even hostile India. This prompted them to identify a further, and significantly negative, requirement: that on no account could they countenance a Soviet-occupied India. On 13 September 1946 the planners explained to a rather sceptical India Office official that their view was derived largely from their thinking on the Middle East defence:

> The members of the JPS committee ... admitted that the situation was that we could not afford to have India occupied by a hostile power. If that happened we should not be able to maintain our position in the Middle East. They seemed to think that even if we could hold the Middle East in a war with Russia, our position could be demolished if the Russians entered India through Afghanistan and Iraq [sic]. Consequently, the rock bottom position appears to be that we have in our own imperial interests to assist India to defend herself. I observed that this was not a very comfortable basis on which to go into negotiations with negotiators as skilled as the Indians.[31]

The immediate cause of this was a marked increase in the perceived Soviet threat to the Middle East in early 1946 in the wake of the crisis in Iran. Intelligence estimates of Soviet intentions in the Middle East and South Asia, prepared by the Joint Intelligence Committee (JIC) during the period April to July 1946, identified an eastward shift of Soviet emphasis away from Turkey towards Iran, which they believed would culminate in 'the domination of Persia by securing a port and a base in the Persian Gulf'.[32]

As a consequence, the JPS were clearly planning in detail, not only for the possibility that India refuse a bare minimum of obligations – responsibility for the defence of her own frontiers – but also that India might eventually align with or be occupied by a hostile power. It was against this latter eventuality that they proposed that an India outside the Commonwealth should not be given the Andaman and Nicobar islands in the eastern Bay of Bengal. Britain would require these 'to defend Malaya against attack from India'. It was also concluded that Ceylon would be 'untenable in the face of an India dominated by Russia'. By March 1947 the COS had concluded that in a future war, if only to deny crucial Indian resources to an enemy, they would have to try and defend a neutral India against the Soviets whether the Indian Government liked it or not! There was thus no sense in which the JPS were refusing to consider a range of unsavoury possibilities.[33]

Specific concern about Soviet ambitions in the Middle East was reinforced during the first months of 1947 by the alarm of both Montgomery and Bevin at the position of the British Empire generally *vis-à-vis* the Soviet Union. Montgomery feared that simultaneous imperial retreat in Cyprus, Cyrenaica, Egypt and India suggested that Britain was about to 'lose the airbases vital for the retaliatory action which alone can decrease the weight of attack on the United Kingdom. . . . When viewed as a whole the repercussions are immense . . . the agreed fundamental principles of our defence strategy are being swept away.' Meanwhile Bevin felt that Attlee's attempts to resolve political problems within the Empire were undermining Britain's prestige. On 1 January 1947 he put his case to Attlee in firm language, 'not only is India going, but Malaya, Ceylon and the Middle East is going with it, with a tremendous repercussion on the African territories. I do beg of you to take a stronger line and not give way to this awful pessimism'. Yet these men were out of step with the priorities held by Attlee and the full Cabinet. Attlee offered Bevin a typically laconic reply: 'you must offer a practical alternative, I fail to find one in your letter'.[34] This disparity between desired strategic facilities in South Asia and the reality of accelerating political developments there was underlined by events in India during late 1946 and early 1947.

In late 1946 the political future of India remained uncertain with continuing impasse between the rival Indian political parties, Congress and the Muslim League. There was also disagreement between the British government and the Viceroy, Lord Wavell, whose plan for a phased British withdrawal had been rejected out of hand by the Cabinet. At the same time, decisions had already been taken which were to transform the situation, for Attlee was planning to replace Wavell as Viceroy by Lord Louis Mountbatten, hitherto Supreme Allied Commander South East Asia.

Important precedents were also being set with regard to defence arrangements with neighbouring successor states. Attlee had acceded to the demands of Burmese political leaders that there should be no preconditions for the discussions on the future of Burma. In view of the precarious security situation within that country, and the known commitments of the Burmese leaders, the latter decision had increased the probability of the early independence of Burma and her withdrawal from the Common-wealth, factors which were bound to have an influence on subsequent independence settlements elsewhere. Negotiations in January 1947 produced an agreement which would indeed clearly lead to the rapid independence of Burma, leaving the question of her possible membership of the Commonwealth still unsettled, while her future defence relationship with Britain was deferred for subsequent agreement.[35] While the Chiefs of Staff considered that Burma was of limited strategic importance and were confident of eventually achieving their requirements there, this was certainly not true of India.

The extent to which Attlee's priority in India was a political settlement rather than strategic considerations was demonstrated by the Cabinet decision announced by Attlee on 20 February 1947 that the British would leave India by June 1948. This was made without any reference to the COS. They were further dismayed when Mountbatten subsequently received an assurance from Attlee that it would be for the British govern-ment, not him as Viceroy, to negotiate with the future Indian government regarding the defence relationship between Britain and India. This was re-emphasized at Mountbatten's insistence in his written instructions from Attlee, which underlined that defence requirements would not form part of independence negotiations and instead should be delayed to some later date.[36] Montgomery complained of the Cabinet's 'wobbly and hesitant' attitude. Nevertheless, before his departure for India, Mountbatten met with the COS to be briefed on their ideas about the future defence arrangement which would follow independence, with great importance being attached by them to India remaining unified in defence matters.[37]

Most British planning proceeded on the basis of hopes for continuing close defence ties between Britain and India. Yet Nehru was now making clear to Baldev Singh, who would become independent India's first Minis-ter of Defence, his own belief that India would leave the Commonwealth and that her security would be endangered only as a result of 'entangle-ment in the power politics of Great Powers'. He noted that there was no major threat to India except possibly from the Soviet Union and that Britain was anyway incapable of defending India.[38]

SEARCHING FOR DEFENCE AGREEMENTS, MAY 1947 TO MAY 1948

In May 1947 the British COS still remained optimistic regarding their aims on the subcontinent even to the extent of believing that Pakistan would necessarily co-operate with India in defence matters.[39] But although Jinnah, like the British COS, was at pains to underline the disproportionate burden of Pakistan's future strategic responsibilities and appealed for some sort of future defence agreement with India, his main objective was in fact the *division* of the Indian Army. His drive for military parity, with its implications for the permanent partition of India, was unacceptable to much of Congress. Any future defence organization was therefore likely to be imperilled by a basic struggle over the separation of the resources of the Indian Services. An irritated Montgomery noted 'Jinnah is fanatical and unbalanced. . . . Herein lies the tragedy . . . Jinnah will not accept a joint command for the two Dominions'.[40] This was compounded by the determination of Mountbatten, with the approval of London, to ignore such difficulties and to pursue a rapid settlement with minimal attention to defence issues. Indeed, during the first six months of 1947, and following their *démarche* over the Middle East, the COS seem to have been increasingly excluded by Attlee from Indian affairs. In so far as Attlee discussed the military dimension he continued to emphasize that the settlement should meet not British interests but 'the defence requirements of India'.[41] Nevertheless, Mountbatten made full use of the mutual fears of both Jinnah and Nehru of the availability of British assistance to their opponent in persuading them to join the Commonwealth. Therefore Pakistan's desire for a defence agreement with Britain remained a lever in the search for co-operation with India.[42]

The question of the Indian Army had important repercussions outside the subcontinent. Mountbatten's wartime South East Asia Command had consisted largely of Indian troops with American logistic support. After demobilization in 1945 the large forces of post-war occupation in Japan, Hong Kong, Thailand, Indo-China, Indonesia, Burma and Malaya were almost entirely Indian. Moreover they had been engaged in extensive fighting against Asian nationalists in Indo-China and Indonesia.[43] During 1946 their use had been justified by the Cabinet Defence Committee with the transparently thin argument that participation in the Allied occupation of South East Asia and Japan would confirm India's 'rightful status' in international affairs. By 1947 the Cabinet recognized that, despite the consequences, if Congress pressed for the withdrawal of Indian troops this could not be resisted on either legal or moral grounds.[44]

On 3 June 1947 Nehru and Jinnah announced acceptance of the proposals which, by granting Dominion status to both parts of India, facilitated the rapid transfer of power that Mountbatten deemed essential. Officials in Britain charged with preparing the formal means of implementing the decision now found that their ability to accommodate the requests of the COS was very limited. Moreover Attlee's 20 February announcement had not included *any conditions* for independence, nor would the Indian Independence Bill be enforceable, thus military requirements were likely to go by default unless a military mission was dispatched to India.[45] The COS sent a telegram to Mountbatten seeking his assistance in obtaining assurances about their requirements. But in India officials held the conviction that, with the important exception of air transit rights to the Far

East, defence issues should be left until new governments were formed. In India, W. H. Morris-Jones, attached to Mountbatten's staff to advise on joint organizations, recalls that it was at this moment that he dutifully proffered a plan for a common defence organization but 'no-one seemed to want a paper on this subject'.[46] Neither Mountbatten nor Attlee dared prejudice a successful political solution.

Following the acceptance by Mountbatten of the post of Governor-General of India, to take effect upon independence, the opportunity of securing the defence requirements subsequently seemed to lie in the Joint Defence Council (JDC) which was established in India to oversee the partition of the Indian forces. The leaders of both India and Pakistan were members of the JDC and Mountbatten was optimistic that his own position as chairman would enable him to influence defence negotiations in favour of the outcome favoured by the COS.[47] But by July 1947 the JPS had come to accept that there no longer seemed to be any possibility of central defence machinery or co-operation between Britain and India in foreign policy. They now noted that the temporary nature of Dominion status to be enjoyed by India and Pakistan suggested the necessity for written agreements on defence matters, evoking uncomfortable parallels with treaty relations with Middle Eastern states. Nevertheless, Britain's basic requirements seem to have been little changed by the advent of Pakistan. The JPS continued to call for both India and Pakistan to be retained in the Commonwealth to ensure the use of the Indian subcontinent as a major support base in war, with the co-operation of its armed forces and the use of its resources of personnel and industrial potential. Airbases in Pakistan were singled out as required for use in the event of a major war. This latter point was underlined by the fact that the COS were increasingly inclined to emphasize that most of their requirements could be met through an agreement with Pakistan only.[48]

India and Pakistan gained independence on 15 August 1947 without any of these strategic requirements being achieved. Yet there was optimism in London that they would still be obtained by means of a COS mission which would negotiate with the JDC under the chairmanship of Mountbatten. In addition, while the Indian Army had been divided, its stores remained in India, a device which Mountbatten and Auchinleck mistakenly believed would assist in bringing the two sides into a common defence arrangement. Certainly India and Pakistan had not reacted negatively to the suggestion of such a mission, and Nehru and Jinnah accepted the necessity of continuing defence assistance from Britain. Britain took further comfort from Nehru's moderate line at the Asian Relations Conference of April 1947.[49]

British optimism was further increased by auspicious defence arrangements with Burma and Ceylon. Although Burma eventually opted to leave the Commonwealth, nevertheless a defence agreement on 29 August 1947 gave the COS all their requirements.[50] In January 1947 Montgomery, the CIGS, had informed Aung Sang in a typically brusque manner that 'if Burma left the Commonwealth she would receive no help from us, but if she remained in it then we would . . . do our best to meet her needs'. This had proved to be an idle threat and under the new agreement a British military mission was to be provided by Britain free of charge for three years, partly to assist in maintaining internal security. In return, Burma agreed to accept a mission from Commonwealth countries only and to allow Britain the use of various airbases, ports and air transit rights.[51] This met the limited needs previously outlined by the COS, namely internal stability, a Commonwealth monopoly of defence relations and transit facilities.[52]

Given the uncertain attitude of India and Pakistan, facilities in Ceylon were of supreme importance for Britain's continued presence in the Indian Ocean. Accordingly, Ceylon's decision to stay within the Commonwealth and the generous agreements reached on 11 November 1947 regarding defence and foreign policies were a significant achievement. Ceylon, which had provided the wartime headquarters for Mountbatten's SEAC Command, agreed to allow continued use of its extensive bases and to consult with the Commonwealth on foreign policy. The attitude of Ceylon's Prime Minister, Senanayake, which the COS found 'very satisfactory', owed much to his concern at possible Indian aggrandizement. Ceylon, he asserted, 'did not want to be drawn from Britain into the Indian sphere'.[53]

By contrast, any prospect of defence co-operation between India and Pakistan was initially nullified by the large-scale communal violence which followed partition and relations deteriorated further during the subsequent crisis and military conflict over the question of Kashmir. Yet for at least two more years COS planning in London held out hope of co-operation. Meanwhile in mid-1947 Britain had been overtaken by economic crisis. Symptomatic of these problems was a Treasury-inspired reassessment of the size of the armed forces calling for, among other things, a reduction by half in the size of the bomber force, a proposal which should have further weakened the validity of the Pakistan airbase concept since the report made clear that, in the Far East and India, reliance in future would have to be placed on Dominion and Allied Air Forces. A subsequent Cabinet paper recommended that the bomber force be reduced to 160 bombers, a far cry from the 600 aircraft strategic bomber force which had been envisaged as a minimum by the Air Ministry only four months previously.[54]

Distracted by intractable problems in the Middle East and the economic difficulties at home, the true extent of the deterioration in the situation in India was only slowly appreciated by the defence planners in London, who continued to anticipate an early dispatch of their mission until persuaded otherwise by a forthright telegram from Ismay. None the less, planning for the mission continued, with a provisional brief being drawn up for mission members listing the requirements which should be sought and noting once again the value of airbases in West Pakistan.[55] At the same time an undercurrent of realism was detectable in the increasing emphasis on access to an offensive base in Pakistan only, rather than the value of increasingly elusive general defence co-operation on the subcontinent.[56] This increasing focus upon the weaker and hence more pliant Pakistan prefigured American regional policy during the 1950s.

In November 1947 this latter point was apparently stressed by the COS to Mountbatten, who had returned from India to attend the wedding of Princess Elizabeth, but Mountbatten considered the idea of the military planners to make a base of Pakistan and to let India out of the Commonwealth to be 'suicidal'. Despite briefing the COS on the difficult state of relations between India and Pakistan – 'neither side trusts or believes the other'[57] – Mountbatten appears to have been reminded by the COS of the importance which they attached to maintaining pressure for the mission to proceed for, on his return to India, he convened a meeting of the JDC on 22 December. At this he obtained the concurrence of the leaders of both countries for Mountbatten to write on their behalf to enquire what topics the mission would wish to discuss.[58] Ironically, and as if to underline Mountbatten's warnings about the political volatility of Pakistan and India, during the three months that had elapsed the JDC had ceased to exist, necessitating copies of the COS reply being handed direct to the Prime Ministers of the two Dominions. Despite the controversial nature of the contents, which called upon both Dominions to make commitments in the event of war far more concrete than the 'old' Dominions had ever done, there is no record of any adverse reaction. Nor, however, was there any positive response at that time and the dispatch of a mission remained an elusive goal.

The relatively leisurely approach of the COS to defence co-operation with India and Pakistan, and indeed with the Commonwealth generally, was transformed in the spring of 1948. The Communist coup in Czechoslovakia in February 1948 and contemporaneous Soviet pressure upon Scandinavia reinforced fears of Soviet expansionism, leading to the speedy conclusion of the Brussels Treaty and the opening of discussions regarding a North Atlantic Treaty.[59] Equally important to the British, in view of their wish for closer defence co-ordination with the USA, was an invitation for detailed joint planning talks. Subsequent discussions represented an attempt by the British and Americans to agree on the basic strategy with which a conflict with the Soviet Union would be fought.[60] American planning at this stage anticipated mounting a strategic air offensive from bases in Pakistan (in addition to others in England and Okinawa but *not* the Middle East) for which the use of American airborne commandos to secure the airfields on the outbreak of war was envisaged.[61] In the course of the joint talks in Washington the British argued against planning on this basis, pointing out the adverse effect on opinion in the Middle East and India were America to introduce troops against Pakistan's wishes, advocating instead the British plan for an air strategy utilizing 'the Suez/ Cairo/Khartoum area as the primary area in the Middle East for an air base', with Pakistan bases as 'an alternative only'. American acceptance of this strategy was marked by its inclusion in the US Short-Range Emergency War Plan (HALFMOON), as well as in its British equivalent, Plan DOUBLEQUICK.[62] Nevertheless the British themselves remained convinced of the necessity for developing additional offensive bases, including aircraft carriers, since the range of bombers at that time was insufficient for all target areas of the Soviet Union to be reached from the UK, the Middle East, Okinawa or Pakistan (even if bases there were available).[63]

FROM BERLIN TO THE COMMONWEALTH CONFERENCE, JUNE 1948 TO JULY 1949

During the late spring of 1948 British planners were forced to recognize that their previous comfortable presumption that war appeared unlikely before 1956, stood in need of substantial revision. The danger of war by accident appeared considerable and the prevailing atmosphere was one of alarm and uncertainty. After a visit to Germany the CIGS recorded:

> In this electrical atmosphere of suspicion and mistrust there are many varying opinions.
>
> General Clay [US Commander in Germany] considers that World War III will begin in six months time; indeed he might well bring it on himself by shooting his way up the autobahn if the Russians become difficult about things, he is a real 'He-man' . . .
>
> General Koenig [French Commander in Germany] thinks World War III will begin in about two years time or perhaps a little sooner . . . and spends a good deal of time on the Riviera.[64]

In mid-1948 the United States decided to dispatch B-29 bombers to British bases in response to tensions over Berlin. This demonstration of the USA's commitment to the defence of Europe seemed to indicate for the first time that a joint strategic air offensive, so long at the heart of British planning, could become a reality. The JIC firmly believed that this atomic capability would act as a deterrent to Soviet aggression. Whether this was so is a matter for conjecture, for it has recently been revealed that these bombers were only conventionally armed. Yet American reassurance was invaluable, given that British planners repeatedly stressed their inability to fight a major war at that time, due to lack of resources.[65]

In July 1948 the JIC completed its annual review of all intelligence relating to the 'Interests, Intentions and Capabilities' of the Soviet Union. This important paper stated, in relation to India and Pakistan, that the Soviet Union's main aim was seen to be the denial of the subcontinent's manpower and resources to any potential enemy, particularly the use of strategic airbases. Without access to Soviet records it is uncertain how valid a representation of Soviet thinking this was at that time, but it was undoubtedly a reflection of British perceptions of the strategic value of the subcontinent. Equally, this concept of deniability to a potential enemy also represented an important element in allied planning in this period when Soviet access to the bases and ports of the subcontinent would have permitted the interdiction of communications to the Far East and Australasia on the outbreak of war.[66]

With the success of the Berlin airlift in late 1948 the planners turned their attention to the forthcoming Commonwealth Prime Ministers' Conference. Here they hoped to capitalize upon the prevailing atmosphere of international tension to pursue improved Commonwealth defence cooperation.[67] This supposition seemed justified in the case of Pakistan when, shortly before the opening of the conference, General Cawthorn, Deputy Chief of Staff of the Pakistan Army, arrived in London on what he claimed was a secret mission to sound out British opinion on the appropriateness of the timing of defence talks between Britain and Pakistan. He described Pakistan as being alarmed by Communism and determined to play its part in collective resistance against Soviet aggression.[68] This was but one, albeit important, of a stream of emissaries to Britain, the United States and even Czechoslovakia during 1948 in search of arms for Pakistan's hard-pressed army, denied military stores during the partition of 1947. They sought a security guarantee, nominally against the Soviet Union but in reality against India. Cawthorn met with political and military leaders, including Attlee and the COS, who generally welcomed the suggestion of defence talks. However, despite the possibility that India or Pakistan might turn to the Eastern bloc for support, they remained anxious to appear evenhanded between the two Dominions, particularly with the Kashmir dispute still unresolved. They were unwilling to undertake defence talks without Indian participation, a condition confirmed by Attlee himself. In response Cawthorn argued that, unlike India, Pakistan was unequivocal about continuing Commonwealth membership and was being unfairly prejudiced by unnecessary restrictions.[69]

Yet privately the COS were alarmed by Kashmir and the JIC asserted that open war between India and Pakistan was a real possibility. While Britain was not prepared to irritate India by extending a formal guarantee to the weak state of Pakistan, privately Britain was prepared to go some way to restore the balance on the subcontinent. Britain bolstered Pakistan's morale by stating that its military advisers would remain in the event of an Indian attack and, moreover, that the UN would apply sanctions.[70]

Ironically, this support to Pakistan came just as her relative strategic importance to Britain was being reassessed and indeed devalued.

Britain's rejection of Pakistan's offer of a defence agreement not only reflected a desire to avoid contradictory obligations or giving offence to India, but also indicated that by the end of 1948 facilities in Pakistan were no longer valued over and above the continued political co-operation of India. For the first time the COS had been presented with a real chance to obtain the defence facilities which they had long coveted, yet the circumstances had now changed markedly. This was an indication of the British perception of the potential influence that India might enjoy, to the advantage of the Commonwealth, in South and South East Asian affairs, acting as a bulwark against Communism in the context of the 'Emergency' in Malaya and Communist gains in China. This approach to South Asia's potential value to the West as a means of influencing affairs in South East Asia had coincided with closer Anglo-American strategic co-operation, with its promise of longer-range aircraft and bases in Japan, Alaska and elsewhere, undermining the value of facilities in Pakistan.

All this was underlined by growing efforts during late 1948 and 1949 to accommodate a republican and neutralist India within the Commonwealth. This decision had not been taken lightly, generating acrimonious debate among the COS, and the Foreign, Commonwealth and Colonial Offices. The Foreign Office in particular wondered whether relations might not be better if carefully defined in a treaty relationship, rather than left to individual feelings of governments under the Commonwealth system. However, it was concluded that, while Nehru advocated anti-colonialism and non-alignment, nevertheless, if only to maintain the prestige and credibility of the Commonwealth, particularly in Asia, India was valuable.[71] This held special significance for the information campaign conducted by Britain's Colonial Information Department, projecting the image of a liberal power that bridged the aspirations of both East and West. The COS were therefore concerned to achieve a politically co-operative India in South East Asia, regardless of the precise form this might take.[72]

The possibility of Pakistan and India co-operating in defence matters therefore remained as remote as ever. During the Commonwealth Prime Ministers' Conference the Pakistani Prime Minister, Liaquat Ali Khan, suggested that direct talks should be opened between Britain and Pakistan, but stressed that the latter was unwilling to be linked in defence matters with India.[73] British leaders should hardly have found this surprising given the continued possibility of open war over the Kashmir issue. Even Senanayake, who declared stridently at this conference that Ceylon 'would take her full share in fighting the "cold" war', was, like Pakistan, alarmed by possible Indian hegemonic ambitions and thus refused to be included in regional defence planning with India and Pakistan.[74]

British planners nevertheless continued to attach some residual importance to airbases in Pakistan. Confirmation that the Americans also retained
an interest in the use of the bases is provided by records of the US War
Plan HARROW, which dealt extensively with the potential use of Karachi.
Subsequently the CIA emphasized that of all bases in Asia, Karachi was
'particularly significant from the standpoint of target proximity'.[75] Yet
while Pakistan expressed willingness to co-operate, British reservations
about the value of her airbases continued to increase. By January 1949,
in the face of a perennial crisis of resources and personnel, there was
recognition in London that the forces required to defend these bases were
beyond the capacity of the allies. Moreover, the expectation that their use
would provoke Soviet retaliation was confirmed by the COS, who also
noted that the USA had once again been persuaded of British reservations
regarding these bases. By March 1949 the COS advised Cabinet that the
prospect of Soviet retaliation, which the allies could not prevent, would
ensure that Pakistan airbases would not be made available.[76]

In March 1949 it was anticipated that no means would be found of
retaining a republican India in the Commonwealth, so planning once more
reverted to the assumption that a military treaty would eventually be
negotiated between Britain and India. Even though it was recognized that
Pakistan would remain in the Commonwealth, regardless of the Indian
decision, there was initial reluctance in London to agree to bilateral defence
negotiations with Pakistan, pending the outcome of the decision on India's
membership. Eventually, at the prompting of the COS, Attlee agreed to
the dispatch of a letter to Liaquat Ali Khan on the opening of such talks.
In anticipation of this the JIC prepared a report on the estimated Soviet
threat to Pakistan, noting that the most likely danger would be from
Soviet air attack to counter or prevent allied use of Pakistan's airbases.
Britain could not offer guarantees on this point; moreover the Cabinet
Defence Committee had already declined to give a commitment to Pakistan
of assistance in the event of an Afghan attack on the North West Frontier.
Pakistan believed, without dissent from the COS, that this should be a
Commonwealth responsibility, guarding as it did access to the Indian
subcontinent in the interests of the Commonwealth.[77]

The decision of the Commonwealth Conference on 27 April 1949 to
accept a formula which facilitated India's continuing Commonwealth membership led to a reassessment of British policy towards India, Pakistan and
Ceylon. Hitherto, their access to classified defence information and defence
training establishments had been restricted. At the direction of Attlee, who
refused to continue the policy of treating the new Commonwealth states
as less than full members, a new 'honesty' was determined upon and, with
the COS noting that Nehru had expressed willingness for defence talks,
there was optimism that the climate was now appropriate for the long-
awaited defence negotiations to take place. Circumstances were further

improved in January 1950 when Britain reached a new agreement with the United States on sharing sensitive information with the Commonwealth.[78]

Accordingly, the planners once again prepared reports in anticipation of such discussions, concluding that, in addition to the main air offensive which would still be directed against the Soviet Union from Britain, Okinawa and the Middle East: 'Air attack from India or Pakistan would cause the Russians considerable air defence problems, and the existence of even potential Allied air bases in the sub-continent might force them to disperse or increase their air defence systems.' However, the large-scale development of airbases was precluded in the short term by lack of resources for airfields or air defence. It was decided that only limited base development and air defence cover would be necessary to maintain air-fields, which could be used as advanced refuelling bases for small numbers of atom bomb carriers only.[79] In any case, it was now considered that an 'inability to operate from Pakistan would only prevent us from reaching a small proportion of major Russian targets'.[80]

Yet when an answer to Attlee's message was finally received from the Prime Minister of Pakistan it was clear that even this more modest goal was unlikely to be attained. Liaquat Ali Khan appeared to make it a precondition of defence negotiations that Britain should be prepared to assist Pakistan in the event of her security being threatened by *any* country. This would have involved Britain giving a guarantee to assist Pakistan against attack by India, a fellow Commonwealth member, and British officials reflected that they might find themselves 'in the ridiculous and impossible situation of being called upon to advise each country on the preparation of its defence plans against the other'. Defence discussions were therefore postponed.[81] This was a decision which, without an improvement in Indo-Pakistani relations, would effectively close the door on any remaining prospect of a formal agreement.

AMERICAN ASCENDANCY AND INDIAN NEUTRALITY, 1949–51

The last years of the Attlee governments were characterized by gradual British strategic eclipse on the subcontinent. Ironically, Britain found herself locked out of close military agreements with either India or Pakistan, by the dual nature of her Commonwealth relationship with these states which she had striven hard to achieve. Reluctant to conclude a defence agreement with Pakistan only, for fear of losing Indian political support, Britain nevertheless found Nehru's neutral stance rendered India an only intermittently satisfactory ally in her search for political co-operation against Communism in South East Asia. There were problems elsewhere. In Ceylon, despite the conclusion of a most satisfactory defence treaty, Senanayake asked for increasing British commitments in the light of developments in China, which the COS could ill afford. Meanwhile, in Burma, unofficial aid to the Karen rebels hampered delicate attempts to build defence relations with independent Burma. In contrast US policy in the region was not hampered by contradictory Commonwealth relationships and, moreover, enjoyed the economic resources to offer attractive partnership. This, along with divergence between Britain and the United States over strategic priorities, pointed the way to continued disagreements and subsequent American ascendancy in South West Asia during the 1950s.

Post-independence military relations with Burma were generally good and from 1948 a British military mission assisted the Burmese Army, often in actions against Communist or Karen rebels. Britain clearly supported the central government, although periodically contemplated applying financial pressure to persuade them to reach a settlement with the Karen minority.[82] However, as early as the summer of 1948 the Foreign Office was shocked by an approach from senior ex-staff officers of a British wartime special operations unit who had worked with the Karens against the Japanese and who now outlined a plan for Karen domination of all Burma. Despite attempts by Bevin and the Foreign Office to distance British policy from these renegades, continued sightings of British officers with the Karen rebels, followed by the capture of a British renegade ex-colonel in Rangoon, exploded in the Burmese press in 1948. Although Britain, with Indian assistance, arranged for the removal of the key British figure assisting the Karens, further reports of unofficial British and Australian assistance soured relations during 1949 and 1950.[83] After a visit in 1949 Strang, the Foreign Office PUS, described the Burmese Prime Minister as 'suspicious, credulous, stubborn and slow'. Conversely, in May 1950 the latter stated that the British military mission was itself under suspicion for assisting the rebels and might have to be withdrawn.[84] Although Burma was not critical to the defence of South or South East Asia, the news was received in London with dismay. Ceylon too became restive after the outbreak of the Korean War. While content to continue to provide bases, she asked for British forces stationed there to be increased. If India remained neutral in any future war, complained Senanayake, Ceylon would be Britain's main regional base and would thus be singled out for 'punitive' attacks.[85]

Arguably, it was from 1949 that Britain felt most keenly the strategic embarrassment resulting from the loss of Indian military personnel, not only in terms of peacetime commitments, but also in terms of India's almost infinite capacity for expansion of her forces in war. With rapidly growing commitments in South East Asia and an increasingly apparent reluctance on the part of the USA to commit her troops to the Middle East in a future war (emphasizing instead the European and Asian theatres) the question of personnel became critical. Britain, with more hope than confidence, looked to the Commonwealth to ease her personnel problems.

New Zealand was persuaded to introduce conscription and Australia extended her commitments in South East Asia. It was the extreme nature of this predicament that perpetuated rather pathetic hopes of eventual Indian participation, denoted by plans for a proposed ANZIM (Australia, New Zealand, India, Malaya) defence area covering British responsibilities in the Far East.[86]

Although British planners held out long-term hopes of drawing India into some pattern of military co-operation, their immediate objectives were political. In the face of insurgencies in South East Asia, Britain concluded that the situation called for an Asian regional organization to counter Communism in the short term, while in the long term it would aim to build a post-colonial partnership between the West and Asia. This was not a new idea, indeed the origins of the concept of South East Asian regionalism, as other historians have demonstrated, lay in Mountbatten's wartime South East Asia Command. However, regional co-operation now enjoyed a new importance. Officials advanced Britain's close relationship with India, Pakistan and Ceylon as well as the European colonial states, as reason for Britain to head such a grouping. India's large industrial capacity and political prestige seemed indispensable, so much so that India was increasingly perceived as a key factor in the defence of South East Asia. India seemed to offer a symbol of co-operation between Asia and the West while augmenting Britain's image as a liberal leader of the Commonwealth. It has been suggested that Britain's decision to break with American policy and recognize China in 1949 was partly motivated by a desire to retain Asian, particularly Indian, sympathies and maintain Commonwealth unity.[87] After the outbreak of the Korean War it was often asserted that 'India ... has undoubted influence on Asian opinion'.[88] Nevertheless, it was hoped that the USA would provide the financial resources for this exercise in regionalism designed to preserve what remained of British hegemony.[89]

Meanwhile until 1949, contrary to the universal rhetoric of the Truman doctrine, the USA had concerned herself primarily with the security of Europe and the Mediterranean. The limited nature of American interest in South Asia pleased Ernest Bevin, who had repeatedly emphasized to Cabinet the importance of Asian markets. As late as 1948, Bevin had held out hopes of a 'third force' consisting of Europe and the Empire-Commonwealth that would be free from dependency on the United States. However, by 1949 this idea was increasingly questioned in favour of 'Western consolidation', responding to heightened East–West tension and Europe's continued weakness. Pakistan too, recognized Europe's debility, turning instead to the United States with a request for a $2 billion loan.[90]

All these factors played their part in Britain's continuing reluctance during 1949 and 1950 to accept Pakistan's repeated offers of defence co-operation in return for a public security guarantee. Although Pakistan offered the best bases for the defence or even recapture of Middle East oil, and useful bases for action against the Soviet Union or for operations in the Indian Ocean, the Kashmir crisis rendered the price too high. The Foreign Office in particular would not contemplate irritating India as an emerging leader of non-aligned Asian nations. Bevin concluded shortly after the outbreak of the Korean War that, until the settlement of the Kashmir crisis, there was no possibility of favouring either party.[91]

Yet at the same time the COS privately concluded that they could never allow a future Indian attack on Pakistan to succeed. Indeed remarkable documents reveal that in late 1950 British planners noted with approval that Air Vice-Marshal Atcherley, the British Chief of the Pakistan Air Force, 'has a plan for bombing Indian cities with the Pakistan Air Force' if attacked. Moreover, they promised air support to Pakistan in such an eventuality. British planners hoped that such air support could be offered under UN auspices adding 'complete air superiority on the side of Pakistan . . . should maintain the Pakistani position long enough to enable hostilities to be brought to an end'. The COS considered this necessary because of the likely adverse reaction of Middle East opinion to an attack on Pakistan, yet any *public* extension of this *de facto* guarantee would have wrecked British relations with India.[92]

Initially prompted by fears about the weakness of Middle East defence after the outbreak of the Korean War, during late 1950 and early 1951 the USA turned to address the same familiar South Asian dilemma as Britain, namely alignment with India or with Pakistan. However, American officials adopted different solutions driven by their rejection of British plans for Middle Eastern defence, based upon an illusive base system in the Cairo/Suez/Khartoum area continually obstructed by increasingly radical nationalists. Instead they looked to a 'northern tier' of more co-operative states, Turkey, Iran, Iraq and Saudi Arabia. To support these countries without committing large numbers of American troops, officials looked to Pakistan's Army and by August 1950, Acheson, the US Secretary of State, was advocating linking the 'northern tier' and South Asia.[93]

During early 1951, like Britain, the United States debated the problem of alienating India if Pakistani co-operation was secured by offering her a military guarantee. Although anxious not to offend India, the USA remained pessimistic about relations with Nehru, who desired leadership of a neutral bloc of Middle Eastern and South East Asian states. These views had been confirmed by a notably unsuccessful visit by Nehru to the USA during October 1949 during which disagreements over China were particularly marked.[94] Nor did the USA share Britain's South East Asian priorities to the same degree. To the dismay of British Foreign Office officials, the USA therefore favoured a guarantee to Pakistan against Indian attack. Pakistan's importance in the Middle East context was further confirmed in 1952 after the fall of the monarchy in Egypt, when the ruling nationalists refused to participate in a Middle East defence organization.[95]

Britain reacted to American policy with hostility. Anglo-American strategy had been diverging over Middle East issues since 1949. During conversations held in April 1951 Britain even disputed (in contradiction to her own past assertions) that Pakistan could contribute to Middle East defence. Britain's obvious pique at closer relations between Pakistan and the USA was compounded by the possibility of India being driven into the arms of the Soviets against the background of a new conflict in East Asia.[96] Moreover, there were separate indications that Pakistan would take an increasing interest in Middle East defence without such costly inducements. In September 1951 Pakistan's Foreign Minister confided:

> political leaders in Pakistan had 'boosted Islam' to such an extent over recent years that if there was aggression on the Islamic countries in the Middle East public opinion in Pakistan would be in such a state of clamour that the Prime Minister would, within six hours, be under the strongest pressure to participate actively in the defence of the Middle East. It was true that this 'boosting of Islam' had been undertaken by politicians largely for their own political needs, but the emotional force which had been created would sweep them along on a wave even though the defence of the Middle East had not been in the minds of many when they exploited this theme.[97]

A serious rift was appearing in Anglo-American policy in South Asia as a consequence of divergent strategies and priorities in the Middle East, East and South East Asia. Thus, while Britain shared India's perspective on Sino-Soviet relations during the Korean War and co-operated in attempting to localize the conflict, the USA viewed Britain's preoccupation with India as an obstacle to constructive Middle East defence.[98]

CONCLUSION

During the 1940s British hopes for military and political co-operation in South Asia, in common with ideas of territorial expansion in South East Asia, or of drawing on the economic resources of Africa, all represented attempts to redeploy imperial assets to counter-balance, even reverse, her decline. Retreat in South Asia was itself to be employed as a political weapon to resist pressure to capitulate in Malaya.[99] The strategic dimension of the transfer of power in South Asia was therefore symptomatic of a wider contradiction that bedevilled Britain's post-war experience. While the conclusion of the Second World War left Britain as one of the victorious allies, the reality as perceived by British defence planners left little room for optimism. Not only had Britain been economically drained by the cost of the war itself, but also in Europe the Soviet Union had emerged as the dominant military power. Furthermore Britain was burdened by onerous post-war occupations and lacked any immediate guarantee of American support, exacerbated by Britain's perceived vulnerability to new weapons of war. In the face of these problems, it was ironic that the radical strategy adopted by the COS, based upon a strategic air offensive, resulted in a renewed dependence upon the traditional pattern of imperial bases. For paradoxically, within the British Empire itself, the Second World War had accelerated nationalist demands for change, with movements in both Asia and the Middle East seeking an early British commitment to independence.[100]

Contrary to the suggestion of some historians, and in spite of the importance of facilities in South Asia, there was never any question of Britain trading independence for strategic desiderata. In India the Cripps mission had removed any remaining doubts about the inevitability of independence, while the paucity of resources available to Britain in the post-war period ensured that the option of repression was scarcely credible militarily, even if there had been the political will within Attlee's Labour administration to employ it. Attlee and Mountbatten were more conscious of this than Bevin or the military planners. But by 1946 even the COS recognized only too clearly the limitations upon their own position and, while they actively sought to maintain significant parts of the imperial edifices, they none the less accepted that political considerations would be the ultimate determinant in South Asia.

Between 1945 and 1949, and despite a volatile political situation in South Asia, the military devoted much of their planning to the best-case scenario of eventually acquiring facilities. This view was driven by the accurate presumption that the successor states would require at least some residual military co-operation to maintain their forces. At the same time, substantial account was taken of the possibility of a hostile subcontinent, typified by thinking on the Andoman and Nicobar islands. The British preoccupation with airbases abated in late 1948 with the acceleration of joint Anglo-American strategic planning, a catalyst for which was the Berlin crisis. By 1949 use of Pakistan's airbases, susceptible to Soviet counterattack, seemed to entail a level of defence commitment which Britain was unable or unwilling to provide. More secure Anglo-American alternatives were available in Britain and Japan.[101]

Ironically this decline in British interest in the airbases took place even as Pakistan pressed forward with eager offers of defence co-operation, albeit motivated by the Kashmir crisis. But by then developments in South East Asia had led to a belief in London that it was more important to retain the support of a potentially influential India than to obtain a defence treaty with Pakistan. By 1949, against the backdrop of the 'Emergency' in Malaya and the success of the Communists in China, the emphasis of Britain's policy in South Asia had shifted to take account of the benefit of India's political leadership in Asia as a whole. South Asia's value had become perceived less in terms of a strategic adjunct to the 'hot war' that Tedder believed would be won 'west of Oman', than as a reservoir of political support for the West in the face of the protracted conflicts that were already developing in South East Asia.

Britain's emphasis on Indian political co-operation ensured a degree of military eclipse in South Asia, particularly by the USA. Yet it might also be noted that the long lists of strategic desiderata drawn up by the COS in the 1940s were not as forlorn as some have sought to suggest. A generous military agreement was concluded with Ceylon and a defence treaty was also achieved with neighbouring Burma. An agreement that would have satisfied most of the COS's requirements was offered by Pakistan from 1949, but rejected by Britain for fear of offending India. In contrast the USA was not hamstrung by contradictory Commonwealth commitments and enjoyed the resources to capitalize on this advantage, drawing closer to Karachi in the early 1950s. It was especially ironic that Britain had privately concluded that, if only to satisfy her Arab allies, she would in any case have to intervene against any Indian attempt to absorb Pakistan. Conversely, Karachi knew that popular sentiment would require Pakistan's involvement in any external attack on the Middle East. *De facto* commitments therefore seemed to exist that were not enshrined in formal treaties.

What then of the much vaunted Indian co-operation in Asia, the objective which persuaded Britain to forgo an alliance with Pakistan in 1949? British officials recognized that extensive Indian *military* assistance in the Far East was not a realistic objective. On 30 June 1950, shortly after the outbreak of the Korean War, the British High Commissioner in India reported to London that he had asked Nehru 'whether India was going to give any practical assistance to the Republic of Korea' but then added mischievously, 'to twist his tail rather than in expectation of a favourable reply . . . the process of educating Nehru and the Government of India will clearly be a long and tortuous one'. But at the same time, the Indian contribution that Britain sought in Asia was primarily *political* in nature, emphasizing Britain's commitment to co-operation between the West and Asia through regional organizations aimed primarily at the defeat of Communism in South East Asia. Therefore, avoiding the severe embarrassment of Indian departure from the Commonwealth in 1949 may have been a negative achievement, but it was hardly insignificant against the background of the struggle for hearts and minds in Malaya. Moreover, overt Indian strategic neutrality was not quite what it seemed. By April 1951 covert Anglo-Indian defence co-operation in the Indian Ocean was considerable, even extending to the joint development of bases. In this sensitive matter, both sides were anxious to 'do everything possible to ensure no publicity is given'.[102]

ACKNOWLEDGEMENTS

The author wishes to thank the Harry S. Truman Library, Independence, Missouri, and the British Academy for awards that facilitated the writing of this chapter. The sections of this chapter dealing with airbases draw on a previous paper written in conjunction with Michael Coleman of Clare College, Cambridge. Responsibility for errors remains with the author.

NOTES

1 This can partly be explained in terms of the political focus of Professor Mansergh's magisterial *Transfer of Power* series.

2 See in particular A. I. Singh's four articles, 'Imperial Defence and the Transfer of Power in India', *International History Review* Vol. IV, No. 4 (November 1982), pp. 568–88; 'Keeping India in the Commonwealth: British Political and Military Aims, 1947–9', *Journal of Contemporary History* Vol. 20 (1985), pp. 469–81; 'Post Imperial British Attitudes to India: The Military Aspect, 1947–51', *The Round Table* Vol. 296 (1985), pp. 360–75. See also P. S. Gupta, 'British Strategic and Economic Priorities During the Negotiations for the Transfer of Power in S. Asia, 1945–7', *Bangladesh Historical Studies* Vol. VII (1983), pp. 39–51. A refreshing exception to this concentration upon India and political matters is A. Jalal, 'India's Partition and the Defence of Pakistan: An Historical Perspective', *Journal of Imperial and Commonwealth History* Vol. XV, No. 3 (May 1987) pp. 289–310.

3 J. Lewis, *Changing Direction: British Military Planning for Post War Strategic Defence, 1942–7*, (London: Sherwood, 1988); R. Ovendale, *The English Speaking Alliance: Britain, the United States, the Dominions and the Cold War, 1945–51* (London: George Allen & Unwin, 1985); D. Smith, *Diplomacy of Fear: Canada and the Cold War, 1941–8* (Toronto: University of Toronto Press, 1989). For an exception see D. K. Fieldhouse, 'The Labour Governments and the Empire-Commonwealth, 1945–51', in R. Ovendale (ed.) *The Foreign Policy of the British Labour Governments, 1945–51* (Leicester: Leicester University Press, 1984). More wide-ranging overviews are offered by P. Darby, *British Defence Policy East of Suez* (Oxford: Oxford University Press, 1973); R. F. Holland, 'The Imperial Factor in British Strategies, 1947–68: From Attlee to Macmillan', *Journal of Imperial and Commonwealth History* Vol. XII, No. 2 (January 1984), pp. 168–86.

4 R. J. McMahon, 'United States Cold War Strategy in South Asia: Making a Military Commitment to Pakistan, 1947–54', *Journal of American History* Vol. 74, No. 3, (December 1988), pp. 813–40; see also H. W. Brands, 'India and Pakistan in American Strategic Planning, 1947–54: Commonwealth Collaborator', *Journal of Imperial and Commonwealth History* Vol. 15 (October 1986), pp. 41–54; A. Jalal, 'Towards the Baghdad Pact: South Asia and the Middle East in the Cold War, 1947–55', *International History Review* Vol. 11, No. 3 (August 1989) pp. 409–33. The American perspective is also explored in P. I. Cheema, *Pakistan's Defence Policy, 1947–58* (London: Macmillan, 1990).

5 For a contrary view see Singh, 'Imperial Defence', pp. 568–78.

6 PHP (44) 17 (0) Final, 'Security in Western Europe and the Northern Atlantic', 6 June 1944, CAB 81/45, Public Record Office, Kew, Surrey (hereafter PRO); PHP (44) 27 (Draft) 'Report on Work Done – August 1943 to May 1944', 17 April 1944, CAB 81/42, PRO; PHP (45) 29 (0) Final, 'The Security of the British Empire', 29 June 1945, CAB 81/46, PRO. On India see PHP (45) 15 (0) Final, 'Security of India and the Indian Ocean', 19 May 1945, CAB 81/46, PRO.

7 The work of the PHPS has attracted considerable attention. The fullest account is given in Lewis, *Changing Direction*, pp. 98–122. See also V. Rothwell, *Britain and the Cold War, 1941–7* (London: Jonathan Cape: 1982), pp. 114–23; M. Kitchen, *Britain and the Soviet Union, 1941–5*, (London: Macmillan, 1986), pp. 198–204 and 215–18; J. Baylis, 'British Wartime Thinking About a Post War West European Security Group', *Review*

of International Studies, Vol. 9, No. 4, (1983), pp. 273–7; H. Rahman, 'British Post Second World War Planning for the Middle East', *Journal of Strategic Studies*, Vol. 5, No. 4 (December 1982), pp. 511–31.

8 COS (45) 402 (0), 'Future Developments in Weapons and Methods of War', 16 June 1945, CAB 80/94, PRO. See also R. Aldrich and M. Coleman, 'Britain and the Strategic Air Offensive Against the Soviet Union: The Question of South Asian Airbases, 1945–9', *History* Vol. 74, No. 242 (October 1989), pp. 400–7.

9 TWC (46) 15 (Revise), 'Future Developments in Weapons and Methods of War', 6 July 1946, DEFE 2/1252, PRO. For more details on this matter see the DCOS papers for 1946 in L/WS/1/989–93, India Office Library and Records, Blackfriars, London (hereafter IOLR.)

10 The value of bateriological weapons was increased by their 'comparative ease of production' and the view that they would be 'complementary to operations with Atomic Bombs', TWC (45) 45, 'Future Developments in Biological Warfare', 6 December 1945, DEFE 2/1252, PRO. See also TWC (45) 44 (Revise), 'Target Ranges' and Annex 1 'Size and Range of Target Cities in the USSR', 5 January 1946, ibid.; TWC (45) 42, 'Potentialities of [Biological] Weapons of War in the Next Ten Years', 12 November 1945, DEFE 2/1251, PRO; TWC (45) 38, 'Effect of Atomic Bombs on Warfare in the Next Few Years', 24 October 1945, ibid.

11 TWC (45) 38, 'Effect of Atomic Bombs on Warfare in the Next Few Years', 24 October 1945, ibid.

12 DO (45) 38, 'US Request for Military Bases', 29 November 1945, *Documents on British Policy Overseas*, (London: HMSO, 1985), Series I, Vol. III, doc. 135, pp. 399–402 (hereafter *DBPO*); see also State Department to British Embassy, 6 November 1945, *Foreign Relations of the United States* (Washington DC: United States Government Printing Office, 1969), 1945, Vol. VI, pp. 206–10 (hereafter *FRUS*). Bevin consulted both Eden and Churchill on this matter, Churchill to Bevin, 13 November 1945, *DBPO*, Series I, Vol. III, doc. 102, pp. 316–18.

13 Halifax to Bevin No. 1264, 27 February 1946, AN3932/101/45, FO 371/51684, PRO. The US JCS seem to have been especially interested in the airfields at Agra, Calcutta and Karachi. See JCS 570/34, 'Overall Examination of US Requirements for Military Bases and Rights', 5 October 1945, CCS 360 (12–9–42) Sec. 8, RG 218, National Archives and Records Administration, Washington DC (hereafter NARA). See also SWNCC–4640, 'Withdrawal of US Forces from Bases on the Territory of Foreign Nations', 6 October 1945, RG 353, NARA. DO (46) 58, 'United States Request for Bases', memorandum by Bevin, 13 April 1946, *DBPO*, Series I, Vol. IV, doc. 69, pp. 233–40.

14 Campbell to Bevin, 8 August 1945, *DBPO*, Series I, Vol. II, doc. 186, pp. 516–17; Anderson to Attlee, 9 February 1946, *DBPO*, Series I, Vol. II, doc. 27, pp. 96–103; unsigned memorandum on COS (46) 229 (0) 'The Strategic Value of India to the British Commonwealth of Nations', 8 September 1946, L/WS/1/985, IOLR.

15 cf. pp. 238–40 and also Lewis, *Changing Direction*; R. Smith and J. Zametica, 'The Cold Warrior: Clement Attlee Reconsidered, 1945–7', *International Affairs* Vol. 61, No. 2 (spring 1985), pp. 237–52.

16 COS (46) 54 (0), 22 February 1946, CAB 80/100, PRO; JP (46) 45 (Final), 'Strategic Position of the British Commonwealth', 27 March 1946, CAB 80/100, PRO.

17 cf. pp. 250–3; Smith and Zametica, 'Cold Warrior', p. 251.

18 Monteath minute, 13 October 1944, on COS (44) 58, L/WS/1/1340, IOLR; Hollis to Monteath, COS 300/6, 13 March 1946, L/WS/1/1044, IOLR.

19 COS (46) 47th mtg (8), 2 October 1946, L/WS/1/1045; DO (47) 44, 'Future Defence Policy', 22 May 1947, CAB 21/1800, PRO. The same reticence was expressed in the earlier drafts, see JP (47) 55, 'Future Defence Policy', 7 May 1947, AIR 9/267, PRO and L/P&O/428, IOLR.

20 Singh, 'Imperial Defence', p. 576.

21 ibid., pp. 573, 575.

22 Cabinet India and Burma Committee mtg, 14 January 1946, *TOP* Vol. VI, No. 355, pp. 788–9.

23 Monteath to Ismay, 1 March 1946, L/WS/1/1044, IOLR; also available as COS (46) 63 (0), 'India: Future Defence Requirements', CAB 80/100, PRO.

24 JP (46) 50 Final, 'India – Future Defence Requirements', 11 March 1946, CAB 84/79, PRO.

25 Enclosure 2 in Wavell to Pethick-Lawrence, 13 July 1946, *TOP* Vol. VIII, No. 26, pp. 49–57.

26 J. Connell, *Auchinleck* (London: Collins, 1959), pp. 830–1.

27 Cabinet Mission to Attlee, 15 May 1946, *TOP* Vol. VII, No. 285, pp. 557–8.

28 Wavell to Pethick-Lawrence, 13 July 1946, *TOP* Vol. VIII, No. 26, pp. 56–7; JP (46) 103 (Final), 'Withdrawal of British Forces from India – Effect on Strategic Requirements', 20 June 1946, CAB 84/82, PRO; COS (46) 133rd mtg, 30 August 1946, *TOP* Vol. VIII, No. 224, pp. 348–9.

29 Aldrich and Coleman, 'Strategic Air Offensive', pp. 410–11; Note by Croft and Turnbull, 9 April 1946, *TOP* Vol. VII, No. 78, p. 197.

30 JIC (46) 10 (0) Final, 'Threat to India's Land Frontiers', 15 April 1946, L/WS/1/987, IOLR; 'Appreciation of the Defence Problems of Pakistan', 1 February 1946, L/WS/1/ 1029, IOLR. See also Jalal, 'India's Partition', p. 291; Singh, 'Imperial Defence', p. 577.

31 Turnbull to Monteath, 13 September 1946, L/WS/1/1045, IOLR. The reference to 'Iraq' in this document should probably read 'Iran'.

32 JIC (46) 64 (0) (Final), Limited Circulation, 'Russia's Strategic Interests and Intentions in the Middle East', 6 July 1946, L/WS/1/1050, IOLR. Monthly reviews of this subject began in May 1946 – see JIC (46) 38 (0) Final Revise, 'Russia's Strategic Interests and Intentions in the Middle East', 14 June 1946, DO 35/1604, PRO. See also JIC (46) 10 (0) Final, Limited Circulation, 'Threat to India's Land Frontiers', 15 April 1946, L/WS/ 1/987, IOLR.

33 Hollis to Monteath, 4 October 1946, *TOP* Vol. VIII, No. 408, pp 661–2; Brief No. 11, 'Future of the Andaman and Nicobars', July 1946, L/WS/1/985, IOLR. For other examples of planning against a hostile India see COS (46) 146th mtg (3), 27 September 1946, L/WS/1/1045, IOLR; JP (46) 205 Final, 'Future of the Andoman and Nicobar Islands', 20 February 1947, ibid. COS (47) 59 (0), 'India: Defence Arrangements', 18 March 1947, ibid.

34 Memorandum by Montgomery to COS, 3 March 1947, WO 216/204, PRO, see also Killearn Diary, entry for 28 June 1947, Middle East Centre, St Anthony's College, Oxford; Bevin to Attlee, 1 January 1947, *TOP* Vol. IX, No. 236, pp. 431–2; Attlee to Bevin, 2 January 1947, ibid., No. 243, pp. 445–6.

35 R. J. Moore, *Escape from Empire: The Attlee Government and the India Problem*, (London: Oxford University Press, 1983), pp. 215–35; Cmd 7029, 'Conclusions reached in the Conversations between His Majesty's Government and the Delegation from the Executive Council of the Governor of Burma, January 1947', 27 January 1947, reproduced as document No. 225 in H. Tinker (ed.) *Burma: The Struggle for Independence, 1944–1948*, Vol. II (London: HMSO, 1984), (hereafter *Struggle*), pp. 378–82.

36 Meeting of Ministers on Indian Questions, GEN 174, 1st mtg, 13 March 1947, *TOP* Vol. IX, No. 530, pp. 940–5; Attlee to Mountbatten, 18 March 1947, *TOP* Vol. IX, No. 543, pp. 973–4.

37 Montgomery diary, Ch. 39, BLM 1/180/1, (3 February to 21 June 1947), Imperial War Museum, London (hereafter IWM); COS (47) 59 (0), 'India Defence Arrangements', 18 March 1947, *TOP* Vol. IX, No. 544, pp. 974–81; Meeting of Ministers, Misc/M (47) 8, 18 March 1947, *TOP* Vol. IX, No. 545, pp. 982–5.

38 Nehru to Baldev Singh, 8 April 1947, in S. Gopal (ed.) *Selected Works of Jawaharlal Nehru*, Second Series, Vol. II (New Delhi: Jawarharlal Memorial Fund, 1984), p. 369.

39 COS (47) 62nd mtg, 12 May 1947, *TOP* Vol. X, No. 416, pp. 786–92.

40 Jalal, 'India's Partition', p. 293; Monty to Simbo, 26 June 1947, Montgomery papers, BLM 1/181/1, IWM.

41 This disregard for military conditions was also apparent in the government's statement of intent of 20 February 1947, which was drawn up without reference to the COS and made no mention of a defence agreement. Statement of 20 February 1947, *TOP* Vol. IX, No. 438, pp. 773–4; Stapleton (Secretary to COS) to Alexander, 19 February 1947,

ibid., No. 432, p. 766. For an alternative explanation that views this as 'a momentary lapse' see Singh, 'Imperial Defence', p. 583.

42 Attlee to Mountbatten, 18 March 1947, *TOP* Vol. IX, No. 543, pp. 973–4; R. J. Moore, 'Mountbatten, India and the Commonwealth', *Journal of Commonwealth and Comparative Politics* Vol. XII (1981), pp. 5–43.

43 Pethick-Lawrence to Wavell, 26 September 1946, *TOP* Vol. VIII, No. 371, pp. 598–604; JP (47) 47 (Final), 'Withdrawal of Indian Forces', 22 May 1947, DEFE 4/4, PRO. Vietminh appealed in vain to Indian troops to fight the 'imperialists and colonisators', Vietminh leaflets, [c. 1945], File 37, papers of General Gracey, Liddell Hart Centre for Military Archives, King's College, London.

44 P. Dennis, *Troubled Days of Peace: Mountbatten and South East Asia Command, 1945–46* (Manchester: Manchester University Press, 1987), pp. 188–9; Singh, 'Imperial Defence', pp. 582–3; Pethick-Lawrence to Wavell, 26 September 1946, *TOP* Vol. VIII, No. 371, pp. 597–8.

45 Scoones to Simpson, 11 June 1947, L/WS/1/1032, IOLR; Turnbull to Carter, 16 June 1947, WS 17061/3 [old style reference, file not re-indexed], IOLR; Scoones to Monteath, 16 June 1947, ibid.

46 Ismay to Mountbatten, 4 July 1947, R/3/1/161, IOLR. Mountbatten seems to have favoured the 1944 Australian-New Zealand Treaty as a model, W. H. Morris-Jones, 'The Transfer of Power, 1947: A View from the Sidelines', *Modern Asian Studies* Vol. 16, No. 1 (1982), p. 25.

47 Viceroy's Personal Report No. 16, 8 August 1947, *TOP* Vol. XII, No. 385, p. 599; minutes of Meeting of Provisional Joint Defence Board, 6 August 1947, *TOP* Vol. XII, No. 352, pp. 545–7.

48 JP (47) 90 (Final), 'India – Strategic Requirements', 7 July 1947, DEFE 4/5, PRO; and annex to above, 'Draft Memorandum from COS to Minister of Defence', *TOP* Vol. XI, No. 554, pp. 957–61; COS to Minister of Defence, July 1947, *TOP* Vol. XI, p. 960.

49 Jalal, 'India's Partition', p. 294. Both the Soviets and the British hoped that India would not establish leadership over an Asian bloc at this conference, T. Remme, 'Great Britain and the International Significance of the Asian Relations Conference, 1947', in A. Gorst, L. Jonman and W. S. Lucas (eds) *British Postwar History: Themes and Perspectives* (London: Pinter, 1989).

50 'Britain–Burma Defence Agreement', 29 August 1947, annexed to IB (47) 168, in *Struggle* Vol. II, No. 503, pp. 734–6.

51 ibid.; Montgomery diary, Ch. 34, BLM1/178/1, IWM. An account of this meeting is also available in a note by Laithwaite for Secretary of State for Burma, 16 January 1947, *Struggle* Vol. II, No. 194, pp. 277–8.

52 IB (47) 145, 24 July 1947, summarized in IB (47) 43rd mtg, 28 July 1947, *Struggle* Vol. II, No. 468, pp. 462–3. See also BUK (47) 13, 9 January 1947, ibid., No. 173, pp. 245–7.

53 D. K. Fieldhouse, 'The Labour Governments and the Empire-Commonwealth, 1945–51', in R. Ovendale (ed.) *The Foreign Policy of the British Labour Governments, 1945–51* (Leicester: Leicester University Press, 1984), p. 94.

54 DO (47) 68, 'Defence Requirements', 15 September 1947, CAB 21/1861, PRO; CP (47) 272, 'Defence Requirements', 30 September 1947, CAB 129/21, PRO; 'The 30 Squadron (600 a/c) Strategic Bomber Force', Annex A, 4 May 1947, AIR 9/268, PRO.

55 Ismay to COS, 15 September 1947, R/3/1/161, IOLR; JP (47) 115 (Final), 'Defence Negotiations with India and Pakistan', 5 September 1947, DEFE 6/3, PRO.

56 Minute by Slessor to Tedder (Chief of the Air Staff), 28 September 1947, AIR 20/7021, PRO; 'Use of Strategic Airfields in N.W. India in the event of a major war', 7 October 1947, AIR 20/7038, PRO.

57 P. Moon (ed.) *Wavell: The Viceroy's Journal* (London: Oxford University Press, 1973), entry for 20 November 1947, p. 437; Erskine-Crum to Hollis, 30 January 1948, DEFE 11/31, PRO.

58 Stapleton to Hollis, 23 February 1948, ibid.

59 CP (48) 71, Memorandum by Bevin 'Coup in Czechoslovakia', 3 March 1948, N2591/157/12, FO 371/71286, PRO; J. Baylis, 'Britain, the Brussels Pact and the Continental

Commitment', *International Affairs* Vol. 60, No. 4 (autumn, 1984), pp. 615–29; C. Wiebes and B. Zeeman, 'The Pentagon Negotiations, March 48', *International Affairs* Vol. 59, No. 3 (summer, 1983), pp. 351–65.

60 JP (48) 35 (Final), 'Discussions with the Americans', 30 March 1948, AIR 20/8101, PRO; COS (48) 58 (0), 'Strategy', 17 March 1948, DEFE 5/10, PRO.

61 Brief of Short Range Emergency War Plan – Short Title 'GRABBER', 17 March 1948, 'USSR' series 3–2–46, Section 12, US JCS Records, RG 165, NARA. On this see G. Herken, *The Winning Weapon* (New York: Alfred Knopf, 1980), p. 248.

62 JP (48) 54 (Final), 'Use of Pakistan as an Air Base during the next eighteen months', 10 May 1948, DEFE 6/6, PRO; Plan HALFMOON, reproduced in T. H. Etzold and J. L. Gaddis (eds) *Containment: Documents on American Policy and Strategy, 1945–50* (New York: Columbia University Press, 1978), p. 315; JP (48) 63 (Final), 26 June 1948, DEFE 6/6, PRO.

63 Aldrich and Coleman, 'Strategic Air Offensive', pp. 418–19.

64 Montgomery diary, Ch. 67, BLM 1/184, (Germany 3–7 April 1948), IWM.

65 See for example DO (48) 49, 'Preparation for Defence', 29 July 1948, CAB 131/6, PRO. On the Berlin crisis see A. Schlaim, 'Britain and the Berlin Blockade', *International Affairs* Vol. 60, No. 1 (1983–4) pp. 1–14.

66 JIC (48) 9 (0) (Final), 'Russian Interests, Intentions and Capabilities', [70 printed pages], 23 July 1948, L/WS/1/1173, IOLR. See also R. Aldrich and M. Coleman, 'The Cold War, the JIC and British Signals Intelligence, 1948', *Intelligence and National Security* Vol. 4, No. 3 (July 1989), pp. 535–49.

67 COS (49) 128th mtg (1), 14 September 1948, DEFE 4/16, PRO; DO (48) 19th mtg, 16 September 1948, CAB 131/5, PRO.

68 Record of a conversation between Noel-Baker and Cawthorn, 18 September 1948, L/WS/1/1047, IOLR.

69 COS (48) 136th mtg (1), 24 September 1948, DEFE 4/16, PRO; Private Secretary of Tedder, to Secretary of COS, covering note by Cawthorn to Tedder, 28 September 1948, DEFE 11/31, PRO. See also Jalal, 'India's Partition', p. 300 and Cheema, *Pakistan's Defence Policy*, pp. 23–45.

70 Jalal, 'India's Partition', p. 303; JIC (48) 112 (Final), 'Possibility of Open War Between India and Pakistan', 27 November 1948, L/WS/1/1135, IOLR.

71 Singh, 'Keeping India in the Commonwealth', pp. 475–7.

72 cf. pp. 85–111; COS (49) 53rd mtg, 8 April 1949, DEFE 4/21, PRO. On Britain's information projection campaign in India during this period see R. Fletcher, 'British Propaganda Since World War II: A Case Study', *Media, Culture and Society* Vol. IV, No. 9 (1982), pp. 97–109.

73 PMM (48) 11th mtg, Confidential Annex, 20 October 1948, CAB 133/88, PRO; Cawthorn to Scoones (CRO), 4 November 1948, DEFE 11/31, PRO; Scoones to Price (MoD), 10 November 1948, ibid.

74 PMM (48) 12th mtg, 20 October 1948, CAB 133/88, PRO; JP (48) 117 (0), 'Defence Appreciation as a Basis for Military Planning by Commonwealth States', 6 December 1948, L/WS/1/1214, IOLR.

75 JP (48) 142 (0) (Preliminary), 'Contribution by Pakistan to Commonwealth Defence', 20 January 1949, L/WS/1/1214, IOLR; Presentation on Operation DUALISM, by Major General Anderson at Maxwell Air Force Base, 6–8 December 1948, Operation DUAL-ISM File, 5–81–45, OPD 337, Sec. 2, RG 341, NARA; ORE 17-(49), 'The Strategic Importance of the Far East to the US and the USSR', 4 May 1949, PSF Intelligence File 17–24, Box 256, Harry S. Truman Memorial Library.

76 Jago, Secretary of JPS (MoD), to Barker (CRO), 21 January 1949, f. 56, L/WS/1/1214, IOLR; COS (49) 13th mtg (7), 27 January 1949, DEFE 11/31, PRO; 'Military Impli-cations of India's possible future status' – Appendix to Annex C of CP (49) 58, 'India's Future Relations with the Commonwealth', 14 March 1949, CAB 129/33, PRO.

77 Secretary of State for Commonwealth Relations to UK High Commissioner, Pakistan, 14 April 1949, DEFE 11/31, PRO; JIC (49) 16 (Final), 'Estimated Russian Threat to Pakistan – 1949 and 1957', 28 April 1949, L/WS/1/1173, IOLR; DO (49) 11th mtg (1), 19 April 1949, CAB 131/8, PRO.

78 cf. pp. 37–8; COS (49) 182, 'Certain Implications Arising out of the Decision that India should Remain in the Commonwealth', 18 May 1949, DEFE 5/14, PRO.

79 JP (49) 67 (0) (Preliminary Draft), 'Place of India and Pakistan in Allied Strategy', 30 June 1949, L/WS/1/1215, IOLR.

80 JP (48) 117 (0) Revised Draft, 'Defence Appreciation as a Basis for Military Planning by Commonwealth Staffs', 13 January 1949, L/WS/1/1214, IOLR.

81 COS (49) 100th mtg (3), 13 July 1949, DEFE 4/22, PRO.

82 CM (49) 15, 24 February 1949, CAB 128/84, PRO.

83 On this see R. Aldrich, 'Unquiet in Death: The Post War Survival of the "Special Operations Executive", 1945–51', in A. Gorst and W. S. Lucas (eds) *Politics and the Limits of Policy* (London: Pinter, 1991).

84 CP (49) 67, 'Sir William Strang's Tour of Southeast Asia and the Far East, 17 March 1949, CAB 129/33, PRO; Bowker to FO No. 366, 3 May 1950, AIR 20/7030, PRO.

85 Memorandum handed by Senanayake to Gordon-Walker, 30 August 1950, AIR 20/2417, PRO. See also minutes of a meeting with the High Commissioner for Ceylon at the CRO, 6 January 1951, ibid.

86 cf. pp. 143–65; DO (49) 66, 'The Requirements of National Defence: Size and Shape of the Armed Forces 1950–1953', 18 October 1949, CAB 131/7, PRO; JP (49) 36 Final, 'Responsibility of Commonwealth Countries in the Far East', 13 May 1949, L/WS/1/1215, IOLR.

87 PUSC (32) Final, 28 July 1949; PUSC (53) Final, 'Regional Co-operation in Southeast Asia', 20 August 1949, F1055/ FO 371/76030; P. Lowe, *The Origins of the Korean War* (London: Longman, 1986), pp. 109–10.

88 CP (50) 200, 'Review of the International Situation in the Light of the Korean Conflict', 30 August 1950, CAB 129/41, PRO.

89 PUSC 53 'Regional Co-operation in Southeast Asia', 20 August 1949, W5572/3/500G, FO 371/76386, PRO.

90 J. Kent, 'The British Empire and the Origins of the Cold War', in A. Deighton (ed.) *Britain and the First Cold War* (London: Macmillan, 1990), pp. 165–84; McMahon, 'Military Commitment to Pakistan', p. 818.

91 CP (50), 'Review of the International Situation in Asia in the Light of the Korean Conflict', 30 August 1950, CAB 129/41, PRO.

92 Brief for VCOS mtg, 'Action in Event of Possible Hostilities Between India and Pakistan', 27 November 1950 (Limited Circulation), AIR 20/7038, PRO; VCOS mtg, 15 December 1950, ibid.

93 Jalal, 'Towards the Baghdad Pact', p. 418.

94 NSC 48/1, 'The Position of the United States with Regard to Asia', 23 December 1949, PSF, Box 211, Harry S. Truman Library, Independence, Missouri, USA; Merrill, 'Indo-American Relations', p. 222.

95 *FRUS*, 1950, Vol. V, pp. 217–18; Jalal, 'Towards the Baghdad Pact', pp. 417–19; McMahon, 'Military Commitment to Pakistan', p. 822; Hahn, 'Containment and Egyptian Nationalism', pp. 27–8.

96 'India and Pakistan in Relation to Middle East Defence', April 1951, DO 35/3008, PRO; Jalal, 'Towards the Baghdad Pact', p. 423.

97 Minutes of a conversation between Laithwaite and Ikramullah, 18 September 1951, DO 35/3008, PRO.

98 McMahon, 'Military Commitment to Pakistan', p. 826; Singh, 'Britain India and the Asian Cold War', pp. 226–7. On East Asia see P. Lowe, 'The Frustrations of Alliance: Britain, the United States and the Korean War, 1950–1951', and M. Dockrill, 'The Foreign Office, Anglo-American Relations and the Korean Truce Negotiations July 1951-July 1953', in J. Cotton and I. Neary (eds) *The Korean War in History* (Manchester: Manchester University Press, 1989), pp. 81–119.

99 On the problem of 'decline' see J. Darwin, 'British Decolonization since 1945: A Pattern or a Puzzle?', *Journal of Contemporary History* Vol. 12, No. 2 (January 1984), pp. 187–209. On South East Asia see R. Aldrich, 'A Question of Expediency: Britain, the United States and Thailand', *Journal of Southeast Asian Studies* Vol. XIX, No. 2 (September 1988), pp. 209–10, 242–4. On Africa see J. Kent, 'Imperialism and the Idea of

Euro-Africa', in J.W. Young and M. Dockrill (eds) *British Security Policy Since 1945* (London: Macmillan, 1988), pp. 47–77.
100 Aldrich and Coleman, 'Strategic Air Offensive', pp. 424–8.
101 See for example W. R. Louis's discussion of Libya during 1949–50 in 'American Anti-colonialism and the Dissolution of the British Empire', *International Affairs* Vol. 61, No. 3 (summer 1985), pp. 404–9.
102 UK High Commissioner India to London, 30 June 1950, annexed to CP (50) 159, 'Korea: Reactions of Other Asian Countries', 5 July 1950, CAB 129/41, PRO; UK High Commissioner India to London, 27 April 1951, AIR 20/7033, PRO.

12

South East Asia and British strategy, 1944–51

Karl Hack

This chapter seeks to place British South East Asian strategy within a wide historical context, establishing the relationship between pre-war and post-war strategies. Pre-war illusions of a 'Main fleet to Singapore' strategy sank with the *Prince of Wales* and the *Renown* on 10 December 1941.[1] Post-war plans instead envisaged a 'minor fleet from Singapore' strategy, in which most eastern naval and air units would be withdrawn to the Middle East on the outbreak of major war. Ironically, however, the calamitous fall of Singapore, in February 1942, only reinforced the belief that the narrow Kra Isthmus, just across the border with Thailand, was essential to Malayan defence. Thus this chapter will begin and end with Churchill, as Prime Minister, presiding over planning for the pre-emptive seizure of southern Thai territory. South East Asia Command's 1945–7 reoccupation of South East Asia and the Malayan Emergency are not discussed in detail.[2] Instead a thematic treatment will be used to create an overview of British strategy.

Darby has argued that South East Asia formed a military and trading periphery to the Indian Empire, and so India's independence on 15 August 1947 should have augured the demise of Britain's regional role.[3] In fact as early as 1937 Malaya and Singapore had taken a central place in balancing the Empire's trade, Britain having a dollar deficit of $591 million in that year, and Malaya a surplus of $247 million, based on sales of rubber and tin.[4] By 1941 Malaya was seen as the Empire's dollar 'arsenal'. Its loss to Japan, wartime debt and trade disruption only accentuated its post-war importance in earning dollars for the Empire and Sterling Area.[5] In 1948 the Colonial Secretary could state that 'It is by far the most important source of dollars in the dependant Empire', and serious interference with its exports 'would gravely worsen the whole dollar balance of the Sterling Area'. After unfavourable market conditions for rubber in 1949, the Korean War raised demand and prices for raw materials, so that in 1950 Malaya earned $350 million of the Sterling Area's $1,285 million.[6] Thus unlike Burma, where the threat of disorder led to accelerated independence in January 1948, Malaya was economically vital.[7]

Singapore and Malaya also played vital roles, however, in Commonwealth relations, Britain's regional prestige, and ultimately the Cold War. From the original 1921 decision to develop it, the Singapore base was recognized as of vital concern to Australia and New Zealand, whose forward naval defence it would provide.[8] By 1926 provisional defence planning envisaged Malaya defended by volunteer battalions only. In the so-called 'Period-of-Relief' before a relieving British fleet could arrive no landward attack would have time to succeed against Singapore, even from nearby Johore. Singapore was thus viewed as a naval fortress, North Malaya as a distinct strategic area, though one which the enemy might seize as a forward logistics base for the main assault on Singapore. In the estimated forty-two days before relief Singapore would rely on 15-inch naval guns, a few aircraft and a small garrison.[9]

By late 1940 aircraft ranges had increased, and Malaya's infrastructure developed. This made overland attack, through Thailand, possible from newly acquired Japanese bases in northern Indo-China. This would remain possible even after the arrival of any relieving fleet (though, after setting a period-of-relief of 180 days in September 1939, the Chiefs of Staff (COS) were now admitting they were, at least temporarily, unable to send a fleet). In response, 1940–1 planning developed based on the defence of possible East Coast landing sites, and to seize, at twenty-four hours' notice, the southern Thai port of Songkhla, around fifty miles from the nearest point on the Malayan border.[10] The latter plan was eventually code-named MATADOR. In contrast to the long, indefensible border, this offered a line of defence less than fifty miles across the Kra peninsula, and guarding the aerodromes in north Malaya. Malaya's geography explains why such a plan was to be central to strategy in both 1941 and 1950–5.

Most of the Malayan peninsula is dominated by a range of hills rising to 7,000 feet, with no lateral communications from about halfway between Singapore and Thailand. The central backbone of hills dies away soon after crossing the Siamese border, with good lateral communications in the vicinity of Songkhla, and sites for aerodromes. Songkhla also possessed road and rail communications to both east and west Malaya.[11] Consequently the 'Songkhla' position alone offered a narrow front, lateral communications, and adequate lines of communication back to east and west Malaya.

Japanese convoys were spotted heading towards Malaya on 6 December 1941. Under pressure not to violate Thai neutrality unless essential, however, the regional Commander-in-Chief failed to authorize Operation MATADOR. Facing Japanese air and naval superiority, and landings north and south, the Matador position might anyway have proved little better than the Maginot Line. Its defenders would have risked serious interdiction of their lines of communication, if not isolation. In 1941 Churchill had assumed Japan would not risk war against the United States and sent all available aircraft and tanks to the Middle East. Over 600 Japanese aircraft soon asserted superiority over 158 inferior allied adversaries. With never more than one squadron of obsolescent British tanks it was 'a battle of flesh and blood against equipment'. As one official historian put it, in global war, 'British strategy, then as now, was concerned with winning the last battle: if Malaya had to be lost to this end, it was for ... the British Commonwealth to stomach it, and ... to learn the lesson'.[12]

The 'lessons' that stuck, however, were that Britain could not hide behind the illusion of a two-ocean Navy, and that failure to hold the Songkhla position had been a serious mistake.[13] In addition the indecent haste with which it seemed the Thai Prime Minister, Phibul Songkram, came to terms with the Japanese destroyed all faith in Thailand as a neutral buffer. The use of forward airfields in Indo-China against Malaya also confirmed that Singapore's strategic frontiers lay as far afield as the Kra Isthmus (southern Thailand) and Tonkin (northern Indo-China).

Thailand's declaration of war in July 1942, and acceptance of four Malay states from Japan in 1943, encouraged the belief that Thailand should be treated as an enemy state after the war. During 1942–3 Churchill and the Vice-Chiefs of Staff decided that Britain would require a free hand over the Kra Isthmus. By mid-July 1945 suggested terms had included the right of British military advice to Thailand, of entry and facilities if there was a threat of war, and even the possibility of stationing British troops on the Kra Isthmus. By August 1945 a committee under Bevin had also decided on rights for securing a steady supply of rice during post-war scarcity, and for war damage compensation and the full restoration of Britain's commercial interests.[14] After the USA supported Thai objections to Britain's original proposals, the final 'Formal Agreement' of 1 January 1946 replaced British with United Nations advice. Thailand acknowledged that 'Thailand was of great importance for the defence of Malaya, Burma, Indonesia and Indo-China. . . . Therefore Thailand must co-operate in all respects to assure international security, as would be considered appropriate by the ... United Nations'. Thailand also agreed not to cut a canal across the Kra Isthmus without the Great Powers' permission. Controls to secure rice for South East Asia, both the most vital and controversial of Britain's demands, were retained.[15]

By 1947 London was considering revising the Formal Agreement, and the COS thought that Thailand might agree to a separate regional security scheme.[16] Continuing nationalist struggles in Indonesia and Indo-China made Asian participation in such arrangements unlikely, however. By 1948 Britain was considering cancelling the Formal Agreement in return for a global payment of reparations. Also the Emergency in Malaya required the active co-operation of Thailand. In 1949 Britain secured an Anglo-

Thai agreement allowing 'hot pursuit' of terrorists across the border, was helping to procure arms for Thailand, and made available security force training facilities in Malaya. By November 1949 the British ambassador to Thailand was anxious that Britain should counter Thai fears of becoming 'cannon fodder in the war against communism', by practical assistance.[17]

During 1948–9 negotiations leading to the cancellation of the Formal Agreement the primary concern was to ensure for the Commonwealth adequate war damage compensation, strategic considerations being insignificant. More important now was Britain's aspiration to form a bridge between East and West, to win Asia away from Communism.[18] The Kra continued to be considered the natural line of resistance for Malaya, but until spring 1950 there was no obvious conventional warfare threat, and insufficient danger of Communist domination of Thailand, to justify planning its defence.[19]

A DOMINION OF SOUTH EAST ASIA

The post-war political reconstruction of South East Asia was a vital part of overall strategic planning.[20] Britain's pre-war Far Eastern territories included nine Malay states, only the four federated Malay states having some functions centralized. The five unfederated Malay states, their treaties with Britain involving less obligation for their Sultans to follow the 'advice' of British officials, were averse to centralization. The Straits Settlements (Penang, Malacca and Singapore) were under a governor in Singapore, who was also High Commissioner for the Malay states, and represented British interests in Sarawak, the Brunei Sultanate and North Borneo.

In advancing up to 600 miles in 70 days to force the surrender of nearly 130,000 (allied) imperial troops in Singapore on 15 February 1942, the Japanese appeared to confirm the need for the strategic unity of these territories. The predominance of the Chinese, previously considered temporary economic workers in Malaya, in the Malayan People's Anti-Japanese Army (MPAJA), also confirmed that the new nation must be built on the basis of common citizenship. Initial plans in 1942 envisaged a united Dominion of South East Asia, but Singapore was eventually excluded because its free port status and predominantly Chinese population made immediate inclusion premature.[21] Sarawak and North Borneo would become Crown Colonies, but initially required separate treatment because of their lack of development. By 1944 plans envisaged a united Malayan Union, with the removal of the Sultans' sovereignty making possible a generous common citizenship, and so the nurturing of gradually increasing self-government, in a non-communal political environment. Wider federation was now to be fostered by appointing a Governor-General to co-ordinate policy in South East Asian territories. This, in essence, was the plan embodied in the White Paper on Malaya and Singapore, published in January 1946, by which time the MPAJA had apparently peacefully disarmed. Malayan federation was seen as vital to political advance and it asserted 'International relations as well as the security and other interests of the British Commonwealth require that Malaya should be able to exercise an influence as a united and enlightened country appropriate to her economic and strategic importance.'[22]

The needs of both defence and self-government, Britain's declared aim for her colonies from July 1942, seemed to demand larger units capable of supporting everything from tertiary educational institutions to armies. As regional centres of influence these would sustain rather than sap Commonwealth power. By 1945–7 Britain was moving towards the creation of federations in South East Asia, the West Indies and East Africa, albeit over an extended time-scale.

By December 1945 the Malay Sultans had, under some duress, all signed new treaties ceding sovereignty to the Crown, paving the way for the inauguration of the Malayan Union as a strong central state under a governor on 1 April 1946. The Malay response was rapid, with the United Malay's National Organization (UMNO) established at an 11–12 May Conference. Initially the Colonial Office and Colonial Secretary refused to contemplate demands to restore Malay sovereignty. The Crown was 'the necessary control, to enable Malaya to be welded into a progressive and united country'. Any restoration would make the Sultans a potential block to wider federation, Chinese integration and the introduction of democratic government.[23]

In order to avert possible disorder and win Asian support in Malaya and abroad the government ultimately negotiated the substitution of the Malayan Federation for the Malayan Union, on 1 February 1948. This restored sovereignty to the Sultans in their states, though retaining a strong central state and a common, but less liberal citizenship. Stockwell states this retained the essence of the original plans, but it also represented a significant blow to British strategy. The British attempt to impose a radical plan had left the Sultans and UMNO in no mood to assimilate the Chinese. Creating a common community in Malaya, let alone the incorporation of Singapore, was going to be difficult.[24] The British long-term plan, perhaps best styled 'unite and quit' rather than 'divide and rule', had got off to an indifferent start.[25]

Malcolm MacDonald was installed as Governor-General in May 1946. In June and July North Borneo and Sarawak respectively became Crown Colonies, passing under his general direction. In May 1948 MacDonald, now Commissioner-General for South East Asia, met with the High Commissioner of Malaya and the Governor of Singapore to discuss ways of creating 'a climate of opinion in Malaya favourable to the incorporation of Singapore in some sort of constitutional union'.[26] At first UMNO's chairman, Dato Onn, felt constrained by his party's opinion not to attend private functions including Tan Cheng Lock, a prominent Chinese leader. It took careful preparation before it was possible to assemble community leaders together in late 1948. By February 1949 a team of fourteen community leaders, later known as the Communities Liaison Committee (CLC), was meeting in private. Even so, early meetings were often tense.[27]

Arguably only the Emergency encouraged a real desire by these essentially conservative community leaders to co-operate against the radical Communist threat. By August 1949 the CLC was reaching some agreement on citizenship and Malay rights, but MacDonald still discouraged discussion of the incorporation of Singapore for fear it would cause a row.[28] The CLC was eventually eclipsed as political leaders were drawn onto bodies dealing with the Emergency. Dato Onn formed the cross-communal Independence of Malaya Party (IMP) in September 1951, after failing to persuade UMNO to accept Chinese members, but the Colonial Office realized his support was uncertain.[29]

In September 1950 the High Commissioner revealed that the high Emergency workload precluded the option of having one governor for Malaya and Singapore. By late 1951 the policy of fusing different communities into one nation, and several territories into one Dominion, was progressing at about stalling pace, even for the anticipated fifteen to twenty years before independence. In Malaya the failure of the Chinese to lend whole-hearted support to the Emergency was causing resentment. Some Singaporean politicians felt that Singapore, where the first elections for Legislative Councillors took place in 1948, might be held back by the Federation. The municipal elections in the Federation, at Kuala Lumpur in February 1952, saw the alliance of the communal UMNO and Malayan Chinese Association vanquish the IMP.[30] The Colonial Office shared the military belief that federation was essential because Singapore could not be defended 'as a kind of hedgehog', but by late 1952 the military were becoming impatient with the 'judicious' approach of the colonial authorities. Of necessity, however, British officials could only play supporting parts in forming attitudes between local communities.[31]

SOUTH EAST ASIA AND ANGLO-AUSTRALIAN PLANNING

The Japanese occupation of Java and Rabaul, culminating in the bombing of Darwin on 19 February 1942, confirmed that for Australia 'What Great Britain calls the Far East is to us the Near North'.[32] The subsequent American domination of the Pacific confirmed to both Australia and Britain that an American Pacific security guarantee was necessary. A combined Anglo-Australian effort would also be necessary if there was to be hope of influencing American post-war Pacific policy. In January 1944 the Australia–New Zealand Agreement demanded the Dominions' representation in any post-war settlement, and aspired to 'a regional zone of defence comprising the South West and South Pacific Area ... based in Australia'.[33] At the October 1944 Commonwealth Conference, an Australian paper stated Australia's desire to co-ordinate Commonwealth Pacific planning, envisaging its defence 'on the island screen to the north of these Dominions'.[34] Britain was looking to increase the Commonwealth defence contributions. Since South Africa and Canada opposed any centralized defence planning, regional arrangements seemed the way forward.[35]

In October 1945 Attlee agreed to apply the concept of a Dominion acting as a Commonwealth instrumentality to Japan, where Australia was particularly anxious for a stringent peace treaty. Australia provided the command for the British Commonwealth Occupation Force in Japan and represented Britain, New Zealand and India on the Allied Council for Japan. Bevin and the Foreign Office, however, were determined that Australia should not detract from Britain's diplomatic presence, and fretted about loss of prestige.[36] The military by contrast were hoping that the co-ordinating body for the occupation forces, the Joint Chiefs of Staff Organization Australia (JCOSA), might provide a model for Commonwealth co-operation. This consisted of the Australian Chiefs of Staff and representatives from New Zealand and all three British Services, and was dissolved after the withdrawal of British forces in 1947.[37]

Britain thus approached the April–May 1946 Commonwealth Prime Ministers' Conference hoping to gain greater Dominions' defence contributions by some sharing of responsibility for regional defence. Each Dominion should assume responsibility for joint defence planning in its area, assisted by Service liaison representatives from other countries. It was agreed that Bevin should approach the US Secretary of State to try and link the United States' desire for base rights in Commonwealth Pacific islands to a regional defence arrangement, but this was firmly rebuffed. Chifley, Prime Minister of Australia, and his Minister of External Affairs, Evatt, thus wanted Commonwealth co-ordination, to include the USA when possible. Chifley believed that there should be a larger Australian defence effort, directed to the Pacific, but was wary of British suggestions that Australia accept responsibility for South East Asian planning. He didn't want to imply Australian responsibility for finding the necessary resources, and current Australian strategy envisaged island defence lines passing between Malaya and the Philippines, not necessarily embracing Malaya.[38]

Chifley also reserved his position on Service liaison, since he wanted the three British COS representatives in the JCOSA system reduced to one.[39] After much discussion Attlee endorsed the principle of one Service representative, not three, in December 1947, facilitating the establishment in 1948 of a British Service Liaison Staff in Australia.[40]

The 1946 conference also saw the COS expound their strategy for countering the Soviet Union in a major war. United States involvement was axiomatic. The atomic bomb seemed to offer the prospect of destroying the enemy's ability to wage war by a strategic air offensive, the only effective answer or deterrent to the Soviet Union's overwhelming numerical superiority. 'Main Support Areas', each capable of planning and sustaining war, were the American continent, southern Africa, western Europe, Australia and New Zealand and, hopefully, India. Bases beyond these were necessary, 'from which areas of importance to Russia can be brought under threat of attack by our long range weapons [which] may be our only means of defence at the onset of war'. From the Middle East, the Caucasus and South Russia could be targeted, and from North West India, the Urals and Siberia.[41] Attlee's opposition to expending effort in the Middle East was overcome by the Chiefs of Staff and Bevin, and its role as a base confirmed in a staff conference of 11 June 1947.[42] Anglo-American planning discussions in March 1948 also revealed that the United States was planning air offensives from Okinawa, Britain and Pakistan, but not the Middle East.[43] This encouraged the Chiefs of Staff to seek greater Commonwealth planning and Middle East commitments, in the hope that this might encourage American co-operation in planning its defence.[44]

For Britain, one original reason for encouraging defence co-ordination in the Pacific, to maximize influence on regional American planning or operational arrangements, was now overshadowed by the need for an Antipodean ANZAC commitment. The knowledge that Okinawa (in the Ryukyu Islands) would be a major American strategic base confirmed that any Soviet danger in the Far East would be neutralized by American air and naval power, preventing southward attack.[45] With China in turmoil and Japan occupied there was no other major threat. In May 1948 an Australian paper suggested Australian planning responsibility in an area stretching from Malaya, to the Pacific waters surrounding New Zealand.[46] This later became known as the ANZAM area.

A November COS paper recommended accepting the proposal, since while American power would render South East Asia secure in war, Australian planning responsibility would encourage them to commit resources to the Middle East.[47] Fraser, Prime Minister of New Zealand, agreed in December that Service-level planning could immediately commence, and in a September 1949 letter confirmed that the New Zealand COS had been instructed to plan their wartime deployment in co-operation with Britain.[48] Attlee informed Chifley of British agreement to Australian initiative for the ANZAM area in December 1948. The Australian Defence machinery, with representation of Britain and New Zealand, was to initiate ANZAM regional air and naval plans, but home defence, including that of the British territories, remained outside its scope. The Australian government formally endorsed the ANZAM arrangement in 1950, and in February 1951 the United States recognized the ANZAM region for certain limited naval purposes.

Australia remained reluctant to commit forces to the Middle East without a clear indication of American plans for the Pacific, and stated this view as late as the Colombo Conference of January 1950.[49] The events of 1942, when Britain and Australia tried to divert Australian troops, returning from the Middle East, to Burma, had left Australia acutely aware of the need to guarantee its own defence. Nevertheless, a June 1950 visit to Australia by Slim (CIGS), in which he emphasized the contrast between Japanese sea power and Pacific ambitions in 1942, and the Soviet Union's orientation towards Europe and the Middle East, resulted in Australia drawing up plans for initial reinforcement both of the Middle East and of South East Asia.[50] On 14 July Menzies reassured a meeting of ministers in London that he personally believed that keeping Australian forces at home in total war played into Soviet hands; 'Menzies agreed with this view, which he said had governed his policy in 1939–40', but Australian public opinion must be courted, and the final decision taken at the time. Though his assurances masked the opposition of Spender and Casey within his Cabinet, Australian priorities in July 1950 can be described as the Middle East in total war, with reservations, and Malaya in the Cold War.[51] The Menzies government decided in May to send to Malaya a small number of transport planes, and in June, bombers, though the Korean War prevented any consideration of a ground commitment.[52]

The Korean War, however, encouraged the United States to show more sympathy towards Australian desires for a Pacific security arrangement. Initially the United States proposed an offshore island pact, avoiding commitments in Hong Kong or the mainland, and including Japan and the Philippines. Australia, however, wanted a guarantee against Japan, not a pact including it, to compensate for an anticipated soft peace treaty. Britain opposed any wider pact from which it was excluded, and believed that any Pacific Pact was premature while wider Asian, particularly Indian, support was unlikely. On 15–17 February 1951, however, John Foster Dulles, American envoy on the Japanese peace treaty negotiations, agreed with Australia and New Zealand a tripartite pact. After initial doubts that it might detract from their commitment to the Middle East in war the COS decided that an American guarantee might actually make Australia more amenable over the Middle East, and felt that Britain should rely on normal Commonwealth liaison to secure its interests. On 12 March the Cabinet agreed not to oppose the agreement, with some reservations about the effect of the exclusion of Hong Kong and Malaya, though some ministers were clearly disturbed by the possibility of losing British prestige.[53]

Signed in September 1951, and operative on 29 April 1952, ANZUS was both the Australian 'price' for a soft Japanese treaty, and one part of increasing American efforts to encourage allied assistance against Communism in Asia.[54] It was not unwelcome to Attlee or the COS, and by late 1951 had made Australia more sympathetic to a Middle East priority in global war.[55]

In 1952, however, the deteriorating situation in Indo-China, and a COS global review which anticipated a short, atomic war, made both less likely, and less valuable, any slow Australian reinforcement of the Middle East. ANZAM proceeded to plan regional naval and air defence, but Britain's long-term aim was a regional pact embracing Asian countries, and the new Conservative government's attempts to gain British association with ANZUS were to cause much Australian anxiety in 1952–3.

INDEPENDENCE FOR THE 'ENGLISH BARRACK IN THE ORIENTAL SEAS'

If Britain hoped to commit Australia to the Middle East, in 1946 it had still been possible to hope that India would follow British diplomacy, and co-operate with Asian defence. During the reoccupation of the Far East Indian troops had been the mainstay of South East Asia Command (SEAC).[56] The emergence of two Dominions, India and Pakistan, on 15 August 1947, and the subsequent outbreak of hostilities over Kashmir in October 1947, meant that little effective defence of the Indian subcontinent could be expected, let alone assistance in South East Asia. Nevertheless, a formula was found to keep a Republican India within the Commonwealth at the April 1949 Commonwealth Conference, and it was still hoped that India might play a role in the diplomatic war against Communism and, ultimately, give material support. Although in April 1950 the Joint Planning Staff saw little hope of this while the Kashmir dispute persisted, they noted that 'India is the only country in South Asia or in South East Asia whose resources are in any way adequate to a major military effort [and] should Burma or Tibet come under communist control India might adopt a different attitude'. It was hoped that the Colombo organization might, through economic co-operation, help to 'educate' Asian countries and eventually facilitate a regional security arrangement enjoying Asian political and material support. For the moment any such pact could only be a 'White Man's Pact'. Consequently, from 1949 to 1954, when the Indo-Chinese crisis precipitated the South East Asia Treaty Organization (SEATO) embracing only two South East Asian countries (Thailand and the Philippines), Britain worked to create the conditions for a wider pact. With the Korean War and implacable American opposition to Communist China it was to be a forlorn aspiration.

A MORE EXPENSIVE ORIENTAL BARRACK: DEFENDING MALAYA

If India remained determined to develop a non-aligned approach to diplomacy, and if Britain intended to draw Australia into a global commitment, what plans were there for South East Asia? Some light is thrown upon this by an April 1946 paper on Far Eastern foreign policy incorporating a Joint Planning Staff Study on strategy. This assumed containment of the Soviet Union along a line of bases running from the Aleutians, through Formosa to the Philippines, making the United States position north of the Tropic of Cancer primarily responsible for defence. Britain would predominate south of the Tropic of Cancer where 'Sea and air power are the dominating factors in the protection of our interests'. French Indo-China was 'of particular importance to the defence of South-East Asia as a whole'.[57]

In the absence of any serious conventional threat the War Office ultimately hoped to 'dispense with white troops East of India', returning to a situation reminiscent of pre-1936, with Singapore protecting vital communications to Australia, and unlikely to form the base for large-scale army operations.[58] They also intended to retain an imperial force, even if the traditional 'English Barrack in the Oriental Seas', India, could no longer be controlled or counted upon.[59] In 1946 a plan was devised for three 'imperial' brigades in northern Burma each comprising one British, one Gurkha and one Burmese hill tribe batallion.[60] The promise of Burmese independence overtook this plan in January 1947, and during 1946–8 plans developed for a mobile Gurkha division in Malaya, and just one brigade of British troops at Singapore, providing for an eventual complement of 4,000–5,000 British and 12,000 Gurkhas. After negotiations an agreement was signed with India on 9 November 1947 to allow the formation of eight Gurkha battalions.[61] As British and Indian troops returned home Allied Land Forces South East Asia (ALFSEA) Army forces dropped from nearly 250,000 in October 1945 to just under 30,000 in July 1947.[62] By late 1948 there were seven partially effective Gurkha battalions in Malaya. Thus the British kept a part of the old Indian Army, one of the so-called 'martial races', albeit at British expense now, to sustain their eastern interests.

Race was not unimportant in British military thinking. The Malay Regiment had been formed in 1934 to test the 'martial' qualities of the Malays, partly in response to the Sultans' dislike for funding Malaya's garrison of alien Asians. Its two battalions were thought to have proven themselves in the war. In January 1946 ALFSEA headquarters suggested 'in line with political plans for fusing states of the Malay peninsula', opening the Malay Regiment to all races. The eventual aim would be six mixed battalions, relieving imperial troops of internal security tasks. Initially, however, individual battalions would not be mixed, though technical arms would to 'utilise the higher intellect available in minority races'. The quick reconstruction of the Malay Regiment would also be a counter-blast to Japanese locally raised forces, and to their wartime appeals to Asian sentiment.[63] It was not clear how far Malay opposition to Malayan Union and citizenship proposals was responsible, but by June 1946 it was proposed to restrict the Malay Regiment to Malays only. Ultimately this would be within a 'Malayan Army' of a division, also incorporating mixed supporting arms. By using non-Malays only in supporting units, 'it will be possible to gauge the military quality of all races', and then further consider the possibility of non-Malay infantry battalions.[64]

In March 1947 the Overseas Defence Committee would authorize only an initial two battalions, but progressive expansion to six was authorized after the outbreak of the Emergency, the target date being October 1950.[65] In fact, despite the need to minimize imperial battalions in Malaya, there were only four battalions operational or forming at the end of 1949, five in April 1951, and the full six by November 1952. This compares to eight Gurkha battalions. Difficulties in financing expansion, in training sufficient Malay NCOs, and in attracting quality British officers, all slowed down progress. Recruiting of the first mixed race battalion 'Federation Regiment' of the Malayan Army, and of a 'Federation' Armoured Car Regiment, began only in late 1952. By November 1953 the former had raised only 469 men, just 71 of them Chinese.[66] Given greater economic opportunities open to many Chinese, the Emergency, and the pre-existing tradition of Malay recruitment, this was understandable, but still represented poor progress towards a united nation of Malaya.

Singapore was allotted responsibility for the small Royal Malayan Navy in 1946 on the grounds of geography, tradition and in the belief its predominantly Chinese population was antipathetic to military service. Logical enough when the two territories were intended to merge, this left Singapore without even one battalion of its own as late as 1956.[67] Financial constraints and unwillingness to make available Royal Air Force training also meant that the Malayan Auxiliary Air Squadrons formed in mid-1950 were constrained to fly Tiger Moth and Harvard trainers until after independence.

In summary, by early 1948 the aim was just one British brigade group in Singapore, six Malay battalions mainly for internal security, and a Gurkha division, at least one brigade of it forming a fully mobile theatre reserve. In March 1946 the Defence Committee decided Hong Kong was indefensible against a major attack by any Asian power controlling the mainland. There three battalions would hold against all other contingencies, and eventually the pre-war Hong Kong Volunteer Reserve would reform.[68] In the United Kingdom there should be a strategic reserve of three brigade groups.

In March–May 1948 the Malayan Communist Party (MCP), responding to increasing government action against trade union disruption, adopted a policy of 'defensive' war against imperialism, thus falling into line with the Soviet 'line', expounded by Zhdanov at the September 1947 Cominform meeting. This assumed two incompatible camps, the imperialist and the democratic. Already in February 1948 there had been a Communist coup in Czechoslovakia, and Britain assumed that the Soviet Union would use all means short of war to encourage local Communists in the Far East. In June mounting tension over Berlin culminated in its blockade.[69] Thus when the 'Emergency' was declared in Malaya on 16–18 June 1948, in response to escalating violence, it was natural that Britain should blame the influence of the two Communist meetings, held in New Delhi in February 1948. These were followed by Communist uprisings in Burma (March), Malaya (June), Indonesia and the Philippines. It was assumed that, forestalled by the Marshall plan in the West, the Soviet Union had opened a new front in the East.[70] In Malaya the MCP could draw on the mainly Chinese veterans of the wartime MPAJA, in which it had played a major organizing role.

The Army was ordered to assist the civil power under police direction, and it was hoped that an early victory in Malaya would encourage resistance to Communism elsewhere. The main emphasis was on increasing the police and raising part-time 'Special Constables'. In August 1948 there were just four British battalions in Malaya. With only one of the three brigades of the United Kingdom strategic reserve formed the COS decided to send it to Malaya, the only active fight against Communism, and the possibility of Australian assistance was unsuccessfully investigated in September.[71] It seemed by early 1949 that the Malayan situation might be coming under control.[72]

In China the Communists were consolidating their hold on the north, and on 9 December 1948 the Cabinet took a paper on the implications of Communist control in the south. Hong Kong, whose theoretical garrison was one British and two Gurkha battalions, though not under immediate threat of attack, would be 'living on the edge of a volcano'. Increased refugees and possible disorder required this garrison be brought up to strength (from two battalions) and a further brigade kept available. In May 1949, with the Communists now sweeping south, the Cabinet concurred with the COS view that Hong Kong might become the object of a trial of strength, making a demonstration of Britain's will to defend it necessary. A brigade was to be sent. In June the Minister of Defence visited Hong Kong, and returned confident that the Colony could be held.[73] It was essential for British prestige in South East Asia. Troops were needed for internal security since the local (Chinese) police could not be counted upon. By late 1949 the Hong Kong garrison was the equivalent of one and one-third divisions and two air squadrons.

Ironically the declaration of the People's Republic of China on 1 October 1949 was followed by a deterioration not in Hong Kong but in Malaya, where the Communists had regrouped, and there was a still insufficient ability to gather intelligence from the Chinese community. This was compounded by shortages of material such as mobile radio sets. Up to 500,000 Chinese squatters on the jungle fringes provided a ready source of Communist support. By February 1950 the local authorities were blaming the deterioration on the external march of Communism and calling for reinforcements to cover units needing retraining, boost morale, and help with the squatter problem. The High Commissioner reported that 'Recently . . . a Chinese who was elected Chairman of [a] village by secret ballot wept on learning of his election', such people must be protected. 'The confidence of the Chinese has not recovered from 1941, and they see a similar situation developing now'.[74]

By late April 1950 26 Infantry Brigade, a squadron of aircraft and a Royal Marine Commando had moved, or had been scheduled to move, from Hong Kong to Malaya, and were not to be replaced because of the importance of building the strategic reserve.[75] With no immediate danger perceived for the colony, Britain's display of determination in Hong Kong turned out to be a passing thing. The British Defence Co-ordinating Committee, Far East (BDCC), were warned there would be no more reinforcements, otherwise 'Malaya would devolve into a bottomless pit devouring all our resources and thus playing straight into Russia's hands'.[76]

General Briggs, given new co-ordinating powers over army and police as Director of Operations, Malaya, in March 1950, drew up a plan to resettle the squatters, deprive the Communists of support, and gradually clear areas of Malaya from south to north. By mid-1951 there were again hopes that some British troops might be released by the year's end. The Korean War prices boom increased rubber and tin income and associated tax revenue, allowing resettlement to proceed quickly, and sustaining the large police forces and Home Guard.[77] For the BDCC, however, a wider regional strategy was necessary to combat Communism.

REGIONAL PLANNING, 1942–50

During 1942–4 the Colonial Office considered regional commissions for areas such as Africa and South East Asia. These might facilitate American co-operation in post-war reconstruction and defence. They might deflect American proposals for the accountability of colonial authorities to an international body. As American diplomacy became more accommodating the Colonial Office lost interest in the idea, fearing foreign, and possibly Foreign Office, interference in colonial territories.

SEAC, however, briefly imposed one authority from India to Indo-China under Mountbatten, assisted by Dening as his political adviser. The

321

Foreign Office had no intention of allowing a return to the pre-war 'parochialism', when very little co-ordination had existed between territories. By 1945 the Colonial Office was resisting the Foreign Office's more ambitious schemes, including the suggestion of a regional Resident Minister.[78] By SEAC's dissolution in November 1946 there was Malcolm MacDonald, Governor-General from May, co-ordinating colonial policy, and Lord Killearn, Special Commissioner for South East Asia from March, representing the Foreign Office in Singapore. The latter appointment had occurred while the overall debate was unresolved because food, and especially rice, scarcity was threatening famine in India and South East Asia.[79]

Lord Killearn held conferences on food, agriculture and transport, and his organization co-ordinated rice allocation until this ceased in late 1949. He assumed Archibald Clark-Kerr's role of mediating between the Indonesian Republic, proclaimed on 17 August 1945, and the Dutch, whom the British were cautiously reinstalling. He viewed South East Asia as 'an essential bastion of the Commonwealth', and with Mountbatten's support sought greater regional co-ordination.[80] At the April–May 1946 Commonwealth Conference the Colonial Secretary still doubted the time was ripe for a formal regional agreement, and so Bevin stressed that Lord Killearn's organization might form the kernel for future developments, with Evatt enthusiastically agreeing on the need for regional co-operation.[81]

By February 1947 the Foreign Office were also moving away from their original concept of co-operating with regional colonial authorities, eventually placing an embargo on arms for the Dutch in Indonesia after the Dutch 'police action' in July.[82] With the French also actively fighting Ho Chi Minh's Viet Minh in Indo-China from late 1946, and Burma and India already promised independence, Dening argued that

> the degree of co-operation [with the French and Dutch] must depend largely on the extent to which [they] are able to settle their differences with the Indonesians and the Viet Nam . . . our aim should be to contrive a general partnership between independent or about-to-be independent Eastern peoples and the Western powers who by their past experience are best able to give them help.

The Governor-General, as a colonial official, was unsuitable for co-ordinating policy for foreign territories; the continuation of the Special Commissioner was vital, 'With our imminent withdrawal from India and Burma, South East Asia becomes of even greater importance [and] its focus will be in Singapore'.[83]

Colonial Office and Foreign Office regional ambitions were partially reconciled when the posts of Special Commissioner and Governor-General were amalgamated, to achieve economies, in May 1948. Malcolm MacDonald became Commissioner-General for South East Asia, responsible to both departments. He also chaired the BDCC, established in December 1946 to replace South East Asia Command. The outbreak of Communist insurrections in the area in 1948 intensified the need for action. At the October 1948 Commonwealth Conference there was an air of crisis over the area. Nehru stated that a broad 'regional understanding', including Australia and New Zealand, was necessary, also stressing his sympathy for Asian nationalist struggles and his suspicion of America. Bevin floated the idea of regional co-operation to establish a firm regional political and economic footing, but it was economic action which received most attention. In Evatt's opinion, 'The most efficacious weapon against communism was the improvement of the standard of living of the peoples'.[84]

The military broadly agreed. A late 1948 Commanders-in-Chief, Far East (CIC, FE), paper saw no threat of military invasion of South East Asia, but stressed the psychological importance of demonstrating the will to resist Communism in Hong Kong.[85] Any penetration of Chinese Communism south of the Yangtse was seen primarily as increasing the threat from indigenous or minority Communist movements, including in Malaya. A March 1949 revision of Far East strategy anticipated little more than the threat, in war, of sporadic Soviet air and sea attacks southwards, even if all China fell. In global war, except the American strategic air bombardment from Okinawa, the allied effort in South East Asia would be defensive. Land communications were 'inadequate for an overland attack on South East Asia by large, fully equipped forces' and their development to such a level was unlikely. There was a railway line but no main road link between the Kra Isthmus and Bangkok. 'As long as the Allies retain control of the sea communications, no serious invasion could develop.' The area was anyway not vital in global war, and the main role of the garrisons was still 'to give the necessary backing to the . . . civil power'. In Cold War a 'half-hearted policy will achieve nothing since only a firm direction and the visible signs of power are likely to convince the oriental mind'. This was the same psychological approach visible in the temporary 1949–50 swelling of Hong Kong's garrison. Simultaneously, however, Britain limited supplies to the Burmese as a part of a policy of encouraging them to accommodate the rebellious Karens, perceived as dependable anti-Communists, and had little money to offer even for the hard-pressed Malayan government.[86]

The Cabinet in December agreed a policy of keeping 'a foot in the door' in China, while consulting allies on how to counter Communism. By February 1949 it was obvious that the United States was reluctant to become involved in the area, and by spring 1949 MacDonald was emphasizing the political need to involve India, and the possibility of an Asian equivalent to the Marshall plan.[87] Bevin sent the Prime Minister a memorandum dated 14 April on recent speeches by Nehru on increasing agrarian revolution in Asia, and the West's neglect of the region, adding 'If we wait too long, we may find ourselves no longer able to influence the situation, since a tendency is already developing, on the part of Nehru, to issue invitations to conferences without asking the United Kingdom'. Clearly India's attempts to organize Asian opinion, from the Asian Relations Conference in March 1947, to the convening of the Asian Conference on Indonesia in January 1949 (in response to the second Dutch 'police action' of December 1948), had convinced Britain that she must prompt Asian countries to act, rather than giving overt political leadership. Nehru's repeated interest in economic action pointed the way.[88]

Sir William Strang (Permanent Secretary at the Foreign Office, 1949–53) also reported that Britain's post-war record left her in a unique position to co-ordinate a policy using 'British experience and American resources'. Little had come of Bevin's attempt to discuss the area at the April 1949 Commonwealth Conference, but in May a working party was set up to study the Far East in the context of President Truman's January 1949 suggestion that some Point Four aid might be available for Asia.[89]

The discovery in September that the United States was not contemplating further funds for the area only made it more necessary to try and organize Asian and Commonwealth countries, and so convince the United States to commit itself. On 27 October the Cabinet endorsed a policy of working towards regional political and, if necessary, military co-operation by first encouraging economic co-ordination, since the Indo-Chinese, Kashmiri and perhaps the Indonesian problem prevented a short-term political approach. In January 1950 the Australians, who had always viewed welfare as the key to fighting Communism, took the initiative at the Colombo Commonwealth Foreign Ministers' conference.[90] In May this resulted in a Consultative Council of the 'Colombo plan', as the organization to co-ordinate assistance for economic development became known. Though it persists into the 1990s, now relying on Japanese funds, it involved no significant new cash funds, and was politically overshadowed by Korea, the United States' China policy, and an Asian tendency to view the Viet Minh as nationalists. Its economic approach was also dwarfed by increasing United States aid, mainly military, to front-line states. The US aid programme to Indo-China was $164 million military aid in 1950–1, and $274 million, mostly military, in 1952.[91] In its main aims the Colombo plan was unsuccessful.

In fact the declaration of the People's Republic of China on 1 October 1949 accentuated differences in British and American approaches, and led Britain, eager both to protect Hong Kong and to avoid driving China into Soviet arms, into recognizing China on 6 January 1950. The United States, constrained by public opinion, its record of supporting the Kuomintang, and a powerful China lobby, would not extend recognition. The Bukit Serene meeting of British regional representatives under MacDonald on

2–4 November 1949 endorsed not only recognition of China, the long-term pursuit of regional organization through economic co-operation, but also the recognition of Bao Dai's government. The French were trying to build up this ex-Emperor of Annam into a credible nationalist alternative to the Viet Minh, and British recognition of Bao Dai on 7 February 1950, though accompanied by the offer of equipment only on repayment terms, indicated British acceptance that a Viet Minh victory would 'be a victory for communism not for nationalism'.[92]

At this point British plans envisaged withdrawing from the Far East, on the outbreak of global war, virtually all British naval units, sixty-four aircraft (to leave just forty-eight), and all troops in excess of internal security needs.[93] In August 1949 the Commanders in Chief, Far East (CIC, FE), had warned that 'the battle for the defence of Malaya . . . in a war with Russia in 1957 has already begun. Success for the enemy in this "cold" war may well make our whole position in South East Asia untenable'.[94] An April 1950 Joint Planning Staff (JPS) study still envisaged the defence of Siam, Burma and Indo-China in war as depending on internal security, and discounted the chances of any successful Communist attack southwards. The struggle in Indo-China was crucial, and with significant Chinese aid now expected for the Viet Minh, time was vital. If France could not quickly deprive the Viet Minh of the rice areas its eventual defeat was likely, leading to a serious threat to its neighbours. The Colombo plan, given American support, might in the long term combat poverty and so Communism.[95] As early as March, however, the CIC Far East were ordering an examination into the possibility that Cold War policy would fail, and of a defence on the remaining frontier, presumably the Kra Isthmus.[96]

The Korean War, which deprived Hong Kong of another brigade late in the year, appeared to offer a victory which would help the Cold War by late September, and then caused near panic in early December as Chinese armies pushed back United Nations forces, but its effect on specifically South East Asian strategy is unclear.

Against this background an August 1950 BDCC paper suggested that Tonkin was the ideal global war defensive line, securing the rice-producing countries, but the United States later proved willing only to support Indo-China with air and naval, not ground forces. The alternative line was on the Kra, and studies quickly ruled out the possibility of including the Thais in planning since the position effectively abandoned Bangkok. The JPS and Vice-Chiefs of Staff continued to stress the contrast between Japanese naval superiority in 1941, and Communist naval inferiority. Combined with long, difficult land communications this might still render any conventional attack southwards ineffective.

The BDCC, however, believed it would be possible to sustain an attack by land alone. They were also increasingly anxious to have a contingency plan in case Indo-China was abandoned or fell. In this case they believed it was possible that 'Thailand will follow the same course of action as in 1941' and certainly that if Phibul Songkram fell any replacement government might sympathize with the Communists. Phibul himself, despite his apparent anti-Communism, was regarded with the circumspection due to a man who was not above suspicion for his role in the rapid Thai collapse to the Japanese in 1941.[97] On 18 December the BDCC urged that if Thailand began to turn Communist the occupation of the Songkhla position was vital. Not only would it seal the border to Communist infiltration helping Malayan terrorists, but timing was essential to its success since

> The Communists as well as ourselves well realise that the Songkhla position is the key to the defence of Malaya. It was realised to be this in 1941 and [its rapid seizure] would have an immensely valuable effect on the Malays, Chinese and others in Malaya. . . . It would be an indication of our determination to defend Malaya and not as in 1942 to be driven from the country.[98]

Planning for seizing the position with a brigade group, hopefully giving the four months necessary to prepare it before any major Chinese attack became possible, had begun by January 1951. On 28 February the Defence Committee endorsed planning both for unopposed and opposed entry, but final authorization was retained in London, and it was recognized that timing intervention could be difficult in the event of Thailand sliding gradually towards communism. Also, the BDCC's estimate of two to three divisions to hold the position against full Chinese attack could not be met in global war, and even in limited war their request would be, as the General Officer Commanding, Malaya described his needs in 1940, 'like asking for the moon'.[99] Geography, and the inability to guarantee 'faraway countries' dictated planning a Kra defensive line in both 1941 and 1951.

CONCLUSION

To place the above in perspective, in a March 1952 Defence Committee discussion it was suggested that the threat of a Communist attack on Malaya would not develop until two years after the loss of Indo-China, and possibly not at all. By this point, however, Britain was involved in Anglo-American discussions on fundamental differences in strategies to counter any Chinese aggression. The Americans favoured blockade and bombing communications in China. Britain worried that this would be ineffective, might invoke the Sino-Soviet alliance of February 1950, and possibly precipitate world war.[100]

By late 1951 the tide had turned in the Emergency, as squatter resettlement progressed and incidents fell.[101] However, doubts in London developed into a sense of crisis when the new Conservative government came to power just after the murder of the High Commissioner, Sir Henry Gurney, in October. With the once dynamic French High Commissioner of Indo-China, General de Lattre de Tassigny, also a sick man in Paris, the period ends with a sense of crisis. An official in the Commissioner-General's Office wrote that 'it is difficult to see what is coming here – whether Communist China will stage an all-out drive . . . or just pursue its present (successful) tactics'. General Montgomery believed that 'The contest between East and West, between Communism and Democracy, between evil and Christianity, is approaching its climax [and the] main objectives of Stalin are today in the East'.[102] General Templer's arrival in February 1952 undoubtedly raised morale in an improving situation, but in late 1951 the sense of anxiety was real.

By 1951 Britain viewed Indo-China as the key to South East Asia, but felt unable to give even material assistance. Britain's most ardent desire had been for American involvement. Once entangled, however, the United States' aggressive deterrence of China undermined Britain's policy of 'sweet reasonableness', of pulling China into the international community. Many Asian countries became increasingly worried by America's zealous anti-communism. Consequently, the Columbo Plan failed to foster significant Asian political or military co-operation against communism.

Despite MacDonald's characteristic optimism, the long-term aim of a Dominion of South East Asia was also progressing slowly, if at all. Stockwell has called the period 1945–57 'Britain's moment in South East Asia', and in terms of the region's economic value, and of the Emergency (which, in contrast to the Indo-Chinese struggle, was now being won) perhaps it was.[103] Overall, however, Britain was increasingly unable to influence events decisively, even in her own territories. Though Britain's influence had always known limits, in this period we are entering the twilight of her influence.

NOTES

1 R. Grenfell, *Main Fleet to Singapore* (Oxford, 1987).
2 See A. H. Short, *The Communist Insurrection in Malaya, 1948–60* (London, 1975); R. Stubbs, *Hearts and Minds in Guerilla Warfare: The Malayan Emergency* (Oxford, 1989); F. S. V. Donnison, *British Military Administration in the Far East* (London, 1956). P. Dennis, *Troubled Days of Peace, Mountbatten and SEAC, 1945–46* (Manchester, 1987).
3 P. Darby, *British Defence Policy East Of Suez, 1947–68* (London, 1973), pp. 2–10. An excellent introduction covering 1600–1960 is in S. Rose, *Britain and South East Asia* (London, 1962).
4 A. J. Rotter, *The Path to Vietnam, Origins of America's Commitment to Southeast Asia* (Ithaca, NY, and London, 1987), p. 56.
5 During and after the war imperial countries held their foreign earnings as sterling balances in London, which pooled and distributed foreign exchange. The Sterling Area also included countries such as Egypt. See Rotter, *Path to Vietnam*; A. P. Dobson, *The Politics of the Anglo-American Economic Special Relationship* (London, 1990).

6 CAB129/CP(48)161, 23 June 1948. CAB129/CP(48)171, 1 July 1948, The Situation in Malaya. CAB129/C(51)26, 20 Nov. 1951, The Situation in Malaya.

7 R. B. Smith, 'Some Contrasts Between Burma and Malaya in British Policy in South-East Asia, 1942–46', in R. B. Smith and A. J. Stockwell, *British Policy and the Transfer of Power in Asia* (London, 1988) pp. 30–76, esp. 32–3, 47–8. Professor Smith's works and comments have been invaluable.

8 J. Neidpath, *The Singapore Naval Base and the Defence of Britain's Far Eastern Empire, 1919–41* (Oxford, 1981) p. 55.

9 Neidpath, *Singapore Naval Base*; W. D. MacIntyre, *The Rise and Fall of the Singapore Naval Base, 1914–42* (London, 1979). For pre-1921 Singapore as a small defended port see Nadzon Haron, 'Colonial Defence and the British Approach to the Problems in Malaya', *Modern Asian Studies* Vol. 24, No. 2 (May 1990) pp. 275–95.

10 WO106/2440 and 2441. Neidpath, *Singapore Naval Base;* MacIntyre, *Singapore Naval Base.* C. C. Ong, 'Major General Dobbie and the Defence of Malaya, 1935–38', *Journal of South East Asian Studies* Vol. V, No. 2 (Sept. 1986) pp. 282–306, and his PhD thesis, ' "Operation Matador" and the Outbreak of the War in the Far East' (LSE, London, 1985). Songkhla is sometimes denoted Singora.

11 Adapted from Air Chief Marshal Brooke Popham, 'Operations in the Far East', *Supplement to the London Gazette* (London: HMSO, 22 Jan. 1948) p. 537. See F. S. V. Donnison, *British Military Administration*, Map 5, pp. 152–3.

12 I. Morrison, *Malayan Postscript* (London, 1942) pp. 187–8. Heath Papers, Dep 233, National Library of Scotland, 'History of the 11th Indian Division', by Colonel A. M. Harrison, Vol. 1, p. 34.

13 Morrison, *Malayan Postscript* pp. 55–6 for 1942 criticism of the failure to launch Matador; also W. D. MacIntyre, *The Singapore Base*, p. 212; Ong, Operation Matador, pp. 414–19.

14 C. Thorne, *Allies of a Kind: The United States, Britain and the War Against Japan, 1941–45* (London, 1978) pp. 346–7, 356, 461–2, 586–7, 614–20, 679–80. Thailand's rice was essential, N. Tarling, 'Rice and Reconciliation', *Journal of the Siam Society (JSS)* Vol. LXVI, No. 2 (July 1978). Attlee's July 1945 Labour government may have been less unsympathetic, as Mountbatten later was in negotiations. N. Tarling's 'Atonement before Absolutism, British Policy towards Thailand in the Second World War', *JSS* Vol. LXVI, No. 1 (Jan. 1978) pp. 22–65 and 'The British and Siamese Rice, 1944–47', *JSS* Vol. LXXV (1987).

15 M. L. Manich Jurmsai, *History of Anglo-Thai Relations* (Bangkok, 1970) pp. 274–84. Britain took an interest in the possibility of a Kra Canal as early as 1843, and thereafter were determined to exclude any other power from the area.

16 Various in CAB134/282–4, especially CAB134/282, FE(0) (47) 9th and 10th meetings, of 22 Oct. 1947 and 21 Nov. 1947. CAB134/284, FE(0) (47) 75.

17 CAB134/288, FE(0) (49) 82 Final, 8 Dec. 1949, Minutes of Day Three, Siam.

18 PREM8/1072, 1073, Siam; FO371/76285, Revision of Formal Agreement 1949. PREM8/1072 noted, 'The advent of a Soviet Mission to Siam is a further argument in favour of a speedy settlement'.

19 CO537/6264, JP(50)47(F) 6 April 1950, Strategy and Defence Policy in South East Asia. Internal Security was the main threat.

20 'Operations in the Far East', *Supplement to the London Gazette* (22 Jan. 1948) pp. 569–74, 575–6. Figures exclude Burma.

21 Malcolm MacDonald Papers, Durham University, MMP 39/8/35, suggests Mountbatten gave military reasons for Singapore's exclusion. However, in 1945–51 the military regarded its federation as important. A. K. H. Lau, 'The Colonial Office and the Malayan Union Policy 1942–43', in Smith and Stockwell (eds) *British Policy and the Transfer of Power in Asia*, pp. 95–126; A. Lau, *'Malayan Citizenship: Constitutional Change and Controversy in Malaya 1942–48'*, in ibid.; CO825/35 No. 55104/1/43 is the central document; W. R. Louis, *Imperialism at Bay: The United States and the Decolonisation of the British Empire, 1941–45* (New York, 1978) for American influence.

22 *Command 6724*, 'Malayan Union and Singapore . . . Future Constitution,' (London: HMSO, 1946).

23 Creech Jones Papers, Rhodes House, Oxford, 57/2. PREM8/459, G. Hall to Prime Minister, 31 May 1946.
24 A. J. Stockwell, *British Policy and Malay Politics During the Malayan Union Experiment* (Kuala Lumpur, 1979). PREM8/459, Malayan Policy, 1945–7.
25 Furedi argues Britain played the ethnic card, see n. 70.
26 A. J. Stockwell, 'British Imperial Policy and the Decolonisation of Malaya 1942–52', *Journal of Imperial and Commonwealth History* Vol. XIII, No. 1 (Oct. 1984), p. 71, quoting CO537/3669, Minute by Morrison, 8 Sept. 1948.
27 MMP 103/ 'Constant Surprise', pp. 306–15.
28 MMP 22/8/19, 19 August 1949 Commissioner-General to Colonial Secretary. MMP, Box 120, 'Constant Surprise', pp. 275–315.
29 CO1022/81, Report on Recent Developments, Mr M. V. Del Tufo, Officer-Administering-Government.
30 CO1022/61, 62 and 63.
31 CO1022/61, J. Paskin, note for T. Lloyd, 5 March 1953, 'the virus of separatism is rife among officials', CO1022/62, comments on Mr Dodds Parker's Memo, for 'hedgehog' quotation. DEFE5/46, COS(53)223, 14 May 1953, for COS and association.
32 A. Watts, *The Evolution of Australian Foreign Policy 1936–63* (London, 1968) pp. 15, 19–20, Menzies, 26 April 1939.
33 ibid., pp. 73ff; T. R. Reese, *Australia, New Zealand and the United States* (Cambridge, 1967), pp. 35–7.
34 The Future of ANZAM in DEFE5/43, COS(52)68, 17 Dec. 1952.
35 J. J. Albert, 'Attlee, the Chiefs of Staff and the Planning of Commonwealth Defence between V. J. Day and the Outbreak of the Korean War', DPhil (Oxford, 1986) pp. 17–19.
36 FO800/461, Minutes from Bevin to Prime Minister, 13 June 1946 and 2 Oct. 1946.
37 R. Buckley, *Occupation Diplomacy* (Cambridge, 1982).
38 CAB133/86, PMM(46)7, 23 April 1946, Australian Defence Policy; ibid., PMM(46)3 and 17th meetings of 24 April and 22 May.
39 CAB133/86, Prime Ministers' Conference, April–May 1946, Meetings 1–5, 10–16, 19–20, Memoranda 3–8. For American interest in Pacific bases, T. R. Reese, *Australia, N.Z. and U.S.*, pp. 52–4.
40 PREM8/743, Defence Organisation 1948, letters between Attlee and Chiffley, May–December 1947.
41 CAB133/86, PMM(46)1, Memoranda, Strategic Position of the British Commonwealth, PMM(46)5, Responsibility for Commonwealth Defence, both by COS. CAB131/4, DO(47)23, 7 March 1947 shows the COS insisting against Attlee's criticism that without the Middle East war would open from 'the last ditch' with survival in doubt. J. M. Lewis, *Changing Direction: British Military Planning for Postwar Strategic Defence 1942–47* (London, 1988).
42 Albert, Commonwealth Defence Planning, pp. 121–3, DO (47) 44, passed on 11 June 1947. For strategic planning, see D. Devereux, *The Formulation of British Defence Policy Towards the Middle East, 1948–56* (London, 1990).
43 Aldrich and Coleman, 'The South Asian Air Bases', *History* Vol. 74, No. 242, p. 418.
44 CAB131/6, DO(48)62, 14 Sept. 1948.
45 DEFE6/5, JP(48)101 (0) (Terms of Reference), 8 Sept. 1948, ordering a comprehensive Far Eastern survey.
46 DEFE5/24, COS(50)392, 4 Oct. 1950, Appendix A, Annex II.
47 CAB131/6, DO(48)79, 18 Nov. 1948, Australian Defence Co-operation, by COS, especially Annex II. Endorsed in CAB131/5, DO(48)22 meeting, 2, 24 Nov. 1948, without apparent controversy.
48 DEFE4/18, COS(48)179 meeting, DEFE5/17.
49 FO800/449, Conversation with Spender and Doidge at Colombo, 13 Jan. 1950. For British responses to Australian attitudes, DEFE11/1, COS(50)27 meeting, 15 Feb. 1950, this document is useful for Commonwealth defence in general, 1949/50.
50 R. O. Neill, *Australia and the Korean War 1950–53* (Canberra, 1981) Vol. 1, pp. 39–44.
51 See n. 48. PREM8/1148, Meeting with Australian Prime Minister, 14 July 1950. D. Lowe, 'Australia, South East Asia and the Cold War 1948–54', DPhil (Cambridge,

1990), pp. 145–200, pp. 176–7 for Australian Cabinet divisions. T. Kaplan, 'Britain's Asian Cold War: Malaya', in A. Deighton (ed.) *Britain and the Cold War* (London, 1990), p. 215, might mislead on this.

52 For Australia's commitment see n. 71 on Edwards.

53 CAB128/CM(51)13, 12 Feb. 1951; CM(51)16, 1 March 1951, CM(51)19, 12 March 1951, minute 8, all meetings. CAB129/CP(51)64, 27 Feb. 1951 and CP(51)47.

54 For an alternative to the 'Spender-centric' view of ANZUS of his *Exercises in Diplomacy* (Sydney, 1969) see D. McClean, 'Anzus Origins: a reassessment', *Australian Historical Studies* No. 94 (April 1990) pp. 64–82.

55 Lowe, 'Australia, South East Asia and the Cold War', pp. 280–1.

56 H. Tinker, 'The Contraction of Empire in Asia 1945–48, the Military Dimension', *Journal of Imperial and Commonwealth History* Vol. XVI (Jan. 1988), pp. 218–33. A. Inder Singh, 'Imperial Defence and the Transfer of Power in India 1940–47', *International History Review* Vol. IV (Nov. 1989) pp. 568–88.

57 CO537/1478, FE(0) (46)52, 16 April 1946, British Foreign Policy in the Far East. The strategic section ultimately derived from a Post Hostilities Planning Committee paper of February 1945, still not approved by the COS.

58 WO216/226, minutes of special Singapore meeting, 3 August 1947. FO371/63547, Dening Memo. of South East Asia, 7 Feb. 1947.

59 K. Jeffrey, 'An English Barrack in the Oriental Seas? India in the Aftermath of the First World War', *Modern Asian Studies* Vol. 5 (1981) pp. 370–87.

60 H. Tinker, 'The Contraction of Empire in Asia', *Journal of Imperial and Commonwealth History* Vol. XVI, No. 2 (Jan. 1988), p. 226.

61 CAB131/14, D(54)24, 28 May 1954, Recruitment of Gurkhas. This plan was emerging from 1946, see CAB131/4, DO(47)22, 7 March 1947, The Future of the Gurkhas; CO537/4085.

62 N. Haron, 'The Malay Regiment 1933–55', PhD thesis (Essex, 1988), p. 60.

63 Haron, ibid. WO32/10835, (17A), Alfsea to War Office, 5 Jan. 1946, passim, WO268/1, Alfsea Qtly Report, 31 Dec. 1946.

64 WO32/10835, (60A), Headquarters Alfsea to HQ Supreme Allied Commander, South East Asia, 14 June 1946.

65 WO268/8, Qtly Report, Far East Land Forces, July–Sept. 1948.

66 Haron, 'The Malay Regiment', pp. 237–9.

67 AIR8/2132, 3 May 1956, Telegrams 155, 156 of 3 May 1956.

68 CAB131/6, DO(48)36, 8 May 1948, Hong Kong, Permanent Garrison. WO268/8 for the Hong Kong Defence Volunteer Force.

69 WO268/8, SEC(48)19/1, 12 April 1948 List of Assumptions.

70 For summaries of the arguments: works in n. 1; C. B. McLane, *Soviet Policies in South East Asia* (Princeton, NJ, 1966) pp. 385–401; for the Soviet line, R. Smith, 'China and South East Asia: The Revolutionary Perspective 1951', *Journal of South East Asian Studies* Vol. XIX, No. 1 (March 1988), pp. 97–110, see pp. 97–8 arguing it was the Indian Communist Party, not the Calcutta Youth Conference, which was vital. F. Furedi, 'Britain's Colonial Wars', *Journal of Commonwealth and Comparative Politics* Vol. XXVIII, No. 1 (March 1990) argues Britain played the racial card to isolate radical nationalism. Contrast this to Britain's conscious policy of 'unite and quit' as portrayed above. FO371/69694 and 5 for Foreign Office views.

71 CAB131/5, DO(48)16 meeting, 13 August 1948, the defence committee noted that one-third of the Burmese army had defected to rebellious Communists. For Australia see P. Edwards, 'The Australian Commitment to the Malayan Emergency 1948–50', *Historical Studies* Vol. 22, No. 89 (Victoria, Oct. 1987) pp. 604–17.

72 AIR20/10377, 'Review of the Emergency in Malaya from June 1948 to August 1957, by Director of Operations, Malaya'. Unless otherwise stated, I have used this document for the Emergency.

73 Hong Kong was vital to British Far Eastern insurance and shipping and second only to Shanghai in British investments. The prestige factor of holding Hong Kong was seen as vital to defence elsewhere, CAB134/287, FE(0) (49) 25 (Revise), 16 May 1949, Colonial Secretary memorandum on Hong Kong.

74 DEFE11/34, High Commissioner to Secretary of State, on resettlement as necessary to

protect and control and the need to retrain police, 15 Feb. 1950. Also DEFE11/34, passim.

75 CAB131/9, DO(50)14, March 1950. CAB131/9, DO(50)32, 29 April 1950. DEFE11/34.
76 DEFE11/35, telegrams between COS and BDCC, April 1950.
77 R. Stubbs, *Counter-Insurgency and the Economic Factor: The Impact of the Korean War Prices Boom on the Malayan Emergency*, Institute of South East Asian Studies (Singapore, 1974).
78 T. Remme, 'Britain and Regional Co-operation in South-East Asia 1945–49', PhD (LSE, 1990), makes Colonial Office opposition to Foreign Office schemes a predominating theme. Understandable rivalry existed, especially before their regional posts were amalgamated, but by 1948–9 Colonial Office doubts were a subtext to the main story. Also N. Tarling, 'Some Rather Nebulous Capacity, Lord Killearn in South East Asia', *Modern Asian Studies* Vol. 20 (1986) pp. 559–98; R. B. Smith, 'Some Contrasts between Burma and Malaya', in Smith and Stockwell, *British Policy and the Transfer of Power in Asia*, pp. 30–76.
79 See n. 80, and the section above on Thailand. PREM8/211, Food Supplies, conveys the critical world food situation of 1946. FO800/461, telegrams between Cairo and the Foreign Office, Feb. 1946. The Cabinet decision was in February.
80 FO800/461, Killearn to London, No. 285, 21 April 1946.
81 CAB131/86, PMM(46)11 meeting, 3 May 1946. Tarling, 'Some Nebulous Capacity', pp. 583–4.
82 Compare CO537/1478, FE(O)(46)52, 16 April 1946, para 29.
83 FO371/63547, Dening note on South East Asia, 7 Feb. 1947.
84 CAB133/88, PMM(48)3 meeting, minute 2.
85 DEFE5/9, COS(48)200, 10 Dec. 1948, China, Annex III.
86 DEFE6/6, JP(48)101 (0) (terms of reference), 8 September 1948 (final revise), 17 March 1949, Far East Strategy.
87 R. Ovendale, *The English-Speaking Alliance: Britain, the United States, the Dominions and the Cold War 1945–51* (London, 1985) p. 156. Part Four is the best available work on 'The Cold War in Asia'. CAB129/CP(48)299, 9 Dec. 1948. Also N. Tarling, 'The United Kingdom and the Origins of the Colombo Plan', *Journal of Commonwealth and Comparative Politics* Vol. XXIV, No. 1 (March 1986) pp. 3–28.
88 For the Asian Relations Conference, T. Remme, 'Britain, the 1947 Asian Relations Conference and regional co-operation in South East Asia', in T. Gorst, L. Johnman and W. S. Lucas (eds) *Postwar Britain 1945–64: Themes and Perspectives* (London, 1989) pp. 109–33. FO800/462, PM/49/71, 14 April 1949, minute from Bevin.
89 CAB129/CP(49)67, 17 March 1949. CAB134/288 for the working party on the Far East set up on 12 May 1949.
90 US funds were recognized as ultimately essential, the Treasury even hoping the provision of such funds might be linked to the reduction of India's sterling balances (British debt in effect). See PREM8/1407, Economic Development in South East Asia; Ovendale, *The English-Speaking Alliance* pp. 165ff.
91 Figures from *FRUS*, Vol. VI, Part I (Washington DC, 1977) pp. 16–26; *FRUS*, Vol. XII, I (Washington DC, 1984) p. 290. Cmd 8529, 'The Colombo Plan', (London: HMSO, 1952) for low Colombo assistance levels.
92 CAB133/288, FE(O) (49)79 (final), 15 Dec. 1949, MacDonald unsuccessfully tried to convince India at Colombo. Ovendale, *The English-Speaking Alliance* pp. 185–210 for the recognition of China. PREM8/1221, for Indo-China. CAB129/CP(50)18, 22 Feb. 1950, 'The Colombo Conference', by Bevin. CAB129/CP(49)244, South East Asia and the Far East, Conference of His Majesty's Representatives.
93 DEFE6/11, JP(49)134 (final), 1 March 1950, Plan GALLOPER.
94 Quoted in CO537/6264, COS(50)89, 9 March 1950.
95 CO537/6264, JP(50)47, 6 April 1950.
96 CO537/6264, COS(50)89, 9 March 1950.
97 DEFE11/42, COS(50)478, 18 Nov. 1950, section on Thailand. DEFE5/24, COS(50)376, 28 Sept. 1950, COS(50)353, 12 Sept. 1950.
98 DEFE11/42, SEACOS 142 for London COS, 18 Dec. 1942.
99 CAB131/11, DO(51)16, 23 Feb. 1951. CAB131/10, DO(51)4 meeting, 28 Feb. 1951.

WO32/2440, CRMC3/406, 13 April 1940, appreciation on Malayan defence by General Bond.
100 CAB131/12, D(52)2 meeting, minute 1, 19 March 1952.
101 AIR20/10377, Appendix A.
102 PREM11/121, letter from Montgomery to Oliver Lyttleton, Colonial Secretary, 27 Dec. 1951: one of several letters.
103 A. J. Stockwell, 'Britain's Imperial Strategy and Decolonisation in South East Asia 1947–57', in D. K. Bassett and V. T. King (eds) *Britain and South East Asia* (Hull, 1986) p. 88.

Select bibliography

BOOKS

(Place of publication is London unless otherwise stated.)

Abadi, J. *Britain's Withdrawal from the Middle East, 1947–71: The Economic and Strategic Imperatives* (Princeton, NJ: Kingston, 1982).

Andrew, C. M. *Secret Service: The Making of the British Intelligence Community* (Heinemann, 1985).

Andrew, C. M. and Dilks, D. (eds) *The Missing Dimension: Governments and Intelligence Communities in the Twentieth Century* (Macmillan, 1984).

Andrew, C. M. and Gordievsky, O. (eds) *KGB: The Inside Story* (Hodder & Stoughton, 1990).

Bartlett, C. J. *The Long Retreat: A Short History of British Defence Policy* (Macmillan, 1972).

Baylis, J. *Anglo-American Defence Relations, 1939–1984* (Macmillan, 1984).

Best, R. *'Co-operation with Like-minded Peoples': British Influence on American Security Policy* (Westport, Conn.: Greenwood, 1986).

Bethell, N. *The Great Betrayal: The Untold Story of Kim Philby's Biggest Coup* (Hodder & Stoughton, 1984).

Bloch, J. and Fitzgerald, P. *British Intelligence and Covert Action* (Junction, 1983).

Botti, T. J. *The Long Wait: The Forging of the Anglo-American Nuclear Alliance, 1945–58* (New York: Columbia, 1987).

Bullock, A. *Ernest Bevin: Foreign Secretary* (New York: Norton, 1983).

Cecil, R. *A Divided Life: A Biography of Donald Maclean* (Bodley Head, 1988).

Clark, I. and Wheeler, N. J. *The British Origins of Nuclear Strategy, 1945–1955* (Oxford: Oxford University Press, 1989).

Cotton, J. and Neary, I. *The Korean War in History* (Manchester: Manchester University Press, 1989).

Danchev, A. *Very Special Relationship* (Brassey's, 1986).

Darby, P. *British Defence Policy East of Suez, 1947–68* (Oxford Unversity Press for RIIA, 1973).

Deighton, A. (ed.) *Britain and the First Cold War* (Macmillan, 1990).

Dockrill, M. and Young, J. W. *British Foreign Policy, 1945–56* (Macmillan, 1989).

Dockrill, S. *British Policy for West German Rearmament* (Cambridge: Cambridge University Press, 1991).

Etzold, T. H. and Gaddis, J. L. *Containment: Documents on American Foreign Policy and Strategy, 1945–50* (New York: Columbia University Press, 1978).

Foot, M. R. D. *SOE in France: An Account of the Work of the Special Operations Executive in France* (HMSO, 1966).
— *SOE: The Special Operations Executive, 1940–46* (BBC, 1984).
Gaddis, J. L. *Strategies of Containment* (New York: Oxford University Press, 1985).
Gowing, M. *Britain and Atomic Energy, 1939–45* (Macmillan, 1964).
— *Independence and Deterrence: Britain and Atomic Energy, 1945–52* (Macmillan, 1974).
Groom, A. J. R. *British Thinking about Nuclear Weapons* (Pinter, 1974).
Grove, E. *From Vanguard to Trident* (Bodley Head, 1987).
Harris, K. *Attlee* (Weidenfeld and Nicholson, 1982).
Hathaway, R. M. *Ambiguous Partnership: Britain and America, 1944–7* (New York: Columbia University Press, 1981).
Hennessy, P. and Jeffrey, K. *States of Emergency: British Governments and Strike-breaking Since 1919* (Routledge & Kegan Paul, 1983).
Heuser, B. *Western 'Containment' Policies in the Cold War: The Yugoslav Case* (Routledge, 1990).
Heuser, B. and O'Neill, R. *Securing the Peace in Europe, 1945–62: Thoughts for the 1990s* (Macmillan, 1991).
Hinsley, F. H. *British Intelligence During the Second World War: Its Influence Upon Operations* (HMSO, 1979–90).
Ireland, T. *Creating the Entangling Alliance: The Origins of the North Atlantic Treaty Organization* (Westport, Conn.: Greenwood Press, 1981).
Jones, R. V. *Most Secret War: British Scientific Intelligence, 1939–45* (Hamish Hamilton, 1978).
— *Reflections on Intelligence* (Heinemann, 1988).
Kaplan, L. S. *The United States and NATO: The Formative Years* (Lexington, Ky: University Press of Kentucky, 1984).
Kovrig, B. *The Myth of Liberation* (Baltimore, Md: Johns Hopkins University Press, 1973).
Lewis, J. *Changing Direction: British Military Planning for Post War Strategic Defence* (Sherwood, 1988).
Louis, W. R. *The British Empire in the Middle East, 1945–51* (Oxford: Clarendon Press, 1984).
Louis, W. R. and Bull, H. *The Special Relationship: Anglo-American Relations Since 1945* (Oxford: Oxford University Press, 1986).
Lucas, W. S. *Divided We Stand: Britain, the United States and the Suez Crisis* (Hodder & Stoughton, 1991).
Manne, R. W. *The Petrov Affair: The Politics of Espionage* (Sydney: Pergamon, 1987).
Masters, A. *The Man Who was M: The Life of Maxwell Knight* (Oxford: Blackwell, 1984).
Osgood, R. E. *NATO: The Entangling Alliance* (Chicago: University of Chicago Press, 1962).
Ovendale, R. *The English-Speaking Alliance: Britain, the United States, the Dominions and the Cold War 1945–51* (Allen & Unwin, 1985).
Ovendale, R. (ed.) *The Foreign Policy of the British Labour Governments, 1945–1951* (Leicester: Leicester University Press, 1984).
Philby, K. *My Silent War* (MacGibbon & Kee, 1968).
Pierre, A. J. *Nuclear Politics: The British Experience with an Independent Strategic Force* (Oxford University Press, 1972).

Reid, E. *Time of Fear, Time of Hope: The Making of the North Atlantic Treaty* (Toronto: McClelland & Stuart, 1977).

Richelson, J. and Ball, D. *The Ties that Bind: Intelligence Co-operation Between the UKUSA Countries* (Allen & Unwin, 1985).

Riste, O. (ed.) *Western Security: The Formative Years – European and Atlantic Security* (Oslo: Norwegian University Press, 1985).

Short, A. *The Communist Insurrection in Malaya, 1948–60* (Muller, 1975).

Sillitoe, Sir Percy *Cloak Without Dagger* (Cassell, 1955).

Smith, B. F. *Shadow Warriors: OSS and the Origins of the CIA* (André Deutsch, 1982).

—— *The War's Long Shadow: World War II and its Aftermath* (André Deutsch, 1986).

Stafford, D. *Britain and the European Resistance, 1940–45: SOE* (St Anthony's/Macmillan, 1980).

Strong, K. *Men of Intelligence: A Study of the Roles of Chiefs of Intelligence from World War II to the Present Day* (Cassell, 1970).

Stubbs, R. *Hearts and Minds in Guerilla Warfare: The Malayan Emergency, 1948–60* (Singapore: Oxford University Press, 1990).

Verrier, A. *Through the Looking Glass: British Foreign Policy in the Age of Illusions* (Cape, 1983).

Wark, W. *The Ultimate Enemy: British Intelligence and Nazi Germany, 1933–1939* (I. B. Tauris, 1985).

West, N. *The Friends: Britain's Post War Secret Intelligence Operations* (Weidenfeld & Nicolson, 1988).

Young, J. *Britain, France and the Unity of Europe, 1945–1951* (Leicester: Leicester University Press, 1984).

—— *France, the Cold War and the Western Alliance, 1944–49* (Leicester: Leicester University Press, 1990).

Zametica, J. (ed.) *British Officials and British Foreign Policy, 1945–50* (Leicester: Leicester University Press, 1990).

ARTICLES

Aldrich, R. 'Imperial Rivalry: British and American Intelligence in Asia, 1942–7', *Intelligence and National Security* 3, 1 (1988) 5–57.

—— 'A Question of Expediency: Britain, the United States and Thailand 1941–2', *Journal of SE Asian Studies XIX*, 2 (1988) 209–44.

—— 'Unquiet in Death: The Post War Survival of the "Special Operations Executive", 1945–51', in A. Gorst and W. Scott Lucas (eds) *Contemporary British History 1931–61: Politics and the Limits of Policy* (London: Pinter, 1991) 193–217.

—— 'Soviet Intelligence, British Security and the End of the Red Orchestra: The Fate of Alexander Rado', *Intelligence and National Security* 6, 1 (1991) 196–218.

Aldrich, R. and Coleman, M. 'The Cold War, the JIC and British Signals Intelligence, 1948', *Intelligence and National Security* 3, 3 (1989) 535–49.

—— 'Britain and the Strategic Air Offensive Against the Soviet Union: The Question of South Asian Air Bases, 1945–9', *History* 74, 242 (1989) 400–27.

Andrew, C. M. 'F. H. Hinsley and the Cambridge Moles: Two Patterns of Intelligence Recruitment', in R. Langhorne (ed.) *Diplomacy and Intelligence During the Second World War* (Cambridge: Cambridge University Press, 1985) 22–40.

—— 'Churchill and Intelligence', *Intelligence and National Security* 3, 1 (1988) 181–93.

Baylis, J. 'Britain and the Dunkirk Treaty: The Origins of NATO', *Journal of Strategic Studies* 5, 2 (1982) 236–47.

—— 'British Wartime Thinking About a Postwar European Security Group', *Review of International Studies* 9, 4 (1983) 265–81.

—— 'Britain, the Brussels Pact and the Continental Commitment', *International Affairs* 60, 4 (1984) 615–29.

Boyle, P. G. 'Britain, America and the Transition from Economic to Military Assistance, 1940–51', *Journal of Contemporary History* 22, 3 (1987) 521–37.

Brands, H. W. 'India and Pakistan in American Strategic Planning, 1947–52', *Journal of Imperial and Commonwealth History* 15 (1986) 41–54.

Cain, F. 'Missiles and Mistrust: US Intelligence Responses to British and Australian Missile Research', *Intelligence and National Security* 3, 4 (1988) 5–23.

Cecil, R. 'The Cambridge Comintern', in Andrew and Dilks, *Missing Dimension*, 169–99.

—— 'C's War', *Intelligence and National Security* 1, 2 (1986) 170–89.

Danchev, A. 'Diplomacy's Wise Man?', *Wilson Quarterly* XIII, 4 (1989) 104–6.

—— 'Taking the Pledge: Oliver Franks and the Negotiation of the North Atlantic Treaty', *Diplomatic History* 15, 2 (1991) 199–221.

Deighton, A. 'The "frozen front": the Labour Government, the Division of Germany and the Origins of the Cold War, 1945–7', *International Affairs* 63, 3 (1987) 449–65.

Devereux, D. 'Britain, the Commonwealth and the Defence of the Middle East, 1948–56', *Journal of Contemporary History* 24 (1989) 327–45.

Dockrill, M. 'The Foreign Office, Anglo-American Relations and the Korean War', *International Affairs* 62, 3 (1986) 459–76.

—— 'British Attitudes Towards France as a Military Ally', *Diplomacy and Statecraft* 1, 1 (1990) 49–71.

Dockrill, S. 'The Evolution of Britain's Policy Towards a European Army, 1950–4', *Journal of Strategic Studies* 12, 1 (1989) 38–63.

Fieldhouse, D. 'The Labour Government and the Empire-Commonwealth', in Ovendale, *Foreign Policy of the British Labour Governments*, 83–121.

Fletcher, R. 'British Propaganda Since World War II: A Case Study', *Media, Culture and Society* IV, 9 (1982) 97–109.

Folly, M. 'Britain and the Issue of Italian Membership of NATO, 1948–9', *Review of International Studies* XIII (1987) 177–96.

—— 'Breaking the Vicious Circle: Britain, the United States and the Genesis of the North Atlantic Treaty', *Diplomatic History* 12, 1 (1988) 59–77.

Gaddis, J. L. 'Intelligence, Espionage and Cold War Origins', *Diplomatic History* 13, 2 (1989) 191–213.

Gorst, A. 'British Military Planning for Postwar Defence', in A. Deighton (ed.) *Britain and the First Cold War* (Macmillan, 1990) 91–108.

Gorst, A. and Lucas, W. S. 'The Other "Collusion": Operation STRAGGLE and Anglo-American Intervention in Syria, 1955–6', *Intelligence and National Security* 4, 3 (1989) 576–96.

Gowing, M. 'Britain, America and the Bomb', in D. Dilks (ed.) *Retreat for Power*, II (Macmillan, 1981) 126–38.

Greenwood, S. 'Return to Dunkirk: The Origins of the Anglo-French Treaty of March 1947', *Journal of Strategic Studies* 6 (1983) 49–65.

Hahn, P. L. 'Containment and Egyptian Nationalism: The Unsuccessful Attempt to Establish a Middle East Command, 1950–53', *Diplomatic History* 11, 1 (1987) 23–40.

Hennessy, P. and Brownfeld, G. 'Britain's Cold War Security Purge: The Origins of Positive Vetting', *Historical Journal* 25, 4 (1982) 965–75.

Hennessy, P. and Townshend, K. 'The Documentary Spoor of Burgess and Maclean', *Intelligence and National Security* 2, 2 (1987) 291–302.

Heuser, B. 'Western Perceptions of the Tito–Stalin Split', *The South Slav Journal* 10, 3 (1987) 336–54.

—— 'NSC 68 and the Soviet Threat: A New View on Western Threat Perception', *Review of International Studies* 17, 1 (1991) 17–41.

Holland, R. F. 'The Imperial Factor in British Strategies, 1947–68', *Journal of Imperial and Commonwealth History* XII, 2 (1984) 168–86.

Jalal, A. 'India's Partition and the Defence of Pakistan', *Journal of Imperial and Commonwealth History* XV, 3 (1987) 289–310.

—— 'Towards the Baghdad Pact: South Asia and Middle Eastern Defence in the Cold War, 1947–55', *International History Review* XI, 3 (1989) 409–33.

Jeffrey, K. 'Intelligence and Counter-Insurgency Operations: Some Reflections on the British Experience', *Intelligence and National Security* 2, 1 (1987) 118–50.

Jervis, R. 'The Impact of the Korean War on the Cold War', *Journal of Conflict Resolution* 24, 4 (1980) 563–92.

Kent, J. 'Imperialism and the Idea of Euro-Africa', in Dockrill and Young, *British Foreign Policy*, 47–77.

—— 'The British Empire and the Origins of the Cold War', in Deighton, *Britain and the First Cold War*, 165–84.

Kerr, S. 'Roger Hollis and the Dangers of the Anglo-Soviet Treaty of 1942', *Intelligence and National Security* 5, 3 (1990) 148–58.

—— 'The Secret Hotline to Moscow: Donald Maclean and the Berlin Crisis of 1948', in Deighton, *Britain and the First Cold War*, 71–87.

—— 'NATO's First Spies: The Case of the Disappearing Diplomats – Guy Burgess and Donald Maclean', in Heuser and O'Neill, *Securing the Peace in Europe*.

Louis, W. R. 'The Special Relationship and Decolonisation: American Anti-Colonialism and the Dissolution of the British Empire', *International Affairs* 61, 3 (1985) 395–420.

Lowe, P. 'The Frustrations of Alliance: Britain, the United States and the Korean War, 1950–1951', in Cotton and Neary, *The Korean War in History*, 81–99.

McLean, D. 'ANZUS Origins: a Reassessment', *Australian Historical Studies* 24, 94 (1990) 64–83.

McMahon, R. J. 'United States Cold War Strategy in South Asia: Making a Military Commitment to Pakistan, 1947–54', *Journal of American History* 74, 3 (1988) 813–40.

Merrick, R. 'The Russia Committee of the British Foreign Office and the Cold War, 1946–7', *Journal of Contemporary History* 20, 3 (1985) 453–68.

Myers, F. 'Conscription and the Politics of Military Strategy in the Attlee Government', *Journal of Strategic Studies* 7, 1 (1984) 55–73.

Ovendale, R. 'William Strang and the Permanent Under Secretaries Committee' in Zametica, *British Officials and British Foreign Policy*, 212–28.

Petersen, N. 'Britain, Scandinavia and the North Atlantic Treaty', *Review of International Studies* 8 (1982) 251–68.

Rahman, H. 'British Post Second World War Planning for the Middle East', *Journal of Strategic Studies* 5, 4 (1982) 511–31.

Schlaim, A. 'Britain, the Berlin Blockade and the Cold War', *International Affairs* 61, 1 (1983/4) 1–15.

Singh, A. I. 'Imperial Defence and the Transfer of Power in India', *International History Review* IV, 4 (1982) 568–88.

—— 'Keeping India in the Commonwealth: British Political and Military Aims, 1947–9', *Journal of Contemporary History* 20, 3 (1985) 469–81.

—— 'Post Imperial British Attitudes to India: The Military Aspect, 1947–51', *The Round Table* 296 (1985) 360–75.

Siracusa, J. M. and Barclay, G. 'Australia, the United States and the Cold War, 1945–51: From VJ Day to ANZUS', *Diplomatic History* 5, 1 (1981) 39–53.

Smith, B. F. 'A Note on the OSS, Ultra and World War II's Intelligence Legacy for America', *Defense Analysis* 3, 2 (1987) 184–9.

—— 'Sharing Ultra in World War II', *International Journal of Intelligence and Counter-Intelligence* 11, 1 (1988) 59–72.

Smith, L. 'Covert British Propaganda: The Information Research Department, 1944–77', *Millennium* 9, 1 (1980) 67–83.

Smith, R. 'A Climate of Opinion: British Officials and the Development of British Soviet Policy, 1945–7', *International Affairs* 64, 4 (1988) 635–47.

Smith, R. and Zametica, J. 'The Cold Warrior: Clement Attlee Reconsidered, 1945–7', *International Affairs* 61, 2 (1985) 237–52.

Taylor, P. M. 'The Projection of Britain Abroad, 1945–51', in Dockrill and Young, *British Foreign Policy*, 9–30.

Thomas, A. 'British Signals Intelligence After the Second World War', *Intelligence and National Security* 3, 4 (1988) 103–11.

Wark, W. K. 'Coming in from the Cold: British Propaganda and the Red Army Defectors', *International History* IX, 1 (1987) 48–73.

—— 'Cryptographic Innocence: The Origins of Signals Intelligence in Canada in the Second World War', *Journal of Contemporary History* 22, 4 (1987) 558–9.

Warner, G. 'The Study of Cold War Origins', *Diplomacy and Statecraft* 1, 3 (1990) 13–26.

Watt, D. C. 'Rethinking the Cold War: A Letter to a British Historian', *Political Quarterly* 49, 4 (1978) 446–56.

—— 'British Military Perceptions of the Soviet Union as a Strategic Threat, 1945–50', in J. Becker and F. Knipping (eds) *Power in Europe?* (Berlin: Walter de Gruyter, 1986) 325–338.

—— 'Intelligence Studies: The Emergence of a British School', *Intelligence and National Security* 3, 2 (1988) 338–42.

—— 'Intelligence and the Historian: A Comment on John Gaddis's "Intelligence, Espionage and Cold War Origins"', *Diplomatic History* 14, 2 (1990) 199–204.

Wheeler, N. 'British Nuclear Weapons and Anglo-American Relations, 1945–54', *International Affairs* 62, 1 (1985/6) 76–86.

—— 'The Attlee Government's Nuclear Strategy, 1945–51', in Deighton *Britain and the First Cold War*, 130–45.

Whitaker, R. 'Origins of the Canadian Government's Internal Security System, 1946–1952', *Canadian Historical Review* LXV, 2 (1984) 154–83.

Wiebes, C. and Zeeman, B. 'Baylis on Post-War Planning', *Review of International Studies* 10, 3 (1983) 242–51.

—— 'The Pentagon Negotiations of March 1948: The Launching of the North Atlantic Treaty', *International Affairs* 59 (1984) 351–63.

Young, J. W. 'The Foreign Office and the Departure of General de Gaulle, June 1945–January 1946', *Historical Journal* 25 (1982) 209–16.

—— 'The Foreign Office, the French and the Post-War Division of Germany', *Review of International Studies* 12, 3 (1986) 223–35.

Index

339